AMERICAN
SOUTHWEST

1st Edition

**Where to Stay and Eat
for All Budgets**

**Must-See Sights
and Local Secrets**

Ratings You Can Trust

Fodor's Travel Publications   New York, Toronto, London, Sydney, Auckland
www.fodors.com

FODOR'S AMERICAN SOUTHWEST

Editors: Michael Nalepa, Eric B. Wechter, lead editors; Paul Eisenberg, Debbie Harmsen, Maria Teresa Hart

Editorial Contributor: John Blodgett

Production Editor: Evangelos Vasilakis

Maps & Illustrations: David Lindroth, Mark Stroud, *cartographers*; Bob Blake, Rebecca Baer, *map editors*; William Wu, *information graphics*

Design: Fabrizio LaRocca, *creative director*; Guido Caroti, Siobhan O'Hare, *art directors*; Tina Malaney, Chie Ushio, Ann McBride, Jessica Walsh, *designers*; Melanie Marin, *senior picture editor*; Moon Sun Kim, *cover designer*

Cover Photo: (The Colorado River seen from the Toroweep Overlook, Grand Canyon National Park, Arizona): George H.H. Huey

Production Manager: Matthew Struble

1st Edition

ISBN 978-1-4000-0732-5

ISSN 1942-874X

SPECIAL SALES

This book is available at special discounts for bulk purchases for sales promotions or premiums. Special editions, including personalized covers, excerpts of existing books, and corporate imprints, can be created in large quantities for special needs. For more information, write to Special Markets/Premium Sales, 1745 Broadway, MD 6-2, New York, New York 10019, or e-mail specialmarkets@randomhouse.com.

AN IMPORTANT TIP & AN INVITATION

Although all prices, opening times, and other details in this book are based on information supplied to us at press time, changes occur all the time in the travel world, and Fodor's cannot accept responsibility for facts that become outdated or for inadvertent errors or omissions. So **always confirm information when it matters,** especially if you're making a detour to visit a specific place. Your experiences—positive and negative—matter to us. If we have missed or misstated something, **please write to us.** We follow up on all suggestions. Contact the American Southwest editor at editors@fodors.com or c/o Fodor's at 1745 Broadway, New York, NY 10019.

PRINTED IN THE UNITED STATES OF AMERICA

10 9 8 7 6 5 4 3 2 1

Be a Fodor's Correspondent

Your opinion matters. It matters to us. It matters to your fellow Fodor's travelers, too. And we'd like to hear it. In fact, we need to hear it.

When you share your experiences and opinions, you become an active member of the Fodor's community. That means we'll not only use your feedback to make our books better, but we'll publish your names and comments whenever possible. Throughout our guides, look for "Word of Mouth," excerpts of your unvarnished feedback.

Here's how you can help improve Fodor's for all of us.

Tell us when we're right. We rely on local writers to give you an insider's perspective. But our writers and staff editors—who are the best in the business—depend on you. Your positive feedback is a vote to renew our recommendations for the next edition.

Tell us when we're wrong. We're proud that we update most of our guides every year. But we're not perfect. Things change. Hotels cut services. Museums change hours. Charming cafés lose charm. If our writer didn't quite capture the essence of a place, tell us how you'd do it differently. If any of our descriptions are inaccurate or inadequate, we'll incorporate your changes in the next edition and will correct factual errors at fodors.com immediately.

Tell us what to include. You probably have had fantastic travel experiences that aren't yet in Fodor's. Why not share them with a community of like-minded travelers? Maybe you chanced upon a beach or bistro or B&B that you don't want to keep to yourself. Tell us why we should include it. And share your discoveries and experiences with everyone directly at fodors.com. Your input may lead us to add a new listing or highlight a place we cover with a "Highly Recommended" star or with our highest rating, "Fodor's Choice."

Give us your opinion instantly at our feedback center at www.fodors.com/feedback. You may also e-mail editors@fodors.com with the subject line "American Southwest Editor." Or send your nominations, comments, and complaints by mail to American Southwest Editor, Fodor's, 1745 Broadway, New York, NY 10019.

You and travelers like you are the heart of the Fodor's community. Make our community richer by sharing your experiences. Be a Fodor's correspondent.

Happy traveling!

Tim Jarrell, Publisher

CONTENTS

About this Book 7
What's Where 8
Quintessential
American Southwest 12
If You Like 14
Great Itineraries 16
When to Go 20

1 ALBUQUERQUE 21
Orientation & Planning 22
Exploring Albuquerque 26
Where to Eat 42
Where to Stay 52
Nightlife & the Arts 61
Sports & the Outdoors 64
Shopping 67
Side Trips from Albuquerque 72

2 SANTA FE 83
Orientation & Planning 84
Exploring Santa Fe 90
Where to Eat 100
Where to Stay 116
Nightlife & the Arts 126
Sports & the Outdoors 131
Shopping 135
Side Trips from Santa Fe 144

3 TAOS 163
Orientation & Planning 164
Exploring Taos 167
Where to Eat 176
Where to Stay 181
Nightlife & the Arts 189
Sports & the Outdoors 191
Shopping 193
Taos Ski Valley 198
Side Trips from Taos 200

4 PHOENIX, SCOTTSDALE &
TEMPE 207
Exploring the Valley of the Sun 208
Sports & the Outdoors 221
Where to Eat 226
Where to Stay 236
Nightlife & the Arts 244
Shopping 249
Valley of the Sun Essentials 251

5 NORTH-CENTRAL ARIZONA . . 253
Flagstaff 255
Side Trips near Flagstaff 263
Sedona & Oak Creek Canyon . . . 264
The Verde Valley, Jerome
& Prescott 271
North-Central Arizona
Essentials 277

6 NORTHEAST ARIZONA 303
The Petrified Forest & the Painted
Desert 305
Navajo Nation East 310
The Hopi Mesas 313
Monument Valley 316
Glen Canyon Dam & Lake Powell 319
Northeast Arizona Essentials . . . 325

7 TUCSON 327
Exploring Tucson 328
Sports & the Outdoors 342
Where to Eat 345
Where to Stay 351
Nightlife & the Arts 354
Shopping 356
Tucson Essentials 357

8 SOUTHERN ARIZONA 359
Southeast Arizona 361
Southwest Arizona 370
Southern Arizona Essentials 376

9 **MOAB & SOUTHEASTERN
  UTAH** **377**
  Moab 380
  Canyonlands National Park 387
  Southeastern Utah 395
  Southeastern Utah Essentials . . 403

10 **SOUTHWESTERN UTAH** **415**
  Utah's Dixie 417
  Along U.S. 89 428
  Grand Staircase–Escalante
  National Monument 431
  Southwestern Utah Essentials . . 433

11 **SOUTHWEST COLORADO** **455**
  Telluride 458
  Purgatory 465
  Durango 468
  Pagosa Springs 474
  Cortez 476
  Southwest Colorado Essentials . . 478

12 **WEST TEXAS** **491**
  El Paso 494
  Guadalupe Mountains
  National Park 500
  Alpine, Marfa & the Davis
  Mountains 502
  Midland-Odessa 505
  San Angelo 507
  West Texas Essentials 508

13 **LAS VEGAS** **527**
  Exploring Las Vegas 528
  Best Bets 538

**AMERICAN SOUTHWEST
ESSENTIALS** **553**
  Getting Started 554
  Booking Your Trip 556

Fodor's Features

Grand Canyon National Park 279
Arches National Park 405
Bryce Canyon National Park 435
Zion National Park 445
Mesa Verde National Park 481
Big Bend National Park 509
Carlsbad Caverns National Park 517

  Transportation 561
  On The Ground 564
INDEX **565**
ABOUT OUR WRITER **576**

MAPS

United States of America 10–11
Albuquerque Old Town 28
Albuquerque 30–31
Where to Eat in Albuquerque . . 44–45
Where to Stay in Albuquerque . . 54–55
Albuquerque Side Trips 73
Santa Fe 88–89
Downtown Santa Fe 93
Where to Eat in Downtown
Santa Fe 103

CONTENTS

Where to Stay & Eat in
Greater Santa Fe 114–115

Where to Stay in Downtown
Santa Fe 123

Side Trips from Santa Fe 145

Taos 170

Where to Eat in Taos 175

Where to Stay in Taos 182

Taos Side Trips 202

Downtown & Central Phoenix 210

Greater Phoenix 213

Scottsdale. 217

Tempe & Around. 220

Where to Eat in the
Valley of the Sun 224–225

Where to Stay in the
Valley of the Sun 238–239

North-Central Arizona 256

Flagstaff & Environs 258

Sedona & Oak Creek Canyon. 265

The Verde Valley, Jerome &
Prescott. 272

Prescott. 276

Grand Canyon South Rim. 285

Grand Canyon Village &
The Rim Trail. 289

Grand Canyon North Rim. 292

Northeast Arizona 306

Petrified Forest National Park 308

Hopi Mesas. 314

Glen Canyon Dam & Lake Powell. . 319

Tuscon. 330

Downtown Tucson 332

Saguaro National Park West Unit. . 339

Saguaro National Park East Unit. . 340

Where to Stay &
Eat in Tucson 348–349

Southern Arizona 362

Southeast Arizona 364

Southwest Arizona 371

Southeastern Utah 379

Canyonlands Needles District 392

Southwestern Utah. 420

St. George. 422

Central Bryce Canyon 440

Southwest Colorado. 458

West Texas 493

El Paso 495

Subterreanean Trail Network,
Carlsbad Caverns NP 522

The Las Vegas Strip 531

ABOUT THIS BOOK

Our Ratings

Sometimes you find terrific travel experiences and sometimes they just find you. But usually the burden is on you to select the right combination of experiences. That's where our ratings come in.

As travelers we've all discovered a place so wonderful that its worthiness is obvious. And sometimes that place is so experiential that superlatives don't do it justice: you just have to be there to know. These sights, properties, and experiences get our highest rating, **Fodor's Choice**, indicated by orange stars throughout this book.

Black stars highlight sights and properties we deem **Highly Recommended**, places that our writers, editors, and readers praise again and again for consistency and excellence.

By default, there's another category: any place we include in this book is by definition worth your time, unless we say otherwise. And we will.

Disagree with any of our choices? Care to nominate a place or suggest that we rate one more highly? Visit our feedback center at www.fodors.com/feedback.

Budget Well

Hotel and restaurant price categories from ¢ to $$$$ are defined in the opening pages of each chapter. For attractions, we always give standard adult admission fees; reductions are usually available for children, students, and senior citizens. Want to pay with plastic? **AE, D, DC, MC, V** after restaurant and hotel listings indicate if American Express, Discover, Diners Club, MasterCard, and Visa are accepted.

Restaurants

Unless we state otherwise, restaurants are open for lunch and dinner daily. We mention dress only when there's a specific requirement and reservations only when they're essential or not accepted—it's always best to book ahead.

Hotels

Hotels have private bath, phone, TV, and air-conditioning and operate on the European Plan (aka EP, meaning without meals), unless we specify that they use the Continental Plan (CP, with a Continental breakfast), Breakfast Plan (BP, with a full breakfast), or Modified American Plan (MAP, with breakfast and dinner) or are all-inclusive (including all meals and most activi-

ties). We always list facilities but not whether you'll be charged an extra fee to use them, so when pricing accommodations, find out what's included.

Many Listings
- ★ Fodor's Choice
- ★ Highly recommended
- ⊠ Physical address
- ✛ Directions
- 🕮 Mailing address
- ☎ Telephone
- 🖷 Fax
- 🌐 On the Web
- 🖄 E-mail
- 🕮 Admission fee
- ⊙ Open/closed times
- Ⓜ Metro stations
- 🖃 Credit cards

Hotels & Restaurants
- 🏨 Hotel
- ⤸ Number of rooms
- ⚲ Facilities
- ⦿ Meal plans
- ✕ Restaurant
- ⚑ Reservations
- ⤫ Smoking
- 🍸 BYOB
- ✕🏨 Hotel with restaurant that warrants a visit

Outdoors
- 🏌 Golf
- ⛺ Camping

Other
- ☾ Family-friendly
- ⇨ See also
- 🖃 Branch address
- ☞ Take note

WHAT'S WHERE

ALBUQUERQUE	With the state's international airport, Albuquerque is the gateway to New Mexico and the state's business, finance, education, and industry capital. Its architecture, food, and art reflect a confluence of Native American, Hispanic, and Anglo culture.
SANTA FE	At the base of the Sangre de Cristo Mountains, Santa Fe has an abundance of museums, cultural events, art galleries, first-rate restaurants, and shops.
TAOS	World-famous museums and galleries, stunning views of the Sangre de Cristo Mountains, and charming streets lined with adobe buildings are a few of the attractions of this town. Nearby historic Taos Pueblo and Ranchos de Taos are other draws.
PHOENIX, SCOTTSDALE & TEMPE	Rising where the Sonoran Desert butts up against the Superstition Mountains, the Valley of the Sun is filled with resorts and spas, more than 200 golf courses, and nearby mountains and trails.
NORTH-CENTRAL ARIZONA	Cool, laid-back towns here are as bewitching as the landscape they inhabit. There are quaint escapes like Prescott and Jerome, New Age Sedona, and the vibrant university town of Flagstaff. The area is also home to Grand Canyon National Park's popular South Rim or more remote North Rim. Don't just peer over the edge—take the plunge into the canyon on a mule train, on foot, or on a raft trip.
NORTHEAST ARIZONA	This remote area includes the stunning Monument Valley. Alongside today's Navajo and Hopi communities, the breathtaking Canyon de Chelly and Navajo National Monument are reminders of how ancient peoples lived with the land.
TUCSON	The history of Arizona begins here, where Hispanic, Anglo, and Native American cultures became intertwined in the 17th century and still are today. Nearby are luxurious guest ranches and spas, as well as Saguaro National Park.
SOUTHERN ARIZONA	Mountain and desert scenery evokes the romanticized spirit of the Wild West. Enduring pockets of westward expansion are the largest draw: infamous Tombstone and the mining boomtown Bisbee.

MOAB & SOUTHEASTERN UTAH	Moab is a world-class mountain bike and river-running destination. On the state's southern edge, stretching into Arizona, Monument Valley's iconic spires and buttes enchant and energize. Sage-brush flats may suddenly drop away into deep and narrow slot canyons. Snow-capped mountains rise like a verdant mirage above the desert. Nearby Arches National Park has the largest collection of natural sandstone arches in the world—more than 2,000. Canyonlands National Park is seldom crowded, making it a place where you can hike, mountain bike, raft, or drive through some of the wildest, most untouched country in the United States.
SOUTHWESTERN UTAH	St. George is a regional hub for shopping, dining, sporting, and cultural events, but the best way to experience this part of the state is to get out of your car and venture onto one of the many and varied trails, or to explore the mostly roadless, expansive Grand Staircase–Escalante National Monument. Another way to view the region is by boat from Lake Powell. Known for its sheer 2,000-foot-high cliffs and river-carved canyons, Zion National Park's world-class trails include Angels Landing and the Narrows. Nearby Bryce Canyon National Park's bizarrely shaped, bright red-orange rocks, or hoodoos, are its signature formation. If you can take to the trails at sunrise or sunset, your reward will be amazing colors.
SOUTHWEST COLORADO	Colorado's southwest quadrant descends from evergreen-clad peaks to red desert speckled with impressive sandstone formations. Durango has a historic downtown and lively nightlife, as well as the Silverton Narrow Gauge Railroad. Mesa Verde National Park provides a peek into the lives of the Ancestral Puebloan people who made their homes among the cliffs.
WEST TEXAS	To say West Texas is desolate is putting it mildly. You're likely to encounter more tumbleweeds than people, especially if you're on a long drive on I–10. But if you get off the Interstate you find civilization, in such towns as El Paso, Midland and Odessa, and San Angelo. The area's number-one attraction is Big Bend National Park, where visitors can experience the Rio Grande River, take in the rough beauty of the Chisos Mountains, or hike through desert, forest, or river valley in silence. Just over the border from West Texas is New Mexico's Carlsbad Caverns National Park, a series of underground caverns that can be reached via an elevator that plunges 75 stories to an underworld of shadows and eerily twisted rock.

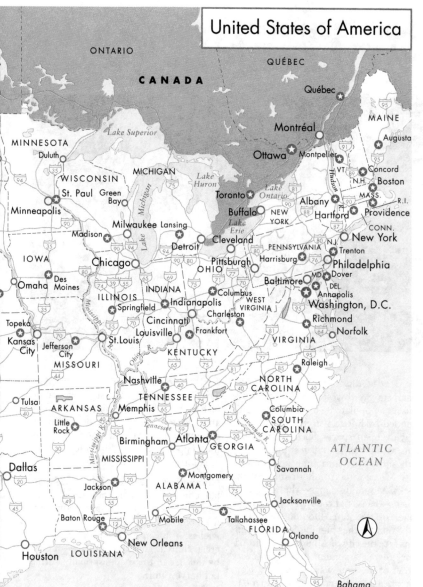

United States of America

QUINTESSENTIAL AMERICAN SOUTHWEST

The Great Outdoors

American Southwest urban centers are densely populated—but they're surrounded by horizon-stretching expanses of wide open spaces filled with mountains as high as 14,000 feet and capped with snow well into June and July. In New Mexico, the southern spine of the Rocky Mountain range—the Sangre de Cristos—runs right down through the center of the state, looming over Taos and Santa Fe; the stunning Sandia Mountains face the city of Albuquerque. In Arizona, there's a summit or path in every corner of the state waiting for you, from Bright Angel trail in the Grand Canyon to iconic Camelback Mountain in Phoenix. In Utah, outdoor recreationists do it all, from mountain biking to backpacking to hiking and trail running to snow-sports of all sorts.

Are You Feeling Chili?

The American Southwest is known to be a warm, often downright hot, region, and we're not just talking outdoor temperatures. We're talking food, specifically the pepper in all its glory and rainbow of colors.

Nothing sets New Mexican food apart like chili pepper, permutations of which locals will heap upon just about any dish, from blue-corn enchiladas to turkey sandwiches. You can often find fresh roasted green chilis at fairs and festivals—or even by the side of the road, especially during fall harvest time.

In Arizona, you can join the quest to find the perfect salsa. No two are the same, and every city and town boasts its own local favorite. Spicy and chunky? Tangy and juicy? Tear-inducing? They run the gamut.

The American Southwest is known for its rich history, captivating cuisine, and breathtaking natural landmarks. Arizonans, New Mexicans, Coloradans, Nevadans, and Texans have developed distinctive cultures all their own, which you can delve into by doing as the natives do.

The Night Sky

Away from the American Southwest's metropolitan areas, the night sky is clear and unpolluted by lights or smog. In December, in the desert, the Milky Way stretches like a chiffon scarf across the celestial sphere. Lie on your back on the hood of your car at night, allow your eyes time to adjust to the darkness, and you'll see more stars than you could possibly have imagined.

Myriad astronomy books and websites have star charts that you can use to explore the cosmos; *National Geographic* has a cool interactive version with images from the Hubble Space Telescope (*www. nationalgeographic.com/stars/chart*). To search for planets, visit *www.stardate.org* or *www.space.com/nightsky* before your trip. Or better yet, take a closer look at one of the Southwest's many observatories.

Cowboy Heritage

People take rodeo seriously in Arizona, whether it's a holiday extravaganza like in Prescott or Payson (which draw top cowboys from around the country), a bull-riding competition at Camp Verde, or a bunch of working cowboys gathered for a team-roping contest in Williams.

These days, particularly with the emergence of bull riding as a stand-alone event—and the crowds often cheer as much for the bulls as the cowboys—rodeos are no longer the hayseed and cowpokey events Arizona grandpa might have enjoyed. Rock-and-roll rodeo has arrived and there is frequently live music as well as roping. So, if you see a flyer posted in a shop window advertising a rodeo, take a walk on the wild side and check out the fine arts of riding and roping. You might be surprised how graceful it is.

IF YOU LIKE

National Wonders

Grand Canyon National Park, Arizona. With an average width of 10 mi, a length of 277 mi, and a depth of 1 mi, the enormity of the Grand Canyon is nearly impossible to fathom. Whether exploring the area on foot, by mule, by raft, or by the plane, the journey is one worth savoring.

Arches National Park, Utah. This park near Moab has the largest concentration of natural sandstone arches in the world. Awe-inspiring scenery and thrilling walks on the top of sandstone fins make this place hard to forget.

Zion National Park, Utah. Sheer 2,000-foot cliffs and river-carved canyons make Zion a must-see Southern Utah attraction.

Carlsbad Caverns National Park, New Mexico. Most of this park's attractions are underground, reachable via an elevator that plunges 75 stories down into a veritable underworld of shadows and eerily twisted rock. (It's also home to 300,000 bats.)

Bryce Canyon National Park, Utah. The park's namesake claimed it was a "Hell of a place to lose a cow," but failed to say anything about how great a place it is to explore on horseback. Sign up for a guided tour at Ruby's Red Canyon Horseback Rides near the park entrance. Orange-pink spires and hoodoos offer a ride unmatched anywhere else.

Big Bend National Park, Texas. This mammoth park in West Texas is all about playing outdoors in every way imaginable, from hiking, bicycling, and horseback riding to fishing, bird-watching, and getting out on the water. Avoid this park at the height of summer or you'll feel like you've stepped into a furnace.

Hiking & Biking

Wheeler Peak, New Mexico. It's one of the more strenuous hiking challenges in the state, but the 8-mi trek to New Mexico's highest point, Wheeler Peak (elevation 13,161 feet), rewards visitors with stunning views of the Taos Ski Valley.

Angels Landing Trail, Utah. One of the Zion National Park's most popular hikes, Angels Landing also happens to be one of the most spectacular. Stop at Scout's Lookout for a breathtaking view. This isn't the trail to take, though, if you are afraid of heights.

Grand Canyon National Park, Arizona. You could spend the rest of your life hiking here and never cover all the trails. Bright Angel trail is the most famous, but it's tough: with an elevation change of more than 5,000 feet, don't try to hike it to the Colorado River and back in one day. Less strenuous is the 9-mi Rim Trail, a paved, generally horizontal walk. Other outstanding choices are the South Kaibab Trail and the Hermit Trail. If waterfalls are your thing, check out Havasu Canyon, an 8-mi hike that descends 3,000 feet to splashing pools of turquoise water.

Moab, Utah. Many consider Moab the mountain biking capital of the world. Test your mettle on popular routes like the Slickrock Trail, Gemini Bridges, or Monitor and Merrimac trails.

Durango, Colorado. Bikes seem to be more popular than cars in Durango, another fabled biking mecca. You can bike around town or into the mountains with equal ease, and there are plenty of locals ready to advise you as to their favorite routes.

Historic Sites

Mesa Verde National Park, Colorado. Established in 1906, Mesa Verde was the first national park to "preserve the works of man," according to President Theodore Roosevelt. The ancestral Pueblo people lived here from AD 600 to AD 1300, and to date more than 4,000 archeological sites—including 600 cave dwellings—have been unearthed. Today, researchers continue to discover and catalog artifacts here on a regular basis.

Taos Pueblo, New Mexico. A United Nations World Heritage Site, Taos Pueblo has the largest collection of multistory pueblo dwellings in the United States. These mud-and-straw structures have sheltered Tiwa-speaking Native Americans for almost 1,000 years (about 100 Taos Native Americans still live here full-time, practicing traditional ways of life, while 2,000 others live nearby in conventional homes).

Montezuma Castle National Monument, Arizona. Located south of Flagstaff, this national monument features one of the best-preserved prehistoric ruins in North America.

Palace of the Governors, New Mexico. The oldest public building in the United States anchors Santa Fe's historic plaza. It has served as the residence for 100 Spanish, Native American, Mexican, and American governors, but today it is New Mexico's state history museum.

Heard Museum, Arizona. This world-class Phoenix museum houses an impressive array of Native American cultural exhibits.

Water Sports & Fly Fishing

Colorado River, Utah. The Grand Poobah of river rafting in Utah. There are numerous outfitters in the Moab area with a wide assortment of half-, full-, and multiday trips of the river. Even in periods of low water, the infamous Cataract Canyon section still provides plenty of thrills and spills.

Grand Canyon National Park, Arizona. There are nearly two-dozen commercial rafting companies offering trips as short as three days or as long as three weeks through the Grand Canyon. Options include motorized rafts or dories rowed by Arizona's version of the California surfer—the Colorado River boatman.

Lake Powell, Utah/Arizona. Formed by the construction of Glen Canyon Dam, this popular recreational attraction is the second largest man-made body of water in the country. (Lake Powell has 2,000 mi of shoreline—that's longer than America's Pacific coastline.) The lake, which straddles the Arizona/Utah border, is a boating paradise; you can see it on a guided excursion, or rent a boat (or houseboat) and explore on your own. It's also home to a wide variety of fish, including striped, smallmouth, and largemouth bass; bluegill; and channel catfish.

GREAT ITINERARIES

NEW MEXICO MOUNTAIN HIGH

Day 1: Albuquerque

Start out by strolling through the shops of Old Town Plaza, then visit the New Mexico Museum of Natural History and Science. Also be sure to check out the Albuquerque Museum of Art and History, and also try to make your way over to the Albuquerque Biological Park, which contains the aquarium, zoo, and botanic park. For lunch, try the atmospheric Monica's or the sophisticated St. Clair Winery and Bistro, both near the Old Town center.

Later in the afternoon, you'll need a car to head east a couple of miles along Central to reach the University of New Mexico's main campus and the nearby Nob Hill District. Start with a stroll around the UNM campus with its many historic adobe buildings; if you have time, pop inside either the Maxwell Museum of Anthropology or the University Art Museum. When you're finished here, walk east along Central into Nob Hill and check out the dozens of offbeat shops. If it's summer, meaning that you still have some time before the sun sets, it's worth detouring from Old Town to Far Northeast Heights (a 15-minute drive), where you can take the Sandia Peak Aerial Tramway 2.7 mi up to Sandia Peak for spectacular sunset views of the city. Either way, plan to have dinner back in Nob Hill, perhaps at Graze or Flying Star. If you're still up for more fun, check out one of the neighborhood's lively lounges; head back downtown for a bit of late-night barhopping.

Days 2 & 3: Santa Fe

On Day 2, head to Santa Fe early in the morning by driving up the scenic Turquoise Trail; once you arrive in town, explore the adobe charms of the downtown central Plaza. Visit the Palace of the Governors and browse the wares of the Native American vendors there. At the Museum of Fine Arts you can see works by Southwestern artists, and at the Museum of International Folk Art you can see how different cultures in New Mexico and elsewhere in the world have expressed themselves artistically. Give yourself time to stroll the narrow, adobe-lined streets of this charming downtown, and treat yourself to some fine New Mexican cuisine in the evening, perhaps with a meal at La Choza or Maria's.

On your second day in town, plan to walk a bit. Head east from the Plaza up to Canyon Road's foot, perusing the galleries. Have lunch at one of the restaurants midway uphill, such as Sol or El Farol. From here, you can either continue walking 2 mi up Canyon, and then Upper Canyon, roads to the Randall Davey Audubon Center, or you can take a cab there. If you're up for some exercise, hike the foothills—there are trails within the center's property and also from the free parking area (off Cerro Gordo Road) leading into the Dale Ball Trail Network. You might want to try one of Santa Fe's truly stellar, upscale restaurants your final night in town, either Geronimo on Canyon Road, or the restaurant at the Inn of the Anasazi, a couple of blocks from the Plaza. Later in the evening, enjoy cocktails at the city's swankest lounge, Swig.

Day 4: Abiquiu

From Santa Fe, drive north up U.S. 285/84 through Española, and then take U.S. 84 from Española up to Abiquiu, the fabled community where Georgia O'Keeffe lived and painted for much of the final five decades of her life. On your way up, before you reach Española, make the detour toward Los Alamos and spend the morning visiting Bandelier National Monument. In Abiquiu, plan to tour Georgia O'Keeffe's home.

Days 5 & 6: Taos

Begin by strolling around Taos Plaza, taking in the galleries and crafts shops. Head south two blocks to visit the Harwood Museum. And then walk north on Paseo del Pueblo to the Taos Art Museum at the Fechin House. In the afternoon, drive out to the Rio Grande Gorge Bridge. Return the way you came to see the Millicent Rogers Museum on your way back to town. In the evening, stop in at the Adobe Bar at the Taos Inn and plan for dinner at Joseph's Table. On the second day, drive out to the Taos Pueblo in the morning and tour the ancient village while the day is fresh. Return to town and go to the Blumenschein Home and Museum, lunching afterward at the Dragonfly Café. After

lunch drive out to La Hacienda de los Martinez for a look at early life in Taos and then to Ranchos de Taos to see the San Francisco de Asís Church.

Day 7: The High Road

On your final day, drive back down toward Albuquerque and Santa Fe via the famed High Road, which twists through a series of tiny, historic villages—including Peñasco, Truchas, and Chimayó. In the latter village, be sure to stop by El Santuario de Chimayó. Have lunch at Léona's Restaurante or Rancho de Chimayó, and do a little shopping at Ortega's Weaving Shop. From here, it's a 30-minute drive to Santa Fe, where you can spend a final night, or a 90-minute drive to Albuquerque.

GREAT ITINERARIES

VALLEY OF THE SUN
1–2 Days

Phoenix and the Valley of the Sun is the best place to begin your trip to Arizona, with a wealth of hotels and resorts. Reserve a day in the Valley and visit the Heard Museum and Desert Botanical Garden. Select one of the area's popular Mexican restaurants for dinner. If time permits, stroll through Old Town Scottsdale's tempting art galleries. Depending on your remaining time in the Valley, you can escape to a spa for a day of pampering, get out your clubs and hit the links, or—if the season is right—catch a major-league baseball spring-training game.

Logistics: Sky Harbor International Airport is located at the center of the city and is 20 minutes away from most of the Valley's major resorts. Plan on driving everywhere in the greater Phoenix area, as public transportation is nearly nonexistent. Phoenix is a remarkably simple area to navigate. Designed on a grid, numbered streets run north–south and named streets (Camelback Road, Glendale Avenue) run east–west. If you need to know which direction you're facing, you can see South Mountain, conveniently located at the south side of Phoenix, from nearly any point in the city.

GRAND CANYON
1–2 Days

The sight of the Grand Canyon's immense beauty has taken many a visitor's breath away. Whatever you do, though, make sure you catch a sunset or sunrise view of the canyon. A night, or even just dinner at the grand El Tovar Hotel won't disappoint, but book your reservation early. Outdoors enthusiasts will want to reserve several days to hike and explore the canyon; more reserved travelers can comfortably see the area in one or two days.

Logistics: Arizona is a large state; the drive north from Phoenix to the Grand Canyon will take several hours, so budget at least a half day to make the 225-mi trip. Take Interstate 17 north from Phoenix into Flagstaff. The best way to reach the South Rim of the canyon is via U.S. 180 northwest from Flagstaff. It's best to travel to the canyon from the city during the week—Interstate 17 fills with locals on Friday and Saturday who are looking to escape the heat. If you have specific plans, whether it's a mule ride and rafting trip or dining and lodging, be sure to book early for the canyon—reservations are necessary.

RED ROCKS & SPECTACULAR SIGHTS
3–4 Days
Option 1: Sedona & Surrounding Area

The unusual red-rock formations in Sedona are sole destinations for most visitors to Arizona, and it's no wonder. Spend at least a day exploring the town and its beauty, whether on a calm stroll or a thrilling Jeep tour. The surrounding area includes Flagstaff, a college town with a love for the outdoors and the stars; Prescott, with its Whiskey Row and Victorian homes; and Jerome, a charming artists' community that thrives more with every passing year.

Logistics: If possible, visit Sedona midweek, before the city folk fill the streets on the weekends. If Sedona is too pricey for your stay, consider Flagstaff or Prescott, which have ample motels and budget hotels.

Option 2: Landmarks of Indian Country

The majestic landscapes in Monument Valley and Canyon de Chelly are among

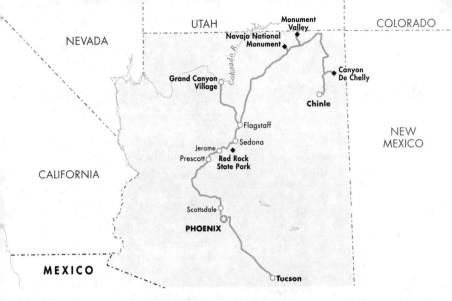

the biggest draws to Arizona. Made famous in countless Westerns and photographs, the scenes are even more astounding in person. This northeast corner of the state is worth several days of exploration. The famous Four Corners where Arizona, New Mexico, Colorado, and Utah meet are within a short drive. For a brief trip, make Monument Valley and Canyon de Chelly the priorities. With added days, you can visit a Native American trading post, Lake Powell and Glen Canyon, and the Four Corners. On your drive toward Interstate 40, be sure to spend an hour or two at Petrified Forest National Park where you'll see a prehistoric forest.

Logistics: Approximately 100 mi from Sedona, the fascinating sites of northeast Arizona are a destination unto themselves. Don't be fooled: this is a remote area and will take hours to reach, whether you're coming from Phoenix, Sedona, or the Grand Canyon. Most travelers view this corner of the state as a road-trip haven, as the highways offer one scenic drive after the other. Plan on making one of the main towns—Tuba City, Page, Window Rock—your base, and take day trips from there. No matter what your itinerary, plan ahead and make reservations

early: the best way to see these popular sites is via guided tour.

TUCSON, THE OLD WEST & HISTORIC SITES
2–4 Days

If culture and shopping are a bit more attractive, consider spending time in Tucson and visiting its neighboring historic communities. Spend at least a day in Tucson proper, visiting Mission San Xavier del Bac, the Saguaro National Park, and the Arizona-Sonora Desert Museum. If hiking is your game, don't miss Sabino Canyon, which offers gorgeous views of the area. With Tucson as your hub, take a day trip just a bit farther south to historic Tombstone and Bisbee. On the way back to the interstate, stop by Kartchner Caverns State Park for a view of the series of spectacular wet caves. Hour-long guided tours are available by reservation.

Logistics: Phoenix is two hours away via Interstate 10, a relatively unscenic drive. Casa Grande is the midway point between the two cities and is a good place to stop for a rest. History buffs may want to stop at Picacho Peak, site of the westernmost battle of the Civil War.

WHEN TO GO

Arizona

High season at the resorts of Phoenix and Tucson is winter. Expect the best temperatures—and the highest prices—from December through March, when nearly every weekend is filled with outdoor festivals. If you're on a budget, the posh desert resorts drop their prices from June through September. The South Rim of the Grand Canyon and Sedona are busy year-round, but least busy during the winter months. Statewide, Arizona's climate is extreme. While a winter visit might be most comfortable in Phoenix, the Grand Canyon, Flagstaff, and Sedona will be quite cold then.

New Mexico

The cool, dry climates of Santa Fe and Taos are a lure in summer, as is the skiing in Taos and Santa Fe in winter. Most Native American ceremonial dances at the pueblos occur in summer, early fall, and at Christmas and Easter. Other major events—including the Santa Fe Opera, Chamber Music Festival, and Native American and Spanish markets—are geared to the heavy tourist season of July and August. The Santa Fe Fiesta and New Mexico State Fair in Albuquerque are held in September, and the Albuquerque International Balloon Fiesta in October. Hotel rates are generally highest during the peak summer season. You can avoid the heaviest crowds by coming in spring or fall.

Southern Utah

Utah's national parks can become crowded and hot in summer. Southern Utah's weather can be ideal any time of year, though hot in summer. Be especially aware of the potential for flash floods in late summer in southern Utah parks, avoiding narrow canyons if there is any threat at all of a thunderstorm.

Southwest Colorado

Summer in Colorado begins in late June or early July. Daytime highs are often in the 80s; nighttime temperatures fall to the 40s and 50s. Fall begins in September, winter creeps in during November, and deep snows arrive by December. Winter tapers off in March, though snow lingers into April on valley bottoms and into July on mountain passes.

West Texas

Though the temperatures can reach 100° in the summer, nights are beautifully cool, combed by winds from the north. Snows carpet the area a few times each winter. Visitors are bound to find something going on each month—from rodeos to art festivals to Cinco de Mayo and Diez y Seis dde Septiembre (Mexican Independence Day) celebrations.

Las Vegas

The Vegas climate is pretty wonderful most of the year, with an average of 300 days of sunshine annually. Even during the warmer months (June–September), it's entirely bearable. Summer highs hover around 100°F with no humidity. The rest of the year, expect still more sun and only the occasional rainy days (the average annual rainfall is 4 inches), with highs in the 70s and 80s in spring and fall, and in the upper 50s and 60s in winter. Freezing temperatures are rare, but desert nights can get chilly between late fall and early spring.

Albuquerque

WORD OF MOUTH

"I always take a ride on the Sandia Peak Tramway. Every time is like the first. You get on at the base, you look up and think to yourself well it couldn't be all that bad . . . then you reach the top of the foothill, and the whole world bursts open like a dream!"
—BeachBoi

"Definitely go to a pueblo! Preferably after visiting the Cultural Center in Albuquerque."
—laurieb_nyny

Updated by
Lynne Arany

At first glance, Albuquerque appears to be a typical Sun Belt city, stretching out more than 100 square mi with no grand design, architectural or otherwise, to hold it together. The city's growth pattern seems as free-spirited as all those hot-air balloons that take part in the Albuquerque International Balloon Fiesta every October. In reality though, this spread-out city bears the distinction of more than 300 years of habitation (2006 ushered in a jubilant year of Tricentennial celebrations). With a bit of exploration, your initial impression of an asphalt maze softens. The distinctive blend of Spanish, Mexican, Native American, Anglo, and Asian influences spread throughout its neighborhoods making Albuquerque a vibrant multicultural metropolis.

Today Albuquerque is the center of New Mexico's educational institutions and financial, manufacturing, and medical industries. It's an unpretentious, practical city with a metro population of nearly 850,000 remarkably easygoing folks. Albuquerque's economy continues to diversify. Intel, the world's largest computer-chip maker, has one of its biggest manufacturing centers here, in the fast-growing northern suburb of Rio Rancho. To the south, the immense Mesa del Sol project has taken root. In addition to a progressive, planned community, it brings with it key international solar-power developers and two very heavy anchors for the state's burgeoning film industry: Albuquerque "Q" Studios and Sony Pictures Imageworks.

The city's substantial arts scene, proudly distinctive from that of Santa Fe and Taos, is apparent the moment you step off a plane at Albuquerque International Sunport and see the works of New Mexican artists throughout the terminal. Significant museums and galleries draw much local support, and feed off the creative energy of the many artists, writers, poets, filmmakers, and musicians who call this area home.

Outdoor enthusiasts will also find plenty of options both in town and a very short drive away as well. Engaging mountainside frontier towns, unique wilderness areas, and the Indian pueblos of the high desert and the Rio Grande Valley are all just beyond Albuquerque's city limits.

ORIENTATION & PLANNING

GETTING ORIENTED

Colorful Historic Route 66 is Albuquerque's Central Avenue, unifying, as nothing else, the diverse areas of the city—Old Town cradled at the bend of the Rio Grande; the downtown business, government, arts, and entertainment center to the east; the University of New Mexico farther east (and EDo, or East Downtown, in-between), and the Nob Hill strip of restaurants and shops past the university. Uptown and the Heights are north and east of Nob Hill. And the North Valley area is back west again, sitting above Old Town. The South Valley and Barelas are just below it and Downtown. The railroad tracks and Central Avenue divide the city into quadrants—Southwest, Northwest, Southeast, and Northeast.

TOP REASONS TO GO

For a drive up the Camino Real (North Fourth St.) or south into Barelas where you'll glimpse vintage shops and taqueria with hand-painted signage in a wonderfully idiosyncratic script and blazing hot colors. Be sure to pause for a bite at Red Ball, Barelas Coffeehouse, or Mary & Tito's. To visit the **KiMo Theatre**, in the center of downtown right on old Rte. 66—a spectacularly embellished Pueblo Deco. A tour inside is a must, as is a sigh of thanks that the city found the funds to restore this palace.

To walk or bike the **Paseo del Bosque** along the Rio Grande. The scenery along the 16-mile trail is a menagerie of cottonwoods, migrating birds, and the ever-present river rippling quietly at your side.

To experience **The National Hispanic Cultural Center**, a one-of-a-kind music and arts venue.

To witness the sunset over the volcanoes in the western desert—a brilliant pink flood that creeps over the valley making its way east to illuminate the Sandias before disappearing. Even better when the scent of roasting green chili fills the late August air.

Old Town, Downtown, EDo (East Downtown), and Barelas. Old Town, Downtown, EDo, and Barelas each represent distinct moments in the city's growth, and you're not likely to find a richer range of architecture in such a small area anywhere. Each of these historic enclaves—we're talking early 1800s through modern times—carries the charms of cultures past and a sense of respect for their place in Albuquerque's future.

University of New Mexico & Nob Hill. The spirit of the University neighborhood has its heart in the campus itself, though its early 20th-century roots are harder to find as the school continues to grow. Nob Hill was an empty landscape until mid-century, when local developers had a vision. Its many remaining Route 66–vintage structures are a fine counterpoint to those you'll find in downtown and Old Town.

North Valley & Northeast Heights. The North Valley and its sister South Valley are the agrarian heart of Albuquerque. It is here one experiences the deepest sense of tradition, where generation after generation of Hispanic families have resided. Change comes slowly, and most would never dream of leaving. The Northeast Heights, however, is all about growth, and can feel like a town apart. Homes here often belong to folks from elsewhere, and are certain to capitalize on their almost startling proximity to the Sandias.

WHEN TO GO

Fall is the season of choice. On just about any day, come late August through November, big balloons waft across the sharp blue sky and the scent of freshly roasting green chiles permeates the air. While Balloon Fiesta brings in the crowds in early October, things are plenty nice—and way cheaper too—after the hot-air hullabaloo. Usually 10°F warmer than Santa Fe's, Albuquerque's winter days are often mild enough for most outdoor activities. The occasional frigid spike is usually gone by morning. Spring brings winds, though it's lovely too, and rates stay low until the summer crowds flock in. Avoid them—late June through July can be brutally hot. August brings cooler temperatures, humidity, and the spectacular cloud formations that herald the brief "monsoon" season.

GETTING HERE & AROUND

BY AIR   The major gateway to New Mexico is Albuquerque International Sunport (ABQ), which is 65 mi southwest of Santa Fe and 130 mi south of Taos.

BY BUS   Buses are practical for getting between Old Town, downtown, and Nob Hill (and all the way to Uptown); the bus system's expedited RapidRide service plies this route and runs until about 8PM Sun–Thurs., and till the wee hours on Fri. and Sat. For routes throughout the city, the friendly folks at ABQ Ride will even provide you with a customized trip plan. The Alvarado Transportation Center downtown is ABQ Ride's central hub, and offers direct connections to the NM Rail Runner train service north to Bernalillo and Santa Fe, as well as points south. Buses accept bicycles, although space is limited. Service is free on the "Downtown Circulator" shuttle route, or if you are transferring (to any route) from the Rail Runner; otherwise fare is $1 (bills or coins, exact change only; 25-cent transfers may be requested on boarding). Bus stops are well marked. *See also Bus Travel in the Essentials chapter.*

BY CAR   Although the city's public bus service, ABQ Ride, provides good coverage, this is still a city where a car is the easiest and most convenient way to get around. Albuquerque sprawls out in all directions, but getting around town is not difficult. The main highways through the city, north–south I–25 and east–west I–40, converge just northeast of downtown and generally offer the quickest access to outlying neighborhoods and the airport. Rush-hour jams are common in the mornings and late afternoons, but they're still far less severe than in most big U.S. cities. All the major car-rental agencies are represented at Albuquerque's Sunport Airport.

BY TAXI   Taxis are metered in Albuquerque, and service is around-the-clock. Given the considerable distances around town, cabbing it can be expensive; figure about $9 from downtown to Nob Hill, and about $20 from the airport to an Uptown hotel. There's also a $1 airport fee.

BY TRAIN   In summer 2006 the City of Albuquerque launched the state's first-ever commuter train line, the *New Mexico Rail Runner Express.* As of this writing, convenient service from Downtown Albuquerque to Santa Fe is on-schedule for completion in early winter 2009. Currently service is from Bernalillo south through the city of Albuquerque, continuing south through Los Lunas to the suburb of Belén, covering a distance of about 50 mi. *In-town stops are currently Downtown, at the Alvarado Transportation Center, and at the north end of town at Journal Center/Los Ranchos. Generally service is limited to commuting hours Mon.–Fri., though it expands to late nights and weekends for special events (such as Balloon Fiesta), but plans are in place for it to run on Saturdays beginning in 2009, and eventually on Sundays.*

Fares are zone-based (one-way, from $1 to $7); discounted day passes ($2–$9) are available; bicycles ride free. Connections to local bus service are available at most stations. *For information on Amtrak service, see Train Travel in New Mexico Essentials.*

TOURS The Albuquerque Museum of Art and History leads free, hour-long historical walks through Old Town at 11 AM except Monday, from March through November.

A back-country and local history expert, Roch Hart owner of **NM Jeep Tours** offers jeep tours and guided hikes that start out from Albuquerque and go as far as time—and permits—allow. He can suggest an itinerary (ghost towns, rock formations, petroglyphs), or tailor one to your interests and timeframe.

ESSENTIALS **Air Contact Albuquerque International Sunport** (☎ *505/244-7700* ⊕ *www. cabq.gov/airport*).

Bus Contact ABQ Ride (☎ *505/243-7433 (RIDE)* ⊕ *www.cabq.gov/transit*).

Taxi Contact Albuquerque Cab (☎ *505/883-4888*). **Yellow Cab** (☎ *505/247-8888*).

Train Contact *New Mexico Rail Runner Express* (☎ *505/245-7245* ⊕ *www. nmrailrunner.com*).

Tour Contacts Albuquerque Museum of Art and History (☎ *505/243-7255* ⊕ *www.cabq.gov/museum.*) **NM Jeep Tours** ☎ *505/252-0112* ⊕ *nmjeeptours.com*).

VISITOR INFORMATION

The Albuquerque CVB operates tourism information kiosks at the airport (on the baggage claim level) and in Old Town on Plaza Don Luis, across from San Felipe de Neri church.

Albuquerque Convention and Visitors Bureau (✉ *PO Box 26866* ☎ *505/ 842-9918 or 800/284-2282* ⊕ *www.itsatrip.org*). **State Information Center** (✉ *Indian Pueblo Cultural Center, 2401 12th St. NW,* ☎ *505/843-7270* ⊕ *www. newmexico.org*).

PLANNING YOUR TIME

Although the city stretches out over considerable sprawl, it conveniently breaks down into a few distinct regions. The Rio Grande River corridor is a great place to start. Many of the best museums are clustered near Rio Grande Boulevard. A trip across the river takes you to Petroglyph National Monument. With a car, neighborhoods just east such as Old Town and Downtown are easily traversed.

I-25 defines a central north-south route. From University of New Mexico on the south, consider ditching the car for awhile and switching to Central Avenue's RapidRide bus. It's just a short spin—by car or bus—east to Nob Hill and its enclave of shops and restaurants, or west to EDo. From downtown, it's a short drive (or bus ride) due south on 4th Street to the National Hispanic Cultural Center. Back in the car now, on I-25 heading north and approaching I-40, consider a shopping detour to Indian Jewelers Supply. Further north, take in the Gruet Winery, then venture a bit west for the Balloon Museum, or a bit east to the

Bien Mur Indian Market. Heading further east, to catch the breathtaking sunset from the Sandia Peak Tram, is quite convenient from here.

Running through the Sandia foothills, is Tramway Boulevard. Not only your access point to side-trips to the crest, the Turquoise Trail to Santa Fe, and Mountainair to the south, this route takes you directly to the Sandia Tram base terminal. A day's worth of hiking and mountain-bike trails and wooded picnic grounds (Elena Gallegos is especially nice) pepper this area, which is part of the Cibola National Forest. From here you are ideally situated to visit a place that explores another essential component of Albuquerque's history and heritage, the National Museum of Nuclear Science and History, nearby on Eubank Boulevard.

EXPLORING ALBUQUERQUE

Albuquerque's terrain is diverse. Along the river in the north and south valleys, the elevation hovers at about 4,800 feet. East of the river, the land rises gently to the foothills of the Sandia Mountains, which rise to higher than 6,000 feet; the 10,378-foot summit is a grand spot from which to view the city below. West of the Rio Grande, where much of Albuquerque's growth is taking place, the terrain rises abruptly in a string of mesas topped by five volcanic cones. The changes in elevation from one part of the city to another result in corresponding changes in temperature, as much as 10°F at any time. It's not uncommon for snow or rain to fall on one part of town but for it to remain dry and sunny in another. ■ TIP➡ **Although it's generally easy to negotiate the city's grid-like geography, and local bus service is quite good, many attractions are a considerable distance apart, making a car a necessity for at least part of your stay (car-rental rates are quite reasonable here, however—especially if you can pick yours up at an off-airport site).**

Numbers correspond to the Albuquerque and Albuquerque Old Town maps.

OLD TOWN, DOWNTOWN, EDO & BARELAS

Albuquerque's social and commercial anchor since the settlement was established in 1706, Old Town and the surrounding blocks contain the wealth of the city's top cultural attractions, including several excellent museums. The action extends from the historic Old Town Plaza for several blocks in all directions—most of the museums are north and east of the Plaza. In this area you'll also find a number of restaurants and scads of shops. Some of these places are touristy and should be overlooked, but the better ones are included in the Where to Eat and Shopping sections of this chapter. The artsy Saw Mill and Wells Park/Mountain Road neighborhoods extend just east of Old Town's museum row; the Duranes section, where the Indian Pueblo Cultural Center commands attention, is just a bit beyond walking distance to the northeast of Old Town.

To reach Albuquerque's up-and-coming downtown from Old Town, it's a rather drab (though quick) 1¼-mi bus ride, walk, or drive southeast along Central Avenue. Although downtown doesn't have many formal attractions short of its anchor (and definitely destination-worthy) art gallery scene, this bustling neighborhood is one of the West's great urban comebacks. It's a diverting place to wander, gallery-hop, shop, snack (or dine), or simply soak in some fine remnants from its Route 66–era boom years for a couple of hours. From here, you're a skip away on the south to the historic Barelas neighborhood, and its superb must-see, the National Hispanic Cultural Center. And to the east is another revitalizing section of town; now known as EDo (East Downtown) and encompassing the historic Huning Highland District, this is where Albuquerque's Old Main Library—an architectural gem—and Gothic Revival high school (now condo's) still stand, and restaurants and shops seem to sprout-up daily.

WHAT TO SEE

⑤ Albuquerque BioPark. This city's foremost outdoor attraction and nature center, the park comprises the recently restored Tingley Beach as well as three distinct attractions, Albuquerque Aquarium, Rio Grande Botanic Garden, and Rio Grande Zoo. The garden and aquarium are located together (admission gets you into both facilities); the zoo is a short drive southeast. You can also ride the scenic *Rio Line* vintage narrow-gauge railroad between the zoo and gardens and aquarium complex; rides are free if you purchase a combination ticket to all of the park's facilities.

Two main components of the Albuquerque Biological Park, **Albuquerque Aquarium** and **Rio Grande Botanic Garden** (✉*2601 Central Ave. NW west of Old Town, north of Central Ave and just east of the Central Ave. bridge*) are a huge draw with kids but also draw plenty of adult visitors. At the aquarium, a spectacular shark tank with floor-to-ceiling viewing is among the most popular of the marine exhibits here. The Spanish-Moorish garden is one of three walled gardens near the entrance of the 36-acre botanic garden. The exquisite Sasebo Japanese Garden joins other specialty landscapes including the Curandera Garden, exhibiting herbs used by traditional Spanish folk medicine practitioners, and the Children's Fantasy Garden, complete with walk-through pumpkin, a 14-foot dragon, and giant bees. The seasonal PNM Butterfly Pavilion is open late May through late September, and year-round, the glass conservatory holds desert and Mediterranean plantings. In summer there are music concerts given on Thursday at the Botanic Garden. And from late November through late December, the Botanic Garden comes alive each evening from 6 to 9 PM for the River of Lights festival, a walk-through show of holiday lights and decorations.

The 64-acre **Rio Grande Zoo** (✉*903 10th St. SW87102*) is an oasis of waterfalls, cottonwood trees, and naturalized animal habitats. More than 250 species of wildlife from around the world live here, including giraffes, camels, polar bears, elephants, zebras, and koalas. The Tropical America exhibit offers a bit of contrast for dry Albuquerque,

Albuquerque
BioPark **5**

Albuquerque
Museum of Art
and History **6**

American
International
Rattlesnake
Museum **3**

¡Explora! **9**

Indian Pueblo
Cultural
Center **10**

National Atomic
Museum **8**

New Mexico
Museum of
Natural History
and Science **7**

Old Town Plaza ..**1**

San Felipe
de Neri
Catholic
Church **2**

Turquoise
Museum **4**

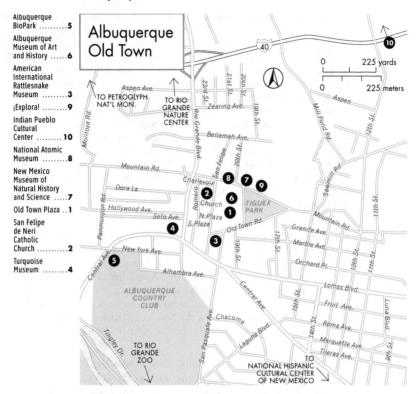

Albuquerque
Old Town

replicating a jungle rain forest and containing toucans, spider monkeys, and brilliant orchids and bromeliads. In keeping with its mission of wildlife care and conservation, the zoo has established captive breeding programs for more than a dozen endangered species. Concerts are performed on the grounds on summer Friday evenings. There's a café on the premises. The *Thunderbird Express* is a ¾-scale train that runs in a nonstop loop within the zoo, and during the 20-minute ride, conductors talk in depth about the creatures and their habitats. Running Tues.–Sun. only, it's free with combo tickets, or $2 otherwise (buy tickets onboard or at the Africa exhibit). **Tingley Beach** (⊠*1800 Tingley Dr. SW, south of Central Ave. and just east of Central Ave. bridge*) is a recreational arm of the biological park that consists of three ponds, created in the 1930s by diverting water from the Rio Grande. You can rent paddle boats (or bicycles; both seasonally), fish the trout-stocked ponds, (gear and fishing licenses available for purchase at the fishing-tackle shop on premises), or sail your model electric- or wind-powered boats. To the west of the ponds, the cottonwood bosque (wetlands forest) fringes the river. Ecological tours of the bosque are given in summer. It's part of the popular 16-mi Paseo del Bosque bike path that is open year-round. There's also a snack bar and a *Rio Line* station; the ¾-scale passenger trains make a stop here en route between the aquarium and garden complex and the zoo. ⊠*903 10th St. SW* ☎*505/764–*

1

6200 ⊕*www.cabq.gov/biopark* ✉*Free Tingley Beach and grounds, $7 Albuquerque Aquarium and Rio Grande Botanic Garden (combined ticket), $7 Rio Grande Zoo, $12 combination ticket for all attractions is available for entries Tues.–Sun. 9–noon, and includes unlimited rides on the Rio Line and Thunderbird Express trains ⊘Daily 9–5, until 6 on weekends, June–Aug. No trains Mon.*

❻ **Albuquerque Museum of Art and History.** This modern structure, which completed a key phase in a spectacular 40,000-square-foot expansion in the mid-2000s, houses the largest collection of Spanish-colonial artifacts in the nation, along with a superb photo archive and other relics of the city's birth and development. The "Common Ground" galleries represent an important permanent collection of primarily 20th-century paintings, all by world-renowned artists with a New Mexico connection. Changing exhibits also reveal a commitment to historically important artists and photographers of the 20th century and later. The centerpiece of "Four Centuries: A History of Albuquerque," is a pair of life-size models of Spanish conquistadors in original chain mail and armor. Perhaps the one on horseback is Francisco Vásquez de Coronado, who, in search of gold, led a small army into New Mexico in 1540—a turning point in the region's history. A multimedia presentation chronicles the development of the city since 1875. The sculpture garden contains more than 50 contemporary works by southwestern artists that include Glenna Goodacre, Michael Naranjo, and Luís Jiménez. Visitors may also take advantage of three tours, all offered at no additional charge with admission: Museum galleries Tues.–Sun. 2 pm; Sculpture Garden Tues.–Sat. 10 am, April through November; Old Town Tues.–Sun. 11 am, mid-March through mid-December. Each takes 45 minutes to an hour. ✉*2000 Mountain Rd. NW, Old Town* ☎*505/243–7255 Shop: 505/242–0434 Café: 505/242–5316* ⊕*www.albuquerquemuseum.com* ✉*$4 (NM residents $3); all tours included with admission. Free Sun. 9–1* ⊘*Tues.–Sun. 9–5 Store: 10–5 Café:.*

FodorśChoice
★

NEED A BREAK? At the Museum of Art & History an intimate outdoor amphitheater is home to live jazz and other musical programming on summer evenings. And year-round, perhaps after a bit of shopping in the sunlit Gallery Store, visitors can dine inside or out at the museum's **City Treats Café** (⊘10:30–4). The wood-lined café is very pleasant, and fresh offerings—grilled chicken salad with spinach and snap peas, and a homemade Mexican brownie—make this a good refueling stop here at the north end of Old Town.

❸ **American International Rattlesnake Museum.** Included in the largest collection of different species of living rattlers in the world are such rare and unusual specimens as an albino western diamondback. Looking for all the world like a plain old shop from the outside, inside the museum's informative exhibit labels, engaging staff, and an educational video supply visitors with the lowdown on these venomous creatures—for instance, they can't hear their own rattles, and the human death rate from rattlesnake bites is less than 1%. The mission here is to educate the public on the many positive benefits of rattlesnakes, and to con-

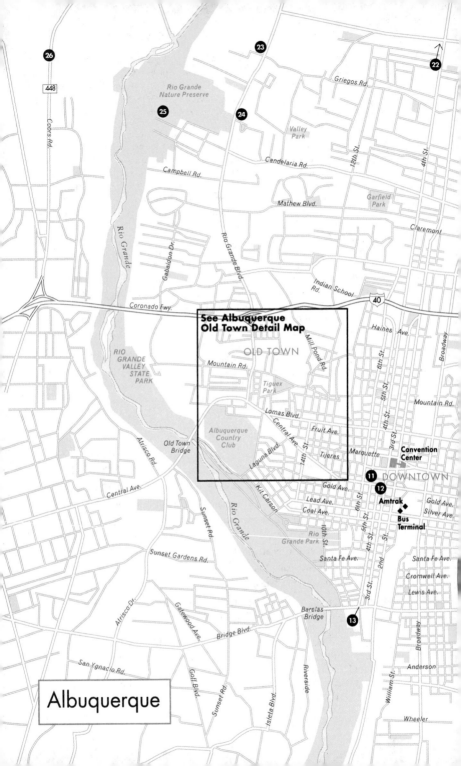

See Albuquerque Old Town Detail Map

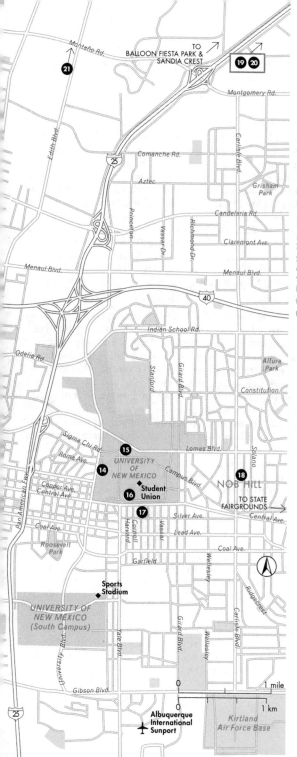

Anderson-Abruzzo
International Ballon Museum 21

Anderson Valley Vineyards 23

Casa Rondeña Winery 24

Gruet Winery 19

Jonson Gallery 15

Kimo Theater 11

Maxwell Museum
of Anthropology 14

National Hispanic
Cultural Center 13

New Mexico
Holocaust & Intolerance
Museum 12

Nob Hill 18

Petroglyph
National Monument 26

Rio Grande Nature Center
State Park 25

Sandia Peak
Aerial Tramway 20

Tamarind
Institute 17

UNM Art Museum 16

Unser Racing Museum 22

tribute to their conservation. ⊠*202 San Felipe St. NW, just off the southeast corner of the Plaza Old Town* ☎*505/242–6569* ⊕*www. rattlesnakes.com* ⊠*$3.50* ⊙*Mon.–Sat. 10–6, Sun. noon–5 (hrs sometimes shorter in winter, call ahead).*

❾ ★ ☋ ¡Explora! Albuquerque's cultural corridor received another jewel in 2003, when this imaginatively executed science museum—its driving concept is "Ideas You Can Touch"—opened right across from the New Mexico Museum of Natural History and Science. ¡Explora! bills itself as an all-ages attraction (and enthralled adults abound) but there's no question that many of the innovative hands-on exhibits—from a high-wire bicycle to kinetic sculpture—are geared especially to children, and offer big fun in addition to big science (and a good dose of art as well). While its colorful Bucky dome is immediately noticeable from the street, Explora also features a playground, theater, and a freestanding staircase that appears to "float" between floors. Like a recent visitor said, "Me encanta el museo." Waaaay cool. Ideas, their gift shop, is too. ⊠*1701 Mountain Rd. NW, Old Town* ☎*505/224–8300 Shop: 505/224–8349* ⊕*www.explora.us* ⊠*$7* ⊙*Mon.–Sat. 10–6, Sun. noon–6.*

❿ ★ ☋ Indian Pueblo Cultural Center. The multilevel semicircular design at this museum was inspired by Pueblo Bonito, the prehistoric ruin in Chaco Canyon in northwestern New Mexico. That layout is emphasized now that the museum entryway has been moved to the east-facing (and sacred) exposure. This phase of a 2008 renovation has made the entire space more welcoming, and suitable to its purpose of evoking the rich history and cultural traditions explored within. Start by watching the museum's video, which discusses the history of the region's Pueblo culture. Then move to the upper-level alcove, where changing exhibits feature different aspects of the arts and crafts of each of the state's 19 pueblos. Lower-level exhibits trace the history of the Pueblo people. Youngsters can touch Native American pottery, jewelry, weaving, tools, and dried corn at the Hands-On Corner and also draw petroglyph designs and design pots. Paintings, sculptures, jewelry, leather crafts, rugs, souvenir items, drums, beaded necklaces, painted bowls, and fetishes are for sale. Ceremonial dances are performed on weekends at 11 and 2, and there are also arts-and-crafts demonstrations each weekend. The Pueblo Harvest Café has been spruced up as well, and is a great spot for lunch (or any meal), where you can try such Native American fare as blue-corn pancakes and Indian tacos, or Native Fusion items like Picuris Pasta. ⊠*2401 12th St. NW, Los Duranes* ☎*505/843–7270 or 800/766–4405* ⊕*www.indianpueblo.org* ⊠*$6* ⊙*Daily 9–5.*

⓫ ★ KiMo Theatre. At the time the KiMo was built, in 1927, Route 66 was barely established and running on its original alignment: north-south on 4th St. Downtown was the center of community activity. And movie palaces were the national rage. Local merchant Oreste Bachechi saw his moment, and hired architect Carl Boller to design a theater that would reflect the local zeitgeist. And he certainly did. Decorated with light fixtures made from buffalo skulls (the eye sockets glow amber in the dark), Navajo symbols, and nine spectacular Western-themed wall murals by Carl Von Hassler, the KiMo represents Pueblo Deco at its apex. Luckily, it was saved from the wrecking ball in 1977 and so, now fully restored, it still stands—one of the few notable early-20th-century structures in downtown Albuquerque remaining. The self-guided tour is a must, or even better, catch a live performance. ✉*423 Central Ave. NW at 5th St., 87102Downtown* ☎*505/768–3522 Event info: 505/768–3544* ⊕*www.cabq.gov/kimo* ✍*Free self-guided tours* ⊙*Tues.–Fri. 8:30–4:30, Sat. 11–5.*

⑧ National Museum of Nuclear Science & History (aka National Atomic Museum).

⟳ Moved in 2009 from a temporary space in Old Town, and renamed as well, this popular museum traces the history of the atomic age and how nuclear science has dramatically influenced the course of modern history. Exhibits include replicas of Fat Man and Little Boy (the bombs dropped on Japan at the end of World War II), and there are children's programs and an exhibit about X-ray technology. With its renaming—and much larger facility—come even larger changes. Eight years after 9/11 security issues pushed them off of Kirtland Air Force Base, they are finally again able to display their mothballed B-29 and other mega-airships germane to their mission. All-new exhibits are also on view. A particularly notable one—and one that brings the scale of the Manhattan Project down to human level—is a restoration of the 1942 Plymouth that was used to transport the "Gadget"'s (as that first weapon was known) plutonium core down from Los Alamos, to the Trinity Site for testing. ✉*601 Eubank Blvd. SE, just a few blocks south of the Eubank Blvd. exit from I-40 SE Heights* ☎*505/245–2137* ⊕*www.atomicmuseum.org* ✍*$5* ⊙*Daily 9–5.*

NEED A BREAK? On the eastern fringe area of Old Town, in a nascent arts district, **Golden Crown Panaderia** (✉ *1103 Mountain Rd. NW, Old Town* ☎ *505/243–2424 or 877/382–2924)* is an aromatic, down-home style bakery known for two things: the ability to custom-design and bake unbelievably artful breads that can depict just about any person or place, and hearty green-chili bread (made with tomatoes, cilantro, Parmesan, green chili, and onions). You can also order hot cocoa, cappuccino, bizcochito (the official state cookie, they are also known as New Mexican wedding cookies), pumpkin-filled empanadas, and plenty of other sweets and sandwiches too (ask what bread is fresh and hot for yours). There's seating on a small patio. It's closed Sunday and Monday.

⑬ National Hispanic Cultural Center. A showpiece for the city, and a show-

Fodor's Choice case for Latino culture and genealogy in Albuquerque's old Barelas
★ neighborhood, this exciting, contemporary space contains a museum and art galleries, multiple performance venues, a 10,000-volume genealogical research center and library, a restaurant, and an education center. Exhibits include dynamic displays of photography and paintings by local artists as well as by internationally known names. The center mounts performances of flamenco dancing, bilingual theater, traditional Spanish and New Mexican music, world music, the symphony, and

more. This is the largest Latino cultural center in the country, and with a $10 million programming endowment (Rita Moreno and Edward James Olmos are among the notables on the national board), the center provides top-notch entertainment in its stunning and acoustically superb Roy E. Disney Center for Performing Arts and smaller Albuquerque Journal Theatre, and it hosts major traveling art exhibits in its first-rate museum, which also houses an esteemed permanent collection. Architecturally, the center borrows from a variety of Spanish cultures, from Moorish Spain (including a re-creation of a defensive tower, or Torreón; the finely detailed fresco that embellishes the interior's 45-foot-tall walls and ceiling depicts Hispanic cultural heritage through time) to Mexico and the American Southwest. One historic feature is a vintage WPA-era school that now contains the research library and La Fonda del Bosque restaurant (open for breakfast and lunch only), which serves solid New Mexican fare indoors and out on the patio; Sunday brunch, live music included, draws a big family crowd. The gift shop, La Tiendita, has a particularly well-chosen and impeccably sourced selection of books, pottery, and artwork. ⊠*1701 4th St. SW, at Avenida César Chavez (Bridge Blvd., Barelas* ☏*505/246–2261; Restaurant: 505/247–9480; Gift Shop: 505/766–6604; Box Office: 505/724–4771* ⊕*www.nhccnm.org* ⊠*$3* ⊗*Tues.–Sun. 10–5.*

⑫ **New Mexico Holocaust & Intolerance Museum.** Although it occupies a rather modest (especially when compared to the over-the-top KiMo Theatre next door) storefront in downtown Albuquerque, this moving museum packs plenty of punch with its low-budget but irrefutably poignant exhibits that document genocide and persecution against persons throughout history, with special emphasis, of course, placed upon the Holocaust carried out by the Nazis before and during World War II. Exhibits inside touch on child slave labor, the rescue of Bulgarian and Danish Jews, a re-created gate from a concentration camp, the Nuremburg Trials, and many artifacts related to Holocaust survivors and the Nazis. There are also areas that discuss other genocides throughout history, from the Bataan Death March to the extinguishing of indigenous cultures. ⊠*415 Central Ave. NW, Downtown* ☏*505/247–0606* ⊕*www.nmholocaustmuseum.org* ⊠*Donation suggested* ⊗*Tues.– Sat. 11–3:30.*

⑦ **New Mexico Museum of Natural History and Science.** The world of wonders
★ at Albuquerque's most popular museum includes the simulated vol-
☾ cano (with a river of bubbling hot lava flowing beneath the see-through glass floor), the frigid Ice Age cave, and new in 2008, "Dawn of the Dinosaurs." The only Triassic exhibit in North America, this permanent hall features some of the state's own rare finds. The Evolator— short for Evolution Elevator—a six-minute high-tech ride, uses video, sound, and motion to whisk you through 35 million years of New Mexico's geological history. A film in the Extreme Screen DynaTheater makes viewers feel equally involved. Arrive via the front walkway, and you'll be greeted by life-size bronze sculptures of a 21-foot-long horned pentaceratops and a 30-foot-long carnivorous albertosaur. Then, on the flip side of time, the Paul Allen-funded "Start-Up!" gal-

leries explore the silicon age. Point-
ing to the details of the birth of the
PC right here in the Duke City
(Allen and a very young Bill Gates
came here in the mid-1970s to create software for the Altair kits that
Ed Roberts designed down on the
south end of town, and the rest,
well, you know), these permanent

halls are a fascinating tour through the early garage days of many
such start-ups. It's a fun way to view Albuquerque history, too, as
well as appreciate the fair job they've done with the Apple side of the
story. Also at the museum is The LodeStar Science Center, which features a state-of-the-art planetarium; it's also used for the wildly popular First Friday Fractals program. ⊠*1801 Mountain Rd. NW, Old
Town* ☎*505/841–2800* ⊕*www.nmnaturalhistory.org* ✉*Museum $7,
DynaTheater $7, planetarium $7; combination ticket for any 2 attractions $12, for any 3 attractions $15* Friday Fractals tickets available
online only. ⊙*Daily 9–5.*

❶ Old Town Plaza. Don Francisco Cuervo y Valdés, a provincial governor
★ of New Mexico, laid out this small plaza in 1706. No slouch when it
☼ came to political maneuvering, he named the town after the duke of
Albuquerque, viceroy of New Spain. He hoped flattery would induce
the duke to waive the requirement that a town have 30 families before
a charter was issued—there were only 15 families living here in 1706.
The duke acquiesced. (Albuquerque is nicknamed "The Duke City," so
he's hardly been forgotten.) Today the plaza is an oasis of tranquility
filled with shade trees, wrought-iron benches, a graceful white gazebo,
and strips of grass. Roughly 200 shops, restaurants, cafés, galleries, and
several cultural sites in *placitas* (small plazas) and lanes surround Old
Town Plaza. During fiestas Old Town comes alive with mariachi bands
and dancing señoritas. ■TIP➡**Seasonally, the Albuquerque Museum
(⇨ above) offers an excellent guided walking tour that details local history and the range of historic architecture that remains intact here.** Mostly
dating back to the late 1800s, styles from Queen Anne to Territorial
and Pueblo Revival, and even Mediterranean, are apparent in the one-
and two-story (almost all adobe) structures. Event schedules and maps,
which contain a list of public restrooms and many Old Town shops and
sights (but by no means all), are available at the **Old Town Visitors
Center** (⊠*303 Romero St. NW, Old Town* ☎*505/243–3215* ⊕*www.
itsatrip.org*), which is somewhat hidden in the rear of Plaza Don Luis,
across the street from the San Felipe de Neri Catholic Church. The
center, an outpost of the Albuquerque Convention & Visitors Bureau,
also offers a wide selection of tourism brochures for attractions city-
wide and beyond. It is open daily, typically 9–4:30 but usually a bit
later in summer.

❷ San Felipe de Neri Catholic Church. More than two centuries after it first
welcomed worshippers, this structure, erected in 1793, is still active.
The building, which replaced Albuquerque's first Catholic church, has

been enlarged and expanded several times, but its adobe walls and other original features remain. Small gardens front and flank the church; the inside is a true respite from the tourism bustle beyond its doorstep—the painting and iconography is simple, authentic, and lovely, the atmosphere hushed. Next to it is a shop and small museum that displays relics—vestments, paintings, carvings—dating from the 17th century. ■TIP→ **There's a hidden treasure behind the church: inside the gnarled tree is a statue that some speculate depicts the Virgin Mary.** ⊠*2005 Plaza NW, Old Town* ☎*505/243–4628* ⊙*Church open to public daily 8* AM*–dusk; museum Mon.–Sat. 1–4. Call ahead to confirm hrs.*

❹ **Turquoise Museum.** Located just west of the hub-bub of Old Town, this strip-mall museum focuses on the beauty, mythology, and physical properties of turquoise, a semiprecious but widely adored gemstone that many people understandably associate with the color of New Mexico's skies. A self-guided tour, entered via a simulated mine shaft, leads to one-of-a-kind showpieces and examples from more than 65 mines on four continents. Displays show how turquoise is formed, talk about the importance of individual mines, and highlight its uses by Native Americans in prehistoric times. At the education center you can learn how to distinguish the real McCoy from plastic. The museum's proprietors are a multi-generation family of longtime traders, and they know whereof they speak; if you retain nothing else, do remember that only turquoise specified as "natural" is the desirable, and most importantly, unadulterated stuff. There is an active silversmith's shop adjacent to the display area; a small gift shop offers historic and contemporary pieces. ⊠*2107 Central Ave. NW, on the west side of Rio Grande Blvd, in a modern shopping center across the street from the main Plaza area Old Town* ☎*505/247–8650* ⊡*$4* ⊙*Weekdays 9:30–5, Sat. 9:30–4 (last tour entries are one hour before closing).*

▌ NEED A
BREAK?

On the east side of downtown in the historic Huning Highland district (though this stretch along Central Avenue is now commonly called EDo), the many temptations of **The Grove Cafe & Market** (⊠ *600 Central Ave. SE, EDo* ☎*505/248–9800*) await you. Perfect for breakfast or lunch (sorry, no dinner), among a flock of interesting options in this short strip, it's a good stop as you continue east to the University of New Mexico and Nob Hill districts. This airy, modern establishment is a local favorite that features locally grown, seasonal specials at coolly reasonable prices. Enjoy such supremely fresh and best-quality treats as Grove Pancakes with fresh fruit, crème fraiche, local honey, and real maple syrup or a Farmers Salad with roasted golden beets, marcona almonds, goat cheese, and lemon basil vinaigrette, or an aged genoa salami sandwich with olive tapanade, arugula, and provolone on an artisan sourdough bread. You can dine on the arbored patio. Or come by for a loose-leaf tea or latte with a cupcake.

UNIVERSITY OF NEW MEXICO & NOB HILL

Established in 1889, the University of New Mexico is the state's leading institution of higher education, with internationally recognized programs in anthropology, biology, Latin American studies, and medicine. Its many outstanding galleries and museums are open to the public free of charge. The university's

> **GOOD TERM**
>
> Kiva fireplace: A corner fireplace whose round form resembles that of a kiva, a ceremonial room used by Native Americans of the Southwest.

Pueblo Revival–style architecture is noteworthy, particularly the old wing of Zimmerman Library and the Alumni Chapel, both designed by John Gaw Meem, a Santa Fe–based architect whose mid-20th century work dominates the campus.

Off-campus life is focused directly to the south and east of school, stretching along Central Avenue from University Blvd. east through the Nob Hill neighborhood. Low-budget eateries, specialty shops, and music and arts venues are tightly clustered within the college-named streets just to the south of Central; things get more upscale as you head further east.

WHAT TO SEE

⑮ Jonson Gallery. The home and studio of Raymond Jonson (1891–1982) house the abstract, colorful works of this pioneering Modernist (and founder, in 1938, of the Transcendental Painting Group) whose paintings and drawings focused on mass and form. The gallery was designed by John Gaw Meem in 1950 to show off the then-new modernism in an appropriately tailored setting. Each summer it mounts a major Jonson retrospective and also exhibits 21st-century works of sculpture, video, and photography, as well as maintaining an important archive on the founding artist and his contemporaries. The Jonson is expected to relocate to a space within the UNM Art Museum by early 2010. ✉ *1909 Las Lomas Rd. NE, mid-campus, to the east of Yale Blvd. University of New Mexico* ☎ *505/277–4967* ⊕ *www.unm.edu/~jonsong* 💲 *Free* ⊙ *Tues.–Fri. 9–4 and by appointment.*

⑭ Maxwell Museum of Anthropology. Many of the more than 2½ million artifacts at the Maxwell, the first public museum in Albuquerque (established in 1932), come from the Southwest. Two permanent exhibitions chronicle 4 million years of human history and the lifeways, art, and cultures of 11,500 years of human settlement in the Southwest. The photographic archives contain more than 250,000 images, including some of the earliest photos of Pueblo and Navajo cultures. The museum shop sells traditional and contemporary southwestern Native American jewelry, rugs, pottery, basketry, and beadwork, along with folk art from around the world. In the children's section are inexpensive books and handmade tribal artifacts. Parking permits for adjacent UNM lots are available inside the museum. ✉ *Redondo West Dr. on the west end of campus, just east of University Blvd. NE, between Las Lomas Rd. NE and Dr. Martin Luther King Blvd. NE, University of*

New Mexico, ☎*505/277–4405* ⊕*www.unm.edu/~maxwell* ⊠*Free* ⊘*Tues.–Fri. 9–4, Sat. 10–4.*

⓲ Nob Hill. The heart of Albuquerque's Route 66 culture and also its hippest, funkiest retail and entertainment district, Nob Hill is the neighborhood just east of UNM, with its commercial spine extending along Central Avenue (old Route 66). Along this stretch you'll find dozens of offbeat shops, arty cafés, and student hangouts, and on the blocks just north and south of Central Avenue, you'll see an eclectic assortment of building styles. Most of the hipper and more gentrified businesses are along the stretch of Central between UNM and Carlisle Boulevard, but the activity is gradually moving east. Old art deco strip malls and vintage motels along this stretch are slowly being transformed into new restaurants and shops. The neighborhood was developed during the 1930s and '40s, peaked in prosperity and popularity during the 1950s, and then fell into a state of decline from the 1960s through the mid-'80s. It was at this time that a group of local business and property owners formed a neighborhood group and banded together to help turn the neighborhood around, and Nob Hill has been enjoying great cachet and popularity ever since. ⊠*Central Ave., from University of New Mexico campus east to Washington St., Nob Hill.*

⓱ Tamarind Institute. This world-famous institution played a major role in reviving the fine art of lithographic printing, which involves working with plates of traditional stone and modern metal. Tamarind certification is to a printer what a degree from Juilliard is to a musician. A small gallery within the facility exhibits prints and lithographs by well-known masters like Jim Dine, and up-and-comers in the craft as well. Guided tours (reservations essential) are conducted on the first Friday of each month at 1:30. Plans are in place for Tamarind to move around the corner to freshly outfitted space in the old UNM architecture building in time for their 50th anniversary in 2010. ⊠*110 Cornell Dr. SE, University of New Mexico 87106* ☎*505/277–3901* ⊕*tamarind.unm. edu* ⊠*Free* ⊘*By appt., Tues.–Fri. 9–5.*

⓰ UNM Art Museum. A handsome facility inside the UNM Center for the Arts, the museum holds New Mexico's largest collection of fine art. Works of old masters share wall space with the likes of Picasso and O'Keeffe, and many photographs and prints are on display. Lectures and symposia, gallery talks, and guided tours are regularly scheduled. ⊠*University of New Mexico Center for the Arts, north of Central Ave. entrance opposite Cornell Dr. SE* ☎*505/277–4001* ⊕*unmartmuseum. unm.edu* ⊠*Free* ⊘*Tues. 9–4 and 5–8, Wed.–Fri. 9–4, Sat.–Sun. 1–4.*

NEED A BREAK?

The definitive student hangout, the **Frontier Restaurant** (⊠*2400 Central Ave. SE 87106at Cornell Dr. SE* ☎*505/266–0550*) is across from UNM and open daily for inexpensive diner-style American and New Mexican chow. Arguably a notch up from a fast-food joint, they are open later than most such spots in town and their breakfast burritos are just fine. Featured along with the John Wayne and Elvis artwork in this sprawling '70s spot are their oversize cinnamon buns. We won't fault you if you cave in and order one.

NORTH VALLEY & INTO THE HEIGHTS

Most of the other attractions in the city lie north of downtown, Old Town, and the University of New Mexico and Nob Hill areas. Quite a few, including the Anderson and Casa Rodeña wineries and the Rio Grande Nature Center, are clustered in two of the city's longest-settled areas: the more rural and lush cottonwood-lined North Valley and Los Ranchos, along the Rio Grande. Early Spanish settlers made their homes here, building on top of even earlier Pueblo homesteads. Historic adobe houses abound. This area is a natural gateway to the West Side. Drive across the lovely Montaño Road bridge and Petroglyph National Monument is moments away, as is the highly recommended side-trip destination, Corrales (⇨ *Side Trips from the Cities chapter*). The Northeast Heights is another matter, with east being the operative word. Here, you are in the foothills of the Sandia Mountains, in upscale neighborhoods that surprise your senses with the sudden appearance of foliage like piñon and ponderosa, which are seen nowhere else in the city. Trips to this area are best combined with more north-central venues like the Bien Shur market or the Balloon museum.

WHAT TO SEE

㉑ **Anderson-Abruzzo International Balloon Museum.** Opened in 2005 at Bal-
★ loon Fiesta Park, the dramatic museum celebrates the city's legacy as the hot-air ballooning capital of the world. This dashing, massive facility is named for Maxie Anderson and Ben Abruzzo, who pioneered ballooning in Albuquerque and were part of a team of three aviators who made the first manned hot-air balloon crossing of the Atlantic Ocean in 1978. You can understand the reason for constructing such a large museum when you examine some of the exhibits inside—these include several actual balloons of important historic note as well as both large- and small-scale replicas of balloons and zeppelins. You'll also see vintage balloon baskets, actual china and flatware used from the ill-fated *Hindenburg* as well as an engaging display on that tragic craft, and dynamic displays that trace the history of the sport, dating back to the first balloon ride, in 1783. Kids can design their own balloons at one particularly creative interactive exhibit. There's a large museum shop offering just about any book or product you could imagine related to hot-air ballooning.

★ The museum anchors Albuquerque's Balloon Fiesta Park, home to the legendary **Albuquerque International Balloon Fiesta** (☎ *505/821–1000 or 888/422–7277* ⊕ *www.balloonfiesta.com*), which began in 1972 and runs for nearly two weeks in early October. Albuquerque's long history of ballooning dates from 1882, when Professor Park A. Van Tassel, a saloon keeper, ascended in a balloon at the Territorial Fair. During the fiesta, which is the largest hot-air-balloon gathering anywhere, you can watch the Special Shapes Rodeo, when hundreds of unusual balloons, including depictions of the old lady who lived in the shoe, the pink pig, and dozens of other fanciful characters from fairy tales and popular culture, soar high above the more than a million spectators. There are night flights, obstacle races, and many other surprising balloon events. Book your hotel far in advance if you plan to attend, and note that hotel rates also rise during the fiesta. ✉ *9201 Balloon Museum Dr. NE, off Alameda Blvd. west of I–25, Northeast Heights* ☎ *505/768–6020* ⊕ *www.balloonmuseum.com* ☞ *$4* ⊙ *Tues.–Sun. 9–5.*

> **DID YOU KNOW?**
>
> Franciscan monks first planted their grapevines in New Mexico before moving more successfully to northern California.

㉓ Anderson Valley Vineyards. A low-key winery that was established in 1973 and enjoys a dramatic, pastoral North Valley setting not far from the Rio Grande, Anderson Valley specializes in chardonnay and cabernet sauvignon. The staff in the intimate tasting room is friendly and knowledgeable, and you can sip your wine while relaxing on an enchanting patio with wonderful views of the Sandia Mountains in the distance. In this agrarian, tranquil setting, it's hard to imagine that you're just a little more than 3 mi north of the bustle of Old Town and downtown. ✉ *4920 Rio Grande Blvd. NW, between Montaño and Chavez Rds. NW North Valley* ☎ *505/344–7266* w *www.nmwine.com* ☞ *Free* ⊙ *Tues.–Sun. noon–5.*

㉔ Casa Rondeña Winery. Perhaps the most architecturally stunning of New
★ Mexico's wineries, Casa Rondeña—which is technically in the burg of Los Ranchos de Albuquerque, not the Duke City proper—strongly resembles a Tuscan villa, with its green-tile roof winery and verdant grounds laced with gardens and fountains. To look at it all, it is hard to believe that most of the structures here went up with the winery's founding in 1995. Casa Rondeña produces a superb cabernet franc, one of the most esteemed vintages in New Mexico. Features that you can see during your visit include a vintage oak fermentation tank and a Great Hall with soaring ceilings, where tastings are conducted. The winery hosts a number of events, including a chamber music festival with wine receptions and dinners. ✉ *733 Chavez Rd. NW, between Rio Grande Blvd. and 4th St. NW North Valley* ☎ *505/344–5911 or 800/706–1699* ⊕ *www.casarondena.com* ☞ *Free* ⊙ *Wed.–Sat. 10–6, Sun. noon–6.*

⑲ Gruet Winery. It's hard to imagine a winetasting experience with less curb
★ appeal. Gruet Winery sits along an ugly access road paralleling I–25, sandwiched between an RV showroom and a lawn-furniture store. But behind the vaguely chalet-like exterior of this otherwise modern industrial building, you're afforded the chance to visit one of the nation's most acclaimed producers of sparkling wines (to see its actual vineyards though, you will have to head south to Truth or Consequences). Gruet had been famous in France since the 1950s for its champagnes. Here in New Mexico, where the Gruet family has been producing wine since 1984, it's earned nationwide kudos for its Methode Champenoise, as well as for impressive pinot noirs, syrahs, and chardonnays. Many of the state's top restaurants now carry Gruet vintages. Tastings include the chance to sample five wines and to take home a souvenir glass. ✉ *8400 Pan American Freeway NE (north frontage rd for I–25), on the east side of I–25, between Alameda Blvd. and Paseo del Norte Northeast Heights* ☎ *505/821–0055 or 888/857–9463* ⊕ *www.*

gruetwinery.com 🎟*Free; $6 for a 5-wine tasting* ⏲*Weekdays 10–5, Sat. noon–5; tours Mon.–Sat. at 2.*

26 ★ **Petroglyph National Monument.** Beneath the stumps of five extinct volcanoes, this park encompasses more than 25,000 ancient Native American rock drawings inscribed on the 17-mi-long West Mesa escarpment overlooking the Rio Grande Valley. For centuries, Native American hunting parties camped at the base, chipping and scribbling away. Archaeologists believe most of the petroglyphs were carved on the lava formations between the years 1100 and 1600, but some images at the park may date as far as 1000 BC. Walking trails provide access to them. A paved trail at **Boca Negra Canyon** (north of the visitor center on Unser Boulevard, beyond Montaño Road) leads past several dozen petroglyphs. The trail at **Rinconado Canyon** (south of the visitor center on Unser) is unpaved. The rangers at the visitor center will supply maps and help you determine which trail is best for the time you have. ✉*Visitor center, 6001 Unser Blvd. NW, at Western Trail Rd., 3 mi north of I-40 Exit 154; from I-25 take Exit 228 and proceed west on Montaño Rd. across the bridge, then south on Unser 1 mi West Side* ☎*505/899–0205* 🌐*www.nps.gov/petr* 🎟*$1 weekdays, $2 weekends* ⏲*Daily 8–5.*

25 **Rio Grande Nature Center State Park.** Along the banks for the Rio Grande, this year-round 170-acre refuge in a portion of the Bosque (about midway up on the Paseo del Bosque trail) is the nation's largest cottonwood forest. If bird-watching is your thing, you've come to the right place: this is home to all manner of birds and migratory waterfowl. Constructed half aboveground and half below the edge of a pond, the park's glass-walled interpretive center (an interesting small-scale building by noted NM architect Antoine Predock) has viewing windows that provide a look at what's going on at both levels, and speakers broadcast the sounds of the birds you're watching into the room. You may see birds, frogs, ducks, and turtles. The park has active programs for adults and children and trails for biking, walking, and jogging. **TIP→ Keep your eye out for what appears to be a game of jacks abandoned by giants: these jetty jacks were built in the 1950s to protect the Rio Grande levees from flood debris.** ✉*2901 Candelaria Rd. NW, 1 ½ mi north on Rio Grande Blvd. from I-40 exit 157A North Valley* ☎*505/344–7240* 🌐*www.rgnc.org or www.nmparks.com* 🎟*$3 per vehicle; grounds free* ⏲*Nature Center daily 10–5, park daily 8–5.*

20 ★ **Sandia Peak Aerial Tramway.** Tramway cars climb 2.7 mi up the steep western face of the Sandias, giving you a close-up view of red rocks and tall trees—it's the world longest aerial tramway. From the observation deck at the 10,378-foot summit you can see Santa Fe to the northeast and Los Alamos to the northwest—all told, you're able to see some 11,000 square feet of spectacular scenery. Cars leave from the base at regular intervals for the 15-minute ride to the top. If you're lucky, you can see birds of prey soaring above or mountain lions roaming the cliff sides. An exhibit room at the top surveys the wildlife and landscape of the mountain, as well as some trails. Narrators point out what you're seeing below, including the barely visible remnants of a 1953 plane crash that killed all 16 passengers onboard.

If you want to tie a meal in to the excursion, there's the upscale **High Finance Restaurant** (☎505/243–9742 ⊕*www. highfinancerestaurant.com*) on top of the mountain (serving steaks, lobster tail, and good burgers at lunch), and a more casual spot, **Sandiago's** (☎505/856–6692 ⊕*www. sandiagos.com*), at the tram's base. High Finance affords clear views from every table, making it a favorite destination for a romantic dinner—the food isn't bad, but it's more about the scenic experience here. ■**TIP**➔ **It's much colder and windier at the summit than at the tram's base, so pack an appropriate jacket, as it would be a shame to spend most of your time at the top huddling inside the visitor center rather than walking around it to drink up the views.** You can also use the tram as a way to reach the Sandia Peak ski and mountain-biking area (⇨*the Sandia Park section of the Side Trips from the Cities chapter*). ⊠*10 Tramway Loop NE, Far Northeast Heights* ☎*505/856-7325* ⊕*www.sandiapeak.com* ⊠*$15* ☉*Memorial Day–Labor Day, daily 9–9; Sept.–May, daily 9–8.*

> **DID YOU KNOW?**
>
> The mean altitude of the entire state of New Mexico is more than a mile above sea level.

㉒ **★** **🝚** **Unser Racing Museum.** Albuquerque is home to the illustrious auto-racing family, the Unsers, whose four generations of drivers have dominated the sport since the early 20th century. The most famous of the clan include Bobby Unser Sr. and Al Unser Sr., and their assorted children and grandchildren. Exhibits at this spiffy museum include a display on Pikes Peak, Colorado, and the legendary hairpins where they first got serious about racing; a study of their legacy at the Indianapolis 500; and a goodly selection of vintage racers, including a few you can test-drive (virtually, that is). ⊠*1776 Montaño Rd. NW, just east of the Rio Grande Blvd. overpass, near the Montaño Rd. Bridge, North Valley* ☎*505/341–1776* ⊕*www.unserracingmuseum.com* ⊠*$7* ☉*Daily 10–4.*

WHERE TO EAT

Here's some news that might surprise foodies: when you get right down to it, Albuquerque has nearly as many sophisticated, inspired restaurants as vaunted Santa Fe. The trick is finding them all amid Albuquerque's miles of ubiquitous chain options and legions of other less-than-savory dives, but if you look, you'll be rewarded with innovative food, and generally at prices much lower than in Santa Fe or other major Southwestern cities. The Duke City has long been a place for hearty home-style cooking in big portions, and to this day, it's easy to find great steak-and-chops houses, BBQ joints, retro diners, and authentic New Mexican restaurants, most them offering plenty of grub for the price.

Until the early 2000s, it had been a bit more challenging to find truly memorable independent restaurants serving contemporary and creative fare, but the scene has changed a lot since then and continues to evolve. Particularly in Nob Hill, downtown, and Old Town, hip new restaurants have opened, offering swank decor and complex and artful variations on modern Southwest, Mediterranean, Asian, and other globally inspired cuisine. A significant Vietnamese population has made that cuisine a star, but Indian, Japanese, Thai, and South American traditions all have a presence, making this New Mexico's best destination for ethnic fare.

WHAT IT COSTS					
	¢	$	$$	$$$	$$$$
Restaurants	under $10	$10–$17	$18–$24	$25–$30	over $30

Prices are per person for a main course at dinner, excluding 8.25% sales tax.

$
AMERICAN
✕ **66 Diner.** Dining at this '50s-style art deco diner is a must for fans of Route 66 nostalgia, and the upbeat decor and friendly service also make it a hit with families. The specialties here are many: chicken-fried steak, burgers, malted milk shakes, enchiladas. Plenty of breakfast treats are available, too. ⊠ *1405 Central Ave. NE, University of New Mexico* ☎ *505/247–1421* ⊕ *www.66diner.com* ⊟ *AE, D, MC, V.*

$$$
Fodor'sChoice
★
CONTEMPORARY
✕ **Artichoke Cafe.** Locals praise the Artichoke for its service and French, contemporary American, and Italian dishes prepared, whenever possible, with organically grown ingredients. Specialties include house-made ravioli stuffed with ricotta and butternut squash with a white wine, sage, and butter sauce; and pan-seared sea scallops wrapped in prosciutto with red potatoes, haricots vert, and wax beans. The appetizers are so tasty you may want to make a meal out of them. The building is about a century old, in the historic Huning Highland district on the eastern edge of downtown, but the decor is uptown modern. The two-tier dining room spills out into a small courtyard. ⊠ *424 Central Ave. SE, EDo* ☎ *505/243–0200* ⊕ *www.artichokecafe.com* ⊟ *AE, D, DC, MC, V* ⊗ *Closed Sun. No lunch Sat.*

★ **¢**
NEW MEXICAN
✕ **Barelas Coffee House.** Barelas may look like a set in search of a script, but it's the real deal: diners come from all over the city to sup in this old-fashioned chili parlor in the Hispanic Historic Route 66 neighborhood south of downtown. You may notice looks of quiet contentment on the faces of the many dedicated chili eaters as they dive into their bowls of Barelas's potent red. There's also tasty breakfast fare. The staff treats everybody like an old friend—indeed, many of the regulars who come here have been fans of Barelas for decades. ⊠ *1502 4th St. SW, Barelas* ☎ *505/843–7577* ⇗ *Reservations not accepted* ⊟ *D, MC, V* ⊗ *Closed Sun. No dinner.*

$
FRENCH
✕ **Brasserie La Provençe.** Classic French bistro dishes—think moules frites, couscous merguez, and croque Madame—are served along with a nice wine list in this pleasant corner spot on the west edge of Nob Hill. Service is good, and the food—which is very good, but not superior—is improved by the congenial atmosphere. Try the patio in fair weather, or the lemon-colored back room when it's not. There are specials each day, and the less-expected menu items such as *Poulet du Midi* (seared chicken breast stuffed with chevre and figs) are palate- and budget-pleasing as well. ⊠ *3001 Central Ave. NE, Nob Hill*

Where to Eat
in Albuquerque

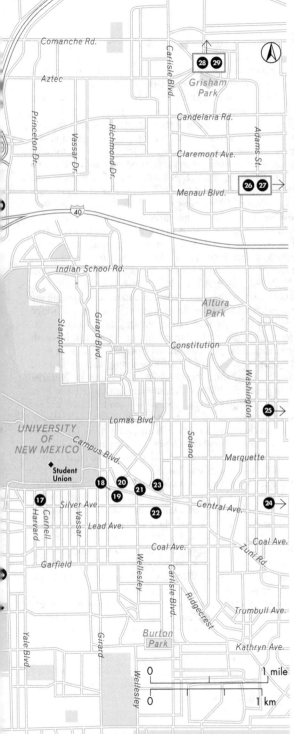

Artichoke Cafe	**13**
Barelas Coffee House	**8**
Bien Shur	**31**
Brasserie La Provençe	**18**
Casa de Benavidez	**33**
Church Street Cafe	**5**
Duran's Cenral Pharmacy	**6**
El Camino Dining Room	**35**
El Patio	**17**
Flying Star	**1, 14, 22, 26, 29, 32**
Gold Street Caffe	**11**
Gruet Steakhouse	**21**
Il Vicino	**23, 28**
Loc Cuates	**25**
Mary & Tito's	**37**
May Cafe	**24**
Monica's El Portal	**4**
Quarters BBQ	**16**
Rancher's Club	**30**
Sadie's	**34**
St. Clair Winery and Bistro	**2**
Seasons Rotisserie & Grill	**3**
66 Diner	**15**
Sophia's Place	**36**
Slate Street Cafe	**7**
Standard Diner	**12**
Thai Crystal	**10**
Tucanos Brazilian Grill	**9**
Viet Taste	**27**
Yanni's Mediterranean Grill & Opa Bar	**19**
Zinc Wine Bar & Bistro	**20**

☎ *505/254–7644* ⊕ *www.laprovencenobhill.com* ▤ *AE, D, MC, V* ⊘ *Closed from 3PM–5 PM.*

$$$$
CONTEMPORARY
Fodor'sChoice
★

✕**Bien Shur.** The panoramic city and mountain views are an essential part of this quietly refined restaurant on the ninth floor of the Sandia Casino complex, but Bien Shur also aspires to be one of the most sophisticated restaurants in the city. Alas, the service can be as uneven as its contemporary fare. You might start with black mission figs and brie, before moving on to pan-roasted sea bass with edamame, shitake mushrooms, jasmine rice, and celery root mousse, or char-grilled buffalo tenderloin with roasted yellow pepper-onion confit. ⊠ *Sandia Resort & Casino, Tramway Rd. NE just east of I–25, Far Northeast Heights* ☎ *505/796–7500 or 800/526–9366* ⊕ *www.sandiacasino.com* ▤ *AE, D, MC, V* ⊘ *Closed Mon. and Tues. No breakfast or lunch.*

$$
NEW MEXICAN

✕**Casa de Benavidez.** The fajitas at this sprawling local favorite with a romantic patio are among the best in town, and the chili is faultless; the burger wrapped inside a sopaipilla is another specialty, as are the chimichangas packed with beef. The charming restaurant occupies a late-19th-century Territorial-style house. ⊠ *8032 4th St. NW, North Valley* ☎ *505/897–7493* ⊕ ▤ *AE, D, MC, V* ⊘ *No dinner Sun.*

★ $
NEW MEXICAN

✕**Church Street Café.** Built in the early 1700s, this structure is among the oldest in New Mexico. Renovations have preserved the original adobe bricks to ensure that this spacious eatery remains as authentic as its menu, which features family recipes spanning four generations—with fresh, local ingredients and spirits employed to satiate streams of hungry tourists. Request the courtyard for alfresco dining amid trellises of sweet grapes and flowers, and where classical and flamenco guitarist José Salazar often performs. Buttery guacamole, with just a bit of bite, is the perfect appetizer to prep one's palate for tender carne asada, redolent and sumptuously spiced. Or try house specialty chili relleno, stuffed with beef and cheese, or a portabella and bell pepper fajita. Traditional desserts and hearty breakfast choices are also offered. ⊠ 2111 Church St. NW, *Old Town* ☎ *505/247–8522* ⊕ *www.churchstreetcafe. com* ▤ *AE, D, MC, V* ⊘ *No dinner Sun.*

¢
NEW MEXICAN

✕**Duran's Central Pharmacy.** This expanded Old Town lunch counter with a dozen tables and a tiny patio just might serve the best tortillas in town. A favorite of old-timers who know their way around a blue-corn enchilada, Duran's is an informal place whose patrons give their food the total attention it deserves. Be sure to leave some browsing time for the pharmacy's book section: Duran's has a good selection of not easily found history and coffee-table volumes covering the Duke City and its storied envrions. ⊠ *1815 Central Ave. NW, Old Town* ☎ *505/247–4141* ▤ *No credit cards* ⊘ *No dinner.*

$
NEW MEXICAN

✕**El Camino Dining Room.** Dating back to 1950, after the Route 66 alignment had already been moved to Central, El Camino seems virtually unchanged over time, and if we didn't know better, we'd think it had been built to cater to folks traveling the Mother Road. It remains a standard bearer of a timeless place. Closing at 2 PM daily, folks come here for their daily fix of perfectly balanced red (rumor is Sadie of Sadie'seven gets a regular dose here), fine green chili stew, light and airy sopapillas, and a setting that evokes another era with its vintage counter, booths, linoleum, and warm and speedy service. ✉ *6800 4th St. NW, North Valley* ☎ *505/344–0448* ⚄ *No reservations accepted* ▤ *AE, D, MC, V* ☯ *Breakfast and lunch daily. Closed for dinner.*

¢ ✗ **El Patio.** A university-area hang-
NEW MEXICAN out, this sentimental favorite
Fodor's Choice has good—sometimes great—food
★ served in the funky patio (the service itself could be described as a student-ghetto gamble). Go for the green-chili chicken enchiladas or any of the heart-healthy and vegetarian selections. But watch out for the fiery green chiles served at harvest time. Note that liquor isn't served, but beer and wine are—they do make decent-tasting "margaritas" using wine. ✉ *142 Harvard St. NE, University of New Mexico* ☎ *505/268–4245* ⚄ *Reservations not accepted* ▤ *MC, V.*

★–$ ✗ **Flying Star.** Flying Star has become a staple and mini-phenom for
CAFE many Albuquerqueans, and although it's a chain, it's locally owned and—just like their Satellite Coffee spots around town—each outpost offers something a little different. The cavernous downtown branch opened in 2005, and it's become a favorite for its striking setting inside the historic Southern Union Gas Co. building, designed by John Gaw Meem in 1950 in an unexpected Modernist mode; the North Valley locale is notable for its comfy and shaded outdoor patio. At Nob Hill the crowd is hip, and the space tighter. The concept works on many levels: it's a newsstand, late-night coffeehouse (there's free Wi-Fi), and an order-at-the-counter restaurant serving a mix of creative Asian, American, and New Mexican dishes (plus several types of wine and beer). Options include Greek pasta with shrimp, green-chili cheeseburgers, Thai-style tofu salad with tangy lime dressing, turkey and Jack cheese melt sandwiches, and an egg and chili-packed *"graburrito."* Desserts change often, but count on a tantalizing array. For a winning pick-me-up, employ some strong hot coffee to wash down a tall slice of the fantastic coconut cream pie. We list a few of our favorite locations. ✉ *723 Silver Ave., Downtown* ☎ *505/244–8099* ✉ *3416 Central Ave. SE, Nob Hill* ☎ *505/255–6633* ✉ *4026 Rio Grande NW, North Valley* ☎ *505/344–6714* ⊕ *www.flyingstarcafe.com* ▤ *AE, D, MC, V.*

★ $ ✗ **Gold Street Caffè.** A culinary cornerstone of downtown Albuquer-
CAFE que's renaissance, this dapper storefront café with exposed-brick walls and high ceilings serves breakfast fare that is truly a cut above, plus equally satisfying lunch and dinner entrées. In the morning, go with eggs Eleganza (two poached eggs atop a green-chili brioche with local goat cheese), along with a side of chili-glazed bacon. Later in the day, consider polenta-dusted tilapia with a sundried-tomato cream sauce, or seared-beef chopped salad with fried rice noodles and chili-lime vinaigrette. You can also just hang out among the hipsters and office workers, sipping a caramel latte and munching on one of the tasty desserts, or enjoy a glass of wine from their short but well-selected list. ✉ *218 Gold Ave. SW, Downtown* ☎ *505/765–1633* ▤ *MC, V* ☯ *No dinner Sun. and Mon.*

$$$$ ✗**Gruet Steakhouse.** The acclaimed Gruet winemaking family operates
STEAK this chic but casual steak house inside the historic Monte Vista Fire
Station, a 1930s WPA-built beauty in the heart of Nob Hill. More
than a mere showcase for promoting Gruet's outstanding sparkling
wines, pinot noirs, and chardonnays, the steak house presents consistently good food (including an addictive side dish, lobster-whipped
potatoes). Among the apps, try the panfried Dungeness crab cake
with a traditional rémoulade sauce. The flat-iron steak topped with
chunky Maytag blue cheese is a favorite main dish, along with the
rare ahi tuna Wellington with wild mushroom duxelle and seared foie
gras. Finish off with a distinctive rose-water-infused ricotta cheesecake
topped with candied oranges and toasted-almond sugar. A kiva fireplace warms the patio in back. The same owners run Gruet Grille, a
contemporary bistro in Northeast Heights. ⊠*3201 Central Ave. NE,
Nob Hill* ☎*505/256–9463* ⊕*www.gruetsteakhouse.com* ▤*AE, D,
MC, V* ⊘*No lunch.*

¢ ✗**Il Vicino.** The pizzas at Il Vicino are baked in a European-style wood-
PIZZA fired oven. If a suitable combination of the 25 possible toppings eludes
you, try the rustica pie, a buttery cornmeal crust topped with roasted
garlic, artichokes, kalamata olives, and capers. The competent kitchen
also turns out Caesar salad, spinach lasagna, and designer sandwiches.
One of their house-brewed beers, say the Wet Mountain India Pale
Ale, which consistently wins awards at the Great American Beer Festival, rounds out the experience. There's another branch, usually less
crowded, in a shopping center not too far from Sandia Peak Aerial
Tramway. ⊠*3403 Central Ave. NE, Nob Hill* ☎*505/266–7855*
⊠*11225 Montgomery Blvd., Far Northeast Heights* ☎*505/271–0882*
⊕*www.ilvicino.com* ♠*Reservations not accepted* ▤*MC, V.*

$ ✗**Los Cuates.** A short drive northeast of Nob Hill and UNM, Los
NEW MEXICAN Cuates (a 3-location local mini-chain) doesn't get as much attention
as some of the city's more touristy New Mexican restaurants, but the
food here is reliable, and prepared with pure vegetable oil rather than
lard, which is one reason it's never as greasy as at some competitors.
Also, the green chili stew is vegetarian (unless you request meat). All
the usual favorites are served here, but top picks include the roast-
beef burrito covered with melted cheese, and the tostada *compuesta*
(a corn tortilla stuffed with beef, beans, rice, potatoes, carne adovada, and chili con queso). ⊠*4901 Lomas Blvd. NE, near Nob Hill*
☎*505/255–5079* ⊕*www.loscuatesrestaurants.com* ♠*Reservations
not accepted* ▤*AE, D, MC, V.*

$ ✗**Mary & Tito's.** Locals can go on about who's got the best chili, be it red
NEW MEXICAN or be it green. What they don't dispute is that Mary & Tito's, an institution for many a decade, and run by the same family since it opened,
is as tasteful as they come. Casual, friendly, and the real deal. Grab a
booth and try the rellenos or the enchiladas. They don't do sopapillas
here, but you won't miss them. A bonus is they make their chili vegetarian, and the red is always sm-o-o-o-th. ⊠*2711 Fourth St. NW,
2 blocks north of Menaul Blvd. NWNorth Valley* ☎*505/344-6266*
♠*No reservations accepted* ▤*AE, D, MC, V*

★ ¢ ✗**May Café.** Few tourists ever make their way to this astoundingly inex-
VIETNAMESE pensive and wonderfully authentic Vietnamese restaurant a short drive
east of Nob Hill, in an uninspired neighborhood just off old Route
66. Favorites from the extensive menu include rare-beef noodle soup;
stir-fried noodles with veggies, fish balls, chicken, barbecue pork, and
pork; spicy fish in baked in a hot pot; and catfish with lemongrass
sauce. You'll also find plenty of vegetarian options, including knockout spring rolls. Friendly, prompt service and a simple, attractive dining room add to the experience. ✉*111 Louisiana Blvd. SE, Southeast*
☎*505/265–4448* ▤*AE, MC, V* ⊘*Closed Sun.*

★ $ ✗**Monica's El Portal.** Locals in the know favor this rambling, assuredly
NEW MEXICAN authentic New Mexican restaurant on the west side of Old Town over
the more famous, though less reliable, standbys around Old Town
Plaza. Monica's has a prosaic dining room plus a cute tiled patio, and
the service is friendly and unhurried yet efficient. If you've never had
chicharrones (fried pork skins), try them here with beans stuffed inside
a flaky sopaipilla. Or consider the traditional blue-corn chicken or beef
enchiladas, and the savory green-chili stew. This is honest, home-style
food, and lunch here may just fill you up for the rest of the day. ✉*321
Rio Grande Blvd. NW, Old Town* ☎*505/247–9625* ▤*AE, D, MC, V*
⊘*Closed Mon. No dinner weekends.*

$ ✗**Quarters BBQ.** This Albuquerque institution, going strong since the
SOUTHERN early '70s, certainly has its followers. Style-wise, their smoky ribs and
chicken, brisket, and sausage may not be your cuppa, but you will need
a fistful of napkins, that's for sure. The sauce is more tangy than sweet,
and slow smoking with a secret recipe makes for the winning combination. Top steaks and Alaskan king crab legs are also available. ✉*801
Yale Blvd. SE, University of New Mexico* ☎*505/843–7505* ▤*AE,
MC, V* ⊘*Closed Sun.*

$$$$ ✗**Rancher's Club.** Hotel restaurants in Albuquerque aren't generally
STEAK special dining destinations in and of themselves, but this clubby, old-
world steak house in the Albuquerque Hilton earns raves among
deep-pocketed carnivores for its delicious aged steaks and ribs. The
dining room is hung with saddles, mounted bison heads, and ranch-
ing-related art. If you're looking to impress a date or clients, order
the fillet of Kobe beef with cream spinach, lobster-mashed potatoes,
and morel-mushroom jus. Other standbys include elk chops, fillet of
ostrich, porterhouse steak, and the Hunter's Grill of antelope, venison,
and wild boar sausage. ✉*Albuquerque Hilton, 1901 University Blvd.
NE, Midtown* ☎*505/889–8071* ⊕*theranchersclubofnm.com* ▤*AE,
D, DC, MC, V* ⊘*No lunch weekends.*

$ ✗**Sadie's.** One of the city's longtime favorites for simple but spicy no-
NEW MEXICAN nonsense New Mexican fare, Sadie's—remembered fondly by old-
timers for the era when it made its home in the Lucky 66 bowling
alley next door—now occupies a long, fortresslike adobe building.
Specialties include carne adovada, spicy beef burritos, and chiles rellenos. The service is always prompt, though sometimes there's a wait
for a table. While you're waiting, try one of the excellent margaritas.
Sadie's salsa is locally renowned and available by the jar for takeout.

✉6230 4th St. NW, North Valley ☎505/345–5339 ⊕www.sadies-
salsa.com ⊟AE, D, MC, V.

$$$ ✗ **Seasons Rotisserie & Grill.** Upbeat yet elegant, this Old Town eatery
CONTEMPORARY is an easy place to have a business lunch or a dinner date, and oeno-
philes will revel in its well-chosen cellar. The kitchen serves innovative
grills and pastas, such as wood-roasted duck breast with Gorgonzola–
sweet potato gratin and grilled prime New York strip steak with garlic-
mashed potatoes and black-truffle butter; great starters include seared
raw tuna with cucumber-ginger slaw, and pecan-crusted three-cheese
chiles rellenos with butternut squash coulis. The rooftop patio and
bar provides evening cocktails and lighter meals. ✉2031 Mountain
Rd. NW, Old Town ☎505/766–5100 ⊕www.seasonsonthenet.com
⊟AE, D, DC, MC, V ⊗No lunch weekends.

★ $$ ✗ **Slate Street Cafe.** An airy, high-ceiling dining room with a semi-cir-
CONTEMPO- cular central wine bar and modern lighting, this stylish restaurant sits
RARY amid pawn shops and bail bond outposts on a quiet, unprepossess-
ing side street downtown. But once inside, you'll find a thoroughly
sophisticated, colorful space serving memorable, modern renditions of
classic American fare, such as fried chicken and meat loaf. The starters
are especially notable, including Japanese-style fried rock shrimp with
orange habañero sauce, and bruschetta topped with honey-cured ham
and Brie. Banana-stuffed brioche French toast is a favorite at breakfast and Saturday brunch. More than 30 wines by the glass are served.
✉515 Slate St. NW, Downtown ☎505/243–2210 ⊕www.slatestreet-
cafe.com ⊟AE, D, MC, V ⊗Closed Sun.

$ ✗ **Sophia's Place.** Muy buenos berry pancakes (and real maple
NEW MEXICAN syrup)…and breakfast burritos (papas on the inside, so be sure to ask
if you'd like them out instead), enchiladas (sprinkled with cojita), and
just about anything the kitchen whips up. You'll find everything from
creative and generous salads and chipotle-chili bacon cheeseburgers to
Udon noodles and fish tacos. Up in Los Ranchos de Albuquerque, in
the heart of the North Valley, Sophia's (named after the Alice Waters–
trained chef/owner's daughter) is a simple, humble-appearing neighborhood spot, yet one that people drive out of their way for—especially
for the weekend brunch. Everything is fresh, often organic, prettily
presented, and always made to order. ✉6313 Fourth St. NW, 2 blocks
north of Osuna/Chavez Rd. NW North Valley ☎505/345–3935 ⊜No
reservations accepted ⊟AE, D, MC, V ⊗No dinner Sun.–Wed.

$ ✗ **St. Clair Winery & Bistro.** The state's largest winery, located in the
CONTINENTAL southern New Mexico town of Deming, St. Clair Winery has a charming and affordable restaurant and tasting room in Old Town. It's part
of a small shopping center on the west side of the neighborhood, just
south of I–40. You enter a shop with a bar for winetasting and shelves
of wines and gourmet goods, which leads into the dark and warmly
lighted dining room. There's also a large, attractive patio. At lunch,
sample the panini sandwich of New Mexico goat cheese and roasted
peppers. Dinner treats include crab-and-artichoke dip, garlic chicken
slow-cooked in chardonnay, and pork tenderloin with merlot and rasp-
berry-chipotle sauce. On weekends, St. Clair serves a popular Sun-

day brunch. ⊠ *901 Rio Grande Blvd., Old Town* ☎ *505/243–9916 or 888/870–9916* ⊕ *www.stclairvineyards.com* ☐ *AE, D, MC, V.*

$$ ✕ **Standard Diner.** In the historic Huning Highland district just east of downtown, the Standard opened in 2006 inside a 1930s Texaco station with high ceilings, massive plate-glass windows, and rich tile floors—it's at once thoroughly elegant yet totally casual, serving upscale yet affordable takes on traditional diner standbys. The long, interesting menu dabbles in meal-size salads (try the chicken-fried-lobster Caesar salad), burgers (including a terrific one topped with crab cakes and hollandaise sauce), sandwiches, and traditional diner entrées given nouvelle flourishes (Moroccan-style pot roast, mac and cheese with smoked salmon and green chiles, flat-iron steak with poblano cream sauce and bell pepper–ginger puree). Kick everything up with a side of wasabi-mashed potatoes, and save room for the twisted tiramisu (espresso-soaked lady fingers), dulce de leche mascarpone, agave-poached pears, and candied pine nuts. ⊠ *320 Central Ave. SE, EDo* ☎ *505/243–1440* ☐ *AE, D, MC, V.*

CONTEMPO-
RARY

¢–$ ✕ **Thai Crystal.** In a state that's sorely lacked good Thai restaurants until recently, this beautiful space filled with Thai artwork and decorative pieces has been a welcome addition to the downtown scene. The extensive menu includes a mix of typical Thai specialties (pineapple fried rice, chicken satay, beef panang curry) as well as some less predictable items, such as steamed mussels topped with red coconut curry, and pork sautéed with a spicy mint, chili, and onion sauce. ⊠ *109 Gold Ave. SW, Downtown* ☎ *505/244–3344* ☐ *AE, MC, V.*

THAI

$–$$ ✕ **Tucanos Brazilian Grill.** There isn't much point in going to Tucanos if you don't love meat. Sure, they serve some vegetables, but the real focus is on *churrascos,* South American–style grilled skewers of beef, chicken, pork, and turkey that parade endlessly out of the open kitchen on the arms of enthusiastic waiters. Carnivority aside, one unexpected treat, if it's available, is the grilled pineapple. The noisy, high-ceiling spot next to the downtown Century 14 Downtown movie theater is a good place to go for drinks, too, and if you're looking for either a stand-alone cooler or a liquid partner for your hearty fare, look no further than a bracing *caipirinha,* the lime-steeped national cocktail of Brazil. ⊠ *110 Central Ave. SW, Downtown* ☎ *505/246–9900* ⊕ *www.tucanos.com* ☐ *AE, D, MC, V.*

BRAZILIAN

$ ✕ **Viet Taste.** Come here for another side of spicy hot. Excellent authentic Vietnamese food is served up in this compact, modern, bamboo-accented restaurant. Ignore the fact that it's within one of Abq's ubiquitous strip-malls. Consider their popular pho variations, order the tofu (or chicken or shrimp) spring rolls with their tangy peanuty sauce, dig into the spicy lemongrass with chicken, and all will be well. ⊠ *5721 Menaul Blvd. NE, on the north side, just west of San Pedro NE, between Cardenas and Valencia Rds. NE Uptown* ☎ *505/888–0101* ☐ *AE, D, MC, V.*

VIETNAMESE

$$ ✕ **Yanni's Mediterranean Grill.** Yanni's is a popular place where the food can run second to its refreshing azure-tiled ambiance. Serving marinated grilled lamb chops with lemon and oregano, grilled yellowfin sole encrusted with Parmesan cheese, pastitsio (a Greek version of mac

GREEK

and cheese), and spinach, feta, and roasted garlic pizzas, Yanni's also offers a vegetarian plate with surprisingly good meatless moussaka, tabouleh, spanakopita, and stuffed grape leaves. There's a huge patio off the main dining room, and next door you can sip cocktails and mingle with locals at Opa Bar. ⊠*3109 Central Ave. NE, Nob Hill* ☎*505/268–9250* ⊕*www.yannisandopabar.com* ⊟*AE, D, MC, V.*

★ $$$
CONTEMPORARY

✕**Zinc Wine Bar & Bistro.** A snazzy spot in lower Nob Hill, fairly close to UNM, Zinc captures the essence of a San Francisco neighborhood bistro with its high ceilings, hardwood floors, and white tablecloths and dark-wood straight-back café chairs. You can drop in to sample wine from the long list or listen to live music downstairs in the Blues Cellar. From the kitchen, consider the starter of asparagus-and-artichoke tart with baby greens and spicy dried-fruit tapenade; or the main dish of oven-roasted wild Alaskan halibut with a Parmesan-asparagus risotto cake, braised leek, and fennel, with a roasted–red pepper vinaigrette. The kitchen uses organic ingredients whenever available. ⊠*3009 Central Ave. NE, Nob Hill* ☎*505/254–9462* ⊕*www.zincabq.com* ⊟*AE, D, MC, V* ☉*No lunch Sat.*

WHERE TO STAY

With a few exceptions, Albuquerque's lodging options fall into two categories: modern chain hotels and motels, and distinctive and typically historic inns and B&Bs. Of larger hotels, you won't find many that are independently owned, historic, or especially rife with personality, although Central Avenue—all across the city—is lined with fascinating old motor courts and motels from the 1930s through the '50s, many of them with their original neon signs and quirky roadside architecture. Alas, nearly all of these are run-down and substandard; they should be avoided unless you're extremely adventurous and can't resist the super-low rates (often as little as $18 a night).

If you're seeking charm and history, try one of the many excellent inns and B&Bs (including those in Corrales and Bernalillo, just north of Albuquerque, listed in the Side Trips from the Cities chapter). Although the cookie-cutter chain hotels may appear largely interchangeable, there are several properties that stand out above the rest, and many of these are described below. Two parts of the city with an excellent variety of economic plain-Jane franchise hotels (Hampton Inn, Comfort Inn, Courtyard Marriott, etc.) are the Airport and the north I–25 corridor. As opposed to many other cities, Albuquerque's airport is extremely convenient to attractions and downtown, and the north I–25 corridor also offers easy access to sightseeing and dining as well as the Balloon Fiesta Park. Wherever you end up staying in Albuquerque, you can generally count on finding rates considerably lower than the national average, and much cheaper than in Santa Fe and Taos.

WHAT IT COSTS					
	¢	$	$$	$$$	$$$$
Hotels	under $70	$70–$130	$131–$190	$191–$260	over $260

Prices are for two people in a standard double room in high season, excluding 12%–13% tax.

DOWNTOWN & OLD TOWN

★ **$$$**   **Andaluz.** Opened in 1939 by Conrad Hilton (who honeymooned here with Zsa Zsa Gabor), this glamorous 10-story hotel on the National Register of Historic Places was known as La Posada de Albuquerque until it was re-invented (and completely redone inside) as a high-end boutique hotel in 2009. Its new name, Andaluz, and its new décor, are meant to serve as a nod to the Moroccan and Spanish colonial influences of the original Hilton design. Its pursuit of Silver LEED certification reflects the hotel's interest in offering state-of-the art amenities to its guests and corporate clients, who will take advantage of multiple meeting rooms, a ballroom, and the on-site restaurant. **Pros:** Historic caché with all the benefits of a complete overhaul. **Cons:** Parking can be a challenge. ⌧*125 2nd St. NW, Downtown* ☎*505/242–9090 or 800/777–5732* ⊟*505/242–8664* ⇱*107 rooms, suites* ⚟*In-hotel: Wi-Fi, restaurant, room service, bars, laundry service, parking (fee)* ⊟*AE, D, DC, MC, V.*

$ **Best Western Rio Grande Inn.** Although part of the Best Western chain, this contemporary four-story low-rise just off I–40—a 10-minute walk from Old Town's plaza—has an attractive Southwestern design and furnishings, plus such modern touches as free high-speed Internet. The heavy handcrafted wood furniture, tin sconces, and artwork in the rooms come from local suppliers and artisans. That locals are familiar with the Albuquerque Grill is a good indicator of the restaurant's reputation. It's a good value. **Pros:** 100-percent non-smoking. Airport shuttle. **Cons:** It's a hike from the rear rooms to the front desk. ⌧*1015 Rio Grande Blvd. NW, Old Town* ☎*505/843–9500 or 800/959–4726* ⊟*505/843–9238* ⊕*www.riograndeinn.com* ⇱*173 rooms* ⚟*In-room: refrigerator, Wi-Fi (some), Ethernet (some). In-hotel: restaurant, room service, bar, pool, gym, laundry facilities, parking (no fee), pets allowed (some)* ⊟*AE, D, DC, MC, V.*

$ **Böttger Mansion of Old Town.** Charles Böttger, a German immigrant, built this pink two-story mansion in 1912. The lacy, richly appointed rooms vary greatly in size and decor; some have four-poster beds, slate floors, claw-foot tubs, or pressed-tin ceilings. All have down comforters, fluffy pillows, and terry robes—and a few are said to be haunted by a friendly ghost or two. The Wine Cellar Suite, in the basement, can accommodate up to six guests and has a kitchenette. A grassy courtyard fronted by a patio provides an escape from the Old Town crowds. Breakfast might consist of stuffed French toast or perhaps burritos smothered in green chili, which you can also enjoy in your room. **Pros:** Balloon, golf, and tour packages are available. **Cons:** Not for the floral-and-frilly phobic ⌧*110 San Felipe St. NW, Old Town*

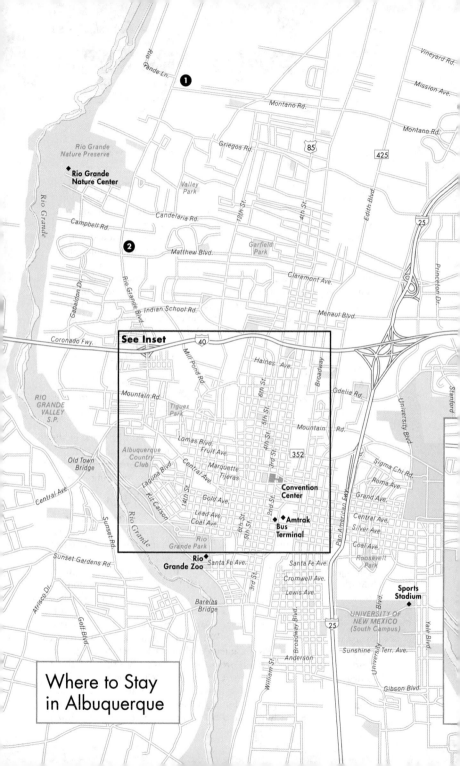

Where to Stay
in Albuquerque

Albuqerque Marriott 13

Andaluz 10

Best Western
Rio Grande Inn 3

Böttger Mansion
of Old Town 5

Casas de Suenos 6

Cinnamon Morning B&B 2

Doubletree Hotel 11

Embassy Suites Hotel
Albuquerque 12

Hotel Albuquerque
of Old Town 4

Hotel Blue 8

Hyatt Regency
Albuquerque 9

Los Poblanos Inn 1

Marriott Pyramid 17

Mauger Estate B&B 7

Nativo Lodge Hotel 16

Sandia Resort & Casino 15

Sheraton Albuquerque
Uptown 14

☎*505/243–3639 or 800/758–3639* ⊕*www.bottger.com* ⤶*7 rooms, 1 2-bedroom suite* ⟐*In-room: kitchen (some), VCR. In-hotel: parking (fee), no-smoking rooms* ▭*AE, MC, V* ⭕*BP.*

★ $ ▦**Casas de Sueños.** This historic compound of 1930s- and '40s-era adobe casitas is perfect if you're seeking seclusion and quiet yet seek easy proximity to museums, restaurants, and shops—Casas de Sueños (sueños means dreams in Spanish) is a few blocks south of Old Town Plaza, but on a peaceful residential street fringing the lush grounds of Albuquerque Country Club. The individually decorated units, which open onto a warren of courtyards and gardens, come in a variety of shapes and configurations. Typical features include Saltillo-tile floors, wood-burning kiva-style fireplaces, leather or upholstered armchairs, skylights, and contemporary Southwestern furnishings. Many rooms have large flat-screen TVs with DVD players and CD stereos, and some sleep as many as four adults. The full breakfast is served outside in the garden when the weather permits, and inside a lovely artists' studio at other times. **Pros:** Charming and tucked away. Some private patios. **Cons:** Ask which rooms have the newest beds, and which have full baths. ✉*310 Rio Grande Blvd. SW, on the south side of Central Ave. Old Town* ☎*505/247–4560 or 800/665–7002* 🖷*505/242–2162* ⊕*www.casasdesuenos.com* ⤶*21 casitas* ⟐*In-room: kitchen (some), DVD (some), VCR (some), hot tub (some). In-hotel: parking (no fee)* ▭*AE, MC, V* ⭕*BP.*

$ ▦**Doubletree Hotel.** A two-story waterfall splashes down a marble backdrop in the lobby of this 15-story downtown hotel, with attractive, pale gold rooms that contain classical mid-century-inspired furnishings and complementary art. The restaurant at the foot of the waterfall is called, appropriately, La Cascada (The Cascade). Breakfast, a lunch buffet, and dinner, from fresh seafood to Southwestern specialties, are served. **Pros:** Old Town shuttle service available. Recent renovation brought Sweet Dreams beds to each room and sleek upgrades throughout. **Cons:** Not all rooms have mountain views. ✉*201 Marquette Ave. NW, Downtown* ☎*505/247–3344 or 800/222–8733* 🖷*505/247–7025* ⊕*www.doubletree.com* ⤶*295 rooms* ⟐*In-room: Ethernet. In-hotel: Wi-Fi, restaurant, room service, bar, pool, laundry service, parking (fee)* ▭*AE, D, DC, MC, V.*

$$$ ▦**Embassy Suites Hotel Albuquerque.** This all-suites high-rise with a
Fodor's Choice   striking contemporary design sits on a bluff alongside I–25, affording
★   guests fabulous views of the downtown skyline and vast desert mesas to the west, and the verdant Sandia Mountains to the east. Rooms are large and done in soothing Tuscan colors; the living areas have pull-out sleeper sofas, refrigerators, dining and work areas, microwaves, and coffeemakers. You'll also find two phones and two TVs in each suite. Included in the rates is a nightly reception with hors d'oeuvres and cocktails, and a full breakfast each morning. With so much living and sleeping space and a great location accessible to downtown, Nob Hill, and the airport, this is a great option if you're staying in town for a while or traveling with a family. **Pros:** Quiet but convenient location adjacent to I-25 and just south of I-40. Congenial staff. **Cons:** Suite setup attracts families in addition to business travelers; the occasional child

run rampant may not appeal to all. ✉*1000 Woodward Pl. NE, Downtown* ☎*505/245–7100 or 800/362–2779* 🖷*505/247–1083* ⊕*www.embassysuitesalbuquerque.com* 🖙*261 suites* ♿*In-room: refrigerator, Wi-Fi. In-hotel: restaurant, bar, fitness facilities, spa, parking (no fee)* ⊟*AE, D, MC, V* ⍥*BP.*

$$ 🏨**Hotel Albuquerque at Old Town.** This appropriately styled 11-story Southwestern hotel rises distinctly above Old Town's ancient structures. The large rooms have desert-color appointments, hand-wrought furnishings, and tile bathrooms; most rooms have a small balcony with nice views. Cristobal's serves commendable Spanish-style steaks and seafood; Café Plazuela & Cantina offers more casual American and New Mexican food; and a fine flamenco guitarist entertains in the Q-Bar & Gallery Lounge. Treatments and facials are available. **Pros:** The high-ceilinged, rustically furnished territorial-style lobby makes for a comfy place to sit a spell. **Cons:** No furniture on balconies. ✉*800 Rio Grande Blvd. NW, Old Town* ☎*505/843–6300 or 877/901–7666* 🖷*505/842–8426* ⊕*www.hotelabq.com* 🖙*168 rooms, 20 suites* ♿*In-room: Wi-Fi, refrigerator (some). In-hotel: 2 restaurants, room service, bar, pool, gym, spa, parking (no fee)* ⊟*AE, D, DC, MC, V.*

¢ 🏨**Hotel Blue.** Formerly a bland chain hotel, this 1960s four-story hotel received a makeover in the early 2000s, hoping to make its name in the boutique market. In reality, its reasonable rates draw more of a party crowd, and the art deco–inspired rooms can pick-up street noise as well; based on the (decidedly basic) services alone it would be a serious stretch to call this place hip or truly of the boutique genre. Still, people rave about the beds, and it is ideally located, especially for those with business downtown. It overlooks a small park, is a short stroll from downtown's music clubs and restaurants, and is a short drive or bus ride, or 15-minute walk from Old Town. In summer, a lively Saturday growers' market (including arts vendors, music, and more) sets up in Robinson Park next door. **Pros:** Tempurpedic beds. Complimentary shuttle. **Cons:** While Blue has a secure main entrance, individual rooms face onto exterior halls. This can be a fringe neighborhood by night. ✉*717 Central Ave. NW, Old Town* ☎*505/924–2400 or 877/878–4868* 🖷*505/924–2465* ⊕*www.thehotelblue.com* 🖙*125 rooms, 10 suites* ♿*In-hotel: Wi-Fi, restaurant, bar, pool, gym, parking (no fee)* ⊟*AE, D, MC, V* ⍥*CP.*

$$ 🏨**Hyatt Regency Albuquerque.** Adjacent to the Albuquerque Convention Center, the city's most sumptuous hotel comprises a pair of soaring, desert-color towers that figure prominently in the city's skyline. The gleaming art deco–inspired interior benefited from a 2008 top-to-bottom renovation; the ambience is refined and not overbearing. The contemporary rooms in mauve, burgundy, and tan combine Southwestern style with all the amenities you'd expect of a high-caliber business-oriented hotel, including Wi-Fi, iPod docking stations, flat-screen TVs, plush pillow-top mattresses, and fluffy bathrobes. McGrath's Bar and Grill serves steaks, chops, chicken, and seafood (and breakfast to the power crowd), and there's also a Starbucks on-site. Bigwigs of all stripes stay in the Penthouse. **Pros:** Easy walking distance from the KiMo Theatre and downtown's art galleries and restaurants, and a quick cab (or bus)

ride elsewhere. The views, the lap pool and the well-equipped 24/7 fitness center (massage service is available there or in rooms). **Cons:** Until you get your bearings, the layout can seem somewhat maze-like. Lack of views on lower floors. ✉ *330 Tijeras Ave. NW, Downtown* ☎ *505/842–1234 or 800/233–1234* 📠 *505/766–6710* 🌐 *albuquerque.hyatt.com* *395 rooms, 14 suites* *In-room: Wi-Fi. In-hotel: restaurant, bars, pool, gym, parking (fee)* 💳 *AE, D, DC, MC, V.*

$$ FodorsChoice ★ **Mauger Estate B&B Inn.** This 1897 Queen Anne mansion—now on the National Register of Historic Places—was the first home in Albuquerque to have electricity. While the mercantile Mauger (pronounced "major") family is long gone (and the electric long since upgraded, along with a detailed restoration throughout), this well-run B&B has retained many of the building's original architectural elements, such as oval windows with beveled and "feather-pattern" glass, hardwood floors, high ceilings, a redbrick exterior, and a front veranda. Rooms—cleanly and contemporarily decorated with a restrained Victorian touch (seen best in the dark woods)—have refrigerators and baskets stocked with munchies, triple-sheeted beds with soft feather duvets, irons and boards, and fresh flowers. There's also a two-bedroom, two-bathroom town house next door. Guests have access to a full-service health club a few blocks away. **Pros:** Pleasant common room, with a library and a late afternoon cookies-and-wine spread. Responsive and informed innkeeper. Good breakfasts, which they will pack to go if needed. Convenient location. **Cons:** Rooms could use more task lighting. At night, on the northern fringe of downtown, it can feel a bit sketchy for walking, but parking is secure. ✉ *701 Roma Ave. NW, Downtown* ☎ *505/242–8755 or 800/719–9189* 📠 *505/842–8835* 🌐 *www.maugerbb.com* *8 rooms, 1 2-bedroom town house* *In-room: Wi-Fi, refrigerator. In-hotel: parking (no fee), some pets allowed* 💳 *AE, D,MC, V* *BP.*

UPTOWN

$$ **Albuquerque Marriott.** This 17-story upscale uptown property draws a mix of business and leisure travelers; it's close to three shopping malls and not too far from Nob Hill. Kachina dolls, Native American pottery, and other regional artworks decorate the elegant public areas. The rooms are traditional American, with walk-in closets, armoires, and crystal lamps, but have Southwestern touches. Rooms on all but the first few floors enjoy staggering views, either of Sandias to the east or the vast mesas to the west. Cielo Sandia specializes in steaks and contemporary New Mexican fare. **Pros:** A top-to-bottom renovation completed in 2007 spruced the place up quite nicely. Cozy Lobby Lounge. **Cons:** Fee for Internet access in rooms. ✉ *2101 Louisiana Blvd. NE, Uptown* ☎ *505/881–6800 or 800/228–9290* 📠 *505/888–2982* 🌐 *www.marriott.com/abqnm* *405 rooms, 6 suites* *In-room: refrigerator, VCR (some), Ethernet. In-hotel: Wi-Fi, restaurant, room service, bar, pool, gym, laundry facilities, laundry service, executive floor, parking (no fee)* 💳 *AE, D, DC, MC, V.*

$ **Sheraton Albuquerque Uptown.** Within easy distance of the airport and Albuquerque's newest shopping malls, this 2008-renovated property meets the consistent Sheraton standard with a pleasant lobby with a cozy bar area and a gift shop. Earthy and muted reds, oranges, and sand-shaded colors accent the lobby and functional but ample rooms, whose nicer touches include a second sink outside the bathroom, comfy mattresses, and bathrobes. **Pros:** Central location with easy highway (and shopping) access. **Cons:** At a heavily-trafficked intersection. ⊠*2600 Louisiana Blvd. NE, Uptown* ☎*505/881–0000 or 800/252–7772* 🖷*505/881–3736* ⊕*sheratonabq.com* 🖵*294 rooms* ⅊*In-room: refrigerator, Wi-Fi. In-hotel: restaurant, room service, pool, gym, executive floor* ⊟*AE, D, DC, MC, V.*

NORTH SIDE

★ **$$** 🏠 **Cinnamon Morning B&B.** A private, beautifully maintained, pet-friendly compound set back from the road and a 10-minute drive north of Old Town, Cinnamon Morning is just south of Rio Grande Nature Center State Park and a perfect roost if you want to be close to the city's wineries and the launching areas used by most hot-air-ballooning companies. Three rooms are in the main house, a richly furnished adobe home with colorful decorations and a lush garden patio. Additionally, there's a secluded two-bedroom guest house with a bath, full kitchen, private entrance, living room, and fireplace; and a colorfully painted one-bedroom casita with a private patio, Mexican-style furnishings, a viga ceiling, a living room with a sleeper sofa. The full breakfasts here are filling and delicious, served by a roaring fire in winter or in the courtyard in summer. **Pros:** Hosts will gladly help with travel ideas and planning. **Cons:** Cancellations must be made 14 days ahead. ⊠*2700 Rio Grande Blvd. NW, North Valley* ☎*505/345–3541 or 800/214–9481* 🖷*505/342–2283* ⊕*www.cinnamonmorning.com* 🖵*3 rooms, 1 casita, 1 guest house* ⅊*In-room: kitchen (some), VCR, Wi-Fi. In-hotel: some pets allowed* ⊟*AE, D, MC, V* ⅋*BP.*

$$$$ 🏠 **Los Poblanos Inn.** Designed by acclaimed architect John Gaw Meem,
Fodor'sChoice this rambling, historic inn lies outside of Albuquerque's sprawl, on
★ 25 acres of organic farm fields, lavender plantings, and gardens in Los Ranchos on the town's north side, near the Rio Grande and just across the street from Anderson Valley Vineyards—with all the greenery and the quiet pace of life here, you'd never know you're in the desert, or in the middle of one of the Southwest's largest cities. You reach the inn via a spectacular tree-lined lane. Every accommodation has a private entrance and contains folk paintings, painted viga ceilings, and high-quality linens. Rooms also contain bath products made on-site, including lavender soap and oils; all have kiva fireplaces, too. The property also includes the 15,000-square-foot La Quinta Cultural Center, a conference space available for meetings that contains a dramatic fresco by Peter Hurd. There's also a library with beautiful artwork. **Pros:** The lavender fields are especially lovely. Personal trainer and day spa service available. **Cons:** None come to mind, if you can afford it. ⊠*4803 Rio Grande Blvd. NW, North Valley* ☎*505/344–9297 or 866/344–9297* 🖷*505/342–1302* ⊕*www.los poblanos.com* 🖵*3 rooms, 4 suites, 2 guest houses* ⅊*In-room: kitchen*

(some), refrigerator (some), DVD (some), VCR (some), Wi-Fi (some). In-hotel: parking (no fee) ☰*AE, MC, V* ⑩*BP.*

$$ ⊞**Marriott Pyramid.** This curious ziggurat-shape 10-story building fits in nicely with the other examples of postmodern architecture that have sprung up in northern Albuquerque in recent years. It's the most upscale of a slew of reputable chain hotels in the area, and it's an excellent base for exploring the North Valley or even having somewhat easier access to Santa Fe than the hotels downtown or near the airport. Rooms have sponge-painted walls and dapper country French decor. They open onto a soaring atrium lobby. Perks include evening turndown service and newspapers delivered to the room each morning. **Pros:** Easy access to I-25. **Cons:** Service is uneven. The lobby is as maze-like and confusing, as you might expect inside a pyramid. ✉*5151 San Francisco Rd. NE, Journal Center* ☎*505/821–3333 or 800/466–8356* 🖷*505/828–0230* ⊕*www.albuquerquemarriottnorth. com* 🛏*248 rooms, 54 suites* ♿*In-room: refrigerator, Wi-Fi. In-hotel: restaurant, room service, bar, pool, gym, laundry facilities, laundry service, parking (no fee)* ☰*AE, D, DC, MC, V.*

★ **$$** ⊞**Nativo Lodge Hotel.** Although it's priced similarly to a number of generic midrange chain properties on the north side, this five-story property has more character than most, especially in the expansive public areas, bar, and restaurant, which have an attractive Southwestern motif that includes hand-carved panels depicting symbols from Native American lore and river-rock walls. Rooms have wing chairs, work desks, Wi-Fi, and dual-line phones. The hotel is just off I–25, but set back far enough to avoid highway noise; several movie theaters and a bounty of restaurants are nearby. **Pros:** Nicely scaled, relaxing atmosphere. **Cons:** If your primary business is down in town, this is a bit far north. ✉*6000 Pan American Freeway NE, Northeast* ☎*505/798– 4300 or 888/628–4861* ⊕*hhandr.com/nativo* 🛏*147 rooms, 3 suites* ♿*In-room: refrigerator, Wi-Fi. In-hotel: restaurant, room service, bar, pool, gym, laundry facilities, parking (no fee)* ☰*AE, D, DC, MC, V.*

$$$ ⊞**Sandia Resort & Casino.** Completed in early 2006 after much antici-
Fodor's Choice pation, this seven-story casino resort set a new standard for luxury
★ in Albuquerque; unfortunately the service here doesn't always quite match the promise. Nevertheless, appointments like 32-inch plasma TVs, handcrafted wooden furniture, louvered wooden blinds, and muted, natural color palettes lend elegance to the spacious rooms, most of which have sweeping views of the Sandia Mountains or the Rio Grande Valley. The 700-acre grounds, which are in the Far Northeast Heights, just across I–25 from Balloon Fiesta Park, ensure privacy and quiet and include a superb golf course and an amphitheater that hosts top-of-the-line music and comedy acts. The Green Reed Spa offers a wide range of treatments, many of them using local clay and plantlife. One of the city's best restaurants for mountain views, Bien Shur, occupies the casino's top floor, and there are three other places to eat on-site. The casino is open 24 hours. **Pros:** 24/7 room service. **Cons:** Smoking is allowed on premises, pool not open year-round. ✉*Tramway Rd. NE just east of I–25, Northeast Heights* ☎*505/796–7500 or 800/526– 9366* ⊕*www.sandiacasino.com* 🛏*198 rooms, 30 suites* ♿*In-room:*

Wi-Fi. In-hotel: 4 restaurants, room service, bars, golf course, pool, gym, spa, laundry service, parking (no fee).

NIGHTLIFE & THE ARTS

For the 411 on arts and nightlife, consult the Venue section of the Sunday edition of the *Albuquerque Journal* (⊕*www.abqjournal.com*), the freebie *weekly Alibi* (⊕*www.alibi.com*), and the Arts Alliance's richly inclusive Arts & Cultural Calendar (⊕*www.abqarts.org/calendar.htm*). For highlights on some of the best music programming in town, go to ⊕*ampconcerts.org*.

NIGHTLIFE

BARS & LOUNGES

Atomic Cantina (✉*315 Gold Ave. SW, Downtown* ☎*505/242–2200*), a funky-hip downtown lounge popular for its cool juke box and extensive happy hours, draws a mix of students, yuppies, and music fans. Many nights there's live music, from punk to rockabilly to trance.

Like its neighbor Atomic Cantina, **Burt's Tiki Lounge** (✉*313 Gold Ave. SW,* ☎*505/247–BURT*), is a place to mingle with real Albuquerque folk who do not suffer from pretense.

Graham Central Station (✉*4770 Montgomery Blvd. NE, Northeast Heights* ☎*505/883–3041*), part of a rowdy regional chain of massive nightclubs, consists of four distinct bars under one roof: country-western, rock, dance, and Latin. It's open Wednesday–Saturday.

Martini Grille (✉*4200 Central Ave. SE, Nob Hill* ☎*505/242–4333*) offers live piano in a swank setting; this gay-popular spot is also a respectable restaurant serving burgers, sandwiches, pastas, and salads.

O'Niell's Pub (✉*4310 Central Ave. SE, Nob Hill* ☎*505/256–0564*) moved into a handsome new space in summer 2006, where it continues to serve good Mexican and American comfort food and present jazz, bebop, and other musicians in a cheery neighborhood bar near the University of New Mexico.

CASINOS

If you love to gamble, the Albuquerque area has a surfeit of options, including Santa Ana, San Felipe, Sandia, Isleta, Laguna, and Acoma pueblos.

Isleta Casino & Resort (✉*11000 Broadway SE, Exit 215 from I-25 Isleta Pueblo* ☎*877/747–5382* ⊕*www.isleta-casino.com*) is located just "7 lucky minutes" south of the Albuquerque airport. Here you can belly up to over 30 table games, sit down at one of 1,600 slots (reel and video styles), or join a high-stakes bingo or poker tournament. The smoke is thick wherever you go (despite designated non-smoking zones), but you can seek respite in their swank new hotel (or spurn it all and take in a show). Live music here ranges from cabaret acts in the Showroom, and headliners like the Neville Brothers and Dr. John in their 2,500-seat outdoor amphitheater. (F *see Side-Trips from Albuquerque for more on Isleta Pueblo*).

Sandia Resort & Casino (⊠*Tramway Rd. NE at I–25, Far Northeast Heights* ☎*505/796–7500 or 800/526–9366* ⊕*www.sandiacasino. com*) is a light, open, airy resort with an enormous gaming area brightened up by soaring ceilings and big windows. In addition to 1,700 slot machines, you'll find craps, blackjack, mini baccarat, and several versions of poker. The 4,200-seat casino amphitheater hosts rock-circuit stalwarts such as Earth, Wind & Fire; Kenny Rogers; Chicago; the occasional big-name comedian; and other acts.

COMEDY CLUBS

Laff's Comedy Club (⊠*6001 San Mateo Blvd. NE, Northeast Heights* ☎*505/296–5653*) serves up the live laughs (and dinner) Wednesday–Sunday.

LIVE MUSIC

People are always surprised to hear what a rich and varied music scene Albuquerque has—and at reasonable prices to boot. With world-class world-music festivals like Globalquerque! and the NM Jazz Festival, to norteño roots, heartstring-tearing country, blues, folk, and the latest rock permutations—and all manner of venues in which to hear (or dance to) them—there's even room for the big-arena warhorses, who mostly play the casinos these days.

¡Globalquerque! (⊕*www.globalquerque.com or ampconcerts.org*), a 2-day world music festival held at the National Hispanic Cultural Center, has been running annually in late September since 2005, and the acts and auxiliary programming just keep getting better. Festival producer AMP Concerts is also the organization that lures folks like David Byrne and the Cowboy Junkies to intimate venues downtown.

The 12,000-seat **Journal Pavilion** (⊠*5601 University Blvd. SE, Mesa del Sol* ☎*505/452–5100 or 505/246–8742* ⊕*www.journalpavilion. com*) amphitheater attracts big-name acts such as Green Day, Nine Inch Nails, Stevie Nicks, and the Dave Matthews Band.

Outpost Performance Space (⊠*210 Yale Blvd. SE, University of New Mexico* ☎*505/268–0044* ⊕*www.outpostspace.org*) programs an inspired, eclectic slate, from local nuevo-folk to techno, jazz, and traveling East Indian ethnic. Some surprisingly big names—especially in the jazz world—show up at this special small venue.

THE ARTS

Albuquerque has a remarkable wealth of local talent, but it also draws a surprising number of world-class stage performers from just about every discipline imaginable. Check the listings mentioned at the introduction to this section for everything from poetry readings, impromptu chamber music recitals, folk, jazz, and blues festivals, and formal symphony performances to film festivals, Flamenco Internacional, and theater.

MUSIC

The well-respected **New Mexico Symphony Orchestra** (☎*505/881–8999 or 800/251–6676 ⊕www.nmso.org)* plays pops, Beethoven, and, at Christmas, Handel's *Messiah*. Most performances are at 2,000-seat Popejoy Hall.

Popejoy Hall (⊠ *University of New Mexico Center for the Arts, Central Ave. NE at Stanford Dr. SE* ☎*505/277–4569 or 800/905–3315 ⊕www.popejoyhall.com)* presents concerts, from rock and pop to classical, plus comedy acts, lectures, and national tours of Broadway shows. UNM's Keller Hall, also in the Center for the Arts, is a small venue with fine acoustics, a perfect home for the University's excellent chamber music program.

THEATER

Albuquerque Little Theatre (⊠*224 San Pasquale Ave. SW, Old Town* ☎*505/242–4750 ⊕www.albuquerquelittletheatre.org)* is a nonprofit community troupe that's been going strong since 1930. Its staff of professionals teams up with local volunteer talent to produce comedies, dramas, musicals, and mysteries. The company theater, across the street from Old Town, was built in 1936 and designed by John Gaw Meem. It contains an art gallery, a large lobby, and a cocktail lounge.

★ The stunning **KiMo Theatre** (⊠*423 Central Ave. NW, Downtown* ☎*505/768–3522 or 505/768–3544 ⊕www.cabq.gov/kimo)*, an extravagantly ornamented 650-seat Pueblo Deco movie palace, is one of the best places in town to see anything. Jazz, dance—everything from traveling road shows to local song-and-dance acts—might turn up here. Former Albuquerque resident Vivian Vance of *I Love Lucy* fame once performed on the stage; today you're more likely to see Wilco or a film-festival screening.

While Popejoy Hall draws the numbers with its huge Broadway touring shows, UNM's **Rodey Theater** (⊠ *University of New Mexico Center for the Arts, Central and Stanford SE* ☎*505/277–4569 or 800/905–3315)*, a smaller house in the same complex, stages experimental and niche works throughout the year, including student and professional plays and dance performances such as the acclaimed annual Summerfest Festival of New Plays during July and the June Flamenco Festival.

Often working in conjunction with the National Hispanic Cultural Center (NHCC), the **Teatro Nuevo México** (⊠*107 Bryn Mawr SE, University of New Mexico* ☎*505/265–5200 ⊕www.teatronm.com)* is dedicated to presenting works created by Latino artists. In addition to plays by the likes of Federico García Lorca and Nilo Cruz, notable in their production roster is a revival of the Spanish operetta form known as zarzuela. These crowd-pleasing pieces may be comedies or drama, and are presented in collaboration with NHCC and the New Mexico Symphony Orchestra.

Come January and February of each year, theater fans of the fresh and new flock to the **Tricklock Company's** (✉ *1705 Mesa Vista Dr. NE, Nob Hill* ☎ *505/254–8393* ⊕ *www.tricklock.com*) REVOLUTIONS International Theatre Festival. Recognized internationally themselves, Tricklock's productions tour regularly, and emphasize works that take them—and their audience—to the edge of theatrical possibility.

SPORTS & THE OUTDOORS

Albuquerque is blessed with an exceptional setting for outdoor sports, backed by a favorable, if unpredictable, climate. Usually 10°F warmer than Santa Fe's, Albuquerque's winter days are often mild enough for most outdoor activities. The Sandias tempt you with challenging mountain adventures (⇨ *see the Sandia Park section of the Side Trips from Albuquerque section for details on mountain biking and skiing in the Sandia Mountains*); the Rio Grande and its Cottonwood forest, the Bosque, provide settings for additional outdoors pursuits.

PARTICIPANT SPORTS

The **City of Albuquerque** (☎ *505/768–5300* ⊕ *www.cabq.gov/living. html*) maintains a diversified network of cultural and recreational programs. Among the city's assets are more than 20,000 acres of open space, four golf courses, 200 parks, 68 paved tracks for biking and jogging, as well as swimming pools, tennis courts, ball fields, playgrounds, and a shooting range.

AMUSEMENT PARK

☺ Drive down San Mateo Northeast in summer and you can't help but glimpse a roller coaster smack in the middle of the city. **Cliff's Amusement Park** (✉ *4800 Osuna Rd. NE, off I–25 at San Mateo Blvd. NE, Northeast Heights* ☎ *505/881–9373* ⊕ *www.cliffsamusementpark.com*) is a clean, well-run attraction for everyone from two-year-olds on up. It features a wooden-track roller coaster as well as rides for all ages and state fair–type games of chance. The park also has a large water-play area. Cliff's is open early April through September, but days and hours vary greatly, so call first.

BALLOONING

Albuquerque is blessed with a high altitude, mild climate, and steady but manageable winds, making it an ideal destination for ballooning. A wind pattern famously known as the "Albuquerque Box," created by the city's location against the Sandia Mountains, makes Albuquerque a particularly great place to fly.

If you've never been ballooning, you may have a notion that it's an inherently bumpy experience, where changes in altitude replicate the queasiness-inducing feeling of being in a tiny propeller plane. Rest assured, the experience is far calmer than you'd ever imagine. The balloons are flown by licensed pilots (don't call them operators) who deftly switch propane-fueled flames on and off, climbing and descending to find winds blowing the way they want to go—thus, there's no real "steering" involved, which makes the pilots' control that much more admirable. The norm is for pilots to land balloons wherever the wind dictates—thus creating the need for "chase vehicles" that pick you up and return you to your departure point—but particularly skilled pilots can use conditions created by the "Box" to land precisely where you started. But even without this "door-to-door" service, many visitors rank a balloon ride soaring over the Rio Grande Valley as their most memorable experience while in town.

Fodor'sChoice
★ There are several reliable companies around metro Albuquerque that offer tours. A ride will set you back about $160–$180 per person. One of the best outfitters in town is **Rainbow Ryders** (☎505/823–1111 or 800/725–2477 ⊕www.rainbowryders.com), an official Ride Concession for the Albuquerque International Balloon Fiesta. Part of the fun is helping to inflate and, later on, pack away the balloon. And if you thought it best not to breakfast prior to your flight, a continental breakfast and champagne toast await your return.

BICYCLING

With the creation of many lanes, trails, and dedicated bike paths, Albuquerque's city leaders are recognized for their bike-friendly efforts—a serious challenge to the committed car culture of its residents. The city's public works department produces an elaborately detailed **bike map,** which can be obtained free by calling ☎505/768–3550 or downloaded from ⊕www.cabq.gov/bike.

Albuquerque has miles of bike lanes and trails crisscrossing and skirting the city as well as great mountain-biking trails at Sandia Peak Ski Area *(⇨See the Sandia Park section of the Side Trips from the Cities chapter).*

While mountain bikes may be rented up in the Sandias, bike rental sources are scarce around town. **Northeast Cyclery** (⊠8305 *Menaul Blvd. NE, Northeast Heights* ☎505/299–1210) has a good range of road and mountain bikes for rent. Most are unisex styles, and they carry kid sizes as well.

Seasonally, at **Tingley Beach** (⊕www.cabq.gov) balloon tire and mountain bikes are available by the hour (⇨ *see What to See, under Albu-*
★ *querque BioPark).*The **Paseo del Bosque Bike Trail** (⊕www.cabq.gov) runs right through Tingley. It's flat as a pancake for most of its 16-mile run, but it is one of the loveliest rides in town.

BIRD-WATCHING

The Rio Grande Valley, one of the continent's major flyways, attracts many migratory bird species. Good bird-viewing locales include the **Rio Grande Nature Center State Park** (⊠2901 *Candelaria Rd. NW, North Valley* ☎505/344–7240 ⊕www.nmparks.com).

GOLF

Most of the better courses in the region—and there are some outstanding ones—are just outside of town *(⇨See the North-Central New Mexico chapter for details).* The four courses operated by the city of

Albuquerque actually hold their own pretty nicely, and the rates are extremely fair. Each course has a clubhouse and pro shop, where clubs and other equipment can be rented. Weekday play is first-come, first-served, but reservations are taken for weekends. Contact the **Golf Management Office** (☎ *505/888–8115* ⊕*www.cabq.gov/golf*) for details. Of the four city courses, **Arroyo del Oso** (⊠*7001 Osuna Rd. NE, Northeast Heights* ☎*505/884–7505*) earns high marks for its undulating 27-hole layout; greens fees are $26 for 18 holes. The 18-hole **Los Altos Golf Course** (⊠*9717 Copper Ave. NE, Northeast Heights* ☎*505/298–1897*), one of the region's most popular facilities, has $26 greens fees. There's also a short, par-3, 9-hole "executive course."

★ **Sandia Golf Club** (⊠*Tramway Rd. NE just east of I–25, Far Northeast Heights* ☎*505/798–3990* ⊕*www.sandiagolf.com*), opened in 2005 at the swanky Sandia Resort & Casino, offers 18 holes set amid lush hilly fairways, cascading waterfalls, and desert brush. Greens fees are $51–$61. The University of New Mexico has two superb courses. Both are open daily and have full-service pro shops, instruction, and snack bars. Greens fees for out-of-staters run about $60 to $70, with cart. **UNM North** (⊠*Tucker Rd. at Yale Blvd., University of New Mexico* ☎*505/277–4146*) is a first-class 9-hole, par-36 course on the north side of campus. The 18-hole facility at **UNM South** (⊠*3601 University Blvd., just west of airport off I–25, Southeast Heights* ☎*505/277–4546* ⊕*www.unmgolf.com*) has garnered countless awards from major golf magazines and hosted PGA and LPGA qualifying events; there's also a short par-3 9-hole course.

HIKING

In the foothills in Albuquerque's Northeast Heights, you'll find great hiking in **Cíbola National Forest**, which can be accessed directly from Tramway Road Northeast, about 4 mi east of I–25 or 2 mi north of Paseo del Norte. Just follow the road into the hillside, and you'll find several parking areas (there's a daily parking fee of $3). This is where you'll find the trailhead for the steep and quite challenging **La Luz Trail**, which climbs some 9 mi (an elevation of more than 3,000 feet) up to the top of Sandia Crest. You can take the Sandia Peak Aerial Tram (⇨ *see Exploring Albuquerque, above*) to the top and then hike down the trail, or vice versa (keep in mind that it can take up to six hours to hike up the trail, and four to five hours to hike down). Spectacular views of Albuquerque and many miles of desert and mountain beyond that are had from the trail. And you can still enjoy a hike along here without going the whole way—if your energy and time are limited, just hike a mile or two and back. No matter how far you hike, however, pack plenty of water.

SPECTATOR SPORTS

BASEBALL

Since 2003 the city has hosted Triple A minor league baseball's **Albuquerque Isotopes** (⊠*University Ave. SE at Ave. Cesar Chavez SE, Southeast* ☎*505/924–2255* ⊕*www.albuquerquebaseball.com*), the farm club of the Major League Florida Marlins; the season runs April through August.

BASKETBALL

It's hard to beat the excitement of home basketball games of the **University of New Mexico Lobos** (✉ *University Ave. at Ave. Cesar Chavez, Southeast* ☎ *505/925–5626* ⊕ *http://golobos.cstv.com*), when 18,000 rabid fans crowd into the school's arena, "the Pit," from November to March. Both the women's and men's teams enjoy huge success every year.

FOOTBALL

The competitively ranked **University of New Mexico Lobos** (✉ *University Ave. at Ave. Cesar Chavez, Southeast* ☎ *505/925–5626* ⊕ *golobos.cstv. com*) play at the 40,000-seat University Stadium in the fall.

SHOPPING

Albuquerque's shopping strengths include a handful of cool retail districts, including Nob Hill, Old Town, and the rapidly gentrifying downtown. These are good neighborhoods for galleries, antiques, and home-furnishing shops, bookstores, and offbeat gift shops. Otherwise, the city is mostly the domain of both strip and indoor malls, mostly filled with ubiquitous chain shops, although you can find some worthy independent shops even in these venues.

SHOPPING NEIGHBORHOODS & MALLS

The **Uptown** (✉ *Louisiana Blvd. NE, between I-40 and Menaul Blvd. NE*) neighborhood is Albuquerque's mall central. From worst to best the big 3 are: Winrock (on the east side of Louisiana Blvd., just north of I-40), which is in a major slump; Coronado (at Louisiana Blvd. NE and Menaul Blvd. NE), which has a big Barnes & Noble and new Sephora; and the newest, and definitely best of the lot, ABQ Uptown (east side, closer to Menaul), which is all outdoors and sports an Apple Store, MAC cosmetics shop, and Williams-Sonoma.

On the far northwest outskirts of town, **Cottonwood Mall** (✉ *Coors Blvd. NW at Coors Bypass, West Side* ☎ *505/899–7467*), is anchored by Dillard's, Foley's, Mervyn's, JCPenney, and Sears Roebuck and has about 130 other shops, including Williams-Sonoma, Aveda, Cache, and Abercrombie & Fitch. There are a dozen restaurants and food stalls, plus a 14-screen theater complex.

Albuquerque's **Downtown** (✉ *Central and Gold Aves. from 1st to 10th Sts.*) has had its highs and lows, but local developers are firm on renting strictly to independent businesses, making an effort to keep downtown from turning into just another collection of chain outlets. In the meantime, stroll along Central and Gold avenues (and neighboring blocks) to admire avant-garde galleries, cool cafés, and curious boutiques.

Funky **Nob Hill** (⊠*Central Ave. from Girard Blvd. to Washington St.*), just east of University of New Mexico and anchored by old Route 66, pulses with colorful storefronts and kitschy signs. At night, neon-lighted boutiques, galleries, and performing-arts spaces encourage foot traffic. Many of the best shops are clustered inside or on the blocks near Nob Hill Business Center, an art deco structure containing several intriguing businesses and La Montañita Natural Foods Co-op, an excellent spot for a snack.

Old Town (⊠*Central Ave. and Rio Grande Blvd.*) has the city's largest concentration of one-of-a-kind retail shops, selling clothing, home accessories, Native American art, and Mexican imports…and a predictable wealth of schlock targeted at tourists.

ART GALLERIES

In addition to Tamarind Institute and Jonson Gallery, both at UNM (⇨ *see University of New Mexico & Nob Hill "What to See" section, above*), Albuquerque has a solid and growing gallery scene. For comprehensive gallery listings, pickup a copy of the *freebie annual Collector's Guide* (⊕*www.collectorsguide.com); for current shows and ArtsCrawl schedules,* lookup the Arts & Cultural Calendar online (⊕*www.abqarts.org/calendar.htm or* ⊕*www.artscrawlabq.org*).

516 Arts (⊠*516 Central Ave. SW, Downtown* ☎*505/242–1445* ⊕*www.516arts.org*) holds a special place in the Duke City's artworld. They offer world-class contemporary art in changing shows that not only cross media boundaries (their collaborative—with AMP Concerts and the KiMo—2008 Guerrilla Girls performance is an example), but challenge a viewer's expectations of what art is, and what it means to them. Exhibits mine the work of local and national artists, and are as likely to speak to issues as they are offer to a powerfully appealing visual presence. LAND/ART, a 2009 series on site-specific environmental art, and the recent "Trappings: Stories of Women, Power, and Clothing," which combined gallery pieces with projections on buses and buildings, are a few examples of 516's commitment.

Every few weeks the exhibits at **Artspace 116** (⊠*116 Central Ave. SW, 2nd FloorDowntown* ☎*505/245–4200* ⊕*www.artspace116.org*) are switched out in order to display the work of yet another New Mexico artist. The small gallery's mission is to present highly selective one-time shows—of prints, oils, sculpture, and any other media—that will help expose an artist to a new audience. Geometric clay vessels by Elizabeth Fritzsche, moody black-and-white photographs by Steven M. Williams, and Allan Rosenfield's large-scale color-driven acrylic and mixed-media pieces are highlights of recent years.

Harwood Art Center(⊠*1114 7th St. NW, off Mountain Rd.Old Town* ☎*505/242–6367* ⊕*www.harwoodartcenter.org*), on the fringe of Downtown and Old Town in the Sawmill/Wells Park neighborhood, is a remarkable resource for its huge roster of community-oriented art classes, and a gallery in its own right. Shows—predominantly of

NM–based artists working in non-traditional forms—take place in their historic brick school building and change monthly.

★ **Coleman Gallery Contemporary Art** (✉ *4115 Silver Ave. SE, Nob Hill* ☎ *505/232–0224* ⊕ *www.colemancontemporary.com*) has emerged as one of Nob Hill's leading art spaces, showing works by a number of the state's top contemporary talents who work largely in an abstract vein.

DSG (✉ *510 14th St. SW, Old Town* ☎ *505/266–7751 or 800/474–7751* ⊕ *www.dsg-art.com*), owned by John Cacciatore, handles works of paint, tapestry, sculpture, and photography by leading regional artists, including Frank McCulloch, Carol Hoy, Leo Neufeld, Larry Bell, Angus Macpherson, Jim Bagley, Nancy Kozikowski, and photographer Nathan Small.

Mariposa Gallery (✉ *3500 Central Ave. SE, Nob Hill* ☎ *505/268–6828* ⊕ *www.mariposa-gallery.com*) sells contemporary fine crafts, including jewelry, sculptural glass, works in mixed media and clay, and fiber arts. The changing exhibits focus on upcoming artists; their buyer's sharp eyes can result in real finds for the serious browser.

★ **Weyrich Gallery** (✉ *2935–D Louisiana Blvd. NE, Uptown* ☎ *505/883–7410* ⊕ *www.weyrichgallery.com*) carries distinctive jewelry, fine art, Japanese tea bowls, woodblocks, hand-color photography, and other largely Asian-inspired pieces.

SPECIALTY STORES

ANTIQUES

FodorśChoice **Classic Century Square Antique Mall** (✉ *4516 Central Ave. SE, Nob*
★ *Hill* ☎ *505/268–8080*) is a three-story emporium of collectibles and antiques. The emphasis is on memorabilia from the early 1880s to the 1950s. (When the set designers for the television miniseries *Lonesome Dove* needed props, they came here.) Items for sale include art deco and art nouveau objects, retro-cool '50s designs, Depression-era glass, Native American goods, quilts and linens, vintage clothes, and Western memorabilia.

Cowboys & Indians (✉ *4000 Central Ave. SE, Nob Hill* ☎ *505/255–4054*) carries Native American and cowboy art and artifacts.

BOOKS

One of the last of the great independents, **Bookworks** (✉ *4022 Rio Grande Blvd. NW, one block north of Griegos Rd. NW, North Valley* ☎ *505/344–8139* ⊕ *www.bkwrks.com*) maintains an ecelectic stock of regional coffee-table books, a well-culled selection of modern fiction and non-fiction, architecture and design titles, and a (small) playground's worth of kids books. Regular signings and readings draw some very big guns to this tiny treasure.

Massive **Page One** (✉ *11018 Montgomery Blvd. NE, Far Northeast Heights* ☎ *505/294–2026*), arguably the best bookstore in Albuquerque, specializes in technical and professional titles, maps, globes, children's titles, and 150 out-of-state and foreign newspapers. Book signings, poetry readings, and children's events are frequently scheduled.

GIFTS, FOOD & TOYS

Beeps (✉*Nob Hill Shopping Center, 3500 Central Ave. SE, Nob Hill* ☎*505/262–1900*), a Nob Hill favorite, carries cards, T-shirts, and amusing, if bawdy, novelties.

Candy Lady (✉*Mountain Rd. at Rio Grande Blvd., Old Town* ☎*505/224–9837 or 800/214–7731*) is known as much for its scandalous adult novelty candies as for its tasty red- and green-chili brittle, plus the usual fudge, chocolates, piñon caramels, and candies. A small room, to the right as you enter, displays the "adult" candy, so you can easily pilot any kids in your party past it.

La Casita de Kaleidoscopes (✉*Poco A Poco Patio, 326–D San Felipe St. NW, Old Town* ☎*505/247–4242*) carries both contemporary and vintage kaleidoscopes of all styles, by more than 80 top artists in the field.

Theobroma Chocolatier (✉*12611 Montgomery Blvd. NE, Far Northeast Heights* ☎*505/293–6545*) carries beautifully handcrafted, high-quality chocolates, truffles, and candies (most of them made on premises), as well as Taos Cow ice cream.

HOME FURNISHINGS

FodorśChoice
★
A (✉*3500 Central Ave. SE, Nob Hill* ☎*505/266–2222*) is a Nob Hill stop for housewares, soaps, candles, body-care products, and jewelry.

A branch of a popular regional chain, **El Paso Import Co.** (✉*3500 Central Ave. SE, Nob Hill* ☎*505/265–1160*) carries distressed and "peely-paint" antique-looking chests and tables loaded with character. If you love the "shabby chic" look, head to this Nob Hill furniture shop.

Hey Jhonny (✉*3418 Central Ave. SE, Nob Hill* ☎*505/256–9244*) is an aromatic store full of exquisite candles, soaps, pillows, fountains, and other soothing items for the home; there's also a branch that carries more furniture and larger pieces around the corner, at 118 Tulane Street.

Jackalope (✉*6400 San Mateo Blvd. NE, Northeast Heights* ☎*505/349–0955*), the favorite Southwestern furniture and bric-a-brac shop in Bernalillo and Santa Fe now has two Albuquerque branches, one here in the Heights, and the other in Old Town. Both of these new franchises aren't quite up to par with the mother ship up north, but they are still a good source of garden furniture, pottery, folk art, and rugs.

Objects of Desire (✉*3225 Central Ave. NE, Nob Hill* ☎*505/232–3088*) is the place to find that special lamp or table from a whimsical and worldly collection of furnishings that appeal to individualized tastes.

Peacecraft (✉*3215 Central Ave. NE, Nob Hill* ☎*505/255–5229*) supports fair trade and stocks handmade folk art and crafts from all around the world—wooden boxes from Kenya, clothing from Guatemala, hats from Honduras. The store also employs a number of university students on work-study.

HISPANIC IMPORTS & TRADITIONS

An Old Town stalwart since the late 1970s, **Casa Talavera** (✉ *621 Rio Grande Blvd., Old Town* ☎ *505/243–2413* ⊕ *www.casatalavera.com*) is just outside the Plaza area, across Rio Grande Blvd. Do venture across to peruse their wide selection of hand-painted Mexican Talavera tiles. Prices are reasonable, making the colorful geometrics, florals, mural patterns, and solids, close to irresistible. Tin lighting fixtures as well as ceramic sink and cabinet knobs fill in the rest of the space in this DIY-inspiring shop (they can hook you up with installation information too).

Hispanaie (✉ *410 Romero St. NW, Old Town* ☎ *505/244–1533* ⊕ *www. hispanaie.com*) is like the Jackalope of yore, and then some. Sure they have every permutation of Our Lady of Guadalupe imaginable (switchplates, tin tokens, etc.), but Nuestra Señora is just the tip of it. This long narrow space is packed with finds of the Latino craft kind, from inexpensive cake toppers in the shape of sweet little pigs to painted tin Christmas ornaments and hand-carved hardwood furnishings.

La Piñata (✉ *No. 2 Patio Market, 206 San Felipe St. NW, Old Town* ☎ *505/242–2400*) specializes in piñatas and papier-mâché products, plus Native American jewelry and leather goods.

Saints & Martyrs (✉ *404 San Felipe NW, Old Town* ☎ *505/224–9323* ⊕ *www.saints-martyrs.com*) has almost a gallery feel to it. Their hand-painted retablos and other saintly images are displayed so well that it's easy to imagine how they might look in your own home. This is an excellent place to lay in a supply of milagros; they have an unusually high-quality selection in sterling.

MUSIC

Natural Sound (✉ *3422 Central Ave. SE, Nob Hill* ☎ *505/255–8295*) is an eclectic record store with a large selection of new and used CDs.

NATIVE AMERICAN ARTS & CRAFTS

Andrews Pueblo Pottery (✉ *303 Romero St. NW, Suite 116, Old Town* ☎ *505/243–0414*) carries a terrific selection of Pueblo pottery, fetishes, kachina dolls, and baskets for the beginning and seasoned collector.

Bien Mur Indian Market Center (✉ *Tramway Rd. NE east of I–25, Northeast Heights* ☎ *505/821–5400 or 800/365–5400*) in Sandia Pueblo showcases the best of the best in regional Native American rugs, jewelry, and crafts of all kinds. You can feel very secure about what you purchase at this trading post, and prices are fair for what you get.

Gertrude Zachary (✉ *1501 Lomas Blvd. NW, Old Town* ☎ *505/247–4442* ✉ *3300 Central Ave. SE, Nob Hill* ☎ *505/766–4700* ✉ *416 2nd St. SW, Downtown* ☎ *505/244–1320*) dazzles with its selection of Native American jewelry. Don't let her screaming billboards around town deter you—this may be your best place to get a bargain on a good bracelet or ring. Locals buy here, too. The 2nd Street branch carries antiques.

To get a feel for what goes into the copious amounts of Native American jewelry you see around town (or if you have a mind to learn the craft yourself), a stop at the fascinating **Indian Jewelers Supply** (✉ *2105 San Mateo Blvd. NE, 1 block south of Indian School Rd. NE, at Haines Ave. NE Uptown* ☎ *505/265–3701* ⊕ *www.ijsinc.com*) is a must. Trays of gemstones (finished and not), silver by weight, all manner of findings, and of course the tools to work them with, fill this large space. Open 8–6, it's best to go mid-mornings after the early rush.

★ **Margaret Moses Gallery.** (✉ *326 San Felipe St. NW, Old Town* ☎ *505/842–1808 or 888/842–1808*) stocks Pueblo pottery, including the black earthenware pottery of San Ildefonso, as well as the work of potters from Acoma, Santa Clara, Isleta, and Zía. Rare Zuñi and Navajo jewelry is on display, as are Navajo weavings from 1900 to the present.

SIDE TRIPS FROM ALBUQUERQUE

SOUTH OF ALBUQUERQUE

When Francisco Vásquez de Coronado arrived in what is now New Mexico in 1540, he found a dozen or so villages along the Rio Grande in the ancient province of Tiguex, between what is now Bernalillo to the north of Albuquerque and Isleta to the south. Of those, only Sandia and Isleta survive today. The Salinas Pueblo Missions ruins, about 65 mi southeast of Albuquerque, remain a striking example of the Spanish penchant for building churches on sites inhabited by native people.

ISLETA PUEBLO
13 mi south of Albuquerque, via I–25 (Exit 213) and NM 47.

Of the pueblos in New Mexico when the Spanish first arrived, Isleta Pueblo is one of two Tiwa-speaking communities left in the middle of the Rio Grande Valley. It was also one of a handful of pueblos that didn't participate in the Pueblo Revolt of 1680, during which Isleta was abandoned. Some of the residents fled New Mexico with the Spanish to El Paso, where their descendants live to this day on a reservation called Ysleta del Sur. Other members went to live with the Hopi of Arizona but eventually returned and rebuilt the pueblo.

Facing the quiet plaza is Isleta's church, **St. Augustine,** built in 1629. One of the oldest churches in New Mexico, it has thick adobe walls, a viga-crossed ceiling, and an austere interior. Legend has it that the ground beneath the floor has the odd propensity to push church and community figures buried under the floor back up out of the ground; bodies have supposedly been reburied several times, only to emerge again.

Polychrome pottery with red and black designs on a white background is a specialty here. The pueblo celebrates its feast days on August 28

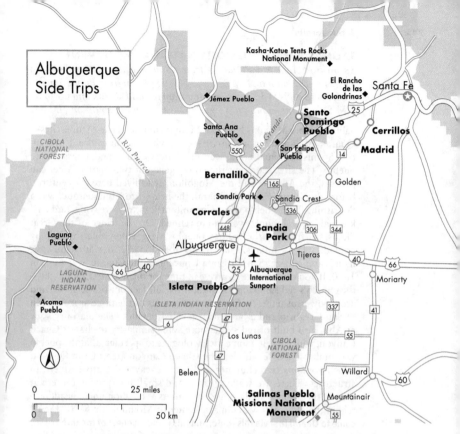

and September 4, both in honor of St. Augustine. The tribal government maintains picnicking and camping facilities, several fishing ponds, and a renowned 18-hole golf course. It also runs the **Isleta Casino & Resort** (⊠*11000 Broadway SE (NM 47)87105* ☎*505/724–3800 or 877/747–5382* ⊕*www.isletacasinoresort.com*), which ranks among the state's most popular gaming facilities. It's a large and handsome space with plenty of slots and myriad gaming tables; the concert hall hosts a mix of oldies, pop stars, and country-western acts—past numbers have included Tom Jones, Vince Gill, and Tony Bennett. There's also boxing held throughout the year. A full-service, upscale 201-room hotel and spa opened in 2008 making Isleta more competitive with other high-profile Native American resorts in the Rio Grande region, including Sandia, Santa Ana, and Pojoaque. Although Isleta is wonderfully picturesque—beehive ovens stand beside adobe homes bedecked with crimson chiles—camera use is restricted here. Only the church may be photographed. ⊠*Tribal Rd. 40* ☎*505/869–3111* ⊕*www. isletapueblo.com* ⊠*Free.*

SPORTS & THE OUTDOORS One of the most esteemed facilities in the state, **Isleta Eagle Golf Course** (⊠*4001 NM 47 SE87105* ☎*505/848–1900 or 866/475–3822* ⊕*www. isletaeagle.com*) consists of three 9-hole layouts set around three lakes; greens fees are $40–$55 for 18 holes.

SALINAS PUEBLO MISSIONS NATIONAL MONUMENT

58 mi (to Punta Agua/Quarai) from Albuquerque, east on I–40 (to Tijeras Exit), south on NM 337 and NM 55; 23 mi from Punta Agua to Abó, south on NM 55, west (at Mountainair) on U.S. 60, and north on NM 513; 34 mi from Punta Agua to Gran Quivira, south on NM 55.

Salinas Pueblo Missions National Monument is made up of three sites— **Quarai, Abó, and Gran Quivira**—each with the ruins of a 17th-century Spanish-colonial Franciscan missionary church and an associated pueblo. The sites represent the convergence of two Native American peoples, the Anasazi and the Mogollon, who lived here for centuries before the Spanish arrived. Quarai, the nearest to Albuquerque, was a flourishing Tiwa pueblo whose inhabitants' pottery, weaving, and basket-making techniques were quite refined. On the fringe of the Great Plains, all three of the Salinas pueblos were vulnerable to raids by nomadic Plains Indians. Quarai was abandoned about 50 years after its mission church, **San Purísima Concepción de Cuarac,** was built in 1630. If you can arrange it, arrive in time for the late afternoon light— the church's red sandstone walls still rise 40 feet out of the earth, and are a powerful sight. At Abó are the remains of the three-story church of San Gregorio and a large unexcavated pueblo. (The masonry style at Abó, also built of red stone, bore some similarity to that at Chaco Canyon, which has led some archaeologists to speculate that the pueblo was built by people who left the Chaco Canyon area.) Gran Quivira, which contains two churches and some excavated Native American structures. There are walking trails and small interpretive centers at each of the pueblos, and expanded exhibits at the monument headquarters in the old cowtown cum arts center of Mountainair. ■TIP→You'll come to Quarai first via this route, and this is the loveliest of the three, with Abó—which you can swing by easily enough if you loop back to Albuquerque via US 60 west (through Mountainair), then north on either NM 47 (for the scenic back route through Isleta); or I-25—a close second. Gran Quivira is more of a detour, and you might find yourself wanting to take a little time to stroll down Mountainair's quaint main street then getting a bite at Pop Shaffer's Café (below) instead. ⊠*N. Ripley Ave. at W. Broadway (U.S. 60), Mountainair* ☎*505/847–2585* ⊕*www.nps.gov/sapu* ⊠*Free* ☉*Late May–early Sept., daily 9–6; early Sept.–late May, daily 9–5.*

BEYOND THE NORTH VALLEY

The land north of Albuquerque is a little bit cooler, a little bit greener, and a lot more pastoral than the city. Drive slowly through Bernalillo and Corrales, and you're bound to see lots of horses, cows, and llamas.

CORRALES

2 mi north of Albuquerque. Take Paseo Del Norte (NM 423) or Alameda Blvd. (NM 528) west from I-25 and head north on Corrales Rd. (NM 448).

Serene Corrales is an ancient agricultural community now inhabited by artists, craftspeople, and the affluent—plus a few descendants of the old families. Small galleries, shops, and places to eat dot the town, and in fall, roadside fruit and vegetable stands open. Bordered by Albuquerque and Rio Rancho, Corrales makes a pleasant escape to winding dirt roads, fields of corn, and apple orchards. On summer weekends visit the Corrales Farmers' Market; in October, the village holds a Harvest Festival. The village's main drag, NM 448, is one of New Mexico's official scenic byways, lined with grand estates and haciendas and shaded by cottonwoods. Just off the byway, you can break for a stroll through Corrales Bosque Preserve, a shaded sanctuary abutting the Rio Grande that's a favorite spot for bird-watching—some 180 species pass through here throughout the year. You can also catch a glimpse of historic hacienda life when you take a tour of the exquisitely restored 19th-century adobe compound of Casa San Ysidro. (⊠*973 Old Church Rd., Corrales* ☎*505/898–3915* ⊕*www.cabq.gov* ☜*$4* ⊗ *Wed.–Sun., call for times*).

WHERE TO EAT & STAY

$$$ ✕ **The Old House Gastropub.** Set in a rambling early-18th-century com-
ECLECTIC pound along the Corrales Scenic Byway, this purportedly haunted hacienda was, for many years, the esteemed Casa Vieja. It hit a rough patch after charismatic chef Jim White sold it in 2005, but it seems to be finding itself again under its new Brit owners. They have re-purposed it as a casual pub with an unusually meaty twist: you'll find burgers of yak, ostrich, wild boar, and more—all supposedly not on the endangered species list. Stick with the simple dishes and go here knowing its historic vibe is a key part of your meal. ⊠*4541 Corrales Rd.87048* ☎*505/898–7489* ⊟*AE, D, MC, V.*

¢–$ ✕ **Village Pizza.** A Chicago native with a knack for baking runs this
PIZZA ordinarily named joint that serves extraordinarily good pizza. Crusts come in different styles (including Chicago-style deep dish), and a wide range of toppings are offered, including such gourmet fixings as artichoke hearts and smoked oysters. In back is an adobe-walled courtyard with a couple of big leafy trees and lots of seating. You get a 10 percent discount if you ride in on horseback. ⊠*4266 Corrales Rd.87048* ☎*505/898–0045* ⊟*AE, D, MC, V.*

★ $ 🏠 **Chocolate Turtle B&B.** Hosts Nancy and Dallas Renner run this light-filled four-room hideaway in a quiet neighborhood in West Corrales. It's a short drive from Rio Rancho and 20-minutes from downtown Albuquerque, but the setting is as peaceful as can be, this Territorial-style home's large windows and neatly landscaped grounds affording sweeping views of the Sandia Mountains. Fresh flowers further brighten the colorfully painted Southwestern-themed rooms, which range from a cozy single to three more substantial doubles, the most desirable with its own private terrace. **Pros:** Service is always good. **Cons:** Decor may be a little too bright for some. ⊠*1098 W. Meadowlark La., Corrales* ☎*505/898–1800 or 877/298–1800* ⊕*www. chocolateturtlebb.com* ➴*4 rooms* ⚿*In-room: no phone, no TV, Wi-Fi* ⊟*AE, D, MC, V* ⦿*BP.*

BERNALILLO

17 mi north of Albuquerque via I–25, 8 mi north of Corrales via NM 448 to NM 528.

Once a rather tranquil Hispanic village, Bernalillo is today one of New Mexico's fastest-growing towns—it's increasingly absorbing the suburban growth northward from Albuquerque. The town holds a Wine Festival each Labor Day weekend, but the most memorable annual event is the Fiesta of San Lorenzo, which has honored the town's patron saint for nearly 400 years. On August 10, San Lorenzo Day, the entire town takes to the streets to participate in the traditional masked *matachine* dance. Matachines, of Moorish origin, were brought to this hemisphere by the Spanish. In New Mexico various versions are danced to haunting fiddle music, in both Native American pueblos and old Spanish villages at different holidays. Though interpretations of the matachines are inexact, one general theme is that of conquest. One dancer, wearing a devil's mask and wielding a whip, presides over the others. A young girl, dressed in white, is also present.

The town's leading attraction, **Coronado State Monument,** is named in honor of Francisco Vásquez de Coronado, the leader of the first organized Spanish expedition into the Southwest, from 1540 to 1542. The prehistoric **Kuaua Pueblo,** on a bluff overlooking the Rio Grande, is believed to have been the headquarters of Coronado and his army, who were caught unprepared by severe winter weather during their search for the legendary Seven Cities of Gold. A worthy stop, the monument has a museum in a restored kiva, with copies of magnificent frescoes done in black, yellow, red, blue, green, and white. The frescoes depict fertility rites, rain dances, and hunting rituals. The original artworks are preserved in the small visitor center. Adjacent to the monument is **Coronado State Park,** which has campsites and picnic grounds, both open year-round. In autumn the views at the monument and park are especially breathtaking, with the trees turning russet and gold. There's also overnight camping at the adjacent Coronado Campground (505/980–8256). ⊠*485 Kuaua Rd., off NM 44/U.S. 550* ☎*505/867–5351* ⊕*www.nmstatemonuments.org* ⊠*$3* ☉ *Wed.–Mon. 8:30–5.*

WHERE TO EAT & STAY

★ **$$$$**
ECLECTIC
✗ **Prairie Star.** Albuquerque residents often make the drive to this 1920s Pueblo Revival hacienda, renowned for the sunset views from its patio. The menu combines contemporary American, Southwestern, and classical cuisine, including duck-confit crepes with red-chili-infused blueberries, lemon chèvre, mint, and pistachios, and dry-aged prime New York steak with black truffle potatoes, cheesy collard greens, and roasted garlic–tomato confit. The culinary quality has become consistently outstanding over the years, and the setting is gorgeous. Prairie Star is on the Santa Ana reservation, right beside the Santa Ana Golf Club. ⊠*288 Prairie Star Rd., Santa Ana Pueblo* ☎*505/867–3327* ⊕*www.santaanagolf.com* ⊟*AE, D, DC, MC, V* ☉ *Closed Mon. No lunch.*

1

$ **✕ Range Cafe & Bakery.** Banana pancakes, giant cinnamon rolls, Asian
ECLECTIC spinach salad, grilled portobello burgers, homemade meat loaf with
Fodor's Choice garlic mashed potatoes, steak-and-enchilada platters, and the signature
★ dessert, Death by Lemon, are among the highlights at this quirky spot
known for down-home fare with creative touches. All the above, plus
a full complement of rich, decadent Taos Cow ice cream, is served in a
refurbished mercantile building with a dead-center view of the Sandia
Mountains. You can order breakfast fare until 3 PM. There are also two
newer branches in Albuquerque, but the original has the best ambience.
✉ *925 Camino del Pueblo* ☎ *505/867–1700* ⊕ *www.rangecafe.com*
⌫ *Reservations not accepted* ☰ *AE, D, MC, V.*

$$$$ ▨ **Hyatt Regency Tamaya.** This spectacular large-scale resort, on 500
Fodor's Choice acres on the Santa Ana Pueblo, includes a top-rated golf course, state-
★ of-the-art spa, and cultural museum and learning center. Most rooms,
swathed in natural stone, wood, and adobe and filled with pueblo-
inspired textiles and pottery, overlook the Sandia Mountains or cottonwood groves; many have balconies or patios. Cultural events include
bread-baking demonstrations (in traditional adobe ovens), storytelling,
and live tribal dance and music performances. Other amenities include
waterslides over two of the outdoor pools, atmospheric bars, guided
nature walks, and hot-air ballooning nearby. The Hyatt's outstanding **Corn Maiden Restaurant** (⊙ *Closed Sun. and Mon. No lunch.*)
serves outstanding contemporary fare that mixes New Mexican, Asian,
regional American influences and ingredients. Try buffalo topped with
foie gras and a truffle demi-glace, or crispy-skin duck served with an
apple–green chili pancake and orange-whiskey sauce. The Santa Ana
Star Casino is a free shuttle ride away. And if you're looking for an
exceptional horseback ride, arrange one with the Tamaya stables. As
you drink in eyefuls of the spectacular pueblo backcountry and weave
among trees and plantings, you'll wonder why you ever settled for the
dull nose-to-butt riding experiences of yesteryear. If you're too suave to
wear the helmet or gloves offered, by all means do not forego a heavy
layer of sunscreen, especially on your face, ears, and neck. **Pros:** This
is the place to come to get away. **Cons:** Occasionally quirky front-
desk service, but that's it. ✉ *1300 Tuyuna Trail, Santa Ana Pueblo,*
☎ *505/867–1234 or 800/633–7313* ☎ *505/771–6180* ⊕ *www.tamaya.
hyatt.com* ⇄ *331 rooms, 19 suites* ⌂ *In-room: Wi-Fi, refrigerator. In-
hotel: 3 restaurants, room service, bars, golf course, tennis courts,
pools, gym, spa, concierge, children's programs (ages 2–14)* ☰ *AE, D,
DC, MC, V.*

SANTO DOMINGO PUEBLO

*40 mi northeast of Albuquerque via I–25; exit on NM 22 and drive
4½ mi west.*

Santo Domingo Pueblo craftspeople sell outstanding *heishi* (shell) jewelry and pottery, along with other traditional arts and crafts, year-
round, but the pueblo's three-day Labor Day Arts and Crafts Fair brings
out artists and visitors in full force. The colorful, dramatic Corn Dance,
held in honor of St. Dominic, the pueblo's patron saint, on August 4,
attracts more than 2,000 dancers, clowns, singers, and drummers.

Painter Georgia O'Keeffe supposedly said the Corn Dance was one of the great events in her life. Still and video cameras, tape recorders, and sketching materials are prohibited. It's quite easy to visit the pueblo as part of a trip to Tent Rocks, covered in the South of Santa Fe section. ⊠*Off NM 22, 4½ mi west of I–25* ☎*505/465–2214* 🎫*Donations encouraged* ☉ *Daily dawn–dusk.*

THE TURQUOISE TRAIL

Fodor'sChoice
★
Etched out in the early 1970s and still well traveled is the scenic Turquoise Trail (or more prosaically, NM 14), a National Scenic Byway which follows an old route between Albuquerque and Santa Fe that's dotted with ghost towns now being restored by writers, artists, and other urban refugees. This 70 mi of piñon-studded mountain back road along the eastern flank of the sacred Sandia Mountains is a gentle roller coaster that also affords panoramic views of the Ortiz, Jémez, and Sangre de Cristo mountains. It's believed that 2,000 years ago Native Americans mined turquoise in these hills. The Spanish took up turquoise mining in the 16th century, and the practice continued into the early 20th century, with Tiffany & Co. removing a fair share of the semiprecious stone. In addition, gold, silver, tin, lead, and coal have been mined here. There's plenty of opportunity for picture-taking and picnicking along the way. The pace is slow, the talk is about the weather, and Albuquerque might as well be on another planet. The entire loop of this trip takes a day, the drive up the Sandia Crest a half day. Two Web sites offer good information: ⊕*www.turquoisetrail.org* and *www.byways.org*

SANDIA PARK

7 mi north of Tijeras. From Tijeras, take I–40 east and exit north on the Turquoise Trail (NM 14); proceed 6 mi and turn left onto NM 536.

Driving east from Albuquerque, before you head up the Turquoise Trail drop down south from I-40 first, and stop at the **Sandia Ranger Station** for a bit of orientation on the Cibola National Forest and the mountains you're about to drive through. Pick up pamphlets and trail maps, and—if there are enough kids in the audience—witness a fire-prevention program with a Smokey the Bear motif. From here you can also embark on a short self-guided tour to the nearby **fire lookout tower** and **Tijeras Pueblo ruins.** ⊠*11776 NM 337, Tijeras, south of I–40, off Exit 175* ☎*505/281–3304* ⊕*www.fs.fed.us/r3/cibola/ districts/sandia.shtml* 🎫*Free, $3 for parking in Cibola National Forest* ☉ *Mon.–Sat. 8–4:30.*

In Cedar Crest, just off NM 14 a couple of miles south of Sandia Park, the modest but nicely laid-out **Museum of Archaeology & Material Culture** chronicles archaeological finds and contains artifacts dating from the Ice Age to the Battle of Wounded Knee. Exhibits shed light on prehistoric man, buffalo hunting, a history of turquoise mining in north-central New Mexico, and the 1930s excavations of Sandia Cave (about 15 mi away) that offered evidence of some of the earliest human life in North America. ⊠*22 Calvary Rd. turn west 5 mi north* *of I–40 Exit 175 in Cedar Crest* ☎*505/281–2005* 💲*$3* ⊙*May–Oct., daily noon–7.*

⏱ It may take months for this odyssey of a place to completely sink in:
Fodor'sChoice quirky and utterly fascinating, **Tinkertown Museum** contains a world of
★ miniature carved-wood characters. The museum's late founder, Ross
Ward, spent more than 40 years carving and collecting the hundreds
of figures that populate this cheerfully bizarre museum, including an
animated miniature Western village, a Boot Hill cemetery, and a 1940s
circus exhibit. Ragtime piano music, a 40-foot sailboat, and a life-size
general store are other highlights. The walls surrounding this 22-room
museum have been fashioned out of more than 50,000 glass bottles
pressed into cement. This homage to folk art, found art, and eccentric
kitsch tends to strike a chord with people of all ages. As you might
expect, the gift shop offers plenty of fun oddities. ✉*121 Sandia Crest
Rd. (NM 536) , take Cedar Crest exit175 north off I–40 east and follow signs on NM 14 to Sandia Crest turnoff* ☎*505/281–5233* ⊕*www.
tinkertown.com* 💲*$3* ⊙*Apr.–Oct., daily 9–6.*

For awesome views of Albuquerque and half of New Mexico, take
NM 536 up the back side of the Sandia Mountains through Cibola
★ National Forest to **Sandia Crest.** At the 10,378-foot summit, explore
the foot trails along the rim (particularly in summer) and take in the
breathtaking views of Albuquerque down below, and of the so-called
Steel Forest—the nearby cluster of radio and television towers. Always
bring an extra layer of clothing, even in summer—the temperature at
the crest can be anywhere from 15 to 25 degrees cooler than down in
Albuquerque. If you're in need of refreshments or are searching for
some inexpensive souvenirs, visit the **Sandia Crest House Gift Shop and
Restaurant** (☎*505/243–0605*), on the rim of the crest.

As you continue north up NM 14 from Sandia Park, after about 12 mi
you pass through the sleepy village of **Golden,** the site of the first gold
rush (in 1825) west of the Mississippi. It has a rock shop and a mercantile store. The rustic adobe church and graveyard are popular with
photographers. Be aware that locals are very protective of this area and
aren't known to warm up to strangers.

WHERE TO STAY

★ **$$** 🏠**Elaine's, A Bed and Breakfast.** This antique-filled three-story log-and-
stone home is set in the evergreen folds of the Sandia Mountain foot-
hills. Four acres of wooded grounds beckon outside the back door. The
top two floors have rooms with balconies and big picture windows that
bring the lush mountain views indoors. The third-floor room also has
cathedral ceilings and a brass bed; some rooms have fireplaces, and one
has its own outside entrance. Breakfast, served in a plant-filled room or
outside on a patio with a fountain, often includes fresh fruit, pancakes,
or waffles with sausage. **Pros:** A real getaway. ✉*Snowline Estate, 72
Snowline Rd.* 🏷*Box 444, Cedar Crest87008* ☎*505/281–2467 or
800/821–3092* ⊕*www.elainesbnb.com* 🛏*5 rooms* ⚄*In-room: no
phone, no TV. In-hotel: no-smoking rooms* ▤*AE, D, MC, V* ⊙❘*BP.*

⚠ **Turquoise Trail Campground and RV Park.** Pine and cedar trees dot this 14-acre park in the Sandias, which has hiking trails with access to the Cibola National Forest. Adjacent to the premises is the Museum of Archaeology & Material Culture. Campsite rates are calculated per person; you will need reservations in October. ✉ *22 Calvary Rd., 5 mi north of I–40 Exit 175 in Cedar Crest* 📞 *505/281–2005* ♿ *Laundry facilities, flush toilets, full hookups, partial hookups (electric and water), dump station, drinking water, showers, fire grates, fire pits, grills, picnic tables, electricity, public telephone, general store, play area* ⏎ *57 sites, 45 with hookups.*

SPORTS & THE OUTDOORS

The 18-hole **Paa-Ko Ridge Golf Course** (✉ *1 Club House Dr.Sandia Park,* 📞 *505/281–6000 or 866/898–5987* ⊕ *www.paakoridge.com*) has been voted "The Best Place to Play Golf in New Mexico" by *Golf Digest.* Golfers enjoy vistas of the mesas and the Sandia Mountains from any of five tee placements on each hole. Greens fees are $59–$99, and tee-time reservations may be made a month ahead. The course is just off NM 14, 3½ mi north of the turnoff for Sandia Crest (NM 536).

Although less extensive and challenging than the ski areas farther north in the Sangre de Cristos, **Sandia Peak** (✉ *NM 536* 📞 *505/242–9052, 505/857–8977 snow conditions* ⊕ *www.sandiapeak.com*) is extremely popular with locals from Albuquerque and offers a nice range of novice, intermediate, and expert downhill trails; there's also a ski school. Snowboarding is welcome on all trails, and there's cross-country terrain as well, whenever snow is available. Snowfall can be sporadic, so call ahead to check for cross-country; Sandia has snow-making capacity for about 30 of its 200 acres of downhill skiing. The season runs from mid-December to mid-March, and lift tickets cost $43. Keep in mind that you can also access the ski area year-round via the Sandia Peak Aerial Tramway *(see Chapter 1, Albuquerque)*, which is faster from Albuquerque than driving all the way around. In summer, the ski area converts into a fantastic mountain-biking and hiking terrain. The ski area offers a number of packages with bike and helmet rentals and lift tickets. Other summer activities at Sandia Peak include sand-pit volleyball, horseshoes, and picnicking.

MADRID
37 mi northeast of Albuquerque, 12 mi north of Golden on NM 14.

Totally abandoned when its coal mine closed in the 1950s, Madrid has gradually been rebuilt and is now—to the dismay of some longtime locals—on the verge of trendiness (some would say it's already there). The entire town was offered for sale for $250,000 back then, but there were no takers. Finally, in the early 1970s, a few artists fleeing big cities settled in and began restoration. Weathered houses and old company stores have been repaired and turned into boutiques and galleries, some of them selling high-quality furniture, paintings, and crafts. Big events here (where folks put the emphasis on the first syllable: "Maa'- drid) include Old Timers Days on July 4 weekend, and the Christmas open house, held weekends in December, when galleries and studios are open and the famous Madrid Christmas lights twinkle brightly.

NEED A BREAK?
Aged hippies, youthful hipsters, and everyone in between congregate at **Java Junction** (⊠ *2855 NM 14* ☎ *505/438-2772*) for lattes, chai, sandwiches, pastries, and other toothsome treats. Upstairs there's a pleasantly decorated room for rent that can sleep up to three guests.

Madrid's **Old Coal Mine Museum** is a remnant of a once-flourishing industry. Children can explore the old tunnel, climb aboard a 1900 steam train, and poke through antique buildings full of marvelous relics. Museum tickets are available at the Mine Shaft Tavern out front. On weekends at 3 PM from late May to mid-October you can cheer the heroes and hiss the villains of the old-fashioned melodramas performed at the **Engine House Theatre.** The theater, inside a converted roundhouse machine shop, has a full-size steam train that comes chugging onto the stage. ⊠ *2814 NM 1487010* ☎ *505/438-3780* ⊕ *www. turquoisetrail.org/oldcoalmine* ▢ *Museum $4, melodrama $10* ☉ *Late May–mid-Oct., weekdays 9:30–5, weekends 9:30–6; mid-Oct.–late May, daily 10–4 (weather permitting; call ahead).*

WHERE TO EAT

★ ¢ ✕**Mineshaft Tavern.** A rollicking old bar and restaurant adjacent to the
CAFE Old Coal Mine Museum, this boisterous place was a miners' commissary back in the day. Today it serves what many people consider to be the best green-chili cheeseburger in New Mexico, along with ice-cold beer and a selection of other pub favorites and comfort foods. ⊠ *2846 NM 1487010* ☎ *505/473-0743* ▭ *D, MC, V* ☉ *No dinner Mon., Tues., and Thurs.*

SHOPPING

The town of Madrid has only one street, so the three-dozen-or-so shops and galleries are easy to find.

You can watch live glassblowing demonstrations at **Al Leedom Studio** (☎ *505/473-2054*); his vibrant vases and bowls are sold alongside the beautiful handcrafted jewelry of wife Barbara Leedom. The Leedoms' friendly cat and dancing dog are also big crowd pleasers. In a pale-blue cottage in the center of town, the **Ghost Town Trading Post** (☎ *505/471-7605*) is a great bet for fine Western jewelry fashioned out of local gemstones (not just turquoise but opal, amber, and onyx). **Johnsen & Swan** (☎ *505/473-1963*) stocks fine leather belts, bags, and wallets; beadwork; custom-made chaps; and Western-inspired jewelry and gifts. **Johnsons of Madrid** (☎ *505/471-1054*) ranks among the most prestigious galleries in town, showing painting, photography, sculpture, and textiles created by some of the region's leading artists. You could spend hours browsing the fine rugs and furnishings at **Seppanen & Daughters Fine Textiles** (☎ *505/424-7470*), which stocks custom Zapotec textiles from Oaxaca, Navajo weavings, Tibetan carpets, and fine Arts and Crafts tables, sofas, and chairs.

CERRILLOS

3 mi northeast of Madrid on NM 14.

Cerrillos was a boomtown in the 1880s—its mines brimmed with gold, silver, and turquoise, and eight newspapers, four hotels, and 21 taverns flourished. When the mines went dry the town went bust. Since then, Cerrillos has served as the backdrop for feature-film and television westerns, among them *Young Guns* and *Lonesome Dove*. Today, it might easily be mistaken for a ghost town, which it's been well on the way to becoming for decades. Time has left its streets dry, dusty, and almost deserted, although it is home to a number of artist-types and the occasional passing Amtrak or freight train roaring through town serves as a reminder of what century you're in.

Casa Grande (⊠*17 Waldo St.87010* ☎*505/438–3008*), a 28-room adobe (several rooms of which are part of a shop), has a small museum ($2) with a display of early mining exhibits. There's also a clean and neat, but oddly out-of-place petting zoo ($2) and a genuinely scenic overlook. Casa Grande is open daily 8 AM–sunset.

Pack rats and browsers alike ought not to miss the **What-Not Shop** (⊠*15B 1st St.87010* ☎*505/471–2744*), a venerable secondhand–antiques shop of a half-century's standing packed floor to ceiling with Native American pottery, cut glass, rocks, political buttons, old postcards, clocks, and who knows what else.

WHERE TO EAT

$ ✕ **San Marcos Cafe.** In Lone Butte, about 6 mi north of Cerrillos, this CAFE restaurant is known for its creative fare and nontraditional setting—an Fodor's Choice actual feed store, with roosters, turkeys, and peacocks running about ★ outside. In one of the two bric-a-brac–filled dining rooms, sample rich cinnamon rolls and such delectables as burritos stuffed with roast beef and potatoes and topped with green chili, and the classic eggs San Marcos, tortillas stuffed with scrambled eggs and topped with guacamole, pinto beans, melted Jack cheese, and red chili. Hot apple pie à la mode with rum sauce is a favorite. Expect a wait on weekends unless you make a reservation. ⊠*3877 NM 14* ☎*505/471–9298* ▤*MC, V* ☉*No dinner.*

SPORTS & THE OUTDOORS

★ Rides with **Broken Saddle Riding Co.** (⊠*Off NM 14, Cerrillos* ☎*505/424–7774* ⊕*www.brokensaddle.com*) take you around the old turquoise and silver mines the Cerrillos area is noted for. On a Tennessee Walker or a Missouri Fox Trotter you can explore the Cerrillos hills and canyons, 23 mi southeast of Santa Fe. This is not the usual nose-to-tail trail ride.

Santa Fe

WORD OF MOUTH

"Santa Fe is one of my all-time favorite cities to visit. We've enjoyed the food at Tia Sophia's on San Francisco Street just off the Plaza, Geronimo (expensive), and Santacafe (excellent with outdoor dining if you like). If you enjoy al fresco dining, go to La Posada Hotel...and check out their restaurant Fuego in the lovely courtyard. Bliss!"

—schoolmarm

Updated by
Georgia de
Katona

With its crisp, clear air and bright, sunny weather, Santa Fe couldn't be more welcoming or more unique. On a plateau at the base of the Sangre de Cristo Mountains—at an elevation of 7,000 feet—the city is brimming with reminders of nearly four centuries of Spanish and Mexican rule, and of the Pueblo cultures that have been here for hundreds more. The town's placid central Plaza, which dates from the early 17th century, has been the site of bullfights, public floggings, gunfights, political rallies, promenades, and public markets over the years. A one-of-a-kind destination, Santa Fe is fabled for its rows of chic art galleries, superb restaurants, and diverse shops selling everything from Southwestern furnishings and cowboy gear, to Tibetan textiles and Moroccan jewelry.

ORIENTATION & PLANNING

GETTING ORIENTED

Park your car and grab a map; this town is best explored on foot.

I–25 cuts just south of Santa Fe, which is 62 mi northeast of Albuquerque. U.S. 285/84 runs north–south through the city. The NM 599 bypass, also called the Santa Fe Relief Route, cuts around the city from I–25's Exit 276, southwest of the city, to U.S. 285/84, north of the city; it's a great shortcut if you're heading from Albuquerque to Española, Abiquiu, Taos, or other points north of Santa Fe. The modest flow of water called the Santa Fe River runs west, parallel to Alameda Street, from the Sangre de Cristo Mountains to the open prairie southwest of town, where it disappears into a narrow canyon before joining the Rio Grande. There's a *dicho,* or saying, in New Mexico: *"agua es vida"*— "water is life"—and every little trickle counts.

Santa Fe Plaza The heart of historic Santa Fe, the Plaza has been the site of a bullring, fiestas, and fandangos. Despite the buildup of tourist shops, the Plaza retains its Old World feel and is still the center of many annual festivities and much of the town's activity.

Canyon Road. One of the city's oldest streets, Canyon Road is lined with galleries, shops and restaurants housed in adobe compounds, with thick walls, and lush courtyard gardens. The architectural influence of Old Mexico and Spain, and the indigenous Pueblo cultures, make this street as historic as it is artistic.

Lower Old Santa Fe Trail. In the 1800s wagon trains from Missouri rolled into town from the Old Santa Fe Trail, opening trade into what had been a very insular Spanish colony and forever changing Santa Fe's destiny. This street joins the Plaza on the south side after passing the state capitol and some of the area's oldest neighborhoods.

Upper Old Santa Fe Trail & Museum Hill. What used to be the outskirts of town became the site of gracious, neo-Pueblo style homes in the mid-20th century, many of them designed by the famed architect John Gaw

TOP EXPERIENCES

A winter stroll on Canyon Road- There are few experiences to match walking this ancient street when it's covered with snow, scented by piñon fires burning in luminarias along the road, and echoing with the voices of carolers and happy families. It's particularly magical on Christmas Eve.

A culinary adventure. Start with rellenos for breakfast and try tapas for dinner. Enjoy some strawberry habañero gelato or sip an Aztec Warrior Chocolate Elixir. Take a cooking lesson. Try things you've never heard of and won't find anywhere else.

Into the wild. Follow the lead of locals and take any one of the many easy access points into the incredible, and surprisingly lush, mountains that rise out of Santa Fe. Raft the Rio Grande, snowboard, snowshoe, or try mountain biking.

Market mashup. Summer offers the phenomenal International Folk Art Market, the famed Indian Market, and the two-for-one weekend of Traditional Spanish Market and Contemporary Hispanic Market. The offerings are breathtaking and the community involvement yet another aspect of Santa Fe to fall in love with.

Meem. Old Santa Fe Trail takes you to Camino Lejo, aka Museum Hill, where you'll find four excellent museums and a café.

Guadalupe District. Also known as the Railyard, this bustling area has undergone a major transformation in the last decade. The brand-new Railyard Park is a model for urban green space and houses the vibrant Farmers' Market. The redevelopment along Guadalupe Street has added dozens of shops, galleries and restaurants to the town's already rich assortment.

SANTA FE PLANNER

WHEN TO GO

The city's population, an estimated 70,000, swells to nearly double that figure in summer. In winter the skiers arrive, lured by the challenging slopes and fluffy, powdery snow of Ski Santa Fe and Taos Ski Valley. Prices are highest June–August. Between September and November and between April and May they're lower, and (except for the major holidays) from December to March they're the lowest. Santa Fe has four distinct seasons, though the sun shines nearly every day of the year. June through August temperatures are high 80s to low 90s during the day, 50s at night, with afternoon rain showers—monsoons—cooling the air. During this season it's advisable to keep a lightweight, waterproof jacket with you. The monsoons come suddenly and can quickly drench you. September and October bring beautiful weather and a marked reduction in crowds. Temperatures, and prices, drop significantly after Halloween. December through March is ski season. Spring comes late at this elevation. April and May are blustery, with daily warm weather (70s and above) finally arriving in May. ■TIP→ **The high elevation here catches people unawares and altitude sickness can utterly ruin a day of fun. Drink water, drink more water, and then have a little more.**

GETTING HERE & AROUND

BY AIR   Among the smallest state capitals in the country, Santa Fe has no major airport (Albuquerque's is the nearest, about an hour away). Tiny Santa Fe Municipal Airport offers limited services, although there's some talk of expanding the facility and its runways to help lure additional airlines. The airport is 9 mi southwest of downtown.

BY BUS   The city's bus system, Santa Fe Trails, covers 10 major routes through town and is useful for getting from the Plaza to some of the outlying attractions. Route M is most useful for visitors, as it runs from downtown to the museums on Old Santa Fe Trail south of town, and Route 2 is useful if you're staying at one of the motels out on Cerrillos Road and need to get into town (if time is a factor for your visit, a car is a much more practical way to get around). Individual rides cost $1, and a daily pass costs $2. Buses run about every 30 minutes on weekdays, every hour on weekends. Service begins at 6 AM and continues until 11 PM on weekdays, 8–8 on Saturday, and 10–7 (limited routes) on Sunday.

BY CAR   Santa Fe is served by several national rental car agencies, including Avis, Budget, and Hertz. Additional agencies with locations in Santa Fe include Advantage, Classy Car Rentals (which specializes in luxury and sports vehicles), Enterprise, Sears, and Thrifty. *See Car Rental in New Mexico Essentials for national rental agency phone numbers.*

BY TAXI   Capital City Cab Company controls all the cabs in Santa Fe. The taxis aren't metered; you pay a flat fee based on how far you're going, usually $6–$10 within the downtown area. There are no cab stands; you must phone to arrange a ride.

BY TRAIN   Amtrak's *Southwest Chief* stops in Lamy, a short drive south of Santa Fe, on its route from Chicago to Los Angeles via Kansas City; other New Mexico stops include Raton, Las Vegas, Albuquerque, and Gallup daily.

ESSENTIALS   **Air Contacts Santa Fe Municipal Airport (SAF)** (✉ *Airport Rd. and NM 599* ☎ *505/473-4118*).

Bus Contacts Greyhound/Texas, New Mexico & Oklahoma Coaches (☎ *505/243-4435 or 800/231-2222* ⊕ *www.greyhound.com*). **Santa Fe Trails** (☎ *505/955-2001* ⊕ *www.santafenm.gov*).

Car Rental Contacts Advantage (☎ *505/983-9470*). **Enterprise** (☎ *505/473-3600*). **Sears** (☎ *505/984-8038*). **Thrifty** (☎ *505/474-3365 or 800/367-2277*).

Taxi Contacts Capital City Cab (☎ *505/438-0000*).

Train Contacts Amtrak (☎ *800/872-7245* ⊕ *www.amtrak.com*). *New Mexico Rail Runner Express* (☎ *505/245-7245* ⊕ *www.nmrailrunner.com*).

VISITOR INFORMATION   **New Mexico Department of Tourism visitor center** (✉ *Lamy Bldg., 491 Old Santa Fe Trail* ☎ *505/827-7400 or 800/733-6396 Ext. 0643* ⊕ *www.newmexico.org*). **Santa Fe Convention and Visitors Bureau** (✉ *201 W. Marcy St., Box 909* ☎ *505/955-6200 or 800/777-2489* ⊕ *www.santafe.org*).

PLANNING YOUR TIME

To make the most of your time it's helpful to think of Santa Fe in zones and to arrange your activities within each. If you've got more than a day or two be sure to explore the northern Rio Grande Valley. Your experience of Santa Fe will gain even more depth once you've gotten out of town to absorb the land and cultures that surround the city

Plan on spending a full day wandering around downtown Santa Fe, strolling down narrow streets, under portals, and across ancient cobbled streets. Sip coffee on the Plaza, take in a museum or two (or three) and marvel at the cathedral. **The New Mexico History Museum** and **Palace of the Governors** are a great place to start to gain a sense of the history and cultures influencing this area. If you are a museum buff, move on to the **New Mexico Museum of Art** where you'll be treated to not only an historic building, but an amazing collection of art from some of the areas most renowned artists, Georgia O'Keeffe and Gustav Baumann being only two of dozens. The changing exhibits here are fantastic and lean to the contemporary. The **Georgia O'Keeffe Museum** is a must-see. This small museum features an impressive array of her works and offers shows featuring other artists, such as Ansel Adams' photography, whose aesthetic was similar to O'Keeffe's and makes a fascinating juxtaposition. ■ TIP➔ **Take one of the docent-led tours offered by the museums.** Almost without exception the docents are engaging and passionate about their subjects. You gain invaluable insight into the collections and their context by taking these free tours. Inquire at the front desk of the museums for more information.

On a stretch called Museum Hill you'll find four world-class museums, all quite different and all highly relevant to the culture of Santa Fe and northern New Mexico. Start at the intimate gem the **Museum of Spanish Colonial Art**, where you'll gain a real sense of the Spanish Empire's influence on the world beyond Spain. **The Museum of International Folk Art** is thoroughly engaging for both young and old. If you have the stamina to keep going, have lunch at the tasty Museum Café and then visit the **Museum of Indian Arts and Culture** and then move on to the **Wheelwright Museum of the American Indian.** There is a path linking all of these museums together and the walk is easy. The museum shops at these four museums are outstanding—if you're a shopper you could easily spend an entire day in the shops alone.

An easy walk from any of the downtown lodgings, **Canyon Road** should definitely be explored on foot. After breakfast at the fabulous Mission Café, the walk up the gently sloping Canyon is pure pleasure. Abundant art festoons the sides of massive-walled adobe compounds on this narrow road., Take any of the side streets and stroll amongst historical homes and ancient acequias (irrigation ditches). When you get hungry, stop at El Farol or the Teahouse to recharge. If you really enjoy walking, keep going up Canyon Road past Cristo Rey Church, where the street gets even more narrow and is lined with residential compounds. At the top is the **Randal Davey Audubon Center**, where birdwatching abounds. If you're tired, take a cab back down the hill where dinner awaits you at any one of dozens of restaurants. If you'd rather

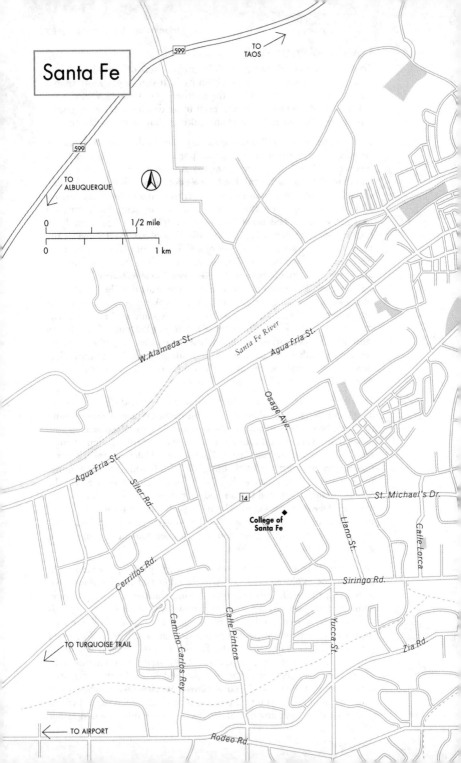

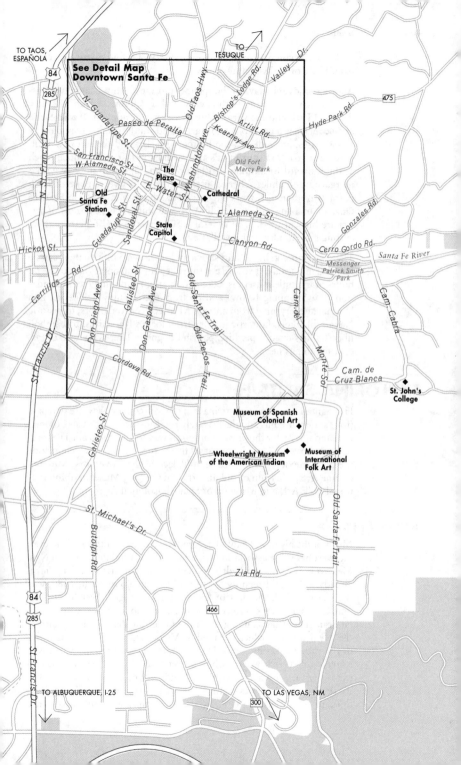

park on Canyon and explore from there, you'll find a pay lot across from El Farol midway up.

Another enjoyable day can be spent exploring the hip Guadalupe District, which is bursting with energy and development from the new Railyard Park and the various businesses surrounding it. **The Santuario de Guadalupe** is a great place to start. Head south from there and enjoy shops, cafés, art galleries, the Farmers Market and the fun new Railyard Park. You can start in this area with breakfast at Zia Diner, lunch at the Railyard Restaurant or El Tesoro, and finish up the day with a margarita and chiles rellenos at the Cowgirl or over a plate of fresh pasta at Andiamo. If you enjoy ceramics, don't miss a stop at **Santa Fe Clay**, an amazing gallery, supply store and studio where dozens of artists are busy at work. The venerable **SITE Santa Fe** is also here, with its cutting edge modern art installations.

There are more galleries and shops in downtown Santa Fe than can be handled in one day. If you've got the time, or if you don't want to spend hours in multiple museums, take a look at our shopping recommendations (⇨ Shopping below) and go from there. Enjoy wandering and looking at everything from antique Moroccan carved doors, to historic Navajo blankets, fantastic jewelry from local silversmiths, to bamboo fiber T-shirts from super-hip Spanish designers. There's a world of fascinating things here.

EXPLORING SANTA FE

Five Santa Fe museums participate in the Museum of New Mexico pass (four state museums and the privately run Museum of Spanish Colonial Art) and it is by far the most economical way to visit them all. The four-day pass costs $18 and is sold at all five of the museums, which include the New Mexico History Museum/Palace of the Governors, Museum of Fine Arts, Museum of Indian Arts and Culture, Museum of International Folk Art, and Museum of Spanish Colonial Art.

SANTA FE PLAZA

Much of the history of Santa Fe, New Mexico, the Southwest, and even the West has some association with Santa Fe's central Plaza, which New Mexico governor Don Pedro de Peralta laid out in 1607. The Plaza, already well established by the time of the Pueblo revolt in 1680, was the site of a bullring and of fiestas and fandangos. Freight wagons unloaded here after completing their arduous journey across the Santa Fe Trail. The American flag was raised over the Plaza in 1846, during the Mexican War, which resulted in Mexico's loss of all its territories in the present southwestern United States. For a time the Plaza was a tree-shaded park with a white picket fence. In the 1890s it was an expanse of lawn where uniformed bands played in an ornate gazebo. Particularly festive times on the Plaza are the weekend after Labor Day, during Las Fiestas de Santa Fe, and at Christmas, when all the trees are filled with lights and rooftops are outlined with *farolitos,* votive candles lit within paper-bag lanterns.

Numbers in the margin correspond to the Downtown Santa Fe map.

WHAT TO SEE

❸ **Georgia O'Keeffe Museum.** One of many East Coast artists who visited ★ New Mexico in the first half of the 20th century, O'Keeffe returned to live and paint here, eventually emerging as the demigoddess of Southwestern art. O'Keeffe's innovative view of the landscape is captured in *From the Plains,* inspired by her memory of the Texas plains, and *Jimson Weed,* a study of one of her favorite plants. Special exhibitions with O'Keeffe's modernist peers are on view throughout the year—many of these are exceptional, sometimes even more interesting than the permanent collection. ⊠*217 Johnson St.* ☎*505/946–1000* ⊕*www.okeeffemuseum.org* ✉*$8, free Fri. 5–8* PM ⊗*Daily Sat.–Thurs. 10–5, Fri. 10–8.*

❹ **Institute of American Indian Arts (IAIA).** Containing the largest collection of contemporary Native American art in the United States, this museum's paintings, photography, sculptures, prints, and traditional crafts were created by past and present students and teachers. The school was founded as a one-room studio classroom in the early 1930s by Dorothy Dunn, a beloved art teacher who played a critical role in launching the careers of many Native American artists. In the 1960s and 1970s it blossomed into the nation's premier center for Native American arts and its alumni have represent almost 600 tribes around the country. Artist Fritz Scholder taught here, as did sculptor Allan Houser. Among their disciples was the painter T. C. Cannon. The gift shop is good enough to warrant a visit all on its own. ⊠*108 Cathedral Pl.* ☎*505/983–1777* ⊕*www.iaia.edu* ✉*$5 (under 16 yrs old free)* ⊗*Mon.–Sat. 10–5, Sun. noon–5.*

❺ **La Fonda.** A *fonda* (inn) has stood on this site, southeast of the Plaza, for centuries. Architect Isaac Hamilton Rapp, who put Santa Fe style on the map, built this area landmark in 1922. Remodeled in 1926 by architect John Gaw Meem, the hotel was sold to the Santa Fe Railway in 1926 and remained a Harvey House hotel until 1968. Because of its proximity to the Plaza and its history as a gathering place for everyone from cowboys to movie stars (Errol Flynn stayed here), it's referred to as "The Inn at the End of the Trail." Major social events still take place here. Have a drink at the fifth-floor Bell Tower Bar (open late spring–early fall), which offers tremendous sunset views. ⊠*E. San Francisco St. at Old Santa Fe Trail* ☎*505/982–5511.*

❷ **New Mexico Museum of Art** (*Museum of Fine Arts*)**.** Designed by Isaac ★ Hamilton Rapp in 1917, the museum contains one of America's finest regional collections. It's also one of Santa Fe's earliest Pueblo Revival structures, inspired by the adobe structures at Acoma Pueblo. Split-cedar *latillas* (branches set in a crosshatch pattern) and hand-hewn vigas form the ceilings. The 8,000-piece permanent collection, of which only a fraction is exhibited at any given time, emphasizes the work of regional and nationally renowned artists, including the early Modernist

Georgia O'Keeffe; realist Robert Henri; the "Cinco Pintores" (five painters) of Santa Fe (including Fremont Elis and Will Shuster, the creative mind behind Zozobra); members of the Taos Society of Artists (Ernest L. Blumenschein, Bert G. Philips, Joseph H. Sharp, and E. Irving Couse, among others); and the works of noted 20th-century photographers of the Southwest, including Laura Gilpin, Ansel

> **FLAME ON!**
>
> Every weekend after Labor Day thousands gather to watch a flailing, 50-foot bogeyman-puppet known as Zozóbra go up in flames amid an incredible display of fireworks, taking troubles of the past year with him. Wildly pagan and utterly Santa Fe.

Adams, and Dorothea Lange. Rotating exhibits are staged throughout the year. Many excellent examples of Spanish-colonial–style furniture are on display. An interior *placita* (small plaza) with fountains, WPA murals, and sculpture, and the St. Francis Auditorium are other highlights. Concerts and lectures are often held in the auditorium. ✉ *107 W. Palace Ave.* ☎ *505/476–5072* ⊕ *www.mfasantafe.org* ✉ *$8, 4-day pass $18 (good at 4 state museums and the Museum of Spanish Colonial Art in Santa Fe), free Fri. 5–8 PM* ⊗ *Tues.–Thurs. and weekends 10–5, Fri. 10–8.*

① **The New Mexico History Museum.** This new museum is the anchor of a campus that encompasses the Palace of the Governors, the Palace Press, the Fray Angelico Chavez History Library, and Photo Archives (an assemblage of more than 750,000 images dating from the 1850s.) Located behind the Palace on Lincoln Avenue, the museum thoroughly encompasses the early history of indigenous people, Spanish colonization, the Mexican Period, and travel and commerce on the legendary Santa Fe Trail. Expected to open in May 2009, the museum has permanent and changing exhibits, such as "Jewish Pioneers of New Mexico," which explores the vital role Jewish immigrants played during the late 19th and early 20th centuries in the state's civic, economic, and cultural development. With advance permission, students and researchers have access to the comprehensive **Fray Angélico Chávez Library** and its rare maps, manuscripts, and photographs (more than 120,000 prints and negatives). The **Museum of New Mexico Press**, which prints books, pamphlets, and cards on antique presses, also hosts bookbinding demonstrations, lectures, and slide shows. The**Palace of the Governors** is a humble one-story neo-Pueblo adobe on the north side of the Plaza, and is the oldest public building in the United States. Its rooms contain period furnishings and exhibits illustrating the building's many functions over the past four centuries. Built at the same time as the Plaza, circa 1610 (scholars debate the exact year), it was the seat of four regional governments—those of Spain, Mexico, the Confederacy, and the U.S. territory that preceded New Mexico's statehood, which was achieved in 1912. The building was abandoned in 1680, following the Pueblo Revolt, but resumed its role as government headquarters when Don Diego de Vargas successfully returned in 1692. It served as the residence for 100 Spanish, Mexican, and American governors, including Governor Lew Wallace, who wrote his epic *Ben Hur* in its then

FodorsChoice
★

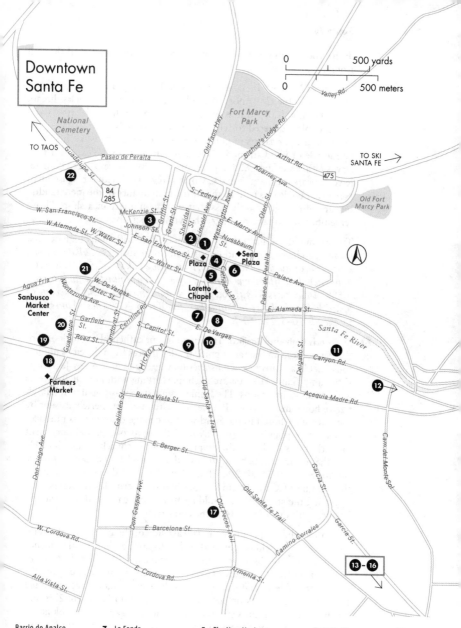

Downtown Santa Fe

National Cemetery

TO TAOS

Fort Marcy Park

TO SKI SANTA FE

Old Fort Marcy Park

Sanbusco Market Center

Plaza

Sena Plaza

Loretto Chapel

Santa Fe River

Canyon Rd.

Farmers Market

Barrio de Analco **7**	La Fonda **5**	**The New Mexico History Museum/Palace of the Governors** **1**	Santa Fe Clay **22**
Cristo Rey Church **12**	Museum of Fine Arts **2**		Santa Fe Southern Railway **20**
El Museo Cultural de Santa Fe **19**	Museum of Indian Arts and Culture **13**	New Mexico State Capitol .. **9**	Santuario de Guadalupe ..**21**
El Zaguan **11**	Museum of International Folk Art **14**	Oldest House **8**	SITE Santa Fe **18**
Georgia O'Keeffe Museum .. **3**		St. Francis Cathedral **6**	Wheelwright Museum of the American Indian **16**
Institute of American Indian Arts **4**	Museum of Spanish Colonial Art **15**	San Miguel Mission **10**	
		Santa Fe Children's Museum **17**	

drafty rooms, all the while complaining of the dust and mud that fell from its earthen ceiling.

Dozens of Native American vendors gather daily under the portal of the Palace of the Governors to display and sell pottery, jewelry, bread, and other goods. With few exceptions, the more than 500 artists and craftspeople registered to sell here are Pueblo or Navajo Indians. The merchandise for sale is required to meet strict standards: all items are handmade or hand-strung in Native American households; silver jewelry is either sterling (92.5% pure) or coin (90% pure) silver; all metal jewelry bears the maker's mark, which is registered with the Museum of New Mexico. Prices tend to reflect the high quality of the merchandise but are often significantly less that what you'd pay in a shop. Please remember not to take photographs without permission.

There's an outstanding gift shop and bookstore with many high quality, locally produced items and books from local authors. ⊠ *Palace Ave., north side of Plaza, Lincoln Ave., west of the Palace.* ☎ *505/476–5100* ⊕ *www.palaceofthegovernors.org or www.nmhistorymuseum.org* ⊠ *$8, 4-day pass $18 (good at all 4 state museums and Museum of Spanish Colonial Art in Santa Fe), free Fri. 5–8* ⊗ *Tues.–Thurs. and weekends 10–5, Fri. 10–8.*

❻ ★ St. Francis Cathedral Basilica. This magnificent cathedral, a block east of the Plaza, is one of the rare significant departures from the city's ubiquitous Pueblo architecture. Construction was begun in 1869 by Jean Baptiste Lamy, Santa Fe's first archbishop, working with French architects and Italian stonemasons. The Romanesque style was popular in Lamy's native home in southwest France. The circuit-riding cleric was sent by the Catholic Church to the Southwest to change the religious practices of its native population (to "civilize" them, as one period document puts it) and is buried in the crypt beneath the church's high altar. He was the inspiration behind Willa Cather's novel *Death Comes for the Archbishop* (1927). In 2005 Pope Benedict XVI declared St. Francis the "cradle of Catholicism" in the Southwestern United States, and upgraded the status of the building from mere cathedral to cathedral basilica—it's one of just 36 in the country.

A small adobe chapel on the northeast side of the cathedral, the remnant of an earlier church, embodies the Hispanic architectural influence so conspicuously absent from the cathedral itself. The chapel's *Nuestra Señora de la Paz* (Our Lady of Peace), popularly known as *La Conquistadora,* the oldest Madonna statue in the United States, accompanied Don Diego de Vargas on his reconquest of Santa Fe in 1692, a feat attributed to the statue's spiritual intervention. Take a close look at the keystone in the main doorway arch: it has a Hebrew tetragram on it. Bishop Lamy had this carved and placed to honor the Jewish merchants of Santa Fe who helped provide necessary funds for the construction of the church. Every Friday the faithful adorn the statue with a new dress. Just south of the cathedral, where the parking lot meets Paseo de Peralta, is the **Archdiocese of Santa Fe Museum** (☎ *505/983–3811*), a small museum where many of the area's historic, liturgical artifacts are on view. ✉ *231 Cathedral Pl.* ☎ *505/982–5619* ☾ *Mon.–Sat. 6–6, Sun. 7–7, except during mass. Mass Mon.–Sat. at 7 and 5:15* PM; *Sun. at 8 and 10* AM, *noon, and 7* PM. *Museum weekdays 8:30–4:30.*

CANYON ROAD

Once a trail used by indigenous people to access water and the lush forest above, and an early-20th-century route for woodcutters and their burros, Canyon Road is now lined with art galleries, shops, and restaurants. The narrow road begins at the eastern curve of Paseo de Peralta and stretches for about 2 mi at a moderate incline toward the base of the mountains. Lower Canyon Road is where you'll find the galleries, shops and restaurants. Upper Canyon Road (above E. Alameda) is narrow and residential, with access to hiking and biking trails along the way, and the Randall Davey Audubon Center at the very top.

Most establishments are in authentic, old adobe homes with thick, undulating walls that appear to have been carved out of the earth. Within those walls is art ranging from cutting-edge contemporary to traditional and even ancient works. Some artists are internationally renowned, like Fernando Botero, others' identities have been lost with time, like the weavers of magnificent Navajo rugs.

There are few places as festive as Canyon Road on Christmas Eve, when thousands of farolitos illuminate walkways, walls, roofs, and even trees. In May the scent of lilacs wafts over the adobe walls, and in August red hollyhocks enhance the surreal color of the blue sky on a dry summer day.

WHAT TO SEE

⑫ **Cristo Rey Church.** Built in 1940 and designed by legendary Santa Fe architect John Gaw Meem to commemorate the 400th anniversary of Francisco Vásquez de Coronado's exploration of the Southwest, this church is the largest Spanish adobe structure in the United States and is considered by many the finest example of Pueblo-style architecture anywhere. The church was constructed in the old-fashioned way by parishioners, who mixed the more than 200,000 mud-and-straw adobe bricks and hauled them into place. The 225-ton stone *reredo* (altar screen) is magnificent. ✉ *Canyon Rd. at Cristo Rey* ☎ *505/983–8528* ☾ *Daily 8–7.*

NEED A BREAK?

Kakawa (*1050 Paseo de Peralta (across the street from Gerald Peters Gallery)*, ☎ *505/982–0388* ⊕ *www.kakawachocolates.com*) is the place to go if chocolate, very good chocolate, is an essential part of your day. Proprietor Mark Sciscenti is a "chocolate historian and chocolate alchemist" and you're unlikely to ever have tasted anything like the divine, agave-sweetened, artisanal creations that emerge from his kitchen. Historically accurate chocolate drinks, like the Aztec Warrior Chocolate Elixir, delicious coffees, and gluten-free chocolate baked goods are served in this cozy, welcoming shop that's as much a taste experience as an educational one.

El Zaguan. Headquarters of the **Historic Santa Fe Foundation (HSFF)**, this 19th-century Territorial-style house has a small exhibit on Santa Fe architecture and preservation, but the real draw is the small but stunning garden abundant with lavender, roses, and 160-year-old trees. You can relax on a wrought-iron bench and take in the fine views of the hills northeast of town. An HSFF horticulturist often gives free tours and lectures in the garden on Thursday at 1 in summer (call to confirm). Tours are available of many of the Foundation's properties on Mother's Day. ⊠ *545 Canyon Rd.* ☎ *505/983–2567* ⊕ *www.historicsantafe.org* ⊡ *Free* ⊙ *Foundation office weekdays 9–noon and 1:30–5; gardens Mon.–Sat. 9–5.*

LOWER OLD SANTA FE TRAIL

It was along the Old Santa Fe Trail that wagon trains from Missouri rolled into town in the 1800s, forever changing Santa Fe's destiny. This street, off the south corner of the Plaza, is one of Santa Fe's most historic and is dotted with houses, shops, markets and the state capitol several blocks down.

WHAT TO SEE

Barrio de Analco. Along the south bank of the Santa Fe River, the barrio—its name means "district on the other side of the water"—is one of America's oldest neighborhoods, settled in the early 1600s by the Tlaxcalan Indians (who were forbidden to live with the Spanish near the Plaza) and in the 1690s by soldiers who had helped recapture New Mexico after the Pueblo Revolt. Plaques on houses on East De Vargas Street will help you locate some of the important structures. Check the performance schedule at the **Santa Fe Playhouse** on De Vargas Street, founded by writer Mary Austin and other Santa Feans in the 1920s.

New Mexico State Capitol. The symbol of the Zía Pueblo, which represents the Circle of Life, was the inspiration for the capitol, also known as the Roundhouse. Doorways at opposing sides of this 1966 structure symbolize the four winds, the four directions, and the four seasons. Throughout the building are artworks from the outstanding collection of the Capitol Art Foundation, historical and cultural displays, and handcrafted furniture—it's a superb and somewhat overlooked array of fine art. The **Governor's Gallery** hosts temporary exhibits. Six acres of imaginatively landscaped gardens shelter outstanding sculptures. ⊠ *Old Santa Fe Trail at Paseo de Peralta* ☎ *505/986–4589* ⊕ *www.newmexico.gov* ⊡ *Free* ⊙ *Weekdays 7–6; tours weekdays by appt.*

The Oldest House. More than 800 years ago, Pueblo people built this structure out of "puddled" adobe (liquid mud poured between upright wooden frames). This house, which contains a gift shop, is said to be the oldest in the United States. ⊠ *215 E. De Vargas St..*

San Miguel Mission. The oldest church still in use in the United States, this
Fodor'sChoice simple earth-hue adobe structure was built in the early 17th century by the Tlaxcalan Indians of Mexico, who came to New Mexico as servants of the Spanish. Badly damaged in the 1680 Pueblo Revolt, the structure

was restored and enlarged in 1710. On display in the chapel are priceless statues and paintings and the San José Bell, weighing nearly 800 pounds, which is believed to have been cast in Spain in 1356. In winter the church sometimes closes before its official closing hour. Mass is held on Sunday at 5 PM. Next door in the back of the Territorial-style dormitories of the old St. Michael's High School, a **Visitor Information Center** can help you find your way around northern New Mexico. ✉ *401 Old Santa Fe Trail* ☎ *505/983–3974* 💲 *$1* 🕐 *Mission Mon.–Sat. 9-5, Sun. 9-4.*

> ### IFAM
>
> The **International Folk Art Market** (☎ *505/476–1197* ⊕ *www.folkartmarket.org)*., held the second full weekend in July on Milner Plaza, is the grassroots art gathering. Master folk artists from every corner of the planet come together to sell their work amidst a festive array of huge tents, colorful banners, music, food, and delighted crowds. There is a feeling of fellowship and celebration here that enhances the satisfaction of buying wonderful folk art.

UPPER OLD SANTA FE TRAIL & MUSEUM HILL

WHAT TO SEE

⑬ ★ Museum of Indian Arts and Culture. An interactive, multimedia exhibition tells the story of Native American history in the Southwest, merging contemporary Native American experience with historical accounts and artifacts. The collection has some of New Mexico's oldest works of art: pottery vessels, fine stone and silver jewelry, intricate textiles, and other arts and crafts created by Pueblo, Navajo, and Apache artisans. Changing exhibitions feature arts and traditions of historic and contemporary Native Americans. You can also see art demonstrations and a video about the life and work of Pueblo potter Maria Martinez. ✉ *710 Camino Lejo* ☎ *505/476–1250* ⊕ *www.indianartsandculture. org* 💲 *$8, 4-day pass $18, good at all 4 state museums and the Museum of Spanish Colonial Art in Santa Fe* 🕐 *Tues.–Sun. 10–5.*

⑭ ☾ Museum of International Folk Art (MOIFA). A delight for adults and children alike, this museum is the premier institution of its kind in the world. In the Girard Wing you'll find thousands of amazingly inventive handmade objects—a tin Madonna, a devil made from bread dough, dolls from around the world, and miniature village scenes galore. The Hispanic Heritage Wing contains art dating from the Spanish-colonial period (in New Mexico, 1598–1821) to the present. The 5,000-piece exhibit includes religious works—particularly *bultos* (carved wooden statues of saints) and *retablos* (holy images painted on wood or tin), as well as textiles and furniture. The exhibits in the Neutrogena Wing rotate, showing subjects ranging from outsider art to the magnificent quilts of Gee's Bend. Lloyd's Treasure Chest, the wing's innovative basement section, provides a behind-the-scenes look at this collection. You can rummage through storage drawers, peer into microscopes, and, on occasion, speak with conservators and other museum personnel. Check the website or call to see if any of the excellent children's activities are scheduled for the time of your visit. Save time to visit the incredible gift shop and book store. ✉ *706 Camino Lejo* ☎ *505/476–1200* ⊕ *www. moifa.org* 🖼 *$8, 4-day pass $18, good at all 4 state museums and the Museum of Spanish Colonial Art in Santa Fe* ◷ *Tues.–Sun. 10–5.*

⑮ **Museum of Spanish Colonial Art.** Opened in 2002, this 5,000-square-foot
Fodor'sChoice adobe museum occupies a building designed in 1930 by acclaimed
★ architect John Gaw Meem. The Spanish Colonial Art Society formed in Santa Fe in 1925 to preserve traditional Spanish-colonial art and culture. The museum, which sits next to the Museum of New Mexico complex, displays the fruits of the society's labor—one of the most comprehensive collections of Spanish-colonial art in the world. The Hale Matthews Library contains a 1,000-volume collection of books relating to this important period in art history. Objects here, dating from the 16th century to the present, include retablos, elaborate santos, tinwork, straw appliqué, furniture, ceramics, and ironwork. There's also a fine collection of works by Hispanic artists of the 20th century. ✉ *750 Camino Lejo* ☎ *505/982–2226* ⊕ *www.spanishcolonial.org* 🖼 *$6, 4-day pass $18, good at all 4 state museums and the Museum of Spanish Colonial Art in Santa Fe* ◷ *Daily 10–5.*

⑰ **Santa Fe Children's Museum.** Stimulating hands-on exhibits, a solar green-
☾ house, oversize geometric forms, and a simulated 18-foot mountain-climbing wall all contribute to this museum's popularity with kids. Outdoor gardens with climbing structures, forts and hands on activities are great for whiling away the time in the shade of big trees. Puppeteers and storytellers perform often. ✉ *1050 Old Pecos Trail* ☎ *505/989–8359* ⊕ *www.santafechildrensmuseum.org* 🖼 *$8* ◷ *Wed.–Sat. 10–5, Sun. noon–5.* Open Tuesdays June-August.

⑯ **Wheelwright Museum of the American Indian.** A private institution in a building shaped like a traditional octagonal Navajo hogan, the Wheelwright opened in 1937. Founded by Boston scholar Mary Cabot Wheelwright and Navajo medicine man Hastiin Klah, the museum originated as a place to house ceremonial materials. Those items were returned to the Navajo in 1977, but what remains is an incredible collection of 19th- and 20th-century baskets, pottery, sculpture, weavings, metalwork, photography, paintings, including contemporary works by Native American artists, and typically fascinating changing exhibits. The Case Trading Post on the lower level is modeled after the trading posts that dotted the southwestern frontier more than 100 years ago. It carries an extensive selection of books and contemporary Native American jewelry, kachina dolls, weaving, and pottery. ✉ *704 Camino Lejo* ☎ *505/982–4636 or 800/607–4636* ⊕ *www.wheelwright.org* 🖼 *Free* ◷ *Mon.–Sat. 10–5, Sun. 1–5; gallery tours weekdays at 2, Sat. at 1.*

GUADALUPE DISTRICT

WHAT TO SEE

⑲ **El Museo Cultural de Santa Fe.** As much an educational and community gathering space as a museum, the Santa Fe Cultural Museum celebrates Santa Fe's—and New Mexico's—rich Hispanic heritage by presenting a wide range of events, from children's theater, to musical concerts, to a great Dia de Los Muertos celebration at the beginning of November. The museum sponsors the Contemporary Hispanic Market just off the Plaza each July (held the same time as Spanish Market), and the Contemporary Hispanic Artists Winter Market, held at El Museo Cultural in late November. There's a gallery that exhibits contemporary art by Hispanic artists. A great resource to visitors are the many classes and workshops, which are open to the public, and touch on everything from guitar and Mexican folkloric dance to children's theater and art. The museum occupies what had been a dilapidated liquor warehouse before El Museo took over the space in the late '90s. ⊠ *1615 Paseo de Peralta* ☎ *505/992–0591* ⊕ *www.elmuseocultural.org* ⊠ *Free; prices vary for events and shows* ⊘ *Tues.–Fri. 1–5, Sat. 10–5; additionally for events and shows.*

㉒ **Santa Fe Clay.** Occupying 10,000 square feet of space this combination clay studio, supply shop and gallery has, for the past fourteen years, become more and more respected in the community for the artists producing works and the quality of the classes taught. Regular classes and studio space are available for adults and children alike, and classes are taught by highly respected ceraminc artists. Gallery shows change regularly and are worth stopping in for a look. ⊠ *1615 Paseo de Peralta, Guadalupe District* ☎ *505/984–1122* ⊕ *www.santafeclay.com* ⊘ *Closed Sundays.*

㉑ **Santa Fe Southern Railway.** For a leisurely tour across the Santa Fe plateau and into the vast Galisteo Basin, where panoramic views extend for up to 120 mi, take a nostalgic ride on the antique cars of the Santa Fe Southern Railway. The train once served a spur of the Atchison, Topeka & Santa Fe Railway. Today the train takes visitors on 36-mi round-trip scenic trips to Lamy, a sleepy village with the region's only Amtrak service, offering picnics under the cottonwoods (bring your own or buy one from the caterer that meets the train) at the quaint rail station. Shorter runs travel down to the scenic Galisteo Basin. Aside from day trips, the railway offers special events such as a Friday-night "High Desert High Ball" cash bar with appetizers and a Saturday Night Barbecue Train ($58). Trains depart from the Santa Fe Depot, rebuilt in 1909 after the original was destroyed in a fire. There's talk of eventually opening a regional transportation and rail museum here, as part of the efforts to redevelop this part of the Guadalupe District. ⊠ *410 S. Guadalupe St.* ☎ *505/989–8600 or 888/989–8600* ⊕ *www.sfsr.com* ⚘ *Reservations essential* ⊠ *Day-trips from $32* ⊘ *Call for schedule.*

㉑ **Santuario de Guadalupe.** A humble adobe structure built by Franciscan missionaries between 1776 and 1795, this is the oldest shrine in the United States to Our Lady of Guadalupe, Mexico's patron saint. The sanctuary, now a nonprofit cultural center, has adobe walls nearly 3 feet thick. Among the sanctuary's religious art and artifacts is a priceless 16th-century work by Venetian painter Leonardo de Ponte Bassano that depicts Jesus driving the money changers from the Temple. Also of note is a portrait of Our Lady of Guadalupe by the Mexican colonial painter José de Alzíbar. Other highlights are the traditional New Mexican carved and painted altar screen, an authentic 19th-century sacristy, a pictorial-history archive, a library devoted to Archbishop Jean Baptiste Lamy that is furnished with many of his belongings, and a garden with plants from the Holy Land. ⊠*100 Guadalupe St.* 🖭 ✉*Donation suggested* ⊙*May–Oct., Mon.–Sat. 9–4; Nov.–Apr., weekdays 9–4.*

⑱ **SITE Santa Fe.** The events at this nexus of international contemporary art
★ include lectures, concerts, author readings, performance art, and gallery shows. The facility hosts a biennial exhibition every even-numbered year. There are always provocative exhibitions here, however, and the immense, open space is ideal for taking in the many larger-than-life installations. ⊠*1606 Paseo de Peralta* 🖭*505/989–1199* ⊕*www.site-santafe.org* ✉*$10, free Fri.* ⊙*Wed., Thurs., and Sat. 10–5, Fri. 10–7, Sun. noon–5.*

WHERE TO EAT

Eating out is a major pastime in Santa Fe and it's well worth coming here with a mind to join in on the fun Restaurants with high-profile chefs stand beside low-key joints, each offering unique and intriguing variations to regional and international cuisine. You'll find restaurants full of locals and tourists alike all over the downtown and surrounding areas. People often comment that food prices rival those in San Francisco or New York. Don't fret. There is wonderful food available for reasonable prices if you look around a bit. Waits for tables are very common during the busy summer season, so it's a good idea to call ahead even when reservations aren't accepted, if only to get a sense of the waiting time. Reservations for dinner at the better restaurants are a must for much of the year.

WHAT IT COSTS					
	¢	$	$$	$$$	$$$$
Restaurants	under $10	$10–$17	$18–$24	$25–$30	over $30

Prices are per person for a main course at dinner, excluding 8.25% sales tax.

$$$ ✕**315 Restaurant & Wine Bar.** As if it were on a thoroughfare in Paris
CONTEMPORARY rather than on Old Santa Fe Trail, 315 has a Continental, white-table-
★ cloth sophistication, but the offbeat wall art gives it a contemporary feel. Chef-owner Louis Moskow, who also owns the popular Railyard Restaurant (⇨ below) prepares refreshingly uncomplicated fare using organic vegetables and locally raised meats. Seasonal specialties on the ever-evolving menu might include squash blossom beignets with local goat cheese, basil-wrapped shrimp with apricot chutney and curry sauce, or grilled boneless lamb loin with crispy polenta, spring vegetables, and green peppercorn sauce. The garden patio opens onto the street scene. There's also a wine bar with an exceptional list of vintages. ⊠*315 Old Santa Fe Trail* 🖭*505/986–9190* ⊕*www.315santafe.com* ▤*AE, MC, V* ⊙*Closed Sun. No lunch Mon.*

2

$ ✕**Andiamo.** Produce from the farmers' market down the street adds to
ITALIAN   the seasonal surprises of this intimate northern Italian restaurant set
★   inside a sweet cottage in the Guadalupe District. Start with the delectable crispy polenta with rosemary and Gorgonzola sauce; move on to the white pizza with roasted garlic, fontina, grilled radicchio, pancetta, and rosemary; and consider such hearty entrées as crispy duck legs with grilled polenta, roasted turnips, and sautéed spinach. ⊠ *322 Garfield St.* ☎ *505/995–9595* ⊕ *www.andiamoonline.com* ⊟ *AE, DC, MC, V* ⊗ *No lunch.*

$$$ ✕**Aqua Santa.** Brian Knox, the charming, gregarious chef at the helm
CONTEMPORARY   of this locals' favorite, is a devotee of the slow-food philosophy. His
Fodor'sChoice   love and appreciation of food is palpable; some of the finest, simplest,
★   yet most sophisticated dishes in town come from the open kitchen in this tiny, one-room gem of a restaurant. The creamy, plastered walls of the intimate dining room are hung with art from local artists, and the ramada-covered patio open in summer feels like dining at a chic friend's house. Diners enjoy dishes like the fabulously tangy Caesar salad, pan-fried oysters with bitter honey and a balsamic reduction, Tuscan bean soup with white-truffle oil, and braised organic New Mexico lamb with olives and summer squash. Brian can be spotted shopping around town for fresh, local ingredients, and the menu changes regularly based on his gastronomic discoveries. Save room for dessert; the silky pannacotta may be the best on the continent. There's an extensive, reasonable wine list, too; ask the friendly staff for their current favorites ⊠ *451 W. Alameda St. (entrance off Water St.)* ☎ *505/982–6297* ⊟ *MC, V* ⊗ *Closed Sun. and Mon. No lunch Tues. or Sat.*

¢   ✕**Atomic Grill.** Burgers, salads, pizzas, sandwiches, and other light fare
AMERICAN   are served at this tiny late-night café a block off the Plaza. The food is decent and the service can be brusque. The best attributes are the comfy patio overlooking pedestrian-heavy Water Street, the huge list of imported beers, and the late hours (it's open until 3 most nights)—an extreme rarity in Santa Fe. You'll be glad this place exists when the bars let out and you're famished. ⊠ *103 Water St.* ☎ *505/820–2866* ⊟ *MC, V.*

¢   ✕**Aztec.** If a cup of really tasty, locally-roasted, non-corporate coffee
CAFÉ   in a funky, creaky-wood-floored old adobe sounds like nirvana to you,
★   then this is the place. Cozy, colorful rooms inside are lined with local art (and artists), the staff is laid back and friendly, and the little patio outside is a busy meeting ground for locals. Food is homemade, healthy, and flavorful. The menu includes sandwiches such as the Martin-roast turkey, green apples, and swiss cheese; fabulous, fluffy quiches; soups, breakfast burritos, and ice cream in the warm season. They're open until 7 (6 PM Sundays) in case you get late afternoon munchies. Free Wi-Fi and a public computer with Internet access. ⊠ *317 Aztec St., Guadalupe District* ☎ *505/820–0025* ⬸ *No reservations* ⊟ *AE, MC, V* ⊗ *closed.*

$ ✕**Bert's la Taqueria.** Fans of interior-Mexican cuisine love this upbeat
MEXICAN   spot with multiple rooms in an old adobe building that was once the nun's cloister for the Santuario de Guadalupe across the street. Colorful paintings hang on the white-washed walls. The menu mixes the expected

Mexican fare—enchiladas, excellent soft tacos—with more unusual regional recipes, such as *chapulines* (grasshoppers—yes, you read that correctly—sautéed with garlic butter) on tostaditas, or cuitlacoche (a delicious mushroom-like fungus that grows on corn) with black beans and fresh corn tortillas. The margaritas are made from scratch and are *muy delicioso.* ⊠ *416 Agua Fria St.* ☎ *505/474–0791* ⊟ *AE, MC, V* ☯ *Closed Sun.*

$ × **Bobcat Bite.** It'll take you 15 easy
AMERICAN   minutes to drive to this tiny road-
Fodor'sChoice   house southeast of town and it's
★   worth it. Folks drive a lot farther for Bobcat Bite's steaks and chops ($17) but especially for one thing: the biggest and juiciest burgers in town. Locals prefer them topped with cheese and green chili. Only early dinners are available, as the place closes by 8 most nights, and you'll want to arrive early to get a seat. No desserts and no credit cards. ⊠ *Old Las Vegas Hwy., 4½ mi south of Old Pecos Trail exit off I–25* ☎ *505/983–5319* ⌁ *Reservations not accepted* ⊟ *No credit cards* ☯ *Closed Sun.–Tues.*

$ × **Body Cafe.** There is a world of things to do inside the contempo-
CAFÉ   rary, Asian-inspired Body. A holistically minded center 5 minutes from downtown, you'll find a spa offering a full range of treatments, a yoga studio (with a good range of classes open to visitors), a child-care center, and boutique selling a wide range of beauty, health, and lifestyle products, plus jewelry, clothing, music, tarot cards, and all sorts of interesting gifts. The café uses mostly organic, local ingredients and serves three meals a day, with an emphasis on vegan and raw dishes. Their breakfast smoothies and homemade granola are delicious. At lunch try soba noodles with peanuts and ginger-soy vinaigrette, and at dinner there's an unbelievably good vegan lasagna layered with basil-sunflower pesto, portobello mushrooms, spinach, squash, tomatoes, nut cheese, and marinara sauce. Beer and wine are served. ⊠ *333 Cordova Rd.* ☎ *505/986–0362* ⊟ *AE, D, MC, V.*

$ × **Bumble Bee's Baja Grill.** A bright, vibrantly colored restaurant with
MEXICAN   closely spaced tables, piñatas, and ceiling fans wafting overhead, Bumble
Fodor'sChoice   Bee's (it's the nickname of the ebullient owner, Bob) delights locals with
★   its super-fresh Cal-Mex style food. If you like fish tacos, their mahimahi ones with creamy, non-dairy slaw are outstanding; try them with a side of salad instead of beans and rice. What a meal! Mammoth burritos with a wide range of fillings (including asparagus—yum!), roasted chicken with cilantro-lime rice, char-grilled trout platters, and a wide variety of vegetarian options keep folks pouring through the doors. You order at

Where to Eat in Downtown Santa Fe

Agua Santa **4**
Andiamo **34**
Atomic Grill **26**
Aztec **31**
Bumble Bee's Baja Grill **3**
Cafe Pasqual's **25**
Clafoutis **2**
Cleopatra Cafe **30**
The Compound **18**
The Cowgirl **32**
Coyote Cafe **29**
Diego's Cafe **1**

El Farol **20**
El Mesón **13**
El Tesoro **33**
Fuego **17**
Geronimo **19**
Guadalupe Cafe **22**
Il Piatto **10**
India Palace **28**
Inn of the Anasazi **15**
La Boca **11**
La Casa Sena **16**
La Choza **38**

Maria's New Mexican
Kitchen **39**
Mariscos la Playa **40**
Mission Cafe **21**
O'Keeffe Cafe **6**
Pink Adobe **23**
Plaza Café **9**
Railyard Restaurant
& Saloon **37**
Rooftop Pizzeria **27**
Santacafé **12**
The Shed **14**

Shohko **7**
Tia Sophia's **8**
315 Restaurant & Bar **24**
Tomasita's **36**
Trattoria Nostrani **5**
Zia Diner **35**

the counter, grab some chips and any one of a number of freshly made salsas from the bar, and wait for your number to come up. Beer, wine, and Mexican soft drinks are served. Try a homemade Mexican chocolate brownie for dessert. Live jazz on Saturday nights. ⊠*301 Jefferson St.* ☎*505/820–2862 www.bumblebeesbajagrill.com* ⊠*3701 Cerrillos Rd.* ☎*505/988–3278* ▤*AE, D, MC, V.*

$$$$
CONTEMPORARY
Fodor'sChoice
★

✕**Cafe Pasqual's.** A perennial favorite, this cheerful cubbyhole dishes up Southwestern and Nuevo Latino specialties for breakfast, lunch, and dinner. Don't be discouraged by lines out front—it's worth the wait. The culinary muse behind it all is Katharine Kagel, who championed organic, local ingredients, and whose expert kitchen staff produces mouth-watering breakfast and lunch specialties like *chili relleno picadillo*, *huevos motuleños*, and the sublime grilled free-range chicken sandwich average $14. Dinner is a more formal, though still friendly and easy-going, affair: char-grilled lamb with pomegranate-molasses glaze, steamed sugar-snap peas, and pan-seared potato cakes is a pleasure; the kicky starter of spicy Vietnamese squid salad with tamarind, garlic, and tomato over arugula is also fantastic. Mexican folk art, colorful tiles, and murals by Oaxacan artist Leovigildo Martinez create a festive atmosphere. Try the chummy communal table, or go late-morning or after 1:30 pm to (hopefully) avoid the crush. ⊠*121 Don Gaspar Ave.* ☎*505/983–9340* ⊕*www.pasquals.com* ▤*AE, MC, V. No reservations for breakfast and lunch.*

$
CAFÉ
★

✕**Chocolate Maven.** Although the name of this cheery bakery suggests sweets, and they do sweets especially well, Chocolate Maven produces impressive savory breakfast and lunch fare. Favorite treats include wild mushroom–and–goat cheese focaccia sandwiches, eggs ménage à trois (one each of eggs Benedict, Florentine, and Madison—the latter consisting of smoked salmon and poached egg), and Caprese salad of fresh mozzarella, basil, and tomatoes. Pizzas are thin-crusted and delicate. Some of the top desserts include Belgian chocolate fudge brownies, mocha-buttercream torte with chocolate-covered strawberries, and French lemon raspberry cake. Don't let the industrial building put you off; the interior is light, bright, and cozy. Try their Mayan Mocha, espresso mixed with steamed milk and a delicious combo of chocolate, cinnamon and red chili—heavenly! ⊠*821 W. San Mateo St.* ☎*505/984–1980* ⊕ www.*chocolatemaven*.com ▤*AE, D, MC, V* ⊗*No dinner.*

¢
CAFÉ
★

✕**Clafoutis.** Undeniably French, this bustling café serves authentic, delicious food. Walk through the door of this bright, open space and you'll almost certainly be greeted with a cheery "bon jour" from Anne Laure, who owns it with her husband, Philippe. Start your day with a crêpe, one of their fluffy omelettes, or *les gauffres* (large house waffles). Lunch offers quiches with perfectly flaky crusts, an enticing selection of large salads (the *salade de la maison* has pears, pine nuts, blue cheese, Spanish chorizo, tomatoes, and cucumbers atop mixed greens), and savory sandwiches, like the classic croque madame, on homemade bread. Their classic onion soup is amazingly comforting on a cold day. The café's namesake dessert, clafoutis, is worth saving room for. Fantastic espresso. ✉ *402 N. Guadalupe St., near Santa Fe Plaza* ☎*505/988–1809* ⟨⟩*no reservations* ▤*AE, MC, V* ⊗*No dinner Closed Sundays.*

¢ ✕**Cleopatra Cafe.** A no-fuss, order-at-the-counter Middle Eastern café
MIDDLE inside the Design Center home-furnishings mall, Cleopatra serves up
EASTERN ultrafresh Egyptian, Lebanese, and Greek food at bargain prices. You
might start with *besara* (fava beans with cilantro, garlic, fried onion,
and pita bread). Popular entrées include the falafel plate, with hummus
and tabouleh salad, and grilled organic-lamb kebabs with onions, bell
peppers, rice, tahini, and Greek salad. Tangy fresh-squeezed lemonade,
and potent Turkish coffee are also offered. The friendly owner, Jack,
greets everyone as though they are friends. He's opened a new, sit-down
restaurant on the Southside of town at 3482 Zafarano St. ✉*418 Cer-*
rillos Rd. ☎*505/820–7381* ▤*MC, V* ⊗*Closed Sun.*

$$$$ ✕**The Compound.** Mark Kiffin, winner of the James Beard Foundation's
CONTEMPORARY "Best Chef of the Southwest," has transformed this gracious, folk art–
Fodor'sChoice filled old restaurant into one of the state's culinary darlings. No longer
★ white glove–formal, it's still a fancy place thanks to a decor by famed
designer Alexander Girard and highly attentive staff, but it also has an
easygoing feel. From Chef Kiffin's oft-changing menu, devoted to ingredients based on those introduced to the area by the Spanish, consider
a starter of warm flan of summer sweet corn, with lobster succotash
and radish sprouts. Memorable entrées include Alaskan halibut with
orange lentils, summer squash, and piquillo peppers in a smoked ham
hock broth; and buttermilk roast chicken with creamed fresh spinach and foie gras pan gravy. The extensive and carefully chosen wine
list will please the most discerning oenophile. Lunch is as delightful
as dinner, while considerably less expensive—about $14 per person.
✉*653 Canyon Rd.* ☎*505/982–4353* ⊕*www.compoundrestaurant.*
com ▤*AE, D, DC, MC, V* ⊗*No lunch weekends.*

☺ $ ✕**The Cowgirl Hall of Fame (aka The Cowgirl).** A rollicking, popular bar
AMERICAN and grill with several rooms overflowing with Old West memorabilia,
Cowgirl has reasonably priced Southwestern, Tex-Mex, barbecue, and
southern fare. Highlights include barbecue, buffalo burgers, chiles rellenos, and salmon tacos with tomatillo salsa. A real treat for parents
is the outdoor-but-enclosed Kiddie Corral where kids have swings, a
climbing structure, and various games to entertain themselves. So what's
the bad news? Frequently subpar service and food that doesn't stand
out in a town of stellar food. Nevertheless, the crowd is friendly and
diverse, the drinks are cold, and if you catch one of the nightly music
acts—usually rock or blues—you're likely to leave smiling. Grab a seat
on the spacious patio in warm weather. The attached pool hall adds a
fun dimension to a night out and has a great juke box to keep toes tapping. ✉*319 S. Guadalupe St.* ☎*505/982–2565* ▤*AE, D, MC, V.*

$$$$ ✕**Coyote Cafe.** Santa Fe went through a culinary shake-up in 2007
CONTEMPORARY with several celebrity chefs changing restaurants. Eric DiStefano, formerly of Geronimo, took over Coyote Café with three other local
industry veterans, and the results have been mixed so far. The famed
locus of Southwestern Cuisine, the restaurant is still the place to go to
taste variations on the beloved green chili, but the menu has evolved
to include the flavors of French and Asian cuisine. Menu offerings
include griddled buttermilk corn cakes with chipotle prawns, Distefa-

no's signature dish, a peppery elk tenderloin, and the five spice rotisserie rock hen with green chili "mac 'n cheese." Service and food quality have varied widely, both in the main dining room and at the Rooftop Cantina, the fun outdoor gathering spot next door where cocktails and under-$15 fare is served April through October. ⊠*132 W. Water St.* ☎*505/983–1615* ⊕*www.coyotecafe.com* ⊟*AE, D, DC, MC, V* ⊘*No lunch except at Rooftop Cantina.*

$ ✕**Diego's Cafe.** Just north of downtown, in De Vargas Mall, you can
NEW MEXICAN sample some of the most authentic and spicy New Mexican food in
★ Santa Fe. Once inside the cheery, casual dining room, you forget the location, especially when relaxing with one of the potent (even by local standards) margaritas. Best bets here include blue-corn enchiladas, bean-and-chicken-stuffed sopaipilla, posole, and outstanding chiles rellenos. Standards like green chili chicken enchiladas are also excellent. Service is typically quick and cheerful. ⊠*DeVargas Center, 193 Paseo de Peralta* ☎*505/983–5101* ⊟*MC, V.*

$$$ ✕**El Farol.** In this crossover-cuisine town, owner David Salazar sums up
SPANISH his food in one word: "Spanish." Order a classic entrée like paella or make a meal from the nearly 30 different tapas—from tiny fried squid to wild mushrooms. Dining is indoors and out. Touted as the oldest continuously operated restaurant in Santa Fe, El Farol (built in 1835) has a relaxed ambience, a unique blend of the western frontier and contemporary Santa Fe. People push back the chairs and start dancing at around 9:30. The restaurant books outstanding live entertainment 7 nights a week, from blues and Latin to border-reggae, and there's a festive flamenco performance on Wednesdays. ⊠*808 Canyon Rd.* ☎*505/983–9912* ⊟*AE, D, MC, V* ⊘

$$$ ✕**El Mesón & Chispa Tapas Bar.** This place is as fun for having drinks and
SPANISH tapas or catching live music (from tango nights to Sephardic music)
★ as for enjoying a full meal. The dignified dining room with an old-world feel has simple dark-wood tables and chairs, white walls, and a wood-beam ceiling—unpretentious yet elegant. Livelier but still quite handsome is the Chispa bar. The delicious tapas menu includes Serrano ham and fried red potatoes with garlic aioli. Among the more substantial entrées are a stellar paella as well as cannelloni stuffed with veal, smothered with béchamel sauce, and served with manchego cheese au gratin. ⊠*213 Washington Ave.* ☎*505/983–6756* ⊟*AE, MC, V* ⊘*Closed Sun. and Mon. No lunch.*

¢ ✕**El Tesoro.** One of the Guadalupe District's better-kept secrets, this
CAFÉ small café occupies a spot in the high-ceilinged center of the Sanbusco Center, steps from several chic boutiques. The tiny kitchen turns out a mix of Central American, New Mexican, and American dishes, all of them using super-fresh ingredients. Grilled tuna tacos with salsa fresca, black beans, and rice; and Salvadorian chicken tamales wrapped in banana leaves are among the tastiest treats. El Tesoro also serves pastries, gelato, lemon bars, hot cocoa, and other snacks, making it a perfect break from shopping. ⊠*Sanbusco Market Center, 500 Montezuma Ave.* ☎*505/988–3886* ⊟*MC, V* ⊘*No dinner.*

$$$$ ✕**Fuego.** An elegant yet comfortable dining room inside the oasis of La
CONTEMPORARY Posada resort, Fuego has become a local favorite for fantastic, inventive food and flawless service. It is one of Santa Fe's top culinary secrets,

2

albeit with sky-high prices. You might start with seared foie gras with apple pie au poivre, before trying free-range *poussin* (young chicken) over a nest of braised leeks and salsify, or roast rack of Colorado elk with parsnip dumplings and a dried-cherry mole. Perhaps the most astounding offering is the artisanal cheese plate—Fuego has one of the largest selections of cheeses west of Manhattan. The wine list is similarly impressive and the helpful sommelier is always on hand to advise. Le Menu Découverte allows you to sample a five-course meal of chef's specialties for $125 (additional $65 for wine pairing). The spectacular Sunday brunch, at $45 per person, is a bargain. ⊠ *330 E. Palace Ave.* ☎ *505/986–0000* ⊕ *www.laposadadesantafe.com* ⊟ *AE, D, DC, MC, V* ☺.

$ ✕ **Gabriel's.** This restaurant has got location (convenient for pre-opera
NEW MEXICAN and post-high road tours), a gorgeous setting (the Spanish-colonial style art, the building, the flower-filled courtyard, and those mountain views!) and the made-to-order guacamole going for it. Their margaritas are stellar. The caveat? The quality of their entrees tends to be wildly uneven. Service is friendly, but as uneven as the food. If you're content with a gorgeous setting and making the stellar guacamole and margaritas your mainstay, with little care as to whether or not the entrée is memorable, this is a great place to go for sunset. Prices are reasonable and the setting truly is spectacular. ⊠ Exit 176, U.S. 285/84, just north of Camel Rock Casino, 5 mi north of Santa Fe Opera ☎ 505/455–7000 ⊕ www.gabrielsrestaurante.com ⊟ AE, D, DC, MC, V.

$$$$ ✕ **Geronimo.** Renowned Chef Martin Rios (formerly at the Inn of the
CONTEMPORARY Anasazi) and two seasoned managing partners took over New Mexico's
Fodor'sChoice only Mobil 4 star-rated restaurant in 2008. Bringing classical French
★ training, a fondness for Asian and Southwestern flavors, and an eye on molecular gastronomy. Rios' menu changes frequently, with dishes ranging from coriander cured semi-boneless quail, served with seared foie gras, harissa French toast, and Pedro Jiminez roasted grapes, to the New York strip, served with a gratin of crushed golden potato, carrot confit, pearl onions, and sauce Bordelaise. Desserts are artful and rich and the Sunday brunch is impressive. Located in the Borrego House, a massive-walled adobe dating from 1756, the intimate, white dining rooms have beamed ceilings, wood floors, fireplaces, and cushioned *bancos*. The new team is easier going and Rios clearly enjoys experimenting with new flavors and techniques. In summer you can dine under the front portal; in winter the bar with fireplace is inviting. ⊠ 724 Canyon Rd. ☎ 505/982–1500 ⊕ www.geronimorestaurant.com ⊟ AE, MC, V ☺ No lunch Mon.

$ ✕ **Guadalupe Cafe.** Come to this informal café for hefty servings of New
NEW MEXICAN Mexican favorites like enchiladas—vegetarian options are delicious—and quesadillas, or burritos smothered in green or red chili, topped off with sopaipilla and honey. The seasonal raspberry pancakes are one of many breakfast favorites as are eggs Benedict with green chili Hollandaise sauce. Service is hit or miss and the wait for a table considerable—but the food keeps 'em coming back for more. ⊠ 422 Old Santa Fe Trail ☎ 505/982–9762 ⚐ Reservations not accepted ⊟ DC, MC, V ☺ Closed Mon. No dinner Sun.

☾ $ ✕**Harry's Roadhouse.** This busy, friendly, art-filled compound just south-
ECLECTIC   east of town consists of several inviting rooms, from a diner-style space
Fodor'sChoice   with counter seating to a cozier nook with a fireplace—there's also an
★   enchanting courtyard out back with juniper trees and flower gardens.
The varied menu of contemporary diner favorites, pizzas, New Mexican fare, and bountiful salads is supplemented by a long list of daily
specials—which often include delicious ethnic dishes. Favorites include
smoked-chicken quesadillas and grilled-salmon tacos with tomatillo
salsa and black beans. Breakfast is fantastic. On weekends, if you're
there early, you might just get a chance at one of owner/pastry chef
Peyton's phenomenal cinnamon rolls. Desserts here are homey favorites, from the chocolate pudding to the blueberry cobbler. ⊠96-B *Old
Las Vegas Hwy., 1 mi east of Old Pecos Trail exit off I–25* ☎*505/989–
4629* ▤*AE, D, MC, V.*

$$ ✕**Il Piatto.** Creative pasta dishes like pappardelle with braised duckling,
ITALIAN   caramelized onions, sun-dried tomatoes, and mascarpone-duck au jus,
and homemade pumpkin ravioli with pine nuts and brown sage but-
ter grace the seasonally changing menu here. Entrées include grilled
salmon with spinach risotto and tomato-caper sauce, and a superb
pancetta-wrapped trout with rosemary, wild mushrooms, and polenta.
It's a crowded but enjoyable trattoria with informal ambience, reason-
able prices, and a snug bar. Service has been sporadic, but is generally
good. ⊠*95 W. Marcy St.* ☎*505/984–1091* ⊕ ▤*AE, D, MC, V* ☉*No
lunch weekends.*

$$ ✕**India Palace.** Even seasoned veterans of East Indian cuisine have been
INDIAN   known to rate this deep-pink, art-filled restaurant among the best in the
★   United States. The kitchen prepares fairly traditional recipes—tandoori
chicken, lamb vindaloo, *saag paneer* (spinach with farmer's cheese),
shrimp *biryani* (tossed with cashews, raisins, almonds, and saffron
rice)—but the presentation is always flawless and the ingredients fresh.
Meals are cooked as hot or mild as requested. Try the Indian buffet at
lunch. ⊠*227 Don Gaspar Ave., enter from parking lot on Water St.*
☎*505/986–5859* ⊕ *www.indiapalace.com* ▤*AE, MC, V.*

$$$$ ✕**Inn of the Anasazi.** This romantic, 90-seat restaurant with hardwood
CONTEMPORARY   floors, soft lighting, and beam ceilings feels slightly less formal than the
Fodor'sChoice   other big-ticket dining rooms in town. A patio is open during the sum-
★   mertime and makes for fun streetside people-watching. New Executive
Chef Oliver Ridgeway has redone the menu using a global approach
to local and seasonally available ingredients, serving dishes like molé
glazed veal medallions with white and green asparagus, Oregon morels
and elephant garlic, and Hawaiian tuna with wasabi nut crust. Patio
fare is lighter and just as interesting—the ahi tuna gyro and fennel
salad with a kalamata tapenade are just two of the terrific dishes. Sunday brunch is a sure bet. ⊠*Inn of the Anasazi, 113 Washington Ave.*
☎*505/988–3030* ▤*AE, D, DC, MC, V.*

$$ ✕**La Boca.** This little restaurant, a clean, bright room within an old
SPANISH   adobe building, has quickly gained rave reviews and become a local
Fodor'sChoice   favorite for its intriguingly prepared Spanish food and excellent wine
★   list. Chef James Campbell Caruso has created a menu just right for
Santa Fe's eating style; a wide, changing array of delectable tapas and

2

an edited selection of classic entrees, like the paella. The friendly, efficient staff is happy to advise on wine and food selections. The chef's tasting menu for $55 per person (additional $25 for wine or sherry pairings) is a fun way to experience Caruso's well-honed approach to his food. Desserts, like the rich chocolate pot au feu, are sumptuous. The room tends to be loud and can get stuffy during winter when the Dutch door and windows are closed, but crowds are friendly and you never know who you'll end up next to in this town of low-key luminaries and celebrities. Half price Tapas en la Tarde from 3 to 5 during the week make a perfect late lunch. ⊠ *72 W. Marcy St, Santa Fe Plaza* ☎*505/982–3433* ◿*Reservations recommended* ▤*AE, D, DC, MC, V* ⊘*No lunch Sundays.*

$$$
CONTEMPORARY

✕**La Casa Sena.** The Southwestern-accented and Continental fare served at La Casa Sena is beautifully presented if not consistently as delicious as it appears. Weather permitting get a table on the patio surrounded by hollyhocks, flowering shrubs, and centuries-old adobe walls. A favorite entrée is the braised Colorado lamb shank with huitlacoche-chipotle demi-glace, roasted purple and Yukon gold potatoes, braised cippolini onions and orange gremolata. There's a knockout lavender crème brûlée on the dessert menu. For a musical meal (evenings only), sit in the restaurant's adjacent, less-pricey Cantina ($23), where the talented and perky staff belt out Broadway show tunes. There's also a wine shop, which sells many of the estimable vintages offered on the restaurant's wine list. ⊠*Sena Plaza, 125 E. Palace Ave.* ☎*505/988–9232* ⊕*www.lacasasena.com* ▤*AE, D, DC, MC, V.*

¢
NEW MEXICAN
★

✕**La Choza.** The less touristy, harder-to-find, and less expensive sister to the Shed, La Choza (which means "the shed" in Spanish) serves super-tasty, super-traditional New Mexican fare. Chicken or pork *carne adovada* burritos, white clam chowder spiced with green chiles, huevos rancheros, and wine margaritas are specialties. The dining rooms are dark and cozy, with vigas set across the ceiling and local art on the walls. The staff is friendly and competent. ⊠*905 Alarid St., near Cerrillos Rd. at St. Francis Dr., around the corner from the Railyard Park* ☎*505/982–0909* ▤*AE, DC, MC, V* ⊘*Closed Sun.*

$
NEW MEXICAN
★

✕**Maria's New Mexican Kitchen.** Serving more than 100 kinds of margaritas is but one of this rustic restaurant's claim to fame. Their house margarita is one of the best in town (and you may have surmised that we take our margaritas seriously here). Get the silver coin if you want to go top shelf and leave the rest of the super tequilas to sip on without intrusion of other flavors. The place holds its own as a reliable, super-tasty source of authentic New Mexican fare, including chiles rellenos, blue-corn enchiladas, and green-chili tamales. The Galisteo chicken, par-boiled and covered in red chili, is simple and satisfying. ⊠*555 W. Cordova Rd.* ☎*505/983–7929* ⊕*www.marias-santafe.com* ▤*AE, D, DC, MC, V.*

$
SEAFOOD
★

✕**Mariscos la Playa.** Yes, even in landlocked Santa Fe, it's possible to find incredibly fresh and well-prepared seafood served in big portions. This cheery, colorful Mexican restaurant surrounded by strip malls is just a short hop south of downtown. Favorite dishes include the absolutely delicious shrimp wrapped in bacon with Mexican cheese. and *caldo* *vuelve a la vida,* a hearty soup of shrimp, octopus, scallops, clams, crab, and calamari. There's also shrimp soup in a tomato broth, fresh oysters on the half shell, and grilled salmon with pico de gallo. The staff and service are delightful. ⊠*537 W. Cordova St.* ☎*505/982–2790* ▤*AE, DC, MC, V.*

¢ ✕**Mission Cafe.** Tucked down the alley behind the San Miguel Mis-

CAFÉ sion, this sunny, art-filled gem of a café inside an 1850s adobe serves

★ super-tasty and satisfying breakfast and lunch fare. The food is American and New Mexican–inspired, with excellent breakfast burritos, delicious pies and cakes from Josie's (hard to come by, longtime local favorites), strong espresso drinks, and locally produced Taos's Cow Ice Cream. Local, natural and organic meats and ingredients are used. During the warmer months, dine on the big front patio, shaded with leafy trees. ⊠*237 E. DeVargas St.* ☎*505/983–3033* ▤*MC, V* ⊘*No dinner.* Closed Sunday.

$$$$ ✕**O'Keeffe Cafe.** This swanky but low-key restaurant next to the Geor-

CONTEMPORARY gia O'Keeffe Museum turns out some delicious and creative fare, including what may be the town's best soups. This is much more than a typical museum café, although the lunches do make a great break following a jaunt through the museum. Dinner is the main event, however, showcasing such tempting and tasy selections as sweetbreads with shallots and cherry demi-glace; cashew-encrusted mahimahi over garlic-mashed potatoes with a mango-citrus–butter sauce; and Colorado lamb chops with red chili–honey glaze; and mint-infused couscous. Chef Laurent Rea's tasting menu with wine pairing for $120 is a very good deal. Patios shaded by leafy trees are great dining spots during warm weather. ⊠*217 Johnson St.* ☎*505/946–1065* ⊕*www.okeeffecafe.com* ▤*AE, D, MC, V.*

$$$ ✕**Pink Adobe.** Rosalea Murphy opened this restaurant in 1944, and the

ECLECTIC place still reflects a time when fewer than 20,000 people lived here. The intimate, rambling rooms of this late-17th-century house have fireplaces and artwork and are filled with conversation made over special-occasion meals. The ambience of the restaurant, rather than the mediocre food and spotty service, accounts for its popularity. The steak Dunigan, smothered in green chili sauce and mushrooms, the lobster, crab, and shrimp enchiladas in green chili lobster bisque, and the Southern fried chicken are among the eclectic dishes served. The apple pie drenched in rum sauce is a favorite. Excellent, top-shelf margaritas are mixed in the adjacent Dragon Room bar. ⊠*406 Old Santa Fe Trail* ☎*505/983–7712* ⊕*www.thepinkadobe.com* ▤*AE, D, DC, MC, V* ⊘*No lunch weekends.*

$ ✕**Plaza Café.** Run with homespun

ECLECTIC care by the Razatos family since

★ 1947, this café has been a fixture on the Plaza since 1918. The decor— red leather banquettes, black

> **WORD OF MOUTH**
>
> "I live here. The Shed can be crowded. Here's a secret. About a mile away (near the railyard, on Alarid St.) is La Choza. La Choza means "the Shed" in Spanish, and—you got it—it's owned by the same family. But while The Shed caters to tourists (it's right on the plaza and can be crowded), La Choza caters to locals.
> —LuccaBrazzi

2

Formica tables, tile floors, a coffered tin ceiling, and a 1940s-style ser-vice counter—hasn't changed much in the past half century. The food runs the gamut, from cashew mole enchiladas to New Mexico meat loaf to Mission-style burritos, but the ingredients tend toward South-western. You'll rarely taste a better tortilla soup. You can cool it off with an old-fashioned ice cream treat from the soda fountain. It's a good, tasty stop for breakfast, lunch, or dinner. ⊠ *54 Lincoln Ave.* ☎ *505/982–1664* &*Reservations not accepted* ⊟*AE, D, MC, V.*

$ ✕ **Pyramid Cafe.** Tucked into a strip mall 5 minutes south of downtown,
MIDDLE this restaurant, with photos of Tunisia, Kilim rugs, and North African
EASTERN textiles on the walls, delights locals with flavors not available anywhere
★ else in town. The Tunisian owner and his staff are adept at preparing classic dishes with the Mediterranean flavors of Lebanon and Greece, but when they turn their attention to home flavors, and those of neigh-boring Morocco, your tastebuds will sing. Try the specials, like the Moroccan tajin with chicken, prunes, raisins, and spices served with rice in a domed, terracotta dish. The brik a l'oeuf, a turnover-like Tuni-sian specialty in phyllo dough with an egg and creamy herbed mashed potatoes tucked inside, is as wonderful as it is unusual. The Tunisian plate, a sampler, is incredible. Free Wi-Fi if you if need it; local, organic ingredients, excellent vegetarian options. The lunch buffet is fresh and satisfying. ⊠ *505 W. Cordova, near Sav-On south of Guadalupe Dis-trict* ☎ *505/989–1378* ⊟*AE, MC, V*

$$ ✕ **Railyard Restaurant & Saloon.** Set inside a bustling, handsome ware-
AMERICAN house in the railyard at the Guadalupe District, this trendy spot oper-ated by the same talented management that runs 315 Restaurant & Wine Bar serves relatively affordable, well-prepared American favor-ites that have been given nouvelle twists. Good bets include steamed bistro black mussels in fresh tomato and basil broth, fried butter-milk-chicken strips with Creole rémoulade dipping sauce, sesame-and-panko-crusted tuna with a soy-honey sauce, and barbecued baby back ribs. If the soft-shell crab is available, order it. Many patrons sit in the casual bar, where both the full and lighter menus are available, and sip on pomegranate margaritas or well-chosen wines by the glass. The patio out front, with breathtaking views of the Sangre de Cristo mountains, is a great spot to sit in the summer. Lunch prices average about $10. ⊠ *530 S. Guadalupe St.* ☎ *505/989–3300* ⊟*AE, D, MC, V* ☉*No lunch Sun.*

$ ✕ **Rooftop Pizzeria.** Santa Fe got its first truly sophisticated pizza parlor
PIZZA in 2006 with the opening of this slick indoor-outdoor restaurant atop
★ the Santa Fe Arcade. The kitchen here scores high marks for its rich and imaginative pizza toppings: consider the one topped with lobster, shrimp, mushrooms, apple-smoked bacon, caramelized leeks, truffle oil, Alfredo sauce, and four cheeses on a blue-corn crust. Antipasti and salads are impressive, too, as there's a wonderful smoked-duck confit–and–pepper-corn spread, or the smoked-salmon Caesar salad. There's also an exten-sive beer and wine list. Although the Santa Fe Arcade's main entrance is on the Plaza, it's easier to access the restaurant from the arcade's Water Street entrance, a few doors up from Don Gaspar Avenue. ⊠ *60 E. San Francisco St.* ☎ *505/984–0008* ⊟*AE, D, MC, V.*

$$$ ✗**Santacafé.** Minimalist elegance marks the interior of Santacafé, one
CONTEMPORARY of Santa Fe's vanguard "food as art" restaurants, two blocks north of
★ the Plaza in the historic Padre Gallegos House. Seasonal ingredients are
included in the inventive dishes, which might include Alaskan halibut
with English peas, saffron couscous, capers, and preserved lemon. Shii-
take-and-cactus spring rolls with ponzu sauce make a terrific starter, as
does the sublime crispy-fried calamari with a snappy lime-chili dipping
sauce—which is big; add a salad for a couple of dollars and you've got
a meal. The patio is a joy in summer, and the bar makes a snazzy spot to
meet friends for drinks just about any time of year. If you're on a tight
budget, consider the reasonably priced lunch menu. Sunday brunch
is a favorite among locals. ⊠*231 Washington Ave.* ☎*505/984–1788*
⊕*www.santacafe.com* ⊟*AE, MC, V* ⊘*No lunch Sun.*

$$ ✗**The Shed.** The lines at lunch attest to the status of this downtown
NEW MEXICAN New Mexican eatery. The rambling, low-doored, and atmospheric
Fodor's Choice adobe dating from 1692 is decorated with folk art, and service is down-
★ right neighborly. Even if you're a devoted green chili sauce fan, you
must try the locally grown red chili the place is famous for; it is rich
and perfectly spicy. Specialties include red-chili enchiladas, green-chili
stew with potatoes and pork, comforting posole, and their charbroiled
Shedburgers. The mushroom bisque is a surprising and delicious offering. Homemade desserts, like the mocha cake, are fabulous. There's
a full bar, too. ⊠*113½ E. Palace Ave.* ☎*505/982–9030* ⊟*AE, DC,
MC, V* ⊘*Closed Sun. Dinner Mon.–Sat*

$$$ ✗**Shohko.** After a brief hiatus Shohko and her family have returned
JAPANESE and once again this is the place for the freshest, best prepared sushi
★ and sashimi in town. On any given night there are two dozen or more
varieties of fresh fish available. The softshell crab tempura is feather-
light, and the Kobe beef with Japanese salsa is tender and delicious.
Sit at the sushi bar and watch the expert chefs work their magic, or at
one of the tables in this old adobe with whitewashed walls, dark wood
vigas, and Japanese decorative details. Table service is friendly, but can
be slow. ⊠ *321 Johnson St., near Santa Fe Plaza* ☎*505/982–9708*
⊸*Reservations recommended for dinner.* ⊟*AE, D, DC, MC, V* ⊘*No
lunch on weekends.*

¢ ✗**Tecolote Cafe.** The mantra here is "no toast" and you won't miss it.
ECLECTIC Since 1980, owners Alice and Bill Jamison have filled the bellies of
★ locals and tourists alike with their delicious breakfasts and lunches
founded, primarily, on northern New Mexican cuisine. The simple
rooms and comfortable seating allow you to focus on such dishes as
the sheepherder's breakfast (red potatoes browned with jalapeños and
topped with red and green chili and two eggs), delicious carne adovada
(lean pork slow-cooked in their homemade red chili), and a green chili
stew that locals swear by to cure colds. French toast is prepared with
homemade breads. When the server asks if you'd like a tortilla or the
bakery basket, go for the basket—full of warm, fresh muffins and bis-
cuits that are heavenly. ⊠ *1203 Cerrillos Rd* ☎*505/988–1362* ⊸ *no
reservations* ⊟*AE, D, DC, MC, V* ⊘*No dinner.*

¢ ✗**Tia Sophia's.** This downtown joint serves strictly New Mexican break-
NEW MEXICAN fasts and lunches (open until 2 PM). You're as likely to be seated next
★ to a family from a remote village in the mountains as you are to a leg-

islator or lobbyist from the nearby state capitol. Tia's ("Auntie's") delicious homemade chorizo disappears fast on Saturdays; if you're an aficionado, get there early. Order anything and expect a true taste of local tradition. Mammoth chili-smothered breakfast burritos will hold you over for hours on the powdery ski slopes during winter. Be warned, though: the red

and green chiles are spicy and you're expected to understand this elemental fact of local cuisine. No alcohol. ⊠ *210 W. San Francisco St.* ☎ *505/983–9880* ▤ *V, MC* ⊗ *No dinners. Closed Sundays.*

$ ✕**Tomasita's.** Always voted a favorite, yet in the scheme of the amazing
NEW MEXICAN   New Mexican food available in this town, it's not a stand-out (though the food is reliable). Located in one of the old railroad depots, the interior is nondescript, though the yellow glass windows cast a strange light over the place. It's almost always busy, full of locals and tourists who line up at the door for spicy green chili dishes. Their full bar is an interesting place to watch a local, not-for-tourists, scene unfold. ⊠ *500 S. Guadalupe St, Guadalupe District* ☎ *505/983–5721* ⊘ *No reservations* ▤ *A, D, DC, MC, V.*

$$$$ ✕**Trattoria Nostrani.** Recognized as one of the 50 best restaurants in the
ITALIAN   country by *Gourmet* magazine, this restaurant earns kudos for stellar seasonal Northern Italian fare as fried squash blossoms and baby artichokes with salsa verde and griddled montasio cheese, and taglierini with shaved summer truffles. The cozy dining room occupies a late-19th-century Territorial-style house a few blocks from the Plaza; dining on the front porch is especially pleasant. Their wine list is extensive and meticulously selected. The caveat: despite excellent service, widespread complaints about the arrogant management persist, and there are extremely rigid no-scent, and no-cellphone policies. ⊠ *304 Johnson St.* ☎ *505/983–3800* ⊕ *www.trattorianostrani.com* ▤ *AE, DC, MC, V* ⊗ *Closed Sun. No lunch.*

¢   ✕**Tune Up.** The local favorite formerly known as Dave's Not Here has
ECLECTIC   become Tune Up. After a fairly extensive renovation of what is still a
★   very small space, the new room has a cozier feel with colorful walls and wood details, booths, a few tables and a community table. The shaded patio out front is a great summertime spot to enjoy the toothsome breakfasts and lunches served. Start the day with savory, and surprisingly delicate, breakfast rellenos, fluffy buttermilk pancakes, or the huevos Salvadoreños (eggs scrambled with scallions and tomatoes, served with refried beans, panfried bananas, and a tortilla). Lunch offerings include the super-juicy Dave Was Here burger served with crispy home-cut fries, a ginger-chicken sandwich on ciabatta bread, and Salvadoran treats called pupusas, which are most like griddled, flattened, soft tamales—delicious! Homemade baked goods include a peanut butter cookie sandwich filled with Nutella. The staff is friendly and efficient and the care of the new owners, Chuy and Charlotte

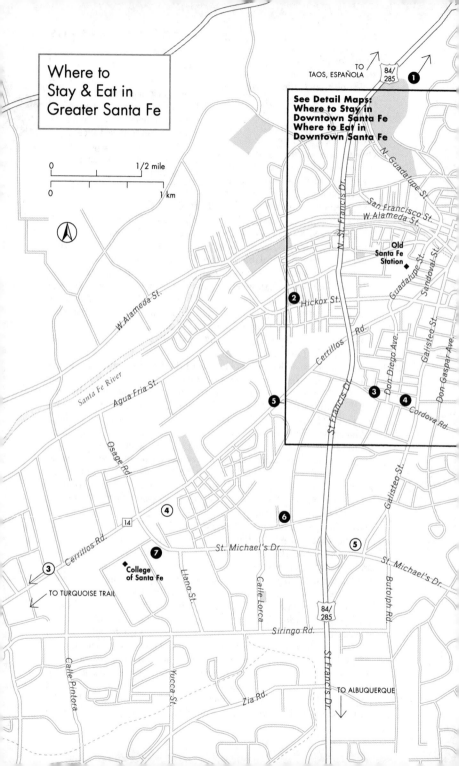

Where to Stay & Eat in Greater Santa Fe

0   1/2 mile
0   1 km

See Detail Maps:
Where to Stay in Downtown Santa Fe
Where to Eat in Downtown Santa Fe

TO
TAOS, ESPAÑOLA

84/285

1

N. Guadalupe St.

San Francisco St.
W. Alameda St.

Old Santa Fe Station

Guadalupe St.

Sandoval St.

Galisteo St.

Don Gaspar Ave.

2 Hickox St.

Cerrillos Rd.

N. St. Francis Dr.

St. Francis Dr.

Don Diego Ave.

3

4

Cordova Rd.

5

W. Alameda St.

Santa Fe River

Agua Fria St.

Osage Rd.

Galisteo St.

(4)

14

Cerrillos Rd.

(3)

TO TURQUOISE TRAIL

7

♦ College of Santa Fe

Llano St.

St. Michael's Dr.

6

Calle Lorca

5

St. Michael's Dr.

Butolph Rd.

84/285

Siringo Rd.

Calle Pintora

Yucca St.

Zia Rd.

St. Francis Dr.

TO ALBUQUERQUE

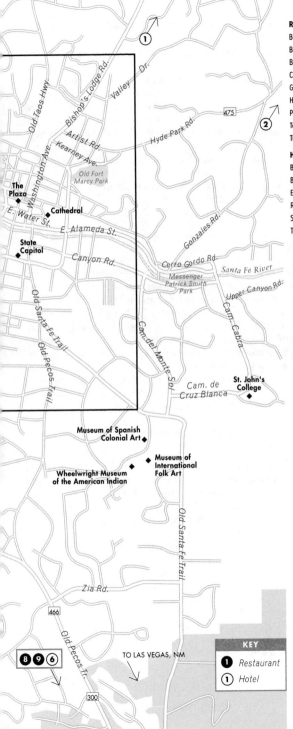

Restaurants ▼

Bert's la Taqueria **7**
Bobcat Bite **8**
Body Cafe **4**
Chocolate Maven **6**
Gabriel's **1**
Harry's Roadhouse **9**
Pyramid Cafe **3**
Tecolate Cafe **5**
Tune Up **2**

Hotels & Campgrounds ▼

Bishop's Lodge Resort & Spa **1**
Bobcat Inn **6**
El Rey Inn **4**
Residence Inn **5**
Santa Fe Courtyard by Marriott **3**
Ten Thousand Waves **2**

2

Rivera, is evident. ⊠*115 Hickox St.* ☎*505/983–7060* ⌖*No reservations* ▱*AE, V, MC* ⊗*No dinner.*

$ ✕ **Zia Diner.** Located in a renovated coal warehouse from the 1880s, this
AMERICAN   slick diner with a low-key, art deco–style interior serves comfort food
★   with a twist (green chili–piñon meat loaf, for example). Stop in for a
full meal or just snack on their classic banana split with homemade
hot fudge sauce. Zia's Cobb salad is one of the best in town, and the
amazingly fluffy corn, green chili, and asiago pie served with a mixed
green salad is hard to match. Service is friendly, and the food is fresh
with lots of local ingredients. There's a small patio and a friendly bar
known for its tasty mixed drinks and personable bartenders. Breakfast
here is great start to the day: try the Nutty New Mexican, a take on
eggs Benedict with green-chili corned beef hash, poached eggs, and
Hollandaise sauce. Yum! ⊠*326 S. Guadalupe St.* ☎*505/988–7008*
⊕*www.ziadiner.com* ▱*AE, MC, V.*

WHERE TO STAY

In Santa Fe you can ensconce yourself in quintessential Santa Fe style
or anonymous hotel-chain decor, depending on how much you want
to spend—the city has costlier accommodations than anywhere in the
Southwest. Cheaper options are available on Cerrillos (pronounced
sir-*ee*-yos) Road, the rather unattractive business thoroughfare southwest of downtown. Quality varies greatly on Cerrillos, but some of
the best-managed, most attractive properties are (from most to least
expensive) the Holiday Inn, the Courtyard Marriott, and the Motel
6. You pay more as you get closer to the Plaza, but for many visitors
it's worth it to be within walking distance of many attractions. Some
of the best deals are offered by B&Bs—many of those near the Plaza
offer much better values than the big, touristy hotels. Rates drop, often
from 30 to 50 percent from November to April (excluding Thanksgiving and Christmas).

In addition to the usual array of inns and hotels here, Santa Fe has
a wide range of **long- and short-term vacation rentals,** some of them
available through the **Management Group** (☎866/982–2823 ⊕*www.
santaferentals.com*). Rates generally range from $100 to $300 per night
for double-occupancy units, with better values at some of the two- to
four-bedroom properties. Many have fully stocked kitchens. Another
route is to rent a furnished condo or casita at one of several compounds
geared to travelers seeking longer stays. The best of these is the luxurious **Campanilla Compound** (☎*505/988–7585 or 800/828–9700* ⊕*www.
campanillacompound.com*), on a hill just north of downtown; rates
run from about $1,400 to $1,800 per week in summer. Another good,
similarly priced bet is **Fort Marcy Suites** (☎ *888/570–2775* ⊕*www.
fortmarcy.com*), on a bluff just northeast of the Plaza with great views.
The individually furnished units accommodate two to six guests and
come with full kitchens, wood fireplaces, VCRs, and CD stereos—these
can be rented nightly or weekly.

WHAT IT COSTS					
	¢	$	$$	$$$	$$$$
Hotels	under $70	$70–$130	$131–$190	$191–$260	over $260

Prices are for a standard double room in room in high season, excluding 13.5%–14.5% tax.

DOWNTOWN VICINITY

★ **$$$** **Alexander's Inn.** Once a B&B, Alexander's now rents two 2-story cottages. It remains an excellent lodging option. Located just a few blocks from the Plaza and Canyon Road, it exudes the charm of old Santa Fe. Cottages are cozy, with Southwest and American country–style furnishings, ethnic heirlooms, skylights, tall windows, and fireplaces. Each has a kitchen, fireplace, full bathroom and private bedroom upstairs. The grounds are dotted with tulips, hyacinths, lilac and apricot trees. Guests receive discounts at the nearby Absolute Nirvana Spa (⇨ Spas below) and full access to El Gancho Health Club, a 15-minute drive away. You'll find a generous welcome basket with wine and snacks and attentive service. **Pros:** Private, homey retreat in the heart of historic Santa Fe, an excellent value. **Cons:** Shares open yard with private home. ⊠529 E. Palace Ave. ☎505/986–1431 or 888/321–5123 ⊕www.alexanders-inn.com ⇔2 cottages ♿In-room: kitchen, CableTV, parking (no fee), Wi-Fi, some pets allowed (fee) ⊟D, MC, V ⓄⅠCP.

$$ **Don Gaspar Inn.** One of the city's best-kept secrets, this exquisitely
Fodor'sChoice landscaped and decorated compound is on a pretty residential street a
★ few blocks south of the Plaza. Its three historic houses have three distinct architectural styles: Arts and Crafts, Pueblo Revival, and Territorial. Floral gardens and aspen and cottonwood trees shade the tranquil paths and terraces, and both Southwest and Native American paintings and handmade furnishings enliven the sunny rooms and suites. The Arts and Crafts main house has two fireplaces, two bedrooms, and a fully equipped kitchen. Staff is attentive without hovering. Considering the setting and amenities, it's a great value. **Pros:** Beautiful décor, generous breakfasts, lush gardens. **Cons:** Some rooms close to elementary school can be noisy in the a.m. when school is in. ⊠623 Don Gaspar Ave. ☎505/986–8664 or 888/986–8664 ☎505/986–0696 ⊕www.dongaspar.com ⇔5 rooms, 5 suites, 1 cottage ♿In-room: kitchen (some), refrigerator, Wi-Fi. In-hotel: parking (no fee), no-smoking rooms ⊟AE, MC, V ⓄⅠCP.

$$$ **El Farolito.** All the beautiful Southwestern and Mexican furniture in this small, upscale compound is custom-made, and all the art and photography original. Rooms are spacious and pleasant with fireplaces and separate entrances; some are in their own little buildings. El Farolito has a peaceful downtown location, just steps from the capitol and a few blocks from the Plaza. Some have CD players. The same owners run the smaller Four Kachinas inn, which is close by and has one handicapped-accessible room (rare among smaller Santa Fe properties). The continental breakfast here is a real treat, featuring a tempting range of delicious baked goods. **Pros:** Attentive service; special dietary requests accommodated. **Cons:** No onsite pool or hot tub. ⊠*514 Galisteo St.* ☎*505/988–1631 or 888/634–8782* ⊕*www.farolito.com* ⟿*7 rooms, 1 suite* ⌂*In-room: VCR (some Wi-Fi. In-hotel: no-smoking rooms* ⊟*AE, D, MC, V* ⧖*CP.*

$$

Fodor's Choice

★

Hacienda Nicholas. It is rare to find classic Santa Fe accommodations—this actually *is* an old hacienda—blocks from the Plaza for reasonable prices. This is one such place. The thick adobe walls surrounding the building create a peace and solitude that belies its central location. Southwest décor

mixes with French country and Mexican details to create an ambience perfectly suited to this city. Homemade, organic breakfasts are deluxe; afternoon snacks will leave you begging for the recipes (which they'll cheerfully provide). The rooms are extremely comfortable and quiet, with details like plush comforters and sheets, and cozy robes. Several rooms open on to the interior courtyard, which has a kiva fireplace and offers a perfect respite after a long day of exploring. This is a real find. **Pros:** Rates are significantly lower than one would expect for the level of service and amenities here; the inn is one of the most "eco-friendly" in town. **Cons:** No hot tub or pool, though guests have privileges at El Gancho Health & Fitness Club 15 minutes away. ⊠*320 E. Marcy St., Santa Fe Plaza* ☎*888/284–3170* ⊕*www.haciendanicholas. com* ⟿*7 rooms* ⌂*In room: cable TV, some fireplaces. In hotel: Wi-Fi* ⊟*A, D, MC, V.*

$$

Fodor's Choice

★

Hotel Santa Fe. Picurís Pueblo has controlling interest in this handsome Pueblo-style three-story hotel on the Guadalupe District's edge and a short walk from the Plaza. The light, airy rooms and suites are traditional Southwestern, with locally handmade furniture, wooden blinds, and Pueblo paintings; many have balconies. The hotel gift shop, Santa Fe's only tribally owned store, has lower prices than many nearby retail stores. The 35 rooms and suites in the posh Hacienda wing have corner fireplaces and the use of a London-trained butler. Amaya is one of the better hotel restaurants in town. Informal talks about Native American history and culture are held in the lobby, and Native American dances take place May–October. **Pros:** Professional, helpful staff, lots of amenities. **Cons:** Some rooms are cramped; standard rooms only slightly above chain-hotel decor. ⊠*1501 Paseo de Peralta* ☎*505/982–1200 or 800/825–9876* ▦*505/984–2211* ⊕*www.hotelsantafe.com* ⟿*40 rooms, 91 suites* ⌂*In-hotel: restaurant, bar, pool, concierge, laundry service, parking (no fee)* ⊟*AE, D, DC, MC, V.*

$$$

Hotel St. Francis. Listed on the National Register of Historic Places, this three-story building, parts of which were constructed in 1923, has walkways lined with turn-of-the-20th-century lampposts and is one block south of the Plaza. The simple, elegant rooms with high ceilings, casement windows, brass-and-iron beds, marble and cherry antiques, and original artworks suggest a refined establishment, though this isn't always the case. Afternoon tea, with scones and finger sandwiches, is served daily (not complimentary) in the huge lobby, which rises 50 feet from a floor of blood-red tiles. **Pros:** The hotel bar is among the few places in town where you can grab a bite to eat until midnight. **Cons:** Service can be spotty and many of the rooms (and especially bathrooms) are quite tiny. ⊠ *210 Don Gaspar Ave.* ☎ *505/983–5700 or 800/529–5700* 🖷 *505/989–7690* ⊕ *www.hotelstfrancis.com* 📞 *80 rooms, 2 suites* ⚲ *In-room: refrigerator, Wi-Fi. In-hotel: restaurant, room service, bar, gym, concierge, laundry service, parking (fee)* ▭ *AE, D, DC, MC, V.*

$$$$ 🏨 **Inn at Loretto.** This plush, oft-photographed, pueblo–inspired property attracts a loyal clientele, many of whom swear by the friendly staff and high decorating standards. The lobby opens up to the gardens and large pool, and leather couches and high-end architectural details make the hotel a pleasure to relax in. Rooms are among the largest of any downtown property and contain vibrantly upholstered handcrafted furnishings and sumptuous slate-floor bathrooms—many have large balconies overlooking downtown. The new restaurant, Luminaria, serves creative Southwestern fare. The spa offers a wide range of Balinese and Thai-style treatments and services. **Pros:** The location, 2 blocks from the Plaza, is ideal. **Cons:** Fairly expensive parking/resort fees. ⊠ *211 Old Santa Fe Trail* ☎ *505/988–5531 or 800/727–5531* 🖷 *505/984–7988* ⊕ *www.hotelloretto.com* 📞 *134 rooms, 5 suites* ⚲ *In-hotel: restaurant, bar, pool, gym, spa, parking (fee)* ▭ *AE, D, DC, MC, V.*

$$$$
Fodor'sChoice
★

🏨 **Inn of the Anasazi.** Unassuming from the outside, this first-rate boutique hotel is one of Santa Fe's finest, with superb architectural detail. The prestigious Rosewood Hotel group took over the property in 2005, carefully upgrading the already sumptuous linens and furnishings. Each room has a beamed viga-and-latilla ceiling, kiva-style gas fireplace, antique Indian rugs, handwoven fabrics, and organic toiletries (including sunblock). Other amenities include full concierge services, twice-daily maid service, exercise bikes upon request, and a library. Especially nice touches in this desert town are the humidifiers in each guest room. A few deluxe rooms have balconies. The restaurant is excellent. **Pros:** The staff is thorough, gracious, and highly professional. **Cons:** Few rooms have balconies to take advantage of the lovely views; no hot tub or pool. ⊠ *113 Washington Ave.* ☎ *505/988–3030 or 800/688–8100* 🖷 *505/988–3277* ⊕ *www.innoftheanasazi.com* 📞 *58 rooms* ⚲ *In-room: safe, VCR, Wi-Fi. In-hotel: restaurant, bar, parking (fee), some pets allowed (fee), minibar* ▭ *AE, D, DC, MC, V.*

$$$$
Fodor'sChoice
★

🏨 **Inn of the Five Graces.** There isn't another property in Santa Fe to compare to this sumptuous, yet relaxed inn with an unmistakable East-meets-West feel. The management and staff at this hotel have created a property that fits right in with the kind of memorable properties you hear about in Morocco and Bali. The décor differs from the cliché Santa Fe style yet locals would tell you that this melding of styles is what true Santa Fe style is all about. The suites have Asian and Latin American antiques and art, kilim rugs, jewel-tone throw pillows, and mosaic-tile bathrooms; most have fireplaces, and many have soaking tubs or walk-in steam showers. The personal service stands out:

dream catchers and ghost stories are left on your pillow, refrigerators are stocked, and afternoon margarita and wine-and-cheese spreads, an exquisite breakfast, and even daily walking tours are all available. A new spa treatment room has been added and there are plans to add a small pool. **Pros:** Tucked into a quiet, ancient neighborhood, the Plaza is only minutes away; fantastic staff, attentive but not overbearing. **Cons:** The cost of a room limits a stay here to all but the very fortunate. ⊠*150 E. DeVargas St.* ☎*505/992–0957 866/992-0957* 🖷*505/955–0549* ⊕*www.fivegraces.com* ⇆*22 suites* ♿*In-room: kitchen (some), refrigerator, Wi-Fi. In-hotel: parking (no fee), some pets allowed (fee)* ⊟*AE, MC, V* ⏀*BP.*

★ $$$ 🏨 **Inn of the Governors.** This rambling hotel by the Santa Fe River received a major makeover in 2004, and is staffed by a polite, enthusiastic bunch. Rooms have a Mexican theme, with bright colors, hand-painted folk art, feather pillows, Southwestern fabrics, and handmade furnishings; deluxe rooms also have balconies and fireplaces. Perks include a complimentary tea and sherry social each afternoon and a quite extensive breakfast buffet along with free Wi-Fi and newspapers. New Mexican dishes and lighter fare like wood-oven pizzas are served in the very popular and very reasonably priced (¢) bar/restaurant, Del Charro. **Pros:** Close to Plaza; friendly, helpful staff. **Cons:** Standard rooms tend to be small and cramped. ⊠*101 W. Alameda St.* ☎*505/982–4333 or 800/234–4534* 🖷*505/989–9149* ⊕*www. innofthegovernors.com* ⇆*100 rooms* ♿*In-room: refrigerator, Wi-Fi. In-hotel: restaurant, room service, bar, pool, concierge, parking (no fee)* ⊟*AE, D, DC, MC, V* ⏀*BP.*

★ $$ 🏨 **Inn of the Turquoise Bear.** In the 1920s, poet Witter Bynner played host to an eccentric circle of artists and intellectuals, as well as some wild parties in his mid-19th-century Spanish–Pueblo Revival home, which is now a B&B. Rooms are simple but have plush linens. The inn's style preserves the building's historic integrity, and there's plenty of ambience and a ranchlike lobby. You might sleep in the room where D.H. Lawrence slept, or perhaps Robert Oppenheimer's room. The terraced flower gardens provide plenty of places to repose, away from the traffic on Old Santa Fe Trail, which borders the property. This is the quintessential Santa Fe inn. **Pros:** Gorgeous grounds and a house steeped in local history; gracious, knowledgable staff. **Cons:** No pool or hot tub onsite. ⊠*342 E. Buena Vista* ☎*505/983–0798 or 800/396–4104* ⊕*www.turquoisebear.com* ⇆*8 rooms, 2 with shared bath; 3 suites* ♿*In-room: VCR, Wi-Fi. In-hotel: parking (no fee), pet friendly.* ⊟*AE, D, MC, V* ⏀*CP.*

$$$
Fodor'sChoice
★
🏨 **Inn on the Alameda.** Near the Plaza and Canyon Road is one of the Southwest's best small hotels. Alameda means "tree-lined lane," and this one perfectly complements the inn's location by the gurgling Santa Fe River. The adobe architecture and enclosed courtyards strewn with climbing rose vines combine a relaxed New Mexico country atmosphere with the luxury and amenities of a top-notch hotel, from afternoon wine and cheese to free local and toll-free calls to triple-sheeted beds with 300-count Egyptian bedding. Rooms have a Southwestern color scheme, handmade armoires and headboards, and ceramic lamps

and tiles—many have patios and kiva fireplaces. **Pros:** The solicitous staff is first-rate; excellent breakfasts. **Cons:** No pool. ⊠*303 E. Alameda St.* ☎*505/984–2121 or 888/984–2121* 🖶*505/986–8325* ⊕*www. innonthealameda.com* ⇥*59 rooms, 10 suites* ⚒*In-room: refrigerator (some). In-hotel: bar, gym, concierge, laundry facilities, parking (no fee), some pets allowed (fee), Wi-Fi* ⊟*AE, D, DC, MC, V* ⦿*CP.*

$$$$ 🏨 **La Fonda.** History and charm are more prevalent in this sole Plaza-front hotel than first-class service and amenities. The pueblo-inspired structure was built in 1922 and enlarged many times. Antiques and Native American art decorate the tiled lobby, and each room has hand-decorated wood furniture, wrought-iron light fixtures, beamed ceilings, and high-speed wireless. Some suites have fireplaces. The 14 rooftop rooms are the most luxurious and include Continental breakfast and private concierge services; there's also an exercise room, garden, and outdoor hot tub there. La Plazuela Restaurant, with its hand-painted glass tiles, serves good and creative Southwestern food. Folk and R&B bands rotate nightly in the bar. **Pros:** Great building and location, steeped in history. **Cons:** For the price, facilities don't stand up to comparison against other downtown properties. ⊠*100 E. San Francisco St.* ☎*505/982–5511 or 800/523–5002* 🖶*505/988–2952* ⊕*www. lafondasantafe.com* ⇥*143 rooms, 24 suites* ⚒*In-room: Wi-Fi. In-hotel: restaurant, bars, pool, gym, concierge, laundry service, parking (fee)* ⊟*AE, D, DC, MC, V.*

$$$$ 🏨 **La Posada de Santa Fe Resort and Spa.** Rooms on the beautiful, quiet grounds of this hotel vary, but extensive renovations have enhanced all rooms to a level of luxury previously lacking. Many have fireplaces, all have flat-screen TVs, CD players, leather couches, marble bathrooms, and Navajo-inspired rugs. The main building contains a handful of luxurious, high-ceiling Victorian rooms. The property boasts excellent bar, spa, and common areas, including the fantastic contemporary restaurant Fuego ($$$$), and the Staab House Lounge. Guests are offered numerous complimentary events throughout the week, like margarita Mondays, wine & cheese pairings on Wednesdays, and chef's receptions on Fridays. **Pros:** Numerous amenities, 2 blocks from the Santa Fe Plaza. **Cons:** Resort can sometimes feel overrun with tour bus crowds. ⊠*330 E. Palace Ave.* ☎*505/986–0000 or 866/331–7625* 🖶*505/982–6850* ⊕*www.laposadadesantafe.com* ⇥*120 rooms, 39 suites* ⚒*In-room: Wi-Fi. In-hotel: restaurant, bar, pool, gym, spa, parking (fee)* ⊟*AE, D, DC, MC, V.*

$$$ 🏨 **Las Palomas.** It's a pleasant 10-minute walk west of the Plaza to reach this group of properties, consisting of two historic, luxurious compounds, one of them Spanish Pueblo–style adobe, the other done in the Territorial style, with a Victorian ambience, as well as the 15 rooms in the recently acquired La Tienda & Duran House compound. A network of brick paths shaded by mature trees leads past the casitas, connecting them with secluded courtyards and flower gardens. Each casita has a bedroom, full kitchen, living room with pull-out sofa, and fireplace, and each opens onto a terrace or patio. Locally handcrafted wooden and leather sofas, desks, and tables fill these spacious accommodations, along with Native American artwork and sculptures. It's

an elegant alternative to the city's upscale full-service hotels, affording guests a bit more privacy and the feel of a private cottage rental—though it is managed by the Hotel Santa Fe. **Pros:** Kid-friendly, with swings and a play yard; on-site fitness center. **Cons:** Big variation in accommodations; no hot tub or pool on site (guests may use pool at the Hotel Santa Fe). ⌧*460 W. San Francisco St.* ☎*505/982–5560 or 877/982–5560* 🖷*505/982–5562* ⊕*www.laspalomas.com* ⇖*38 units* ⌂*In-room: kitchen, VCR, Wi-Fi. In-hotel: gym* ¶⊙*CP.*

$$ 🏠 **Madeleine Inn.** Santa Fe hasn't always been a town of pseudo-
Fodor'sChoice pueblo buildings and this lovely Queen Anne Victorian is living proof.
★   Built by a railroad tycoon in 1886, this beautifully maintained B&B is nestled amongst mature trees and gardens just 4 blocks from the Plaza. Plush beds, lovely antiques and art adorn the rooms. Fireplaces grace four rooms and the smells of freshly baked goodies welcome you in the afternoon. Organic breakfasts here are worth sticking around for, and the staff is professional and gracious. The amazing Absolute Nirvana spa is on the premises. Guests have privileges to El Gancho Health & Tennis Club 15 minutes away. **Pros:** Like its companion inn, Hacienda Nicholas, the rates at this committed "eco-friendly" business are a bargain for the services and amenities provided. **Cons:** Steep stairs, no elevators in this three-story Victorian. ⌧*106 Faith-way St., Santa Fe Plaza* ☎*505/982–3465 or 888/877–7622* ⊕*www. madeleineinn.com* ⇖*7 rooms* ⌂*In room: cable TV, some fireplaces In hotel: Wi-Fi* ▭*A, D, MC, V.*

★ **$$**   🏠**Old Santa Fe Inn.** About four blocks south of the Plaza, in the hip Guadalupe District, this contemporary inn, which opened in 2001 and looks like an attractive, if fairly ordinary, adobe motel, has stunning and spotless rooms with elegant Southwestern furnishings. Tile baths, high-quality linens, and upscale furnishings fill every room, along with two phone lines and CD stereos; many have kiva fireplaces, or balconies and patios. Small business center and gym are open 24 hours. Most rooms open onto a gravel courtyard–parking lot, although chili ristras hanging outside each unit brighten things up. The make-your-own-breakfast-burrito buffet is a nice touch. **Pros:** Rooms are more inviting than several more-expensive downtown hotels and it's a short walk to the Plaza. **Cons:** Minimal, though friendly and professional, staffing. ⌧*320 Galisteo St.* ☎*505/995–0800 or 800/745–9910* 🖷*505/995–0400* ⊕*www.oldsantafeinn.com* ⇖*34 rooms, 9 suites* ⌂*In-room: refrigerator (some), VCR, Wi-Fi. In-hotel: gym, parking (no fee)* ▭*AE, D, DC, MC, V* ¶⊙*CP.*

$$ 🏠**Pueblo Bonito B&B Inn.** Rooms in this 1873 adobe compound have handmade and hand-painted furnishings, Navajo weavings, brick and hardwood floors, sand paintings and pottery, locally carved santos (Catholic saints), and Western art. All have kiva fireplaces and private entrances, and many have kitchens. Breakfast is served in the main dining room. Afternoon tea also offers complimentary margaritas. The Plaza is a five-minute walk away. **Pros:** Intimate, cozy inn on peaceful grounds. **Cons:** Bathrooms tend to be small; breakfast is more Continental, not home-cooked. ⌧*138 W. Manhattan Ave.* ☎*505/984–8001 or 800/461–4599* 🖷*505/984–3155* ⊕*www.pueblobonitoinn.*

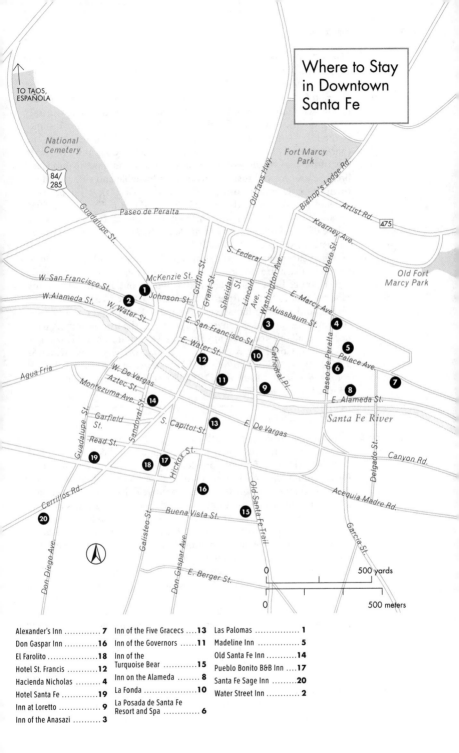

Where to Stay in Downtown Santa Fe

Alexander's Inn **7**

Don Gaspar Inn **16**

El Farolito **18**

Hotel St. Francis **12**

Hacienda Nicholas **4**

Hotel Santa Fe **19**

Inn at Loretto **9**

Inn of the Anasazi **3**

Inn of the Five Gracecs **13**

Inn of the Governors **11**

Inn of the
Turquoise Bear **15**

Inn on the Alameda **8**

La Fonda **10**

La Posada de Santa Fe
Resort and Spa **6**

Las Palomas **1**

Madeline Inn **5**

Old Santa Fe Inn **14**

Pueblo Bonito B&B Inn **17**

Santa Fe Sage Inn **20**

Water Street Inn **2**

com ♥13 *rooms, 5 suites* &*In-room: kitchen (some), refrigerator (some). In-hotel: restaurant, laundry facilities, parking (no fee), no-smoking rooms* ▤*AE, DC, MC, V* ¶⊙¶*CP.*

★ $ ▦ **Santa Fe Sage Inn.** On the southern edge of the Guadalupe District, this motel offers affordable low-frills comfort and surprisingly attractive (given the low rates) Southwestern decor within walking distance of the Plaza (six blocks). Special packages are available for three- and four-day stays during peak-season events. Get a room upstairs and in one of the rear buildings for the most privacy and quiet. Continental breakfast is served. **Pros:** Comfortable, affordable and close to downtown **Cons:** Rooms on corner of Cerrillos and Don Diego can be noisy; unrenovated rooms lackluster. ✉*725 Cerrillos Rd.* ☎*505/982–5952 or 866/433–0335* ⊕*www.santafesageinn.com* ♥162 *rooms* &*In-room: Wi-Fi. In-hotel: restaurant, pool, parking (no fee), some pets allowed* ▤*AE, DC, MC, V* ¶⊙¶*CP.*

$$$ ▦ **Water Street Inn.** The large rooms in this restored adobe 2½ blocks from the Plaza are decorated with reed shutters, antique pine beds, viga-beam ceilings, hand-stenciled artwork, and a blend of cowboy, Hispanic, and Native American art and artifacts. Most have fireplaces, and all have flat-screen TVs with DVD players and CD stereos. Afternoon hors d'oeuvres are served in the living room. A patio deck is available for relaxing. **Pros:** Close to restaurants, Plaza; gracious staff. **Cons:** Inn overlooks a parking lot. ✉*427 W. Water St.* ☎*505/984–1193 or 800/646–6752* ⊕*www.waterstreetinn.com* ♥8 *rooms, 4 suites* &*In-room: DVD, Wi-Fi. In-hotel: parking (no fee)* ▤*AE, DC, MC, V* ¶⊙¶*CP.*

SOUTH OF DOWNTOWN

★ $ ▦ **Bobcat Inn.** A delightful, affordable, country hacienda that's a 15-minute drive southeast of the Plaza, this adobe B&B sits amid 10 secluded acres of piñon and ponderosa pine, with grand views of the Ortiz Mountains and the area's high-desert mesas. John and Amy Bobrick run this low-key retreat and prepare expansive full breakfasts as well as high tea on Saturday during the summer high season (these are by reservation only). Arts and Crafts furniture and Southwest pottery fill the common room, in which breakfast is served and guests can relax throughout the day. The unpretentious rooms are brightened by Talvera tiles, folk art, and colorful blankets and rugs; some have kiva fireplaces. The Lodge Room is outfitted with handcrafted Adirondack furniture, and its bathroom has a whirlpool tub. Guests have access to El Gancho Health & Fitness center (fee) nearby. **Pros:** Gracious, secluded inn; wonderful hosts. **Cons:** Located outside town, a drive is required for all activities except eating at Bobcat Bite, which is right next door. No pets; no children under age 6. ✉*442 Old Las Vegas Hwy.* ☎*505/988–9239* ⊕*www.nm-inn.com* ♥5 *rooms* &*In-room: no TV, Wi-Fi. In-hotel: parking (no fee)* ▤*D, MC, V* ¶⊙¶*BP.*

$$ ▦ **El Rey Inn.** The kind of place where Lucy and Ricky might have
Fodor's Choice stayed during one of their cross-country adventures, the El Rey was
★ built in 1936 but has been brought gracefully into the 21st century, its rooms and bathrooms handsomely updated without losing any

period charm. Rooms are individually decorated and might include antique television armoires, beamed ceilings, upholstered wing chairs and sofas; some have kitchenettes. Each unit has a small covered front patio with wrought-iron chairs. Beautifully landscaped grounds are covered with flowers in the summer and towering trees shade the parking lot. There's a landscaped courtyard with tables and chairs by the pool. **Pros:** Excellent price for a distinctive, charming property. **Cons:** Rooms closest to Cerrillos can be noisy; some rooms are quite dark. ✉*1862 Cerrillos Rd.* ☎*505/982–1931 or 800/521–1349* 🖷*505/989–9249* ⊕*www.elreyinnsantafe.com* ➾*86 rooms* 🛆*In-room: kitchen (some) Wi-Fi. In-hotel:continental breakfast, pool,2 hot tub, laundry facilities, parking (no fee), no-smoking in rooms, fitness room* ☰*AE, DC, MC, V* �†⊙†*CP.*

$$$ 🖷**Residence Inn.** This compound consists of clusters of three-story adobe town houses with pitched roofs and tall chimneys. Best bets for families or up to four adults traveling together are the one-room suites, which each have a loft bedroom and then a separate sitting area (with a curtain divider) that has a Murphy bed. All units have wood-burning fireplaces. It's right off a major intersection about 3 mi south of the Plaza, but it's set back far enough so that there's no traffic noise. Ask for one of the second-floor end units for the best mountain views. **Pros:** Complimentary full breakfast, evening socials, and grocery-shopping service are provided. **Cons:** Not within walking distance of any restaurants or attractions. ✉*1698 Galisteo St.* ☎*505/988–7300 or 800/331–3131* 🖷*505/988-3243* ⊕*www.marriott.com/safnm* ➾*120 suites* 🛆*In-room: kitchen,. In-hotel:Wi-Fi, parking (no fee)* ☰*AE, D, DC, MC, V* ⊙*BP.*

$ 🖷**Santa Fe Courtyard by Marriott.** Of the dozens of chain properties along gritty Cerrillos Road, this is the only bona fide gem, even though it looks like all the others: clad in faux adobe and surrounded by parking lots and strip malls. Don't fret—it's easy to forget about the nondescript setting once inside this glitzy miniature resort, which comprises several buildings set around a warren of lushly landscaped interior courtyards. Aesthetically, the rooms look Southwestern, with chunky carved-wood armoires, desks, and headboards reminiscent of a Spanish-colonial hacienda. **Pros:** Rooms have the usual upscale-chain doodads: mini-refrigerators, coffeemakers, hair dryers, clock radios—there's also high-speed Internet. **Cons:** Location on Cerrillos is a little out of the way for sightseeing ✉*3347 Cerrillos Rd.* ☎*505/473–2800 or 800/777–3347* 🖷*505/473–4905* ⊕*www.santafecourtyard.com* ➾*213 rooms* 🛆*In-room: refrigerator, Wi-Fi. In-hotel: restaurant, room service, bar, pool, gym, laundry facilities, laundry service, parking (no fee)* ☰*AE, D, DC, MC, V.*

NORTH OF SANTA FE

$$$$ 🖷**Bishop's Lodge Resort and Spa.** Although this historic resort is just five minutes from the Plaza, its setting in a bucolic valley at the foot of the Sangre de Cristo Mountains makes it feel worlds apart. Outdoor activities abound including hiking, horseback riding, skeet-shooting, tennis (professional lessons available) and trapshooting. History runs

deep here with the nearly 150-year-old chapel built by Archbishop Jean Baptiste Lamy—a figure lionized by writer Willa Cather—at the resort's center. Rooms have antique and reproduction Southwestern furnishings—shipping chests, Mexican tinwork, and Native American and Western art. Many offer balconies or patios with spectacular mountain vistas. The Las Fuentes Restaurant & Bar specializes in inventive Nuevo Latino fare. Locals often descend on the excellent Sunday brunch. **Pros:** Service with a smile—every member of the staff is trained in the art of hospitality, and it shows in their genuine eagerness to please. The tranquil SháNah Spa and the beautiful grounds make this place a special getaway only minutes from downtown. **Cons:** Resort is spread out over 700 acres and some rooms seem rather far flung. The narrow, windy roads throughout make driving around the property a bit precarious. ⊠*Bishop's Lodge Rd., 2½ mi north of downtown* ☎*505/983–6377 or 800/419–0492* ⊕*www.bishopslodge.com* ➫*92 rooms, 19 suites* ♿*In-room: refrigerator. In-hotel: 2 restaurants (one open during summer only), bar, tennis courts, pool, fitness center, spa, children's programs (ages 5–13), airport shuttle, parking (no fee)* ▤*AE, D, MC, V.*

$$$$
Fodor'sChoice
★
🌀 **Ten Thousand Waves.** Devotees appreciate the Zenlike atmosphere of this Japanese-style health spa and small hotel above town. Nine light and airy hillside cottages are settled down a piñon-covered hill below the first-rate spa, which is tremendously popular with day visitors. The sleek, uncluttered accommodations have marble or stone wood-burning fireplaces, CD stereos, fine woodwork, low-slung beds or futons, and courtyards or patios; two come with full kitchens. There's also a cozy, vintage Airstream Bambi trailer available at much lower rates ($139 nightly)—it's a kitschy, fun alternative to the much pricier cottages. The facility has private and communal indoor and outdoor hot tubs and spa treatments. Overnight guests can use the communal tubs for free. The snack bar serves sushi and other healthful treats. Ask about the Japanese movie nights. **Pros:** This is a delightfully sensuous experience all the way around. **Cons:** You might not want to leave the premises, but you'll have to because there is no on-site restaurant. ⊠*3451 Hyde Park Rd., 4 mi northeast of the Plaza* 🗑*Box 10200,* ☎*505/982–9304* 🖨*505/989–5077* ⊕*www.tenthousandwaves.com* ➫*12 cottages, 1 trailer* ♿*In-room: no a/c, kitchen (some), refrigerator, VCR (some), no TV (some), Wi-Fi (some). In-hotel: spa, parking (no fee), some pets allowed (fee)* ▤*D, MC, V.*

NIGHTLIFE & THE ARTS

Few, if any, small cities in America can claim an Arts scene as thriving as Santa Fe's—with opera, symphony, and theater in splendid abundance. The music acts here tend to be high-caliber, but rather sporadic. Nightlife, as in dance clubs, is considered fairly "bleak." When popular acts come to town the whole community shows up and dances like there's no tomorrow. A super, seven-week series of music on the Plaza bandstand runs through the summer with performances four nights a week. Gallery openings, poetry readings, plays, and dance concerts take place year-round, not to mention the famed opera and chamber-music festivals. Check the arts and entertainment listings in Santa Fe's daily newspaper, the *New Mexican* (⊕*www.santafenewmexican.com*), particularly on Friday, when the arts and entertainment section, "Pasatiempo," is included, or check the weekly *Santa Fe Reporter* (⊕*www. sfreporter.com*) for shows and events. As you suspect by now, activities peak in the summer.

NIGHTLIFE

Culturally endowed though it is, Santa Fe has a pretty mellow nightlife scene; its key strength being live music, which is presented at numerous bars, hotel lounges, and restaurants. Austin-based blues and country groups and other acts wander into town, and members of blockbuster bands have been known to perform unannounced at small clubs while vacationing in the area. But on most nights your best bet might be quiet cocktails beside the flickering embers of a piñon fire or under the stars out on the patio.

Catamount Bar (⊠*125 E. Water St.* ☎*505/988–7222*) is popular with the postcollege set; jazz and blues-rock groups play on weekends and some weeknights. The dance floor is small, but there's an enjoyable second-story balcony with seating. The pool tables are a big draw.

★ The **Cowgirl** (⊠*319 S. Guadalupe St.* ☎*505/982–2565*) is one of the most popular spots in town for live blues, country, rock, folk, and even comedy, on occasion. The bar is friendly and the drinks are great. Their pool hall is fun and can get wild as the night gets late.

Dragon Room (⊠*406 Old Santa Fe Trail* ☎*505/983–7712*), at the Pink Adobe restaurant (⇨ Where to Eat above), long a hot-spot in town, has been tidied up and, consequently, it's no longer the fun, lively destination for colorful locals and curious tourists. Good drinks and bar food, though.

Eldorado Court and Lounge (⊠*309 W. San Francisco St.* ☎*505/988–4455*), in the lobby of the classy Eldorado Hotel, is a gracious lounge where classical guitarists and pianists perform nightly. It has the largest wines-by-the-glass list in town.

★ **El Farol** (⊠*808 Canyon Rd.* ☎*505/983–9912*) is where locals go to have a drink at the end of the day; the front porch being a particularly choice spot to enjoy the afternoon and evenings of summer. The roomy, rustic bar has a true old West atmosphere, and you can order some fine Spanish brandies and sherries in addition to cold beers and tasty mixed drinks (particularly those margaritas locals are so fond of). It's a great place to see a variety of music; the dancefloor fills up with a friendly crowd.

Evangelo's (⊠*200 W. San Francisco St.* ☎*505/982–9014*) is an old-fashioned, street-side bar, with pool tables downstairs, 200 types of imported beer, and rock bands on many weekends.

★ **Matador** (⊠*116 W. San Francisco St. Ste 113, enter down stairs on Galisteo St. Santa Fe Plaza* ☎*No phone*) is exactly what Santa Fe needed: a dark, subterranean dive bar right downtown. Owners Frank and César, both entertaining characters, have banished any notions of

Southwest-style decor by painting the place black and covering the walls with old punk posters, and locals love it. You'll find a decent selection of beers, stiff mixed drinks, and some fine tequilas (this is Santa Fe, after all). The music is all-over-the-place loud, with local DJs spinning on various nights, and campy flicks play on a wall screen. The early crowd is older, and gets younger and hipper as the night goes on. Cash only!

Santa Fe Brewing Company (✉ *35 Fire Place, on NM 14, the Turquoise Trail* ☎ *505/424–3333* ⊕ *www.santafebrewing.com*) hosts all sorts of music and serves fine micro-brews and food (and Taos Cow ice cream!) from its location about 15 minutes south of downtown. Recent acts have included X, Sierra Leone Refugee All-Stars, Taj Mahal, and local stars Hundred-Year Flood and Goshen. Very kid-friendly, the venue has an indoor room for the cold months, and a great outdoor stage where the performers, and the sunset, are on full view.

Second Street Brewery (✉ *1814 2nd St.* ☎ *505/982–3030*), a short drive south of downtown, packs in an eclectic, easygoing bunch for their own microbrewed ales, pretty lackluster pub fare, live rock, folk, and some great local DJs. There's an expansive patio, and the staff is friendly.

Tin Star Saloon (✉ *411B W. Water St., near Santa Fe Plaza* ☎ *505/984–5050* ⊕ *www.tinstarsaloon.com*) is a welcome addition to Santa Fe's nightlife, with a great bar in a cozy room and live music almost every night. They book a wide range of music, from hard rock to R&B. The crowd here likes to dance.

Tiny's (✉ *Cerrillos Rd. and St. Francis Dr.* ☎ *505/983–9817*), a retro-fabulous restaurant serving steaks and New Mexican fare, is a legend in this town with politicos, reporters, and deal-makers. The real draw is the kitsch-filled '50s cocktail lounge.

WilLee's Blues Club (✉ *401 S. Guadalupe St.* ☎ *505/982–0117*) presents poundin' blues, rock and hip hop showsseveral nights a week in an intimate, often-packed space in the Guadalupe District.

THE ARTS

The performing arts scene in Santa Fe blossoms in summer. Classical or jazz concerts, Shakespeare on the grounds of St. John's campus, experimental theater at Santa Fe Stages, or flamenco—"too many choices!" is the biggest complaint. The rest of the year is a bit quieter, but an increasing number of off-season venues have developed in recent years. The Pasatiempo section of the *Santa Fe New Mexican*'s Friday edition or the *Santa Fe Reporter*, released on Wednesdays, are great sources for current happenings.

The city's most interesting multiuse arts venue, the **Center for Contemporary Arts (CCA)** (✉ *1050 Old Pecos Trail* ☎ *505/982–1338* ⊕ *www. ccasantafe.org*) presents indie and foreign films, art exhibitions, provocative theater, and countless workshops and lectures.

2

CONCERT VENUES

A 10-minute drive north of town, **Camel Rock Casino** (⊠ *U.S. 285/84* ☎ *800/462–2635* ⊕ *www.camelrockcasino.com*) hosts a fairly wide variety of performers such as Buju Banton, the Marshall Tucker Band, and Chubby Checker.

Santa Fe's vintage downtown movie house was fully restored and converted into the 850-seat **Lensic Performing Arts Center** (⊠ *211 W. San Francisco St.* ☎ *505/988–1234* ⊕ *www.lensic.com*) in 2001. The grand 1931 building, with Moorish and Spanish Renaissance influences, hosts the Santa Fe Symphony, theater, classic films, lectures and readings, noted world, pop, and jazz musicians, and many other noteworthy events.

On the campus of the Santa Fe Indian School, the **Paolo Soleri Outdoor Amphitheater** (⊠ *1501 Cerrillos Rd.* ☎ *505/989–6318*) is a fantastic venue and hosts pop, blues, rock, reggae, and jazz concerts spring–fall; past performers have included Ozomatli, Bonnie Raitt, and Chris Isaak. Watching the sunsets play across the sky is as spectacular as the shows onstage.

The **St. Francis Auditorium** (⊠ *Museum of Fine Arts, northwest corner of Plaza*) is the scene of cultural events such as theatrical productions and varied musical performances.

DANCE

The esteemed **Aspen Santa Fe Ballet** (☎ *505/983–5591 or 505/988–1234* ⊕ *www.aspensantafeballet.com*) presents several ballet performances throughout the year at the Lensic Performing Arts Center.

Fans of Spanish dance should make every effort to see **Maria Benitez Teatro Flamenco** (⊠ *P.O. Box 8418 , back of the Children's Museum Building.* ☎ *505/955–8562 or 888/435–2636* ⊕ *www.mariabenitez. com*), who performs from late June through August. Maria Benitez is one of the world's premier flamenco dancers, and her performances often sell out well in advance.

MUSIC

★ The acclaimed **Santa Fe Chamber Music Festival** (☎ *505/983–2075* ⊕ *www. sfcmf.org*) runs mid-July through late August, with performances nearly every night at the St. Francis Auditorium, or, occasionally, the Lensic Performing Arts Center. There are also free youth-oriented concerts given on several summer mornings. You can also attend many rehearsals for free; call for times.

Performances by the **Santa Fe Desert Chorale** (☎ *505/988–2282 or 800/244–4011* ⊕ *www.desertchorale.org*) take place throughout the summer at a variety of intriguing venues, from the Cathedral Basilica St. Francis to Loretto Chapel. This highly regarded singing group, which was started in 1982, also performs a series of concerts during the December holiday season.

Fodor'sChoice **Santa Fe Opera** (☎505/986–5900 or 800/280–4654 ⊕*www.santa*
★ *feopera.org*) performs in a strikingly modern structure—a 2,126-seat,
indoor-outdoor amphitheater with excellent acoustics and sight lines.
Carved into the natural curves of a hillside 7 mi north of the city on
U.S. 285/84, the opera overlooks mountains, mesas, and sky. Add some
of the most acclaimed singers, directors, conductors, musicians, designers, and composers from Europe and the United States, and you begin
to understand the excitement that builds every June. The company,
which celebrated its 50th anniversary in 1996, presents five works in
repertory each summer—a blend of seasoned classics, neglected master-
pieces, and world premieres. Many evenings sell out far in advance, but
inexpensive standing-room tickets are often available on the day of the
performance. A favorite pre-opera pastime is tailgating in the parking
lot before the evening performance—many guests set up elaborate picnics of their own, but you can also preorder picnic meals ($32 per meal)
by calling ☎505/983–2433 24 hours in advance; pick up your meal
up to two hours before the show, at the Angel Food Catering kiosk on
the west side of the parking lot. Or you can dine at the Preview Buffet,
set up 2½ hours before each performance by the Guilds of the Santa
Fe Opera. These meals include a large spread of very good food along
with wine, held on the opera grounds. During dessert, a prominent
local expert on opera gives a talk about the evening's performance. The
Preview Buffet is by reservation only, by calling the opera box office
number listed above, and the cost is $50 per person.

Orchestra and chamber concerts are given at St. Francis Auditorium
and the Lensic Performing Arts Center by the **Santa Fe Pro Musica**
(☎505/988–4640 or 800/960–6680 ⊕*www.santafepromusica.com*)
from September through April. Baroque and other classical compo-
sitions are the normal fare; the annual Christmas performance is a
highlight.

The **Santa Fe Symphony** (☎505/983–1414 or 800/480–1319 ⊕*www.
sf-symphony.org*) performs seven concerts each season (from October
to April) in the Lensic Performing Arts Center.

THEATER
The **Greer Garson Theatre Company** (✉*College of Santa Fe, 1600 St.
Michael's Dr.* ☎505/473–6511 or 800/456–2673 ⊕*www.csf.edu*)
stages student productions of comedies, dramas, and musicals from
October to May.

The oldest extant theater company west of the Mississippi, the **Santa
Fe Playhouse** (✉*142 E. De Vargas St.* ☎505/988–4262 ⊕*www.santa
feplayhouse.org*) occupies a converted 19th-century adobe stable and
has been presenting an adventurous mix of avant-garde pieces, classical drama, and musical comedy since 1922. The Fiesta Melodrama—a
spoof of the Santa Fe scene—runs late August–mid-September.

Theaterwork (✉*James A. Little Theater at the New Mexico School for
the Deaf, 1060 Cerrillos Rd* ☎505/471–1799 ⊕*www.theaterwork.
org*) is a well-respected community theater group that performs five
plays each season, which runs from September through May.

Santa Fe Performing Arts (☎*505/984–1370* ⊕*www.sfperformingarts. org*), running since 1986, has become a local favorite for its professional productions and adult resident company as well as its commitment to outreach education in the schools and for community youth in its after-school programs. The theater is committed to developing new works; call or check the website for the current schedule.

SPORTS & THE OUTDOORS

The Santa Fe National Forest is right in the city's backyard and includes the Dome Wilderness (5,200 acres in the volcanically formed Jémez Mountains) and the Pecos Wilderness (223,333 acres of high mountains, forests, and meadows at the southern end of the Rocky Mountain chain). The 12,500-foot Sangre de Cristo Mountains (the name translates as "Blood of Christ," for the red glow they radiate at sunset) fringe the city's east side, constant and gentle reminders of the mystery and power of the natural world. To the south and west, sweeping high desert is punctuated by several less formidable mountain ranges. The dramatic shifts in elevation and topography around Santa Fe make for a wealth of outdoor activities. Head to the mountains for fishing, camping, and skiing; to the nearby Rio Grande for kayaking and rafting; and almost anywhere in the area for bird-watching, hiking, and biking.

PARTICIPANT SPORTS

For a one-stop shop for information about recreation on public lands, which includes national and state parks, contact the **New Mexico Public Lands Information Center** (⊠*1474 Rodeo Rd.* ☎*505/438–7542* 🖷*505/438–7582* ⊕*www.publiclands.org*). It has maps, reference materials, licenses, permits—just about everything you need to plan an adventure in the New Mexican wilderness.

★ ☺ The huge **Genoveva Chavez Community Center** (⊠*3221 Rodeo Rd.* ☎*505/955–4001* ⊕*www.chavezcenter.com*) is a reasonably priced (adults $4 per day) facility with a regulation-size ice rink (they rent ice skates for the whole family), an enormous gymnasium, indoor running track, 50-meter pool, leisure pool with waterslide and play structures, aerobics center, fitness room, two racquetball courts, and a child-care center.

BICYCLING

You can pick up a map of bike trips—among them a 30-mi round-trip ride from downtown Santa Fe to Ski Santa Fe at the end of NM 475— from the New Mexico Public Lands Information Center, or at the bike shops listed below. One excellent place to mountain-bike is the Dale Ball Trail Network, which is accessed from several points.

Bike N' Sport (⊠*530 W. Cordova Rd.* ☎*505/820–0809*) provides rentals and information about guided tours.

Mellow Velo (✉638 Old Santa Fe Trail,Lower Old Santa Fe Trail ☎505/995–VELO (8356)) is a friendly, neighborhood bike shop offering group tours, privately guided rides, bicycle rentals ($35.50 per day—make reservations!) and repairs. These guys offer a great way to spend a day.

Santa Fe Mountain Sports (✉607 Cerrillos Rd. ☎505/988–3337 ⊕www. santafemountainsports.com ✆Mon.–Sat. 9–6, Sun. 9–5) has a good selection of bikes for rent (⇨ Skiing below).

BIRD-WATCHING

At the end of Upper Canyon Road, at the mouth of the canyon as it wends into the foothills, the 135-acre **Randall Davey Audubon Center** harbors diverse birds and other wildlife. Guided nature walks are given many weekends; there are also two major hiking trails that you can tackle on your own. The home and studio of Randall Davey, a prolific early Santa Fe artist, can be toured on Monday afternoons in summer. There's also a nature bookstore. ✉1800 Upper Canyon Rd. ☎505/983–4609 ⊕www.audubon.org/chapter/nm/nm/rdac ⬚$2, house tour $5 ✆Weekdays 9–5, weekends 10–4; grounds daily dawn–dusk; house tours Mon. at 2.

For a knowledgeable insider's perspective, take a tour with **WingsWest Birding** Tours(☎800/583–6928 ⊕http://home.earthlink.net/~wingswestnm). Gregarious and knowledgable guide Bill West leads four- to eight-hour early-morning or sunset tours that venture into some of the region's best bird-watching areas, including Santa Fe Ski Basin, Cochiti Lake, the Jémez Mountains, the Upper Pecos Valley, and Bosque del Apache National Wildlife Refuge.

FISHING

There's excellent fishing spring through fall in the Rio Grande and the mountain streams that feed into it, as well as a short drive away along the Pecos River. **High Desert Angler** (✉453 Cerrillos Rd. ☎505/988–7688 or 888/988–7688 ⊕www.highdesertangler.com) is a superb fly-fishing outfitter and guide service. This is your one-stop shop for equipment rental, fly-fishing tackle, licenses, and advice.

GOLF

Marty Sanchez Links de Santa Fe (✉205 Caja del Rio Rd., off NM 599, the Santa Fe Relief Rte. ☎505/955–4400 ⊕www.linksdesantafe.com), an outstanding municipal facility with beautifully groomed 18- and 9-hole courses, sits on high prairie west of Santa Fe with fine mountain views. It has driving and putting ranges, a pro shop, and a snack bar. The greens fees are $31 for the 18-hole course, $22 on the par-3 9-holer.

HIKING

Hiking around Santa Fe can take you into high-altitude alpine country or into lunaresque high desert as you head south and west to lower elevations. For winter hiking, the gentler climates to the south are less likely to be snow packed, while the alpine areas will likely require snowshoes or cross-country skis. In summer, wildflowers bloom in the high country, and the temperature is generally at least 10° cooler than

2

in town. The mountain trails accessible at the base of the Ski Santa Fe area (end of NM 475) stay cool on even the hottest summer days. Weather can change with one gust of wind, so be prepared with extra clothing, rain gear, food, and lots of water. Keep in mind that the sun at 10,000 feet is very powerful, even with a hat and sunscreen.

For information about specific hiking areas, contact the New Mexico Public Lands Information Center. Any of the outdoor gear stores in town can also help with guides and recommendations. The **Sierra Club** (⊕*www.riogrande.sierraclub.org*) organizes group hikes of all levels of difficulty; a schedule of hikes is posted on the Web site.

Aspen Vista is a lovely hike along a south-facing mountainside. Take Hyde Park Road (NM 475) 13 mi, and the trail begins before the ski area. After walking a few miles through thick aspen groves you come to panoramic views of Santa Fe. The path is well marked and gently inclines toward Tesuque Peak. The trail becomes shadier with elevation—snow has been reported on the trail as late as July. In winter, after heavy snows, the trail is great for intermediate-advanced cross-country skiing. The round-trip is 12 mi and sees an elevation gain of 2,000 feet, but it's just 3½ mi to the spectacular overlook. The hillside is covered with golden aspen trees in late September.

A favorite spot for a ramble, with a vast network of trails, is the **Dale Ball Foothills Trail Network,** a network of some 20 mi of paths that winds and wends up through the foothills east of town and can be accessed at a few points, including Hyde Park Road (en route to the ski valley) and the upper end of Canyon Road, at Cerro Gordo. There are trail maps and signs at these points, and the trails are very well marked.

★ Spurring off the Dale Ball trail system, the steep but rewarding (and dog-friendly) **Atalaya Trail** runs from the visitor parking lot of St. John's College (off of Camino de Cruz Blanca, on the East Side) up a winding, ponderosa pine–studded trail to the peak of Mt. Atalaya, which affords incredible 270-degree views of Santa Fe. The nearly 6-mi round-trip hike climbs a nearly 2,000 feet (to an elevation of 9,121 feet), so pace yourself. The good news: the return to the parking area is nearly all downhill.

HORSEBACK RIDING
New Mexico's rugged countryside has been the setting for many Hollywood westerns. Whether you want to ride the range that Gregory Peck and Kevin Costner rode or just head out feeling tall in the saddle, you can do so year-round. Rates average about $20 an hour. *See the Side Trips section for additional horseback listings in Cerrillos, Galisteo, and Ojo Caliente.*

Bishop's Lodge (✉*1297 Bishop's Lodge Rd.* ☎*505/983–6377*) provides rides and guides year-round. Call for reservations.

RIVER RAFTING
If you want to watch birds and wildlife along the banks, try the laidback Huck Finn floats along the Rio Chama or the Rio Grande's White Rock Canyon. The season is generally between April and September.

Most outfitters have overnight package plans, and all offer half- and full-day trips. Be prepared to get wet, and wear secure water shoes. For a list of outfitters who guide trips on the Rio Grande and the Rio Chama, write the **Bureau of Land Management (BLM), Taos Resource Area Office** (⊠*226 Cruz Alta Rd., Taos* ☎*505/758–8851* ⊕*www.nm.blm. gov*), or stop by the BLM visitor center along NM 68 16 mi south of Taos in Pilar.

Kokopelli Rafting Adventures (⊠*551 W. Cordova Rd.* ☎*505/983–3734 or 800/879–9035* ⊕*www.kokopelliraft.com*) will take you on half-day to multiday river trips down the Rio Grande and Rio Chama. **New Wave Rafting** (⊠*mi 21, Highway 68; 70 CR 84B* ☎ *800/984–1444* ⊕*www.newwaverafting.com*) conducts full-day, half-day, and overnight river trips, as well as fly-fishing trips, from their new location in Embudo, 21 miles north of Española. **Santa Fe Rafting Company and Outfitters** (⊠*1000 Cerrillos Rd.* ☎*505/988–4914 or 888/988/4914* ⊕*www.santaferafting.com*) customizes rafting tours. Tell them what you want—they'll do it.

SKIING

To save time during the busy holiday season you may want to rent skis or snowboards in town the night before hitting the slopes so you don't waste any time waiting during the morning rush. **Alpine Sports** (⊠*121 Sandoval St.* ☎*505/983–5155* ⊕*www.alpinesports-santafe.com*) rents downhill and cross-country skis and snowboards. **Cottam's Ski Rentals** (⊠*Hyde Park Rd., 7 mi northeast of downtown, toward Ski Santa Fe* ☎*505/982–0495 or 800/322–8267*) rents the works, including snowboards, sleds, and snowshoes.

★ **Santa Fe Mountain Sports** (⊠*607 Cerrillos Rd, Guadalupe District* ☎*505/988–3337* ⊕*www.santafemountainsports.com* ⊙*9–6, Sun 9–5*) is a family-owned specialty mountain shop that rents boots, skis and snowboards for the whole family in the winter, as well as bicycles in the summertime. The super-helpful staff is great to work with.

Ski Santa Fe (⊠*End of NM 475, 18 mi northeast of downtown* ☎*505/982–4429, 505/983–9155 conditions* ⊕*www.skisantafe.com*), open roughly from late November through early April, is a fine, mid-size operation that receives an average of 225 inches of snow a year and plenty of sunshine. It's one of America's highest ski areas—the 12,000-foot summit has a variety of terrain and seems bigger than its 1,700 feet of vertical rise and 660 acres. There are some great powder stashes, tough bump runs, and many wide, gentle cruising runs. The 44 trails are ranked 20% beginner, 40% intermediate, and 40% advanced; there are seven lifts. Snowboarders are welcome, and there's the Norquist Trail for cross-country skiers. Chipmunk Corner provides day care and supervised kids' skiing. The ski school is excellent. Rentals, a good restaurant, a ski shop, and Totemoff Bar and Grill round out the amenities.

SHOPPING

Santa Fe has been a trading post for eons. Nearly a thousand years ago the great pueblos of the Chacoan civilizations were strategically located between the buffalo-hunting tribes of the Great Plains and the Indians of Mexico. Native Americans in New Mexico traded turquoise and other valuables with Indians from Mexico for metals, shells, parrots, and other exotic items. After the arrival of the Spanish and the West's subsequent development, Santa Fe became the place to exchange silver from Mexico and natural resources from New Mexico for manufactured goods, whiskey, and greenbacks from the United States. With the building of the railroad in 1880, Santa Fe had access to all kinds of manufactured goods as well as those unique to the region via the old trade routes.

The trading legacy remains, but now downtown Santa Fe caters to those looking for handcrafted goods. Sure, T-shirt outlets and a few major retail clothing shops have moved in, but shopping in Santa Fe consists mostly of one-of-a-kind independent stores. Canyon Road, packed with art galleries, is the perfect place to find unique gifts and collectibles. The downtown district, around the Plaza, has unusual gift shops, clothing, and shoe stores that range from theatrical to conventional, curio shops, and art galleries. The funky, up-and-coming Guadalupe District, less touristy than the Plaza, is on downtown's southwest perimeter and includes the Sanbusco Market Center and the Design Center, both hubs of unique and wonderful boutiques.

ART GALLERIES

The following are only a few of the nearly 200 galleries in greater Santa Fe—with the best of representational, nonobjective, Native American, Latin American, cutting-edge, photographic, and soulful works that defy categorization. The Santa Fe Convention and Visitors Bureau (⇨ *Visitor Information in Essentials, above*) has a more extensive listing. *The Collectors Guide to Santa Fe, Taos, and Albuquerque* is a good resource and is available in hotels and at some galleries, as well as on the Web at ⊕www.collectorsguide.com. Check the "Pasatiempo" pullout in the *Santa Fe New Mexican* on Friday for a preview of gallery openings.

Fodor'sChoice ★ **Andrew Smith Gallery** (⊠*203 W. San Francisco St.* ☎*505/984–1234*) is a significant photo gallery dealing in works by Edward S. Curtis and other 19th-century chroniclers of the American West. Other major figures are Ansel Adams, Edward Weston, O. Winston Link, Henri Cartier-Bresson, Eliot Porter, Laura Gilpin, Dorothea Lange, Alfred Stieglitz, Annie Liebowitz, and regional artists like Barbara Van Cleve.

Bellas Artes (⊠*653 Canyon Rd.* ☎*505/983–2745*), a sophisticated gallery and sculpture garden, has ancient ceramics and represents internationally renowned artists like Judy Pfaff, Phoebe Adams, and Olga de Amaral.

Charlotte Jackson Fine Art (⊠*200 W. Marcy St.* ☎*505/989–8688*) focuses primarily on monochromatic "radical" painting. Florence Pierce, Joe

Barnes, William Metcalf, Anne Cooper, and Joseph Marioni are among the artists producing minimalist works dealing with light and space.

Fodor'sChoice **evo Gallery** (⊠ *554 South Guadalupe St, Guadalupe District* ☎ *505/982–*
★ *4610* ⊕ *www.evogallery.org*) is another gallery that affirms Santa Fe's reputation as a leading center of contemporary art. Powerhouse artists like Jenny Holzer, Ed Ruscha, Donald Judd, Jasper Johns and Agnes Martin are represented in this huge space in the Guadalupe District.

Fodor'sChoice **Gerald Peters Gallery** (⊠ *1011 Paseo de Peralta* ☎ *505/954–5700*) is
★ Santa Fe's leading gallery of American and European art from the 19th century to the present. It has works by Max Weber, Albert Bierstadt, the Taos Society, the New Mexico Modernists, and Georgia O'Keeffe, as well as contemporary artists.

★ **James Kelly Contemporary** (⊠ *1601 Paseo de Peralta., Guadalupe District* ☎ *505/989–1601* ⊕ *www.jameskellycontemporary.com*) mounts sophisticated, high-caliber shows by international and regional artists, such as Agnes Martin, Bruce Nauman, Susan Rothenberg and Richard Tuttle. Located in a renovated warehouse directly across from SITE Santa Fe, James Kelly has been instrumental in transforming the Railyard District into Santa Fe's center for contemporary art.

LewAllen Contemporary (⊠ *129 W. Palace Ave.* ☎ *505/988–8997*) is a leading center for a variety of contemporary arts by both Southwestern and other acclaimed artists, among them Judy Chicago; sculpture, photography, ceramics, basketry, and painting are all shown in this dynamic space.

Fodor'sChoice **Linda Durham Gallery** (⊠ *1101 Paseo de Peralta, near Canyon Rd.*
★ ☎ *505/466–6600* ⊕ *www.lindadurham.com*) has showcased paintings, sculpture and photography of, primarily, New Mexico-based artists. This community-minded gallery has become highly regarded and its artists highly sought.

Monroe Gallery (⊠ *112 Don Gaspar Ave.* ☎ *505/992–0800*) showcases works by the most celebrated black-and-white photographers of the 20th century, from Margaret Bourke-White to Alfred Eisenstaedt.

★ **Nedra Matteucci Galleries** (⊠ *1075 Paseo de Peralta* ☎ *505/982–4631* ⊠ *555 Canyon Rd.* ☎ *505/983–2731*) exhibits works by California regionalists, members of the early Taos and Santa Fe schools, and masters of American Impressionism and Modernism. Spanish-colonial furniture, Indian antiquities, and a fantastic sculpture garden are other draws of this well-respected establishment.

Peyton Wright (⊠ *237 E. Palace Ave.* ☎ *505/989–9888*), tucked inside the historic Spiegelberg house, represents some of the most talented emerging and established contemporary artists in the country, as well as antique and even ancient Chinese, pre-Columbian, Russian, and Latin works.

Photo-eye Gallery (⊠ *376–A Garcia St.* ☎ *505/988–5159*) shows contemporary photography that includes the beautiful and sublime; there's also a stellar bookstore.

Pushkin Gallery (⊠ *550 Canyon Rd.* ☎ *505/982–1990*) is yet more evidence that Santa Fe's art scene is about so much more than regional work—here you can peruse works by some of Russia's leading 19th- and 20th-century talents, with an emphasis on impressionism.

Riva Yares Gallery (⌧ *123 Grant St.* ☏ *505/984–0330*) specializes in contemporary artists of Latin American descent. There are sculptures by California artist Manuel Neri, color field paintings by Esteban Vicente, and works by Santa Feans Elias Rivera, Rico Eastman, and others—plus paintings by such international legends as Hans Hofman, Milton Avery, and Helen Frankenthaler.

Santa Fe Art Institute (⌧ *1600 St. Michael's Dr.* ☏ *505/424–5050*), a nonprofit educational art organization that sponsors several artists in residence and presents workshops, exhibitions, and lectures, has a respected gallery whose exhibits change regularly. The institute is set inside a dramatic contemporary building. Past artists in residence have included Richard Diebenkorn, Larry Bell, Moon Zappa, Henriette Wyeth Hurd, and and Judy Pfaff.

Ⓒ
Fodor'sChoice
★
Shidoni Foundry and Galleries (⌧ *Bishop's Lodge Rd., 5 mi north of Santa Fe, Tesuque* ☏ *505/988–8001*) casts work for accomplished and emerging artists from all over North America. On the grounds of an old chicken ranch, Shidoni has a rambling sculpture garden and a gallery. Self-guided foundry tours are permitted Saturday 9–5 and weekdays noon–1, but the sculpture garden is open daily during daylight hours; you can watch bronze pourings most Saturday afternoons. This is a dream of a place to expose your kids to large-scale art and enjoy a lovely expanse of green grass at the same time.

SPECIALTY STORES

ANTIQUES & HOME FURNISHINGS

Artesanos (⌧ *1414 Maclovia St.* ☏ *505/471–8020*) is one of the best Mexican-import shops in the nation, with everything from leather equipale chairs to papier-mâché *calaveras* (skeletons used in Day of the Dead celebrations), and tinware. They specialize in Talavera and other tiles.

At **Asian Adobe** (⌧ *310 Johnson St.* ☏ *505/992–6846*) browse porcelain lamps, ornate antique baby hats and shoes, red-lacquer armoires, and similarly stunning Chinese and Southeast Asian artifacts and antiques.

Bosshard Fine Art Furnishings (⌧ *340 S. Guadalupe St.* ☏ *505/989–9150*) deals in African ethnographica, which complement the vast selection of tapestries, architectural elements, statues, and ceramics from the Southwest as well as Asia.

Casa Nova (⌧ *530 S. Guadalupe St.* ☏ *505/983–8558*) sells functional art from around the world, deftly mixing colors, textures, and cultural icons—old and new—from stylish pewter tableware from South Africa to vintage hand-carved ex-votos (votive offerings) from Brazil.

Fodor'sChoice
★
The **Design Center** (⌧ *418 Cerrillos Rd.*), which occupies a former Chevy dealership in the Guadalupe District, contains some of the most distinctive antique and decorative arts shops in town, plus a couple of small restaurants. Be sure to browse the precious Latin American antiques at **Claiborne Gallery** (☏ *505/982–8019*), along with the artful contemporary desks, tables, and chairs created by owner Omer Claiborne. **Gloria List Gallery** (☏ *505/982–5622*) specializes in rare 17th- and 18th-century

The Art of Santa Fe

The artistic roots of Santa Fe stretch back to the landscape and the devotion of those who roamed and settled here long before the Santa Fe Trail transplanted goods and people from the East. The intricate designs on Native American pottery and baskets, the embroidery on the ritual dance wear, the color and pattern on Rio Grande weavings, and the delicate paintings and carvings of devotional images called santos all contributed to the value and awareness of beauty that Santa Fe holds as its cultural birthright. The rugged landscape, the ineffable quality of the light, and the community itself continue to draw to Santa Fe a plethora of musicians, writers, and visual artists. The spell of beauty is so powerful here that some people call the town "Fanta Se," but for those who live in Santa Fe the arts are very real (as are economic realities; most artists hold additional jobs—ask your waiter).

With wide-eyed enchantment, visitors often buy paintings in orange, pink, and turquoise that are perfect next to the adobe architecture, blue sky, and red rocks of the New Mexican landscape. When they get home, however, the admired works sometimes end up in a closet simply because it's so hard to integrate the Southwestern look with the tone of the existing furnishings and artwork. Taking the risk is part of the experience. Rather than suffering from buyer's remorse, those who make the aesthetic leap can take the spirit of northern New Mexico home with them. Although it may shake up the home decor, the works are a reminder of a new way of seeing and of all the other values that inspire one to travel in the first place.

Most galleries will send a painting (not posters or prints) out on a trial basis for very interested clients. If looking at art is new to you, ask yourself if your interest is in bringing home a souvenir that says "I was there" or in art that will live in the present and inspire the future, independent of the nostalgia for the "land of enchantment." Santa Fe has plenty of both to offer—use discrimination while you look so you don't burn out on the first block of Canyon Road.

Santa Fe, while holding strong in its regional art identity, emerged in the late 1990s as a more international art scene. Native American and Hispanic arts groups now include the work of contemporary artists who have pressed beyond the bounds of tradition. Bold color and the oft-depicted New Mexico landscape are still evident, but you're just as likely to see mixed-media collages by a Chinese artist currently living in San Francisco. A few Santa Fe outlets, such as the Riva Yares Gallery and evo gallery, are dedicated to representing artists with Latin American roots. "The world is wide here," Georgia O'Keeffe once noted about northern New Mexico. And just as Santa Fe welcomed early Modernist painters who responded to the open landscape and the artistic freedom it engendered, contemporary artists working with edgier media, such as conceptual, performance, and installation art, are finding welcoming venues in Santa Fe, specifically at SITE Santa Fe museum.

devotional and folk art, chiefly from South America, Italy, Spain, and Mexico. And at **Sparrow & Magpie Antiques** (☎ *505/982–1446*), look mostly for East Coast and Midwest folk art and textiles, although the shop carries some Southwestern pieces, too.

Design Warehouse (✉ *101 W. Marcy St.* ☎ *505/988–1555*), a welcome antidote to Santa Fe's preponderance of shops selling Native American and Spanish-colonial antiques, stocks super-hip contemporary sofas, kitchenware, lamps, and other sleek knickknacks, such as those made by the Italian firm Alessi.

Doodlet's (✉ *120 Don Gaspar Ave.* ☎ *505/983–3771*) has an eclectic collection of stuff: pop-up books, silly postcards, tin art, hooked rugs, and stringed lights. Wonderment is in every display case, drawing the eye to the unusual. Delightfully quirky, there's something for just about everyone here, and often it's super-affordable.

Foreign Traders (✉ *202 Galisteo St.* ☎ *505/983–6441*), a Santa Fe institution founded as the Old Mexico Shop in 1927 and still run by the same family, stocks handicrafts, antiques, and accessories from Mexico and other parts of the world.

Jackalope (✉ *2820 Cerrillos Rd.* ☎ *505/471–8539*), a legendary if somewhat overpriced bazaar, sprawls over 7 acres, incorporating several pottery barns, a furniture store, endless aisles of knickknacks from Latin America and Asia, and a huge greenhouse. There's also an area where craftspeople, artisans, and others sell their wares—sort of a mini–flea market.

★ **La Mesa** (✉ *225 Canyon Rd., Canyon Road* ☎ *505/984–1688* ⊕ *www.lamesaofsantafe.com*) has become well-known for showcasing contemporary handcrafted works by more than 50, mostly local, artists including Kathy O'Neill, Gregory Lomayesva, and Melissa Haid. Collections include dinnerware, glassware, pottery, lighting, fine art and accessories.

★ **Montez Gallery** (✉ *Sena Plaza Courtyard, 125 E. Palace Ave.* ☎ *505/982–1828*) sells Hispanic works of religious art and decoration, including retablos (holy images painted on wood or tin), bultos (carved wooden statues of saints), furniture, paintings, pottery, weavings, and jewelry. A number of award-winning local artists' work is shown here.

Pachamama (✉ *223 Canyon Rd.* ☎ *505/983–4020*) carries Latin American folk art, including small tin or silver *milagros,* the stamped metal images used as votive offerings. The shop also carries weavings and Spanish-colonial antiques and other delightful trinkets.

Sequoia (✉ *201 Galisteo St.* ☎ *505/982–7000*) shows the imaginative, almost surreal, furniture creations of its owner, who was born in India. Curvaceous glass shelves, lamps, and candlesticks mix with paintings and fine linens.

BOOKS

More than a dozen shops in Santa Fe sell used books, and a handful of high-quality shops carry the latest releases from mainstream and small presses.

ALLÁ (✉ *102 W. San Francisco St., upstairs* ☎ *505/988–5416*) is one of Santa Fe's most delightful small bookstores. It focuses on hard-to-find

Spanish-language books and records, including limited-edition hand-made books from Central America. It also carries Native American books and music, as well as English translations.

Collected Works Book Store (✉ *208B W. San Francisco St.* ☎ *505/988–4226*) carries art and travel books, including a generous selection of books on Southwestern art, architecture, and general history, as well as the latest in contemporary literature. The proprietor, Dorothy Massey, and her staff are well-loved for their knowledge and helpfulness.

Garcia Street Books (✉ *376 Garcia St.* ☎ *505/986–0151*) is an outstanding independent shop strong on art, architecture, cookbooks, literature, and regional Southwestern works—it's a block from the Canyon Road galleries. They have frequent talks by authors under their portal during the summer.

Nicholas Potter (✉ *211 E. Palace Ave.* ☎ *505/983–5434*) specializes in used, rare, and out-of-print books. The quixotic shop also stocks used jazz and classical CDs.

Photo-eye Books (✉ *376 Garcia St.* ☎ *505/988–5152*) stocks new, rare, and out-of-print photography books.

Travel Bug (✉ *839 Paseo de Peralta* ☎ *505/992–0418*) has a huge array of travel tomes and guidebooks, and USGS and other maps. There's also a cozy coffeehouse with high-speed wireless.

CLOTHING & ACCESSORIES

Fodor'sChoice **Back at the Ranch** (✉ *209 E. Marcy St.* ☎ *505/989–8110 or 888/962–*
★ *6687*) is the place for cowboy boots. The cozy space, in an old, creaky-floored adobe is stocked with perhaps the finest handmade cowboy boots you will ever see—in every color, style, and embellishment imaginable. Other finds, like funky ranch-style furniture, 1950s blanket coats, jewelry, and belt buckles are also sold. The staff is top-notch and the boots are breathtaking.

Fodor'sChoice **O'Farrell Hats** (✉ *111 E. San Francisco St.* ☎ *505/989–9666*) is the
★ domain of America's foremost hat-making family. Founder Kevin O'Farrell passed away in 2006, and the legacy continues with his son Scott and the highly trained staff. This quirky shop custom-crafts one-of-a-kind beaver-lined cowboy hats that make the ultimate Santa Fe keepsake. This level of quality comes at a cost, but devoted customers—who have included everyone from cattle ranchers to U.S. presidents—swear by O'Farrell's artful creations.

★ **Double Take at the Ranch** (✉ *321 S. Guadalupe St.* ☎ *505/820–7775*) ranks among the best consignment stores in the West, carrying elaborately embroidered vintage cowboy shirts, hundreds of pairs of boots, funky old prints, and amazing vintage Indian pawn and Mexican jewelry. The store adjoins Santa Fe Pottery, which carries the works of local artists.

Lucchese (✉ *203 W. Water St.* ☎ *505/820–1883*) has been crafting some of the West's finest handmade cowboy boots since 1883.

Mirá (✉ *101 W. Marcy St.* ☎ *505/988–3585*) clothing for women is hip, eclectic, and funky, combining the adventurous spirit of New Mexico with global contemporary fashion. The shop has jewelry, accessories and collectibles from Latin America, the Flax line of natural-fiber clothing, and knockout dresses and separates not sold anywhere else in town.

Maya (⊠*108 Galisteo St, Santa Fe Plaza* ☎*505/989–7590*) is a groovy assemblage of unconventional and fun women's clothing, jewelry, accessories, select books, shoes, handbags, global folk art, hats, and a small selection of housewares. It's a funky shop with many lines from small design houses and local jewelers. Check out the selection of relicario-style jewelry from Wanda Lobito. The staff isn't always terribly helpful, but they aren't unfriendly.

Origins (⊠*135 W. San Francisco St.* ☎*505/988–2323*) borrows from many cultures, carrying pricey women's wear like antique kimonos and custom-dyed silk jackets. One-of-a-kind accessories complete the spectacular look that Santa Fe inspires.

FOOD & COOKERY

In the DeVargas shopping center, **Las Cosas Kitchen Shoppe** (⊠*N. Guadalupe St. at Paseo de Peralta in the De Vargas Mall* ☎*505/988–3394 or 877/229–7184*) carries a fantastic selection of cookery, tableware, and kitchen gadgetry and gifts. The shop is also renowned for its cooking classes, which touch on everything from high-altitude baking to Asian-style grilling.

★ **The Spanish Table** (⊠*109 N. Guadalupe St., Santa Fe Plaza* ☎*505/986–0243* ⊕*www.spanishtable.com*) stands out as a destination for all things Spanish when it comes to culinary needs. From their cold-case with Spanish meats and cheese, to their cookware and beautiful Majolica pottery, books, dry goods, and wonderful world-music selection, you will be challenged to leave empty-handed. The staff is always ready to help advise on a recipe or gift idea and they'll ship your purchases anywhere you like.

FodorśChoice **Todos Santos** (⊠*125 E. Palace Ave.* ☎*505/982–3855*) is a tiny candy
★ shop in the 18th-century courtyard of Sena Plaza, carrying seen-to-be-believed works of edible art, including chocolate milagros and altar pieces gilded with 23-karat gold or silver leaf. Truffles come in exotic flavors, like tangerine chili, rose caramel and lemon verbena. Amidst the taste sensations and quirky folk art are amazing and delightful customized Pez dispensers from Albuquerque folk artist Steve White. Hayward, the proprietor, is delightful, and he'll ship.

JEWELRY

Eidos (⊠*500 Montezuma Ave (inside Sanbusco Center, Guadalupe District* ☎*505/992–0020* ⊕*www.eidosjewelry.com*) features "concept-led" minimalist contemporary jewelry from European designers and Deborah Alexander and Gordon Lawrie, who own the store. Lovely, contemporary space, fascinating array of materials, good range of prices, and helpful staff.

Golden Eye (⊠*115 Don Gaspar St., Santa Fe Plaza* ☎*505/984–0040*) is a pint-sized shop (even by Santa Fe standards) that features fine, hand-crafted jewelry in high-karat gold, often paired with gemstones. Their experienced, helpful staff of artisans can help you pick out something beautiful and unusual.

Jett (✉ *110 Old Santa Fe Trail, Santa Fe Plaza* ☎ *505/988–988–1414*) showcases jewelers and artists, many local, who are remarkable for creative, original approaches to their work. Intriguing selection of surprisingly affordable silver and gold jewelry, modern artistic lighting, and delightful miniature objects like vintage trailers and circus tents made from recycled metal.

LewAllen & LewAllen Jewelry (✉ *105 E. Palace Ave., Santa Fe Plaza* ☎ *800/988–5112* ⊕ *www.lewallenjewelry.com*) is run by father-and-daughter silversmithing team, Ross and Laura LewAllen. Handmade jewelry ranges from whimsical to mystical inside their tiny shop just off the Plaza. There is something for absolutely everyone in here, including delightful charms for your pet's collar.

Fodor's Choice **Patina** (✉ *131 W. Palace Ave, Santa Fe Plaza* ☎ *505/986–3432 or* ★ *877/877–0827* ⊕ *www.patina-gallery.com*) presents outstanding contemporary jewelry, textiles, and sculptural objects of metal, clay and wood, in a airy, museum-like space. With a staff whose courtesy is matched by knowledge of the genre, artists/owners Ivan and Allison Barnett have used their fresh curatorial aesthetic to create a showplace for the 112 American and European artists they represent—many of whom are in permanent collections of museums such as MOMA.

MARKETS

Browse through the vast selection of local produce, meat, flowers,
Fodor's Choice honey, and cheese—much of it organic—at the thriving **Santa Fe Farmers**
★ **Market** (✉ *Guadalupe St. and Cerrillos Rd.* ☎ *505/983–4098* ⊕ *www.santafefarmersmarket.com*)The market is now housed in its new, permanent building in the Railyard and it's open year-round. It's a great people-watching event, and there's storytelling for kids as well as a snack bar selling terrific breakfast burritos and other goodies. With the growing awareness of the importance and necessity of eating locally grown and organic food, this market offers living testimony to the fact that farming can be done successfully, even in a high-desert region like this one.

Tesuque Pueblo Flea Market (✉ *U.S. 285/84, 7 mi north of Santa Fe* ☎ *505/983–2667* ⊕ *www.tesuquepueblofleamarket.com*) was once considered the best flea market in America by its loyal legion of bargain hunters. The Tesuque Pueblo took over the market in the late '90s and raised vendor fees, which increased the presence of predictable, often pricey goods brought in by professional flea-market dealers. In recent years, however, the pueblo has brought in a nice range of vendors, and this market with as many as 500 vendors in peak season is again one of the best shopping events in town. The 12-acre market is next to the Santa Fe Opera and is open Friday–Sunday, mid-March–December.

NATIVE AMERICAN ARTS & CRAFTS

Frank Howell Gallery (✉ *103 Washington Ave.* ☎ *505/984–1074*) stocks lithographs, serigraphs, prints, and posters of the late Frank Howell as well as works by other Native American artists.

Morning Star Gallery (⊠*513 Canyon Rd.* ☏*505/982–8187*) is a veritable museum of Native American art and artifacts. An adobe shaded by a huge cottonwood tree houses antique basketry, pre-1940 Navajo silver jewelry, Northwest Coast Native American carvings, Navajo weavings, and art of the Plains Indians. Prices and quality prohibit casual purchases, but the collection is magnificent.

Niman Fine Arts (⊠*125 Lincoln Ave.* ☏*505/988–5091*) focuses on the prolific work of contemporary Native American artists–Hopi painters Arlo Namingha and Michael Namingha.

Packard's on the Plaza (⊠*61 Old Santa Fe Trail* ☏*505/983–9241*), the oldest Native American arts-and-crafts store on Santa Fe Plaza, also sells Zapotec Indian rugs from Mexico and original rug designs by Richard Enzer, old pottery, saddles, kachina dolls, and an excellent selection of coral and turquoise jewelry. Local favorite Lawrence Baca, whose iconic jewelry has made him a regular prizewinner at Spanish Market, is featured here. Prices are often high, but so are the standards. There's also an extensive clothing selection.

Fodor'sChoice
★ The **Rainbow Man** (⊠*107 E. Palace Ave.* ☏*505/982–8706*), established in 1945, does business in an old, rambling adobe complex, part of which was dates from before the 1680 Pueblo Revolt. The shop carries early Navajo, Mexican, and Chimayó textiles, along with photographs by Edward S. Curtis, a breathtaking collection of vintage pawn and Mexican jewelry, Day of the Dead figures, Oaxacan folk animals, New Mexican folk art, kachinas, and contemporary jewelry from local artists. The friendly staff possesses an encyclopedic knowledge of the art they carry.

Fodor'sChoice
★ **Robert Nichols Gallery** (⊠*419 Canyon Rd, Canyon Road* ☏*505/982–2145* ⊕*www.robertnicholsgallery.com* ☉*Closed Sundays*) represents a remarkable group of Native American ceramics artists doing primarily non-traditional work. Diverse artists such as Glen Nipshank, whose organic, sensuous shapes would be right at home in MoMA, and Diego Romero, whose Cochiti-style vessels are detailed with graphic novel–style characters and sharp social commentary, are right at home here. It is a treat to see cutting-edge work that is clearly informed from indigenous traditions.

Trade Roots Collection (⊠*411 Paseo de Peralta* ☏*505/982–8168*) sells Native American ritual objects, such as fetish jewelry and Hopi rattles. Open by appointment only, this store is an excellent source of fine ethnic crafts materials for artists.

Trader's Collection (⊠*218 Galisteo St, Santa Fe Plaza* ☏*505/992–0441* ⊕*traderscollection.com*). When the venerable Shush Yaz gallery closed in August 2007, several of the key staff members created this new showplace of American Indian arts and crafts. Antique pieces co-mingle with contemporary works here, by artists such as Nocona Burgess and jeweler Kim Knifechief, and the staff is friendly and knowledgeable.

SIDE TRIPS FROM SANTA FE

SOUTH OF SANTA FE

The most prominent side trip south of the city is along the fabled Turquoise Trail, an excellent—and leisurely—alternative route to Albuquerque that's far more interesting than I–25; it's covered in the Side Trips from Albuquerque section. Although the drive down I–25 offers some fantastic views of the Jémez and Sandia mountains, the most interesting sites south of town require hopping off the interstate. From here you can uncover the region's history at El Rancho de las Golondrinas and enjoy one of New Mexico's most dramatic day hikes at Tent Rocks canyon. Conversely, if you leave Santa Fe via I–25 north and then cut down in a southerly direction along U.S. 285 and NM 41, you come to tiny Galisteo, a little hamlet steeped in Spanish-colonial history.

PECOS NATIONAL HISTORIC PARK
★ *25 mi east of Santa Fe on I–25.*

Pecos was the last major encampment that travelers on the Santa Fe Trail reached before Santa Fe. Today the little village is mostly a starting point for exploring the Pecos National Historic Park, the centerpiece of which is the **ruins of Pecos,** once a major Pueblo village with more than 1,100 rooms. Twenty-five hundred people are thought to have lived in this structure, as high as five stories in places. Pecos, in a fertile valley between the Great Plains and the Rio Grande Valley, was a trading center centuries before the Spanish conquistadors visited in about 1540. The Spanish later returned to build two missions.

The Pueblo was abandoned in 1838, and its 17 surviving occupants moved to the Jémez Pueblo. Anglo travelers on the Santa Fe Trail observed the mission ruins with a great sense of fascination (and relief—for they knew it meant their journey was nearly over). A couple of miles from the ruins, **Andrew Kozlowski's Ranch** served as a stage depot, where a fresh spring quenched the thirsts of horses and weary passengers. The ranch now houses the park's law-enforcement corps and is not open to the public. You can view the mission ruins and the excavated pueblo on a ¼-mi self-guided tour in about two hours.

The pivotal Civil War battle of Glorieta Pass took place on an outlying parcel of parkland in late March 1862; a victory over Confederate forces firmly established the Union army's control over the New Mexico Territory. The Union troops maintained headquarters at Kozlowski's Ranch during the battle. Check out the park visitor center for information about guided park tours (in summer only) and to see exhibits on the region's checkered history. ⊠ *NM 63, off I–25 at Exit 307, Pecos* ☎ *505/757-7200 (park info) 505/757-7241 (visitor's center)* ⊕ *www.nps.gov/peco* ≅ *$3* ☉ *Late May–early Sept., daily 8–6; early Sept.–late May, daily 8–5.*

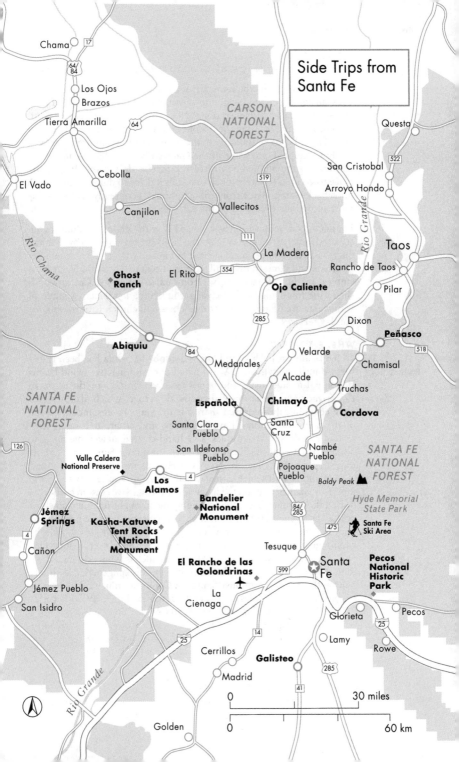

GALISTEO

25 mi south of Santa Fe via I–25 north to U.S. 285 to NM 41 south.

South of Santa Fe lie the immense open spaces and subtle colorings of the Galisteo Basin and the quintessential New Mexican village of Galisteo—a blend of multigenerational New Mexicans and recent migrants who protect and treasure the bucolic solitude of their home. The drive from Santa Fe takes about 30 minutes and offers a panoramic view of the low, sculpted landscape of the Galisteo Basin, which is an austere contrast to the alpine country of the Sangre de Cristos. It's a good place to go for a leisurely lunch or a sunset drive to dinner, maybe with horseback riding. Aside from these options, there really isn't anything more to do here except enjoy the surroundings.

Founded as a Spanish outpost in 1614, with original buildings constructed largely with stones from the large Pueblo ruin nearby that had once housed 1000 people, Galisteo has attracted a significant number of artists and equestrians (trail rides and rentals are available at local stables) to the otherwise very traditional community. Cottonwoods shade the low-lying pueblo-style architecture, a premier example of vernacular use of adobe and stone. The small church is open only for Sunday services.

WHERE TO STAY

$$$ ⬚ **The Galisteo Inn.** This rambling old adobe hacienda has been trans-
Fodor'sChoice   formed into an idyllic inn. Worn pine floors and massive wood beams
★   rich in patina and vistas and patios from which to enjoy them add to the privacy and romance of this upscale refuge, which also has two cozy, economical rooms that share a bath. Many rooms, including one of the inexpensive ones, have fireplaces, and all are decorated with tasteful, understated antiques and hand-crafted newer pieces. The acclaimed La Mancha Restaurant ($$); no dinner Sunday and Monday, reservations essential) serves superb contemporary, Latin-infused cuisine and is well worth a visit whether or not you're staying at the inn. If you can, eat out on the lawn under the massive cottonwood trees during the summer. The often-changing menu might feature pistachio-crusted Dungeness crab cakes with pineapple-caper tartar sauce, and an unusual "mac-and-cheese" with orzo pasta, black truffles, oyster mushrooms, goat cheese, and white-truffle essence. The bar serves light fare and requires no reservation; the Sunday brunch is wonderful and does require reservations. **Pros:** The rustic chic of this congenial, cozy inn is a delightful respite from busy Santa Fe. **Cons:** Not much to do beyond the walls of the inn unless you hire guides to explore. ⊠9 *La Vega St.* ⬧*HC 75, Box 4, Galisteo 87540* ☎*505/466–8200 or 866/404–8200* ⬚*505/466–4008* ⬤*www.galisteoinn.com* ⬚*11 rooms, 9 with bath; 1 suite* ⬧*In-room:. In-hotel: restaurant, pool, no kids under 10, no-smoking rooms, Wi-Fi in public areas* ⊟*D, MC, V* ⫮⊙⫮*BP.*

SPORTS & THE OUTDOORS

Galarosa Stable (⊠*NM 41, Galisteo* ☎*505/466–4654 or 505/670–2467* ⬤*www.galarosastables.com*) offers two hour rides starting at $70 per person, south of Santa Fe in the panoramic Galisteo Basin.

EL RANCHO DE LAS GOLONDRINAS

★ *15 mi south of Santa Fe off I–25's Exit 276 in La Cienega.*

The "Williamsburg of the Southwest," El Rancho de las Golondrinas ("the ranch of the swallows") is a reconstruction of a small agricultural village with buildings from the 17th to 19th century. Travelers on the El Camino Real would stop at the ranch before making the final leg of the journey north, a half-day ride from Santa Fe in horse-and-wagon time. By car, the ranch is only a 25-minute drive from the Plaza. From I–25, the village is tucked away from view, frozen in time. Owned and operated by the Paloheimo family, direct descendants of those who owned the ranch when it functioned as a *paraje,* or stopping place, the grounds maintain an authentic character without compromising history for commercial gain. Even the gift shop carries items that reflect ranch life and the cultural exchange that took place there.

Self-guided tours survey Spanish-colonial lifestyles in New Mexico from 1660 to 1890: you can view a molasses mill, threshing grounds, and wheelwright and blacksmith shops, as well as a mountain village and a *morada* (meeting place) of the order of Penitentes (a religious fraternity known for its reenactment during Holy Week of the tortures suffered by Christ). Farm animals roam through the barnyards on the 200-acre complex. Wool from the sheep is spun into yarn and woven into traditional Rio Grande–style blankets, and the corn grown is used to feed the animals. During the spring and harvest festivals, on the first weekends of June and October, respectively, the village comes alive with Spanish-American folk music, dancing, and food and crafts demonstrations. There are ample picnic facilities and a snack bar that serves a limited number of items on weekends only. ⊠ *334 Los Pinos Rd.* ☎ *505/471–2261* ⊕ *www.golondrinas.org* ⌚ *$5* ☉ *June–Sept., Wed.–Sun. 10–4; some additional weekends for special events.*

WHERE TO STAY

$–$$ Sunrise Springs Inn. Down the road from Las Golondrinas, this eco-resort offers guests holistic-based rest and rejuvenation. The sleek, minimalist accommodations are either in private casitas, with kitchenettes and fireplaces, or in a standard room; four rooms and two suites are located near the Samadhi Spa, which specializes in Asian body work. Other amenities at this lush retreat with bio-dynamic ponds and gardens are a Japanese-style teahouse and the Sages Art Center, which holds a raku-pottery studio and offers classes in raku, yoga, and tai chi. You can enjoy fine, globally inspired cuisine at the Blue Heron restaurant ($$); try the duck confit hot pot with noodles and ginger broth, or house-smoked tofu with sesame-sautéed greens, coconut sweet potatoes, and fresh garden vegetables. **Pros:** Full-service resort is an easy, eco-conscious place to immerse yourself in. **Cons:** Ask about renovation projects and get a room away from them; 15 miles from Santa Fe. ⊠ *242 Los Pinos Rd., Santa Fe* ☎ *505/471–3600 or 800/955–0028* ᐸ *505/471–7365* ⊕ *www.sunrisesprings.com* ⌁ *38 rooms, 20 casitas, 2 suites* ♿ *In-room: kitchen (some), refrigerator (some), DVD (some), no TV (some). In-hotel: restaurant, bar, spa* ☰ *AE, D, MC, V.*

Fodor's Choice   **KASHA-KATUWE TENT ROCKS NATIONAL MONUMENT**
★   *40 mi south of Santa Fe via I–25, Exit 264.*

This is a terrific hiking getaway, especially if you have time for only one hike. The sandstone rock formations look like stacked tents in a stark, water- and wind-eroded box canyon. Located 45 minutes south of Santa Fe, near Cochiti Pueblo, Tent Rocks offers excellent hiking year-round, although it can get hot in summer, when you should bring extra water. The drive to this magical landscape is equally awesome, as the road heads west toward Cochiti Dam and through the cottonwood groves around the pueblo. It's a good hike for kids. The round-trip hiking distance is only 2 mi, about 1½ hours, but it's the kind of place where you'll want to hang out for a while. Take a camera. There are no facilities here, just a small parking area with a posted trail map and a self-pay admission box; you can get gas and pick up picnic supplies and bottled water at Cochiti Lake Convenience Store. ⊠ *I–25 south to Cochiti Exit 264; follow NM 16 for 8 mi, turning right onto NM 22; continue approximately 3½ more mi past Cochiti Pueblo entrance; turn right onto BIA 92, which after 2 mi becomes Forest Service Rd. 266, a rough road of jarring, washboarded gravel that leads 5 mi to well-marked parking area* ☎ *505/761–8700* ⊕ *www.nm.blm.gov* ☑ *$5 per vehicle* ☉ *Apr.–Oct., daily 7–7; Nov.–Mar., daily 8–5.*

SPORTS & THE OUTDOORS
The 18-hole, par-72 **Pueblo de Cochiti Golf Course** (⊠ *5200 Cochiti Hwy., Cochiti Lake* ☎ *505/465–2239* ⊕ *www.pueblodecochiti.org/ golfcourse.html*), set against a backdrop of steep canyons and red-rock mesas, is a 45-minute drive southwest of Santa Fe. Cochiti was designed by Robert Trent Jones Jr. and offers one of the most challenging and visually stunning golfing experiences in the state. Greens fees are $62 (Fri-Sun) and include a cart.

JÉMEZ COUNTRY

In the Jémez region, the 1,000-year-old Ancestral Puebloan ruins at Bandelier National Monument present a vivid contrast to Los Alamos National Laboratory, birthplace of the atomic bomb. You can easily take in part of Jémez Country in a day trip from Santa Fe.

On this tour you can see terrific views of the Rio Grande Valley, the Sangre de Cristos, the Galisteo Basin, and, in the distance, the Sandias. There are places to eat and shop for essentials in Los Alamos and a few roadside eateries along NM 4 in La Cueva and Jémez Springs. There are also numerous turnouts along NM 4, several that have paths leading down to the many excellent fishing spots along the Jémez River.

The 48,000-acre Cerro Grande fire of May 2000 burned much of the pine forest in the lower Jémez Mountains, as well as more than 250 homes in Los Alamos. Parts of the drive are still scarred with char-coaled remains, but most of the vegetation has returned, and many homes have been rebuilt in the residential areas.

LOS ALAMOS
35 mi from Santa Fe via U.S. 285/84 north to NM 502 west.

Look at old books on New Mexico and you rarely find a mention of Los Alamos, now a busy town of 19,000 that has the highest per capita income in the state. Like so many other Southwestern communities, Los Alamos was created expressly as a company town; only here the workers weren't mining iron, manning freight trains, or hauling lumber—they were busy toiling at America's foremost nuclear research facility, Los Alamos National Laboratory (LANL). The facility still employs some 8,000 full-time workers, most who live in town but many others who live in the Española Valley and even Santa Fe. The lab has experienced some tough times in recent years, from the infamous Wen Ho Lee espionage case in the late '90s to a slew of alleged security breaches in 2003 and 2004. The controversies have shed some doubt on the future of LANL.

A few miles from ancient cave dwellings, scientists led by J. Robert Oppenheimer built Fat Man and Little Boy, the atom bombs that in August 1945 decimated Hiroshima and Nagasaki, respectively. LANL was created in 1943 under the auspices of the intensely covert Manhattan Project, whose express purpose it was to expedite an Allied victory during World War II. Indeed, Japan surrendered—but a full-blown Cold War between Russia and the United States ensued for another four and a half decades.

Despite the negative publicity of recent years, LANL works hard today to promote its broader platforms, including "enhancing global nuclear security" but also finding new ways to detect radiation, fighting pollution and environmental risks associated with nuclear energy, and furthering studies of the solar system, biology, and computer sciences. Similarly, the town of Los Alamos strives to be more-well rounded, better understood, and tourist-friendly.

The **Bradbury Science Museum** is Los Alamos National Laboratory's public showcase, and its exhibits offer a balanced and provocative examination of such topics as atomic weapons and nuclear power. You can experiment with lasers; witness research in solar, geothermal, fission, and fusion energy; learn about DNA fingerprinting; and view exhibits about World War II's Project Y (the Manhattan Project, whose participants developed the atomic bomb). ⊠ *Los Alamos National Laboratory, 15th St. and Central Ave.* ☎ *505/667–4444* ⊕ *www.lanl. gov/museum* ⊠ *Free* ☉ *Tues.–Fri. 9–5, Sat.–Mon. 1–5.*

New Mexican architect John Gaw Meem designed **Fuller Lodge,** a short drive up Central Avenue from the Bradbury Science Museum. The massive log building was erected in 1928 as a dining and recreation hall for a small private boys' school. In 1942 the federal government purchased the school and made it the base of operations for the Manhattan Project. Part of the lodge contains an art center that shows the works of northern New Mexican artists; there's a picturesque rose garden on the grounds. This is a bustling center with drop-in art classes, 9 art shows per year, and a gallery gift shop featuring 70 local artisans. The website is updated regularly and is a good reference for current activities. ⊠*2132 Central Ave.* ☎*505/662-9331* ⊕*www.artfulnm.org* ✉*Free* ⊘*Mon.–Sat. 10–4.*

Join the ranks of locals, Los Alamos National Laboratory employees, and tourists who line up each morning at **Chili Works** (⊠*1743 Trinity Dr.* ☎*505/662-7591*) to sample one of the state's best breakfast burritos. This inexpensive, simple take-out spot is also worth a stop to grab breakfast or lunch before heading off for a hike at Bandelier. The burritos are stellar and the chili is hot.

The **Los Alamos Historical Museum,** in a log building beside Fuller Lodge, displays exhibits on the once-volatile geological history of the volcanic Jémez Mountains, the 700-year history of human life in this area, and more on—you guessed it—the Manhattan Project. It's rather jarring to observe ancient Puebloan potsherds and arrowheads in one display and photos of an obliterated Nagasaki in the next. ⊠*1921 Juniper St.* ☎*505/662-4493* ⊕*www.losalamoshistory.org* ✉*Free* ⊘*Mon.–Sat. 9:30–4:30, Sun. 1–4.*

WHERE TO EAT & STAY

★ **$$** ✕**Blue Window Bistro.** Despite its relative wealth, Los Alamos has never cultivated much of a dining scene, which makes this cheerful and elegant restaurant all the more appreciated by foodies. The kitchen turns out a mix of New Mexican, American, and Continental dishes, from a first-rate Cobb salad to steak topped with Jack cheese and green chili to double-cut pork chops with mashed potatoes, applewood-smoked bacon, and red-onion marmalade. In addition to the softly lighted dining room with terra-cotta walls, there are several tables on a patio overlooking a lush garden. ⊠*813 Central Ave.* ☎*505/662-6305* ⊟*AE, D, DC, MC, V* ⊘*Closed Sun.*

$ ⊞**Best Western Hilltop House Hotel.** Minutes from the Los Alamos National Laboratory, this well-kept three-story hotel hosts both vacationers and scientists. It's standard chain-hotel décor here: rooms are done with contemporary, functional furniture and have microwaves, refrigerators, and coffeemakers; deluxe ones have kitchenettes. The La Vista Restaurant on the premises serves tasty, if predictable, American fare. The very good Blue Window Bistro is next door. **Pros:** Great proximity to the restaurants and shops in town; friendly, easygoing staff. **Cons:** This isn't a property with much character; but it's a solid bet for business travelers and those wanting to use Los Alamos as a jumping-off point for excursions beyond Santa Fe. ⊠*400 Trinity Dr.* ☎*505/662-2441 or 800/462-0936* 🖷*505/662-5913* ⊕*www.bwhilltop.com* ⋗*73 rooms, 19 suites* ⟨In-room: kitchen (some), refrigerator/microwave, Wi-Fi. Inhotel: restaurant, room service, bar, pool, gym, laundry facilities, some pets allowed* ⊟*AE, D, DC, MC, V* ⦿|*CP.*

SPORTS & THE OUTDOORS

HIKING   **Tsankawi** (pronounced sank-ah-*wee*) is an Ancestral Puebloan ruin that
★   is actually a part of Bandelier National Monument, although it lies 12 miles from the main park area. The Pueblo people's daily routines cre-

ated trails carved into the soft volcanic rock of the Pajarito Plateau in the 1400s as they made their way from their mesa-top homes to the fields and springs in the canyon below. In the 1½ mi loop you can see petroglyphs and south-facing cave dwellings. There is a large unexcavated pueblo ruin on top of the mesa. Wear good shoes for the rocky path and a climb on a 12-foot ladder that shoots between a crevasse in the rock and the highest point of the mesa. This is an ideal walk if you don't have time to explore Bandelier National Monument in depth. It's on the road toward White Rock, about a 35-minute drive from Santa Fe. ⊠*From NM 502, take turnoff for White Rock, NM 4; continue west for about ¼ mi to sign for Tsankawi on left; trail is clearly marked* ☎*505/672–3861.*

SKIING **Pajarito Mountain Ski Area** (⊠*397 Camp May Rd., off NM 501, just west of downtown Los Alamos* ☎*505/662–5725* ⊕*www.skipajarito. com*), a small, low-key area near Los Alamos, has some excellent long runs and a good selection of wide-open, intermediate mogul runs, plus a terrain park; the base elevation is 9,200 feet, and there's a vertical rise drop of 1,410 feet. There's no artificial snowmaking, so the slopes are barely open during dry winters and the season runs according to conditions (usually about mid-December through April). But there's never a wait for the five lifts. In summer there's mountain biking on Pajarito's trails and occasional concerts and events at the base.

BANDELIER NATIONAL MONUMENT

☾ *10 mi south of Los Alamos via NM 501 south to NM 4 east; 40 mi north*
Fodor'sChoice *of Santa Fe via U.S. 285/84 north to NM 502 west to NM 4 west.*
★
Seven centuries before the Declaration of Independence was signed, compact city-states existed in the Southwest. Remnants of one of the most impressive of them can be seen at **Frijoles Canyon** in Bandelier National Monument. At the canyon's base, near a gurgling stream, are the remains of cave dwellings, ancient ceremonial kivas, and other stone structures that stretch out for more than a mile beneath the sheer walls of the canyon's tree-fringed rim. For hundreds of years the Ancestral Puebloan people, relatives of today's Rio Grande Pueblo Indians, thrived on wild game, corn, and beans. Suddenly, for reasons still undetermined, the settlements were abandoned.

Wander through the site on a paved, self-guided trail. Steep wooden ladders and narrow doorways lead you to the cave dwellings and cell-like rooms. There is one kiva in the cliff wall that is large, and tall enough to stand in.

Bandelier National Monument, named after author and ethnologist Adolph Bandelier (his novel *The Delight Makers* is set in Frijoles Canyon), contains 23,000 acres of backcountry wilderness, waterfalls, and wildlife. Sixty miles of trails traverse the park. A small museum in the visitor center focuses on the area's prehistoric and contemporary Native American cultures, with displays of artifacts from 1200 to modern times as well as displays on the forest fires that have devastated parts of the park in recent years. There is a small café in the wonderful, 1930s CCC-built stone visitors complex. It is worth getting up early to get here when there are still shadows on the cliff walls because the petroglyphs are fantastic and all but disappear in the bright light of the afternoon. If you are staying in the area, ask about the night walks at the visitor center—they're stellar! Pets are not allowed on any trails. *☎505/672–0343 ⊕ www.nps.gov/band/index.htm ⊠$12 per vehicle, good for 7 days ⊙ Late May–early Sept., daily 8–6; early Sept.–Oct. and Apr.–late May, daily 8–5:30; Nov.–Mar., daily 8–4:30.*

JÉMEZ SPRINGS
20 mi west of Valles Caldera on NM 4.

The funky mountain village of Jémez Springs draws outdoorsy types for hiking, cross-country skiing, and camping in the nearby U.S. Forest Service areas. The town's biggest tourist draws are Jémez State Monument and Soda Dam, but many people come here for relaxation at the town's bathhouse.

The geological wonder known as **Soda Dam** was created over thousands of years by travertine deposits—minerals that precipitate out of geo-thermal springs. With its strange mushroom-shape exterior and caves split by a roaring waterfall, it's no wonder the spot was considered sacred by Native Americans. In summer it's popular for swimming. *⊠NM 4, 1 mi north of Jémez State Monument.*

Jémez State Monument contains impressive Spanish and Native American ruins set throughout a 7-acre site and toured via an easy .3-mi loop trail. About 700 years ago ancestors of the people of Jémez Pueblo built several villages in and around the narrow mountain valley. One of the villages was Guisewa, or "Place of the Boiling Waters." The Spanish colonists built a mission church beside it, San José de los Jémez, which was abandoned by around 1640. *⊠NM 4, Jémez Springs ☎505/829-3530 ⊕www.nmstatemonuments.org ⊠$3 ⊙ Wed.–Mon. 8:30–5.*

★ Now owned and operated by the village of Jemez Springs,the original structure at the **Jémez Spring Bath House** was erected in the 1870s near a mineral hot spring. Many other buildings were added over the years, and the complex was completely renovated into an intimate Victorian-style hideaway in the mid-1990s. It's a funky, low-key spot that's far less formal and fancy than the several spa resorts near Santa Fe. You can soak in a mineral bath for $10 (30 minutes) or $15 (60 minutes). Massages cost between $37 (30 minutes) and $95 (90 minutes). An acu-puncturist is available with advance notice. Beauty treatments include facials, manicures, and pedicures. The Jémez Package ($95) includes a half-hour bath, an herbal blanket wrap, and a one-hour massage. You can stroll down a short path behind the house to see where the steaming-hot springs feed into the Jémez River. It's worth noting that the tubs are not communal, but individual, and there are no outdoor tubs. Children under 14 are not allowed. *⊠NM 4 ☎505/829–3303 or 866/204–8303 ⊕www.jemezspringsbathhouse.com ⊙ June–early Oct., daily 10–8; early Nov.–May, daily 10–6.*

Giggling Springs (*⊠040 Abousleman Loop ☎505/829–9175 ⊕www. gigglingsprings.com ⊙ Closed Mondays & Tuesdays*) offers a large, outdoor natural mineral hot spring. Right across the street from the Laughing Lizard, this is a good option for the soakers who want hot water but don't want the individualized treatments at the Bath House. Very accommodating staff; no children under 14. Pool capacity is limited to 8 at a time; reservations are recommended. $15 per hour, $25 for two hours, $35 for the day.

WHERE TO STAY

★ ¢ 🖥 **Laughing Lizard Inn and Cafe.** Consisting of a simple four-room motel-style inn and a cute adobe-and-stone café with a corrugated-metal roof, the Laughing Lizard makes for a sweet and cheerful diversion—it's right in the center of the village. Rooms are cozy and simple with white linens, dressers, books, and porches that look out over the rugged mesa beyond the river valley. Healthful, eclectic fare—apple-walnut sandwiches, sweet potato–and–spinach salads, raspberry-chipotle-chicken burritos, veggie pizzas, herbal teas, offbeat beers, homemade desserts—is served in the homey café (limited hours off-season; call first), which has a saltillo-tile screened porch and an open-air wooden deck. **Pros:** Great staff, beautiful location. **Cons:** Rooms are on the worn side, and fairly small. No a/c. ⊠*NM 4* ☎*505/829–3108* ⊕*www. thelaughinglizard.com* 🛏*4 rooms* ⚘*In-hotel: restaurant, some pets allowed* ▤*D, MC, V.*

$ 🖥 **Cañon del Rio.** On 6 acres along the Jémez River beneath towering mesas, this light-filled, contemporary adobe inn (formerly called the Riverdancer) has rooms with cove ceilings, tile floors, and Native American arts and crafts. All have French doors and open onto a courtyard with a natural-spring fountain. Wellness packages include massage, acupuncture, and aromatherapy. Breakfasts are a big deal here and they're delicious. **Pros:** Property has an abundance of water—a real treat in New Mexico. **Cons:** Though comfortable, room décor looks like a Southwest chain-hotel. ⊠*16445 NM 4* ☎*505/829–4377* ⊕*www.canondelrio.com* 🛏*6 rooms, 1 suite* ⚘*In-room: kitchen (some), no TV, In-hotel: Wi-Fi* 🍴*CP* ▤*AE, D, MC, V.*

GEORGIA O'KEEFFE COUNTRY

It's a 20-minute drive north of Santa Fe to reach the Española Valley, where you head west to the striking mesas, cliffs, and valleys that so inspired the artist Georgia O'Keeffe—she lived in this area for the final 50 years of her life. You first come to the small, workaday city of Española, a major crossroads from which roads lead to Taos, Chama, and Abiquiu. The other notable community in this area is tiny Ojo Caliente, famous for its hot-springs spa retreat.

ESPAÑOLA
20 mi north of Santa Fe via U.S. 285/84.

This small but growing city midway along the Low Road from Santa Fe to Taos is a business hub for the many villages and Pueblos scattered throughout the region north of Santa Fe. The area at the confluence of the Rio Grande and Rio Chama was declared the capital for Spain by Don Juan de Oñate in 1598, but wasn't more than a collection of small settlements until the town was founded in 1880s as a stop on the Denver & Rio Grande Railroad. Lacking the colonial charm of either Santa Fe or Taos Española is known for being pretty "rough and tumble." There are many cheap burger joints, New Mexican–food restaurants, and a few chain motels, but few reasons to stick around for more than a quick meal. The city has become known as the "lowrider capital of the world" because of the mostly classic cars that have been retrofitted with lowered chassis and hydraulics that allow the cars to bump and grind as they cruise the streets on perpetual parade. The cars are often painted spectacularly, with religious murals, homages to dead relatives, and other spectacular scenes adorning them.

You may see a number of people wearing white (and sometimes orange or blue) turbans; they are members of the large American Sikh community that settled on the south end of town in the late '60s. Initially viewed with suspicion by the provincial Hispanics of the area, the Sikhs have become integral members of the community, teaching Kundalini yoga, establishing businesses and medical practices, and influencing many local restaurants to add vegetarian versions of New Mexican dishes to their menus.

All of the main arteries converge in the heart of town amidst a series of drab shopping centers, so watch the signs on the town's south side. Traffic moves slowly, especially on weekend nights when cruisers bring car culture alive.

NEED A BREAK? **Lovin' Oven** serves delicious, homemade donuts, apple fritters and turnovers, and hot coffee amidst all the latest news and gossip shared amongst the hordes of locals who pour through the doors at this sweet little shop on Española's south end. Get there early, once the goodies are gone they're gone. ⊠ *107 N. Riverside Dr., Española* ☎ *505/753-5461.*

The region is known for its longstanding weaving traditions, and one place you can learn about this heritage is the **Española Valley Fiber Arts Center** (⊠ *325 Paseo de Oñate* ☎ *505/747-3577* ⊕ *www.evfac.org* ✉ *Free* ☉ *Mon. 9–8, Tues.–Sat. 9–5, Sun. 12-5*), a nonprofit facility set inside an adobe building in the city's historic section. Here you can watch local weavers working with traditional materials and looms and admire (and purchase) their works in a small gallery. There are also classes offered on spinning, weaving, and knitting, which are open to the public and range from one day to several weeks. Emphasis here is placed on the styles of weaving that have been practiced here in the northern Rio Grande Valley since the Spaniards brought sheep and treadle looms here in the late 16th century. The center also celebrates the ancient traditions of New Mexico's Navajo and Pueblo weavers.

WHERE TO EAT & STAY

★ $$ ✗ **El Paragua Restaurant.** With a dark, intimate atmosphere of wood and stone, this historic place started out as a lemonade-cum-taco stand in the late 1950s but is now known for some of the state's most authentic New Mexican and regional Mexican cuisine. Steaks and fish are grilled over a mesquite-wood fire; other specialties include chorizo enchiladas, panfried breaded trout amadine, and menudo. This restaurant is still a family affair; service is gracious and the food is worth the drive. If you don't have time to sit down for a meal, stop at El Parasol taco stand in the parking lot next door for excellent, cheap Mexican/New Mexican. Vegetarians, ask for the Khalsa special, a super delicious veggie quesadilla created for the local Sikhs. ⊠603 Santa Cruz Rd., NM 76 just east of NM 68 ☎505/753–3211 or 800/929–8226 ⊕www.elparagua. com ☐AE, DC, MC, V.

$$$$ ⛺**Rancho de San Juan.** This secluded 225-acre Relaix & Châteaux
Fodor'sChoice compound hugs Black Mesa's base. Many of the inn's rooms are self-
★ contained suites, some set around a courtyard and others amid the wilderness. All rooms have Southwestern furnishings, Frette robes, Aveda bath products, and CD stereos; nearly all have kiva fireplaces. The top units have such cushy touches as two bedrooms, 12-foot ceilings, Mexican marble showers, kitchens, Jacuzzis, and private patios. The restaurant serves dinner Tuesday through Saturday by reservation only. Featuring spectacular contemporary cuisine, the à la carte menu of appetizers, entrees, and desserts, changes weekly. Past fare has included Texas quail stuffed with corn bread, green chiles, and linguiça sausage, and Alaskan halibut with tomatillo-lime salsa, caramelized butternut squash, and creamed spinach. Hike to a beautiful handcarved sandstone shrine on a bluff above the property. In-suite spa and massage services are available. ⊠U.S. 285, 3½ mi north of U.S. 84 ⬩Box 4140, Española 87533 ☎505/753–6818 ⊕www.ranchodesanjuan. com ⟟4 suites, 9 casitas ⬩In-room: no a/c (some), kitchen (some), no TV. In-hotel: restaurant, no kids under 8, no-smoking rooms ☐AE, D, DC, MC, V.

ABIQUIU
24 mi northwest of Española via U.S. 84.

This tiny, very traditional Hispanic village was originally home to freed *genizaros,* indigenous and mixed-blood slaves who served as house servants, shepherds and other key roles in Spanish, Mexican and American households well into the 1880s. With their mixed blood and Spanish surnames, those once known as genizaros now make up a significant population of the state. Many descendants of original families still live in the area, although since the late 1980s Abiquiu and its surrounding countryside have become a nesting ground for those fleeing big-city lifestyles, among them actresses Marsha Mason and Shirley MacLaine. Abiquiu—along with parts of the nearby Española Valley—is also a hotbed of organic farming, with many of the operations here selling their goods at the Santa Fe Farmers Market and to restaurants throughout the Rio Grande Valley.

A number of artists live in Abiquiu, with several studios showing traditional Hispanic art as well as contemporary works and pottery open regularly to the public; many others open each year over Columbus Day weekend for the **Annual Abiquiu Studio Tour** (☎505/685–4454 ⊕www. abiquiustudiotour.org). A feeling of insider versus outsider and old-timer versus newcomer still prevails. Newcomers or visitors may find themselves shut out by locals; it's best to observe one very important local custom: no photography is allowed in and around the village.

You can visit **Georgia O'Keeffe's home** through advance reservation (at least four months recommended if you plan on visiting during high season) with the **Georgia O'Keeffe Museum** (☎ *505/685–4539* ⊕ *www. okeeffemuseum.org*), which conducts one-hour tours Tuesday, Thursday, and Friday, mid-March–November, additional tours Wednesday, Jul-Aug for $30. In 1945 Georgia O'Keeffe bought a large, dilapidated late-18th-century Spanish-colonial adobe compound just off the Plaza. Upon the 1946 death of her husband, photographer Alfred Stieglitz, she left New York City and began dividing her time permanently between this home, which figured prominently in many of her works, and the one in nearby Ghost Ranch. She wrote about the house, "When I first saw the Abiquiú house it was a ruin...As I climbed and walked about in the ruin I found a patio with a very pretty well house and a bucket to draw up water. It was a good-sized patio with a long wall with a door on one side. That wall with a door in it was something I had to have. It took me 10 years to get it—three more years to fix the house up so I could live in it—and after that the wall with the door was painted many times." The patio is featured in *Black Patio Door* (1955) and *Patio with Cloud* (1956). O'Keeffe died in 1986 at the age of 98 and left provisions in her will to ensure that the property's houses would never be public monuments.

SHOPPING

★ **Bode's** (⊠ *U.S. 84* ☎ *505/685–4422* ⊕ *www.bodes.com*), (pronounced bow dees) across from the Abiquiu post office, is so much more than a gas station. It's a popular stop for newspapers, quirky gifts, locally made products, cold drinks, supplies, fishing gear (including licenses), amazing breakfast burritos, hearty green chili stew, sandwiches, and other short-order fare. The friendly, busy station serves as general store and exchange post for news and gossip.

WHERE TO STAY

$$ ▦ **Abiquiu Inn and Cafe Abiquiu.** Deep in the Chama Valley, the inn has a secluded, exotic feel—almost like an oasis—with brightly decorated rooms, including several four-person casitas, with woodstoves or fireplaces and tiled baths; some units have verandas with hammocks and open views of O'Keeffe Country. The café, open for breakfast lunch and dinner, ($$) serves commendable New Mexican, Italian, and American fare, from blue-corn tacos stuffed with grilled trout to lamb-and-poblano chili stew; it's also known for its seasonal fresh-fruit cobblers. The inn is the departure point for O'Keeffe-home tours, where the O'Keeffe Museum has a small office. It has an exceptional art gallery, crafts shop, and gardens. Two basic, but very comfortable, Traveler's Rooms are available for $80. The RV park on the property offers full hookups and a dump station for $18 per night. ⊠ *U.S. 84* ⊕ *Box 120, Abiquiu 87510* ☎ *505/685–4378 or 888/735–2902* 🖶 *505/685–4931* ⊕ *www.abiquiuinn.com* ➥ *12 rooms, 2 suites, 5 casitas* ⌂ *In-room:*

kitchen (some). In-hotel: restaurant (where free Wi-Fi is available) ⊟*AE, D, DC, MC, V.*

GHOST RANCH
10 mi northwest of Abiquiu on U.S. 84.

For art historians, the name Ghost Ranch brings to mind Georgia O'Keeffe, who lived on but a small parcel of this 20,000-acre dude and cattle ranch. The ranch's owner in the 1930s—conservationist and publisher of *Nature Magazine,* Arthur Pack—first invited O'Keeffe here to visit in 1934; Pack soon sold the artist the 7-acre plot on which she lived summer through fall for most of the rest of her life.

In 1955 Pack donated the rest of the ranch to the Presbyterian Church, which continues to use Pack's original structures and about 55 acres of land as a conference center.

☺ The **Ghost Ranch Education and Retreat Center** (⊠*U.S. 84* ☎*505/685– Fodor'sChoice 4333 or* ⊕*www.ghostranch.org* ⊠*Suggested Donation $3 minimum*), ★ open to the public year-round, is busiest in summer, when the majority of workshops take place. Subjects range from poetry and literary arts to photography, horseback riding, and every conceivable traditional craft of northern New Mexico. These courses are open to the public, and guests camp or stay in semirustic cottages or casitas. If you're here for a day trip, after registering at the main office, you may come in and hike high among the wind-hewn rocks so beloved by O'Keeffe. The **Florence Hawley Ellis Museum of Anthropology** contains Native American tools, pottery, and other artifacts excavated from the Ghost Ranch Gallina digs. Pioneer anthropologist Florence Hawley Ellis conducted excavations at Chaco Canyon and at other sites in New Mexico. Adjacent to the Ellis Museum, the **Ruth Hall Museum of Paleontology** exhibits the New Mexico state fossil, the coelophysis, also known as "the littlest dinosaur," originally excavated near Ghost Ranch. For the art lover, or the lover of the New Mexican landscape, Ghost Ranch offers guided O'Keeffe & Ghost Ranch Landscape Tours of the specific sites on the ranch that O'Keeffe painted during the five decades that she summered here. Her original house is not part of the tour and is closed to the public. These one-hour tours are available mid-March through mid-October, on Tuesday, Wednesday, Friday, and Saturday at 1:30 and 3:00; the cost is $25, and you must call first to make a reservation. The landscape tours are timed to coincide with the tours given at her house in Abiquiu, although they have nothing to do with the O'Keeffe studio tours offered there. Here's a little-known tidbit: limited camping is available on Ghost Ranch for both RVs and tents ($16-$26) and full hookups are available for RVs.

The **Ghost Ranch Piedra Lumbre Education and Visitor Center, which is part of the Ghost Ranch organization,** has a gallery with rotating art presentations, exhibits on New Mexico's natural history, a gift shop, and two museums. ⊠*U.S. 84, just north of main Ghost Ranch entrance* ☎*505/685–4312* ⊕*www.ghostranch.org* ⊠*Donation* ☺ *Visitor Center: Mar.–Oct., daily 9–5. Hawley and Hall museums: Late May–early*

Sept., Tues.–Sat. 9–5, Sun. and Mon. 1–5; early Sept.–late May, Tues.–Sat. 9–5.

The best and most interesting way to reach Ojo Caliente from Ghost Ranch is to return down U.S. 84 just past Abiquiu and then make a left turn (north) onto NM 554 toward El Rito, 12 mi away. This small, rural community known for its crafts making (especially weaving) has a

★ funky general store and **El Farolito** (✉ *1212 Main St.* ☎ *505/581–9509*), a cubbyhole of a restaurant on the town's tree-shaded Main Street that serves State Fair blue-ribbon green chili and other New Mexican specialties, including a terrific posole. This place celebrated their 25th year in 2008 and has somewhat of a cult following, so don't be surprised if you have to wait for dinner. The ride here offers a stunning view back east toward the Sangre de Cristos. Cash only; closed Mondays.

OJO CALIENTE
28 mi northeast of Abiquiu by way of El Rito via NM 554 to NM 111 to U.S. 285, 50 mi north of Santa Fe on U.S. 285.

Ojo Caliente is the only place in North America where five different types of hot springs—iron, lithium, arsenic, salt, and soda—are found side by side. The town was named by Spanish explorer Cabeza de Vaca, who visited in 1535 and believed he had stumbled upon the Fountain of Youth. Modern-day visitors draw a similar conclusion about the restorative powers of the springs. The spa itself, built in the 1920s, is a no-frills establishment that is in the process of extensive renovations; it comprises a hotel and cottages, a restaurant, a gift shop, massage rooms, men's and women's bathhouses, a chlorine-free swimming pool, and indoor and outdoor mineral-water tubs. The hotel, one of the original bathhouses, and the springs are all on the National Register of Historic Places, as is the adjacent and recently restored Round Barn (the only adobe one in the nation), from which visitors can take horseback tours and guided hikes to ancient Pueblo dwellings and petroglyph-etched rocks. Spa services include wraps, massage, facials, and acupuncture. The setting at the foot of sandstone cliffs topped by the ruins of ancient Indian pueblos is nothing short of inspiring.

WHERE TO STAY
$–$$ 🏨 **Ojo Caliente Mineral Springs Spa and Resort.** Accommodations here run the gamut from spartan in the unfussy original 1916 hotel (no TVs, simple furnishings) to rather upscale in the elegant suites, which were added in summer 2006. Rooms in the hotel have bathrooms but no showers or tubs—bathing takes place in the mineral springs (it's an arrangement that pleases most longtime devotees but doesn't sit well with others). The cottages are quite comfy, with refrigerators and TVs; some have kitchenettes, with tile showers in the bathrooms. In summer 2006 Ojo opened 12 spacious suites, which have such luxury touches as kiva fireplaces and patios; half of these have private double soaking tubs outside, which are filled with Ojo mineral waters. All lodgers have complimentary access to the mineral pools and *milagro* (miracle) wraps, and the bathhouse has showers. Horseback tours can be prearranged. The Artesian restaurant serves world-beat fare in a charming

dining room ($$). Four-day and overnight packages are available, from $700 per person. There's also camping on-site, beside the cottonwood-shaded Rio Ojo Caliente—double-occupancy camping rates are $20 for tents, $40 for RVs. **Pros:** This place can feel like a real "getaway" and for fairly reasonable rates. **Cons:** Service and treatments can be disappointing; ask about the construction/renovation happening; as it's ongoing it can get loud and isn't relaxing. ⊠ *50 Los Baños Dr., off U.S. 285, 30 mi north of Española* ✉ *Box 68, 87549* 🕾 *505/583–2233 or 800/222–9162* 🖷 *505/583–2464* ⊕ *www.ojocalientesprings.com* ⟵ *19 rooms, 19 cottages, 12 suites, 3 3-bedroom houses* ⬥ *In-room: no a/c, no phone, kitchen (some), refrigerator (some), no TV (some). In-hotel: restaurant, spa* ⊟ *AE, D, DC, MC, V.*

THE HIGH ROAD TO TAOS

Fodor's Choice The main highway to Taos (NM 68) is a good, even scenic, route if ★ you've got limited time but by far the most spectacular and interesting route is what is known as the High Road. Towering peaks, lush hillsides, orchards and meadows surround tiny, ancient Hispanic villages that are as picturesque as they are historically fascinating. The High Road follows U.S. 285/84 north to NM 503 (a right turn just past Pojoaque), to County Road 98 (a left toward Chimayó), to NM 76 northeast to NM 75 east, to NM 518 north. The drive takes you through the badlands of stark, weathered rock—where numerous Westerns have been filmed—quickly into rolling foothills, lush canyons, and finally into pine forests. Although most of these insular, traditional Hispanic communities offer little in the way of shopping and dining, the region has steadily become more of a haven for artists.

From Chimayó to Peñasco, you can find mostly low-key but often high-quality art galleries, many of them run out of the owners' homes. During the final two weekends in September each year, more than 100 artists in these parts show their work in the **High Road Art Tour** (🕾 *866/343–5381* ⊕ *www.highroadnewmexico.com*); call or visit the Web site for a studio map.

Depending on when you make this drive, you're in for some of the state's most radiant scenery. In mid-April the orchards are in blossom; summer turns the valleys into lush green oases; and in fall the smell of piñon adds to the sensual overload of golden leaves and red-chili ristras hanging from the houses. In winter the fields are covered with quilts of snow, and the lines of homes, fences, and trees stand out like bold pen-and-ink drawings against the sky. But the roads can be icy and treacherous—if in doubt, stick with the Low Road to Taos. If you decide to take the High Road just one way between Santa Fe and Taos, you might want to save it for the return journey—the scenery is even more stunning when traveling north to south.

CHIMAYÓ
28 mi north of Santa Fe, 10 mi east of Española on NM 76.

From U.S. 285/84 north of Pojoaque, scenic NM 503 winds past horse paddocks and orchards in the narrow Nambé Valley, then ascends into the red-sandstone canyons with a view of Truchas Peaks to the northeast before dropping into the bucolic village of Chimayó. Nestled into hillsides where gnarled piñons seem to grow from bare bedrock, Chimayó is famed for its weaving, its red chiles, and its two chapels.

Fodor'sChoice **El Santuario de Chimayó,** a small frontier adobe church, has a fantastically
★ carved and painted reredo (wood altar) and is built on the site where, believers say, a mysterious light came from the ground on Good Friday in 1810 and where a large wooden crucifix was found beneath the earth. The chapel sits above a sacred *pozito* (a small hole), the dirt from which is believed to have miraculous healing properties. Dozens of abandoned crutches and braces placed in the anteroom—along with many notes, letters, and photos—testify to this. The Santuario draws a steady stream of worshippers year-round—Chimayó is considered the Lourdes of the Southwest. During Holy Week as many as 50,000 pilgrims come here. The shrine is a National Historic Landmark, and its altar and artwork underwent an ambitious and much needed restoration in 2004. It's surrounded by small adobe shops selling every kind of religious curio imaginable, and some very fine traditional Hispanic work from local artists. ✉*Signed lane off CR 98* ☎*505/351–4889* ⊕*www.archdiocese santafe.org/AboutASF/Chimayo.html* ✉*Free* ⊙*June–Sept., daily 9–5; Oct.–May, daily 9–4.*

A smaller chapel 200 yards from El Santuario was built in 1857 and dedicated to **Santo Niño de Atocha.** As at the more famous Santuario, the dirt at Santo Niño de Atocha's chapel is said to have healing properties in the place where the *Santo Niño* was first placed. The little boy saint was brought here from Mexico by Severiano Medina, who claimed Santo Niño de Atocha had healed him of rheumatism. San Ildefonso pottery master Maria Martinez came here for healing as a child. Tales of the boy saint's losing one of his shoes as he wandered through the countryside helping those in trouble endeared him to the people of northern New Mexico. It became a tradition to place shoes at the foot of the statue as an offering. Many soldiers who survived the Bataan Death March during WWII credit Santo Niño for saving them, adding to his beloved status in this state where the percentage of young people who enlist in the military remains quite high. ✉*Free* ⊙*Daily 9–5.*

WHERE TO STAY
★ $ ✕**Léona's Restaurante.** This fast-food-style burrito and chili stand under a massive catalpa tree at one end of the Santuario de Chimayó parking lot has only a few tables, and in summer it's crowded. Delicious dishes from the kitchen include homemade posole stew, carne adovada, and green-chili cheese tamales. The specialty is flavored tortillas—everything from jalapeño to butterscotch. The tortillas have become so legendary that owner Léona Medina-Tiede opened a tortilla factory in Chimayó's Manzana Center and now does a thriving mail-order busi-

ness. ⊠*Off CR 98, behind Santuario de Chimayó* ☎*505/351–4569 or 888/561–5569* ⊕*www.leonasrestaurante.com* ⊟*AE, D, DC, MC, V* ⊘*Closed Tues. and Wed. No dinner.*

★ $$ ☷**Casa Escondida.** Intimate and peaceful, this adobe inn has sweeping views of the Sangre de Cristo range. The setting makes it a great base for mountain bikers. The scent of fresh-baked strudel wafts through the rooms, which are decorated with antiques and Native American and other regional arts and crafts. Ask for the Sun Room, in the main house, which has a private patio, viga ceilings, and a brick floor. The separate one-bedroom Casita Escondida has a kiva-style fireplace, tile floors, kitchenette, and a sitting area. A large hot tub is hidden in a grove behind wild berry bushes, there are several covered porches, and a massive bird feeding station that draws dozens and dozens of birds. In-room massage is available by appointment and special packages—romance, birthday, etc—are also available. **Pros:** This b&b is a very good value, with gracious hosts and in beautiful surroundings; there's not a TV on the entire property. **Cons:** Remote setting means you must drive to sights. ⊠*CR 0100, off NM 76* ⊘*Box 142, 85722* ☎*505/351–4805 or 800/643–7201* ⊟*505/351–2575* ⊕*www. casaescondida.com* ⚘*In-room: no phone, kitchen (some), no TV, Wi-Fi. In-hotel: no-smoking rooms, some pets allowed; public computer for guests(w/WiFi)* ⟲*7 rooms, 1 suite* ⊟*MC, V* ⊙*BP.*

SHOPPING

Centinela Traditional Arts-Weaving (⊠*NM 76, 1 mi east of junction with CR 98* ☎*505/351–2180 or 877/351–2180* ⊕*www.chimayoweavers. com*) continues the Trujillo family weaving tradition, which started in northern New Mexico more than seven generations ago. Irvin Trujillo and his wife, Lisa, are both gifted award-winning master weavers, creating Rio Grande–style tapestry blankets and rugs, many of them with natural dyes that authentically replicate early weavings. Most designs are historically based, but the Trujillos contribute their own designs as well. The shop and gallery carries these heirloom-quality textiles, with a knowledgeable staff on hand to demonstrate or answer questions about the weaving technique.

Ortega's Weaving Shop (⊠*NM 76 at CR 98* ☎*505/351–2288 or 877/351–4215* ⊕*www.ortegasdechimayo.com*) sells Rio Grande–and Chimayó-style textiles made by the family whose Spanish ancestors brought the craft to New Mexico in the 1600s. The Galeria Ortega, next door, sells traditional New Mexican and Hispanic and contemporary Native American arts and crafts. In winter the shop is closed on Sunday.

In the plaza just outside the Santuario, **Highroad Marketplace** (⊠*Off CR 98* ☎*505/351–1078 or 866/343–5381*) stocks a variety of arts and crafts created all along the High Road, from Chimayó to Peñasco. Be sure to stop into El Potrero, a treasure-trove of trinkets as well as high-quality arts and crafts from local artists.

CORDOVA
4 mi east of Chimayó via NM 76.

A picturesque mountain village with a small central plaza, a school, a post office, and a church, Cordova is the center of the regional wood-carving industry. The town supports more than 30 full-time and part-time carvers. Many of them are descendants of José Dolores López, who in the 1920s created the village's signature unpainted "Cordova style" of carving. Most of the *santeros* (makers of religious images) have signs outside their homes indicating that santos are for sale. Many pieces are fairly expensive, a reflection of the hard work and fine craftsmanship involved—ranging from several hundred dollars for small ones to several thousand for larger figures, but there are also affordable and delightful small carvings of animals and birds. The St. Anthony of Padua Chapel, which is filled with handcrafted retablos (wood tablets painted with saints) and other religious art, is worth a visit.

PEÑASCO
15 mi north of Truchas on NM 76.

Although still a modest-size community, Peñasco is one of the larger towns along the High Road and a good bet if you need to fill your tank with gas or pick up a snack at a convenience store.

WHERE TO EAT

$ ✕**Sugar Nymphs Bistro.** It's taken a little time for folks to learn about, let alone find, this delightful little place set inside a vintage theater in sleepy Peñasco. You can't miss the vivid murals on the building, it's right on the High Road, and it is hands down the best restaurant along this entire route. If you get an early start from Santa Fe and get through Chimayo in the morning, you'll get here right in time for a fabulous lunch or an early dinner if you've meandered. Chef-owner Kai Harper Leah earned her stripes at San Francisco's famed vegetarian restaurant, Greens, and presents an eclectic menu of reasonably priced, inspired food: creatively topped pizzas, bountiful salads, juicy bacon cheeseburgers, butternut-squash ravioli. Desserts are also memorable—consider the chocolate pecan pie. You can dine on the patio in warm weather. The Sunday brunch is excellent. ⊠ *15046 NM 75* ☎ *505/587–0311* ▤ *MC, V* ☉ *Closed Mon.*

Fodor'sChoice
★

Taos

WORD OF MOUTH

"We both loved Taos—small, but so unassuming. We managed to take in the plaza, Kit Carson Home, Millicent Rogers Museum, Rio Grande Gorge Bridge, Hacienda de los Martínez (hard to find, but worth it!), San Francisco de Asís Church, and, the highlight I think, Taos Pueblo."

—Chele60

"The Taos Pueblo is larger than most, and it does offer some little shops, but it's definitely not a shopping destination. It's more of a place to see how the Indians live/lived."

—JackOneill

Updated by
Barbara Floria

Taos casts a lingering spell. Set on a rolling mesa at the base of the San-gre de Cristo Mountains, it's a place of piercing light and spectacular views, where the desert palette changes almost hourly as the sun moves across the sky. Adobe buildings—some of them centuries old—lie nes-tled amid pine trees and scrub, some in the shadow of majestic Taos Mountain. The smell of piñon wood smoke rises from the valley in winter; in spring and summer, it gives way to fragrant sage.

The magic of the area has drawn people here for hundreds of years. The earliest inhabitants were Native Americans of the Taos–Tiwa tribe; their descendants still live and maintain a traditional way of life at Taos Pueblo, a 95,000-acre reserve 3 mi north of what is now the town's commercial center. Spanish settlers, who arrived in the 1500s, brought both farming and Catholicism to the area; their influence can still be seen today at Ranchos de Taos, 4 mi south of town, and at the San Francisco de Asís Church, whose massive adobe walls and *camposanto* (graveyard) are among the most photographed in the country.

In the early 20th century, another population—artists—discovered Taos and began making the pilgrimage here to write, paint, and take photographs. The early adopters of this movement were paint-ers Bert Phillips and Ernest Blumenschein, who were traveling from Denver on a planned painting trip into Mexico in 1898 when they stopped to have a broken wagon wheel repaired in Taos. Enthralled with the earthy beauty of the region, they abandoned their plan to journey farther south, settled, and eventually formed the Taos Soci-ety of Artists in 1915. Over the following years, many illustrious artists, including Georgia O'Keeffe, Ansel Adams, and D.H. Law-rence also took up residence in the area, and it is still a mecca for creative types today. The downtown area is now filled with galleries and shops that display the work of local artists, and museums that document Taos's artistic history.

These days, Taos has a variable population of about 6,500 (the 2000 U.S. Census officially places it at 4,700, but there's always an influx during the summer and the winter ski season, and these numbers don't include Arroyo Seco, Taos Ski Valley, and other neighboring villages). Many come here for a break from the urban sprawl of larger U.S. cities; the actress Julia Roberts is among the escapees.

ORIENTATION & PLANNING

GETTING ORIENTED

Taos is small and resolutely rustic, and the central area is highly walk-able. Sociable Taoseños make the town a welcoming place to explore. You need a car to reach the Rio Grande Gorge and other places of inter-est beyond Taos proper. Traffic can be heavy in the peak summer and winter seasons (an accident on the main route through town, Paseo del Pueblo, can back up traffic for miles); ask locals about back roads that let you avoid the busy street.

TOP REASONS TO GO

Southwestern style. The simple elegance of adobe architecture balances the vibrancy of Southwestern art. The result? Aesthetic perfection.

American roots. The Taos Pueblo and the proud Navajo Indians that call the area home provide a unique perspective on pre-Columbian culture and accomplishments.

Desert solitaire. Bask in the ultimate stress-reducer of the empty high desert and pine-covered hills.

Green chiles. Piquant, but not overly hot, the ubiquitous green chili shows up in everything from breakfast burritos to stacked blue corn enchiladas to lobster bisque. Smokey and smooth, it's an apt corollary to Proust's madeleines.

Downtown Taos. More than four centuries after it was laid out, the Taos Plaza and adjacent streets remain the center of tourist activity in Taos. Bent Street, where New Mexico's first American governor lived and died, is an upscale shopping area and gallery enclave, and many of the best restaurants and bars are within walking distance.

South of Taos. The first Spanish settlers were farmers and many families continue to till the fertile land south of Taos. Ranchos de Taos, a mall village a few miles south of the plaza centered around the iconic church memorialized by Georgia O'Keefe and photographer Ansel Adams.

Taos Pueblo to Rio Grande Gorge. The Pueblo is the virtual beating heart of the entire valley, setting historic precedents and architectural reference points for everything that Taos has become. The casino aside, the area has been spared commercial development and remains a neighborhood of modest homes and farms. High desert scrub and wide open spaces fall away beneath the elegance of the Rio Grande Gorge Bridge.

TAOS PLANNER

WHEN TO GO

With more than 300 days of sunshine annually, Taos typically yields good weather year-round. The summer high season brings hot days (80s) and cool nights (50s), as well as afternoon thunderstorms. A packed arts and festival schedule in summer means the hotels and B&Bs are filled, lodging rates are high, restaurants are jammed, and traffic anywhere near the plaza is often at a standstill. Spring and fall are stunning and favor milder temperatures, fewer visitors, and shoulder season prices. If the snow is plentiful, skiers arrive en masse but are likely to stay close to the slopes, only venturing into town for a meal or two.

GETTING HERE & AROUND

BY AIR   Albuquerque International Sunport is the nearest (130 mi) major airport to Taos. Taos Municipal Airport is 12 mi west of the city but ceased offering commercial service in 2005 and is just open to charters and private planes. Faust's Transportation offers shuttle service between Albuquerque's airport and Taos, as well as to Taos Ski Valley, Angel Fire, and Red River. The cost is $50 to $60 per person, and the ride takes 2¾–3 hours.

BY BUS   Greyhound Lines runs buses once a day from Albuquerque to Taos.

BY CAR   The main route from Santa Fe to Taos is NM 68, also known as the Low Road, which winds between the Rio Grande and red-rock cliffs before rising to a spectacular view of the plain and river gorge. You can also take the wooded High Road to Taos. From points north of Taos, take NM 522; from points east or west, take U.S. 64. **Cottam Walker** rents cars by the day, week, and month.

BY TAXI   Taxi service in Taos is sparse, but Faust's Transportation, based in nearby El Prado, has a fleet of radio-dispatched cabs.

ESSENTIALS   **Air Shuttle Contacts Faust's Transportation** (☎575/758–3410 or 888/830–3410 ⊕ www.newmexiconet.com/trans/faust/faust.html).

Bus Contacts Greyhound (☎800/231–2222 ⊕ www.greyhound.com).

Car Rental Contacts Cottam Walker Ford (⊠1320 Paseo del Pueblo Sur ☎575/751–3200 ⊕ www.forddetaos.com).

Taxi Contacts Faust's Transportation (☎575/758–3410 or 888-231-2222).

VISITOR
INFORMATION   **Taos Visitors Center** (⊠1139 Paseo del Pueblo Sur ☐ Drawer I, Taos 87571 ☎505/758–3873 or 800/48-0696 ⊕ www.taosvacationguide.com). **Taos Ski Valley Chamber of Commerce** (☎575/776–1413 or 800/517–9816 ⊕ www. taosskivalley.com).

PLANNING YOUR TIME

With its wealth of museums, historical sites, unique restaurants and grand vistas it's a shame so many people consider Taos little more than a stopover on their way to and from Santa Fe. Even so, whether you've got an afternoon or a week in the area, begin by strolling around Taos Plaza and along Bent Street, taking in the galleries, Native American crafts shops, and eclectic clothing stores. Take Ledoux Street south from west Plaza and go two blocks to the Harwood Museum, then walk back to the Plaza and cross over to Kit Carson Road, where you can find more shops and galleries as well as the Kit Carson Home and Museum. Continue north on Paseo del Pueblo to the Taos Art Museum at the Fechin House and you'll have enjoyed much of the best Taos has to offer. If you have time to venture a bit farther afield, head north on Paseo del Pueblo out to the Taos Pueblo, then west to the magnificent Millicent Rogers Museum. If you're headed south stop at the La Hacienda de los Martinez for a look at early life in Taos and then on to Ranchos de Taos to see the stunning San Francisco de Asís Church and channel your inner artist.

EXPLORING TAOS

The Museum Association of Taos includes five properties. Among them are the Harwood Museum, Taos Art Museum at the Fechin House, the Millicent Rogers Museum, the E.L. Blumenschein Home and Museum, and La Hacienda de los Martínez. Each of the museums charges $8–$10 for admission, but you can opt for a combination ticket—$25 for all five, valid for one year.

Numbers in the text correspond to numbers in the margin and on the Taos map.

3

DOWNTOWN TAOS

WHAT TO SEE

② **Blumenschein Home and Museum.** For an introduction to the history of the Taos art scene, start with Ernest L. Blumenschein's residence, which provides a glimpse into the cosmopolitan lives led by the members of the Taos Society of Artists, of which Blumenschein was a founding member. One of the rooms in the adobe-style structure dates from 1797. On display are the art, antiques, and other personal possessions of Blumenschein and his wife, Mary Greene Blumenschein, who also painted, as did their daughter Helen. Several of Ernest Blumenschein's vivid oil paintings hang in his former studio, and works by other early Taos artists are also on display. ⊠ *222 Ledoux St.* ☎ *575/758–0505* ⊕ *www.taoshistoricmuseums.org* ✉ *$8, $25 with Museum Association of Taos combination ticket* ⊗ *May–Dec., daily 10–5; Call for winter hours.*

⑥ **Firehouse Collection.** More than 100 works by well-known Taos artists like Joseph Sharp, Ernest L. Blumenschein, and Bert Phillips hang in the Taos Volunteer Fire Department building. The exhibition space adjoins the station house, where five fire engines are maintained at the ready and an antique fire engine is on display. ⊠ *323 Camino de la Placita* ☎ *575/758–3386* ✉ *Free* ⊗ *Weekdays 9–4:30.*

⑤ **Governor Bent Museum.** In 1846, when New Mexico became a U.S. possession as a result of the Mexican War, Charles Bent, a trader, trapper, and mountain man, was appointed governor. Less than a year later he was killed in his house by an angry mob protesting New Mexico's annexation by the United States. Governor Bent was married to María Ignacia, the older sister of Josefa Jaramillo, the wife of mountain man Kit Carson. A collection of Native American artifacts, western Americana, and family possessions is squeezed into five small rooms of the adobe building where Bent and his family lived. ⊠ *117 Bent St.* ☎ *575/758–2376* ✉ *$3* ⊗ *daily 10–5.*

③ **Harwood Museum.** The Pueblo Revival former home of Burritt Elihu ★ "Burt" Harwood, a dedicated painter who studied in France before moving to Taos in 1916, is adjacent to a museum dedicated to the works of local artists. Traditional Hispanic northern New Mexican artists, early art-colony painters, post–World War II modernists, and contemporary artists such as Larry Bell, Agnes Martin, Ken Price, and

Earl Stroh are represented. Mabel Dodge Luhan, a major arts patron, bequeathed many of the 19th- and early-20th-century works in the Harwoods' collection, including *retablos* (painted wood representations of Catholic saints) and *bultos* (three-dimensional carvings of the saints). In the Hispanic Traditions Gallery upstairs are 19th-century tinwork, furniture, and sculpture. Downstairs, among early-20th-century art-colony holdings, look for E. Martin Hennings's *Chamisa in Bloom*, which captures the Taos landscape particularly beautifully. A tour of the ground-floor galleries shows that Taos painters of the era, notably Oscar Berninghaus, Ernest Blumenschein, Victor Higgins, Walter Ufer, Marsden Hartley, and John Marin, were fascinated by the land and the people linked to it. An octagonal gallery exhibits works by Agnes Martin. Martin's seven large canvas panels (each 5 feet square) are studies in white, their precise lines and blocks forming textured grids. Operated by the University of New Mexico since 1936, the Harwood is the second-oldest art museum in the state. ✉*238 Ledoux St.* ☎*575/758-9826* ⊕*www.harwoodmuseum.org* ✑*$8, $25 with Museum Association of Taos combination ticket* ⊘*Tues.–Sat. 10–5, Sun. noon–5.*

❹ Kit Carson Home and Museum. Kit Carson bought this low-slung 12-room adobe home in 1843 for his wife, Josefa Jaramillo, the daughter of a powerful, politically influential Spanish family. Three of the museum's rooms are furnished as they were when the Carson family lived here. The rest of the museum is devoted to gun and mountain-man exhibits, such as rugged leather clothing and Kit's own Spencer carbine rifle with its beaded leather carrying case, and early Taos antiques, artifacts, and manuscripts. ✉*113 Kit Carson Rd.* ☎*575/758-0505.* ✑*$8,* ⊘*Tues.–Sat., 10–4, Sun., noon–4, closed Mon.*

NEED A BREAK? Let the aroma of fresh-ground coffee draw you into the tiny **World Cup** (✉*102–A Paseo del Pueblo Norte* ☎*575/737-5299*), where you can sit at the counter or wander outside to a bench on the porch. Locals engage in political rhetoric here, often slanted toward the left, so be prepared for a rousing debate if you dare to dissent.

❼ Kit Carson Park. The noted pioneer is buried in the park that bears his name. His grave is marked with a *cerquita* (a spiked wrought-iron rectangular fence), traditionally used to outline and protect burial sites. Also interred here is Mabel Dodge Luhan, the pioneering patron of the early Taos art scene. The 32-acre park has swings and slides for recreational breaks. It's well marked with big stone pillars and a gate. ✉*211 Paseo del Pueblo Norte* ☎*575/758-8234* ✑*Free* ⊘*Late May–early Sept., daily 8–8; early Sept.–late May, daily 8–5.*

❽ Taos Art Museum at the Fechin House. The interior of this extraordinary adobe house, built between 1927 and 1933 by Russian émigré and artist Nicolai Fechin, is a marvel of carved Russian-style woodwork and furniture. Fechin constructed it to showcase his daringly colorful paintings. The house has hosted the Taos Art Museum since 2003, with a collection of paintings from more than 50 Taos artists, including founders

A GOOD WALK

Begin at the gazebo in the middle of **Taos Plaza** ❶. After exploring the Plaza, head south from its western edge down the small unmarked alley (its name is West Plaza Drive). The first cross street is Camino de la Placita. Across it, West Plaza Drive becomes Ledoux Street. Continue south on Ledoux to the **Blumenschein Home and Museum** ❷ and, a few doors farther south, the **Harwood Museum** ❸. (If you're driving, the parking area for the Harwood Foundation is at Ledoux and Ranchitos Road.)

From the Harwood Foundation, walk back north on Ranchitos Road a few blocks, make a left on Camino de la Placita, and go right onto Don Fernando Road. Follow it east along the north side of the Plaza to Paseo del Pueblo Norte (NM 68), which is the main street of Taos. As you cross NM 68, Don Fernando Road changes to Kit Carson Road. On the north side of Kit Carson Road is the **Kit Carson Home and Museum** ❹. After visiting the home, head back to Paseo del Pueblo Norte and walk north past the Taos Inn to browse through Bent Street's shops, boutiques, and galleries.

In a tiny plaza is the **Governor Bent Museum** ❺, the modest home of

the first Anglo governor of the state. Across the street is the John Dunn House. Once the homestead of a colorful and well-respected Taos gambling and transportation entrepreneur, the Dunn House is now a small shopping plaza. At the western end of Bent Street, head north on Camino de la Placita. In about 2½ blocks you'll come to the Taos Volunteer Fire Department building, which doubles as a fire station and the **Firehouse Collection** ❻ exhibition space.

Head east on Civic Plaza and cross Paseo del Pueblo Norte. To the north will be **Kit Carson Park** ❼ and the **Taos Art Museum at the Fechin House** ❽, named for the iconoclastic artist Nicolai Fechin.

TIMING

The entire walk can be done in a half day, a whole day if you stop to lunch along the way and browse in the shops and galleries. The Taos Art Museum at the Fechin House is closed Monday. Hours vary by season, but visits by appointment are welcomed. Some museums are closed on the weekend, so you may want to do this walk on a Wednesday, Thursday, or Friday. You can tour each of the museums in less than an hour.

of the original Taos Society of Artists, among them Joseph Sharp, Ernest Blumenschein, Bert Phillips, E.I. Couse, and Oscar Berninghaus. ⊠ *227 Paseo del Pueblo Norte* ☎ *575/758–2690* ⊕ *www.taosartmuseum.org* ✉ *$8, $25 with Museum Association of Taos combination ticket* ☉ *Tues.–Sun. 10–5.*

 Taos Plaza. The first European explorers of the Taos Valley came here with Captain Hernando de Alvarado, a member of Francisco Vásquez de Coronado's expedition of 1540. Basque explorer Don Juan de Oñate arrived in Taos in July 1598 and established a mission and trading arrangements with residents of Taos Pueblo. The settlement developed into two plazas: the Plaza at the heart of the town became a thriving

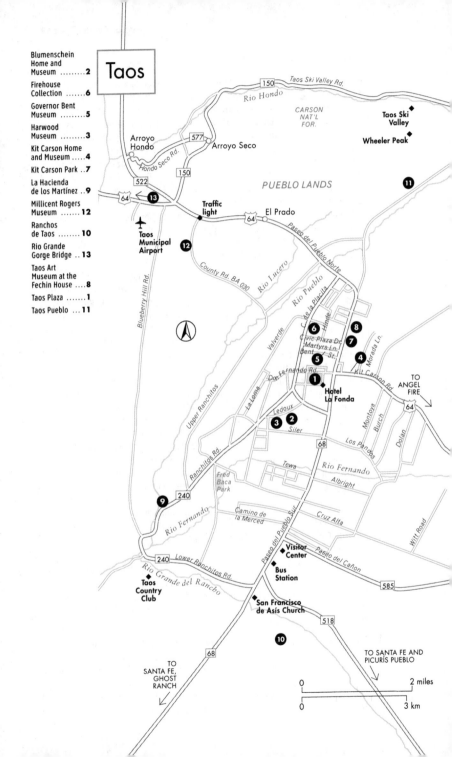

Taos

Blumenschein Home and Museum 2

Firehouse Collection 6

Governor Bent Museum 5

Harwood Museum 3

Kit Carson Home and Museum 4

Kit Carson Park ..7

La Hacienda de los Martínez ..9

Millicent Rogers Museum 12

Ranchos de Taos 10

Rio Grande Gorge Bridge ..13

Taos Art Museum at the Fechin House ...8

Taos Plaza 1

Taos Pueblo ...11

Taos Ski Valley Rd.

Rio Hondo

CARSON NAT'L FOR.

Taos Ski Valley

Wheeler Peak

Arroyo Hondo

Arroyo Seco

Hondo Seco Rd.

PUEBLO LANDS

Traffic light

El Prado

Paseo del Pueblo Norte

Taos Municipal Airport

County Rd. BA 030

Rio Lucero

Rio Pueblo

C. de la Placita

Rio Pueblo

Valverde

Blueberry Hill Rd.

Civic Plaza Dr.

Martyrs Ln.

Bent St.

Hlnde

Kit Carson Rd.

TO ANGEL FIRE

Don Fernando Rd.

Hotel La Fonda

Morada Ln.

Upper Ranchitos

La Loma

Ledoux

Siler

Montoya

Burch

Dolan

Los Pandos

Ranchitos Rd.

Tewa

Rio Fernando

Albright

Fred Baca Park

Rio Fernando

Camino de la Merced

Cruz Alta

Witt Road

Lower Ranchitos Rd.

Rio Grande del Rancho

Paseo del Pueblo Sur

Visitor Center

Paseo del Cañon

Bus Station

Taos Country Club

San Francisco de Asis Church

TO SANTA FE, GHOST RANCH

TO SANTA FE AND PICURÍS PUEBLO

0   2 miles

0   3 km

business district for the early colony, and a walled residential plaza was constructed a few hundred yards behind. It remains active today, home to a throng of gift and coffee shops. The covered gazebo was donated by heiress and longtime Taos resident Mabel Dodge Luhan. On the southeastern corner

> **GOOD TERM**
>
> Retablo: Holy image painted on wood or tin.

of Taos Plaza is the **Hotel La Fonda de Taos.** Some infamous erotic paintings by D. H. Lawrence that were naughty in his day but are quite tame by present standards can be viewed ($3 entry fee for nonguests) in the former barroom beyond the lobby.

NEED A BREAK?

Join the locals at the north or south location of the Bean (✉ *900 Paseo del Pueblo Norte* ☎ ✉ *1033 Paseo del Pueblo Sur* ☎ *575/758-5123*). The Bean roasts its own coffee, and the south-side location (where you can dine on an outside patio) offers good breakfast and lunch fare. The north location, in an adobe building, displays local artwork and is the most atmospheric of the two.

SOUTH OF TAOS

WHAT TO SEE

9 **La Hacienda de los Martínez.** Spare and fortlike, this adobe structure built between 1804 and 1827 on the bank of the Rio Pueblo served as a community refuge during Comanche and Apache raids. Its thick walls, which have few windows, surround two central courtyards. Don Antonio Severino Martínez was a farmer and trader; the hacienda was the final stop along El Camino Real (the Royal Road), the trade route the Spanish established between Mexico City and New Mexico. The restored period rooms here contain textiles, foods, and crafts of the early 19th century. There's a working blacksmith's shop, usually open to visitors on Saturday, and weavers create beautiful textiles on reconstructed period looms. ✉ *708 Hacienda Raod, Off Ranchitos Rd., NM 240* ☎ *575/758–1000* ⊕ *www.taoshistoricmuseums.com/martinez. html* ✉ *$8, $25 with Museum Association of Taos combination ticket* ⊙ *May–Dec., daily 10–4; Call for winter hours. Closed Monday.*

10 **Ranchos de Taos.** A few minutes' drive south of the center of Taos, this village still retains some of its rural atmosphere despite the highway traffic passing through. Huddled around its famous adobe church and dusty plaza are cheerful, remodeled shops and galleries standing shoulder to shoulder with crumbling adobe shells. This ranching, farming, and budding small-business community was an early home to Taos Native Americans before being settled by Spaniards in 1716. Although many of the adobe dwellings have seen better days, the shops, modest galleries, taco stands, and two fine restaurants point to an ongoing revival.

★ The massive bulk of **San Francisco de Asís Church** (✉ *NM 68, 500 yards south of NM 518, Ranchos de Taos* ☎ *575/758–2754*) is an enduring attraction. The Spanish Mission–style church was erected in 1815 as a spiritual and physical refuge from raiding Apaches, Utes, and Comanches. In 1979 the deteriorated church was rebuilt with traditional adobe bricks by community volunteers. Every spring a group gathers to re-mud the facade. The earthy, clean lines of the exterior walls and supporting bulwarks have inspired generations of painters and photographers. The late-afternoon light provides the best exposure of the heavily buttressed rear of the church—though today's image-takers face the challenge of framing the architecturally pure lines through rows of parked cars and a large, white sign put up by church officials; morning light is best for the front. Bells in the twin belfries call Taoseños to services on Sunday and holidays. Monday through Saturday from 9 to 4 you can step inside. In the parish hall just north of the church (and for a $3 fee) you can view a 15-minute video presentation every half hour that describes the history and restoration of the church and explains the mysterious painting *Shadow of the Cross,* on which each evening the shadow of a cross appears over Christ's shoulder (scientific studies made on the canvas and the paint pigments cannot explain the phenomenon). The fee also allows you to view the painting.

TAOS PUEBLO TO RIO GRANDE GORGE

WHAT TO SEE

⑫ **Millicent Rogers Museum.** More than 5,000 pieces of spectacular Native
Fodor'sChoice American and Hispanic art, many of them from the private collec-
★ tion of the late Standard Oil heiress Millicent Rogers, are on display here. Among the pieces are baskets, blankets, rugs, kachina dolls, carvings, paintings, rare religious artifacts, and most significantly, jewelry (Rogers, a fashion icon in her day, was one of the first Americans to appreciate the turquoise-and-silver artistry of Native American jewelers). Other important works include the pottery and ceramics of Maria Martinez and other potters from San Ildefonso Pueblo (23 mi north of Santa Fe). Docents conduct guided tours by appointment, and the museum hosts lectures, films, workshops, and demonstrations. The two-room gift shop has exceptional jewelry, rugs, books, and pottery. ✉ *1504 Millicent Rogers Rd., from Taos Plaza head north on Paseo del Pueblo Norte and left at sign for CR BA030, also called Millicent Rogers Rd.* ☎ *575/758–2462* ⊕ *www.millicentrogers.com* 🎫 *$8, $25 with Museum Association of Taos combination ticket* ⊙ *Apr.–Sept., daily 10–5; Nov.–Mar., Tues.–Sun. 10–5.*

⑬ **Rio Grande Gorge Bridge.** It's a dizzying experience to see the Rio Grande
☍ 650 feet underfoot, where it flows at the bottom of an immense, steep
★ rock canyon. In summer the reddish rocks dotted with green scrub contrast brilliantly with the blue sky, where you might see a hawk lazily floating in circles. The bridge is the second-highest expansion bridge in the country. Hold on to your camera and eyeglasses when looking down, and watch out for low-flying planes. The Taos Municipal Airport is close by, and daredevil private pilots have been known to

A GOOD DRIVE

Drive 2 mi north on Paseo del Pueblo Norte (NM 68), and keep your eyes peeled for the signs on the right, beyond the post office, directing you to **Taos Pueblo** ⓫. To reach the **Millicent Rogers Museum** ⓬ next, return to NM 68 to head north and make a left onto County Road BA030. If you find yourself at the intersection with U.S. 64 and 150, you've gone too far. Continue down the county road to the big adobe wall; the sign for the museum is on the right. This rural road eventually connects back onto Upper Ranchitos Road. After exploring the museum, return to NM 68 north; then make a left on U.S. 64 west to the **Rio Grande Gorge Bridge** ⓭, a stunning marriage of natural wonder and human engineering. Bring along sturdy hiking shoes and plenty of water and snacks for an invigorating walk down into the gorge. But remember, what goes down must come up, and it's an arduous path.

TIMING

Plan on spending 1½ hours at the pueblo. Taos can get hot in summer, but if you visit the pueblo in the morning, you'll avoid the heat and the crowds. Winters can be cold and windy, so dress warmly. If your visit coincides with a ceremonial observance, set aside several hours, because the ceremonies, though they are worth the wait, never start on time. Two hours should be enough time to take in the museum and the grandeur of the Rio Grande Gorge Bridge.

challenge one another to fly under the bridge. Shortly after daybreak, hot-air balloons fly above and even inside the gorge. ⊠ *U.S. 64, 12 mi west of town.*

⓫ **Taos Pueblo.** For nearly 1,000 years the mud-and-straw adobe walls of Taos Pueblo have sheltered Tiwa-speaking Native Americans. A United Nations World Heritage Site, this is the largest collection of multistory pueblo dwellings in the United States. The pueblo's main buildings, Hlauuma (north house) and Hlaukwima (south house), are separated by a creek. These structures are believed to be of a similar age, probably built between 1000 and 1450. But the entire site is covered in the UN World Heritage designation. The dwellings have common walls but no connecting doorways—the Tiwas gained access only from the top, via ladders that were retrieved after entering. Small buildings and corrals are scattered about.

FodorśChoice ★

The pueblo today appears much as it did when the first Spanish explorers arrived in New Mexico in 1540. The adobe walls glistening with mica caused the conquistadors to believe they had discovered one of the fabled Seven Cities of Gold. The outside surfaces are continuously maintained by replastering with thin layers of mud, and the interior walls are frequently coated with thin washes of white clay. Some walls are several feet thick in places. The roofs of each of the five-story structures are supported by large timbers, or vigas, hauled down from the mountain forests. Pine or aspen *latillas* (smaller pieces of wood) are placed side by side between the vigas; the entire roof is then packed with dirt.

Even after 400 years of Spanish and Anglo presence in Taos, inside the pueblo the traditional Native American way of life has endured. Tribal custom allows no electricity or running water in Hlauuma and Hlaukwima, where varying numbers (usually fewer than 100) of Taos Native Americans live full-

time. About 2,000 others live in conventional homes on the pueblo's 95,000 acres. The crystal-clear Rio Pueblo de Taos, originating high above in the mountains at the sacred Blue Lake, is the primary source of water for drinking and irrigating. Bread is still baked in *hornos* (outdoor domed ovens). Artisans of the Taos Pueblo produce and sell (tax-free) traditionally handcrafted wares, such as mica-flecked pottery and silver jewelry. Great hunters, the Taos Native Americans are also known for their work with animal skins and their excellent moccasins, boots, and drums.

Although the population is about 80% Catholic, the people of Taos Pueblo, like most Pueblo Native Americans, also maintain their native religious traditions. At Christmas and other sacred holidays, for instance, immediately after Mass, dancers dressed in seasonal sacred garb proceed down the aisle of St. Jerome Chapel, drums beating and rattles shaking, to begin other religious rites.

The pueblo **Church of San Geronimo**, or St. Jerome, the patron saint of Taos Pueblo, was completed in 1850 to replace the one destroyed by the U.S. Army in 1847 during the Mexican War. With its smooth symmetry, stepped portal, and twin bell towers, the church is a popular subject for photographers and artists (though the taking of photographs inside is discouraged).

The public is invited to certain ceremonial dances held throughout the year: January 1, Turtle Dance; January 6, Buffalo or Deer Dance; May 3, Feast of Santa Cruz Foot Race and Corn Dance; June 13, Feast of San Antonio Corn Dance; June 24, Feast of San Juan Corn Dance; second weekend in July, Taos Pueblo Powwow; July 25 and 26, Feast of Santa Ana and Santiago Corn Dance; September 29 and 30, Feast of San Geronimo Sunset Dance; December 24, Vespers and Bonfire Procession; December 25, Deer Dance or Matachines. While you're at the pueblo, respect the RESTRICTED AREA signs that protect the privacy of residents and native religious sites; do not enter private homes or open any doors not clearly labeled as curio shops; do not photograph tribal members without asking permission; do not enter the cemetery grounds; and do not wade in the Rio Pueblo de Taos, which is considered sacred and is the community's sole source of drinking water.

The small, rather prosaic, and smoke-free Taos Mountain Casino (open daily) is just off Camino del Pueblo after you turn right off Paseo del Pueblo on your way to the main pueblo. ⊠ *Head to right off Paseo del Pueblo Norte just past Best Western Kachina Lodge* ☎ *575/758–1028*

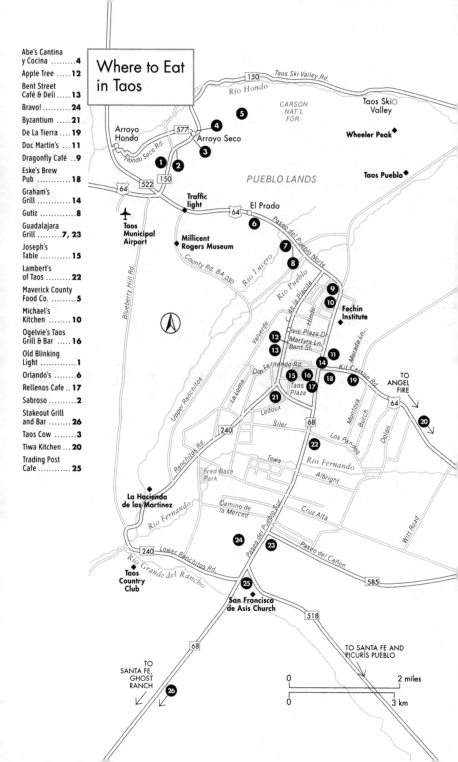

Abe's Cantina
y Cocina **4**

Apple Tree **12**

Bent Street
Café & Deli **13**

Bravo! **24**

Byzantium **21**

De La Tierra **19**

Doc Martin's ...**11**

Dragonfly Café ..**9**

Eske's Brew
Pub **18**

Graham's
Grill **14**

Gutiz **8**

Guadalajara
Grill **7, 23**

Joseph's
Table **15**

Lambert's
of Taos **22**

Maverick County
Food Co. **5**

Michael's
Kitchen **10**

Ogelvie's Taos
Grill & Bar **16**

Old Blinking
Light **1**

Orlando's **6**

Rellenos Cafe ..**17**

Sabroso **2**

Stakeout Grill
and Bar **26**

Taos Cow **3**

Tiwa Kitchen ...**20**

Trading Post
Cafe **25**

Where to Eat in Taos

⊕*www.taospueblo.com* 🖃*Tourist fees $10. Guided tours by appt. Still-camera permit $5; note: cameras that may look commercial, such as those with telephoto lenses, might be denied a permit; video-camera permit $5. Commercial photography, sketching, or painting only by prior permission from governor's office (575/758–1028); fees vary; apply at least 10 days in advance* ☉*Mon.–Sat., 8–5, Sun. 8:30–5. Closed for funerals, religious ceremonies, and for 2-month quiet time in late winter or early spring, and last part of Aug.; call ahead before visiting at these times.*

NEED A BREAK?

Look for signs that read FRY BREAD on dwellings in the pueblo: you can enter the kitchen and buy a piece of fresh bread dough that's flattened and deep-fried until puffy and golden brown and then topped with honey or powdered sugar. You also can buy delicious bread that's baked daily in the clay hornos (outdoor adobe ovens) that are scattered throughout the pueblo.

WHERE TO EAT

For a place as remote as Taos, the dining scene is surprisingly varied. You can find the usual coffee shops and Mexican-style eateries but also restaurants serving creatively prepared Continental, Asian, and Southwestern cuisine.

WHAT IT COSTS				
¢	$	$$	$$$	$$$$
Restaurants under $10	$10–$17	$18–$24	$25–$32	over $32

Prices are for a main course, excluding 8.25% sales tax.

¢
CAFÉ
✕**Abe's Cantina y Cocina.** Family-owned and -operated since the 1940s, Abe's is both store and restaurant. You can have your breakfast burrito, rolled tacos, or homemade tamales at one of the small tables crowded next to the canned goods, or take it on a picnic. ⊠*489 NM 150, Taos Ski Valley Rd., Arroyo Seco* 🕾*575/776–8643* ▭*AE, D, MC, V* ☉*Closed Sun.*

★ $$
ECLECTIC
✕**Apple Tree.** Named for the large tree in its umbrella-shaded courtyard, this terrific lunch and dinner spot is in a historic adobe just a block from the Plaza. Among the well-crafted dishes are mango-chicken enchiladas, vegetarian calabasa quesadillas, and barbecued duck fajitas. The restaurant has an outstanding wine list. Sunday brunch is great fun here—dig into a plate of Papas Tapadas (two eggs any style over seasoned homefries, with red or green chili, and topped with white cheddar. Expect a bit of a wait if you don't have a reservation. ⊠*123 Bent St.* 🕾*575/758–1900* ⊕*www.appletreerestaurant.com* ▭*AE, D, DC, MC, V.*

★ $
CAFÉ
✕**Bent Street Cafe & Deli.** Try for a seat on the cheery, covered outdoor patio next to giant sunflowers. You can enjoy a breakfast burrito, homemade granola, fresh baked goods, dozens of deli sandwiches, tortilla soup and homemade chili. Your meal can be topped off with a

chocolate nut brownie and accompanied by beer, wine, and gourmet coffees. Friendly service is rendered in an old-fashioned country kitchen atmosphere, complete with frilly curtains. Open 8–3. ✉ *120-M Bent St.* ☎*575/758–5787* ⊟*MC, V.*

$ ✕**Bravo!** This restaurant and full
AMERICAN bar inside an upscale grocery, beer, and wine shop, is a great stop for gourmet picnic fixings or an on-site meal on the outdoor patio. You can feast on anything from a turkey sandwich to lobster-and-shrimp ravioli to well-prepared pizzas. The beer and wine selection is formidable. ✉ *1353–A Paseo del Pueblo Sur* ☎*575/758–8100* ⊕*www.bravotaos.com* ⌔*Reservations not accepted* ⊟*AE, MC, V* ⊘*Closed Sun.*

★ **$$** ✕**Byzantium.** Off a grassy courtyard near the Blumenschein and Har-
CONTEMPORARY wood museums, this traditional-looking adobe restaurant offers an eclectic menu. Asian, European, and Middle Eastern influences can be tasted in dishes like Chilean sea bass poached in coconut lemon grass, tandoori quail, and sizzling mussels on the half shell. Service is friendly, and the vibe is low-key—this is a spot relatively few tourists find out about. ✉ *11-C La Placita* ☎*575/751–0805* ⊟*AE, MC, V* ⊘*Closed Tues. and Wed. No lunch.*

★ **$$$** ✕**De La Tierra.** A dashing, dramatic, high-ceiling restaurant inside the
CONTEMPORARY fancifully plush El Monte Sagrado resort, this chic spot presents daring globally influenced cuisine. Top starters include roasted garlic soup and tandoori chicken and a butter lettuce salad with stone fruit and sherry vinaigrette. Among the mains, you can't go wrong with the roasted duck with black bean pilaf and mango mole or the pistachio crusted pork tenderloin with red chili demi-glace. Buttermilk churros with pistachio anglaise makes for a happy ending. It's dressy by Taos standards, but you'll still fit in wearing smartly casual threads. ✉ *317 Kit Carson Rd., El Monte Sagrado Resort* ☎*575/758–3502.* ⊕*www.elmontesagrado.com* ⊟*AE, D, DC, MC, V.*

$$ ✕**Doc Martin's.** The restaurant of the Historic Taos Inn takes its name
CONTEMPORARY from the building's original owner, a local physician who saw patients in the rooms that are now the dining areas. The creative menu includes wild salmon with roasted pepper sauce, pepper-crusted buffalo strip steak with bourbon demi-glace and a pan-seared halibut with mint chipoltle vinaigrette. There's an extensive wine list, and the adjoining Adobe Bar serves up some of the best margaritas in town. In winter ask for a table near the cozy kiva fireplace. ✉ *Historic Taos Inn, 125 Paseo del Pueblo Norte* ☎*575/758–1977* ⊕*www.taosinn.com* ⊟*AE, D, MC, V.*

WORD OF MOUTH

"I just moved to Taos about a year ago and have been trying lots of new restaurants...Here are my recommendations for dining in Taos:

"Orlando's—Just north of the plaza/downtown area. Excellent New Mexican with a few good vegetarian options.

"Graham's Grille—On the main road. Pretty good variety on their menu. A few veg options. Much more affordable at lunch too.

"Guadalajara Grill (southside)— Great taqueria. Great prices too."
—creativejen

3

$ ✕ **Dragonfly Café.** This charming café bakes its own bread and serves
CAFÉ   a variety of ethnic specialties including organic Asian salads, Middle
Eastern lamb served with a Greek salad, hummus and pita bread, cur-
ried chicken salad, bison burgers and Vietnamese chicken salad. You
can sit out front on a shaded outdoor patio with a fountain when it's
warm and watch the tourists go by. Dragonfly also does a brisk mail-
order business with its red chili–infused truffles, delicious granola, and
many other tasty products. Open Wed. to Sat. 11—9, 9–3 on Sunday.
⊠*402 Paseo del Pueblo Norte* ☏*575/737–5859* ⊕*www.dragonfly*
taos.com ▭*MC, V* ☽Closed Mon. and Tues.

$ ✕ **Eske's Brew Pub.** This casual dining and quaffing pub is favored by
AMERICAN   off-duty ski patrollers and river guides. The menu mostly covers hearty
sandwiches (try the grilled bratwurst and sauerkraut sandwich), soups,
and salads. The microbrewery downstairs produces everything from
nutty, dark stout to light ales, but you shouldn't leave without sampling the house specialty—Taos green-chili beer. There's live music on
weekends, and in good weather you can relax on the patio. ⊠*106 Des
Georges La.* ☏*575/758–1517* ⊕*www.eskesbrewpub.com* ▭*MC, V.*

★ **$** ✕ **Guadalajara Grill.** Some of the tastiest Mexican food this side of the
MEXICAN   border makes the well-priced menu of this relaxed and friendly establishment so popular there's a location on both the north and south ends
of town. It's ultracasual here (you select your own beer from a cooler,
and order from the counter). The extensive menu includes grilled fish
tacos served in soft homemade tortillas, shrimp with garlic sauce, bulg-
ing burritos smothered in red or green chili, and for the adventurous,
shark enchiladas. ⊠*822 Paseo del Pueblo Norte* ☏*575/737–0816*
⊠*1384 Paseo del Pueblo Sur* ☏*575/751–0063* ▭*MC, V.*

$ ✕ **Graham's Grille.** The folks who frequent this upscale bar and eatery
CONTEMPORARY   tend to be hip, sophisticated, and good-looking—just like the artful
food served in this minimalist environment. Local, seasonal produce,
cage-free chickens, and homemade stocks are key to the fresh flavors
and creative combinations prepared by chef Leslie Fay, a long-time
Taos restaurateur. Small plates worth sampling include grilled artichoke with lemon aioli, creole crab cakes with green chili remoulade,
and corn and crab chowder. Main courses range from buffalo burgers
to fancy grilled salmon topped with pink grapefruit, orange and avocado salsa. Worthy desserts include a coconut cake with mango cream
and a lemon and pinon pound cake with blueberry coulis. ⊠ *106 Paseo
del Pueblo Norte,* ☏*575/751-1350* ◁*reservations accepted* ▭*AE,
MC, V* ☽ *Closed Sun.*

$ ✕ **Gutiz.** When French, Spanish, and South American culinary influ-
FUSION   ences combine, the result is the menu at Gutiz, a casual eatery on the
north end of town. Best bets for breakfast include cinnamon French
toast made with thick homemade bread or a baked omelet topped with
a green tapenade. Lunch favorites might include a warm salad
nicoise and *chicharon de pollo*—fried chicken tenders topped with
hot aji Amarillo sauce. Dinner is served Wednesday through Sunday
and includes nightly specials. Meals are served on a gravel patio or
inside the small lilac-hued dining room with views of the open kitchen.

✉ *812B Paseo del Pueblo North,* ☎ *575/758-1226* ⚓ *Reservations not accepted* ▭ *No credit cards* ⊙ *Closed Monday.*

★ **$$$**
CONTEMPORARY

✕ **Joseph's Table.** Locally renowned chef Joseph Wrede has moved around the area a bit in recent years, but has settled into what he does best—overseeing his own swank yet friendly restaurant in the La Fonda Hotel on the Taos Plaza. Amid artful surroundings of giant flowers hand-painted on walls, you can sample some of the most innovative and masterfully prepared cuisine tuna tartar with fresh mango and avocado salsa, before moving on to ruby trout with pinot noir reduction and fried capers. But the masterpiece here is pepper-crusted beef tenderloin with madiera mushroom sauce. Lighter fare, including addictive duck-fat fries, are available at the bar, and there's an astounding wine list. ✉ *108–A S. Taos Plaza, La Fonda Hotel* ☎ *575/751–4512* ⊕ *www.josephstable.com* ▭ *AE, D, DC, MC, V.*

$$$
Fodor'sChoice
★
CONTINENTAL

✕ **Lambert's of Taos.** Superb service and creative cuisine define this Taos landmark located 2½ blocks south of the Plaza. Don't miss the marinated roasted beet salad with warm goat cheese and pumpkin seeds, Dungeness crab cakes with Thai curry, or corn and applewood smoked bacon chowder appetizers. Or have all three and call it a night. The signature entrees include, pepper-crusted lamb with a red-wine demiglace, and roasted duck with an apricot chipotle glaze. Memorable desserts are a warm apple and almond crisp topped with white chocolate ice cream and a dark chocolate mouse with raspberry sauce. A small plate bistro menu is available in the cozy bar or in the spacious dining rooms. The lengthy wine list includes some of California's finest vintages. ✉ *309 Paseo del Pueblo Sur* ☎ *575/758–1009* ▭ *AE, D, DC, MC, V* ⊙ *No lunch.*

$
AMERICAN

✕ **Maverick County Food Co.** If you like casual and friendly eateries with unfussy fare and great desserts you'll feel right at home in this out-of-the-way local's choice. Chef Sheila Guzman serves up masterful buffalo and beef burgers, curries, Asian bowls, and simple salads. Save room for the mile-high coconut cake, fresh seasonal fruit pies, and bourbon chocolate cake. Open 11–4. ✉ *480 State Road 150, Arroyo Seco, 87514* ☎ *575/776-0900* ⚓ *No reservations* ▭ *No credit cards* ⊙ *Closed Sun. and Mon.*

$
AMERICAN

✕ **Michael's Kitchen.** This casual, homey restaurant serves up a bit of everything—you can have a hamburger while your friend who can't get enough chili sauce can order up vegetarian cheese enchiladas garnished with lettuce and tomatoes. Brunch is popular with the locals (dig into a plate of strawberry-banana-pecan pancakes), and amusing asides to the waitstaff over the intercom contribute to the energetic buzz. Breakfast, lunch, and dinner are served daily, but you must order dinner by 8:30 PM. ✉ *304 Paseo del Pueblo Norte* ☎ *575/758-4178* ⊕ *www.michaels kitchen.com* ⚓ *Reservations not accepted* ▭ *AE, D, MC, V.*

$$
AMERICAN

✕ **Ogelvie's Taos Grill and Bar.** On the second floor of an old two-story adobe building, touristy but festive Ogelvie's is the perfect spot for people-watching from on high, especially from the outdoor patio in summer. You won't find any culinary surprises here, just dependable meat-and-potato dishes. The sure bets are filet mignon with brandy-cream sauce, lamb sirloin with rosemary aioli, and blue-corn enchiladas stuffed with beef or chicken. There's live music many nights. ⊠*103 E. Plaza* ☎*575/758–8866* ⊕*www.ogelvies.com* ⌕*Reservations not accepted* ⊟*AE, D, MC, V.*

$$
NEW MEXICAN
✕**Old Blinking Light.** Just past the landmark "old blinking light" (now a regular stoplight at Mile Marker 1), this rambling adobe is known for its steaks, ribs, and enormous (and potent) margaritas. There's also a long list of tasty appetizers, such as posole stew and chipotle-shrimp quesadillas. Several huge burgers are available, plus first-rate chicken mole. In summer you can sit out in the walled garden and take in the spectacular mountain view. There's a wineshop on the premises. ⊠*Mile Marker one, Taos Ski Valley Rd., between El Prado and Arroyo Seco* ☎*575/776–8787* ⊕*www.oldblinkinglight. com* ⊟*AE, MC, V* ⊘*No lunch.*

★ ¢
NEW MEXICAN
✕**Orlando's.** This family-run local favorite is likely to be packed during peak hours, while guests wait patiently to devour favorites such as *carne adovada* (red chili–marinated pork), blue-corn enchiladas, and scrumptious shrimp burritos. You can eat in the cozy dining room, outside on the front patio, or call ahead for takeout if you'd rather avoid the crowds. ⊠*114 Don Juan Valdez La., off Paseo del Pueblo Norte* ☎*575/751–1450* ⊟*MC, V* ⊘.

$
NEW MEXICAN
✕**Rellenos Cafe.** Touted as the only organic New Mexican restaurant in town, this casual eatery also serves wheat-free, gluten-free, and vegan menu options on request. Popular specialties served on the casual outdoor patio include killer chiles rellenos topped with a brandy cream sauce, grilled garlic shrimp, and seafood paella. Service is friendly, the clientele largely local. The house drink, a fruity sangria, is served in gargantuan Mexican glasses. ⊠*135 Paseo del Pueblo Sur,* ☎*575/758–7001.* ⌕ *Reservations not accepted* ⊟*MC, V* ⊘ *Closed Sun.*

★ **$$$**
CONTEMPORARY
✕**Sabroso.** Reasonably priced, innovative cuisine and outstanding wines are served in this 150-year-old adobe hacienda, where you can also relax in lounge chairs near the bar, or on a delightful patio surrounded by plum trees. The Mediterranean-influenced contemporary menu changes regularly, but an evening's entrée might be pan-seared sea scallops, risotto cakes, and ratatouille, or ribeye steak topped with a slice of Stilton cheese. There's live jazz and cabaret in the piano bar several nights a week. Order from the simpler bar menu if you're seeking something light—the antipasto plate and white-truffle-oil fries are both delicious. ⊠*470 NM 150, Taos Ski Valley Rd.* ☎*575/776–3333* ⊕*www.sabrosotaos.com* ⊟*AE, MC, V* ⊘ *No lunch.*

$$$$
Fodor'sChoice
★
STEAK
✕**Stakeout Grill and Bar.** On Outlaw Hill in the foothills of the Sangre de Cristo Mountains, this old adobe homestead has 100-mi-long views and sunsets that dazzle. The outdoor patio encircled by a piñon forest has kiva fireplaces to warm you during cooler months. The decadent fare is well-prepared, fully living up to the view it accompanies—try filet mignon with bearnaise, buffalo rib eye with chipotle cilantro butter, almond-crusted wild sockeye salmon with shaved fennel, kurabuta pork rack with red wine sauce. Don't miss the tasty Kentucky bourbon pecan pie and crème brûlée with toasted coconut for dessert. ⊠*Stakeout Dr., 8 mi south of Taos Plaza, east of NM 68, look for cowboy sign* ☎*575-758-2042* ⊟*AE, D, DC, MC, V* ⊘*No lunch.*

★ ¢ ✕**Taos Cow.** Locals, travelers headed up to Taos Ski Valley, and visitors
CAFÉ to funky Arroyo Seco rejoiced when the famed Taos Cow ice-cream
company opened this cozy storefront café in 1994. This isn't merely a
place to sample amazing homemade ice cream (including such innovative flavors as piñon-caramel, lavender, and Chocolate Rio Grande–
(chocolate ice cream packed with cinnamon-chocolate chunks). You
can also nosh on French toast, omelets, turkey-and–Brie sandwiches,
black bean–and–brown rice bowls, organic teas and coffees, natural
sodas, homemade granola, and more. The friendly staff and burning incense lend a hippie-dippie vibe to the place. ✉*485 NM 150*
☎*575/776–5640* ⊕*www.taoscow.com* ▤*MC, V* ⊘*No dinner.*

¢ ✕**Tiwa Kitchen.** This one-of-a-kind restaurant, even for Taos, serves
NATIVE AMERI- authentic Native American food in a casual setting. Ben White Buf-
CAN falo and his wife Debbie Moonlight Flowers organically grow much
of the restaurant's ingredients themselves and use traditional beehive
wood-fired ovens just outside the back door for baking corn and roasting peppers. Try the blue corn taco made with blue corn fry bread or
grilled buffalo sausage served with red or green chili. ✉*328 Veterans
Highway (Taos Pueblo Road),* ☎*575/751-1020.* ⚑*Reservations not
accepted* ▤*No credit cards* ⊘*Closed Tues., and for six weeks in the
spring during the Pueblo's traditional "quiet time."*

★ $$ ✕**Trading Post Cafe.** Local hipsters outnumber tourists at this casual
CONTEMPORARY spot. Intelligent and attentive service along with well-presented con-
temporary Southwestern art makes any meal a pleasure. For starters try
the signature noodle soup or minestrone with smoked ham before mov-
ing on to an oven-roasted duck with seasonal vegetables and creamy
mashed potatoes or any of the traditional pasta dishes. Supurb desserts
include a coconut cream pie and rich strawberry shortcake. To park,
turn east onto NM 518 (Talpa Road) just north of the restaurant, and
then walk back along Talpa Road to get to the entrance. ✉*4179 Paseo
del Pueblo Sur, NM 68, Ranchos de Taos* ☎*575/758–5089* ▤*AE, D,
MC, V* ⊘*Closed Mon. No lunch Sun.*

WHERE TO STAY

The hotels and motels along NM 68 (Paseo del Pueblo Sur and Norte)
suit every need and budget; with a few exceptions, rates vary little
between big-name chains and smaller establishments. Make advance
reservations and expect higher rates during the ski season (usually from
late December to early April) and in the summer. Skiers have many
choices for overnighting, from accommodations in the town of Taos to
spots snuggled up right beside the slopes, although several of the hotels
up at Taos Ski Valley have been converted to condos in recent years,
eroding the supply of overnight accommodations. Arroyo Seco is a
good alternative if you can't find a room right up in the Ski Valley.

The best deals in town are the bed-and-breakfasts. Mostly family-
owned, they provide personal service, delicious breakfasts, and many
extras that hotels charge for. The B&Bs are often in old adobes that
have been refurbished with style and flair. Many have "casitas," private
cottages or lodges separate from the main building.

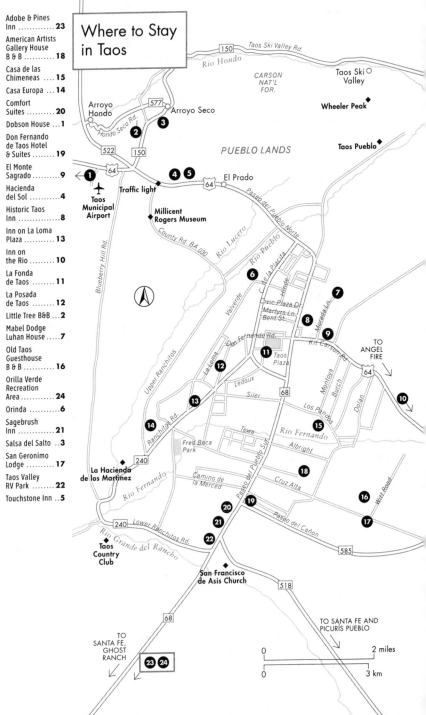

Adobe & Pines Inn **23**

American Artists Gallery House B & B **18**

Casa de las Chimeneas **15**

Casa Europa ... **14**

Comfort Suites **20**

Dobson House ... **1**

Don Fernando de Taos Hotel & Suites **19**

El Monte Sagrado **9**

Hacienda del Sol **4**

Historic Taos Inn **8**

Inn on La Loma Plaza **13**

Inn on the Rio **10**

La Fonda de Taos **11**

La Posada de Taos **12**

Little Tree B&B .. **2**

Mabel Dodge Luhan House **7**

Old Taos Guesthouse B & B **16**

Orilla Verde Recreation Area **24**

Orinda **6**

Sagebrush Inn **21**

Salsa del Salto .. **3**

San Geronimo Lodge **17**

Taos Valley RV Park **22**

Touchstone Inn .. **5**

Where to Stay in Taos

WHAT IT COSTS					
	¢	$	$$	$$$	$$$$
Hotels	under $70	$70–$130	$131–$190	$191–$260	over $260

Prices are for a standard double room in high season, excluding 10%–12% tax.

DOWNTOWN TAOS

3

$$ ▦ **Adobe & Pines Inn.** Native American and Mexican artifacts decorate the main house of this B&B, which has expansive mountain views. Part of the main adobe building dates from 1830. The rooms and suites contain Mexican-tile baths, kiva fireplaces, and fluffy goose-down pillows and comforters, plus such modern touches as flat-screen TVs, DVD players, Wi-Fi, and CD players. Separate casitas and suites are more spacious and offer plenty of seclusion, with private entrances and courtyard access. The owners serve gourmet breakfasts in a sunny glass-enclosed patio. **Pros:** Quiet rural location; fantastic views. **Cons:** Not in town; some bedrooms are small. ⊠ *NM 68* ⌂ *Box 837, Ranchos de Taos 87557* ☎ *575/751–0947 or 800/723–8267* ⊕ *www.adobepines.com* 📞 *4 rooms, 2 suites, 2 casitas* ⚐ *In-room: minirefrigerators (some), kitchenette (some), DVD, Wi-Fi. In-hotel: pets allowed* ⊟ *MC, V* ⦿ *BP.*

★ **$$** ▦ **American Artists Gallery House Bed & Breakfast.** Each of the immaculate adobe-style rooms and suites here is called a "gallery," and owners LeAn and Charles Clamurro have taken care to decorate them with local arts and crafts. Some have Jacuzzis and all have kiva fireplaces; one family-friendly suite has a full kitchen; and all have private entrances, wood-burning fireplaces, and front porches where you can admire the view of Taos Mountain. Sumptuous hot breakfasts—along with conversation and suggestions about local attractions—are served up at a community table in the main house each morning, where you can often see the resident peacock, George, preening outside the windows. **Pros:** Private entrances. True gourmet breakfast. **Cons:** Some rooms have small bathrooms; small common room. ⊠ *132 Frontier La., Box 584,* ☎ *575/758–4446 or 800/532–2041* 🖷 *575/758–0497* ⊕ *www.taosbedandbreakfast.com* 📞 *7 rooms, 3 suites* ⚐ *In-room: Wi-Fi, kitchen (some), refrigerator (some), VCR (some). In-hotel: some pets allowed (fee)* ⊟ *AE, D, DC, MC, V* ⦿ *BP.*

★ **$$$** ▦ **Casa de las Chimeneas.** Tile hearths, French doors, and traditional viga ceilings grace the "House of Chimneys" B&B, 2½ blocks from the Plaza and secluded behind thick walls. Each room in the 1912 structure has a private entrance, a fireplace, handmade New Mexican furniture, bathrooms with Talavera tiles, and a bar stocked with complimentary beverages. All rooms overlook the gardens, and facilities include a small but excellent spa offering a wide range of treatments. Two-course breakfasts are included, as are full evening meals. **Pros:** Private setting. In-house spa. **Cons:** 30-day cancellation policy. ⊠ *405 Cordoba Rd., Box 5303,* ☎ *575/758–4777 or 877/758–4777* 🖷 *575/758–3976* ⊕ *www.visittaos.com* 📞 *6 rooms, 2 suites* ⚐ *In-room: refrigerator* *(some), VCR. In-hotel: gym, spa, laundry facilities, no-smoking rooms, minirefrigerator, Wi-Fi* ☐AE, D, DC, MC, V ⦶MAP.

$$ ☷ **Casa Europa.** The main part of this exquisite 18th-century adobe estate has been tastefully expanded to create an unforgettable B&B with old world romance. Each room is furnished with hand-picked European antiques accented with Southwestern accessories. The two main common areas are light and airy, with comfortable chairs to relax in while the fireplace crackles. Breakfasts are elaborate, and complimentary homemade afternoon baked treats are served. Although the property is under two miles for the plaza, its pastoral setting makes it feel a world away. Innkeepers Lisa and Joe McCutcheon take personal pride in offering their guests every courtesy and assistance. **Pros:** Attentive service; memorable setting and sophisticated style. **Cons:** No elevator to second floor; short drive to town. ⊠*840 Upper Ranchitos Rd.* ⌂*HC 68, Box 3F, 87571* ☎*888/758–9798* 📠*575/758–9798* ⦶*www.casaeuropanm.com* ⦕*5 rooms, 2 suites* &In-room: VCR (some). In-hotel: bars, some pets allowed (fee)* ☐AE, D, MC, V ⦶BP.

$ ☷ **Comfort Suites.** Clean and comfortable rooms make this property one of better chain options in town. The units are large (technically they're not full suites but rather rooms with large sitting areas) and have a sense of Southwestern style. The lobby has a kiva fireplace surrounded by *nichos*—enclaves where statues are placed. Guests have access to the Sagebrush Inn facilities next door. **Pros:** One of the newest chains in town; good value. **Cons:.** Cookie-cutter décor; concrete patio around the pool. ⊠*1500 Paseo del Pueblo Sur, Box 1268,* ☎*575/751–1555 or 888/751–1555* ⦶*www.taoshotels.com/comfortsuites* ⦕*60 rooms* &*In-room: Ethernet, refrigerator. In-hotel: pool, Wi-Fi* ☐AE, D, DC, MC, V ⦶CP.

$$ ☷ **Dobson House.** Guests who book one of the two private suites at this eco-tourist destination can help preserve the environment in style. This eclectic B&B relies primarily on passive heating and cooling and electricity is provided by solar panels. In addition, the 6,000-square-foot residence, within walking distance of the Rio Grande gorge was built by hand by innkeepers Joan and John Dobson using 2,000 old tires, 20,000 recycled aluminum cans, and 28,000 pounds of dry cement and packed earth. Even so, guests live luxuriously with Ralph Lauren linens, and Joan's full-on breakfasts of Texas pecan biscuits, chicken-apple sausage and Mexican baked eggs. The couples' sophisticated art collection adorns the home's authentic adobe walls. **Pros:** Environmentally friendly; one-of-a-kind accommodation; serene and private. **Cons:** A long drive to town for dinner; hard to find. ⊠*475 Tune Drive, El Prado* ☎*575/776-5738* ⦶ *www.new-mexico–Bed-and–Breakfast.com* ⦕*2 suites* &*In-room: no a/c, no phone, no TV. In-hotel, no pets, no kids under 14* ☐*no credit cards* ⦶ BP.

$ ☷ **Don Fernando de Taos Hotel.** The accommodations at this hotel are grouped around central courtyards and connected by walkways. The hotel-style rooms are appointed with Southwestern furnishings, and some rooms have fireplaces. A glassed-in atrium with sliding side doors and roof panels surrounds the pool. There's a free shuttle to take guests to the town center. **Pros:** Large rooms; indoor pool. **Cons:** Spread out; highway noise. ⌧ *1005 Paseo del Pueblo Sur,* ☎ *575/758–4444 or 800/759–2736* 🖷 *575/758–0055* ⊕ *www.donfernandodetaos.com* 🛏 *110 rooms, 14 suites* ♿ *In-room: Wi-Fi, refrigerator (some). In-hotel: restaurant, bar, pool, laundry service* ▤ *AE, D, DC, MC, V.*

$$$$

Fodor'sChoice

★ 🖿 **El Monte Sagrado.** Pricey but classy (although the resort has lowered its rates a bit in recent years), El Monte Sagrado is an eco-sensitive New Age haven offering all manner of amenities, from alternative therapies like milk-and-honey body wraps to cooking and wine classes. A short drive away, the property has an expansive ranch property that's available for you to explore on horseback or on foot. Suites and casitas are accented with exotic themes, ranging from Native American designs to foreign flourishes from faraway lands including Japan or Tibet. A popular outdoor area dubbed the Sacred Circle is a patch of grassy land encircled by cottonwoods. The on-site restaurant, De la Tierra, serves daring cuisine. **Pros:** Eco-friendly. Exotic and sophisticated. **Cons:** Sprawling property not easily walkable. ⌧ *317 Kit Carson Rd.,* ☎ *575/758–3502 or 800/828–8267* 🖷 *575/737–2980* ⊕ *www.elmontesagrado.com* 🛏 *48 rooms, 6 casitas, 30 suites,* ♿ *In-room: kitchen (some), refrigerator (some), VCR, Wi-Fi. In-hotel: 2 restaurants, room service, bar, pool, gym, spa, bicycles, concierge, children's programs (ages 4–12), laundry service, some pets allowed (fee), minibar* ▤ *AE, D, DC, MC, V.*

★ $$$

🖿 **Hacienda del Sol.** Art patron Mabel Dodge Luhan bought this house in the 1920s and lived here with her husband, Tony Luhan, while building their main house. It was also their private retreat and guesthouse for visiting notables; Frank Waters wrote *People of the Valley* here— other guests have included Willa Cather and D. H. Lawrence. Most of the rooms contain kiva fireplaces, Southwestern handcrafted furniture, and original artwork, and all have CD players. Certain adjoining rooms can be combined into suites. Breakfast is a gourmet affair that might include huevos rancheros or Belgian waffles. Perhaps above all else, the "backyards" of the rooms and the secluded outdoor hot tub have a view of Taos Mountain s. **Pros:** Cozy public rooms, Private setting. **Cons:** Traffic noise; some rooms are less private than others. ⌧ *109 Mabel Dodge La., Box 177,* ☎ *575/758–0287 or 866/333–4459* 🖷 *575/758–5895* ⊕ *www.taoshaciendadelsol.com* 🛏 *11 rooms* ♿ *In-room: WiFi, refrigerator (some), no TV* ▤ *AE, D, MC, V* ⍾ *BP.*

★ $$

🖿 **Historic Taos Inn.** Mere steps from Taos Plaza, the inn is listed on the National Register of Historic Places. Spanish-colonial-style architecture including decorative alcoves in rooms provides an authentic feel to this atmospheric property that consists of four buildings, including the upscale Helen's House, which was added in 2006 and contains eight posh rooms. Many rooms have been updated and the older ones have thick adobe walls, viga ceilings, and other elements typical of vintage Taos architecture. In summer there's dining alfresco on the patio. The lobby, which also serves as seating for the Adobe Bar, is built around an old town well from which a fountain bubbles forth. The plaza and many shops and eateries are within walking distance of the inn, and the restaurant, Doc Martin's, is popular with locals. **Pros:** Across from the plaza location; lushly furnished rooms. **Cons:** Street noise; bar noise. ⊠*125 Paseo del Pueblo Norte,* ☎*575/758–2233 or 888/518–8267* 🖷*575/758–5776* ⊕*www.taosinn.com* 📞*43 rooms, 3 suites* ��*In-hotel: restaurant, bar* ⊟*AE, DC, MC, V.*

★ **$$$$** 🖼**Inn on La Loma Plaza.** The walls surrounding this Pueblo Revival building date from the early 1800s; the inn itself is listed on the National Register of Historic Places. The rooms have kiva fireplaces, CD stereos, coffeemakers, and Mexican-tile bathrooms, and many have private patios or decks. The living room has a well-stocked library with books on Taos and art. Owners Jerry and Peggy Davis provide helpful advice about the area and serve a generous breakfast, afternoon snacks, and evening coffee. Guests have privileges at the nearby health club (but the inn has its own hot tub). **Pros:** Towering trees. Inspiring views. **Cons:** Lots of stairs; on a busy street. ⊠*315 Ranchitos Rd., Box 4159,* ☎*575/758–1717 or 800/530–3040* 🖷*575/751–0155* ⊕*www. vacationtaos.com* 📞*5 rooms, 1 suite, 2 studios* ⒒*In-room: kitchen (some), DVD, Wi-Fi* ⊟*AE, D, MC, V* ⦿*BP.*

$ 🖼 **Inn on the Rio.** This property started as a strip motel, but over the years it has been transformed with adobe-style architecture and hand-painted murals into a charming B&B. The overall feel of the rooms can't quite escape their motel roots, but they are tastefully furnished with Southwestern art and linens. A well-tended garden overflowing with wildflowers and herbs surrounds the pool and hot tub area. Innkeepers Robert and Julie Cahalane prepare homemade bread, green chili and egg casseroles, and cinnamon-infused coffee for breakfast. **Pros:** One of the few outdoor heated pools in town; private entrance to each room. **Cons:** Traffic noise; small bathrooms. ⊠*910 E. Kit Carson Road* ☎ *575/758-7199, 800/859-6752* ⊕ *www.innontherio.com* 📞*12 rooms* ⒒*In-room: no a/c, Wi-Fi, some pets allowed. In-hotel: pool, hot tub.* ⊟*AE, D, MC, V.* ⦿ *BP*

$$ 🖼**La Posada de Taos.** A couple of blocks from Taos Plaza, this family-friendly 100-year old inn has beam ceilings, a decorative arched doorway, and the intimacy of a private hacienda. Five guest rooms are in the main house; the sixth is a separate cottage with a king-size bed, sitting room, and fireplace. The rooms all have mountain or courtyard garden views, and some open onto private patios—almost all have kiva-style fireplaces. Breakfasts are hearty. **Pros:** A few blocks from the plaza; historic building. **Cons:** Small rooms; not much privacy in the main house. ⊠*309 Juanita La., Box 1118,* ☎*575/758–8164 or 800/645–4803* 🖷*575/751–4694* ⊕*www.laposadadetaos.com* 📞*5 rooms, 1 cottage* ⒒*In-room: no a/c, no phone, VCR. In hotel: Wi-Fi* ⊟*AE, MC, V* ⦿*BP.*

$$$ 🖼 **La Fonda de Taos.** A much needed interior and exterior renovation has brought this historic property (there's been a hotel on this location since 1840) up to snuff. Its plaza location, upscale rooms and no children under 8 policy make this a great choice for a romantic getaway. The rooms are rustic yet elegant and are furnished in neutral colors with luxury linens and hand-tiled bathrooms. It also the houses the award-winning Joseph's Table restaurant. **Pros:** Location, location, location. **Cons:** Street noise; not family-friendly. ⊠*108 S. Plaza* ☎ *575/758-2211,*

800/833-2211. ⊕*www.hotellafonda.com* ⌫*19 rooms, 5 suites, 1 penthouse* ⟳*In-room: VCR, refrigerator, non-smoking rooms available, Wi-Fi. In-hotel: 2 restaurants, bar, parking (no fee), no kids under 8.* ☰*AE, D, MC, V* ℺ *EP.*

★ $$ ▦**Mabel Dodge Luhan House.** Quirky and offbeat—much like Taos——this National Historic Landmark was once home to the heiress who drew illustrious writers and artists—including D. H. Lawrence, Willa Cather Georgia O'Keeffe, Ansel Adams, Martha Graham, and Carl Jung—to Taos. The main house, which has kept its simple, rustic feel, has nine guest rooms; there are eight more in a modern building, as well as 2 two-bedroom cottages. The house exudes early century elegance and the grounds offer numerous quiet corners for private conversations or solo meditation. Guests can stay in what was Mabel's room, in her hand-carved double bed to be precise; or in the solarium, an airy room at the top of the house which is completely surrounded by glass (and accessible by a ladder). For art-groupies, nothing can quite compare with sleeping in the elegant room Georgia O'Keefe stayed in while visiting. The inn is frequently used for artistic, cultural, and educational workshops, hence the tiny, but exceptional bookstore in the lobby specializing in local authors and artists. **Pros:** Historical relevance; rural setting just blocks from the plaza. **Cons:** Lots of stairs and uneven paths. ✉*240 Morada La.* ☎*575/751–9686 or 800/846–2235* 🖷*575/737–0365* ⊕*www.mabeldodgeluhan.com* ⌫*16 rooms; 1 suite, 2 casitas* ⟳*In-room: no phone, no TV. In-hotel: Wi-Fi.* ☰*AE, MC, V* ℺*BP.*

$$ ▦**Old Taos Guesthouse B&B.** Once a ramshackle 180-year-old adobe hacienda, this homey B&B on 7½ acres has been completely and lovingly outfitted with the owners' hand-carved doors and furniture, Western artifacts, and antiques. There are 80-mi views from the outdoor hot tub and a shady veranda surrounds the courtyard. The owners welcome families. Breakfasts are healthy and hearty. **Pros:** Beautifully appointed; private entrance to each room. **Cons:** Very small bathrooms; some rooms are dark. ✉*1028 Witt Rd., Box 6552,* ☎*575/758–5448 or 800/758–5448* ⊕*www.oldtaos.com* ⌫*7 rooms, 2 suites* ⟳*In-room: no phone (some), kitchen (some), VCR (some). In-hotel: Wi-Fi, some pets allowed (fee)* ☰*D, MC, V* ℺*BP.*

$$$ ▦**Orinda.** Built in 1947, this adobe estate has spectacular views and country privacy. The rustic rooms have separate entrances, kiva-style fireplaces, traditional viga ceilings, and Mexican-tile baths. Some of the rooms can be combined with a shared living area into a large suite. One has a Jacuzzi. The hearty breakfast is served family-style in the soaring two-story sun atrium amid a gallery of artworks, all for sale. **Pros:** Most rooms are spacious; gorgeous views of Taos Mountain. **Cons:** Rooms are a little bland; a bit pricey for what is offered. ✉*461 Valverde,* ☎*575/758–8581 or 800/847–1837* 🖷*575/751–0534* ⊕*www.orindabb.com* ⌫*5 rooms* ⟳*In-room: no a/c (some), refrigerator, VCR (some). In-hotel: no-smoking rooms, some pets allowed (fee)* ☰*AE, MC, V* ℺*BP.*

$$ ▦**Sagebrush Inn.** Georgia O'Keeffe once lived and painted in a third-story room of the original inn. These days it's not as upscale—or expensive—as

many other lodging options in Taos, but it has a shaded patio with large trees, a good restaurant, and a collection of antique Navajo rugs. Many of the guest rooms have kiva-style fireplaces; some have balconies. There's country-western music nightly. **Pros:** Good value; nightly music. **Cons:** Very spread out; many of the rooms are dark; traffic noise. ⊠*1508 Paseo del Pueblo Sur, Box 557,* ☎*575/758–2254 or 800/428–3626* 🖶*575/758–5077* ⊕*www.sagebrushinn.com* 🛏*68 rooms, 32 suites* ♿*In-hotel: 2 restaurants, bar, Wi-Fi, pool* ▭*AE, D, DC, MC, V* ⦿*BP.*

★ $$　🏨 **San Geronimo Lodge.** Built in 1925, this property was one of the first resort hotels in Taos and sits on 2½ acres that front majestic Taos Mountain and adjoin the Carson National Forest. New owners Charles and Pam Montgomery are upgrading the rooms as needed, while preserving the property's historical charm and appeal. An extensive library, attractive grounds, rooms with fireplaces and private decks, two rooms designed for people with disabilities, and 5 rooms for guests with pets are among the draws. Hanging Navajo rugs, Talavera-tile bathrooms, and high viga ceilings provide an authentic Southwestern experience. **Pros:** Serene inside and out; extensive common rooms. **Cons.** Hard to find; some rooms have small bathrooms. ⊠*1101 Witt Rd.,* ☎*575/751–3776 or 800/894–4119* 🖶*575/751–1493* ⊕*www.sangeronimolodge. com* 🛏*18 rooms* ♿*In-room: Wi-Fi, VCR (some). In-hotel: pool, some pets allowed (fee)* ▭*AE, D, MC, V* ⦿*BP.*

★ $$$　🏨 **Touchstone Inn.** D. H. Lawrence visited this house in 1929; accordingly, the inn's owner, Taos artist Bren Price, has named many of the antiques-filled rooms after famous Taos literary figures. The grounds overlook part of the Taos Pueblo lands, all within a mile of Taos Plaza. Some rooms have fireplaces. The enormous Royale Suite has a second-story private deck and large bathroom with Jacuzzi, walk-in shower, and skylight. Early-morning coffee is available in the living room, and breakfasts with inventive vegetarian presentations (such as blueberry pancakes with lemon sauce) are served in the glassed-in patio. The adjacent Spa offers a wide range of beauty and skin treatments. **Pros:** Extensive common rooms; impeccably furnished rooms. **Cons:** Highway noise; lots of stairs. ⊠*110 Mabel Dodge La.,* ☎*575/758–0192 or 800/758–0192* 🖶*575/758–3498* ⊕*www.touchstoneinn.com* 🛏*6 rooms, 3 suites* ♿*In-room: VCR. In-hotel: Wi-Fi, spa* ▭*MC, V* ⦿*BP.*

CAMPING

★　⛺ **Orilla Verde Recreation Area.** You can hike, fish, and picnic among trees and sagebrush at this beautiful area along the banks of the Rio Grande, 10 mi south of Ranchos de Taos, off NM 68 at NM 570. The area has four developed campgrounds with running water, flush toilets, and showers. Three primitive campgrounds have vault toilets only. To pay the camping fee, leave cash in an envelope provided, drop it in a tube, and the rangers will collect it (or a volunteer sometimes is on hand to collect payments). 🏕*Bureau of Land Management, 226 Cruz Alta Rd., Taos 87571* ☎*575/758–4060* ♿*Flush toilets, drinking water, fire grates, picnic tables* 🛏*9 RV sites with hookups, 70 developed sites (tent and RV)* ▭*No credit cards.*

⚠ **Taos Valley RV Park and Campground.** The sites are grassy, with a few shade trees, in this park 2½ mi from Taos Plaza near the junction of NM 68 and NM 518. Some RV supplies are for sale. ⊠ *120 Estes Rd., off Paseo del Pueblo Sur, behind Rio Grande Ace Hardware* ✆ *Box 7204, Taos 87571* ☎ *575/758–2524 or 800/999–7571* ⊕ *www.taosnet.com/rv* ♿ *Flush toilets, full hookups, drinking water, showers, picnic tables, electricity, public telephone, Wi-Fi, general store, play area* 🛏 *92 RV sites, 24 tent sites* ⊟ *AE, MC, V. 575/758–2524*

3

ARROYO SECO

★ $$ 🏨 **Little Tree B&B.** In an authentic adobe house in the open country between Taos and the ski valley, Little Tree's rooms are built around a garden courtyard and have magnificent views of Taos Mountain and the high desert that spans for nearly 100 mi to the west. Some have kiva fireplaces and Jacuzzis, and all are decorated in true Southwestern style. **Pros:** Rare opportunity to stay in a real adobe (not stucco) home. Spotless and beautifully maintained. **Cons:**.15-minute drive to Taos. Isolated. ⊠ *226 Hondo Seco Rd., Arroyo Hondo* ✆ *Box 509, 87571* ☎ *575/776–8467 or 800/334–8467* ⊕ *www. littletreebandb.com* 🛏 *4 rooms* ♿ *In-room: Wi-Fi, VCR (some), no TV (some)* ⊟ *MC, V* ⦿ *BP.*

$$ 🏨 **Salsa del Salto.** Rooms at this handsome compound set back from the road to the Ski Valley, just a short drive up from the funky village of Arroyo Seco, are either in the sunny, contemporary main inn building or in separate units with private entrances and a bit more seclusion. The master suite affords panoramic views of the mountains and has a huge bathroom. The Lobo and Kachina rooms are a great value, not as large as some but with romantic glass–Brick showers, high beam ceilings, Saltillo-tile floors with radiant heating. Friendly and helpful owners Pam and Jim Maisey worked for Marriott hotels for 25 years, and it shows. Breakfast is a substantial affair, where you might enjoy a shrimp, mushroom, and provolone omelet or salmon eggs Benedict, and there's always a hearty soup or snack presented in the afternoon. **Pros:**. Spacious rooms. Good access for skiers. **Cons:** Far from cultural attractions in Taos. Feels more like a hotel than a B&B. ⊠ *543 NM 150, Box 1468, El Prado* ☎ *575/776–2422 or 800/530–3097* 🖷 *575/776–5734* ⊕ *www.bandbtaos.com* 🛏 *10 rooms* ♿ *In-room: Cable TV, DVD (some), Wi-Fi. In-hotel: pool* ⊟ *AE, MC, V* ⦿ *BP.*

NIGHTLIFE & THE ARTS

Evening entertainment is modest in Taos. Some motels and hotels present solo musicians or small combos in their bars and lounges. Everything from down-home blues bands to Texas two-step dancing blossoms on Saturday and Sunday nights in winter. In summer things heat up during the week as well. For information about what's going on around town pick up *Taos Magazine*. The weekly *Taos News*, published on Thursday, carries arts and entertainment information in the

"Tempo" section. The arts scene is much more lively, with festivals every season for nearly every taste.

NIGHTLIFE

Fodor'sChoice
★ The **Adobe Bar** (⊠ *Taos Inn, 125 Paseo del Pueblo Norte* ☎ *575/758–2233*), a local meet-and-greet spot known as "Taos's living room," books talented acts, from solo guitarists to small folk groups and, two or three nights a week, jazz musicians.

★ **Alley Cantina** (⊠ *121 Teresina La.* ☎ *575/758–2121*) has jazz, folk, and blues—as well as shuffleboard, pool and board games for those not moved to dance. It's housed in the oldest structure in downtown Taos.

Caffe Tazza (⊠ *122 Kit Carson Rd.* ☎ *575/758–8706*) presents free evening performances throughout the week—folk singing, jazz, belly dancing, blues, poetry, and fiction readings.

Fernando's Hideaway (⊠ *Don Fernando de Taos Hotel & Suites, 1005 Paseo del Pueblo Sur* ☎ *575/758–4444*) occasionally presents live entertainment—jazz, blues, hip-hop, R&B, salsa, and country music. Complimentary happy-hour snacks are laid out on weekday evenings, 5–7.

The **Kachina Lodge Cabaret** (⊠ *413 Paseo del Pueblo Norte* ☎ *575/758–2275*) usually brings in an area radio DJ to liven up various forms of music and dancing.

The **Sagebrush Inn** (⊠ *1508 Paseo del Pueblo Sur* ☎ *575/758–2254*) hosts musicians and dancing in its lobby lounge. There's usually no cover charge for country-western dancing.

The piano bar at **Sabroso** (⊠ *470 CR 150, Arroyo Seco* ☎ *575/776–3333*) often presents jazz and old standards.

THE ARTS

Long a beacon for visual artists, Taos is also becoming a magnet for touring musicians, especially in summer, when performers and audiences are drawn to the heady high-desert atmosphere. Festivals celebrate the visual arts, music, poetry, and film.

The **Taos Center for the Arts** (⊠ *133 Paseo del Pueblo Norte* ☎ *575/758–2052* ⊕ *www.taoscenterforthearts.org*), which encompasses the Taos Community Auditorium, presents films, plays, concerts and dance performances.

The **Taos Fall Arts Festival** (☎ *575/758–21063 or 800/732–8267* ⊕ *www.taosfallarts.com*), from late September to early October, is the area's major arts gathering, when buyers are in town and many other events, such as a Taos Pueblo feast, take place.

The **Taos Spring Arts Celebration** (☎ *575/758–3873 or 800/732–8267* ⊕ *www.taoschamber.com*), held throughout Taos in May, is a showcase for the visual, performing, and literary arts of the community and allows you to rub elbows with the many artists who call Taos home. The Mother's Day Arts and Crafts weekend during the festival always draws an especially large crowd.

MUSIC

From mid-June to early August the Taos School of Music fills the evenings with the sounds of chamber music at the **Taos School of Music Program and Festival** (☎705/776–2388 ⊕*www.taosschoolofmusic.com*). Running strong since 1963, this is America's oldest chamber music summer program and possibly the largest assembly of top string quartets in the country. Concerts are presented a couple of times a week from mid-June to August, at the Taos Community Auditorium and at Taos Ski Valley. Tickets cost $10–$20. The events at Taos Ski Valley are free.

Solar energy was pioneered in this land of sunshine, and each year in late June the flag of sustainability is raised at the three-day **Taos Solar Music Festival** (⊕*www.solarmusicfest.com*). Top-name acts appear, and booths promote alternative energy, permaculture, and other ecofriendly technologies.

SPORTS & THE OUTDOORS

Whether you plan to cycle around town, jog along Paseo del Pueblo Norte, or play a few rounds of golf, keep in mind that the altitude in Taos is higher than 7,000 feet. It's best to keep physical exertion to a minimum until your body becomes acclimated to the altitude—a full day to a few days, depending on your constitution.

BALLOONING

Hot-air ballooning has become nearly as popular in Taos as in Albuquerque, with a handful of outfitters offering rides, most starting at about $200 per person. **Paradise Balloons** (☎575/751–6098 ⊕*www. taosballooning.com*) will thrill you with a "splash and dash" in the Rio Grande River as part of a silent journey through the 600-foot canyon walls of Rio Grande Gorge. **Pueblo Balloon Company** (☎575/751–9877 ⊕*www.puebloballoon.com*) conducts balloon rides over and into the Rio Grande Gorge.

BICYCLING

Taos-area roads are steep and hilly, and none have marked bicycle lanes, so be careful while cycling. The West Rim Trail offers a fairly flat but view-studded 9-mi ride that follows the Rio Grande canyon's west rim from the Rio Grande Gorge Bridge to near the Taos Junction Bridge.

Gearing Up Bicycle Shop (✉129 *Paseo del Pueblo Sur* ☎575/751–0365) is a full-service bike shop that also has information about tours and guides. **Native Sons Adventures** (✉1033–A *Paseo del Pueblo Sur* ☎575/758–9342 *or* 800/753–7559) offers guided tours on its mountain bikes.

FISHING

Carson National Forest has some of the best trout fishing in New Mexico. Its streams and lakes are home to rainbow, brown, and native Rio Grande cutthroat trout.

In midtown Taos, **Cottam's Ski & Outdoor** (⊠*207–A Paseo del Pueblo Sur* ☎*575/758–2822 or 800/322–8267* ⊕*www.cottamsoutdoor.com*) provides fishing and bike trips and ski and snowboard rentals. **Solitary Angler** (⊠*204–B Paseo del Pueblo Norte* ☎*575/758–5653 or 866/502–1700* ⊕*www.thesolitaryangler.com*) guides fly-fishing expeditions that search out uncrowded habitats. Well-known area fishing guide Taylor Streit of **Taos Fly Shop & Streit Fly Fishing** (⊠*308–C Paseo del Pueblo Sur* ☎*575/751–1312* ⊕*www.taosflyshop.com*) takes individuals or small groups out for fishing and lessons.

GOLF

The greens fees at the 18-hole, PGA-rated, par-72 championship course at **Taos Country Club** (⊠*54 Golf Course Dr., Ranchos de Taos* ☎*575/758–7300*) are $59–$75.

HEALTH CLUBS & FITNESS CENTERS

The **Northside Health & Fitness Center** (⊠*1307 Paseo del Pueblo Norte* ☎*575/751–1242*) is a spotlessly clean facility with indoor and outdoor salt water pools, a hot tub, tennis courts, and aerobics classes. Nonmembers pay $8.50 per day. The center provides paid child care with a certified Montessori teacher. The **Taos Youth and Family Center** (⊠*407 Paseo del Cañon E* ☎*575/758–4160*) has an outdoor Olympic-size ice arena, where rollerblading, volleyball, and basketball take place in summer. There's also a large swimming pool. Admission is $2 per day.

LLAMA TREKKING

As one of the most offbeat outdoor recreational activities in the Taos area, llama trekking is offered by **Wild Earth Llama Adventures** (☎*575/586–0174 or 800/758–5262* ⊕*www.llamaadventures.com*) in a variety of packages, from one-day tours to excursions lasting several days in wilderness areas of the nearby Sangre de Cristo Mountains. Llamas, relatives of the camel, are used as pack animals on trips that begin at $89 for a day hike. Gourmet lunches eaten on the trail are part of the package, along with overnight camping and meals for longer trips.

RIVER RAFTING

The Taos Box, at the bottom of the steep-walled canyon far below the Rio Grande Gorge Bridge, is the granddaddy of thrilling white water in New Mexico and is best attempted by experts only—or on a guided trip—but the river also offers more placid sections such as through the Orilla Verde Recreation Area. Spring runoff is the busy season, from mid-April through June, but rafting companies conduct tours March to November. Shorter two-hour options usually cover the fairly tame section of the river. The **Bureau of Land Management, Taos Resource Area Office** (⊠*226 Cruz Alta* ☎*575/758–8851*) has a list of registered river guides and information about running the river on your own.

Big River Raft Trips (☎*575/758–9711 or 800/748–3760* ⊕*www.bigriverrafts.com*) offers dinner float trips and rapids runs. **Far Flung Adventures** (☎*575/758–2628 or 800/359–2627* ⊕*www.farflung.com*) operates half-day, full-day, and overnight rafting trips along the Rio Grande and the Rio Chama. **Los Rios River Runners** (☎*575/776–8854 or 800/544–1181*

⊕*www.losriosriverrunners.com*) will take you to your choice of spots—the Rio Chama, the Lower Gorge, or the Taos Box. **Native Sons Adventures** (⊠*1335 Paseo del Pueblo Sur* ☎*575/758–9342 or 800/753–7559* ⊕*www.nativesonsadventures.com*) offers several trip options on the Rio Grande.

SHOPPING

Retail options in Taos Plaza consist mostly of T-shirt emporiums and souvenir shops that are easily bypassed, though a few stores, carry quality Native American artifacts and jewelry. The more upscale galleries and boutiques are two short blocks north on Bent Street, including the John Dunn House Shops. Kit Carson Road, also known as U.S. 64, has a mix of the old and the new. There's metered municipal parking downtown, though the traffic can be daunting. Some shops worth checking out are in St. Francis Plaza in Ranchos de Taos, 4 mi south of the Plaza near the San Francisco de Asís Church. Just north of Taos off NM 522 you can find Overland Ranch (including Overland Sheepskin Co.), which has gorgeous sheepskin and leather clothing, along with other shops, galleries, restaurants, and an outdoor path winding through displays of wind sculptures.

ART GALLERIES

For at least a century, artists have been drawn to Taos's natural grandeur. The result is a vigorous art community with some 80 galleries, a lively market, and an estimated 1,000 residents producing art full- or part-time. Many artists explore themes of the western landscape, Native Americans, and adobe architecture; others create abstract forms and mixed-media works that may or may not reflect the Southwest. Some local artists grew up in Taos, but many—Anglo, Hispanic, and Native Americans—are adopted Taoseños.

Envision Gallery (⊠*Overland Ranch Complex, NM 522 north of Taos* ☎*505/751–1344*) has contemporary art and an outdoor exhibit of wind sculptures.

Farnsworth Gallery Taos (⊠*133 Paseo del Pueblo Norte* ☎*575/758– 0776*). Best known for his finely detailed paintings of horses, the work of artist John Farnsworth also includes colorful local landscapes, large-scale still-lifes, and scenes of Native American kiva dancers.

Fenix Gallery (⊠*208–A Ranchitos Rd.* ☎*575/758–9120*) is a showcase for contemporary art, exhibiting paintings, sculpture, ceramics, and lithography by established Taos artists.

Gallery Elena (⊠*111 Morada La.* ☎*575/758–9094*) shows the symbolic and impressionistic works of Veloy, Dan, and Michael Vigil.

Inger Jirby Gallery (✉ *207 Ledoux St.* ☎ *575/758–7333*) displays Jirby's whimsically colored landscape paintings.

★ **J.D. Challenger Gallery** (✉ *221 Paseo del Pueblo Norte* ☎ *575/751–6773 or 800/511–6773*) is the home base of personable painter J.D. Challenger, who has become famous for his dramatically rendered portraits of Native Americans from tribes throughout North America.

Las Comadres (✉ *228–A Paseo del Pueblo Norte* ☎ *575/737–5323*) is a women's cooperative gallery showing arts and crafts.

Lumina Fine Art & Sculpture Gardens (✉ *11 NM 230* ☎ *575/776–0123 or 877/558–6462*) exhibits paintings by worldwide artists and has 3 acres of sculpture gardens, including works of Japanese stone carvers.

Michael McCormick Gallery (✉ *106–C Paseo del Pueblo Norte* ☎ *575/758–1372 or 800/279–0879*) is home to the sensual, stylized female portraits of Miguel Martinez and the iconic portraits of Malcolm Furlow. The gallery also has an extensive collection of Rembrandt etchings.

Mission Gallery (✉ *138 E. Kit Carson Rd.* ☎ *575/758–2861*) carries the works of early Taos artists, early New Mexico Modernists, and important contemporary artists. The gallery is in the former home of painter Joseph H. Sharp.

Navajo Gallery (✉ *210 Ledoux St.* ☎ *575/758–3250*) shows the works of the internationally renowned Navajo painter and sculptor R.C. Gorman, who died in 2005 and who was known for his ethereal imagery—especially his portraits of Native American women.

Nichols Taos Fine Art Gallery (✉ *403 Paseo del Pueblo Norte* ☎ *575/758–2475*) has exhibits of oils, watercolors, pastels, charcoal, and pencils from artists representing many prestigious national art organizations.

Parks Gallery (✉ *127–A Bent St.* ☎ *575/751–0343*) specializes in contemporary paintings, sculptures, and prints. Mixed-media artist Melissa Zink shows here, as well as painter Jim Wagner.

R.B. Ravens Gallery (✉ *4146 NM 68, Ranchos de Taos* ☎ *575/758–7322 or 866/758–7322*) exhibits paintings by the founding artists of Taos, pre-1930s Native American weavings, and ceramics in a spare museum-quality setting.

Robert L. Parsons Fine Art (✉ *131 Bent St.* ☎ *575/751–0159 or 800/613–5091*) shows early Taos art colony paintings, antiques, and authentic antique Navajo blankets.

Six Directions (✉ *129-B N. Plaza* ☎ *575/758–5844*) has paintings, alabaster and bronze sculpture, Native American artifacts, silver jewelry, and pottery. Bill Rabbit and Robert Redbird are among the artists represented here.

Spirit Runner Gallery (✉ *303 Paseo del Pueblo Norte* ☎ *575/758–1132*) exhibits colorful acrylic and gold-leaf paintings by Taos native Ouray Meyers.

Studio de Colores Gallery (✉ *119 Quesnel, El Prado near Taos* ☎ *575/751–3502 or 888/751–3502*) is home to the work of two artists, Ann Huston and Ed Sandoval, who are married to one another but have extremely distinctive styles. Sandoval is known for his trademark *Viejito* (Old Man) images and swirling, vibrantly colored landscapes; Ann specializes in soft-hue still lifes and scenes of incredible stillness.

Two Graces Gallery (⊠*San Francisco Plaza* ☏*575/758–4639*) owner and artist Robert Cafazzo displays an astonishing assortment of traditional Indian pottery and kachinas, contemporary art by local artists, old postcards, and rare books on area artists.

> **DID YOU KNOW?**
>
> For more than a century, clear mountain light, sweeping landscapes, and a soft desert palette have drawn artists to Taos.

SPECIALTY STORES

BOOKS

Brodsky Bookshop (⊠*226-A Paseo del Pueblo Norte* ☏*575/758–9468*) has new and used books—contemporary literature, Southwestern classics, children's titles—piled here and there, but amiable proprietor Rick Smith will help you find what you need.

G. Robinson Old Prints and Maps (⊠*John Dunn House, 124–D Bent St.* ☏*575/758–2278*) stocks rare books, maps, and prints from the 16th to 19th century.

Moby Dickens (⊠*John Dunn House, 124-A Bent St.* ☏*575/758–3050*)specializes in rare and out-of-print books and carries a wide selection of contemporary fiction and nonfiction.

Sustaining Cultures (⊠*114 Doña Luz* ☏*575/751–0959*) stocks spiritual and new-age books and tapes and offers tarot readings.

CLOTHING

Artemisia(⊠*115 Bent St.,* ☏*575/737–9800*) has a wide selection of one-of-a kind wearable art by local artists.

Aventura (⊠*Overland Ranch, 4 mi north of 87571* ☏*575/758–2144*), which opened in 2005, produces stylish (and super-warm) contemporary blanket "wraps" as well as other winter-oriented outdoor wear.

Clarke & Co.(⊠*120-E Bent St.,* ☏*575–758-2696*) is the only store in Taos that sells contemporary, upscale men's clothing.

Coactemalan Art Import (⊠*108 Kit Carson,* ☏*575/751–3775* has Central and South American handmade clothing and gifts.

The Little Place Boutique (⊠*124-H Bent St.,* ☏*575/758–0440*) sells distinctive women's resort clothing, jewelry, and gifts.

Lollipops(⊠*120-D Bent St.,* ☏*575/758–8477*) carries designer children's clothing and accessories.

Mariposa Boutique Inc. (⊠*120-F Bent St.* ☏*575/758–9028*) has handmade women's and children's specialty clothing.

Overland Sheepskin Company (⊠*NM 522, Overland Ranch, 4 mi north of Taos* ☏*575/758–8820 or 888/754–8352*) carries high-quality sheepskin coats, hats, mittens, and slippers, many with Taos beadwork.

Steppin 'Out (⊠*120-K Bent St.,* ☏*575/758–4487* carries European footware, distinctive clothing, handmade handbags, and unique accessories.

COLLECTIBLES & GIFTS

Arroyo Seco Mercantile (⊠*488 State Road 15., Arroyo Seco* ☎*575/776–8806* ⊕*www.secomerc.com*) carries a varied assortment of 1930s linens, handmade quilts, candles, organic soaps, vintage cookware, handthrown pottery, decorated crosses, and souvenirs.

Casa Mia Gift Shop (⊠*San Francisco Plaza* ☎*575/758-1185*) carries authentic Indian jewelry, weavings, drums, and pottery.

Coyote Moon (⊠*120—C Bent St.,* ☎*575/758-4437*) has a great selection of south-of-the-border folk art, painted crosses, jewelry and day-of-the-dead figurines some featuring American rock stars.

Horse Feathers (⊠*109–B Kit Carson Rd.* ☎*575/758-7457*) is a fun collection of cowboy antiques and vintage western wear—boots, hats, buckles, jewelry, and all manner of paraphernalia.

Letherwerks (⊠*124—B Bent St.,* ☎*575/758-2778*) makes and sells handmade leather belts, bags, wallets, and backpacks.

San Francisco de Asis Parish Gift Shop (⊠*San Francisco Plaza,* ☎*575/758-2754*) has a wide range of religious art including handmade retablos, rosaries, crosses painted by local artists, traditional pottery, and retablos.

Taos Drums (⊠*NM 68, 5 mi south of Plaza* ☎*575/758-9844 or 800/424-3786*) is the factory outlet for the Taos Drum Factory. The store, 5 mi south of Taos Plaza (look for the large tepee), stocks handmade Pueblo log drums, leather lamp shades, and wrought-iron and Southwestern furniture.

White Lotus (⊠*122—A/B Paseo del Pueblo Sur,* ☎*751/758–0040*) expatriate Tibetans own this festive shop that has clothing, jewelry, Eastern spiritual books, and crafts from India, Nepal, Tibet, Thailand and Indonesia.

HOME FURNISHINGS

Abydos (⊠*7036 SR 518, Talap, near Ranchos de Taos* ☎*575/758–0483 or 888/900–0863*) sells fine handmade New Mexican–style furniture.

Antiquarius Imports (⊠*487 State Road 150 Arroyo Seco* ☎*575/776–8381* ⊕*www.antiquariusimports.com*)stocks rare Indian, Afgani and African antiques and furniture along with contemporary naturally dyed carpets made in Pakistan.

★ **Alhambra** (⊠*124 Paseo del Pueblo Sur* ☎*575/758–4161*) carries rare antique furniture, rugs and textiles from India, Tibet, Nepal, Thailand and China.

Casa Cristal Pottery (⊠*1306 Paseo del Pueblo Norte* ☎*575/758–1530*), 2½ mi north of the Taos Plaza, has a huge stock of stoneware, serapes, clay pots, Native American ironwood carvings, fountains, sweaters, ponchos, clay fireplaces, Mexican blankets, tiles, piñatas, and blue glassware from Guadalajara.

★ **Country Furnishings of Taos** (✉ *534 Paseo del Pueblo Norte* ☎*575/758–4633*) sells folk art from northern New Mexico, handmade furniture, metalwork lamps and beds, and colorful accessories.

EC-LEK-TIC (✉ *401 Paseo del Pueblo Norte* ☎*575/758-7232)*imports rare Indian, Tibetan and Chinese antique furniture, sculpture, rugs and home furnishings.

Starr Interiors (✉ *117 Paseo del Pueblo Norte* ☎*575/758–3065*) has a striking collection of Zapotec Indian rugs and hangings.

Taos Blue (✉ *101-A Bent St.* ☎*575/758–3561*) carries jewelry, pottery, and contemporary works by Native Americans (masks, rattles, sculpture), as well as Hispanic *santos* (bultos and retablos).

The **Taos Company** (✉ *124-K Bent St.* ☎*575/758–1141, 800/548–1141*) sells magnificent Spanish-style furniture, chandeliers, rugs, and textiles; Mexican *equipal* (wood and leather) chairs; and other accessories.

Taos Tin Works (✉ *1204-D Paseo del Pueblo Norte* ☎*575/758–9724*) sells handcrafted tinwork such as wall sconces, mirrors, lamps, and table ornaments by Marion Moore.

Weaving Southwest (✉ *216-B Paseo del Pueblo Norte* ☎*575/758–0433*) represents 20 tapestry artists who make beautiful rugs, and blankets. The store also sells supplies for weavers, including hand-dyed yarn.

NATIVE AMERICAN ARTS & CRAFTS

Buffalo Dancer (✉ *103-A E. Plaza* ☎*575/758–8718*) buys, sells, and trades Native American arts and crafts, including pottery, belts, kachina dolls, hides, and silver-coin jewelry.

El Rincón Trading Post (✉ *114 E. Kit Carson Rd.* ☎*575/758–9188*) is housed in a large, dark, cluttered century-old adobe. Native American items of all kinds are bought and sold here: drums, feathered head-dresses, Navajo rugs, beads, bowls, baskets, shields, beaded moccasins, jewelry, arrows, and spearheads. The packed back room contains Native American, Hispanic, and Anglo Wild West artifacts.

Taos General Store (✉ *223-C Paseo del Pueblo Sur* ☎*575/758–9051*) stocks a large selection of furniture and decorative items from around the world, as well as American Indian pots, rugs, and jewelry.

SPORTING GOODS

Cottam's Ski & Outdoor (✉ *207-A Paseo del Pueblo Sur* ☎*575/758–2822*) carries hiking and backpacking gear, snowboarding and skateboarding equipment, maps, fishing licenses and supplies, and ski equipment, along with related clothing and accessories.

Mudd 'n' Flood Mountain Shop (✉ *134 Bent St.* ☎*575/751–9100*) has gear and clothing for rock climbers, backpackers, campers, and back-country skiers.

Taos Mountain Outfitters (✉ *114 S. Plaza* ☎*575/758–9292*) has supplies for kayakers, skiers, climbers, and backpackers, as well as maps, books, and handy advice.

TAOS SKI VALLEY

NM 150, 22 mi northeast of Taos.

A trip to Taos Ski Valley begins at the traffic light where you turn right onto NM 150 (Taos Ski Valley Road) from U.S. 64. Along the way, the hamlet of Arroyo Seco, some 5 mi up NM 150 from the

traffic light, is worth a stop for lunch (tryMaverick County Food Co.) and a look at crafts and antiques shops. Beyond Arroyo Seco the road crosses a high plain, then plunges into the Rio Hondo Canyon to follow the cascading brook upstream through the forest to Taos Ski Valley, where NM 150 ends. (It does not continue to Red River, as some disappointed motorists discover.)

Skiers from around the world return to the slopes and hospitality of the Village of Taos Ski Valley every year. This world-class area is known for its alpine village atmosphere, perhaps the finest ski school in the country, and the variety of its 72 runs—it's also slowly but surely becoming more of a year-round destination, as the valley attracts outdoors enthusiasts with spectacular, and often challenging, hiking in summer and fall. Many of the few hotels at the ski valley have been converted to ski-in ski-out condos since the early 2000s, further evidence that the once funky ski area is becoming more of a Colorado-style full-scale resort town. Some of the best trails in Carson National Forest begin at the Village of Taos Ski Valley and go though dense woodland up to alpine tundra. There aren't many summer visitors, so you can have the trails up to Bull-of-the-Woods, Gold Hill, Williams Lake, Italianos, and Wheeler Peak nearly all to yourself. Easy nature hikes are organized by the Bavarian hotel, guided by Shar Sharghi, a botanist and horticulturist. Special events like barn dances and wine tastings occur throughout the nonskiing seasons.

WHERE TO EAT

$$
AMERICAN
✕**Rhoda's Restaurant.** Rhoda Blake founded Taos Ski Valley with her husband, Ernie. Her slope-side restaurant serves pasta, burgers, and sandwiches for lunch. Dinner fare is a bit more substantive, such as veal medallions with pancetta and seafood chiles rellenos with ancho chili sauce. ⊠*Resort Center, on the slope* ☎*575/776–2005* ▤*AE, MC, V.*

$$
SOUTHWESTERN
✕**Tim's Stray Dog Cantina.** This wildly popular spot occupies a chalet-style building in the heart of the Taos ski area, and it's a favorite spot for lunch, and dinner and après-ski cocktails. Favorites include rainbow trout with lemon butter, chiles rellenos, green-chili burgers (both beef and veggie). ⊠*105 Sutton Pl.* ☎*575/776–2894* ▤*MC, V.*

WHERE TO STAY

★ **$$$** **Austing Haus.** Owner Paul Austing constructed much of this handsome, glass-sheathed building, 1½ mi from Taos Ski Valley, along with many of its furnishings. The breakfast room has large picture windows, stained-glass paneling, and an impressive fireplace. Aromas of fresh-baked goods, such as Paul's apple strudel, come from the kitchen. Guest rooms are pretty and quiet with harmonious, peaceful colors; some have four-poster beds and fireplaces. In winter the inn offers ski packages. ⊠*NM 150* ☐*Box 8, Village of Taos Ski Valley 87525* ☎*575/776–2649 or 800/748–2932* ☐*575/776–8751* ⊕*www.austinghaus.net* ➬*22 rooms, 3 chalets* ♿*In-hotel: restaurant* ▭*AE, DC, MC, V* ⏐○⏐*CP.*

★ $$$$　🏨**The Bavarian.** This luxurious, secluded re-creation of a Bavarian lodge has the only mid-mountain accommodations in the Taos Ski Valley. The King Ludwig suite has a dining room, kitchen, marble bathroom, and two bedrooms with canopied beds. Three suites have whirlpool tubs. The restaurant ($$$) serves contemporary Bavarian-inspired cuisine, such as baked artichokes and Gruyère, and braised pork loin with garlic-mashed potatoes and red cabbage. Summer activities include hiking, touring with the resident botanist, horseback riding, rafting, and fishing. Seven-night ski packages are offered. ⊠*100 Kachina Rd.* ☐*Box 653, Taos Ski Valley 87525* ☎*575/776–8020* ☐*575/776–5301* ⊕*www. thebavarian.net* ➬*4 suites* ♿*In-room: kitchen, VCR. In-hotel: restaurant* ▭*AE, MC, V* ☉*Closed May and early Nov.* ⏐○⏐*BP.*

$$$$　🏨**Inn at Snakedance.** This modern condominium resort is right on the slopes. The inn has a handsome library where guests can enjoy an après-ski coffee or after-dinner drink next to a fieldstone fireplace. Some rooms have fireplaces. In summer the hotel offers weeklong vacation packages, including a cooking school and fitness adventure courses. Hondo Restaurant ($$; closed in summer), a frequent winner of the *Wine Spectator* Award of Excellence, turns out esteemed contemporary American cooking, such as smoked Memphis-style ribs. ⊠*110 Sutton Place Rd.* ☐*NM 150; Box 89, Village of Taos Ski Valley 87525* ☎*575/776–2277 or 800/322–9815* ☐*575/776–1410* ⊕*www.innsnakedance.com* ➬*33 condo units.* ♿*In-room: kitchens, Wi-Fi. In-hotel: restaurant* ▭*AE, DC, MC, V* ☉*Closed mid-Apr.– Memorial Day* ⏐○⏐*CP.*

NIGHTLIFE & THE ARTS

The Taos School of Music gives free weekly summer concerts and recitals from mid-June to early August at the **Hotel Saint Bernard** (☎*575/776– 2251*), at the mountain base (near the lifts) of Taos Ski Valley.

SPORTS & THE OUTDOORS

Wheeler Peak is a designated wilderness area of Carson National Forest, where travel is restricted to hiking or horseback riding. Part of the Sangre de Cristo Mountains, this 13,161-foot peak is New Mexico's highest. The 8-mi trail to the top begins at the Village of Taos Ski Valley. Only experienced hikers should tackle this strenuous trail. Dress warmly even in summer, take plenty of water and food, and pay attention to *all* warnings and instructions distributed by the forest rangers. Quite a few shorter and less taxing trails also depart from the ski valley and points nearby; trailheads are usually marked with signs. ⊠ *Twining Campground, next to ski area parking lot* ☎*575/758–6200.*

Fodor's Choice
★
With 72 runs—more than half of them for experts—and an average of more than 320 inches of annual snowfall, **Taos Ski Valley** ranks among the country's most respected—and challenging—resorts. The slopes tend to be tough here (the ridge chutes, Al's Run, Inferno), but 25 percent (e.g., Honeysuckle) are for intermediate skiers, and 24 percent (e.g., Bambi, Porcupine) for beginners. Until recently t was one of the nation's handful of resorts that banned snowboarding. Taos Ski Valley is justly famous for its outstanding ski schools, one of the best in the country—if you're new to the sport, this is a terrific resort to give it a try. ⊠ *Village of Taos Ski Valley* ☎*75/776–2291* ⊕*www.skitaos.org* ⊠*Lift tickets $66* ⊙ *Late Nov.–early Apr.*

SHOPPING

Andean Softwear (⊠*118 Sutton Pl.* ☎*575/776–2508*) carries exotic clothing, textiles, and jewelry. Note the deliciously soft alpaca sweaters from Peru.

SIDE TRIPS FROM TAOS

Surrounded by thousands of acres of pristine Carson National Forest and undeveloped high desert, Taos makes an ideal base for road-tripping. Most of the nearby adventures involve the outdoors, from skiing to hiking to mountain biking, and there are several noteworthy campgrounds in this part of the state. Although these side trips can be done in a day, several of the ski-resort communities mentioned in this section have extensive overnight accommodations.

THE ENCHANTED CIRCLE

Fodor's Choice
★
The Enchanted Circle, an 84-mi loop north from Taos and back, rings Wheeler Peak, New Mexico's highest mountain, and takes you through glorious panoramas of alpine valleys and the towering mountains of the lush Carson National Forest. You can see all the major sights in one day, or take a more leisurely tour and stay overnight.

From Taos, head north about 15 mi via U.S. 64 to NM 522, keeping your eye out—after about 15 mi—for the sign on the right that points to the D. H. Lawrence Ranch and Memorial. You can visit the memorial, but the other buildings on the ranch are closed to the public. Continue north a short ways to reach Red River Hatchery, and then go another 5 mi to the village of Questa. Here you have the option of continuing north on NM 522 and detouring for some hiking at Wild Rivers Recreation Area, or turning east from Questa on NM 38 and driving for about 12 mi to the rollicking ski town of Red River. From here, continue 16 mi east along NM 38 and head over dramatic Bobcat Pass, which rises to a tad under 10,000 feet. You'll come to the sleepy old-fashioned village of Eagle Nest, comprising a few shops and down-home restaurants and motels. From here, U.S. 64 joins with NM 38 and runs southeast about 15 mi to one of the state's fastest-growing communities, Angel Fire, an upscale ski resort that's popular for hiking, golfing, and mountain biking in summer. It's about a 25-mi drive west over 9,000-foot Palo Flechado Pass and down through winding Taos Canyon to return to Taos.

Leave early in the morning and plan to spend the entire day on this trip. During ski season, which runs from late November to early April, you may want to make it an overnight trip and get in a day of skiing. In spring, summer, and fall your drive should be free of snow and ice. A sunny winter day can yield some lovely scenery (but if it's snowy, don't forget your sunglasses).

Carson National Forest surrounds Taos and spans almost 200 mi across northern New Mexico, encompassing mountains, lakes, streams, villages, and much of the Enchanted Circle. Hiking, cross-country skiing, horseback riding, mountain biking, backpacking, trout fishing, boating, and wildflower viewing are among the popular activities here. The forest is home to big-game animals and many species of smaller animals and songbirds. For canyon climbing, head into the rocky Rio Grande Gorge. The best entry point into the gorge is at the Wild Rivers Recreation Area, north of Questa. You can drive into the forest land via NM 522, NM 150, NM 38, and NM 578. Carson National Forest also has some of the best trout fishing in New Mexico. Its streams and lakes are home to rainbow, brown, and native Rio Grande cutthroat trout.

The forest provides a wealth of camping opportunities, from organized campgrounds with restrooms and limited facilities to informal roadside campsites and sites that require backpacking in. If mountains, pines, and streams are your goal, stake out sites in Carson National Forest along the Rio Hondo or Red River; if you prefer high-desert country along the banks of the Rio Grande, consider Orilla Verde or Wild Rivers Recreation Area. Backcountry sites are free; others cost up to $7 per night.

If you're coming from a lower altitude, you should take time to acclimatize, and all hikers should follow basic safety procedures. Wind, cold, and wetness can occur any time of year, and the mountain climate produces sudden storms. Dress in layers and wear sturdy footwear; carry water, food, sunscreen, hat, sunglasses, and a first-aid kit. Contact the Carson National Forest's visitor center for maps, safety guidelines, camping information, and conditions (it's open weekdays 8–4:30). ⊠ *Forest Service Bldg., 208 Cruz Alta Rd., Taos* ☎ *575/758– 6200* ⊕ *www.fs.fed.us/r3/carson.*

The Enchanted Circle Bike Tour takes place in mid-September. The rally loops through the entire 84-mi Enchanted Circle, revealing a brilliant blaze of fall color. In summer you can head up the mountainside via ski lift in Red River and Angel Fire.

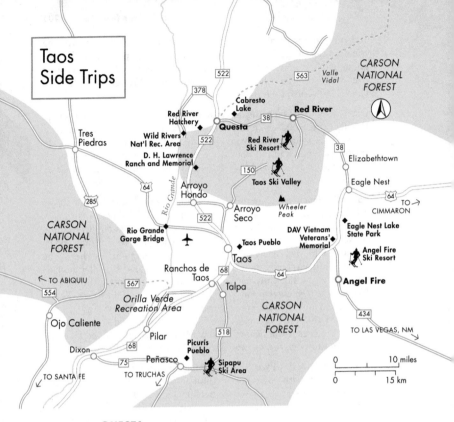

QUESTA

25 mi north of Taos via U.S. 64 to NM 522.

Literally "hill," in the heart of the Sangre de Cristo Mountains, Questa is a quiet village nestled against the Red River itself and amid some of New Mexico's most striking mountain country. **St. Anthony's Church,** built of adobe with 5-foot-thick walls and viga ceilings, is on the main street. Questa's **Cabresto Lake,** in Carson National Forest, is about 8 mi from town. Follow NM 563 northeast to Forest Route 134, then 2 mi of a primitive road (134A)—you'll need a four-wheel-drive vehicle. You can trout fish and boat here from about June to October.

Although it's only a few miles west of Questa as the crow flies, you have to drive about 15 mi north of Questa via NM 522 to NM 378 to reach **Wild Rivers Recreation Area,** which offers hiking access to the dramatic confluence of two national wild and scenic rivers, the Rio Grande and Red River. There are some fairly easy and flat trails along the gorge's rim, including a ½ mi interpretive loop from the visitor center out to La Junta Point, which offers a nice view of the river. But the compelling reason to visit is a chance to hike down into the gorge and study the rivers up close, which entails hiking one of a couple of well-marked but steep trails down into the gorge, a descent of about 650 feet. It's not an especially strenuous trek, but many visitors come without sufficient water and stamina, have an easy time descending into the gorge, and then find it difficult to make it back up. There are also 29 basic campsites, some along the rim and others along the river. ⊠*NM 522, follow signed dirt road from highway, Cerro* ☎*575/770–1600, camping information* ⚒*$3 per vehicle; camping $7 per vehicle* ⊙*Daily 6 AM–10 PM; visitor center late May–early Sept., daily 10–4.*

NEED A BREAK?
Hip coffeehouses are something of a rarity in rural New Mexico, but funky Paloma Blanca (⊠*2322 S. NM 522* ☎*575/586–2261*) **is a hit, not only because of its excellent coffee drinks but owing to the excellent sandwiches, pizza, pastries, homemade bread, and Taos Cow ice cream. It's the perfect place to stock up on food before hiking at Wild Rivers Recreation Area.**

☺ At the **Red River Hatchery,** freshwater trout are raised to stock waters in Questa, Red River, Taos, Raton, and Las Vegas. You can feed them and learn how they're hatched, reared, stocked, and controlled. The visitor center has displays and exhibits, a fishing pond, and a machine that dispenses fish food. The self-guided tour can last anywhere from 20 minutes to more than an hour, depending on how enraptured you become. There's a picnic area and camping on the grounds. ⊠*NM 522, 5 mi south of Questa* ☎*575/586–0222* ⚒*Free* ⊙*Daily 8–5.*

The influential and controversial English writer David Herbert Lawrence and his wife, Frieda, arrived in Taos at the invitation of Mabel Dodge Luhan, who collected famous writers and artists the way some people collect butterflies. Luhan provided them a place to live, Kiowa Ranch, on 160 acres in the mountains. Rustic and remote, it's now known as the **D. H. Lawrence Ranch and Memorial,** though Lawrence never actually owned it. Lawrence lived in Taos on and off for about 22 months during a three-year period between 1922 and 1925. He wrote his novel *The Plumed Serpent* (1926), as well as some of his finest short stories and poetry, while in Taos and on excursions to Mexico. The houses here, owned by the University of New Mexico, are not open to the public, but you can enter the small cabin where Dorothy Brett, the Lawrences' traveling companion, stayed. You can also visit the D. H. Lawrence Memorial, a short walk up Lobo Mountain. A white shed-like structure, it's simple and unimposing. The writer fell ill while in France and died in a sanatorium there in 1930. Five years later Frieda had Lawrence's body disinterred and cremated and brought his ashes back to Taos. Frieda Lawrence is buried, as was her wish, in front of the memorial. ⊠*NM 522, follow signed dirt road from highway, San Cristobal* ☎*575/776–2245* ⚒*Free* ⊙*Daily dawn–dusk.*

RED RIVER
12 mi east of Questa via NM 38.

Home of a major ski resort that has a particularly strong following with folks from Oklahoma and the Texas panhandle, Red River (elevation 8,750 feet) came into being as a miners' boomtown during the 19th century, taking its name from the river whose mineral content gives it a rosy color. When the gold petered out, Red River died, only to be rediscovered in the 1920s by migrants escaping the dust storms in the Great Plains. An Old West flavor remains: Main Street shoot-outs, an authentic melodrama, and square dancing and two-stepping are among the diversions. Because of its many country dances and festivals, Red River is affectionately called "The New Mexico Home of the Texas Two-Step." The bustling little downtown area contains souvenir shops and sportswear boutiques, casual steak and barbecue joints, and a number of motels, lodges, and condos. There's good fishing to be had in the Red River itself, and excellent alpine and Nordic skiing in the surrounding forest.

NEED A BREAK?

In Red River stop by the **Sundance** (⊠ *401 E. High St.* ☎575/754–2971) for Mexican food or a fresh-fruit sangria. The stuffed sopapillas here are particularly good. **Texas Red's Steakhouse** (⊠ *111 E. Main St.* ☎575/754–2964) has charbroiled steaks, chops, buffalo burgers, and chicken. There's also a branch down in Eagle Nest, in the heart of downtown.

About 16 mi southeast of Red River, NM 38 leads to the small village of Eagle Nest, the home of New Mexico's most recently designated state park, **Eagle Nest Lake State Park** (⊠ *42 Marina Way, just south of town* ☎575/377–1594 ⊕*www.emnrd.state.nm.us* ⊠*$5*), which became part of the park system in 2004. This 2,400-acre lake is one of the state's top spots for kokanee salmon and rainbow trout fishing as well as a favorite venue for boating; there are two boat ramps on the lake's northwest side. You may also have the chance to spy elk, bears, mule deer, and even reclusive mountain lions around this rippling body of water, which in winter is popular for snowmobiling and ice-fishing. The park is open 6 AM–9 PM, and camping is not permitted.

Thousands of acres of national forest surround rustic Eagle Nest, population 189, elevation 8,090 feet. The shops and other buildings here evoke New Mexico's mining heritage, while a 1950s-style diner, Kaw-Lija's, serves up a memorable burger; you can also grab some take-out food in town and bring it to Eagle Nest Lake for a picnic.

WHERE TO STAY

Roadrunner Campground. The Red River runs right through this woodsy mountain campground set on 25 rugged acres. There are two tennis courts and a video-game room. ⊠*1371 E. Main St., Box 588, Red River* ☎575/754–2286 or 800/243–2286 ⊕*www.redrivernm. com/roadrunnerrv* ☖ *Laundry facilities, flush toilets, full hookups, drinking water, showers, picnic tables, electricity, public telephone, general store, play area, swimming (river)* ⊅*141 RV sites, 2 cabins* ☉*Closed mid-Sept.–Apr.*

SPORTS & THE OUTDOORS

★ At the **Enchanted Forest Cross-Country Ski Area,** 24 mi of groomed trails loop from the warming hut, stocked with snacks and hot cocoa, through 600 acres of meadows and pines in Carson National Forest, 3 mi east of Red River. ⊠*417 W. Main St.* ☎575/754–2374 or 800/966–9381 ⊕*www.enchantedforestxc.com* ⊠*$14* ☉*Late Nov.–Easter, weather permitting.*

The **Red River Ski Area** is in the middle of the historic gold-mining town of Red River, with lifts within walking distance of restaurants and hotels. Slopes for all levels of skiers make the area popular with families, and there's a snowboarding park. There are 58 trails served by seven lifts, and the vertical drop is about 1,600 feet. Red River has plenty of rental shops and accommodations. ⊠ *400 Pioneer Rd., off NM 38* ☎ *575/754-2223* ⊕ *www.redriverskiarea.com* 🎫 *Lift tickets $58* ☉ *Late Nov.–late Mar.*

ANGEL FIRE

30 mi south of Red River and 13 mi south of Eagle Nest via NM 38 and U.S. 64.

Named for its blazing sunrise and sunset colors by the Ute Indians who gathered here each autumn, Angel Fire is known these days primarily as a ski resort, generally rated the second–Best in the state after Taos. In summer there are arts and music events as well as hiking, river rafting, and ballooning. A prominent landmark along U.S. 64, just northeast of town, is the **DAV Vietnam Veterans Memorial**, a 50-foot-high wing-shaped monument built in 1971 by D. Victor Westphall, whose son David was killed in Vietnam.

WHERE TO STAY

$$$ 🏨 **Angel Fire Resort.** The centerpiece of New Mexico's fastest-growing and most highly acclaimed four-season sports resort, this upscale hotel is set at the mountain's base, a stone's throw from the chairlift. Indeed, winter is the busiest season here, but during the warmer months it's a popular retreat with hikers, golfers, and other outdoorsy types who appreciate retiring each evening to spacious digs. Even the standard rooms are 500 square feet, and the larger deluxe units have feather pillows, ski-boot warmers, and fireplaces. The resort also manages a variety of privately owned condo units, from studios to three-bedrooms, which are available nightly or long-term. **Pros:** Slope-side location; fantastic views. **Cons:** Some rooms are in need of an upgrade. ⊠ *10 Miller La., Box Drawer B,* ☎ *575/377–6401 or 800/633–7463* 🖨 *575/377–4200* ⊕ *www.angelfireresort.com* 🛏 *139 rooms* ♿ *In-room: refrigerator, Wi-Fi. In-hotel: 4 restaurants, bars, golf course, tennis courts, bicycles* 🍴 *AE, D, MC, V.*

🏕 **Enchanted Moon Campground.** In Valle Escondido, off U.S. 64 near Angel Fire, this wooded area with a trout pond has views of the Sangre de Cristos. Features include horse stalls, a chuckwagon, and an indoor recreation area with video games. ⊠ *7 Valle Escondido Rd., Valle Escondido* ☎ *575/758–3338* ⊕ *www.emooncampground.com* ♿ *Flush toilets, full hookups, Wifi, drinking water, showers, grills, picnic tables, electricity, , play area* 🛏 *27 RV sites, 22 tent sites* ☉ *Closed mid-Oct.–Apr.*

NIGHTLIFE & THE ARTS

Music from Angel Fire (☎ *575/377–3233 or 888/377–3300* ⊕ *www. musicfromangelfire.org*) is a nightly series of classical (and occasional jazz) concerts presented at venues around Angel Fire and Taos for about three weeks from late August to early September. Tickets cost $20–$30 per concert, and the festival—begun in 1983—continues to grow in popularity and esteem each year.

SPORTS & THE OUTDOORS

The 18-hole golf course at the **Angel Fire Country Club** (⊠ *Country Club Dr. off NM 434* ☎ *575/377–3055*), one of the highest in the nation, is open May to mid-October, weather permitting. The challenging front 9 runs a bit longer than the back and takes in great views of aspen- and pine-shaded canyons; the shorter back 9 has more water play and somewhat tighter fairways. Greens fees are $75–$85.

★ The fast-growing and beautifully maintained **Angel Fire Resort** is a busy ski destination, with 70 runs for all levels of skiers, five lifts, 19 mi of cross-country trails, and four terrain parks; the vertical drop is about 2,100 feet. Other amenities include a 1,000-foot snow-tubing hill, a well-respected ski and snowboard school, snowbiking (also taught at the school), ice fishing, a children's ski-and-snowboard center, and superb snowmaking capacity. ⊠ *N. Angel Fire Rd. off NM 434* ☎ *575/377– 6401, 800/633–7463, 575/377–4222 snow conditions* ⊕ *www.angel fireresort.com* ☜ *Lift tickets $59* ☻ *Mid-Dec.–early Apr.*

Phoenix, Scottsdale & Tempe

Updated by
JoBeth Jamison

The Valley of the Sun, otherwise known as metro Phoenix (i.e., Phoenix and all its suburbs, including Tempe and Scottsdale), is named for its 325-plus days of sunshine each year. The Valley marks the northern tip of the Sonoran Desert, a prehistoric seabed that reaches from northwestern Mexico with a landscape offering much more than just cacti. Palo verde and mesquite trees, creosote bushes, brittle bush, and agave dot the land, which is accustomed to being scorched by temperatures in excess of 100°F for weeks at a time. Late summer brings precious rain when monsoon storms illuminate the sky with lightning shows and the desert exudes the scent of creosote. Spring sets the Valley blooming, and the giant saguaros are crowned in white flowers for a short time in May—in the evening and cool early mornings—and masses of vibrant wildflowers fill desert crevices and span mountain landscapes.

Although many come to Phoenix for the golf and the weather, the Valley has much to offer by way of shopping, outdoor activities, and nightlife. The best of the latter are in Scottsdale and the East Valley with a variety of hip dance clubs, old-time saloons, and upscale wine bars.

EXPLORING THE VALLEY OF THE SUN

It can be useful to think of Phoenix as a flower with petals (other communities) growing in every direction from the bud of Sky Harbor Airport. The East Valley includes Scottsdale, Paradise Valley, Tempe, Mesa, Fountain Hills, and Apache Junction. To the southeast are Chandler, Gilbert, and Ahwatukee. The West Valley includes Glendale, Sun City, and Litchfield Park. Central Avenue, which runs north and south through the heart of downtown Phoenix, is the city's east–west dividing line. Everything east of Central is considered the East Valley and everything west of Central is the West Valley.

Getting around can be difficult unless you have a car. From Sky Harbor airport, the one-way cab fare to the Four Seasons Resort in North Scottsdale (about 32 mi) can easily cost more than the daily charge for a rental car. Public transit is here in varying degrees and is inexpensive, but services do not connect well within and between communities. Various phases of a light-rail system connecting Mesa, Tempe, and Phoenix will be under construction for years to come, though, as of this writing, Phase I, which spans downtown and central Phoenix, was scheduled to be completed in December 2008. As of this writing, the traffic-paralyzing Phoenix Convention Center expansion project was also slated for December 2008 completion, but it would still be wise to allow extra time when traveling to downtown Phoenix, especially during major sports or entertainment events. Check ⊕ *www.valleymetro. org* for traffic restrictions.

ABOUT THE RESTAURANTS & HOTELS

With each passing year, Phoenix becomes less of a city born of the Old West and more of a modern metropolis. Large luxury resorts offer comforts and conveniences many never imagined could exist in the middle of a desert—including four-star restaurants with celebrity chefs,

TOP REASONS TO GO

Resort spas: With its dozens of outstanding desert spas, Phoenix has massaged and wrapped its way to the top of the relaxation destinations list.

The Heard Museum: This small but world-renowned museum complex elegantly celebrates Native American people, culture, art, and history.

Shopping & dining: From Old Town Scottsdale to the Fashion Squares, the Valley of the Sun is a retail mecca, as well as a melting pot of fine and funky dining establishments.

The Great Outdoors: Sure there's urban sprawl, but Phoenix also has cool and accessible places to get away from it all, like the Desert Botanical Garden, Papago Park, Tempe Town Lake, and the mountain and desert preserves.

Golf: All year long links lovers can take their pick of top-rated, public and private courses—many with incredibly spectacular views.

4

golf courses designed by legendary PGA players, European- and Asian-themed spas, and water parks. The good news is that the kind of land required to build such grandiose accommodations no longer exists in central Phoenix, so to compete, older hotels are renovating, adding amenities, and offering competitive rates. Restaurants are experiencing a similar trend. Local menus have gone from meat and potatoes to pan-seared espresso-crusted fillets and Asian sweet-potato compote, and only the strong survive. Yes, you can still visit an authentic dude ranch, and you can certainly find the old hole-in-the-wall hamburger or Mexican food joint—you just have to look a little harder these days.

WHAT IT COSTS					
	¢	$	$$	$$$	$$$$
Restaurants	under $8	$8–$12	$13–$20	$21–$30	over $30
Hotels	under $100	$100–$150	$151–$225	$226–$350	over $350

Restaurant rrices are per person for a main course. The final tab will include sales tax of 8.1% in Phoenix, 7.95% in Scottsdale. Hotel prices are for a standard double in high season for two people.

■ TIP➔ **First-time visitors are often surprised to discover that some of the area's finest restaurants and shops are tucked into hotels and strip malls.**

DOWNTOWN & CENTRAL PHOENIX

Growth in the Valley over the past two decades has meant the emergence of a real downtown in Phoenix, where people hang out: there are new apartments and loft spaces, cultural and sports facilities—including Chase Field (formerly known as Bank One Ballpark and still affectionately referred to by many locals as BOB) and the US Airways Center, and large areas for conventions and trade shows. It's retained a mix of past and present, too, and restored homes in Heritage Square, from the original townsite, give an idea of how far the city has come

Arizona
Center **4**

Arizona
Mining & Mineral
Museum **8**

Arizona
Science
Center **2**

Encanto Park ...**9**

Heard
Museum **10**

Heritage
Square **1**

Museo
Chicano **5**

Orpheum
Theatre **7**

Phoenix Art
Museum **11**

Phoenix
Museum of
History **3**

Wells Fargo
Museum **6**

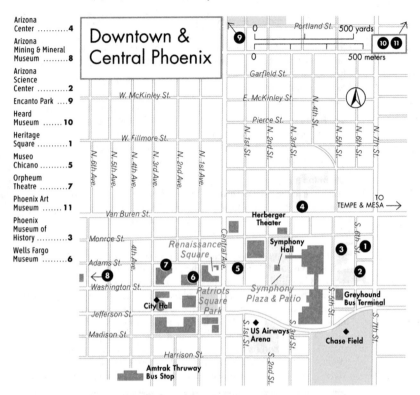

since its inception around the turn of the 20th century. Downtown Phoenix is also known as Copper Square.

There are lots of parking options downtown, and they're listed on the free map provided by Downtown Phoenix Partnership, available in many local restaurants (⊕*www.coppersquare.com*). Many downtown sites are served by DASH (Downtown Area Shuttle), a free bus service. You can use DASH to get around or to get back to your car when you're finished.

Numbers in the margin correspond to numbers on the What to See in Downtown & Central Phoenix map.

WHAT TO SEE

4 **Arizona Center.** Amid dramatic fountains, sunken gardens, and towering palm trees stands this two-tier, open-air structure: downtown's most attractive shopping venue. The center has about 50 shops and restaurants, open-air vendors, a large sports bar, and a multiplex cinema. ⊠*400 E. Van Buren St., Downtown Phoenix* ☎*602/271–4000 or 480/949–4386* ⊕*www.arizonacenter.com.*

2 **Arizona Science Center.** With more than 300 hands-on exhibits, this is the venue for science-related exploration. You can pilot a simulated airplane flight, travel through the human body, navigate your way through the solar system in the Dorrance Planetarium, and watch a movie in the giant, five-story film theater. ✉ *600 E. Washington St., Downtown Phoenix* ☎ *602/716–2000* ⊕ *www.azscience.org* ✉ *Museum $9; combination museum, theater, and planetarium $19* ⊗ *Daily 10–5.*

After visiting the Science center, stop at the Norman Rockwell–like diner MacAlpine's Soda Fountain (✉ *2303 N. 7th St., Downtown Phoenix* ☎ *602/262–5545* **for a decadent malt, sundae, or ice-cream soda. Opened in 1928 as a Rexall Drug Store, it has the oldest operating soda fountain in the Southwest.**

⑧ Arizona Mining and Mineral Museum. Arizona's phenomenal wealth and progress has had a lot to do with what lies beneath the actual land, namely the copper, gold, silver, and other earthbound deposits. This museum offers a mother lode of information and features more than 3,000 rocks, minerals, fossils, and mining equipment, including a 43-foot-tall Boras mine headframe and an 1882 baby-gauge steam train locomotive. ✉ *1502 W. Washington, Downtown Phoenix* ☎ *602/255–3795* ⊕ *www.azminfun.com* ✉ *$2* ⊗ *Weekdays 8–5, Sat. 11–4.*

⑨ Encanto Park. Urban Encanto (Spanish for "enchanted") Park covers 222 acres at the heart of one of Phoenix's oldest residential neighborhoods. There are many attractions, including picnic areas, a lagoon where you can paddleboat and canoe, a municipal swimming pool, a nature trail, the Enchanted Island amusement park, fishing in the park's lake, and two public golf courses. ✉ *1202 W. Encanto Blvd., Central Phoenix* ☎ *602/261–8993 or 602/254–1200* ⊕ *www.enchantedisland.com* ✉ *Park free, Enchanted Island rides $1* ⊗ *Park daily 6–midnight; Enchanted Island Wed.–Fri. 10–4, weekends 7–4.*

> **WORD OF MOUTH**
>
> "The Heard museum is not to be missed. It is one of the largest, most comprehensive collections of Native American art in the Southwest. There's even a large section of the museum which is targeted towards children and their interests (left side as you walk in)."
> —mykidsherpa

⑩ Heard Museum. Pioneer settlers Dwight and Maie Heard built a Spanish colonial–revival building on their property to house their collection of Southwestern art. Today the staggering collection includes such exhibits as a Navajo hogan, an Apache wickie-up (a temporary Native American structure, similar to a lean-to, constructed from branches, twigs, and leaves, sometimes covered with hides), and rooms filled with art, pottery, jewelry, kachinas, and textiles. The Heard also actively supports and displays pieces by working Indian artists. A fabulous long-term exhibition entitled Home: Native People In the Southwest, opened in 2005. Annual events include the Guild Indian Fair & Market and the World Championship Hoop Dance Contest. Children enjoy the interactive art-making exhibits. ■ TIP➜ **The museum also has an incredible gift shop with authentic, high-quality goods purchased directly from native artists.** There's a museum satellite branch in Scottsdale that has

Fodor's Choice ★

rotating exhibits, and another in the West Valley featuring some of the Heard's permanent collection as well as rotating exhibits. ✉2301 N. Central Ave., Central Phoenix ☎602/252–8848 ⊕www.heard.org ✑$10 ⊙Daily 9:30–5 ✉Heard Museum West: 16126 N. Civic Center Plaza, West ValleySurprise ☎623/344–2200 ✑$5 ⊙Tues–Sun. 9:30–5. ✉Heard Museum North: 32633 N. Scottsdale Rd., North Scottsdale ☎480/488–9817 ✑$3 ⊙Mon–Sat. 10–5.

❶ Heritage Square. In a parklike setting from 5th to 7th streets between Monroe and Adams streets, this city-owned block contains the only remaining houses from the original Phoenix townsite. On the south side of the square, along Adams Street, stand several houses built between 1899 and 1901. The Bouvier Teeter House has a Victorian-style tearoom, and the Thomas House and Baird Machine Shop are now Pizzeria Bianco. The one-story brick Stevens House holds the **Arizona Doll and Toy Museum** (✉602 E. Adams St., Downtown Phoenix ☎602/253–9337 ✑$3 ⊙Tues–Sat. 10–4, Sun. noon–4, Closed Mon. and Aug.). **Rosson House,** an 1895 Victorian in the Queen Anne style, is the queen of Heritage Square. Built by a physician who served a brief term as mayor, it's the sole survivor among fewer than two-dozen Victorians erected in Phoenix. It was bought and restored by the city in 1974. ✉6th and Monroe Sts., Downtown Phoenix ☎602/262–5029 ✑$5 ⊙Wed.–Sat. 10–4, Sun. noon–4.

NEED A BREAK?

The Victorian-style tearoom in the **Bouvier Teeter House** (✉622 E. Adams St., Downtown Phoenix ☎602/252–4682), which was built as a private home in 1899, serves authentic teatime fare; there are also heartier sandwiches and salads.

❺ Museo Chicano. Based on and celebrating the culture of Latinos, this unique museum showcases works of artists from the United States and Mexico. Permanent and revolving exhibits include everything from ancient Mayan artifacts to revolutionary works by Frida Kahlo and Diego Rivera, to stirring and colorful pop art that has become a modern signature of Latino style—making this site a premier center for enjoying Latin American art. ✉147 E. Adams St., Downtown Phoenix ☎602/257–5536 ⊕www.museochicano.com ✑$2 ⊙Tues.–Sat. 10–4.

❼ Orpheum Theatre. This Spanish-colonial movie palace has been an architectural focal point of downtown since it was built in 1929. The eclectic ornamental details of the interior have been meticulously restored and the Orpheum is still a venue for live performances, from Broadway shows to ballet to lectures. ✉203 W. Adams St., Downtown Phoenix ☎602/534–5600 ⊕www.friendsoftheorpheumtheatre.org ⊙Tours by appointment only.

⓫ Phoenix Art Museum. This museum is one of the most visually appealing pieces of architecture in the Southwest. Basking in natural light, the museum makes great use of its modern, open space by tastefully fitting more than 17,000 works of art from all over the world—including sculptures by Frederic Remington and paintings by Georgia O'Keeffe, Thomas Moran, and Maxfield Parrish—within its soaring concrete

4

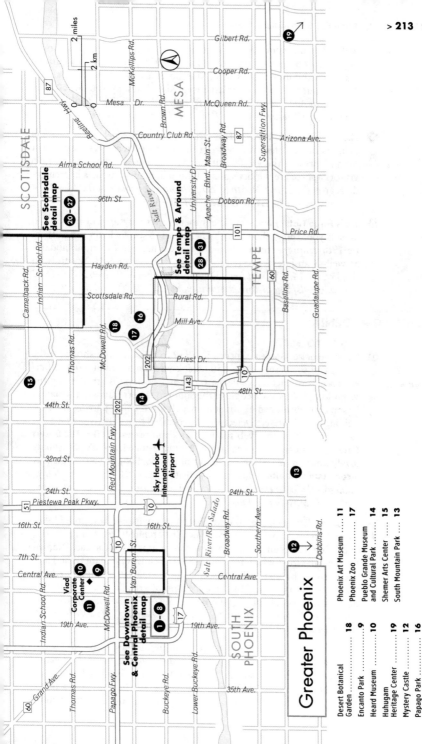

Greater Phoenix

Desert Botanical
Garden 18
Encanto Park 9
Heard Museum 10
Huhugam
Heritage Center 19
Mystery Castle 12
Papago Park 16

Phoenix Art Museum 11
Phoenix Zoo 17
Pueblo Grande Museum
and Cultural Park 14
Shemer Arts Center 15
South Mountain Park ... 13

walls. The museum hosts more than 20 significant exhibitions annually. Daily one-hour tours are included in the price of admission: the featured exhibition tour at 1 PM; Museum Masterworks at 2 PM (also at 11 AM Saturday); both tours are repeated on Tuesday at 6 PM. ⊠*1625 N. Central Ave., Central Phoenix* ☎*602/257–1222* ⊕*www.phxart.org* 🖾*$10; free Tues. 3–9 PM* ⊗ *Wed.–Sat. 10–5, Tues. 10–9.*

❸ **Phoenix Museum of History.** This striking glass-and-steel museum offers exhibits on regional history from the 1860s (when Anglo settlement began) through the 1930s. Interactive exhibits are designed to help visitors appreciate the city's multicultural heritage as well as its tremendous growth. ⊠*105 N. 5th St., Downtown Phoenix* ☎*602/253–2734* ⊕*www.pmoh.org* 🖾*$6* ⊗ *Tues.–Sat. 10–5.*

❻ **Wells Fargo History Museum.** The museum isn't very big but if the Wild West is your thing, there's lots of neat stuff to see, including an authentic 19th-century stagecoach and a replica that you can climb aboard, as well as an interactive telegraph. The artwork of N.C. Wyeth is on display. ⊠*145 W. Adams, Downtown Phoenix* ☎*602/378–1852* ⊕*www.wellsfargohistory.com/museums* 🖾*Free* ⊗ *Weekdays 9–5.*

GREATER PHOENIX

WHAT TO SEE

⑱ **Desert Botanical Garden.** Opened in 1939 to conserve and showcase the ecology of the desert, these 150 acres contain more than 4,000 different species of cacti, succulents, trees, and flowers. A stroll along the ½-mi-long Plants and People of the Sonoran Desert trail is a fascinating lesson in environmental adaptations; children enjoy playing the self-guiding game "Desert Detective." Specialized tours are available at an extra cost; check the Web site for times and prices. ■TIP→**The Desert Botanical Garden stays open late, to 8 PM year-round, and it's particularly lovely when lighted by the setting sun or by moonlight, so you can plan for a cool, late visit after a full day of activities.** ⊠*1201 N. Galvin Pkwy., Papago Salado* ☎*480/941–1225* ⊕*www.dbg.org* 🖾*$10* ⊗ *Oct.–Apr., daily 8–8; May–Sept., daily 7–8.*

⑲ **Huhugam Heritage Center.** Built to harmonize with the land, the Huhugam Heritage Center mixes cool modern architecture with red earth, and as a whole is an impressive new way of looking at the past. Named for the tribe from which the modern-day Akimel O'odham (Pima) and Pee Posh (Maricopa) tribes descended, the small museum and education center is a celebration and collection of arts, culture, and history of the native people of the Gila River. ⊠*4759 N. Maricopa Rd., The Gila River Indian Community, south of Chandler* ☎*520/796–3500* ⊕*www.huhugam.com* 🖾*$5* ⊗ *Wed.–Fri. 10–4.*

⑫ **Mystery Castle.** At the foot of South Mountain lies a curious dwelling built from desert rocks by Boyce Gulley, who came to Arizona to cure his tuberculosis. Boyce's daughter Mary Lou has lived here since her father's death in 1945, and, though she has slowed down a bit in recent years, she still leads tours on request. Full of fascinating oddities, the castle has 18 rooms with 13 fireplaces, a downstairs grotto tavern, a roll-away bed with a mining railcar as its frame, and some original pieces of Frank Lloyd Wright–designed furniture. The pump organ belonged to Elsie, the Widow of Tombstone, who buried six husbands under suspicious circumstances. ✉ *800 E. Mineral Rd., South Phoenix* ☎ *602/268–1581* ▨ *$5* ⏰ *Oct.–June, Thurs.–Sun. 11–4. Call to confirm hrs.*

> **PAPAGO SALADO**
>
> The word Papago, meaning "bean eater," was a name given by 16th-century Spanish explorers to the Hohokam, a vanished native people of the Phoenix area. Farmers of the desert, the Hohokam lived in central Arizona from about AD 1 to 1450, when their civilization abandoned the Salt River (Rio Salado) valley, leaving behind the remnants of their villages and a complex system of irrigation canals.

16 Papago Park. An amalgam of hilly desert terrain, streams, and lagoons, this park has picnic ramadas (shaded, open-air shelters), a golf course, a playground, hiking and biking trails, and even large-mouth bass and trout fishing. (An urban fishing license is required for anglers age 15 and over.) The hike up to landmark **Hole-in-the-Rock** (a natural observatory used by the native Hohokam to devise a calendar system) is steep and rocky, and a much easier climb up than down. **Governor Hunt's Tomb,** the white pyramid at the top of ramada 16, commemorates the former Arizona leader and provides a lovely view. ✉ *625 N. Galvin Pkwy., Papago Salado* ☎ *602/256–3220* ⊕ *www. papagosalado.org* ▨ *Free* ⏰ *Daily 6–11.*

17 Phoenix Zoo. Four designated trails wind through this 125-acre zoo, replicating such habitats as an African savannah and a tropical rain forest. Meerkats, warthogs, desert bighorn sheep, and the endangered Arabian oryx are among the unusual sights. The Forest of Uco is home to the endangered spectacled bear from South America. Harmony Farm on the Discovery Trail introduces youngsters to small mammals, and a stop at the big red barn provides a chance to groom a horse or milk a cow. The Butterfly Pavilion is also enchanting. The 30-minute narrated safari train tour costs $3 and provides a good orientation to the park. ■TIP→ **In December the zoo stays open late (6–10 PM) for the popular "Zoolights" exhibit that transforms the area into an enchanted forest of more than 225 million twinkling lights, many in the shape of the zoo's residents. Starry Safari Friday Nights in summer are fun, too.** ✉ *455 N. Galvin Pkwy., Papago Salado* ☎ *602/273–1341* ⊕ *www.phoenixzoo. org* ▨ *$14* ⏰ *Jan. 7–May and Oct.–Nov. 6, daily 8–5; June–Sept., weekdays 7–2, weekends 7–4; Nov. 7–Jan. 6, daily 8–4.*

14 Pueblo Grande Museum and Cultural Park. Phoenix's only national landmark, this park was once the site of a 500-acre Hohokam village supporting about 1,000 people and containing homes, storage rooms, cemeteries, and ball courts. Three exhibition galleries hold displays on the Hohokam culture and archaeological methods. View the 10-minute orientation video before heading out on the ½-mi Ruin Trail past excavated sites that give a hint of Hohokam savvy: there's a building

Fodor's Choice
★

whose corner doorway was perfectly placed to watch the summer-solstice sunrise. Children particularly like the hands-on, interactive learning center. Guided tours by appointment only. ✉ *4619 E. Washington St., Papago Salado* ☎ *602/495–0901* ⊕ *www.pueblogrande.com* ⌨ *$5* ⊗ *Oct.–Apr., Mon.–Sat. 9–4:45, Sun. 1–4:45; May–Sept., Tues.–Sat. 9–4:45. Closed Sun. and Mon.*

⑮ **Shemer Arts Center.** Near the Phoenician Resort, the Shemer Arts Center ☾ features revolving exhibits of current Arizona artists, who have agreed ★ to donate one of their pieces to the center's permanent collection. The collection is largely contemporary and exhibits change every month or so in this former residence. ✉ *5005 E. Camelback Rd., Greater Phoenix* ☎ *602/262–4727* ⊕ *www.phoenix.gov/shemer* ⌨ *Free* ⊗ *Mon. and Wed.–Fri. 10–5, Tues. 10–9, Sat. 9–1.*

⑬ **South Mountain Park.** This desert wonderland, the world's largest city ☾ park (almost 17,000 acres), offers a wilderness of mountain-desert ★ trails for hikers, bikers, and horseback riders—and a great place to view sunsets. The Environmental Center has a model of the park as well as displays detailing its history, from the time of the ancient Hohokam people to gold-seekers. Roads climb past picnic ramadas constructed by the Civilian Conservation Corps, winding through desert flora to the trailheads. Look for ancient petroglyphs, try to spot a desert cottontail rabbit or chuckwalla lizard, or simply stroll among the desert vegetation. Maps of all scenic drives as well as of hiking, mountain biking, and horseback trails are available at the Gatehouse Entrance just inside the park boundary. ✉ *10919 S. Central Ave., South Phoenix* ☎ *602/495–0222* ⊕ *www.phoenix.gov/parks* ⌨ *Free* ⊗ *Daily 5:30–10:30; Environmental Education Center: Wed.–Sat. 9–3, Sun. 9–2.*

SCOTTSDALE

Nationally known art galleries, souvenir shops, and funky Old Town fill downtown Scottsdale—the third-largest artist community in the United States. Fifth Avenue is known for shopping and Native American jewelry and crafts stores, while Main Street and Marshall Way are home to the international art set with galleries and interior-design shops. Most galleries on Main Street and Marshall Way are open Thursday evenings until 9. Although your tour of downtown can easily be completed on foot, the Ollie the Trolley service operates a trolley with regular service through Scottsdale (☎ *480/970–8130* information). ■ **TIP→If you have limited time in the area, spend a half day in downtown Scottsdale and the rest of the day at Taliesin West.**

Numbers in the margin correspond to numbers on the What to See in Scottsdale map.

WHAT TO SEE

㉖ **5th Avenue.** Whether you seek handmade Native American arts and crafts, casual clothing, or cacti, you'll find it here—at such landmark shops as Adolfos Espoza, Kactus Jock, and Gilbert Ortega. ✉ *5th Ave. between Civic Center Rd. and Stetson Dr., Downtown Scottsdale* ☎ *800/737–0008* ⊕ *www.5thavescottsdale.org.*

5th Avenue ... **26**

Main Street
Arts
District **24**

Marshall Way
Arts
District **25**

Old Town
Scottsdale **23**

Scottsdale
Center for
the Arts **20**

Scottsdale
Historical
Museum **22**

Scottsdale Museum
of Contemporary
Art **21**

Taliesin
West **27**

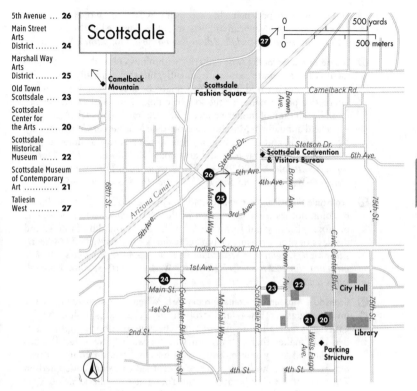

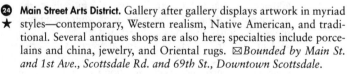

NEED A BREAK?

The **Sugar Bowl Ice Cream Parlor** (✉ *4005 N. Scottsdale Rd., Downtown Scottsdale* ☎ *480/946–0051*) transports you back in time to a 1950s malt shop. In business in the same building since 1958, the Sugar Bowl serves great burgers and lots of yummy ice-cream confections. Valley resident Bil Keane, creator of the comic strip "Family Circus," has often used this spot as inspiration for his cartoons, many of which are on display here.

㉔ **Main Street Arts District.** Gallery after gallery displays artwork in myriad ★ styles—contemporary, Western realism, Native American, and traditional. Several antiques shops are also here; specialties include porcelains and china, jewelry, and Oriental rugs. ✉ *Bounded by Main St. and 1st Ave., Scottsdale Rd. and 69th St., Downtown Scottsdale.*

㉕ **Marshall Way Arts District.** Galleries that exhibit predominantly contemporary art line the blocks of Marshall Way north of Indian School Road, and upscale gift and jewelry stores can be found here, too. Farther north on Marshall Way across 3rd Avenue, are more art galleries and creative stores with a Southwestern flair. ✉ *Marshall Way, from Indian School Rd. to 5th Ave., Downtown Scottsdale.*

㉓ **Old Town Scottsdale.** "The West's Most Western Town," this area has rustic storefronts and wooden sidewalks; it's touristy, but the closest you'll come to experiencing life here as it was 80 years ago. High-quality jewelry, pots, and Mexican imports are sold alongside kitschy souvenirs. ✉ *Main St. from Scottsdale Rd. to Brown Ave., Downtown Scottsdale.*

㉚ Scottsdale Center for the Arts. Galleries within this cultural and entertainment complex rotate exhibits frequently, but they typically emphasize contemporary art and artists. You might be able to catch a comical, interactive performance of the long-running "Late Night Catechism," or an installation of modern dance. The acclaimed Scottsdale Arts Festival is held annually in March. The **Scottsdale Museum of Contemporary Art** is on-site, and there's also a good museum store for unusual jewelry and stationery, posters, and art books. ✉ *7380 E. 2nd St., Downtown Scottsdale* ☎ *480/994–2787* ⊕ *www.scottsdalearts.org* 🎟 *Free* 🕐 *Mon.–Wed., Fri., and Sat. 10–5, Thurs. 10–8, Sun. noon–5.*

㉒ Scottsdale Historical Museum. Scottsdale's first schoolhouse, this redbrick building houses a reconstruction of the 1910 schoolroom, as well as photographs, original furniture from the city's founding fathers, and displays of other treasures from Scottsdale's early days. ✉ *7333 Scottsdale Mall, Downtown Scottsdale* ☎ *480/945–4499* ⊕ *www.scottsdale museum.com* 🎟 *Free* 🕐 *Oct.–May, Wed.–Sat. 10–5, Sun. noon–4; June–Sept., Wed.–Sun. 10–2.*

㉑ Scottsdale Museum of Contemporary Art. When you step through the
🔄 immense glass entryway and stroll through the spaces within the five galleries, you realize it's not just the spacious outdoor sculpture garden that makes this a "museum without walls." New installations are planned every few months, with an emphasis on contemporary art, architecture, and design. Free, docent-led tours are conducted on Thursday at 1:30. Kids can visit the Young at Art gallery. SMoCA, as it's known locally, is connected with the **Scottsdale Center for the Arts**. ✉ *7374 E. 2nd St., Downtown Scottsdale* ☎ *480/994–2787* ⊕ *www.scottsdalearts.org* 🎟 *$7, free Thurs.* 🕐 *Sept.–May, Wed. and Sun. noon–5, Thurs. 10–8, Fri. and Sat. 10–5; June–Aug., Tues., Wed., Fri., and Sat. 10–5, Thurs. 10–8, Sun. noon–5.*

㉗ Taliesin West. Ten years after visiting Arizona in 1927 to consult on
Fodor'sChoice designs for the Biltmore hotel, architect Frank Lloyd Wright chose
★ 600 acres of rugged Sonoran Desert at the foothills of the McDowell Mountains as the site for his permanent winter residence. Today the site is a National Historic Landmark and still an active community of students and architects. Wright and apprentices constructed a desert camp here using organic architecture to integrate the buildings with their natural surroundings. In addition to the living quarters, drafting studio, and small apartments of the Apprentice Court, Taliesin West has two theaters, a music pavilion, and the Sun Trap—sleeping spaces surrounding an open patio and fireplace. Five guided tours are offered, ranging from a one-hour "panorama" tour to a three-hour behind-the-scenes tour, with other tours offered seasonally; all visitors must be accompanied by a guide. In 2005, after a major renovation, Wright's living quarters were opened for the first time to the public.

They include a living space and a private bedroom and work space. ■TIP→ It's a short but very worthwhile side trip from downtown Scottsdale to Taliesin West. Drive 20 minutes north on the 101 Freeway to Frank Lloyd Wright Boulevard. The entrance is at the corner of Frank Lloyd Wright Boulevard and Cactus Road. ✉ *12621 Frank Lloyd Wright Blvd., North Scottsdale* ☎ *480/860–2700* ⊕ *www.franklloydwright.org* 🎫 *$18–$45* ☉ *Sept.–June, daily 8:30–5:30; July and Aug., Thurs.–Mon. 8:30–5:30. Call to confirm.*

TEMPE & AROUND

Tempe is the home of Arizona State University's main campus and a thriving student population. A 20-minute drive from Phoenix, the tree- and brick-lined Mill Avenue is the main drag, filled with student hangouts, bookstores, boutiques, eateries, and a repertory movie house. There are always things to do or see, and plenty of music venues and fun, casual dining spots. This is one part of town where the locals actually hang out, stroll, and sit at the outdoor cafés. The Tempe Festival of the Arts on Mill Avenue is held twice a year (in early December and March–April); it has all sorts of interesting arts and crafts (⊕ *www.tempefestivalofthearts.com*).

The inverted pyramid that is Tempe City Hall, on 5th Street, one block east of Mill Avenue, was constructed by local architects Rolf Osland and Michael Goodwin not just to win design awards (which they have) but also to shield city workers from the desert sun. The pyramid is built mainly of bronzed glass and stainless steel, and the point disappears in a sunken courtyard lushly landscaped with jacaranda, ivy, and flowers, out of which the pyramid widens to the sky: stand underneath and gaze up for a weird fish-eye perspective.

The banks of the Rio Salado in Tempe are the site of a new commercial and entertainment district, and Tempe Town Lake—a 2-mi-long waterway created by inflatable dams in a flood control channel—which is open for boating. There are biking and jogging paths on the perimeter.

Note that Tempe will be an incredible sight when its acres of high-rise condos, lofts, and upscale retail space have been completed. Until then, Tempe, especially downtown and the area surrounding the ASU campus, is largely a traffic-ridden construction site. Allow for plenty of time to get around, especially during special events.

Numbers in the text correspond to numbers on the Tempe & Around map.

WHAT TO SEE

③⓪ Arizona State University. What began as the Tempe Normal School for Teachers—in 1886, a four-room redbrick building and 20-acre cow pasture—is now the 750-acre campus of ASU, the largest university in the Southwest. The **ASU Visitor Information Center** (✉ *215 E. 7th St., at Rural Rd.* ☎ *480/965–0100*) has maps of a self-guided walking tour (it's a long walk from Mill Avenue, so you might opt for the short

4

Arizona State
University **30**

Mesa Southwest
Museum **31**

Tempe
Center for
the Arts **29**

Tempe Town
Lake **28**

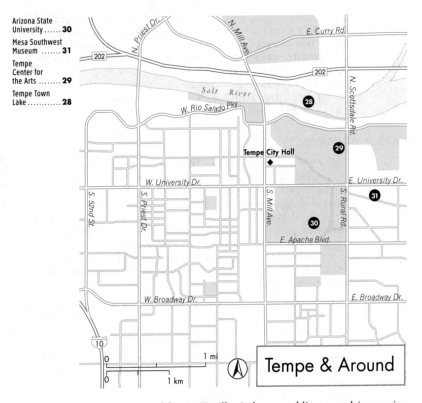

Tempe & Around

version suggested here). You'll wind past public art and innovative architecture—including a music building that bears a strong resemblance to a wedding cake (designed by Taliesin students to echo Frank Lloyd Wright's Gammage Auditorium) and a law library shaped like an open book—and end up at the 71,706-seat **Sun Devil Stadium** (⊠ *ASU Campus, 5th St.* ☎ *800/786–3857*), home to the school's Sun Devils. One of the most outstanding stadiums in the country, it has a spectacular setting. It's literally carved out of a mountain and cradled between the Tempe buttes. While touring the west end of campus, stop into the **Arizona State University Art Museum** (⊠ *Mill Ave. and 10th St.* ☎ *480/965–2787* ⊕ *asuartmuseum.asu.edu* ⊠ *Free* ☉ *Sept.–Apr., Tues. 10–9, Wed.–Sat. 10–5; May–Aug., Tues.–Sat. 11–5, Sun. 1–5*). It's in the gray-purple stucco Nelson Fine Arts Center, just north of the Gammage Auditorium. For a relatively small museum, it has an extensive collection, including 19th- and 20th-century painting and sculpture by masters such as Winslow Homer, Edward Hopper, Georgia O'Keeffe, and Rockwell Kent. Works by faculty and student artists are also on display, and there's a gift shop. In Matthews Hall, the **Northlight Gallery** (⊠ *Matthews Hall, Mill Ave. and 10th St.* ☎ *480/965–6517* ⊠ *Free* ☉ *Mon. 7–9, Tues.–Thurs. 10:30–4:30, Sat. 12:30–4:30*) exhibits works by both renowned and emerging photographers.

③ Mesa Southwest Museum. Kids young and old get a thrill out of the ☺ largest collection of dinosaur fossils in the state at this large museum where you can also pan for gold and see changing exhibits from around the world. ✉ *53 N. Macdonald St., Mesa* ☎ *480/644–2230* ⊕ *www.cityofmesa.org/swmuseum* ✉ *$8* ☉ *Tues.–Fri. 10–5, Sat. 11– 5, Sun. 1–5.*

㉙ Tempe Center for the Arts. This award-winning arts center at the edge of Tempe Town Lake opened in 2007 and has since become a great source of local pride. Visual art, music, theater, and dance, featuring local, regional, and international talent are showcased in a state-of-the-art, 600-seat proscenium theater, a 200-seat studio theater and a 3,500 square-foot gallery. ✉ *700 W. Rio Salada Pkwy.* ☎ *480/350– 2822* ⊕ *www.tempe.gov/arts.*

㉘ Tempe Town Lake. The man-made Town Lake has turned downtown ☺ Tempe into a commercial and urban-living hot spot and attracts college students and Valley residents of all ages. Little ones enjoy the Splash Playground, and fishermen appreciate the rainbow trout–stocked lake. **Rio Lago Cruises** rents boats and has a selection of short cruise options. ✉ *990 W. Rio Salado Pkwy., between Mill and Rural Aves. north of Arizona State University* ☎ *480/350-8625, 480/517–4050 Rio Lago Cruises* ⊕ *www.tempe.gov/lake and www.riolagocruise.com.*

SPORTS & THE OUTDOORS

BALLOONING
Adventures Out West and Unicorn Balloon Company (☎ *480/991–3666 or 800/755–0935* ⊕ *www.adventuresoutwest.com*) has horseback riding, jeep tours, and hot-air-balloon flights that conclude with complimentary champagne, a flight certificate, and video.

The Hot Air Balloon Company (☎ *602/482–6030 or 800/843–5987* ⊕ *www.arizonaballooning.com*) offers private and group sunrise and sunset flights with sparkling beverages and fresh pastries served on touchdown.

Hot Air Expeditions (☎ *480/502–6999 or 800/831–7610* ⊕ *www.hotair expeditions.com*) is the best ballooning in Phoenix. Flights are long, the staff is charming, and the gourmet snacks, catered by the acclaimed Vincent restaurant, are out of this world.

BICYCLING
There are plenty of gorgeous areas for biking in the Phoenix area, but riding in the streets isn't recommended as there are few adequate bike lanes in the city. **Phoenix Parks and Recreation** (☎ *602/262–6861* ⊕ *www. ci.phoenix.az.us/parks*) has detailed maps of Valley bike paths.

ABC/Desert Biking Adventures (☎ *602/320–4602 or 888/249–2453* ⊕ *www.desertbikingadventures.com*) offers two-, three-, and four-hour mountain-biking excursions through the McDowell Mountains and the Sonoran Desert.

AOA Adventures (☎480/945–2881 ⊕www.aoa-adventures.com) leads half-day, full-day, and multiple-day adventures, with their extremely knowledgeable and personable staff.

Wheels N' Gear (⊠16447 N. 91st St., North Scottsdale, Scottsdale ☎480/945–2881) rents bikes by the day or the week.

GOLF

Green fees can run from $35 at a public course to more than $500 at some of Arizona's premier golfing spots. New courses seem to pop up monthly: there are more than 200 in the Valley (some lighted at night), and the PGA's Southwest section has its headquarters here. Call well ahead for tee times during the cooler months. During the summer, fees drop dramatically and it's not uncommon to schedule a round before dawn. ■TIP→ **Some golf courses offer a discounted twilight rate—and the weather is often much more amenable at this time of day.** Check course Web sites for discounts before making your reservations. Also, package deals abound at resorts as well as through booking agencies like **Arizona Golf Adventures** (☎877/841–6570 ⊕www.azteetimes.com), who will plan and schedule a nonstop golf holiday for you. For a copy of the *Arizona Golf Guide*, contact the **Arizona Golf Association** (☎602/944–3035 or 800/458–8484 ⊕www.azgolf.org).

Arizona Biltmore Country Club (⊠Arizona Biltmore Resort & Spa, 24th St. and Missouri Ave., Camelback Corridor ☎602/955–9655 ⊕www.arizonabiltmore.com), the granddaddy of Valley golf courses, has two 18-hole PGA championship courses, lessons, and clinics. Green fees range from $49 (in summer months) to $205.

FodorśChoice   **ASU Karsten Golf Course** (⊠1125 E. Rio Salado Pkwy., Tempe
★   ☎480/921–8070 ⊕www.asukarsten.com) is the Arizona State University 18-hole golf course where NCAA champions train. Green fees are between $35 and $108.

FodorśChoice   **Gold Canyon Golf Club** (⊠6100 S. King's Ranch Rd., Gold Canyon
★   ☎480/982–9449 or 800/624–6445 ⊕www.gcgr.com), near Apache Junction in the East Valley, offers fantastic views of the Superstition Mountains and challenging golf. Green fees range from $54 to $199.

★ **Grayhawk Country Club** (⊠8620 E. Thompson Peak Pkwy., North Scottsdale, Scottsdale ☎480/502–1800 ⊕www.grayhawk.com), a 36-hole course, has beautiful mountain views. The cost for 18 holes ranges from $50 (summer) to $225; 36 holes is $325.

★ **The Phoenician Golf Club** (⊠The Phoenician, 6000 E. Camelback Rd., Camelback Corridor ☎480/423–2449 ⊕www.thephoenician.com) has a 27-hole course. Green fees are $79 to $199. Summer fees after 11 AM start at $29.

★ **Tournament Players Club of Scottsdale** (⊠Fairmont Scottsdale Princess Resort, 17020 N. Hayden Rd., North Scottsdale, Scottsdale ☎480/585–3600 ⊕www.tpc.com), a 36-hole course by Tom Weiskopf and Jay Morrish, is the site of the PGA FBR Open, which takes place in January. Green fees range from $75 to $260.

FodorśChoice   **Troon North** (⊠10320 E. Dynamite Blvd., North Scottsdale, Scotts-
★   dale ☎480/585–7700 ⊕www.troonnorthgolf.com) is a challenge for the length alone (7,008 yards). The million-dollar views add to the

experience at this perfectly maintained 36-hole course. Green fees are $75 to $295.

HIKING

The city's **Phoenix Mountain Preserve System** (✍️ *Phoenix Mountain Preservation Council, Box 26121, Phoenix 85068* ☎️ *602/262–6861* 🌐 *www. phoenixmountains.org*) administers the mountainous regions that surround the city and has its own park rangers who can help plan your hikes. It also publishes a book, *Day Hikes and Trail Rides in and*

around Phoenix. ■**TIP→**No matter the season, be sure to bring sunscreen, a hat, plenty of water, and a camera to capture a dazzling sunset. It's always a good idea to tell someone where you'll be and when you plan to return.

The wonderful folks at **AOA Adventures** (☎️ *480/945–2881* 🌐 *www.aoa-adventures.com*) cater to hikers at different levels of expertise on their half-day, full-day, and multiple-day hikes. The guides are extremely knowledgeable about local flora and fauna.

★ **Camelback Mountain and Echo Canyon Recreation Area** (✉️ *Tatum Blvd. and McDonald Dr., Paradise Valley* ☎️ *602/256–3220 Phoenix Parks & Recreation Dept.*) has intermediate to difficult hikes up the Valley's most outstanding central landmark.

☺ **The Papago Peaks** (✉️ *Van Buren St. and Galvin Pkwy., Central Scottsdale, Scottsdale* ☎️ *602/256–3220 Phoenix Parks & Recreation Dept. Eastern and Central District*) were sacred sites for the Tohono O'odham. The soft-sandstone peaks contain accessible caves, some petroglyphs, and splendid views of much of the Valley. This is a good spot for family hikes.

Piestewa Peak Summit Trail (✉️ *2701 E. Piestewa Peak Dr., Paradise Valley* ☎️ *602/262–7901 North Mountain Preserves Ranger Station*), just north of Lincoln Drive, ascends the landmark mountain at a steep 19% grade, but children can handle the 1¼-mi hike if adults take it slowly—allow about 1½ hours for each direction. No dogs are allowed on the trail.

★ **South Mountain Park** (✉️ *10919 S. Central Ave., South Phoenix* ☎️ *602/534–6324*) is the jewel of the city's Mountain Park Preserves. Its mountains and arroyos contain more than 60 mi of marked and maintained trails—all open to hikers, horseback riders, and mountain bikers. It also has three car-accessible lookout points, with 65-mi sight lines. Rangers can help you plan hikes to view some of the 200 petroglyph sites.

☺ **Waterfall Trail** (✉️ *13025 N. White Tank Mountain Rd., Waddell* ☎️ *623/935–2505*) is a short and easy trail. Part of the 25 mi of trails available at the White Tanks Regional Park, it's kid-friendly, and strollers and wheelchairs roll along easily to Petroglyph Plaza, which boasts

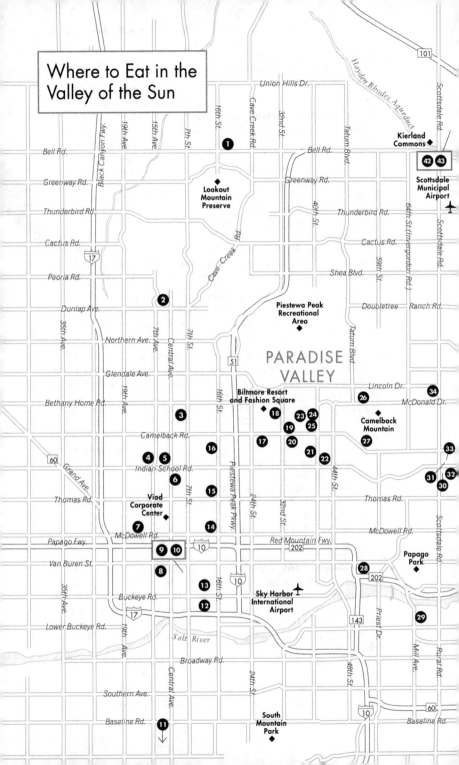

Where to Eat in the Valley of the Sun

**Phoenix &
Paradise Valley** ▼

Barrio Café **15**
Carolina's **12**
Chelsea's Kitchen **24**
Coup Des Tartes **16**
elements **26**
Fate **13**
FEZ **6**
Fry Bread House **4**
Gourmet House
of Hong Kong **14**
La Fontanella **22**
La Grande Orange **21**
Lon's at the Hermosa **23**
Los Dos Molinos **11**
Mrs. White's
Golden Rule Café **8**
My Florist Cafe **7**
Pane Bianco **5**
Pizzeria Bianco **9**
The Rose & Crown **10**
Stockyards Restaurant **28**
Tarbell's **19**
Taste of Inida **1**
Ticoz Resto-Bar **3**
Via Delosantos **2**

Camelback Corridor ▼

Bistro 24 ....**17**
Tomaso's **20**
T. Cook's **27**
Vincent on Camelback **25**
Zen 32 ....**18**

Scottsdale ▼

AZ 88 ....**30**
Bourbon Steak **43**
Carlsbad Tavern **36**
Eddie V's **41**
La Hacienda **42**
L'Ecole **35**
Medizona **33**
Scratch Pastries **32**
Rancho Pinot Grill **34**
Sea Saw **31**

Tempe, Mesa & Chandler ▼

C-Fu Gourmet **37**
Citrus Cafe **38**
El Zocalo Mexican Grill **39**
House of Tricks **29**
Kai **40**

1,500-year-old boulder-carvings—dozens are in clear view from the trail. From there the trail takes a rockier but manageable course to a waterfall, which, depending on area rainfall, can be cascading, creeping, or completely dry. Stop at the visitor center to view desert reptiles such as the king snake and a gopher snake in the aquariums.

HORSEBACK RIDING

More than two dozen stables and equestrian-tour outfitters in the Valley attest to the saddle's enduring importance in Arizona—even in this auto-dominated metropolis. Stables offer rides for an hour, a whole day, and even some overnight adventures.

Cowboy College (✉ *30208 N. 152nd St., North Scottsdale, Scottsdale* ☎ *480/471–3151 or 888/330–8070* ⊕ *www.cowboycollege.com*) has wranglers who will teach you everything you need to know about ridin', ropin', and ranchin'.

MacDonald's Ranch (✉ *26540 N. Scottsdale Rd., North Scottsdale, Scottsdale* ☎ *480/585–0239* ⊕ *www.macdonaldsranch.com*) offers one- and two-hour trail rides and guided breakfast, lunch, and dinner rides through desert foothills above Scottsdale.

★ **OK Corral & Stable** (✉ *2655 E. Whiteley St., Apache Junction* ☎ *480/982–4040* ⊕ *www.okcorrals.com*) offers one-, two-, and four-hour horseback trail rides and steak cookouts as well as one- to five-day horse-packing trips. Ron Feldman, an authority on the history and secrets of the Lost Dutchman Mine, is the guide for historical pack trips through the Superstition Mountains.

WHERE TO EAT

Phoenix and its surroundings have metamorphosed into a melting pot for every type of cuisine imaginable, from northern to Tuscan Italian; from mom-and-pop to Mexico City Mexican; from low-key Cuban to high-end French- and Greek-inspired Southwestern; from Japanese- and Spanish-style tapas to kosher food and American classics with subtle ethnic twists.

DOWNTOWN & CENTRAL PHOENIX

AMERICAN

$$ ✕ **Chelsea's Kitchen.** With its hip, Pacific Northwest–chic interior and a
Fodor'sChoice patio that feels more like a secret garden, Chelsea's Kitchen can easily
★ make you forget you're dining in the desert. This casually sophisticated establishment insists on the freshest ingredients (especially fish), used with equally fresh and flavorful ideas that complement the restaurant's cool but comfortable style. Specials change frequently but regulars love the short-rib hash, shrimp ceviche, and signature tacos, with tortillas and corn chips made on-site. ✉ *5040 N. 40th St., Central Phoenix* ☎ *602/957–2555* ▭ *AE, MC, V* ⊘ *No lunch.*

$ ✕ **Pane Bianco.** Chef-owner Chris Bianco spends his evenings turning out some of the Valley's best pizza at his downtown Pizzeria Bianco, and his days creating to-die-for focaccia sandwiches at this minimalist take-out sandwich shop. Order at the counter, pick up your brown-bagged meal (which always includes a piece of candy), and dine outside at a picnic table. The menu only has a handful of sandwich selections, but each features wood-fired focaccia stuffed with farm-fresh ingredients. ⊠*4404 N. Central Ave., Central Phoenix* ☎*602/234–2100* ⊟*AE, MC, V* ☉*Closed Sun. and Mon. No dinner.*

¢ ✕**La Grande Orange.** This San Francisco–inspired store and eatery sells
Fodor'sChoice artisanal nosh and novelty items, along with a formidable selection
★ of wines. Valley residents flock to LGO, as they call it, to see and be seen, and to feast on mouthwatering sandwiches, pizzas, salads, and decadent breads and desserts. The small tables inside fill up quickly at breakfast and lunch but there's also seating on the patio. Try the Commuter Sandwich on a homemade English muffin or the delicious French pancakes with a Spanish latte that, depending on the barista, might be the most memorable cup of *jose* you'll ever have. ⊠*4410 N. 40th St., Central Phoenix* ☎*602/840–7777* ⊟*AE, MC, V.*

ASIAN

$ **Fate.** In an old house in the evolving downtown arts district, this funky eatery/art gallery/music salon/well-kept secret turns out some of the Valley's best Asian food. Hong Kong–born chef-owner Johnny Chu pairs simple fresh ingredients with fantastic sauces to create popular dishes such as House Dynamite, a spicy stir-fry of pineapple, veggies, and peanuts in a sweet-and-spicy sauce. Dinner is served until 3 AM on weekends, accompanied by a DJ spinning tunes. ⊠*905 N. 4th St., Downtown Phoenix* ☎*602/254–6424* ⊟*MC, V* ☉*Closed Sun.*

BRITISH

$ ✕**The Rose & Crown.** It seems appropriate that next to two of the Valley's major sports complexes, an intriguing new rivalry is afoot. Just north of Chase Field and the US Airways Center, the undefeated heavyweight restaurant champion is Pizzeria Bianco. But now, weighing in on the northwest corner of 7th and Adams streets, is another kind of American restaurant with European roots. The Rose & Crown offers good, hearty, traditional, English pub grub—fish-and-chips, bangers and mash, and shepherd's pie—with equally hearty beers to wash it down. The atmosphere in the historic home is comfortable and inviting, and without the decades of stale smoke, ale, and grease. Expect a wait on game and special-event nights. ⊠*628 E. Adams St., Downtown Phoenix* ☎*602/256–0223* ⚓*Reservations not accepted* ⊟*AE, MC, V*

CAFÉ

$ ✕**My Florist Café.** Cool, classic, and supremely stylish, My Florist is a stunning pacesetter for the future of food and fun in the downtown Phoenix area. The sleek, high-ceiling interior, a wall of windows, hardwood floors, and a pristine jazz piano welcome enlightened locals who know good taste and great-tasting food—the menu consists of gourmet salads and sandwiches made with phenomenal breads baked fresh daily at the adjoining Willo Bakery. ⊠*534 W. McDowell Rd., Downtown Phoenix* ☎*602/254–0333* ⊟*AE, D, DC, MC, V.*

CHINESE

$ ✕**Gourmet House of Hong Kong.** Traditional Chinatown specialties like *chow fun* (thick rice noodles) are excellent at this simple, diner-style place: try the assorted-meat version, with chicken, shrimp, pork, and squid. Dishes with black-bean sauce are among the menu's best. Delights such as five-flavor frogs' legs, duck feet with greens, and beef tripe casserole are offered, if you're feeling adventurous. ⊠*1438 E. McDowell Rd., Downtown Phoenix* ☎*602/253–4859* ⊟*AE, D, MC, V.*

ECLECTIC

$–$$ ✕**FEZ.** It's not a hat—but it does top the list of restaurants in central
Fodor'sChoice   Phoenix. From its sleek interior to its central location and diverse cli-
★   entele, right down to its affordable lunch, happy hour, dinner, Sunday brunch, and late-night menus, FEZ covers everything. "American fare with a Moroccan flair" means bold culinary leaps, with items like the FEZ Burger, *kisras* (flatbread pizza), and the signature crispy rosemary pomegranate chicken—but it all lands safely on the taste buds. Potables include specialty martinis and margaritas and a formidable wine list. ⊠*3815 N. Central Ave., Central Phoenix* ☎*602/287–8700* ⊟*AE, MC, V.*

ITALIAN

$$ ✕**La Fontanella.** Quality and value are a winning combination at this outstanding neighborhood restaurant. The interior is reminiscent of an Italian villa, with antiques, crisp table linens, fresh flowers, and windows dressed in lace curtains, and chef-owner Isabelle Bertuccio turns out magnificent food, often using recipes from her Tuscan and Sicilian relatives. The escargot and herb-crusted rack of lamb top the list. Homemade pasta is served with Sicilian semolina bread and homemade sausages or meatballs. For dessert, Isabelle's husband, Berto, creates sumptuous gelato. ⊠*4231 E. Indian School Rd., Central Phoenix* ☎*602/955–1213* ⊟*AE, D, DC, MC, V* ⊘*No lunch.*

LATIN AMERICAN

$ ✕**Ticoz Resto-Bar.** The slogan "Urban. Latin. Sexy. Chill" fits this place like a stiletto heel. The colorful but dark interior is sleek and cool, the fare has just the right spice, and the happy-hour mojitos have just the right price, making this a hot central Phoenix haunt. Try the Ticoz lettuce wraps, the empanadas, the sweet-corn tamales, or *barbacoa* (simmered) beef. ⊠*5114 N. 7th St., Central Phoenix* ☎*602/200–0160* ⊟*AE, MC, V.*

MEXICAN

$$$ ✕**Barrio Cafe.** Owners Wendy Gruber and Silvana Salcido Esparza have taken Mexican cuisine to a new level. Expect guacamole made to order at your table, and modern Mexican specialties—such as *cochinita pibil,* slow-roasted pork with red achiote and sour orange, and *chiles en Nogada,* a delicious traditional dish from central Mexico featuring a spicy poblano pepper stuffed with fruit, chicken, and raisins—on the menu. The flavor-packed food consistently draws packs of people but you can drink in the intimate atmosphere—and a specialty margarita or *aqua fresca* (fruit water)—while you wait for a table. ⊠*2814 N. 16th St., Downtown Phoenix* ☎*602/636–0240* ⌕*Reservations not accepted* ⊟*AE, MC, V* ⊘*Closed Mon.*

PIZZA

$ ✕**Pizzeria Bianco.** Brooklyn native Chris Bianco makes pizza with a passion in this small establishment on Heritage Square. His wood-fired creations incorporate the finest and freshest ingredients (including homemade mozzarella cheese) in a brick oven imported from Italy. Bar Bianco next door is a good place to relax with a beverage while you wait for your table. ▪TIP➔**Arrive a few minutes before they open at 5 PM to avoid the long wait, especially on Friday and Saturday nights.** ✉623 E. Adams St., Downtown Phoenix ☎602/258–8300 ▤AE, MC, V ☉Closed Sun. and Mon. No lunch.

SOUTHERN

¢ ✕**Mrs. White's Golden Rule Café.** This downtown lunch spot is the best place in town for true Southern cooking. Every entrée—from fried chicken to pork chops—comes with corn bread, and the peach cobbler is legendary. ✉808 E. Jefferson St., Downtown Phoenix ☎602/262–9256 ⌀Reservations not accepted ▤No credit cards ☉Closed weekends. No dinner.

SOUTHWESTERN

¢ ✕**Fry Bread House.** Indian fry bread, a specialty of the Native American culture, is a delicious treat—pillows of deep-fried dough topped with sweet or savory toppings and folded in half. Local fry-bread fanatics get their fix from chef-owner Cecelia Miller of the Tohono O'odham Nation. Choose from culture-crossing combinations like savory shredded chili beef with cheese, beans, green chiles, veggies, and sour cream, or try the sweeter synthesis of honey and sugar, or chocolate with butter. ✉4140 N. 7th Ave., Downtown Phoenix ☎602/351–2345 ▤D, MC, V ☉Closed Sun.

GREATER PHOENIX

AMERICAN

$$$$ ✕**Stockyards Restaurant.** If you're looking for a hearty meal, "Arizona's Original Steak House" is the place to go. Succulent prime rib and steaks, fresh seafood, and poultry are complemented by rib-sticking side dishes such as whiskey-sweet-potato mash, cowboy beans with chorizo, and roasted corn. The handsome dining room decor features Old West heavy wood, etched glass, and pressed-tin ceilings. A beautiful hand-carved mahogany bar and huge cut-glass chandelier adorn the 1889 Saloon in back. ✉5009 E. Washington, South Phoenix ☎602/273–7378 ▤AE, D, DC, MC, V ☉No lunch weekends.

$$$ ✕**Lon's at the Hermosa.** In an adobe hacienda hand-built by cowboy artist Lon Megargee, this romantic spot has sweeping vistas of Camelback Mountain and the perfect patio for after-dinner drinks under the stars.

Fodor'sChoice ★

Megargee's art and cowboy memorabilia decorate the dining room. The menu changes seasonally but includes appetizers like rock shrimp with roasted-corn sauce and juniper-smoked wild Chinook salmon. Wood-grilled, melt-in-your-mouth filet mignon over Gorgonzola mashed potatoes, and more exotic dishes like pecan-grilled antelope are main course options. Phoenicians love the Sunday brunch. ⊠ *Hermosa Inn, 5532 N. Palo Cristi Dr., Paradise Valley* ☎602/955–7878 ⊟*AE, D, DC, MC, V* ⊗ *No lunch Sat.*

ECLECTIC

$$$ ✕ **elements.** Perched on the side of Camelback Mountain at the Sanctuary Resort, this stylish, modern restaurant offers breathtaking desert-sunset and city-light views. There's a cordial community table where you can sit and order such appetizers as the trilogy of duck, wild escargot wontons, and fried calamari with miso-scallion vinaigrette. Entrées are excellent; among the best is the bacon-wrapped fillet of beef with Maytag blue cheese and merlot demi-glace. ⊠ *Sanctuary on Camelback Mountain, 5700 E. McDonald Dr., Paradise Valley* ☎480/607–2300 ⌂ *Reservations essential* ⊟*AE, D, DC, MC, V.*

$$$ ✕ **Tarbell's.** Cutting-edge cuisine is the star at this sophisticated bistro. The grilled salmon glazed with a molasses-lime sauce and served on a crispy potato cake is a long-standing classic; the focaccia with red onion, Romano cheese, and roasted thyme with hummus is excellent; and imaginative designer pizzas are cooked in a wood-burning oven. Your sweet tooth won't be disappointed by Tarbell's warm, rich, chocolate cake topped with pistachio ice cream. Hardwood floors, copper accents, and a curving cherrywood-and-maple bar create a sleek, cosmopolitan look, favored by Biltmore golfers. ⊠ *3213 E. Camelback Rd., Camelback Corridor* ☎602/955–8100 ⌂ *Reservations essential* ⊟*AE, D, DC, MC, V* ⊗ *No lunch.*

FRENCH

$$$$ ✕ **Bistro 24.** Smart and stylish, with impeccable service, the Ritz's Bistro 24 has a parquet floor, colorful murals, an elegant bar, and an outdoor patio. Take a break from shopping at nearby Biltmore Fashion Park and enjoy the largest Cobb salad in town. For dinner, try classic French *steak au poivre* with *frites*, grilled fish, or sushi. Happy hour is every day from 5 to 7 in the bar. Sunday brunch is a local favorite. ⊠ *Ritz-Carlton Hotel, 2401 E. Camelback Rd., Camelback Corridor* ☎602/952–2424 ⊟*AE, D, DC, MC, V.*

$$$ ✕ **Coup Des Tartes.** Tables are scattered among three small rooms of an old house at this country French restaurant. It's BYOB, and there's an $8 corkage fee, but all's forgiven when you taste the delicate cuisine prepared in the tiny kitchen. Offerings may include baked Brie, pineapple-caper *escolar* (a delicious, richer version of sea bass), or herb-crusted chicken with a creamy spinach sauce. The signature dessert, a banana brûlée tart, is delectable. ⊠ *4626 N. 16th St., North Central Phoenix* ☎602/212–1082 ⌂ *Reservations essential* ⊟*AE, D, MC, V* ⋒ *BYOB* ⊗ *Closed Sun. and Mon. No lunch.*

INDIAN

$ ✕**Taste of India.** This perennial favorite in the Valley specializes in northern Indian cuisine. Breads here—*bhatura, naan, paratha*—are superb, and vegetarians enjoy wonderful meatless specialties, including the eggplant-based *benghan bhartha,* and *bhindi masala,* a tempting okra dish. Just about every spice in the rack is used for the lamb and chicken dishes, so be prepared to guzzle extra water—or an English beer. If your server says an item is spicy, *trust him.* ✉1609 E. Bell Rd., North Central Phoenix ☎602/788–3190 ☰AE, MC, V.

ITALIAN

$$$–$$$$ ✕**Tomaso's.** In a town where restaurants can come and go almost overnight, Tomaso's has been a favorite since 1977, and for good reason. Chef Tomaso Maggiore learned to cook at the family's restaurant in Palermo, Sicily, and honed his skills at the Culinary Institute of Rome. The result is authentic Italian cuisine that's consistently well prepared and delicious. The house specialty, *osso buco* (braised veal shank), is outstanding. Other notables include risotto and cannelloni. ✉3225 E. Camelback Rd., Camelback Corridor ☎602/956–0836 ☰AE, D, DC, MC, V ⊗No lunch weekends ✉7341 N. Ray Rd., Chandler ☎480/940–1200.

JAPANESE

$$ ✕**Zen 32.** In the ebb and flow of central Phoenix, Zen 32 has managed to stay afloat while just about every other sushi restaurant has sunk—the convenient location, casually chic atmosphere, and consistently creative rolls make it easy to understand why. The soft-shell crab, rainbow, and caterpillar rolls, and the succulent citrus yellowtail are favorites from the sushi menu while the grill produces plenty of tasty nonfish fare. The covered patio faces the zoom and vroom of 32nd Street, but the soothing mist and meditation music create a tranquil, yes, even Zen-like atmosphere. ✉3160 E. Camelback Rd., Camelback Corridor ☎602/954–8700 ☰AE, MC, V ⊗No lunch weekends.

MEDITERRANEAN

$$$–$$$$
Fodor'sChoice
★ ✕**T. Cook's at the Royal Palms.** One of the finest restaurants in the Valley, T. Cook's oozes romance, from the floor-to-ceiling windows with dramatic views of Camelback Mountain to its 1930s-style Spanish-colonial architecture and decor. The Mediterranean-influenced menu includes grilled "fireplace" fare like pork chops with polenta dumplings, paella, and a changing variety of enticing entrées. Desserts and pastries are works of art. For special-occasion meals, call on the services of the resort's Director of Romance. ✉Royal Palms Resort & Spa, 5200 E. Camelback Rd., Camelback Corridor ☎602/840–3610 ⚑Reservations essential ☰AE, D, DC, MC, V.

MEXICAN

$ ✕**Los Dos Molinos.** In a hacienda that belonged to silent-era movie star Tom Mix, this fun restaurant focuses on New Mexican–style Mexican food. That means *hot.* New Mexico chiles form the backbone and fiery breath of the dishes, and the green-chili enchilada and beef taco are potentially lethal. The red salsa and enchiladas with egg on top are excellent. There's a funky courtyard where you can sip potent margaritas while waiting for a table. Fodors.com users agree, this is a must-do dining experience if you want authentic New Mexican–style food, but be prepared to swig lots of water. ✉ *8646 S. Central Ave., South Phoenix* 🕾 *602/243–9113* ⟐ *Reservations not accepted* ⊟ *AE, D, DC, MC, V* ⊘ *Closed Sun. and Mon.* ✉ *260 S. Alma School Rd., Mesa* 🕾 *480/969–7475*

$ ✕ **Via Delosantos.** The family-owned
Fodor'sChoice restaurant looks a little rough around the edges outside but it's what's inside that counts—an accommodating staff, an enormous and authentic Mexican menu, and one of the best-tasting and best-priced house margaritas in town.

Entrées are ample and include more than just tired combinations of beef, beans, and cheese. Try the fajitas *calabacitas* with a yellow- and green-squash succotash; or the delicious chicken *delosantos,* a cheesy chicken breast and tortilla concoction. Expect to wait on weekends, either at the bar or outside, but also expect that the experience will be worth it. ✉ *9120 N. Central Ave., North Central Phoenix* 🕾 *602/997–6239* ⟐ *Reservations not accepted* ⊟ *AE, D, DC, MC, V.*

¢ ✕ **Carolina's.** This small, nondescript restaurant in South Phoenix makes the most delicious, thin-as-air flour tortillas imaginable. In-the-know locals and downtown working folk have been lining up at Carolina's for years to partake of the homey, inexpensive Mexican food. The tacos, tamales, burritos, flautas, and enchiladas are served on paper plates. ✉ *1202 E. Mohave St., South Phoenix* 🕾 *602/252–1503* ⊟ *AE, D, DC, MC, V* ⊘ *Closed Sun. Dinner on weekdays only until 7:30 PM and Sat. until 6 PM* ✉ *2126 E. Cactus Rd., North Central Phoenix* 🕾 *602/275–8231.*

SOUTHWESTERN

$$$–$$$$ ✕ **Vincent on Camelback.** Chef Guerithault is best known for creating French food with a Southwestern touch. You can make a meal of his famous appetizers: corn ravioli with white-truffle oil, or shrimp beignets with lavender dressing. The dessert menu overflows with intoxicating soufflés. Though the food is renowned, the service is not. ✉ *3930 E. Camelback Rd., Camelback Corridor* 🕾 *602/224–0225* ⟐ *Reservations essential* ⊟ *AE, D, DC, MC, V* ⊘ *Closed Sun. No lunch Sat.*

SCOTTSDALE

AMERICAN

$$$ ✕**Eddie V's.** The DC Ranch area is booming with great restaurants to keep the north Valley locals happy, including this one. By night, Eddie V's appears almost too sophisticated for its upscale-mall location. Sleek lighting filters through massive panes of tinted glass, revealing an elegant, contemporary interior clad in crisp linens. Specializing in fresh seafood done right (try the Hong Kong–style Chilean sea bass or the broiled scallops), grilled meats, and fine wines, the place is great for fine dining. But, with the inviting bar and lounge area and succulent appetizers like kung pao–style calamari and a variety of fresh oysters, Eddie's is also enormously popular (and slightly more affordable) as a happy-hour spot. ✉ *20715 N. Pima Rd., Suite F1, North Scottsdale* ☎*480/538–8468* 🖃*AE, D, DC, MC, V.*

$ ✕**AZ 88.** A great spot for people-watching, this sleek, glassed-in restaurant serves some of the Valley's best cocktails and food at affordable **FodorśChoice** prices. Large portions of tasty salads, sandwiches, sumptuous burgers ★ (try the Au Poivre II), and perfectly poured cosmopolitans never fail to satisfy. If you're seeking quiet, dine outside on the beautiful patio overlooking Scottsdale Mall. ✉*7353 E. Scottsdale Mall, Central Scottsdale* ☎*480/994–5576* 🥢*Reservations not accepted* 🖃*AE, D, DC, MC, V* 🕒*No lunch weekends.*

CAFÉ

$ ✕**Scratch Pastries.** Duc and Noelle Liao are a model couple, literally. The two met in Paris where Duc worked as a fashion photographer and Noelle as a model. Now, the two are the hottest pair in pastry making. A graduate of Le Cordon Bleu, Duc Liao conjures up sublime creations, both salty and sweet, from a savory duck-breast sandwich and a mouthwatering mushroom quiche, to perfectly flaky croissants and a delicately sweet, parfaitlike mont blanc dessert. Don't let the pastry shop's location in a strip mall fool you; this is a flavor trip all the way to France. Expect crowds during peak lunch hours. ✉ *7620 E. Indian School Rd., Suite 103, Downtown Scottsdale* ☎*480/947–0057* 🥢*Reservations not accepted* 🖃*AE, MC, V* 🕒*No dinner.*

ECLECTIC

$$$ ✕**Medizona.** The daring (and pricey) combination of Mediterranean-**FodorśChoice** meets-New Mexican cuisine has been pleasing renowned critics and ★ foodies across the country and all over town for years. Though it appears somewhat lackluster from the outside, the inside is intimate and charming with Saltillo-tile floors, and a mix of brick and yellow walls with accents of dark blue and white that create a pleasant foundation for enjoying the restaurant's marriage of ethnic fare. Where else have you ever had tantalizing rabbit baklava, or achiote-rubbed panfried salmon with crayfish-corn risotto and morel mushroom-baby clam sauce, or Moroccan-spiced chicken with black-bean saffron couscous and cilantro yogurt sauce, or prickly pear tiramisu to top off such a palette-puzzling meal? For something more casual, enjoy the new adjoining wine lounge and tapas bar. ✉ *7217 E. 4th Ave., Scottsdale* ☎*480/947–9500* 🖃*AE, MC, V* 🕒*Closed Sun.*

4

$$$ ✕**Rancho Pinot Grill.** The attention to quality paid by the husband-and-
Fodor'sChoice   wife proprietors here—he manages, she cooks—has made this one of
★   the town's top dining spots. The inventive menu changes daily, depend-
ing on what's fresh. If you're lucky, you might come on a day when
the kitchen has made *posole,* a mouthwatering broth with hominy,
salt pork, and cabbage. Entrées might include quail, chicken with
toasted polenta, scallops with edamame-tomato relish, grilled sea bass,
handmade pasta, or vegetarian antipasto. ⊠*6208 N. Scottsdale Rd.,
northwest of Trader Joe's in Lincoln Village Shops, Central Scottsdale*
☎*480/367–8030* ⊟*AE, D, DC, MC, V* ⊗*Closed Sun. and Mon. mid-
May–Nov. No lunch.*

FRENCH

$$$ ✕**L'Ecole.** You won't regret putting yourself in the talented hands of the
student chefs at the Valley's premier cooking academy. Choose from
an extensive list of French-inspired entrées or the four-course prix-
fixe menu, available for lunch ($30) and dinner ($35). The fine-dining atmosphere is designed to give students (who fill each restaurant
position) and customers the impression of the real thing, which is why
customers keep coming back. The menu changes seasonally but expect
inventive appetizers such as lobster gratin, stuffed rabbit saddle, ricotta
gnocchi, and entrées such as filet mignon. ⊠*Scottsdale Culinary Institute, 8100 E. Camelback Rd., Central Scottsdale* ☎*480/425–3111*
⌃*Reservations essential* ⊟*AE, D, DC, MC, V* ⊗*Closed weekends.*

JAPANESE

$$$ ✕**Sea Saw.** Chef Nobu Fukada is creating some of the Valley's most
Fodor'sChoice   interesting food at this small, simple eatery. "Tapanese" cuisine—small
★   plates of Japanese tapas such as baked black cod marinated in miso,
allow you to sample lots of different items. Other delights include the
white fish carpaccio (served warm) and the sushi foie gras. If you're
feeling really adventurous, try the "Omakase Menu," a 10-course din-
ner created from what's fresh that day. The few tables and bar seats
fill up quickly so if you have to wait, do as the locals do—indulge in a
glass of wine next door at Kazimierz wine bar while you wait. ⊠*7133
E. Stetson Dr., Central Scottsdale* ☎*480/481–9463* ⌃*Reservations
essential* ⊟*AE, D, DC, MC, V* ⊗*No lunch.*

MEXICAN

$$$–$$$$ ✕**La Hacienda.** La Hacienda is widely considered to be among the fin-
Fodor'sChoice   est Mexican-inspired restaurants in North America, and to ensure
★   truly authentic cuisine, executive chef Reed Groban took tasting tours
through Mexican villages and towns and came back with a remarkably
native sense of the country's truly complex palette. You'll find no bur-
ritos or tacos here, but a host of dishes and savory sauces that highlight
the delicate balance of spice, heat, and pure flavor found south of the
border, but rarely in America, making this Mexican food experience
well worth the drive and extra dollars (and the drive to the Fairmont
Scottsdale Princess Resort). Enjoy appetizers like the crab enchilada
with creamy pumpkin-seed sauce, the spinach salad with warm chorizo
dressing, and La Hacienda's signature dish—spit-roasted suckling pig
marinated in tamarind and bitter orange, carved table-side. ⊠*Fair-*

mont Scottsdale Princess Resort, 7575 E. Princess Dr., North Scottsdale ☎*480/585–4848* ⌖*Reservations essential* ▭*AE, D, DC, MC, V* ◷*Closed Wed. No lunch.*

$$ ✗**Carlsbad Tavern.** This busy New Mexico–style eatery serves big portions of such tasty dishes as a half-pound habanero cheeseburger, green-chili mashed potatoes, chipotle barbecue baby back ribs, and *carne adovada,* a spicy, slow-roasted pork specialty. They'll custom mix your margarita with fresh lime and lemon juice and blend it with your choice of some 35 tequilas. There's a late-night menu for the after-10 PM crowd. ⊠*3313 N. Hayden Rd., Central Scottsdale* ☎*480/970–8164* ▭*AE, D, MC, V.*

STEAK

$$$$ ✗**Bourbon Steak.** Formerly the site of the once-renowned Marquesa restaurant, this upscale steak restaurant was opened in February 2008 by top-rated chef Michael Mina and is already living up to the royal reputation of the Scottsdale Princess. Select from American-grade or Japanese Kobe beef. The flaming doughnuts Foster makes a perfect finish to a fine meal. ⊠*Fairmont Scottsdale Princess Resort, 7575 E. Princess Dr., North Scottsdale* ☎*480/585–4848* ⌖*Reservations essential* ▭*AE, D, DC, MC, V* ◷*Closed Mon. and Tues. Brunch only Sun. No lunch.*

TEMPE & AROUND

CHINESE

$–$$ ✗**C-Fu Gourmet.** This is serious Chinese food, the kind you'd expect to find on Mott Street in New York City's Chinatown or Grant Avenue in San Francisco. The large restaurant is generally loud and chaotic but there's a good reason that tons of Valley residents will endure long drives and wait times to be part of it. C-Fu's specialty is fish, and you can watch several species swimming around the big holding tanks. Shrimp are fished out of the tank, steamed, and bathed in a potent garlic sauce. Clams in black-bean sauce and tilapia in a ginger-scallion sauce also hit all the right buttons. If you don't find what you're looking for on the menu, tell them what you want and they'll make it. There's a daily dim sum brunch, too. ⊠*2051 W. Warner Rd., Chandler* ☎*480/899–3888* ▭*AE, D, DC, MC, V.*

ECLECTIC

$$$ ✗**House of Tricks.** There's nothing up the sleeves of Robert and Robin Trick, who work magic on the ever-changing eclectic menu that emphasizes the freshest available seafood, poultry, and fine meats, as well as vegetarian selections, and keeps up with the changing tastes of ASU attendees and visitors. One of the Valley's most unique dining venues, the restaurant encompasses a 1920s home and a separate brick- and adobe-style house originally built in 1903, adjoined by an intimate wooden deck and outdoor patio shaded by a canopy of grapevines and trees. At lunch you can't go wrong with the quiche of the day. ⊠*114 E. 7th St., Tempe* ☎*480/968–1114* ▭*AE, D, MC, V* ◷*Closed Sun.*

FRENCH

$$$ ✕ **Citrus Cafe.** Elegant yet casual, this small restaurant does everything right, from the romantic candlelit dining room to a daily menu featuring what's freshest from the market. For starters, try the baked Brie with almonds and apples or the superb leek-and-potato soup. Main dishes are pure French comfort food: veal kidneys, sweetbreads, leg of lamb, roast pork, and occasionally rabbit. ✉ *2330 N. Alma School Rd., Chandler* ☎ *480/899–0502* ▭ *AE, D, DC, MC, V* ✆ *Closed Mon. No lunch.*

MEXICAN

$$ ✕ **El Zocalo Mexican Grill.** A positively caliente experience that might be one of the key reasons to put Chandler on your map. With high ceilings, plenty of open space and a modern twist, El Zocalo is a far cry from the typical Mexican cantina. Enjoy a huge selection of Mexico's finest tequilas and sip on Spanish wines while savoring some authentic Mexican fare out on the inviting, courtyard-style patio. As the night marches on, push your table aside and put on your dancing shoes for some fantastic salsa music performed live by a top-notch local band. ✉ *28 S. San Marcos Pl., Chandler* ☎ *480/722-0303* ▭ *AE, D, DC, MC, V* ✆ *Closed Sun. and Mon.*

SOUTHWESTERN

$$$$ ✕ **Kai.** Innovative Southwestern cuisine at Kai ("seed" in the Pima language) uses indigenous ingredients from local tribal farms. The seasonal menu reflects the restaurant's natural setting on the Gila River Indian Community. Standout appetizers include lobster tail on Indian fry bread and bacon-wrapped quail. Entrées like seared duck breast with pheasant sausage and the Cheyenne River buffalo tenderloin are excellent. The restaurant is adorned with Native American artifacts and has huge windows that showcase gorgeous mountain and desert views. ✉ *Sheraton Wild Horse Pass Resort & Spa, 5594 W. Wild Horse Pass Blvd., Chandler* ☎ *602/225–0100* ⌂ *Reservations essential* ▭ *AE, D, DC, MC, V* ✆ *Closed Sun. and Mon.*

WHERE TO STAY

Developers and hoteliers have taken advantage of the Valley's wide-open spaces to introduce super-size, luxury resorts that offer everything from their own golf courses and water parks to four-star restaurants and shopping villages. Downtown Phoenix properties tend to be the business hotels, close to the heart of the city and the convention centers—and often closer to the average vacationer's budget. Many properties here cater to corporate travelers during the week but lower their rates on weekends to entice leisure travelers, so ask about weekend specials when making reservations.

DOWNTOWN & CENTRAL PHOENIX

$$$ ⊡ **Hotel San Carlos.** Built in 1927 in an Italian Renaissance design, the seven-story San Carlos is the only historic hotel still operating in downtown Phoenix. Among other distinctions, it was the Southwest's first air-conditioned hotel, and suites bear the names of such movie-star guests as Marilyn Monroe and Spencer Tracy. Big-band music, wall tapestries, Austrian crystal chandeliers, shiny copper elevators, and an accommodating staff transport you to a more genteel era. The rooms are snug by modern standards but have attractive period furnishings. An off-site fitness center accommodates guests for a small fee. **Pros:** A distinctive, character-filled spot for a downtown stay. **Cons:** Old-time charm may not translate well to those used to modern spaciousness and amenities. ⊠ *202 N. Central Ave., Downtown Phoenix,* ☎ *602/253–4121 or 866/253–4121* ⊕ *www.hotelsancarlos.com* ↪ *109 rooms, 12 suites* ☖ *In-room: Wi-Fi. In-hotel: restaurant, pool, room service, laundry service, parking (fee), public Wi-Fi, no-smoking rooms* ▤ *AE, D, DC, MC, V.*

$$$ ⊡ **Hyatt Regency Phoenix.** This convention-oriented hotel efficiently handles the arrival and departure of hundreds of business travelers each day. The seven-story atrium has huge sculptures, colorful tapestries, potted plants, and comfortable seating areas. The revolving restaurant has panoramic views of the Phoenix area. Rooms are spacious, but the atrium roof blocks east views on floors 8 through 10. **Pros:** Business amenities, views from restaurant. **Cons:** Tricky area to navigate, especially during construction; parking gets pricey. ⊠ *122 N. 2nd St., Downtown Phoenix,* ☎ *602/252–1234* ↪ *712 rooms, 25 suites* ☖ *In-room: Wi-Fi. In-hotel: 4 restaurants, bars, pools, gym, concierge, parking (fee), no-smoking rooms* ▤ *AE, D, DC, MC, V.*

$$$ ⊡ **Wyndham Phoenix.** When Wyndham took over this former Crowne Plaza, the chain invested $6 million to create an appealing mix of classic comfort and modern accommodations. Ideally situated for all things downtown (but little else) the hotel stands, with very little competition, in the center of bustling Copper Square within 1 mi of Heritage and Science parks, America West Arena, Chase Field, and the Arizona Center. Spacious rooms with subtle Southwestern tones are designed for the business traveler, and are relatively quiet and well-lit, with large desks and ergonomic desk chairs, but they're also kid-friendly, comfortable, and convenient for pro baseball and basketball fans, as well as theater, symphony, convention, and celebrity concertgoers. **Pros:** Will be prime location for light-rail travel, on-site Starbucks for coffee junkies. **Cons:** Outdated rooms, better for business than pleasure. ⊠ *50 E. Adams St., Downtown Phoenix,* ☎ *602/333–0000* ↪ *532 rooms, 108 suites* ☖ *In-room: refrigerator (some), Ethernet, Wi-Fi (some). In-hotel: restaurant, room service, bar, pool, gym, laundry service, parking (fee), no-smoking rooms* ▤ *AE, D, DC, MC, V.*

GREATER PHOENIX

$$$$ ⊡ **Arizona Biltmore Resort & Spa.** Designed by Frank Lloyd Wright's colleague Albert Chase McArthur, the Biltmore has been Phoenix's premier resort since it opened in 1929. The lobby, with its stained-glass

Fodor'sChoice ★

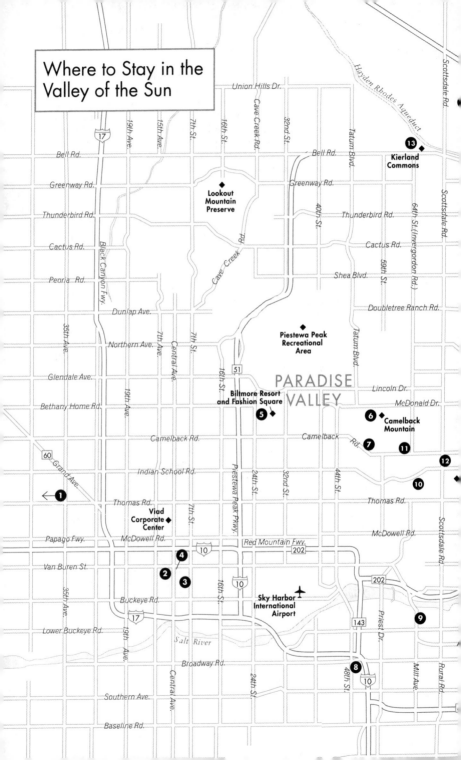

Where to Stay in the Valley of the Sun

I-17

Bell Rd.

Greenway Rd.

Thunderbird Rd.

Cactus Rd.

Peoria Rd.

35th Ave.

Black Canyon Fwy.

19th Ave.

15th Ave.

7th St.

16th St.

Cave Creek Rd.

32nd St.

Union Hills Dr.

Bell Rd.

Greenway Rd.

Lookout Mountain Preserve

Cave Creek Pky.

Tatum Blvd.

40th St.

Thunderbird Rd.

Cactus Rd.

Shea Blvd.

59th St.

Doubletree Ranch Rd.

Hayden Rhodes Aqueduct

Scottsdale Rd.

64th St. (Invergordon Rd.)

Scottsdale Rd.

13 Kierland Commons

Dunlap Ave.

Northern Ave.

7th Ave.

Central Ave.

7th St.

19th Ave.

Piestewa Peak Recreational Area

Tatum Blvd.

51

PARADISE VALLEY

Lincoln Dr.

McDonald Dr.

Glendale Ave.

Bethany Home Rd.

Camelback Rd.

Indian School Rd.

60

Grand Ave.

Piestewa Peak Pkwy.

16th St.

24th St.

32nd St.

44th St.

Biltmore Resort and Fashion Square

5 ◆

6 ◆ Camelback Mountain

Camelback Rd.

7

11

12

10

Thomas Rd.

1 ←

Thomas Rd.

Viad Corporate Center

7th St.

McDowell Rd.

McDowell Rd.

Scottsdale Rd.

Papago Fwy.

Van Buren St.

35th Ave.

19th Ave.

Buckeye Rd.

I-17

Central Ave.

7th St.

10

16th St.

10

Red Mountain Fwy. 202

Sky Harbor International Airport

202

143

Priest Dr.

Mill Ave.

Rural Rd.

4

2

3

9

Lower Buckeye Rd.

Salt River

Broadway Rd.

24th St.

48th St.

10

8

Southern Ave.

Central Ave.

Baseline Rd.

Phoenix & Paradise Valley ▼

Hotel San Carlos **2**

Hyatt Regency Phoenix **3**

Sanctuary on
Camelback Mountain **6**

Wyndham Phoenix **4**

Camelback Corridor ▼

Arizona Biltmore **5**

Royal Palms **7**

Scottsdale ▼

Fairmont Scottsdale Princess **14**

Four Seasons Scottsdale
at Troon North **15**

Hotel Indigo **12**

Hotel Valley Ho **10**

The Phoenician **11**

Westin Kierland **13**

Tempe ▼

The Buttes Marriot Resort **8**

Tempe Mission Palms Hotel **9**

Litchfield Park ▼

Wigwam Resort **1**

4

skylights, wrought-iron pilasters, and cozy sitting alcoves, fills with piano music each evening. Guest rooms are large, with Southwestern-print fabrics and Mission-style furniture. The Biltmore sits on 39 impeccably manicured acres of cool fountains, open walkways, and colorful flower beds. **Pros:** Centrally located; stately, historic charm. **Cons:** In recent years, service has been hit-and-miss and the food is not what it used to be. ⊠*2400 E. Missouri Ave., Camelback Corridor,* ☎*602/955–6600 or 800/950–0086* ⊕*www.arizonabiltmore.com* ⌐*739 rooms, 72 villas* ⌂*In-room: safe, Ethernet, Wi-Fi, refrigerator. In-hotel: 4 restaurants, bar, tennis courts, pools, gym, spa, bicycles, concierge, children's programs (ages 6–12), laundry service, parking (no fee), no-smoking rooms* ▤*AE, D, DC, MC, V.*

$$$$
Fodor'sChoice
★

🏨**Royal Palms Resort & Spa.** Once the home of Cunard Steamship executive Delos T. Cooke, this Mediterranean-style resort has a stately row of the namesake palms at its entrance, courtyards with fountains, and individually designed rooms. Deluxe casitas are all different, though they follow one of three elegant styles—trompe l'oeil, romantic retreat, or Spanish colonial. The restaurant, T. Cook's, is renowned and the open-air Alvadora Spa seems like it has every imaginable amenity, including an outdoor rain shower. **Pros:** A favorite among Fodors.com users in search of romantic getaways. **Cons:** Expensive. ⊠*5200 E. Camelback Rd., Camelback Corridor,* ☎*602/840–3610 or 800/672–6011* ⊕*www.royalpalmsresortandspa.com* ⌐*76 rooms, 62 suites, 44 casitas* ⌂*In-room: safe, refrigerator, Ethernet, Wi-Fi. In-hotel: restaurant, room service, bar, pool, gym, spa, laundry service, parking (fee), no-smoking rooms* ▤*AE, D, DC, MC, V.*

$$$$
Fodor'sChoice
★

🏨**Sanctuary on Camelback Mountain.** This luxurious boutique hotel is the only resort on the north slope of Camelback Mountain. Secluded mountain casitas are painted in desert hues and feature breathtaking views of Paradise Valley. Chic spa casitas surround the pool and are outfitted with contemporary furnishings and private patios. Bathrooms are travertine marble with elegant sinks and roomy tubs. For those who enjoy going *eau* and even *au naturel,* some suites have outdoor tubs. An infinity-edge pool, Zen meditation garden, and Asian-inspired Sanctuary Spa make this a haven for relaxation. The hotel's restaurant, elements, is the hot spot for cocktails at sunset. **Pros:** Inner-city getaway with mountain seclusion, unparalleled views of Camelback's Praying Monk Rock. **Cons:** It can be hard to find your room on the sprawling property, walking between buildings can mean conquering slopes or flights of stairs. ⊠*5700 E. McDonald Dr., Paradise Valley* ☎*480/948–2100 or 800/245–2051* ⊕*www.sanctuaryaz.com* ⌐*98 casitas* ⌂*In-room: kitchen (some), refrigerator (some), Ethernet, Wi-Fi. In-hotel: restaurant, room service, bar, tennis courts, pools, gym, spa, parking (no fee), no-smoking rooms, no elevator, public Wi-Fi* ▤*AE, D, DC, MC, V.*

$$$

🏨**Wigwam Resort.** Built in 1918 as a retreat for executives of the Goodyear Company, the Wigwam has a long and storied history. After significant renovation in 2007 and 2008, the resort maintains its historical character while delivering a modern-day, first-class luxury experience. The property, which can be accessed by chauffeured golf carts, is stunning and features great golf and a true Old West experience that puts less of an emphasis on "old." **Pros:** Now a part of Starwood's Luxury Collection, Wigwam standards are higher than they've ever been. **Cons:** No matter how extreme the renovation, historical properties will always have antiquated elements that don't meet every expectation. ⊠*300 Wigwam Blvd., Litchfield Park* ☎*623/935–3811 or 800/327–0396* ⊕*www.wigwamresort.com* ⟲*261 rooms, 70 suites* ⏃*In-hotel: 3 restaurants, bars, golf courses, tennis courts, pools, gym, spa, children's programs (ages 6–12), parking (no fee)* ⊟*AE, D, DC, MC, V.*

SCOTTSDALE

☾ **$$$$**
Fodor'sChoice
★ 🏨**Fairmont Scottsdale Princess.** Home of the Tournament Players Club Stadium golf course and the FBR Phoenix Open, this resort covers 450 breathtakingly landscaped acres of desert. Willow Stream Spa, one of the top spa spots in the country, has a dramatic rooftop pool and kids love the fishing pond and waterslides. Rooms are done in Southwestern style and service is what you'd expect at a resort of this caliber: excellent and unobtrusive. Even pets get the royal treatment: a specially designated pet room comes with treats and turndown service. **Pros:** Upscale favorite, especially with families. **Cons:** Some rooms are beginning to show some wear and tear for the price. ⊠*7575 E. Princess Dr., North Scottsdale,* ☎*480/585–4848 or 800/344–4758* ⊕*www.fairmont.com/scottsdale* ⟲*458 rooms, 119 casitas, 72 villas, 2 suites* ⏃*In-room: safe, Wi-Fi. In-hotel: 5 restaurants, bars, golf courses, tennis courts, pools, gym, spa, children's programs (ages 6–12), parking (no fee), no-smoking rooms, some pets allowed* ⊟*AE, D, DC, MC, V.*

☾ **$$$$**
Fodor'sChoice
★ 🏨**Four Seasons Scottsdale at Troon North.** This is a logical choice for serious golfers as it's adjacent to two Troon North premier courses where guests receive preferential tee times and free shuttle service. The resort is tucked in the shadows of Pinnacle Peak, near the Pinnacle Peak hiking trail. Large, casita-style rooms have separate sitting and sleeping areas as well as outdoor garden showers, fireplaces, and balconies or patios. Suites come with telescopes and star charts. Talavera, the hotel's main restaurant, is elegant and accommodating. **Pros:** While developments are breathing down its neck this resort remains a true, remote desert oasis. **Cons:** Far from everything. ⊠*10600 E. Crescent Moon Dr., North Scottsdale,* ☎*480/515–5700 or 888/207–9696* ⊕*www.fourseasons.com* ⟲*210 rooms, 22 suites* ⏃*In-room: safe, refrigerator (some), Ethernet, Wi-Fi. In-hotel: 3 restaurants, bar, tennis courts, pools, gym, golf course, spa, children's programs (ages 5–12), laundry service, parking (no fee), no-smoking rooms* ⊟*AE, D, DC, MC, V.*

☾ **$$$$**
Fodor'sChoice
★ 🏨**The Phoenician.** In a town where luxurious, expensive resorts are the rule, the Phoenician still stands apart, primarily in the realm of service. The gilded, marbled lobby with towering fountains is the backdrop for a $25 million fine-art collection. Large rooms, in the main building and outer-lying casitas are decorated with elegant 1960s furniture and have private patios and oversize marble bathrooms. If you'd like a suite that comes with a personal chef and a personally monogrammed robe, book a stay at the new Canyon Suites, an exclusive, boutique resort within the resort, which offers even more luxury and specialized, first-class

Top Spas in the Valley of the Sun

The Valley of the Sun is all about relaxation and there's no better place for it than at one of Phoenix's rejuvenating resort spas. Many feature Native American–inspired treatments and use indigenous ingredients such as agave, desert clay, and neroli oil (derived from orange blossoms). Try to enjoy not only the treatments but the spa amenities, including pools, whirlpools, eucalyptus steam rooms, and relaxation areas with outdoor fireplaces. *For contact information, see Where to Stay in this chapter. Prices are subject to change.*

Alvadora at the Royal Palms Resort & Spa. Romance is not limited to the restaurant and rooms here. Complete with its own pool and salon, Alvadora treatments incorporate herbs, flowers, oils, and minerals indigenous to the Mediterranean. The Orange Blossom Body Buff is a signature treatment: a full-body scrub using neroli oil, and the Fango Mud Wrap promises good cleansing ($135). The massage menu ranges from a 60-minute classic ($135) to the two-therapist Quattro de Palma ($235) and couples' massage sessions ($270–$390). Spa use for nonresort guests is only Sunday through Thursday and requires purchase of a spa package.

Four Seasons Troon North. The elegant Spa at Four Seasons Troon North is a little bit of heaven, hidden in the serene foothills of the Sonoran desert. The list of massages seems endless and includes a 50-minute Head Over Heals rub with two therapists at once ($310), or an 80-minute moonlight balcony massage ($290). Body treatments range from $95 to $310. Try the 80-minute, Four Seasons-In-One package with four treatments for $210, or the Golfers Massage in which

muscles are kneaded with warmed golf balls ($155).

Sanctuary Spa at Sanctuary on Camelback Mountain. This sleek Zen-like spa has 11 Asian-inspired indoor-outdoor treatment rooms nestled against Camelback Mountain. Try a Watsu in-water body massage ($150–$210), a transporting 30-minute Thai Foot Reflexology massage ($95–$170), or a Bamboo Lemongrass Scrub ($90–$210). A 60-minute massage starts at $150.

VH Spa at the Hotel Valley Ho. After seeing the rebirth of the Hotel Valley Ho, guests should feel comfortable entrusting renovation of the body and soul to the hip, colored-glass VH Spa (VH stands for Vitality and Health). Create your own 60-minute spa experience for $130 or go à la carte with the unique Red Flower Hammam Full-Body Treatment Massage, a Turkish-inspired detoxification that scrubs the skin with coffee, olive stones, and fresh lemon ($100–$190).

Willow Stream Spa at the Fairmont Scottsdale Princess. This is one of the Valley's most elaborate spas. Inspired by Havasu Canyon a hidden oasis in the Grand Canyon, there's water everywhere—from the rooftop pool to streams that flow throughout the resort's grounds. Amid this luxury, you can splurge for the two-hour Havasupai Body Treatment ($319), in which aches and pains are kneaded away under three waterfalls of varying pressure. It includes a eucalyptus foot massage, a body scrub, a soak in a private tub, and a body, face, and scalp massage. A 60-minute massage starts at about $160.

service. There's a secluded tennis garden and 27 holes of premier golf. The Centre for Well Being Spa has a meditation atrium and a pool lined with mother-of-pearl tiles where you can drift off to another world. Afterward, you can take in a sophisticated afternoon tea. **Pros:** You get what you pay for in terms of luxury, highest industry standards. **Cons:** High prices, even in the off-season; not a laid-back resort experience. ⊠ *6000 E. Camelback Rd., Camelback Corridor,* ☎ *480/941–8200 or 800/888–8234* ⊕ *www.thephoenician.com* ⮑ *647 rooms, 108 suites* ⌂ *In-room: safe, refrigerator (some), Ethernet, Wi-Fi. In-hotel: 6 restaurants, bars, room service, golf courses, tennis courts, pools, gym, children's programs (ages 5–12), parking (no fee), no-smoking rooms, public Wi-Fi* ☰ *AE, D, DC, MC, V.*

☼ **$$$$**
Fodor'sChoice
★
Westin Kierland Resort & Spa. Original artwork by Arizona artists is displayed throughout the Westin Kierland and the spacious rooms all have balconies or patios with views of the mountains or the resort's water park and tubing river, where kids can enjoy programs like "Club Teen." Kierland Commons, within walking distance, is a planned village of upscale specialty boutiques and restaurants. Of the eight restaurants, Deseo is the star, presided over by well-known chef Douglas Rodriguez, regarded as the inventor of Nuevo Latino cuisine. **Pros:** Bagpipers stroll around the courtyard at sunset, amazing beds. **Cons:** Bagpipers, both Internet access and customer service can be unreliable. ⊠ *6902 E. Greenway Pkwy., North Scottsdale,* ☎ *480/624–1000* ⊕ *www.kierlandresort.com* ⮑ *732 rooms, 63 suites, 32 casitas* ⌂ *In-room: refrigerator (some), Ethernet, Wi-Fi. In-hotel: 8 restaurants, bars, golf courses, tennis courts, pools, gym, spa, children's programs (ages 4–17), parking (no fee), no-smoking rooms, public Wi-Fi* ☰ *AE, D, DC, MC, V.*

$$$
Hotel Indigo. This Scottsdale spot, renovated in 2006, is perfect for what it is: simple, modern, and, most of all, centrally located. Eclectic rooms are colorfully accented with clean lines, with plasma-screen TVs, and exceptionally comfy beds. Suites feature entire walls covered with images of Arizona's spectacular slot canyons. Large, natural-stone showers feature Aveda products. The Golden Bean café serves Starbucks coffee and the Phi Bar offers a nice selection of wine and beer. **Pros:** Great value, ideal Scottsdale location, pet-friendly. **Cons:** Walls aren't thick enough to block out the Top 40 music piped through the entryway. ⊠ *4415 N. Civic Center Plaza, Downtown Scottsdale,* ☎ *480/941–9400* ⮑ *117 rooms, 9 suites* ⌂ *In-room: safe, refrigerator (some), Ethernet, Wi-Fi. In-hotel: restaurant, bar, pool, gym, laundry service, parking (no fee), no-smoking rooms* ☰ *AE, D, DC, MC, V.*

$$$
Hotel Valley Ho. One of Scottsdale's newer hotels is actually one of its oldest. Originally opened in 1956, it was a hangout for celebrities including Natalie Wood, Robert Wagner, and Tony Curtis. In 2001 the hotel was restored to its former '50s fabulousness—complete with Trader Vic's, the hotel's original restaurant. A large pool is at the heart of this Frank Lloyd Wright–inspired hotel, surrounded by lush landscaping, and an outdoor grill and dining area. A 6,000-square-foot spa, a fitness center, and 10,000 square feet of meeting space have been added as well as The Tower, which houses 35 residential suites.

4

Pros: Retro decor, great history, and hip, youthful style. **Cons:** The busy location and retro-hip decor are not for everyone, check pictures online before booking. ⊠*6850 E. Main St., Downtown Scottsdale,* ☎*480/248–2000* ⊕*www.hotelvalleyho.com* ↩*190 rooms, 35 condo (tower) suites, 4 terrace suites, 2 executive suites* ⎣*In-room: Ethernet, Wi-Fi. In-hotel: 3 restaurants, bars, pool, gym, spa, no-smoking rooms, public Wi-Fi* ⊟*AE, D, DC, MC, V.*

TEMPE & AROUND

� $$$ 🏨 **The Buttes Marriott Resort.** Two miles east of Sky Harbor airport, nestled in desert buttes at Interstate 10 and AZ 60, this hotel joins dramatic architecture (the lobby's back wall is the volcanic rock itself) and classic Southwest design (pine and saguaro-rib furniture, works by major regional artists) with stunning Valley views. Recently purchased by Marriott, the Buttes is on its way to become a top relaxation destination with its Naranda "Revive" spa facility. "Radial" rooms are the largest; inside rooms face the huge free-form pools with waterfall, hot tubs, and a poolside cantina. The Top of the Rock restaurant is elegant. Kids can enjoy the new Lazy River and summer activities. **Pros:** Beautiful, centrally located Tempe property, great beds, friendly service. **Cons:** "City views" also include freeway and parking-lot views. ⊠*2000 Westcourt Way, Tempe* ☎*602/225–9000 or 888/867–7492* ↩*345 rooms, 8 suites* ⎣*In-room: refrigerator (some), Wi-Fi. In-hotel: 2 restaurants, bars, tennis courts, pool, gym, spa, laundry service, executive floor, parking (no fee), no-smoking rooms, some pets allowed, public Wi-Fi* ⊟*AE, D, DC, MC, V.*

$$$ 🏨 **Tempe Mission Palms Hotel.** A handsome, casual lobby and an energetic young staff set the tone at this three-story courtyard hotel. Rooms are Southwestern in style, and quite comfortable. Between the Arizona State University campus and Old Town Tempe, this is a convenient place to stay if you're attending ASU sports events, and Harry's Bar becomes a lively sports lounge at game time. **Pros:** Nice hotel with friendly service, right at the center of ASU and Mill Avenue activity. **Cons:** All that activity can be bad for light sleepers. ⊠*60 E. 5th St., Tempe* ☎*480/894–1400 or 800/547–8705* ⊕*www.missionpalms.com* ↩*297 rooms, 6 suites* ⎣*In-room: refrigerator (some), Ethernet, Wi-Fi. In-hotel: restaurant, room service, bar, tennis courts, pool, gym, airport shuttle, parking (no fee), no-smoking rooms, public Wi-Fi* ⊟*AE, D, DC, MC, V.*

NIGHTLIFE & THE ARTS

THE ARTS

For weekly listings of theater, arts, and music, check out "The Rep Entertainment Guide" in Thursday's *Arizona Republic,* pick up a free issue of the independent weekly *New Times,* the weekly *Get Out* in Thursday's *East Valley Tribune* (or free on newsstands), or check out *Where Phoenix/Scottsdale Magazine,* available free in most hotels. A good online source of information on events in the Valley is the *Arizona Republic* Web site (⊕*www.azcentral.com*) which has extensive nightlife and arts listings.

TICKETS **Arizona State University Public Events Box Office** (☎*480/965–6447* ⊕*www.herbergercollege.asu.edu*) sells tickets for ASU events. **Tickets. com** (⊕*www.tickets.com*) sells tickets for ASU Public Events at Grady Gammage Auditorium, Kerr Theatre, and the Maricopa County Events Center, formerly the ASU Sundome. **Ticketmaster** (☎*480/784–4444* ⊕*www.ticketmaster.com*) sells tickets for nearly every event in the Valley and has outlets at Fry's, Wherehouse, and Tower Records stores.

CLASSICAL MUSIC

Arizona Opera (✉*4600 N. 12th St., Downtown Phoenix* ☎*602/266–7464* ⊕*www.azopera.com*) stages an opera season, primarily classical, in both Tucson and Phoenix. The Phoenix season runs from October to March at Symphony Hall.

Phoenix Symphony Orchestra (✉*Arizona Center, 455 N. 3rd St., Suite 390, Downtown Phoenix* ☎*602/495–1999* ⊕*www.phoenixsymphony. org*) is the resident company at Symphony Hall. Its season, which runs September through May, includes orchestral works from classical and contemporary composers, a chamber series, composer festivals, and outdoor Pops concerts.

DANCE

Ballet Arizona (☎*602/381–1096* ⊕*www.balletaz.org*), the state's professional ballet company, presents a full season of classical and contemporary works (including pieces commissioned for the company) in Tucson and Phoenix, where it performs at the Orpheum Theater, downtown. The season runs from October through May.

THEATER

Actors Theatre of Phoenix (✉*Box 1924, Phoenix 85001* ☎*602/253–6701* ⊕*www.atphx.org*) is the resident theater troupe at the Herberger Theater Center. The theater presents a full season of drama, comedy, and musical productions; it runs from September through May.

Arizona Theatre Company (✉*808 N. 1st St.Central Phoenix* ☎*602/252–8497* ⊕*www.aztheatreco.org*) is the only resident company in the country with a two-city (Tucson and Phoenix) operation. Productions, held from September through June, range from classic dramas to musicals and new works by emerging playwrights.

Black Theater Troupe (✉*333 E. Portland St., Downtown Phoenix* ☎*602/258–8128*) performs at its own house, the Helen K. Mason Center, a half block from the city's Performing Arts Building on Deck Park. It presents original and contemporary dramas and musical revues, as well as adventurous adaptations, between September and May.

☾ **Childsplay** (✉*Box 517, Tempe 85280* ☎*480/350–8101* ⊕*www.childs playaz.org*) is the state's theater company for young audiences and families, which runs during the school year. Rotating through many a venue, these players deliver high-energy performances.

☾ **Great Arizona Puppet Theatre** (✉*302 W. Latham St., Downtown Phoenix* ☎*602/262–2050* ⊕*www.azpuppets.org*), which performs in a historic building featuring lots of theater and exhibit space, mounts a yearlong cycle of inventive puppet productions that change frequently.

Phoenix Theatre (⊠*100 E. McDowell Rd., Downtown Phoenix* ☎*602/254–2151* ⊕*www.phxtheatre.org*), across the courtyard from the Phoenix Art Museum, stages musical and dramatic performances as well as productions for children by the Cookie Company.

WILD WEST SHOWS

Fodor'sChoice ★ ☺ **Rawhide Western Town and Steakhouse at the Wildhorse Pass** (⊠*5700 W. North Loop Rd., Gila River Indian Community, Chandler* ☎*480/502–5600* ⊕*www.rawhide.com*) moved from Scottsdale in 2006, and now calls the 2,400-acre master-planned Wild Horse Pass Development in the Gila River Indian Community, home. Large portions of the original Rawhide were moved to the new site, including the legendary steak house and saloon, Main Street and all of its retail shops, and the Six Gun Theater. Exciting additions include canal rides along the Gila River Riverwalk, train rides, and a Native American village honoring the history and culture of the Akimel O'othom and Pee Posh Tribes.

☺ **Rockin' R Ranch** (⊠*6136 E. Baseline Rd., Mesa* ☎*480/832–1539* ⊕*www.rockinr.net*) includes a petting zoo, a reenactment of a Wild West shoot-out, and—the main attraction—a nightly cookout with a Western stage show. Pan for gold or take a wagon ride until the "vittles" are served, followed by music and entertainment.

NIGHTLIFE

You can find nightlife listings and reviews in the *New Times* free weekly newspaper, distributed Wednesday, "The Rep Entertainment Guide" of the *Arizona Republic*, or the entertainment weekly *Get Out* in Thursday's *East Valley Tribune* or free on newsstands (⊕*www.getoutaz. com*). *PHX Downtown*, a free monthly available in downtown establishments, has an extensive calendar of events from art exhibits and poetry readings to professional sports. The local gay scene is covered in *Echo Magazine*, which you can pick up all over town.

BARS & LOUNGES

AZ88 (⊠*7353 Scottsdale Mall, Scottsdale Civic Center, Scottsdale* ☎*480/994–5576*) is great for feasting on huge portions of great food and lavish quantities of liquor, but also for feasting your eyes on the fabulous people who flock here on weekend nights to see and be seen.

Casey Moore's Oyster House (⊠*850 S. Ash Ave., Tempe* ☎*480/968–9935*) is a laid-back institution where rockers, hippies, and families come together in a 1910 house rumored to be haunted by ghosts. Enjoy 28 beers on tap and fresh oysters at this Irish pub–style favorite.

Fez On Central (⊠*3815 N. Central Ave., Central Phoenix* ☎*602/287–8700*) is a stylish restaurant by day and a gay-friendly, hip hot spot by night. The sleek interior and fancy drinks make you feel uptown, while the happy-hour prices and location keep this place grounded.

Fox Sports Bar (⊠*16203 N. Scottsdale Rd., North Scottsdale, Scottsdale* ☎*480/368–0369*) is where trendy, stylish sports fans gather to watch live Fox Sports broadcasts on flat-screen TVs, play pool, and socialize in the sleek VIP room.

★ **Jade Bar** (⊠*5700 E. McDonald Dr., Sanctuary on Camelback Resort, Paradise Valley* ☎*480/948–2100*) has spectacular views of Paradise Valley and Camelback Mountain, an upscale, modern bar lined with windows, and a relaxing fireplace-lit patio.

Kazimierz World Wine Bar (⊠*7137 E. Stetson Dr., Central Scottsdale, Scottsdale* ☎*480/946–3004*) is entered through a door marked THE TRUTH IS INSIDE, beyond which lies a dark, cave-like wine bar with comfy chairs and good music.

Majerle's Sports Grill (⊠*24 N. 2nd St., Downtown Phoenix, Phoenix* ☎*602/253–9004*), operated by former Suns basketball player Dan Majerle, is within striking distance of the major sports facilities and offers a comprehensive menu for pre- and postgame celebrations.

Postino Winebar (⊠*3939 E. Campbell Ave., Central Phoenix, Phoenix* ☎*602/852–3939*) occupies a former post office in the Arcadia neighborhood. More than 40 wines are poured by the glass. Order a few grazing items off the appetizer menu (the bruschetta is unmatched by any in the Valley) and settle in, or carry out a bottle of wine, hunk of cheese, and loaf of bread for a twilight picnic.

The Salty Senorita (⊠*336 N. Scottsdale Rd., Central Scottsdale, Scottsdale* ☎*480/946–7258*) is known more for its extensive margarita selection and lively patio crowd than for its food. The restaurant–bar touts 51 different margaritas—with some recipes so secret they won't tell you what goes in them—try the El Presidente or the Chupacabra.

Seamus McCaffrey's Irish Pub (⊠*18 W. Monroe St., Downtown Phoenix* ☎*602/253–6081*) is a fun and friendly place to enjoy one of the dozen European brews on draft. A small kitchen turns out traditional Irish fare.

Six Lounge and Restaurant (⊠*7316 E. Stetson Dr., Central Scottsdale, Scottsdale* ☎*480/663–6620*) is a crowded see-and-be-seen hot spot attracting the Valley's designer-clad jet-setters who groove to the tunes of a DJ.

BLUES, JAZZ & ROCK

FodorsChoice **Char's Has the Blues** (⊠*4631 N. 7th Ave., Central Phoenix* ☎*602/230– 0205*) is one of the Valley's top blues clubs, with nightly bands.

Marquee Theatre (⊠*730 N. Mill Ave., Tempe* ☎*480/829–0607*) hosts mainly headlining rock-and-roll entertainers.

★ **Rhythm Room** (⊠*1019 E. Indian School Rd., Central Phoenix* ☎*602/265–4842*) attracts excellent local and national rock artists, as well as blues, seven nights a week. The perfect sidekick, Rack Shack Blues BBQ, in the parking lot, cooks up good barbecue Wednesday through Saturday evenings.

Sugar Daddy's Blues (⊠*3102 N. Scottsdale Rd., North Scottsdale, Scottsdale* ☎*480/970–6556*) serves rhythm, blues, and eclectic Cajun-meets-Southwestern food nightly until 2 AM. A gratis graffiti-clad limo will pick you up anywhere within a 7-mi radius of the bar.

COUNTRY & WESTERN

★ **Greasewood Flats** (⊠*27500 N. Alma School Pkwy., North Scottsdale, Scottsdale* ☏*480/585–7277*) isn't fancy; in fact, it's downright ramshackle, but the burgers are delicious and the crowds friendly. There's a dance floor with live music Thursday through Sunday. In winter, wear jeans and a jacket, since everything is outside; to keep warm, folks congregate around fires burning in halved oil drums.

Handlebar-J (⊠*7116 E. Becker La., Central Scottsdale, Scottsdale* ☏*480/948–0110*) is a lively restaurant and bar with a Western linedancing, 10-gallon-hat–wearing crowd.

DANCE CLUBS

Anderson's Fifth Estate (⊠*4224 N. Craftsman Ct., Scottsdale* ☏*480/941–9333*), with two DJs and two dance floors, is one hot night spot. There's live music some Fridays, and a retro-dance party airs live on a local radio station on Saturday.

★ **Axis/Radius** (⊠*7340 E. Indian Plaza Rd., Central Scottsdale, Scottsdale* ☏*480/970–1112*) is the dress-to-impress locale where you can party at side-by-side clubs connected by a glass catwalk.

Cherry Lounge & Pit (⊠*411 S. Mill Ave., Downtown, Tempe* ☏*480/966–3573*) is considered by locals to be the best dance club in the Valley. The fact that it is equipped with plenty of patron-accessible dance poles and that free pole-dancing lessons are offered during nonpeak hours probably gave it a leg up.

Myst (⊠*7340 E. Shoeman La., North Scottsdale, Scottsdale* ☏*480/970–5000*) is an ultraswanky dance club where you can sip cocktails in a sunken lounge or hang out at the white-hot Milk Bar adorned with white-leather seating and an all-white bar. Upstairs is the private VIP lounge, complete with skyboxes overlooking the dance floor.

GAY & LESBIAN BARS

Ain't Nobody's Bizness (⊠*3031 E. Indian School Rd., Central Phoenix* ☏*602/224–9977*) is the most popular lesbian bar in town; you'll also find a few gay men at this male-friendly establishment, well known as one of the most fun in town.

★ **Amsterdam** (⊠*718 N. Central Ave., Downtown Phoenix* ☏*602/258–6122*) attracts a young crowd that wants to see and be seen; it's where Phoenix's beautiful gay people hang out.

B.S. West (⊠*7125 E. 5th Ave., Downtown Scottsdale, Scottsdale* ☏*480/945–9028*) is tucked behind a shopping center on Scottsdale's main shopping drag and draws a stylish, well-heeled crowd.

Charlie's (⊠*727 W. Camelback Rd., West Phoenix* ☏*602/265–0224*), a longtime favorite of local gay men, has a country-western look (cowboy hats are the accessory of choice) and friendly staff.

E Lounge (⊠*4343 N. 7th Ave. Central Phoenix* ☏*602/279–0388*) is for ladies who love live music, drink specials, late-night DJs—and other ladies who love the same.

MICROBREWERIES

★ **Four Peaks Brewing Company** (⊠*1340 E. 8th St., Tempe* ☏*480/303–9967*) is the former redbrick home of Bordens Creamery. Ten different brews are on tap, and pub grub, pizza, and burgers fill the menu.

Rio Salado Brewing Company (✉*1520 W. Mineral Rd., Tempe* ☎*480/755–1590*) brews excellent German-style beers, with at least six on tap regularly. The low-key Tap Room is a great place to relax, shoot darts, or play pool. Complimentary tours of the brewery are available Saturday afternoon.

Rock Bottom Brewery (✉*8668 E. Shea Blvd., North Scottsdale, Scottsdale* ☎*480/998–7777* ✉*21001 N. Tatum Blvd., Desert Ridge Mall, North Phoenix, Phoenix* ☎*480/513–9125* ✉*14205 S. 50th St., Ahwatukee, Phoenix* ☎*480/598–1300*) has tasty pub grub (start with the giant soft pretzels served with spicy spinach dip) and beer brewed on the premises. Watch out: the bill tends to rack up quickly.

San Tan Brewing Company (✉*8 San Marcos Pl., Old Town, Chandler* ☎*480/917–8700*)combines good food with great beer and an energetic pub atmosphere without the tired, hole-in-the-wall or overly commercial feel. Wash down some raspberry mushrooms and a stuffed burger with a San Tan IPA.

Sonora Brewhouse (✉*322 E. Camelback Rd., Central Phoenix, Phoenix* ☎*602/279–8909*) is a great hangout with mediocre pub grub and outstanding locally crafted brews like Light Cream Ale, Trooper IPA, and Brewer's Den Hefeweizen, one of the Valley's best.

SHOPPING

Most of the Valley's power shopping is concentrated in central Phoenix, downtown Scottsdale, and the Kierland area in North Scottsdale but auctions and antiques shops cluster in odd places—and as treasure hunters know, you've always got to keep your eyes open.

SHOPPING CENTERS

Arizona Mills (✉*5000 Arizona Mills Circle, I–10 and Baseline Rd., Tempe* ☎*480/491–7300*), a mammoth "value-oriented retail and entertainment mega mall," features more than 175 outlet stores and sideshows, including Off 5th–Saks Fifth Avenue, Kenneth Cole, and Last Call from Neiman Marcus. When you tire of bargain-hunting relax in the food court, cinemas, or faux rain forest.

★ **Biltmore Fashion Park** (✉*24th St. and Camelback Rd., Camelback Corridor* ☎*602/955–8400*) has a posh, parklike setting. Macy's, Saks Fifth Avenue, and Borders are the anchors for more than 70 stores and upscale shops, such as Betsey Johnson and Cartier. It's accessible from the Camelback Esplanade and the Ritz Carlton by a pedestrian tunnel that runs beneath Camelback Road.

The Borgata (✉*6166 N. Scottsdale Rd., Central Scottsdale, Scottsdale* ☎*602/953–6311*), an outdoor re-creation of the Italian village of San Gimignano, with courtyards, stone walls, turrets, and fountains, is a lovely setting for browsing upscale boutiques or just sitting at an outdoor café.

Chandler Fashion Square (✉ *3111 W. Chandler Blvd., Chandler* ☎*480/812–8488*) features anchor stores Nordstrom, Dillard's, Macy's and Sears, along with more than 180 other national retail chains like Coach, Pottery Barn, and Cheesecake Factory.

⟳ **Desert Ridge Marketplace** (⊠*Tatum Blvd. and Loop 101, North Phoenix* ☎*480/513–7586*), an outdoor megamall, has more than 1 million square feet of shops and restaurants, but it's also a family entertainment destination, with an 18-theater cineplex, bowling alley, rock-climbing wall, and Dave & Buster's, a multivenue entertainment center with a virtual-reality game room and dance club.

★ **Kierland Commons** (⊠*Greenway Pkwy. at Scottsdale Rd., North Scottsdale, Scottsdale* ☎*480/348–1577*), next to the Westin Kierland Resort, is one of the city's newest shopping areas. "Urban village" is the catchphrase for this outdoor pedestrian mall with restaurants and upscale chain retailers, among them J. Crew and Tommy Bahama.

★ **Mill Avenue Shops** (⊠*Mill Avenue, between Rio Salado Pkwy. and University Dr., Downtown, Tempe* ☎*480/967–4877*), named for the landmark Hayden Flour Mill, is an increasingly commercial and construction-laden area, but it's still a fun-filled walk-and-shop experience. Directly west of the Arizona State University campus, Mill Avenue is an active melting pot of students, artists, residents, and tourists. Shops include Borders, Urban Outfitters, a few remaining locally owned stores, and countless bars and restaurants. The Valley Art Theater is a Mill Avenue institution and Tempe's place for indie cinema. Twice a year (in early December and March/April), the Mill Avenue area is the place to find indie arts and crafts when it hosts the Tempe Festival of the Arts.

★ **Old Town Scottsdale** (⊠*Between Goldwater Blvd., Brown Ave., 5th Ave. and 3rd St., Downtown Scottsdale, Scottsdale* ☎*800/737–0008*) is the place to go for authentic Southwest-inspired gifts, clothing, art, and artifacts. Despite its massive modern neighbors, this area and its merchants have long respected and maintained the single-level brick storefronts that embody Scottsdale's upscale cow-town charm. More than 100 businesses meet just about any aesthetic want or need, including Gilbert Ortega, one of the premiere places for fine Native American jewelry and art. Some of Scottsdale's best restaurants are also tucked in this pleasing maze of merchants.

★ **Scottsdale Fashion Square** (⊠*Scottsdale and Camelback Rds., Central Scottsdale, Scottsdale* ☎*480/949–0202*) has a retractable roof and many specialty shops unique to Arizona. There are also Nordstrom, Dillard's, Neiman Marcus, Macy's, Juicy Couture, Anthropologie, Z Gallerie, Louis Vuitton, Tiffany, and Arizona's only Gucci store. A huge food court, restaurants, and a cineplex complete the picture.

VALLEY OF THE SUN ESSENTIALS

To research prices, get advice from other travelers, and book travel arrangements, visit ⊕www.fodors.com.

TRANSPORTATION

BY AIR

Phoenix Sky Harbor International Airport (PHX) is served by most major airlines; it's a hub for US Airways and Southwest Airlines. Just 3 mi east of downtown Phoenix, it's surrounded by freeways linking it to almost every part of the metro area.

The blue vans of SuperShuttle cruise Sky Harbor, each taking up to seven passengers to their individual destinations, with no luggage fee or airport surcharge. Wheelchair vans are also available. Drivers accept credit cards and expect tips. Fares are $7 to downtown Phoenix, around $16 to most places in Scottsdale, and $20 to $35 to places in far north Scottsdale or Carefree. SuperShuttle also operates the upscale and personalized ExecuCar service.

Only a few taxi firms (Checker/Yellow Cab and Courier Cab are good options) are licensed to pick up at Sky Harbor's commercial terminals. All add a $1 surcharge for airport pickups, don't charge for luggage, and are available 24 hours a day. A trip to downtown Phoenix can cost from $8 to $12. The fare to downtown Scottsdale averages about $25. If you're headed to the East Valley, expect to shell out more than $30.

A few limousine firms cruise Sky Harbor, and many more provide airport pickups by reservation. Scottsdale Limousine requires reservations but offers a toll-free number; rates start at $65 (plus tip).

Contacts ExecuCar (☎602/232-4600 or 800/410-4444 ⊕www.supershuttle. com). **Scottsdale Limousine** (☎480/946-8446 or 800/747-8234). **Sky Harbor International Airport (PHX)** (☎602/273-3300 ⊕www.phxskyharbor.com). **SuperShuttle** (☎602/244-9000 or 800/258-3826 ⊕www.supershuttle.com). **Valley Metro buses** (☎602/253-5000).

BY BUS

Greyhound Lines has statewide and national routes from its main terminal near Sky Harbor airport.

Valley Metro routes service most of the Valley suburbs, but these routes are not really suitable for vacationers and offer limited service evenings and weekends.

Phoenix runs a free Downtown Area Shuttle (DASH), with purple minibuses circling the area between the Arizona Center and the state capitol at 15-minute intervals from 6:30 AM to 11 PM weekdays and from 11 AM to 11 PM weekends; this system also serves major thoroughfares in several suburbs—Glendale, Scottsdale, Tempe, Mesa, and Chandler. The city of Tempe operates the Free Local Area Shuttle (FLASH), which serves the downtown Tempe and Arizona State University area from

7 AM until 8 PM. Check the Valley Metro Web site for all public transit options (including DASH and FLASH) in the Valley.

Contacts Greyhound Lines (✉ *2115 E. Buckeye Rd., Phoenix* ☎ *602/389–4200 or 800/229–9424* ⊕ *www.greyhound.com*). **Valley Metro** (☎ *602/262–7433* ⊕ *www.valleymetro.org*).

BY CAR

To get around Phoenix, *you will need a car*. Only the major downtown areas (Phoenix, Scottsdale, Tempe, and Glendale) are pedestrian-friendly. There's no mass transit beyond a commuter-bus system. At the airport most rental companies offer shuttle services to their lots. ■TIP➔**Don't expect to nab a rental car without a reservation, however, especially in the high season, from January to April.**

BY TAXI

Taxi fares are unregulated in Phoenix, except at the airport. The 800-square-mi metro area is so large that one-way fares in excess of $50 are not uncommon; it's a good idea to ask what the damages will be before you get in, since it will often be cheaper to rent a car, even if you are renting for only a day. Except within a compact area, such as central Phoenix, travel by taxi is not recommended. Taxis charge about $3 for the first mile and $1.50 per mile thereafter (not including tips).

Contacts Checker/Yellow Cab (☎ *602/252–5252*). **Courier Cab** (☎ *602/232–2222*).

BY TRAIN

Amtrak provides train service in Arizona with bus transfers to Phoenix. Eastbound train passengers will stop in Flagstaff, where Amtrak buses depart for Phoenix each morning. Westbound train travelers will likely make the transfer in Tucson, where Amtrak-run buses have limited service to Phoenix on Sunday, Tuesday, and Thursday nights. What used to be Phoenix's downtown train terminal is now the Amtrak Thruway Bus Stop.

Information Amtrak (✉ *4th Ave. and Harrison St.* ☎ *602/253–0121 or 800/872–7245* ⊕ *www.amtrak.com*).

CONTACTS & RESOURCES

VISITOR INFORMATION

The Native American Tourism Center aids in arranging tourist visits to reservation lands; it can't afford to send information packets, but you can call or stop in weekdays 8 to 5.

Contacts Arizona Office of Tourism (☎ *602/364–3730 or 888/520–3444* ⊕ *www.arizonaguide.com*). **Greater Phoenix Convention and Visitors Bureau** (☎ *602/254–6500* ⊕ *www.phoenixcvb.com*). **Native American Tourism Center** (✉ *4130 N. Goldwater Blvd., Phoenix* ☎ *480/945–0771* 🖷 *480/945–0264*). **Scottsdale Convention and Visitors Bureau** (☎ *480/421–1004 or 800/782–1117* ⊕ *www.scottsdalecvb.com*).

North-Central Arizona

WORD OF MOUTH

"When we were there we viewed the sunset from the main area outside Bright Angel lodge—beautiful! We caught the sunrise from the South Kaibab trailhead—beautiful! Storm rolled in that night, no sunset just thunder and lightning—awesome! Next day, cloudy, misty, light rain, sun peeking though clouds—beautiful! I guess what I am saying is don't get too hung up on being at the right spot for the sunrise/sunset, it's all spectacular!"

—BlackandGold

"On the way back to Scottsdale, we stopped at 'the Chapel of the Holy Cross.' We got there just as the sun was starting to go down and the views were stunning. A very moving experience."

—RichinPA

Updated by
Mara Levin

A landscape of vast plateaus punctuated by steep ridges and canyons, north-central Arizona is rich in natural attractions. To the north of Flagstaff the San Francisco Peaks, a string of tall volcanic mountains, rises over 12,000 feet, tapering to the 9,000-foot Mount Elden and a scattering of diminutive cinder cones. To the south, a seemingly endless stand of ponderosa pines covers this part of the Colorado Plateau before the terrain plunges dramatically into Oak Creek Canyon. The canyon then opens to reveal red buttes and mesas in the high-desert areas surrounding Sedona. The desert gradually descends to the Verde Valley, crossing the Verde River before reaching the 7,000-foot Black Range, over which lies the Prescott Valley.

Flagstaff, the hub of this part of Arizona, was historically a way station en route to southern California. First the railroads, then Route 66 carried westbound traffic right through the center of town. Many of those who were "just passing through" stayed and built a community. The town's large network of bike paths and parks abuts hundreds of miles of trails and forest roads, an irresistible lure for outdoors enthusiasts.

Down AZ 89A in Sedona, the average age and income rises considerably. This was once a hidden hamlet used by Western filmmakers but New Age enthusiasts flocked to the region in the 1980s believing it was the center of spiritual powers. Well-off executives and retirees followed soon after, building clusters of McMansions throughout the area. Sophisticated restaurants, upscale shops, luxe accommodations, and New Age entrepreneurs cater to both these populations, and to the tourist trade which brings close to 5 million visitors a year.

EXPLORING NORTH CENTRAL ARIZONA

Nestled between the Grand Canyon and Phoenix, north-central Arizona has enough natural beauty and sophisticated attractions to compete with its neighbors to the north and south. Most visitors flock to Sedona, world-renowned for red rocks, pink jeeps, and New Age energy. The surrounding area of Verde Valley may not attract the same hordes, but this means more welcome peace and quiet. Flagstaff is surrounded by the Coconino National Forest and wrapped around the base of the tallest mountains in the state (the San Francisco Peaks). Phoenicians flee the summertime heat to cool off in the mountains and explore Prescott.

WHAT IT COSTS					
	¢	$	$$	$$$	$$$$
Restaurants	under $8	$8–$12	$13–$20	$21–$30	over $30
Hotels	under $70	$70–$120	$121–$175	$176–$250	over $250

Restaurant prices are per person for a main course at dinner. Hotel prices are for a standard double in high season, excluding taxes and service charges.

ABOUT THE RESTAURANTS

You'll find lots of American comfort food in this part of the country: barbecue restaurants, steak houses, and burger joints predominate. If you're looking for something different, Sedona and Flagstaff have the majority of good, multiethnic restaurants in the area, and if you're craving Mexican, you're sure to find something authentic and delicious (note that burritos are often called "burros" around here). Sedona is the best place in the area for fine dining, but foodies can savor meals in neighboring towns as well. Some area restaurants close in January and February—the slower months in the area—so call ahead. Reservations are suggested from April through October.

ABOUT THE HOTELS

Flagstaff and Prescott have the more affordable lodging options, with lots of comfortable motels and B&Bs, but no real luxury. The opposite is true in Sedona, which is filled with opulent resorts and hideaways, most offering solitude and spa services—just don't expect a bargain. Reservations are essential for Sedona and suggested for Flagstaff and Prescott. Little Jerome has a few B&Bs but call ahead if you think you might want to spend the night. If you're in for a thrill, many of the historic hotels in north-central Arizona have haunted rooms that can be booked on request.

TOP REASONS TO GO

The Grand Canyon: This natural wonder, one of nature's longest-running works in progress, both exalts and humbles the human spirit.

Mother Nature: Stunning red rocks, snowcapped mountains, and crisp country air.

Father Time: Ancient Native American sites show life before Columbus "discovered" America.

Main Street charm: Jerome and Prescott exude small-town hospitality.

Let your aura out: The free spirit and energy of Sedona is delightfully infectious, even for skeptics.

FLAGSTAFF

146 mi northwest of Phoenix, 27 mi north of Sedona via Oak Creek Canyon.

Few travelers slow down long enough to explore Flagstaff, a town of 54,000, known locally as "Flag;" most stop only to spend the night at one of the town's many motels before making the last leg of the trip to the Grand Canyon, 80 mi north. Flag makes a good base for day trips to ancient Native American sites and the Navajo and Hopi reservations, as well as to the Petrified Forest National Park and the Painted Desert, but the city is a worthwhile destination in its own right.

In summer, Phoenix residents head here, seeking relief from the desert heat, since at any time of the year temperatures in Flagstaff are about 25°F cooler than in Phoenix. They also come to Flagstaff in winter: to ski at the small Arizona Snowbowl, about 15 mi northeast of town among the San Francisco Peaks.

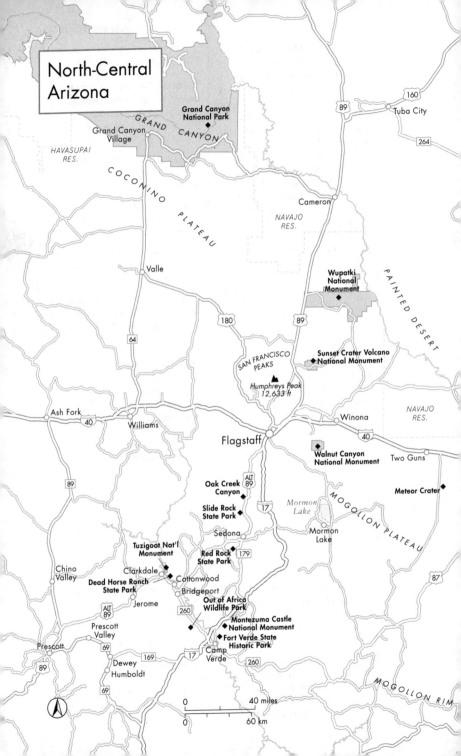

North-Central Arizona

Grand Canyon National Park

Grand Canyon Village

HAVASUPAI RES.

GRAND CANYON

160

89

Tuba City

264

COCONINO PLATEAU

Cameron

NAVAJO RES.

Valle

Wupatki National Monument

PAINTED DESERT

180

89

SAN FRANCISCO PEAKS

Sunset Crater Volcano National Monument

64

▲ *Humphreys Peak 12,633 ft*

NAVAJO RES.

Ash Fork

40

Williams

Flagstaff

Winona

40

Two Guns

Walnut Canyon National Monument

89

Oak Creek Canyon

ALT 89

Meteor Crater

Slide Rock State Park

17

Mormon Lake

MOGOLLON PLATEAU

Sedona

Mormon Lake

Tuzigoot Nat'l Monument

Red Rock State Park

179

Chino Valley

Clarkdale

Cottonwood

87

Dead Horse Ranch State Park

Jerome

Bridgeport

ALT 89

260

Out of Africa Wildlife Park

Montezuma Castle National Monument

Prescott Valley

69

169

17

Fort Verde State Historic Park

Prescott

89

Dewey Humboldt

Camp Verde

260

69

MOGOLLON RIM

0   40 miles

0   60 km

EXPLORING FLAGSTAFF

WHAT TO SEE

8 Arizona Snowbowl. Although still one of Flagstaff's largest attractions, droughts can make snowy slopes a luxury. Fortunately, visitors can enjoy the beauty of the area year-round. The Agassiz ski lift climbs to a height of 11,500 feet in 25 minutes, and doubles as a skyride through the Coconino National Forest in summer. From this vantage point, you can see up to 70 mi; views may even include the North Rim of the Grand Canyon. There's a lodge at the base with a restaurant, bar, and ski school. To reach the ski area, take U.S. 180 north from Flagstaff; it's 7 mi from the Snowbowl exit to the skyride entrance. ⊠ *Snowbowl Rd., North Flagstaff* ☎ *928/779–1951* ⊕ *www.arizonasnowbowl.com* 🖃 *Skyride $10* ⊗ *Skyride: Memorial Day–early Sept., daily 10–4; early Sept.–mid-Oct., Fri.–Sun. 10–4, weather permitting.*

1 Historic Downtown District. Storied Route 66 runs right through the heart of downtown Flagstaff. The late-Victorian, Tudor Revival, and early-art deco architecture in this district recalls the town's heyday as a logging and railroad center. A walking-tour map of the area is available at the visitor center in the Tudor Revival–style **Santa Fe Depot** (⊠ *1 E. Rte. 66, Downtown*), an excellent place to begin sightseeing. Highlights include the 1927 **Hotel Monte Vista** (⊠ *100 N. San Francisco St., Downtown* ⊕ *www.hotelmontevista.com*), built after a community drive raised $200,000 in 60 days. The construction was promoted as a way to bolster the burgeoning tourism in the region, and the hotel was held publicly until the early 1960s. The 1888 **Babbitt Brothers Building** (⊠ *12 E. Aspen Ave., Downtown*) was constructed as a building-supply store and then turned into a department store by David Babbitt, the mastermind of the Babbitt empire. The Babbitts are one of Flagstaff's wealthiest founding families. Most of the area's first businesses were saloons catering to railroad construction workers, which was the case with the 1888 **Vail Building** (⊠ *5 N. San Francisco St., Downtown*), a brick art deco–influenced structure covered with stucco in 1939. It now houses Crystal Magic, a New Age shop. ⊠ *Downtown Historic District, Rte. 66 north to Birch Ave., and Beaver St. east to Agassiz St.*

9 Lava River Cave. Subterranean lava flow formed this mile-long cave roughly 700,000 years ago. Once you descend into its boulder-strewn maw, the cave is spacious, with 40-foot ceilings, but claustrophobes take heed: about halfway through, the cave tapers to a 4-foot-high squeeze that can be a bit unnerving. A 40°F chill pervades the cave throughout the year so take warm clothing. To reach the turnoff for the cave, go approximately 9 mi north of Flagstaff on U.S. 180, then turn west onto FR 245. Turn left at the intersection of FR 171 and look for the sign to the cave. The trip is approximately 45 minutes from Flagstaff. Although the cave is on National Forest Service property, the only thing here is an interpretive sign, so it's definitely something you tackle at your own risk. ■ TIP➔ Pack a flashlight (or two). ⊠ *FR 171B.*

2 Lowell Observatory. In 1894, Boston businessman, author, and scientist Percival Lowell founded this observatory from which he studied Mars. His theories of the existence of a ninth planet sowed the seeds for the

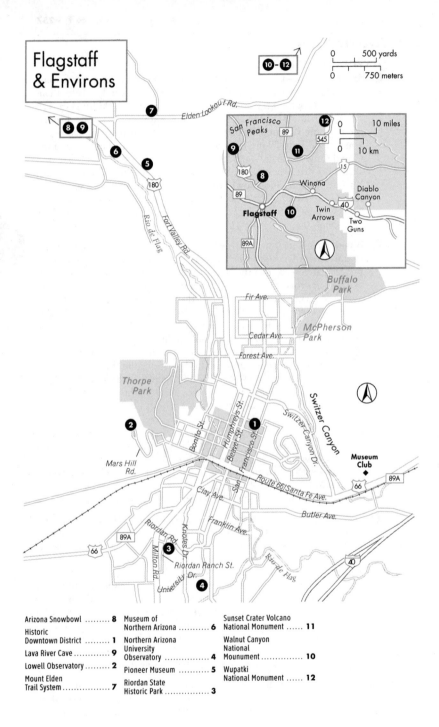

Flagstaff & Environs

| 0 | | 500 yards |
| 0 | | 750 meters |

Elden Lookout Rd.

7

8 **9**

6

5

180

Rio de Flag

Fort Valley Rd.

San Francisco Peaks

89

12

545

0   10 miles

0   10 km

9

11

180

89

8

Winona

15

Diablo Canyon

Flagstaff **10**

Twin Arrows

40

Two Guns

89A

Buffalo Park

Fir Ave.

McPherson Park

Cedar Ave.

Forest Ave.

Thorpe Park

Switzer Canyon

2

Mars Hill Rd.

Bonito St.

Humphreys St.

Beaver St.

San Francisco St.

1

Switzer Canyon Dr.

Museum Club ◆

89A

Route 66 Santa Fe Ave.

66

Clay Ave.

Butler Ave.

Franklin Ave.

89A

Riordan Rd.

Milton Rd.

Knoles Dr.

3

Riordan Ranch St.

Route Flag

40

University Dr.

4

Arizona Snowbowl **8**

Historic Downtown District **1**

Lava River Cave **9**

Lowell Observatory **2**

Mount Elden Trail System **7**

Museum of Northern Arizona **6**

Northern Arizona University Observatory **4**

Pioneer Museum **5**

Riordan State Historic Park **3**

Sunset Crater Volcano National Monument **11**

Walnut Canyon National Mounument **10**

Wupatki National Monument **12**

discovery of Pluto at Lowell in 1930 by Clyde Tombaugh. The 6,500-square-foot Steele Visitor Center hosts exhibits and lectures and has a gift shop. Several interactive exhibits—among them Pluto Walk, a scale model of the solar system—appeal to children. A new Discovery Channel research telescope is anticipated for 2010 and visitors are invited, on some evenings, to peer through the 24-inch Clark telescope. Day and evening viewings are offered year-round, but call ahead for a schedule. ■ TIP➔**The Clark observatory dome is open and unheated, so dress for the outdoors.** To reach the observatory, less than 2 mi from downtown, drive west on Route 66, which resumes its former name, Santa Fe Avenue, before it merges into Mars Hill Road. ✉*1400 W. Mars Hill Rd., West Flagstaff* ☎*928/774–3358, 928/233–3211 recorded info* ⊕*www.lowell.edu* ✉*$6* ⊙*Hrs vary; call ahead.*

❼ Mount Elden Trail System. Most trails in the 35-mi-long Mount Elden Trail System lead to views from the dormant volcanic field, across the vast ponderosa pine forest, all the way to Sedona. The most challenging trail in the Mount Elden system, which happens to be the route with the most rewarding views, is along the steep switchbacks of the **Elden Lookout Trail** (✉*Off U.S. 89, 3 mi east of downtown Flagstaff*). If you traverse the full 3 mi to the top, keep your focus on the landscape rather than the tangle of antennae and satellite dishes that greet you at the top. The 4-mi-long **Sunset Trail** (✉*Off U.S. 180, 3 mi north of downtown Flagstaff, then 6 mi east on FR 420/Schultz Pass Rd.*) proceeds with a gradual pitch through the pine forest, emerging onto a narrow ridge nicknamed the Catwalk. **The access road to this trail is closed in winter.**

❻ Museum of Northern Arizona. This institution, founded in 1928, is respected worldwide for its research and its collections centering on the natural and cultural history of the Colorado Plateau. Among the permanent exhibitions are an extensive collection of Navajo rugs and a Hopi kiva (men's ceremonial chamber). A gallery devoted to area geology is usually a hit with children: it includes a life-size model dilophosaurus, a carnivorous dinosaur that once roamed northern Arizona. Outdoors, a life-zone exhibit shows the changing vegetation from the bottom of the Grand Canyon to the highest peak in Flagstaff. A nature trail, open only in summer, heads down across a small stream into a canyon and up into an aspen grove. Also in summer, the museum hosts exhibits and the works of Native American artists, whose wares are sold in the museum gift shop. ✉*3101 N. Fort Valley Rd., North Flagstaff* ☎*928/774–5213* ⊕*www.musnaz.org* ✉*$7* ⊙*Daily 9–5.*

❹ Northern Arizona University Observatory. The observatory, with its 24-inch telescope, was built in 1952 by Dr. Arthur Adel whose study of infrared astronomy pioneered research into molecules that absorb light passing through the Earth's atmosphere. Today's studies of Earth's shrinking ozone layer rely on some of Dr. Adel's early work. Visitors to the observatory—which houses one of the largest telescopes that the public is allowed to move and manipulate—are usually hosted by friendly students and faculty members of the university's Department of Physics and Astronomy. ✉*Bldg. 47, Northern Arizona Campus*

Observatory, Dept. of Physics and Astronomy, S. San Francisco St., just north of Walkup Skydome, University ☎928/523–7170 ☒*Free* ☉ *Viewings Fri. 7:30–10 PM, weather permitting.*

❺ **Pioneer Museum.** The Arizona Historical Society operates this museum in a volcanic-rock building constructed in 1908. The structure was Coconino County's first hospital for the poor, and the current displays include one of the depressingly small nurses' rooms, an old iron lung, and a reconstructed doctor's office. Most of the exhibits, however, touch on more cheerful aspects of Flagstaff history—like road signs and children's toys. The museum holds a folk-crafts festival on July 4. Those crafts, and ones of other local artisans, are sold in the museum's gift shop. The museum is part of the Fort Valley Park complex, in a wooded residential section at the northwest end of town. ☒*2340 N. Fort Valley Rd., North Flagstaff* ☎*928/774–6272* ⊕*www.arizona historicalsociety.org* ☒*$3* ☉*Mon.–Sat. 9–5.*

❸ **Riordan State Historic Park.** This artifact of Flagstaff's logging heyday is near Northern Arizona University. The centerpiece is a mansion built in 1904 for Michael and Timothy Riordan, The 13,300-square-foot, 40-room log-and-stone structure—designed by Charles Whittlesley, who was also responsible for the El Tovar Hotel at the Grand Canyon—contains furniture by Gustav Stickley, father of the American Arts and Crafts design movement. One room holds "Paul Bunyan's shoes," a 2-foot-long pair of boots made by Timothy in his workshop. Everything on display is original to the house. The mansion may be explored on a guided tour only; reservations are suggested. ☒*409 W. Riordan Rd., University* ☎*928/779–4395* ⊕*www.azstateparks.com* ☒*$6* ☉*May–Oct., daily 8:30–5, with tours on the hr 9–4; Nov.–Apr., daily 10:30–5, with tours on the hr 11–4.*

SPORTS & THE OUTDOORS

HIKING & ROCK CLIMBING

You can explore Arizona's alpine tundra in the San Francisco Peaks, part of the Coconino National Forest, where more than 80 species of plants grow on the upper elevations. The habitat is fragile, so hikers are asked to stay on established trails (there are lots of them). ■**TIP**➔**Flat-landers should give themselves a day or two to adjust to the altitude before lengthy or strenuous hiking.** (Anyone with cardiac or respiratory problems should be cautious about overexertion.)

The rangers of the **Coconino National Forest** (☒*1824 S. Thompson St., North Flagstaff* ☎*928/527–3600* ⊕*www.fs.fed.us/r3/coconino*) maintain many of the region's trails and can provide you with details on hiking in the area; the forest's main office is open weekdays 8 to 4:30.

Flagstaff is in the **Peaks District** (☒*Peaks Ranger Station, 5075 N. U.S. 89, East Flagstaff* ☎*928/526–0866*) of the Coconino National Forest, and there are many trails to explore. The **Humphreys Peak Trail** (☒*Trailhead: Snowbowl Rd., 7 mi north of U.S. 180*) is 9 mi round-trip, with a vertical climb of 3,843 feet to the summit of Arizona's highest mountain

(12,643 feet). Those who don't want a long hike can do just the first mile of the adjacent, 5-mi-long **Kachina Trail** (⊠ *Trailhead: Snowbowl Rd., 7 mi north of U.S. 180*); gently rolling, this route is surrounded by huge stands of aspen and offers fantastic vistas.

Vertical Relief Rock Gym (⊠ *205 S. San Francisco St., Downtown* ☎ *928/556–9909*) has the tallest indoor climbing walls in the Southwest as well as climbing excursions throughout the Flagstaff area.

MOUNTAIN BIKING

The **Coconino National Forest** has some of the best trails in the region. A good place to start is the **Lower Oldham Trail** (⊠ *Trailhead: Cedar St.*), which originates on the north end of Buffalo Park in Flagstaff; there's a large meadow with picnic areas and an exercise path. The terrain rolls, climbing about 800 feet in 3 mi, and the trail is technical in spots but easy enough to test your tolerance of the elevation.

You can rent mountain bikes, get good advice, and purchase trail maps at **Absolute Bikes** (⊠ *200 E. Rte. 66, Downtown* ☎ *928/779–5969*). From mid-June through mid-October, the **Flagstaff Nordic Center** (⊠ *U.S. 180, 16 mi north of Flagstaff, North Flagstaff* ☎ *928/220–0550* ⊕ *www.flagstaffnordiccenter.com*) opens its cross-country trails to mountain bikers. A map of the **Urban Trails System**, available at the Flagstaff Visitor Center (⊠ *1 E. Rte. 66, Downtown* ☎ *928/774–9541 or 800/842–7293*), details biking options in town.

SKIING & SNOWBOARDING

The ski season usually starts in mid-December and ends in mid-April. The **Arizona Snowbowl** (⊠ *Snowbowl Rd., North Flagstaff* ☎ *928/779–1951, 928/779–4577 snow report* ⊕ *www.arizonasnowbowl.com*), 7 mi north of Flagstaff off U.S. 180, has 32 downhill runs, four chairlifts, and a vertical drop of 2,300 feet. There are a couple of good bump runs, but it's better for beginners or those with moderate skill; serious area skiers take a road trip to Telluride. Still, it's a fun place to ski or snowboard. The Hart Prairie Lodge has an equipment-rental shop and a SKIwee center for ages 4 to 7. All-day adult lift tickets are $8. Half-day discounts are available, and group-lesson packages (including two hours of instruction, an all-day lift ticket, and equipment rental) are a good buy at $73. A children's program (which includes lunch, progress card, and full supervision 9–3:30) runs $75. Many Flagstaff motels offer ski packages, including transportation to Snowbowl.

WHERE TO EAT

★ **$$$** ✕ **Cottage Place.** Regarded by locals as one of the best fine-dining venues in the area, this restaurant in a cottage built in 1909 has intimate dining rooms and an extensive wine list. The menu strays slightly from Continental to include some classic American dishes, such as char-broiled lamb chops. The grilled herb salmon and the chateaubriand for two are recommended. Dinner includes soup and salad, but save room for Chocolate Decadence. ⊠ *126 W. Cottage Ave., Downtown* ☎ *928/774–8431* ⊟ *AE, MC, V* ⊗ *Closed Mon. and Tues. No lunch.*

★ ¢ ✕ **La Bellavia.** At this favorite bohemian breakfast and lunch nook, the trout and eggs platter is the standard—two eggs served with Idaho trout flavored with a hint of lemon, rounded off by a buttermilk pancake. Other options include Swedish oat pancakes, seven-grain French toast, and 10 varieties of eggs Benedict. A palette of creative sandwiches and familiar salads makes this a worthwhile lunch stop as well. The café doubles as a gallery for local artists whose work hangs on the walls. ✉18 S. Beaver St., Downtown ☎928/774–8301 ☰MC, V ⊗No dinner.

WHERE TO STAY

■ TIP→ Trains pass through the downtown area along Route 66 (also called Santa Fe Avenue) about every 15 minutes throughout the day and night. Light sleepers may prefer to stay in the south or east sections of town to avoid hearing the train noise.

★ $$ 🏨 **Little America of Flagstaff.** The biggest hotel in town is deservedly popular. It's a little distance from the roar of the trains, the grounds are surrounded by evergreen forests, and it's one of the few places in Flagstaff with room service. Plush rooms have comfortable sitting areas with French provincial–style furniture. Other pluses are an above-average in-house restaurant, courtesy van service to the airport and the Amtrak station, and a gift shop with great Southwestern stuff. **Pros:** Large, very clean rooms; walking trails. **Cons:** Large-scale property can feel impersonal. ✉2515 E. Butler Ave., Downtown, ☎928/779–2741 or 800/352–4386 ⊕www.flagstaff.littleamerica.com ⇨248 rooms ⌂In-room: kitchen, refrigerator, safe. In-hotel: restaurant, room service, bar, pool, gym, laundry facilities, laundry service, public Wi-Fi, no elevator ☰AE, D, DC, MC, V.

THE ARTS

Flagstaff Cultural Partners/Coconino Center for the Arts (✉2300 N. Fort Valley Rd., North Flagstaff ☎928/779–2300 ⊕www.culturalpartners. org) has gallery space for exhibitions, a theater, and performance space. The **Flagstaff Symphony Orchestra** (☎928/774–5107 ⊕www.flagstaff symphony.org) has year-round musical events. The 1917 **Orpheum Theater** (✉15 W. Aspen St., Downtown ☎928/556–1580 ⊕www.orpheum-presents.com) features music acts, films, lectures, and plays. **Theatrikos Theatre Company** (✉11 W. Cherry Ave., Downtown ☎928/774–1662 ⊕www.theatrikos.com) is a highly regarded performance-art group.

A Celebration of Native American Art (✉3101 N. Fort Valley Rd., North Flagstaff ☎928/774–5211), featuring exhibits of work by Zuni, Hopi, and Navajo artists, is held at the Museum of Northern Arizona from late May through September.

SIDE TRIPS NEAR FLAGSTAFF

EAST OF FLAGSTAFF

⑩ **Walnut Canyon National Monument** consists of a group of cliff dwell-
★ ings constructed by the Sinagua people, who lived and farmed in and
around the canyon starting around AD 700. The more than 300 dwellings here were built between 1080 and 1250 and abandoned, like those
at so many other settlements in Arizona and New Mexico, around
1300. Early Flagstaff settlers looted the site for pots and "treasure";
Woodrow Wilson declared this a national monument in 1915, which
began a 30-year process of stabilizing the site.

Part of the fascination of Walnut Canyon is the opportunity to enter
the dwellings, stepping back in time to an ancient way of life. Some of
the Sinagua homes are in near-perfect condition in spite of all the loot-
ing, because of the dry, hot climate and the protection of overhanging
cliffs. You can reach them by descending 185 feet on the 1-mi stepped
Island Trail, which starts at the visitor center. As you follow the trail,
look across the canyon for other dwellings not accessible on the path.
Island Trail takes about an hour to complete at a normal pace. Those
with health concerns should opt for the easier ½-mi **Rim Trail,** which
has overlooks from which dwellings, as well as an excavated, reconstructed pit house, can be viewed. Picnic areas dot the grounds and
line the roads leading to the park. ■TIP→**Wear layers, as the climate
can change quickly.** Guides conduct tours on Wednesday, Saturday, and
Sunday from late May through early September. ✉ *Walnut Canyon
Rd., 3 mi south of I-40, Exit 204, Winona* ☎*928/526–3367* ⊕*www.
nps.gov/waca* ☑*$5* ☉*Nov.–Apr., daily 9–5; May–Oct., daily 8–5.*

SAN FRANCISCO VOLCANIC FIELD

The San Francisco Volcanic Field north of Flagstaff encompasses 2,000
square mi of fascinating geological phenomena, including ancient volcanoes, cinder cones, valleys carved by water and ice, and the San
Francisco Peaks themselves, some of which soar to almost 13,000 feet.
There are also some of the most extensive Native American dwellings
in the Southwest. ■TIP→**The area is short on services, so fill up on gas
and consider taking a picnic.**

⑪ **Sunset Crater Volcano National Monument** lies 14 mi northeast of Flagstaff
★ off U.S. 89. Sunset Crater, a cinder cone that rises 1,000 feet, was an
active volcano 900 years ago. Its final eruption contained iron and sul-
fur, which give the rim of the crater its glow and thus its name. You can
walk around the base, but you can't descend into the huge, fragile cone.
The **Lava Flow Trail,** a half-hour, mile-long, self-guided walk, provides a
good view of the evidence of the volcano's fiery power: lava formations
and holes in the rock where volcanic gases vented to the surface.

If you're interested in hiking a volcano, head to **Lenox Crater,** about
1 mi east of the visitor center, and climb the 280 feet to the top of the
cinder cone. The cinder is soft and crumbly so wear closed, sturdy

shoes. From **O'Leary Peak,** 5 mi from the visitor center on Forest Route 545A, enjoy great views of the San Francisco Peaks, the Painted Desert, and beyond. The road is unpaved and rutted, though, so it's advisable to take only high-clearance vehicles, especially in winter. In addition, there's a gate, about halfway along the route, which is usually closed, and when it is, it means a steep 2½-mi hike to the top on foot. To get to the area from Flagstaff, take Santa Fe Avenue east to U.S. 89, and head north for 12 mi; turn right onto the road marked Sunset Crater and go another 2 mi to the visitor center. ⊠ *Sunset Crater–Wupatki Loop Rd., 14 mi northeast of Flagstaff* ☎ *928/556–0502* ⊕ *www.nps. gov/sucr* ☜ *$5, including Wupatki National Monument and Doney Mountain* ☉ *Nov.–Apr., daily 9–5; May–Oct., daily 8–5.*

⑫
★ Families from the Sinagua and other ancestral Puebloans are believed to have lived together in harmony on the site that is now **Wupatki National Monument,** farming and trading with one another and with those who passed through. The eruption of Sunset Crater may have influenced migration to this area a century after the event, as freshly laid volcanic cinders held in moisture needed for crops.

Other sites to visit are Wukoki, Lomaki, and the Citadel, a pueblo on a knoll above a limestone sink. Although the largest remnants of Native American settlements at Wupatki National Monument are open to the public, other sites are off-limits. If you're interested in an in-depth tour, consider a ranger-led overnight hike to the **Crack-in-Rock Ruin.** The 14-mi (round-trip) trek covers areas marked by ancient petroglyphs and dotted with well-preserved sites. The trips are only conducted in April and October; call by February or August if you'd like to take part in the lottery for one of the 100 available places on these $50 hikes. Between the Wupatki and Citadel ruins, the **Doney Mountain** affords 360-degree views of the Painted Desert and the San Francisco Volcanic Field. It's a perfect spot for a sunset picnic. In summer, rangers give lectures. ⊠ *Sunset Crater–Wupatki Loop Rd., 19 mi north of Sunset Crater visitor center* ☎ *928/679–2365* ⊕ *www. nps.gov/wupa* ☜ *$5, including Sunset Crater National Monument and Doney Mountain* ☉ *Daily 9–5.*

SEDONA & OAK CREEK CANYON

119 mi north of Phoenix, I–17 to AZ 179 to AZ 89A; 60 mi northeast of Prescott, U.S. 89 to AZ 89A; 27 mi south of Flagstaff on AZ 89A.

It's easy to see what draws so many people to Sedona. Red-rock buttes—Cathedral Rock, Bear Mountain, Courthouse Rock, and Bell Rock, among others—reach up into an almost always blue sky, and both colors are intensified by dark-green pine forests. Surrealist Max Ernst, writer Zane Grey, and many filmmakers drew inspiration from these vistas—more than 80 Westerns were shot in the area in the 1940s and '50s alone.

These days, Sedona lures enterprising restaurateurs and gallery owners from the East and West coasts. New Age followers, who believe that the

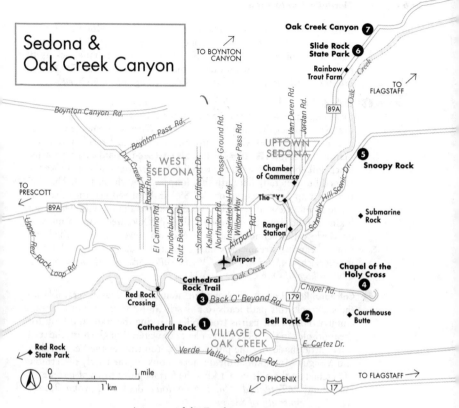

Sedona & Oak Creek Canyon

area contains some of the Earth's more important vortexes (energy centers), also come in great numbers believing that the "vibe" here confers a sense of balance and well-being, and enhances creativity.

Sedona is roughly divided into three neighborhoods: Uptown, which is a walkable shopping district; West Sedona, which is a 4-mi-long commercial strip; and Central Sedona, which encompasses everything south of the "Y" where AZ 179 and AZ 89A intersect.

Sedona Trolley (☎928/282–4211 ⊕*www.sedonatrolley.com*) offers two types of daily orientation tours, both departing from the main bus stop in Uptown and lasting less than an hour. One goes along AZ 179 to the Chapel of the Holy Cross, with stops at Tlaquepaque and some galleries; the other passes through West Sedona to Boynton Canyon (Enchantment Resort). Rates are $11 for one or $20 for both.

EXPLORING SEDONA

MAIN ATTRACTIONS

❷ **Bell Rock.** With its distinctive shape right out of your favorite Western film and its proximity to the main drag ensuring a steady flow of admirers, you may want to arrive early to see this popular butte. The views from here are good, but an easy and fairly accessible path follows mostly gentle terrain for 1 mi to the base of the butte. Mountain bikers, parents with all-terrain baby strollers, and not-so-avid hikers should have little problem getting there. No official paths climb the rock itself, but many forge their own routes (at their own risk). ⊠*AZ 179, several hundred yards north of Bell Rock Blvd., Village of Oak Creek.*

❶ Cathedral Rock. It's almost impossible not to be drawn to this butte's towering, variegated spires. The approximately 1,200-foot-high Cathedral Rock looms dramatically over town. When you emerge from the narrow gorge of Oak Creek Canyon, this is the first recognizable formation you'll spot. ■TIP➔**The butte is best seen toward dusk from a distance.** Hikers may want to drive to the Airport Mesa and then hike the rugged but generally flat path that loops around the airfield. The trail is a ½ mi up Airport Road off AZ 89A in West Sedona; the reward is a panoramic view of Cathedral Rock without the crowds. Those not hiking should drive through the Village of Oak Creek, and 5 mi west on Verde Valley School Road to its end, where you can view the butte from a beautiful streamside vantage point and take a dip in Oak Creek if you wish. ⊠*5 mi to end of Verde Valley School Rd., west off AZ 179, Village of Oak Creek.*

❸ Cathedral Rock Trail. A vigorous but nontechnical 1½-mi scramble up the slickrock, this path leads to a nearly 360-degree view of red rock country. Follow the cairns (rock piles marking the trail) and look for the footholds in the rock. Carry plenty of water: though short, the trail offers little shade and the pitch is steep. You can see the Verde Valley and Mingus Mountain in the distance. Look for the barely discernible "J" etched on the hillside marking the former ghost town of Jerome 30 mi distant. ⊠*Trailhead: About ½ mi down Back O' Beyond Rd. off AZ 179, 3 mi south of Sedona.*

❹ Chapel of the Holy Cross. You needn't be religious to be inspired by the setting and the architecture here. Built in 1956 by Marguerite Brunwige Staude, a student of Frank Lloyd Wright, this modern landmark, with a huge cross on the facade, rises between two red-rock peaks. Vistas of the town and the surrounding area are spectacular. Though there is only one regular service—Monday at 5 PM—all are welcome for quiet meditation. A small gift shop sells religious artifacts and books. A trail east of the chapel leads you—after a 20-minute walk over occasional loose-rock surfaces—to a seat surrounded by voluptuous red-limestone walls, worlds away from the bustle and commerce around the chapel. ⊠*Chapel Rd., off AZ 179, Village of Oak Creek* 🕾*928/282–4069* ⊕*www.chapeloftheholycross.com* 🎫*Free* ⊙*Daily 9–5.*

❼ Oak Creek Canyon. Whether you want to swim, hike, picnic, or enjoy
★ beautiful scenery framed through a car window, head north through the wooded Oak Creek Canyon. It's the most scenic route to Flagstaff and the Grand Canyon, and worth a drive-through even if you're not heading north. The road winds through a steep-walled canyon, where you crane your neck for views of the dramatic rock formations above. Although the forest is primarily evergreen, the fall foliage is glorious. Oak Creek, which runs along the bottom, is lined with tent camp-

grounds, fishing camps, cabins, motels, and restaurants. ⊠*AZ 89A, beginning 1 mi north of Sedona, Oak Creek Canyon.*

6 **Slide Rock State Park.** A good place for a picnic, Slide Rock is 7 mi north of Sedona. On a hot day you can plunge down a natural rock slide into a swimming hole (bring an extra pair of jeans or a sturdy bathing suit and river shoes to wear on the slide). The site started as an early-20th-century apple orchard and the natural beauty attracted Hollywood—a number of John Wayne and Jimmy Stewart movies were filmed here. A few easy hikes run along the rim of the gorge. Fly-fishing for trout is possible when it's too cold for swimming. One downside is the traffic, particularly on summer weekends; you might have to wait to get into the park. Unfortunately, the popularity of the stream has led to the occasional midsummer closing due to E. coli– bacteria infestations; the water is tested daily and there is a water-quality hotline at 602/542–0202. ⊠*6871 N. AZ 89A, Oak Creek Canyon* ☎*928/282–3034* ⊕*www.azstateparks.com* ⊠*$10 per vehicle for up to 4 persons* ☉*Labor Day–Memorial Day, daily 8–5; Memorial Day– Labor Day, daily 8–7.*

5 **Snoopy Rock.** Kids love this: when you look almost directly to the east, this butte really does look like the famed Peanuts beagle lying atop red rock instead of his doghouse. You can distinguish the formation from several places around town including the mall in Uptown Sedona, but to get a clear view, venture up Schnebly Hill Road. Park by the trail-head on the left immediately before the paved road deteriorates to dirt. Marg's Draw, one of several trails originating here, is worthwhile, gently meandering 100 feet down-canyon, through the tortured desert flora to Morgan Road. Backtrack to the parking lot for close to a 3-mi hike. ■TIP➡Always carry plenty of water, no matter how easy the hike appears. ⊠*Schnebly Hill Rd., off AZ 179, Central.*

SPORTS & THE OUTDOORS

■TIP➡A Red Rock Pass is required to park in the Coconino National Forest from Oak Creek Canyon through Sedona and the Village of Oak Creek. Passes cost $5 for the day, $15 for the week, or $20 for an entire year and can be purchased at four visitor centers surrounding and within Sedona. Passes are also available from vending machines at popular trailheads including Boynton Canyon, Bell Rock, and Huckaby. Locals widely resent the pass, feeling that free access to national forests is a right. The Forest Service counters that it doesn't receive enough federal funds to maintain the land surrounding Sedona, trampled by 5 million visitors each year, and that a parking fee is the best way to raise revenue. ☎*928/282–4119 information only* ⊕*www.redrockcountry.org.*

GOLF

Fodor'sChoice ★ **Sedona Golf Resort** (⊠*35 Ridge Trail Dr., Village of Oak Creek* ☎*928/284–9355 or 877/733–6630* ⊕*www.sedonagolfresort.com*) was designed by Gary Panks to take advantage of the many changes in elevation and scenery. Golf courses are a dime a dozen in Arizona, but this one is regarded as one of the best in the state.

HIKING & BACKPACKING

For free detailed maps, hiking advice, and information on camp-grounds, contact the rangers of the **Coconino National Forest** (⊠*Sedona Ranger District, 250 Brewer Rd., West* ☎*928/282–4119* ⊕*www. fs.fed.us/r3/coconino* ⊘*Weekdays 8–4:30*). Ask here or at your hotel for directions to trailheads for Doe's Mountain (an easy ascent, with many switchbacks), Loy Canyon, Devil's Kitchen, and Long Canyon.

Among the paths in Coconino National Forest, the popular **West Fork Trail** (⊠*Trailhead: AZ 89A, 9½ mi north of Sedona*) traverses the Oak Creek Canyon for a 3-mi hike. A walk through the woods in the midst of sheer red-rock walls and a dip in the stream is a great summer combo. The trailhead is about 3 mi north of Slide Rock State Park. Any backpacking trip in the **Secret Mountain Wilderness** near Sedona guarantees stunning vistas, otherworldly rock formations, and Zen-like serenity, but little water, so pack a good supply. ■TIP➜**Plan your trip for the spring or fall: summer brings 100°F heat and sudden thunderstorms that flood canyons without warning.** Most individual trails in the wilderness are too short for anything longer than an overnighter, but several trails can be linked up to form a memorable multiday trip. Contact the Sedona Ranger District for full details.

HORSEBACK RIDING

Among the tour options at **Trail Horse Adventures** (⊠*85 Five J La., Lower Red Rock Loop Rd., West* ☎*800/723–3538* ⊕*www.trailhorse adventures.com*) are a midday picnic, an Oak Creek swim, and a full-moon ride with a campfire cookout. Rides range from about $60 for an hour to about $200 for an entire day.

JEEP TOURS

Several jeep-tour operators headquartered along Sedona's main Uptown drag conduct excursions, some focusing on geology, some on astronomy, some on vortexes, some on all three. You can even find a combination jeep tour and horseback ride. Prices start at about $55 per person for two hours and go upward of $100 per person for four hours. Although all the excursions are safe, many are not for those who dislike heights or bumps.

A Day in the West (☎*928/282–4320 or 800/973–3662* ⊕*www.aday inthewest.com*) can take you to all the prime spots or combine a jeep tour with local wine tasting. The ubiquitous **Pink Jeep Tours** (⊠*204 N. AZ 89A, Sedona* ☎*928/282–5000 or 800/873–3662* ⊕*www.pinkjeep. com*) are a popular choice. **Sedona Red Rock Jeep Tours** (⊠*270 N. AZ 89A, Sedona* ☎*928/282–6826 or 800/848–7728* ⊕*www.redrockjeep. com*) is also a reliable operator.

MOUNTAIN BIKING

As a general rule, mountain bikes are allowed on all trails and jeep paths unless designated as wilderness or private property. The rolling terrain, which switches between serpentine trails of buff red clay and mounds of slickrock, has few sustained climbs but ■TIP➜**be careful of blind drop-offs that often step down several feet in unexpected places.** The thorny trailside flora makes carrying extra inner tubes a must, and an inner tube sealant is a good idea, too. If you plan to ride for several hours, pack a gallon of water and start early in the morning on hot days. Shade is rare, and with the exception of (nonpotable) Oak Creek, water is nonexistent.

For the casual rider, **Bell Rock Pathway** (⊠ *Trailhead: 5 mi south of Sedona on AZ 179*) is a scenic and easy ride traveling 3 mi through some of the most breathtaking scenery in red rock country. Several single-track trails spur off this one making it a good starting point for many other rides in Sedona. **Submarine Rock Loop** is perhaps the most popular single-track loop in the area, and for good reason. The 10-mi trail is a heady mixture of prime terrain and scenery following slickrock and twisty trails up to Chicken Point, a sandstone terrace overlooking colorful buttes. The trail continues as a bumpy romp through washes almost all downhill. Be wary of blind drop-offs in this section. It wouldn't be overly cautious to scout any parts of the trail that look sketchy.

A few hundred yards south of Bell Rock Pathway, **Bike and Bean** (⊠ *6020 AZ 179, Village of Oak Creek* ☎ *928/284–0210* ⊕ *www. bike-bean.com*) offers rentals, tours, trail maps, their own blend of coffee, and advice on trails and conditions.

WHERE TO EAT

Some Sedona restaurants close in January and February, so call before you go; if you're planning a visit in high season (April to October), make reservations.

★ $$$$ ✕**L'Auberge.** The most formal dining room in Sedona, on the L'Auberge de Sedona resort property, promises a quiet, civilized evening of indulgence. Chef Jonathan Agelman offers a fusion of American cuisine with French influences, and among the house favorites is the venison accompanied by wild game cassoulet and broccolini. You can make the most of L'Auberge's 1,200-bottle wine cellar by enjoying the five-course wine-paired meal for $140. The lavish Sunday brunch is well worth the splurge. ⊠ *L'Auberge de Sedona, 241 AZ 89A, Uptown* ☎ *928/282–1667* ▤ *AE, D, DC, MC, V.*

★ $$$ ✕**Heartline Café.** Fresh flowers and innovative cuisine that even the staff struggles to characterize are this attractive café's hallmarks. Local ingredients pepper the menu, giving a Sedona twist to Continental fare, and favorites include pecan-crusted trout with Dijon sauce and oak-grilled salmon marinated in tequila and lime. Appealing vegetarian plates are also available. Desserts include a phenomenal crème brûlée, as well as homemade truffles at the chef's whim. ■TIP→**The owners also do gourmet take-out next door—perfect prep for picnics under the red rocks.** ⊠ *1610 W. AZ 89A, West* ☎ *928/282–0785* ▤ *AE, D, MC, V* ⊙ *No lunch Mon.–Thurs.*

★ $$ ✕**Dahl & DiLuca.** Andrea DiLuca and Lisa Dahl have created one of the most popular Italian restaurants in town: Andrea runs the kitchen, and Lisa meets and greets diners when she's not making delicious homemade soups like white bean with ham and hearty minestrone. Renaissance reproductions and café seating give the impression of a Roman piazza. ⊠*2321 W. AZ 89A, West* ☎*928/282–5219* ▭*AE, D, MC, V* ☾*No lunch.*

★ ¢ ✗**Sally's Mesquite Grill and BBQ.** Although it offers limited indoor seating, this Uptown hideaway behind a long row of tourist shops is worth a visit. It's super casual, with just an ordering window where you can select pulled pork sandwiches and homemade comfort food such as beans or coleslaw. The barbecue sauce has a bit of a kick, and the french fries (also made from scratch) are fabulous. Hours vary with the season, so call ahead. ⊠*250 Jordan Rd., No. 9, Uptown* ☎*928/282–6533* ▭*MC, V.*

WHERE TO STAY

★ $$$$ ▦**Enchantment Resort.** The rooms and suites at this resort are tucked into small, pueblo-style buildings in serene Boynton Canyon. Accommodations come in many configurations, and multiple bedrooms can be joined to create large, elaborate suites. All have beehive gas fireplaces, private decks, and superb views. The resort's world-class spa, Mii Amo, offers all-inclusive packages, along with a myriad of treatments and innovative spa cuisine. **Pros:** Gorgeous setting, state-of-the-art spa, numerous on-site activities. **Cons:** Twenty-minute drive into town. ⊠*525 Boynton Canyon Rd., West,* ☎*928/282–2900 or 800/826–4180* ⊕*www.enchantmentresort.com* ↪*107 rooms, 115 suites* ⌂*In-room: Wi-Fi, safe, kitchen (some). In-hotel: 3 restaurants, bar, tennis courts, pools, gym, spa, bicycles, children's programs (ages 4–12), no elevator* ▭*AE, D, MC, V.*

★ $$$–$$$$ ▦**L'Auberge de Sedona.** This hillside resort consists of a central lodge building; creek-side rooms; and—the major attraction—cabins in the woods along Oak Creek. Rooms in the lodge are decorated in lush country-European style and the cabins have wood-burning fireplaces. Phoenix couples flock to this hideaway and dine in the hotel's French restaurant, one of the most romantic eateries in Arizona. **Pros:** Luxurious rooms and cabins, secluded setting yet close to town. **Cons:** Exclusive feel, in-house restaurant very pricey. ⊠*301 L'Auberge La., Uptown* ☐*Box B, 86336* ☎*928/282–1661 or 800/905–5745* ⊕*www.lauberge.com* ↪*21 rooms, 31 cottages;* ⌂*In-room: refrigerator, safe. In-hotel: 2 restaurants, pool, public Wi-Fi, spa* ▭*AE, D, DC, MC, V.*

★ $$ ▦**The Canyon Wren.** The best value in the Oak Creek Canyon area, this small B&B has freestanding cabins with views of the canyon walls, and hosts Milena and Mike regard guests' privacy first and foremost. It's likely that their two lovable dogs, Zoey and Wookiee, will greet you on arrival. Cabins have private decks and fireplaces. **Pros:** Romantic yet homey, wonderful hosts and breakfast. **Cons:** May be too rustic for some, 6 mi to town. ⊠*6425 N. AZ 89A, Oak Creek Canyon,* ☎*928/282–6900 or 800/437–9736* ⊕*www.canyonwrencabins.com* ↪*4 cabins* ⌂*In-room: no phone, kitchen, no TV. In-hotel: no-smoking rooms, no elevator* ▭*AE, D, MC, V* ⊠|CP.

SHOPPING

With a few exceptions, most of the stores in what is known as the Uptown area (north of the "Y," running along AZ 89A to the east of its intersection with AZ 179) cater to the tour-bus trade with Native American jewelry and New Age souvenirs. If this isn't your style, the largest concentration of stores and galleries is in Central Sedona, along AZ 179, south of the "Y," with plenty of offerings for serious shoppers.

THE VERDE VALLEY, JEROME & PRESCOTT

VERDE VALLEY

Often overlooked by travelers on trips to Prescott or Flagstaff, the Verde Valley offers several enjoyable diversions, including the historical wonders at Montezuma Castle and Tuzigoot.

❶ The military post for which **Fort Verde State Historic Park** is named was built between 1871 and 1873 as the third of three fortifications in this part of the Arizona Territory. To protect the Verde Valley's farmers and miners from Tonto Apache and Yavapai raids, the fort's administrators oversaw the movement of nearly 1,500 Native Americans to the San Carlos and Fort Apache reservations. A museum details the history of the area's military installations, and three furnished officers' quarters show the day-to-day living conditions of the top brass—it's a good break from the interstate if you've been driving for too long. Signs from any of Interstate 17's three Camp Verde exits will direct you to the 10-acre park. ⊠ *125 E. Hollomon St.* ☎ *928/567–3275* ⊕ *www. azstateparks.com* ⊠ *$2* ⊙ *Daily 8–4:30.*

❷ The five-story, 20-room cliff dwelling at **Montezuma Castle National Monument** was named by explorers who believed it had been erected by the Aztecs. Southern Sinagua Native Americans actually built the roughly 600-year-old structure, which is one of the best-preserved prehistoric dwellings in North America—and one of the most accessible. An easy paved trail (⅓ mi round-trip) leads to the dwelling and to adjacent Castle A, a badly deteriorated six-story living space with about 45 rooms. No one is permitted to enter the site, but the viewing area is close by. From Camp Verde, take Main Street to Montezuma Castle Road.

Somewhat less accessible than Montezuma Castle—but equally striking—is the **Montezuma Well** (☎ *928/567–4521*), a unit of the national monument. Although there are some Sinagua and Hohokam sites here, the limestone sinkhole with a limpid blue-green pool lying in the middle of the desert is the park's main attraction. This cavity—55 feet deep and 365 feet across—is all that's left of an ancient subterranean cavern; the water remains at a constant 76°F year-round. It's a short hike up here, but the peace, quiet, and the views of the Verde Valley reward the effort. To reach Montezuma Well from Montezuma Castle, return to Interstate 17 and go north to Exit 293; signs direct you to the well,

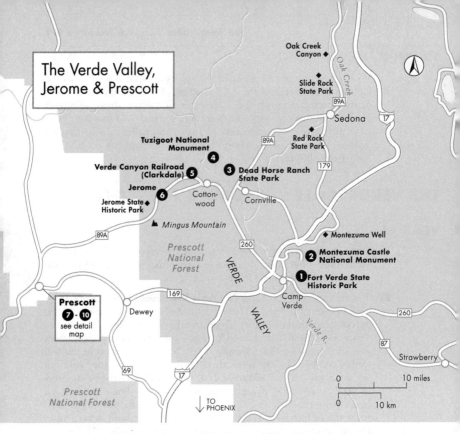

The Verde Valley, Jerome & Prescott

which is 4 mi east of the freeway. The drive includes a short section of dirt road. ⊠ *Montezuma Castle Rd., 7 mi northeast of Camp Verde* ☎ *928/567–3322* ⊕ *www.nps.gov/moca* ⊠ *$5* ⊙ *Labor Day–Memorial Day, daily 8–5; Memorial Day–Labor Day, daily 8–6.*

❸ The 423-acre spread of **Dead Horse Ranch State Park,** which combines high-desert and wetlands habitats, is a pleasant place to while away the day. You can fish in the Verde River or the well-stocked Park Lagoon, or hike on some 6 mi of trails that begin in a shaded picnic area and wind along the river; adjoining forest service pathways are available for those who enjoy longer treks. Birders can check off more than 100 species from the Arizona Audubon Society lists provided by the rangers. Bald eagles perch along the Verde River in winter, and the common black hawks—a misnomer for these threatened birds—nest here in summer. It's 1 mi north of Cottonwood, off Main Street. ⊠ *675 Dead Horse Ranch Rd., Cottonwood* ☎ *928/634–5283* ⊕ *www.azstate parks.com* ⊠ *$6 per car* ⊙ *Daily 8–5.*

❹ **Tuzigoot National Monument** isn't as well preserved as Montezuma Castle but it's more impressive in scope. Tuzigoot is another complex of the Sinagua people, who lived on this land overlooking the Verde Valley from about AD 1000 to 1400. The pueblo, constructed of limestone and sandstone blocks, once rose three stories and housed 110 rooms.

Inhabitants were skilled dry farmers and traded with peoples hundreds of miles away. Items used for food preparation, as well as jewelry, weapons, and farming tools excavated from the site, are displayed in the visitor center. Within the site, you can step into a reconstructed room. ⊠*3 mi north of Cottonwood on Broadway Rd., between Cottonwood's Old Town and Clarkdale, Clarkdale* ☎*928/634–5564* ⊕*www.nps. gov/tuzi* ⊠*$5* ⊙*Sept.–May, daily 8–5; June–Aug., daily 8–6.*

⑤ Train buffs come to the Verde Valley to catch the 22-mi **Verde Canyon**
★ Railroad, which follows a dramatic route through the Verde Canyon, the remains of a copper smelter, and much unspoiled desert that is inaccessible by car. The destination—the city of Clarkdale—might not be that impressive, but the ride is undeniably scenic. Knowledgeable announcers regale riders with the area's colorful history and point out natural attractions along the way—in winter, you're likely to see bald eagles. This four-hour trip is especially popular in fall-foliage season and in spring, when the desert wildflowers bloom; book well in advance. Round-trip rides cost $54.95. For $79.95 you can ride the much more comfortable living-room-like first-class cars, where hot hors d'oeuvres, coffee, and a cocktail are included in the price. ■**TIP→Reservations are required.** ⊠*Arizona Central Railroad, 300 N. Broadway, Clarkdale* ☎*800/320–0718* ⊕*www.verdecanyonrr.com.*

SPORTS & THE OUTDOORS

The **Verde Ranger District** office of the **Prescott National Forest** (⊠*300 E. AZ 260, Camp Verde* ☎*928/567–4121* ⊕*www.fs.fed.us/r3/ prescott*) is a good resource for places to hike, fish, and boat along the Verde River.

The **Black Canyon Trail** (⊠*AZ 260, 4 mi south of Cottonwood, west on FR 359 4½ mi*) is a bit of a slog, rising more than 2,200 feet in 6 mi, but the reward is grand views from the gray cliffs of Verde Valley to the red buttes of Sedona to the blue range of the San Francisco Peaks.

WHERE TO EAT

$$ ✕**Page Springs Restaurant.** Come to these two rustic, wood-paneled rooms in Cornville, on the loop to the town of Page Springs—off AZ 89A—for down-home Western chow: great chili, burgers, and steaks. You'll get an Oak Creek view for much less than you'd pay closer to Sedona. ⊠*1975 N. Page Springs Rd., Cornville* ☎*928/634–9954* ▭*No credit cards.*

JEROME

⑥ *3½ mi southwest of Clarkdale, 20 mi northwest of Camp Verde, 33 mi*
★ *northeast of Prescott, 25 mi southwest of Sedona on AZ 89A.*

Jerome was once known as the Billion Dollar Copper Camp, but after the last mines closed in 1953 the booming population of 15,000 dwindled to 50 determined souls. Although its population has risen back to almost 500, Jerome still holds on to its "ghost town" designation and several B&Bs and eateries regularly report spirit sightings. It's hard to imagine this town was once the location of Arizona's largest JCPenney store and one of the state's first Safeway supermarkets! Jerome saw its first revival during the mid-1960s, when hippies arrived and turned it into an arts colony of sorts, and it has since become a tourist attraction. In addition to its shops and historic sites, Jerome is worth visiting for its scenery: it's built into the side of Cleopatra Hill, and from here you can see Sedona's red rocks, Flagstaff's San Francisco Peaks, and even eastern Arizona's Mogollon Rim country.

Jerome is about a mile above sea level, but structures within town sit at elevations that vary by as much as 1,500 feet, depending on whether they're on Cleopatra Hill or at its foot. Blasting at the United Verde (later Phelps Dodge) mine regularly shook buildings off their foundations—the town's jail slid across a road and down a hillside, where it sits today. And that's not all that was unsteady about Jerome. In 1903 a reporter from a New York newspaper called Jerome "the wickedest town in America," due to its abundance of drinking and gambling establishments; town records from 1880 list 24 saloons. Whether by divine retribution or drunken accidents, the town burned down several times.

Of the three mining museums in town, the most inclusive is part of **Jerome State Historic Park.** Just outside town, signs on AZ 89A will direct you to the turnoff for the park, reached by a short, precipitous road. The museum occupies the 1917 mansion of Jerome's mining king, Dr. James "Rawhide Jimmy" Douglas Jr., who purchased Little Daisy Mine in 1912. You can see some of the tools and heavy equipment used to grind ore, but accounts of the town's wilder elements—such as the House of Joy brothel—are not so prominently displayed. ⊠*State Park Rd.* ☎*928/634–5381* ⊕*www.azstateparks.com* ⊠*$3* ☉*Daily 8–5.*

The **Mine Museum** in downtown Jerome is staffed by the Jerome Historical Society. The museum's collection of mining stock certificates alone is worth the (small) price of admission—the amount of money that changed hands in this town 100 years ago boggles the mind. ⊠*200 Main St.* ☎*928/634–5477* ⊠*$2* ☉*Daily 9–4:30.*

WHERE TO EAT

$ ✕ **Haunted Hamburger/Jerome Palace.** After the climb up the stairs from Main Street to this former boardinghouse, you'll be ready for the hearty burgers, chili, cheese steaks, and ribs that dominate the menu. Lighter fare, including such meatless selections as the guacamole quesadilla, is also available. Eat on the outside deck overlooking Verde Valley or in the upstairs dining room, where "Claire," the resident ghost, purportedly hangs out. ⊠*410 Clark St.* ☎*928/634–0554* ▭*MC, V.*

SHOPPING

Jerome has its share of art galleries (some perched precariously on Cleopatra Hill), along with boutiques, and they're funkier than those in Sedona. Main Street and, just around the bend, Hull Avenue are Jerome's two primary shopping streets. Your eyes may begin to glaze over after browsing through one boutique after another, most offering tasteful Southwestern paraphernalia.

PRESCOTT

33 mi southwest of Jerome on AZ 89A to U.S. 89, 100 mi northwest of Phoenix via I–17 to AZ 69.

In a forested bowl 5,300 feet above sea level, Prescott is a prime summer refuge for Phoenix-area dwellers. It was proclaimed the first capital of the Arizona Territory in 1864 and settled by Yankees to ensure that gold-rich northern Arizona would remain a Union resource. (Tucson and southern Arizona were strongly pro-Confederacy.) Although early territorial settlers thought that the area's original inhabitants were of Aztec origin, today it's believed that they were ancestors of the Yavapai, whose reservation is on the outskirts of town. The Aztec theory—inspired by *The History and Conquest of Mexico,* a popular book by historian William Hickling Prescott, for whom the town was named—has left its mark on such street names as Montezuma, Cortez, and Alarcon.

Despite a devastating downtown fire in 1900, Prescott remains the "West's most Eastern town" with a rich treasure trove of late-19th-century New England–style architecture. With two institutions of higher education, Yavapai College and Prescott College, Prescott could be called a college town, but it doesn't really feel like one, perhaps because so many retirees also reside here, drawn by the temperate climate and low cost of living.

WHAT TO SEE

10 **Phippen Museum of Western Art.** The paintings and bronze sculptures of George Phippen, along with works by other artists of the West, form the permanent collection of this museum, about 5 mi north of downtown. Phippen met with a group of prominent cowboy artists in 1965 to form the Cowboy Artists of America, a group dedicated to preserving the Old West as they saw it. He became the president but died the next year. A memorial foundation set up in his name opened the doors of this museum in 1984. ⊠*4701 U.S. 89N* ☎*928/778–1385* ⊕*www. phippenartmuseum.org* ☜*$5* ⊘*Tues.–Sat. 10–4, Sun. 1–4.*

8 **Sharlot Hall Museum.** Local history is documented at this remarkable museum. Along with the original ponderosa-pine log cabin, which housed the territorial governor, and the museum, named for historian and poet Sharlot Hall, the parklike setting contains three fully restored period homes and a transportation museum. Territorial times are the focus, but natural history and artifacts of the area's prehistoric peoples are also on display. ⊠*415 W. Gurley St., 2 blocks west of Courthouse Plaza, Downtown* ☎*928/445–3122* ⊕*www.sharlot.org* ☜*$5* ⊘*Tues.–Sat. 10–4, Sun. 1–4.*

9 **Smoki Museum.** The 1935 stone-and-log building, which resembles an Indian pueblo, is almost as interesting as the Native American artifacts inside. Baskets, kachinas, pottery, rugs, and beadwork make up the collection, which represents Native American culture from the pre-Columbian period to the present. ⊠*147 N. Arizona St., Downtown* ☎*928/445–1230* ⊕*www.smokimuseum.org* ☜*$5* ⊘*Tues.–Sat. 10–4, Sun. 1–4.*

5

Phippen
Museum of
Western Art ... **10**

Sharlot Hall
Museum **8**

Smoki
Museum **9**

Whiskey
Row **7**

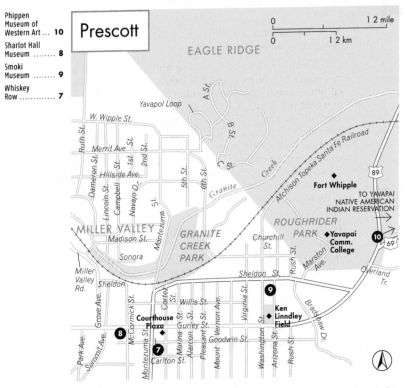

Prescott

0   1 2 mile
0   1 2 km

EAGLE RIDGE

7 **Whiskey Row.** Twenty saloons and houses of pleasure once lined this
stretch of Montezuma Street, along the west side of Courthouse Plaza.
Social activity is more subdued these days, and the historic bars provide
an escape from the street's many boutiques. ⊠*Downtown.*

SPORTS & THE OUTDOORS

HIKING &
CAMPING

More than a million acres of national-forest land surround Prescott.
Contact the **Bradshaw Ranger District** (⊠*2230 E. AZ 69, Hwy. 69*
☎*928/443–8000* ⊕*www.fs.fed.us/r3/prescott*) for information about
hiking trails and campgrounds in the Prescott National Forest south
of town down to Horse Thief Basin. Campgrounds near Prescott are
generally not crowded.

WHERE TO EAT

$ ✕**Prescott Brewing Company.** Good beer, good food, good service, and
good prices—for a casual meal, it's hard to beat this cheerful restaurant on the town square. Fresh-baked beer bread comes with many
entrées. ⊠*130 W. Gurley St., Downtown* ☎*928/771–2795* ▱*AE,
D, DC, MC, V.*

WHERE TO STAY

$$–$$$ ⬚**Prescott Resort Conference Center and Casino.** On a hill on the outskirts of town, this upscale property has views of the mountain ranges surrounding Prescott and the Valley, although many guests hardly notice, so riveted are they by the poker machines and slots in Arizona's only hotel casino. There are plenty of recreational facilities to occupy those able to resist the one-armed bandits. **Pros:** Recently renovated, comfortable rooms. **Cons:** Large-scale property feels impersonal, drive to town center. ✉*1500 AZ 69,* ☎*928/776–1666 or 800/967–4637* ⊕*www.prescottresort.com* ➟*161 rooms* ⧖*In-room: refrigerator. In-hotel: restaurant, bar, tennis courts, pool, gym, no-smoking rooms, public Wi-Fi* ▤*AE, D, DC, MC, V.*

NORTH-CENTRAL ARIZONA ESSENTIALS

To research prices, get advice from other travelers, and book travel arrangements, visit ⊕*www.fodors.com.*

5

TRANSPORTATION

BY AIR

Prescott Municipal Airport is 8 mi north of town on U.S. 89. Flagstaff Pulliam Airport is 3 mi south of town off Interstate 17 at Exit 337. Sedona Airport is in West Sedona.

US Airways Express flies from Phoenix to Flagstaff Pulliam Airport. Sedona Airport is a base for several air tours but has no regularly scheduled flights. United Airlines and Frontier Airlines offer connecting service to Prescott Municipal Airport from Phoenix.

Contacts Flagstaff Pulliam Airport (☎*928/556–1234*). **Prescott Municipal Airport** (☎*928/445–7860*). **Sedona Airport** (☎*928/282–4487*).

BY BUS

Greyhound Lines has daily connections from throughout the West to Flagstaff, but none to Sedona. Buses also run between Prescott and Phoenix Sky Harbor International Airport.

The Sedona–Phoenix Shuttle makes eight trips daily between those cities; the fare is $45 one-way, $85 round-trip. You can also get on or off at Camp Verde, Cottonwood, or the Village of Oak Creek. The bus leaves from three terminals of Sky Harbor International Airport in Phoenix. Reservations are required.

Contacts Greyhound Lines (☎*800/231–2222* ⊕*www.greyhound.com*). **Sedona–Phoenix Shuttle Service** (☎*928/282–2066, 800/448–7988 in Arizona* ⊕*www.sedona-phoenix-shuttle.com*).

BY CAR

Flagstaff lies at the intersection of Interstate 40 (east–west) and Interstate 17 (running south from Flagstaff), 134 mi north of Phoenix via Interstate 17. The most direct route to Prescott from Phoenix is to take

Interstate 17 north for 60 mi to Cordes Junction and then drive northwest on AZ 69 for 36 mi into town. Interstate 17, a four-lane divided highway, has several steep inclines and descents (complete with a number of runaway-truck ramps), but it's generally an easy and scenic thoroughfare. If you want to take the more leisurely route through Verde Valley to Prescott, continue north on Interstate 17 another 25 mi past Cordes Junction until you see the turnoff for AZ 260, which will take you to Cottonwood in 12 mi. Here you can pick up AZ 89A, which leads southwest to Prescott (41 mi) or northeast to Sedona (19 mi).

Sedona stretches along AZ 89A, its main thoroughfare, which runs roughly east–west through town. To reach Sedona more directly from Phoenix, take Interstate 17 north for 113 mi until you come to AZ 179; it's another 15 mi on that road into town. The trip should take about 2½ hours. The 27-mi drive from Sedona to Flagstaff on AZ 89A, which winds its way through Oak Creek Canyon, is breathtaking.

Contacts **Farabee's Jeep Rentals** (☎ 928/282–8700 ⊕ www.sedonajeep rentals.com).

BY TRAIN
Amtrak comes into the downtown Flagstaff station twice daily. There's no rail service into Prescott or Sedona.

Information **Amtrak** (☎ 928/774–8679 or 800/872–7245 ⊕ www.amtrak.com).

VISITOR INFORMATION
Information **Camp Verde Chamber of Commerce** (☎ 928/567–9294 ⊕ www. campverde.org). **Clarkdale Chamber of Commerce** (☎ 928/634–9438 ⊕ www. clarkdalechamber.com). **Cottonwood Chamber of Commerce** (☎ 928/634–7593 ⊕ www.cottonwood.verdevalley.com). **Flagstaff Visitors Center** (☎ 928/774–9541 or 800/842–7293 ⊕ www.flagstaffarizona.org). **Jerome Chamber of Commerce** (☎ 928/634–2900 ⊕ www.jeromechamber.com). **Prescott Area Coalition for Tourism** (☎ 928/708–9336 ⊕ www.visit-prescott.com). **Sedona–Oak Creek Canyon Chamber of Commerce** (☎ 928/282–7722 or 800/288–7336 ⊕ www. sedonachamber.com)

Grand Canyon National Park

When it comes to the Grand Canyon, there are statistics, and there are sensations. While the former are impressive—the canyon measures in at an average width of 10 mi, length of 277 mi, and depth of a mile—they don't truly prepare you for that first impression. Seeing the canyon for the first time is an astounding experience—one that's hard to wrap your head around. In fact, it's more than an experience, it's an emotion, one that is only just beginning to be captured with the superlative "Grand."

WELCOME TO GRAND CANYON

TOP REASONS TO GO

★ **Its status:** This is one of those places where you really want to say, "Been there, done that!"

★ **Awesome vistas:** Painted desert, sandstone canyon walls, pine and fir forests, mesas, plateaus, volcanic features, the Colorado River, streams, and waterfalls make for some jaw-dropping moments.

★ **Year-round adventure:** Outdoor junkies can bike, boat, camp, fish, hike, ride mules, whitewater raft, watch birds and wildlife, cross-country ski, and snowshoe.

★ **Continuing education:** Adults and kids can get schooled, thanks to free park-sponsored nature walks and interpretive programs.

★ **Sky-high and river-low experiences:** Experience the canyon via plane, train, and automobile, as well as helicopter, boat, bike, mule, or on foot.

1 South Rim. The South Rim, on the other hand, is where the action is: Grand Canyon Village's lodging, camping, eateries, stores, and museums, plus plenty of trailheads into the canyon. Visitor services and facilities are open and available every day of the year, including holidays. Three free shuttle routes cover 30-some stops, and visitors who'd rather relax than rough it can treat themselves to comfy hotel rooms and elegant restaurant meals (lodging and camping reservations are essential).

KEY	
🏕	Ranger Station
▲	Campground
🛖	Picnic Area
🍴	Restaurant
🖼	Lodge
🏃	Trailhead
🚻	Restrooms
⇘	Scenic Viewpoint
·····	Walking/Hiking Trails
······	Bicycle Path

KANAB PLATEAU

Kanab Canyon

Tuweep   The Dome

◆ Supai

Havasu Canyon

Toroweap Overlook

← 3

0 _____ 10 mi
0 _____ 10 km

18

2 North Rim. Of the nearly 5 million people who visit the park annually, 90% enter at the South Rim, but many believe the North Rim is even more gorgeous—and worth the extra effort. Accessible only from mid-May to mid-October (or the first good snowfall), the North Rim has legitimate bragging rights: at more than 8,000 feet above sea level (and 1,000 feet higher than the South Rim), it offers precious solitude and three developed viewpoints. Rather than staring into the canyon's depths, you get a true sense of its expanse.

3 **West Rim.** Though technically not in Grand Canyon National Park the west rim of the canyon has some spectacular scenery, and some of the most gorgeous waterfalls in the United States. The recently opened Skywalk, part of the Hualapai Tribe's efforts to expand its tourism offerings on the West Rim, is a U-shaped glass bridge suspended above the Colorado River—not for the faint of heart.

GETTING ORIENTED

ARIZONA

Grand Canyon National Park is a superstar—biologically, historically, and recreationally. One of the world's best examples of arid-land erosion, the canyon provides a record of three of the four eras of geological time. In addition to its diverse fossil record, the park reveals prehistoric traces of human adaptation to an unforgiving environment. It's also home to several major ecosystems, five of the world's seven life zones, three of North America's four desert types, and all kinds of rare, endemic, and protected plant and animal species.

5

GRAND CANYON NATIONAL PARK

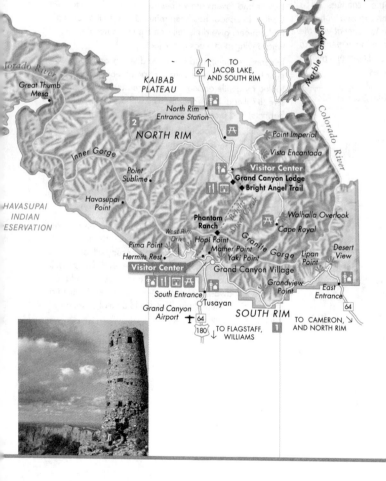

GRAND CANYON PLANNER

When to Go

There's no bad time to visit the canyon, though the busiest times of year are summer and spring break. Visiting during these peak seasons, as well as holidays, requires patience and a tolerance for crowds. Note that weather changes on a whim in this exposed high-desert region. *You cannot visit the North Rim in the winter due to weather conditions and related road closures.*

AVG. HIGH/LOW TEMPS

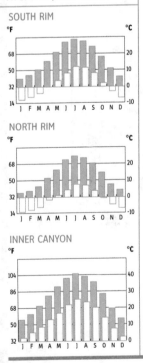

SOUTH RIM

NORTH RIM

INNER CANYON

Flora & Fauna

Eighty-nine mammal species inhabit Grand Canyon National Park, as well as 355 species of birds and 56 kinds of reptiles and amphibians. The rare Kaibab squirrel is found only on the North Rim—you can recognize them by their all-white tails and the long tufts of white hair on their ears. The pink Grand Canyon rattlesnake lives at lower elevations within the canyon.

Hawks and ravens are visible year-round. The endangered California condor has been reintroduced to the canyon. Park rangers give daily talks on the magnificent birds, whose wingspan measures 9 feet.

In spring, summer, and fall, mule deer, recognizable by their large antlers, are abundant at the South Rim. Don't be fooled by gentle appearances; these guys can be aggressive. It's illegal to feed them, as it will disrupt their natural habitats, and increase your risk of getting bitten.

The South Rim's Coconino Plateau is fairly flat, at an elevation of about 7,000 feet, and covered with stands of piñon and ponderosa pines, junipers, and Gambel's oak trees. On the Kaibab Plateau on the North Rim, Douglas fir, spruce, quaking aspen, and more ponderosas prevail. In spring you're likely to see asters, sunflowers, and lupine in bloom at both rims.

The best times to see wildlife are early in the morning and late in the afternoon. Look for out-of-place shapes and motions, keeping in mind that animals occupy all layers in a natural habitat and not just at your eye level. Use binoculars for close-up views. While out and about try to fade into the woodwork by keeping your movements limited and noise at a minimum. Never feed wild animals. Not only is it dangerous, it's illegal as well.

Getting Here & Around

The best route into the park from the east or south is from Flagstaff. Take U.S. 180 northwest to the park's southern entrance and Grand Canyon Village. To go on to the North Rim, go north from Flagstaff on U.S. 89 to Bitter Springs, then take U.S. 89A to the junction of Highway 67 and travel south on the highway for about 40 mi. From the west on Interstate 40, the most direct route to the South Rim is on U.S. 180 and Highway 64.

The South Rim is open to car traffic year-round, though access to Hermits Rest is limited to shuttle buses from March through November. Parking is free once you pay the $25 park entrance fee, but it can be hard to find a spot. Try the large lot in front of the general store near Yavapai Lodge or the Maswik Transportation Center lot. If you visit from October through April, traffic will be lighter and parking less of a problem.

In summer, South Rim roads are congested, and it's easier, and sometimes required, to park your car and take the free shuttle. There are in fact three free shuttle routes in the Grand Canyon: **The Hermits Rest Route** operates March through November, between Grand Canyon Village and Hermits Rest. **The Village Route** operates year-round in the village area; it provides the easiest access to the Canyon View Information Center. **The Kaibab Trail Route** goes from Canyon View Information Center to Yaki Point, including a stop at the South Kaibab Trailhead. Running from one hour before sunrise until one hour after sunset, shuttles arrive every 15 to 30 minutes. The roughly 30 stops are clearly marked throughout the park.

At 8,000 feet, the more remote North Rim is off-limits during winter. From mid-October (or the first heavy snowfall) through mid-May, there are no services, and Highway 67 south of Jacob Lake is closed. Weather information and road conditions for both rims, updated each morning, can be obtained by calling 928/638–7888.

Avoid Crowds

The park is most crowded near the entrances and in Grand Canyon Village, as well as on the scenic drives, especially the 23-mi Desert View Drive. To avoid crowds, go farther into the canyon, and try the mostly paved Rim Trail. In summer, bypass the South Rim for the North Rim if you're looking for more solitude.

Planning Your Trip

The number-one rule for a great trip to the Grand Canyon is to plan ahead. This is especially true if you want to go down the canyon on a mule: mule rides require at least a six-month advance reservation, and up to one or two year's notice for the busy season (they can be reserved up to 23 months in advance). Sometimes cancellations allow riders to join at the last minute, but don't count on it. For lodgings in the park, reservations are also essential; they're taken up to 13 months in advance.

Before you go, get the complimentary *Trip Planner* from the park's official Web site, ⊕ *www.nps.gov/grca*. Also visit ⊕ *www.thecanyon.com*, a commercial site with general park information.

Every person arriving at the South or North Rim is given a detailed map of the area. Once you arrive at the park, pick up *The Guide*, a free newspaper with a detailed area map and a schedule of free park programs. The park also distributes *The Grand Canyon Accessibility Guide*, also free, which can be picked up at visitor centers.

GRAND CANYON'S SOUTH RIM

By Carrie
Frasure &
Jill Koch

Visitors to the canyon converge mostly on the South Rim, and mostly during the summer. Grand Canyon Village is here, with most of the park's lodging and camping, trailheads, restaurants, stores, and museums, along with a nearby airport and railroad depot. Believe it or not, the average stay in the park is a mere four hours; this is not advised! You need to spend several days to truly appreciate this marvelous place, but at the very least, give it a full day.

SCENIC DRIVES

Desert View Drive. This heavily traveled 23-mi stretch of road follows the rim from the East entrance to the Grand Canyon Village. Starting from the less congested entry near Desert View, road warriors can get their first glimpse of the canyon from the 70-foot-tall Watchtower, the top of which provides the highest viewpoint on the South Rim. Along the way are eight overlooks and the secluded and lovely Buggeln picnic area.

Hermit Road. The Santa Fe Company built Hermit Road, formerly known as West Rim Drive, in 1912 as a scenic tour route. Ten overlooks dot this 8-mi stretch, each worth a visit. The road is filled with hairpin turns, so make sure you adhere to posted speed limits. From March through November, Hermit Road is closed to private auto traffic because of congestion; during this period, a free shuttle bus will carry you to all the overlooks. Riding the bus round-trip without getting off at any of the viewpoints takes 75 minutes; the return trip stops only at Mohave and Hopi points. ■TIP→ Take plenty of water with you for the ride—the only water along the way is at Hermits Rest.

WHAT TO SEE

HISTORIC SITES

Kolb Studio. Built in 1904 by the Kolb brothers as a photographic workshop and residence, this building provides a view of Indian Gardens, where, in the days before a pipeline was installed, Emery Kolb descended 3,000 feet each day to get the water he needed to develop his prints. Kolb was doing something right; he operated the studio until he died in 1976 at age 95. The gallery here has changing exhibitions of paintings, photography, and crafts. There's also a bookstore. During the winter months, a ranger-led tour of the studio illustrates the role the Kolb brothers had on the development of the Grand Canyon. Call ahead to sign up for the tour. ⊠ *Grand Canyon Village, near Bright Angel Lodge* ☎928/638–2771 ⊠ *Free* ⊙ *Mid-May–mid-Oct., daily 8–5; mid-Oct.–mid-May, daily 8–6.*

Powell Memorial. A granite statue honors the memory of John Wesley Powell, who measured, charted, and named many of the canyons and creeks of the Colorado River. It was here that the dedication ceremony for Grand Canyon National Park took place on April 3, 1920. ⊠ *About 3 mi west of Hermit Road Junction on Hermit Rd.*

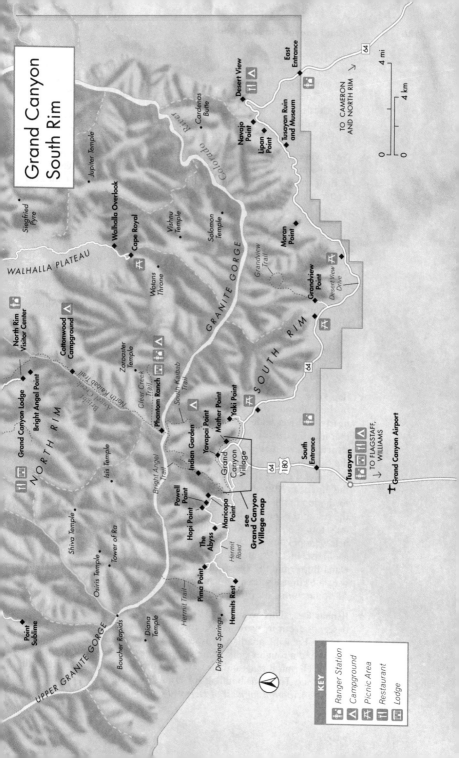

SCENIC STOPS

The Abyss. At an elevation of 6,720 feet, the Abyss is one of the most awesome stops on Hermit Road, revealing a sheer drop of 3,000 feet to the Tonto Platform, a terrace of Tapeats sandstone layers about two-thirds of the way down the canyon. You also can see some isolated sandstone columns, the largest of which is called the Monument. ⊠ *About 5 mi west of Hermit Road Junction on Hermit Rd.*

★ **Desert View and Watchtower.** From the top of the 70-foot stone-and-mortar watchtower, even the muted hues of the distant Painted Desert to the east and the Vermilion Cliffs rising from a high plateau near the Utah border are visible. In the chasm below, angling to the north toward Marble Canyon, an imposing stretch of the Colorado River reveals itself. Up several flights of stairs, the Watchtower houses a glass-enclosed observatory with powerful telescopes. ⊠ *About 23 mi east of Grand Canyon Village on Desert View Dr.* ☎ *928/638–2736* ⊘ *Daily 8–7, hrs may vary.*

Grandview Point. At an elevation of 7,496 feet, the view from here is one of the finest in the canyon. To the northeast is a group of dominant buttes, including Krishna Shrine, Vishnu Temple, Rama Shrine, and Shiva Temple. A short stretch of the Colorado River is also visible. Directly below the point, and accessible by the steep and rugged Grandview Trail, is Horseshoe Mesa, where you can see remnants of Last Chance Copper Mine. ⊠ *About 12 mi east of Grand Canyon Village on Desert View Dr.*

★ **Hopi Point.** From this elevation of 7,071 feet, you can see a large section of the Colorado River; although it appears as a thin line, the river is nearly 350 feet wide below this overlook. The overlook extends farther into the canyon than any other point on Hermit Road. The unobstructed views make this a popular place to watch the sunset. Across the canyon to the north is Shiva Temple, which remained an isolated section of the Kaibab Plateau until 1937. That year, Harold Anthony of the American Museum of Natural History led an expedition to the rock formation in the belief that it supported life that had been cut off from the rest of the canyon. Imagine the expedition members' surprise when they found an empty Kodak film box on top of the temple. Directly below Hopi Point lies Dana Butte, named for a prominent 19th-century geologist. In 1919, an entrepreneur proposed connecting Hopi Point, Dana Butte, and the Tower of Set across the river with an aerial tramway, a technically feasible plan that fortunately has not been realized. ⊠ *About 4 mi west of Hermit Road Junction on Hermit Rd.*

★ **Hermits Rest.** This westernmost viewpoint and Hermit Trail, which descends from it, were named for "hermit" Louis Boucher, a 19th-century French-Canadian prospector who had a number of mining claims and a roughly built home down in the canyon. Views from here include Hermit Rapids and the towering cliffs of the Supai and Redwall formations. The stone building at Hermits Rest sells curios and refreshments. ⊠ *About 8 mi west of Hermit Road Junction on Hermit Rd.*

Lipan Point. Here, at the canyon's widest point, you can get an astonishing visual profile of the gorge's geologic history, with a view of every eroded layer of the canyon. You can also see Unkar Delta, where a creek joins the Colorado to form powerful rapids and a broad beach. Ancestral Puebloan farmers worked the Unkar Delta for hundreds of years, growing corn, beans, and melons. ⊠ *About 25 mi east of Grand Canyon Village on Desert View Dr.*

★ **Mather Point.** You'll likely get your first glimpse of the canyon from this viewpoint, one of the most impressive and accessible (and most crowded!) on the South Rim.

> **GREAT VIEWS**
>
> The best time of day to see the canyon is before 10 AM and after 2 PM, when the angle of the sun brings out the colors of the rock, and clouds and shadows add dimension. Hopi Point and the Yavapai Observation Station are the top spots on the South Rim to watch the sun set; Yaki and Pima Points also offer vivid views. For a grand sunrise, try Mather or Yaki Points. Arrive at least 30 minutes early for sunrise views and as much as 90 minutes for sunset views.

Named for the National Park Service's first director, Stephen Mather, this spot yields extraordinary views of the Grand Canyon, including deep into the Inner Gorge and numerous buttes: Wotan's Throne, Brahma Temple, and Zoroaster Temple, among others. The Grand Canyon Lodge, on the North Rim, is almost directly north from Mather Point and only 10 mi away—yet you have to drive 215 mi to get from one spot to the other. ⊠ *Near Canyon View Information Plaza.*

Moran Point. This point was named for American landscape artist Thomas Moran, who was especially fond of the play of light and shadows from this location. He first visited the canyon with John Wesley Powell in 1873. "Thomas Moran's name, more than any other, with the possible exception of Major Powell's, is to be associated with the Grand Canyon," wrote canyon photographer Ellsworth Kolb. It's fitting that Moran Point is a favorite spot of photographers and painters. ⊠ *About 17 mi east of Grand Canyon Village on Desert View Dr.*

Pima Point. Enjoy a bird's-eye view of Tonto Platform and Tonto Trail, which winds its way through the canyon for more than 70 mi. Also to the west, two dark, cone-shaped mountains—Mount Trumbull and Mount Logan—are visible on the North Rim on clear days. They rise in stark contrast to the surrounding flat-top mesas and buttes. ⊠ *About 7 mi west of Hermit Road Junction on Hermit Rd.*

Trailview Overlook. Look down on a dramatic view of the Bright Angel and Plateau Point trails as they zigzag down the canyon. In the deep gorge to the north flows Bright Angel Creek, one of the region's few permanent tributary streams of the Colorado River. Toward the south is an unobstructed view of the distant San Francisco Peaks, as well as Bill Williams Mountain (on the horizon) and Red Butte (about 15 mi south of the canyon rim). ⊠ *About 2 mi west of Hermit Road Junction on Hermit Rd.*

5

GRAND CANYON NATIONAL PARK

Yaki Point. Stop here for an exceptional view of Wotan's Throne, a flat-top butte named by François Matthes, a U.S. Geological Survey scientist who developed the first topographical map of the Grand Canyon. The overlook juts out over the canyon, providing unobstructed views of inner canyon rock formations, South Rim cliffs, and Clear Creek Canyon. This point marks the beginning of the South Kaibab Trail and is one of the best places on the south rim to watch the sunset. ⊠ *2 mi east of Grand Canyon Village on Desert View Dr.*

FodorsChoice **Yavapai Observation Station.** The word Yavapai means "sun people" in
★ Paiute, a group of nomadic Indians associated with the Grand Canyon. This point offers panoramic views of the mighty gorge through a wall of windows. Exhibits include videos of the canyon floor and the Colorado River, a scaled diorama of the canyon, fossils and rock fragments used to recreate the complex layers of the canyon walls, and a display on the natural forces used to carve the chasm. ⊠ *Adjacent to Grand Canyon Village.*

RANGER PROGRAMS

☾ The National Park Service sponsors all sorts of orientation activities, such as daily guided hikes and talks. The focus may be on any aspect of the canyon—from geology and flora and fauna to history and early inhabitants. For schedules on the South Rim, go to Canyon View Information Plaza, pick up a free copy of *The Guide* to the South Rim, or check online. For youngsters, ages 4 to 14, the Junior Ranger Program provides a free, fun way to look at the cultural and natural history of this sublime destination. These hands-on educational programs include guided adventure hikes, ranger-led "discovery" programs, and book readings.

SPORTS & THE OUTDOORS

AIR TOURS

★ Flights by plane and helicopter over the canyon are offered by a number of companies (*see below*), departing from the Grand Canyon Airport at the south end of Tusayan. Prices and lengths of tours vary, but you can expect to pay about $109–$120 per adult for short plane trips and approximately $130–$235 for brief helicopter tours.

OUTFITTERS &   **Air Grand Canyon** (⊠ *Grand Canyon Airport* ☎ *800/247–4726* ⊕ *www.*
EXPEDITIONS *airgrandcanyon.com*). **Grand Canyon Airlines** (☎ *866/235–9422* ⊕ *www. grandcanyonairlines.com*). **Grand Canyon Helicopters** (☎ *800/541–4537* ⊕ *www.grandcanyonhelicoptersaz.com/gch*), **Maverick Helicopters** (☎ *800/962–3869* ⊕ *www.maverickhelicopters.com*). **Papillon Grand Canyon Helicopters** (☎ *800/528–2418* ⊕ *www.papillon.com*).

HIKING

Although permits are not required for day hikes, you must have a backcountry permit for longer trips (⇨ *See Admission Fees & Permits in the Grand Canyon Essentials section*). Some of the more popular trails

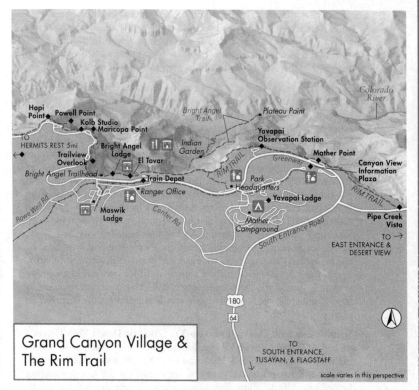

Grand Canyon Village &
The Rim Trail

5

are listed in this chapter; more detailed information and maps can be obtained from the Backcountry Information Center.

Remember that the canyon has significant elevation changes and, in summer, extreme temperature ranges, which can pose problems for people who aren't in good shape or who have heart or respiratory problems. ■TIP➜Carry plenty of water and energy foods. The majority of each year's 400 search-and-rescue incidents result from hikers underestimating the size of the canyon, hiking beyond their abilities, or not packing sufficient food and water. ⚠Under no circumstances should you attempt a day hike from the rim to the river and back. Remember that when it's 80°F on the South Rim, it's 110°F on the canyon floor. Allow two to four days if you want to hike rim to rim (it's easier to descend from the North Rim, as it is more than 1,000 feet higher than the South Rim). Hiking steep trails from rim to rim is a strenuous trek of at least 21 mi and should only be attempted by experienced canyon hikers.

EASY
Fodor'sChoice
★

Rim Trail. The South Rim's most popular walking path is the 9-mi (one way) Rim Trail, which runs along the edge of the canyon from Mather Point (the first overlook on Desert View Drive) to Hermits Rest. This walk, which is paved to Maricopa Point, visits several of the South Rim's historic landmarks. Allow anywhere from 15 minutes to a full day; the Rim Trail is an ideal day hike, as it varies only a few hundred feet in elevation from Mather Point (7,120 feet) to the trailhead at Hermits Rest (6,640 feet). The trail also can be accessed from the major viewpoints along Hermit Road, which are serviced by shuttle buses during the busy summer months. ■TIP➜On the Rim Trail, water is only available in the Grand Canyon Village area and at Hermits Rest.

MODERATE
★

Bright Angel Trail. Well-maintained, this is one of the most scenic hiking paths from the South Rim to the bottom of the canyon (9.6 mi each way). Rest houses are equipped with water at the 1.5- and 3-mi points from May through September and at Indian Garden (4 mi) year-round. Water is also available at Bright Angel Campground, 9.25 mi below the trailhead. Plateau Point, about 1.5 mi below Indian Garden, is as far as you should attempt to go on a day hike; plan on spending six to nine hours. Bright Angel Trail is the easiest of all the footpaths into the canyon, but because the climb out from the bottom is an ascent of 5,510 feet, the trip should be attempted only by those in good physical condition and should be avoided in midsummer due to extreme heat. The top of the trail, a tight set of switchbacks called Jacob's Ladder, can be icy in winter. Originally a bighorn sheep path and later used by the Havasupai, the trail was widened late in the 19th century for prospectors and is now used for both mule and foot traffic. Hikers going downhill should yield to those going uphill. Also note that mule trains have the right-of-way—and sometimes leave unpleasant surprises in your path.

DIFFICULT
★

South Kaibab Trail. This trail starts at Yaki Point on Desert View Drive, 4 mi east of Grand Canyon Village. Because the trail is so steep—descending from the trailhead at 7,260 feet down to 2,480 feet at the Colorado River—and has no water, many hikers return via the less-demanding Bright Angel Trail; allow four to six hours. During this 6.4-mi trek to the Colorado River, you're likely to encounter mule trains and riders. At the river, the trail crosses a suspension bridge and runs on to Phantom Ranch. Along the trail there is no water and very little shade. There are no campgrounds, though there are portable toilets at Cedar Ridge (6,320 feet), 1.5 mi from the trailhead. Toilets and an emergency phone are also available at the Tipoff, 4.6 mi down the trail (3 mi past Cedar Ridge). The trail corkscrews down through some spectacular geology. Look for (but don't remove) fossils in the limestone when taking water breaks. ■TIP➜Even though an immense network of trails winds through the Grand Canyon, the popular corridor trails (Bright Angel and South Kaibab) are recommended for the first overnight trip in the canyon and for hikers new to the region.

MULE RIDES

★ Mule rides provide an intimate glimpse into the canyon for those who have the time, but not the stamina to see the canyon on foot. The treks are not for the faint of heart or people in questionable health. ■TIP➜Reservations are essential and are accepted up to 23 months in advance, or you can check the waiting list for last-minute cancellations.

OUTFITTERS &
EXPEDITIONS

Grand Canyon National Park Lodges Mule Rides. These trips delve into the canyon from the South Rim. Riders must be at least 55 inches tall, weigh less than 200 pounds, and understand English. Children under 15 must be accompanied by an adult. Riders must be in fairly good physical condition, and pregnant women are advised not to take these trips. The all-day ride to Plateau Point costs $153.95 (box lunch included). An overnight with a stay at Phantom Ranch at the bottom of the canyon is $420.09 ($743.03 for two riders). Two nights at Phantom Ranch, an option available from November through March, will set you back $592.83 ($991.38 for two). Meals are included. Reservations, especially during the busy summer months, are a must, but you can check at the Bright Angel Transportation Desk to be placed on the waiting list. *6312 S. Fiddlers Green Circle, Suite 600, N. Greenwood Village, CO 80111 ☎303/297–2757 or 888/297–2757 ⊕www. grandcanyonlodges.com ⊗May–Sept., daily.*

RAFTING

OUTFITTER With a reputation for high quality and a roster of 3- to 13-day trips, **Canyoneers** (☎800/525–0924 ⊕*www.canyoneers.com*) is popular with those who want to do some hiking as well. The five-day trip "Best of the Grand" trip includes a hike down to Phantom Ranch. Three- to 14-day motorized and oar trips, available April through September, cost between $895 and $3,250.

GRAND CANYON'S NORTH RIM

The North Rim stands 1,000 feet higher than the South Rim and has a more alpine climate, with twice as much annual precipitation. Here, in the deep forests of the Kaibab Plateau, the crowds are thinner, the facilities fewer, and the views even more spectacular. Due to snow, the North Rim is off-limits in the winter. The park buildings are closed mid-October through mid-May. The road closes when the snow makes it impassable—usually by the end of November.

SCENIC DRIVES

★ **Highway 67.** Open mid-May to mid-October (and often until Thanksgiving), the two-lane paved road climbs 1,400 feet in elevation as it passes through the Kaibab National Forest. Also called the "North Rim Parkway," this scenic route crosses the limestone-capped Kaibab Plateau—passing broad meadows, sun-dappled forests, and small lakes and springs—before abruptly falling away at the abyss of the Grand Canyon. Wildlife abounds in the thick ponderosa pine forests and lush mountain meadows. It's common to see deer, turkeys, and coyotes as you drive through this remote region. Point Imperial and Cape Royal can be reached by spurs off this scenic drive running from Jacob Lake to Bright Angel Point.

U.S. 89/89A. The route north from Cameron Trading Post on U.S. 89 offers a stunning view of the Painted Desert to the right. The desert, which covers thousands of square miles stretching to the south and east, is a vision of subtle, almost harsh beauty, with windswept plains and mesas, isolated buttes, and barren valleys in pastel patterns. About

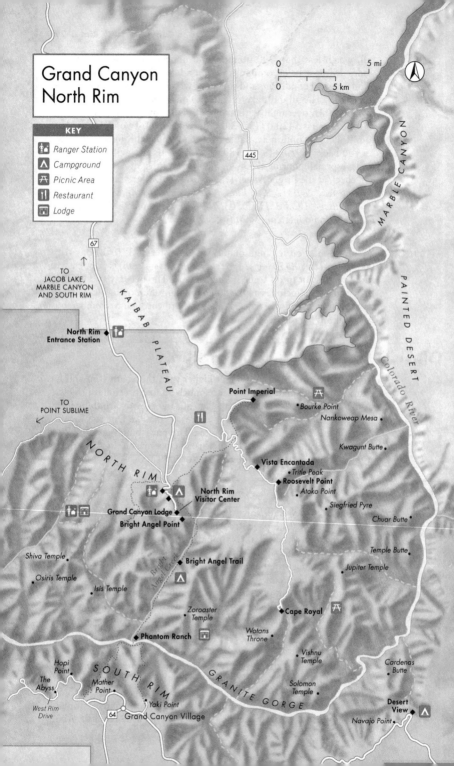

Grand Canyon
North Rim

KEY

🏚	Ranger Station
⛺	Campground
🪧	Picnic Area
🍴	Restaurant
🏠	Lodge

5 mi

5 km

445

67

MARBLE CANYON

PAINTED DESERT

KAIBAB PLATEAU

TO
JACOB LAKE,
MARBLE CANYON
AND SOUTH RIM

North Rim
Entrance Station

TO
POINT SUBLIME

Point Imperial

Colorado River

• Bourke Point

Nankoweap Mesa

Kwagunt Butte •

NORTH RIM

Vista Encantada
• Tritle Peak
Roosevelt Point
• Atoko Point

Siegfried Pyre •

Chuar Butte •

North Rim
Visitor Center

Grand Canyon Lodge
Bright Angel Point

Temple Butte •

Shiva Temple •

Jupiter Temple •

Osiris Temple •

Isis Temple •

Bright Angel Trail

Bright Angel Trail

Cape Royal

Zoroaster
Temple

Phantom Ranch

Wotans
Throne

SOUTH RIM

Vishnu
Temple

Cardenas
Butte •

Hopi
Point

The
Abyss

Mather
Point

GRANITE GORGE

Solomon
Temple •

Desert
View

West Rim
Drive

Yaki Point

64

Grand Canyon Village

Navajo Point •

30 mi north of Cameron Trading Post, the Painted Desert country gives way to sandstone cliffs that run for miles. Brilliantly hued and ranging in color from light pink to deep orange, the Echo Cliffs rise to more than 1,000 feet in many places. At Bitter Springs, 60 mi north of Cameron, U.S. 89A branches off from U.S. 89, running north and providing views of Marble Canyon, the geographical beginning of the Grand Canyon. Traversing a gorge nearly 500 feet deep is Navajo Bridge, a narrow steel span built in 1929 and listed on the National Register of Historic Places. About 18 mi past Navajo Bridge, a sign directs you to the San Bartolome Historic Site, an overlook with plaques that tell the story of the Domínguez-Escalante expedition of 1776.

WHAT TO SEE

HISTORIC SITES

Grand Canyon Lodge. Built in 1928 by the Union Pacific Railroad, the massive stone structure is listed on the National Register of Historic Places. Its huge sunroom has hardwood floors, high-beam ceilings, and a marvelous view of the canyon through plate-glass windows. On warm days, visitors sit in the sun and drink in the surrounding beauty on an outdoor deck, where park personnel deliver free lectures on geology and history. ⊠ *Off Hwy. 67, near Bright Angel Point.*

SCENIC STOPS

★ **Bright Angel Point.** The trail, which leads to one of the most awe-inspiring overlooks on either rim, starts on the grounds of the Grand Canyon Lodge and runs along the crest of a point of rocks that juts into the canyon for several hundred yards. The walk is only 0.5 mi round-trip, but it's an exciting trek accented by sheer drops on each side of the trail. In a few spots where the route is extremely narrow, metal railings ensure visitors' safety. The temptation to clamber out to precarious perches to have your picture taken could get you killed—every year several people die from falls at the Grand Canyon. ⊠ *North Rim Dr.*

Cape Royal. A popular sunset destination, Cape Royal showcases the canyon's jagged landscape; you'll also get a glimpse of the Colorado River, framed by a natural stone arch called Angels Window. In autumn, the aspens turn a beautiful gold, adding even more color to an already magnificent scene of the forested surroundings. At Angels Window Overlook, **Cliff Springs Trail** starts its 1-mi route (round-trip) through a forested ravine. The trail terminates at Cliff Springs, where the forest opens to another impressive view of the canyon walls. ⊠ *Cape Royal Scenic Dr., 23 mi southeast of Grand Canyon Lodge.*

Point Imperial. At 8,803 feet, Point Imperial has the highest vista point at either rim; it offers magnificent views of both the canyon and the distant country: the Vermilion Cliffs to the north, the 10,000-foot Navajo Mountain to the northeast in Utah, the Painted Desert to the east, and the Little Colorado River Canyon to the southeast. Other prominent points of interest include views of Mount Hayden, Saddle Mountain, and Marble Canyon. ⊠ *2.7 mi left off Cape Royal Scenic Dr. on Point Imperial Rd., 11 mi northeast of Grand Canyon Lodge.*

Fodor'sChoice   **Point Sublime.** Talk about solitude. Here you can camp within feet of the
★   canyon's edge. Sunrises and sunsets are spectacular. The winding road,
through gorgeous high country, is only 17 mi, but it will take you at
least two hours, one-way. The road is intended only for vehicles with
high-road clearance (pickups and four-wheel-drive vehicles). It is also
necessary to be properly equipped for wilderness road travel. Check
with a park ranger or at the information desk at Grand Canyon Lodge
before taking this journey. You may camp here only with a permit from
the Backcountry Office. ⇨ *See Admission Fees & Permits in the Essentials section at the end of chapter.* ⊠ *North Rim Dr., Grand Canyon;
about 20 mi west of North Rim Visitor Center.*

Roosevelt Point. Named after the president who gave the Grand Canyon
its national park status in 1919, this is the best place to see the confluence of the Little Colorado River and the Grand Canyon. The cliffs
above the Colorado River south of the junction are known as the Pali-
sades of the Desert. A short woodland loop trail leads to this eastern
viewpoint. ⇨ See "Roosevelt Point Trail" in Hiking. ⊠ *Cape Royal
Rd., 18 mi southeast of Grand Canyon Lodge.*

RANGER PROGRAMS

♻ Daily guided hikes and talks may focus on any aspect of the canyon—
from geology and flora and fauna to history and the canyon's early
inhabitants. For schedules, go to the Grand Canyon Lodge or pick up
a free copy of *The Guide* to the North Rim. Children ages 9 to 14 can
take part in the hands-on Discovery Pack Junior Ranger Program and
earn a Junior Ranger certificate and badge.

SPORTS & THE OUTDOORS

BICYCLING

Mountain bikers can test the many dirt access roads found in this
remote area, including the 17-mi trek to Point Sublime. It's rare to
spot other people on these primitive roads. **North Rim Outfitters Station**
(⊠ *Grand Canyon Lodge, North Rim* ☎ *877/386–4383 Ext. 758*
⊕ *www.grandcanyonforever.com*) offers Schwinn bicycles on a hourly,
half-day, or full-day basis.

HIKING

EASY   **Roosevelt Point Trail.** At Roosevelt Point on Cape Royal Road, this easy
♻   0.2-mi round-trip trail loops through the forest to the scenic viewpoint.
★   Allow 20 minutes for this short, secluded hike.

♻ **Transept Trail.** This 3-mi (round-trip), 1½-hour trail begins at 8,255
feet near the Grand Canyon Lodge's east patio. Well-maintained and
-marked, it has little elevation change, sticking near the rim before
reaching a dramatic view of a large stream through Bright Angel Canyon. The route leads to a side canyon called Transept Canyon, which
geologist Clarence Dutton named in 1882, declaring it "far grander
than Yosemite." It's also a great place to view fall foliage.

DIFFICULT **North Kaibab Trail.** At 8,241 feet, the trailhead to North Kaibab Trail is about 2 mi north of the Grand Canyon Lodge and is open only from May through October. It is recommended for experienced hikers only, who should allow four days for the full hike. The long, steep path drops 5,840 feet over a distance of 14.5 mi to the Colorado River, so the National Park Service suggests that day hikers not go farther than Roaring Springs (5,020 feet) before turning to hike back up out of the canyon. After about 7 mi, Cottonwood Campground (4,080 feet) has drinking water in summer, restrooms, shade trees, and a ranger. It leads to Phantom Ranch. ■TIP➜**For a fee, a shuttle takes hikers to the North Kaibab trailhead twice daily from Grand Canyon Lodge.**

⚠**Flash floods can occur any time of the year, especially from June through September when thunderstorms develop rapidly. Check forecasts before heading into the canyon, never camp in dry washes, and use caution when hiking in narrow canyons and drainage systems.**

MULE RIDES

OUTFITTER **Canyon Trail Rides.** This company leads mule rides on the easier trails of the North Rim. A one-hour ride (minimum age 7) runs $30. Half-day trips on the rim or into the canyon (minimum age 10) cost $65; full-day trips (minimum age 12) go for $125. Weight limits vary from 200 to 220 pounds. Available daily from May 15 to October 15, these excursions are popular, so make reservations in advance. *Box 128, TropicUT 84776* ☎*435/679–8665* ⊕*www.canyonrides.com.*

THE WEST RIM & HAVASU CANYON

Known as "The People" of the Grand Canyon, the Pai Indians—the Hualapai and Havasupai—have lived along the Colorado River and the vast Colorado Plateau for more than 1,000 years. Both tribes traditionally moved seasonally between the plateau and the canyon, alternately hunting game and planting crops. Today, they rely on tourism as an economic base.

THE HUALAPAI TRIBE & GRAND CANYON WEST

70 mi north of Kingman via Stockton Hill Rd., Pierce Ferry Rd., and Diamond Bar Rd.

The plateau-dwelling Hualapai ("people of the tall pines") acquired a larger chunk of traditional Pai lands with the creation of their reservation in 1883. Hualapai tribal lands include diverse habitats ranging from rolling grasslands to rugged canyons, and travel from elevations of 1,500 feet at the Colorado River to more than 7,300 feet at Aubrey Cliffs. In recent years, the Hualapai have been attempting to foster tourism on the West Rim—most notably with the spectacular Skywalk, a glass walkway suspended 4,000 feet above the Colorado River and extending 70 feet from the edge of the canyon rim.

The West Rim is a five-hour drive from the South Rim of Grand Canyon National Park. The dusty, 14-mi stretch of unpaved road leading to Grand Canyon West can be off-putting to some. For a different approach along Diamond Bar Road, visitors can schedule Park & Ride services from the Grand Canyon West Welcome Center on Pierce Ferry Road for a nominal fee; reservations are required (☎702/260–6506).

Visitors aren't allowed to travel in their own vehicles once they reach the West Rim, but must purchase a tour package from **Destination Grand Canyon West** (☎877/716–9378 ⊕*www.destinationgrandcanyon.com* ✉*$29.95 entrance fee; parking $20 per vehicle*). The basic Hualapai Legacy tour package ($29.95 per person) includes a Hualapai visitation permit and shuttle transportation. Stops include Eagle Point, with authentic dwellings; Hualapai Ranch, site of Western performances, cookouts, and horseback and wagon rides; and Guano Point, where the "High Point Hike" offers panoramic views of the Colorado River. For an extra cost you can add a helicopter trip into the canyon, a boat trip on the Colorado, an off-road Hummer adventure, a horseback or wagon ride to the canyon rim, or a walk on the Skywalk ($29.95 per person).

THE HAVASUPAI TRIBE & HAVASU CANYON

141 mi from Williams (to head of Hualapai Hilltop), west on I–40 and AZ 66, north on Indian Hwy. 18.

With the establishment of Grand Canyon National Park in 1919, the Havasupai were confined to their summer village of Supai and the surrounding 518 acres in the 5-mi-wide and 12-mi-long Havasu Canyon. In 1975, the reservation was substantially enlarged, but is still completely surrounded by national park lands on all but its southern border. Each year, about 25,000 tourists fly, hike, or ride into Havasu Canyon to visit the land of this tribe that has lived in this isolated area for centuries. Despite their economic reliance on tourism, the Havasupai take their guardianship of the Grand Canyon seriously, and severely limit visitation in order to protect the fragile canyon habitats.

Dubbed the "Shangri-la of the Grand Canyon," the remote, inaccessible Indian reservation includes some of the world's most beautiful and famous waterfalls. As high as 200 feet, the falls cascade over red cliffs and plunge into deep turquoise pools surrounded by thick foliage and sheltering cottonwood trees. The travertine in the water coats the walls and lines the pools with bizarre, drip-castle rock formations. Centuries of accumulated travertine formations in some of the most popular pools were washed out in massive flooding decades ago, destroying some of the otherworldly scenes pictured in older photos, but the place is still magical.

To reach Havasu's waterfalls, you must hike downstream from the village of Supai, where the 600 tribal members now live (the village is accessible only down the 8-mi-long Hualapai Trail, which drops 2,000 feet from the canyon rim to the tiny town). The first fall, 1½ mi from Supai, is the 75-foot-high **Navajo Falls**, which rushes over red-wall limestone and collects in a beautiful blue-green pool perfect for swimming. Not much farther downstream, the striking **Havasu Falls** dashes over a ledge into another pool of refreshing 70°F water. The last of the enchanting waterfalls is **Mooney Falls,** 2 mi down from Navajo Falls. Named after a prospector who fell to his death here in 1880, Mooney Falls plummets 196 feet down a sheer travertine cliff.

The Havasupai restrict the number of visitors to the canyon; you must have reservations. Contact **Havasupai Tourist Enterprise** (☎928/448–2141 ⊕www.havasupaitribe.com).

WHERE TO STAY & EAT

ABOUT THE RESTAURANTS

Inside the park, you can find everything from cafeteria food to casual café fare to elegant evening specials. There's even a coffeehouse brewing organic joe. The dress code is casual across the board, but El Tovar is your best option if you're looking to dress up a bit and thumb through an extensive wine list.

ABOUT THE HOTELS

The park's accommodations include three "historic rustic" facilities and four motel-style lodges. Outside of El Tovar Hotel, the canyon's architectural crown jewel, frills are hard to find. Rooms are basic but comfortable, and most guests would agree that the best in-room amenity is a view of the canyon. **Reservations are a must, especially during the busy summer season. If you want to get your first choice (especially Bright Angel Lodge or El Tovar), make reservations as far in advance as possible; they're taken up to 13 months ahead.**

ABOUT THE CAMPGROUNDS

Inside the park, camping is permitted only in designated campsites. Some campgrounds charge nightly camping fees in addition to entrance fees, and some accept reservations up to five months in advance. Others are first-come, first-served. The South Rim has three campgrounds, one with RV hookups. The North Rim's single in-park campground does not offer hookups. All four campgrounds are near the rims and easily accessible. In-park camping in a spot other than a developed rim campground requires a permit from the Backcountry Information Center, which also serves as your reservation. For park campground information, call ☎877/444–6777 or go online to ⊕www.recreation.gov; for backcountry camping information, call ☎928/638–7875.

WHAT IT COSTS				
¢	$	$$	$$$	$$$$
Restaurants	under $8	$8–$12	$13–$20	$21–$30	over $30
Hotels	under $70	$70–$120	$121–$175	$176–$250	over $250

Restaurant prices are per person for a main course at dinner. Hotel prices are for a standard double in high season, excluding taxes and service fees.

There is no camping on the West Rim, but you can pitch a tent on the beach near the Colorado River at the primitive campground on Diamond Creek Road. Hikers heading to the falls in Havasu Canyon can stay at the primitive campground in Supai.

WHERE TO EAT

IN THE SOUTH RIM

$$$ ✕**Arizona Room.** The canyon views from this casual Southwestern-style steak house are the best of any restaurant at the South Rim. The menu includes such delicacies as chile-crusted pan-seared wild salmon, chipotle barbecue baby back ribs, roasted vegetable and black bean enchiladas, and mustard and rosemary crusted prime rib. For dessert, try the cheesecake with prickly-pear syrup paired with one of the house's specialty coffee drinks. Seating is first-come, first served, so arrive early to avoid the crowds. ⊠*Bright Angel Lodge, Desert View Dr., Grand Canyon Village* ☎*928/638–2631* ⊕*www.grandcanyonlodges.com* ⚎*Reservations not accepted* ⊟*AE, D, DC, MC, V* ☉*Closed Jan.–mid-Feb. No lunch Nov.–Feb.*

$$$ ✕**El Tovar Dining Room.** No doubt about it—this is the best restaurant
Fodor's Choice for miles. Modeled after a European hunting lodge, this rustic 19th-
★ century dining room built of hand-hewn logs is worth a visit. Breakfast, lunch, and dinner are served beneath the beamed ceiling. The cuisine is modern Southwestern with an exotic flair. Start with the hoisin barbecue sea scallops or the mozzarella roulades of prosciutto and basil pesto. The dinner menu includes such dishes as mesquite smoked pork chops with wild rice stuffing, grilled New York strip steak with buttermilk-cornmeal onion rings, and a salmon tostada topped with organic greens and tequila vinaigrette. The dining room also offers an extensive wine list. ■TIP➜**Dinner reservations can be made up to six months in advance with room reservations and 30 days in advance for all other visitors.** ⊠*El Tovar Hotel, Desert View Dr., Grand Canyon Village* ☎*303/297–2757 or 888/297–2757 (reservations only), 928/638–2631* ⊕*www.grandcanyonlodges.com* ⚎*Reservations essential* ⊟*AE, D, DC, MC, V.*

¢ ✕**Canyon Café.** Fast-food favorites here include pastries, burgers, and pizza. Open for breakfast, lunch, and dinner, the cafeteria also serves specials, chicken potpie, fried catfish, and fried chicken. ⊠*Yavapai Lodge, Desert View Dr., Grand Canyon Village* ☎*928/638–2631* ⊕*www.grandcanyonlodges.com* ⚎*Reservations not accepted* ⊟*AE, D, DC, MC, V* ☉*Closed mid-Dec.–Feb.*

IN THE NORTH RIM

$$$$ ✕ **Grand Cookout.** Dine under the stars and enjoy live entertainment at
☺ this chuckwagon-style dining experience. Fill up on Western favorites including barbecue beef brisket, roasted chicken, baked beans, and cowboy biscuits. Transportation from the Grand Canyon Lodge to the cookout is included. Be sure to call before 4 PM for dinner reservations. ⊠*Grand Canyon Lodge, North Rim* ☎*877/386–4383 Ext. 0* ⚎*Reservations essential* ⊟*AE, D, DC, MC, V* ☉*Closed mid-Oct.–mid-May.*

$$$ ✕**Grand Canyon Lodge Dining Room.** The historic lodge has a huge, high-
★ ceilinged dining room with spectacular views and very good food; you
might find pork medallions, roast chicken, and buffalo steaks on the
dinner menu. It's also open for breakfast and lunch. ⊠*Grand Can-
yon Lodge, Bright Angel Point, North Rim* ☎*877/386–4383 Ext.
760* ⌖*Reservations not accepted* ☰*AE, D, DC, MC, V* ♥*Closed
mid-Oct.–mid-May.*

¢ ✕**Deli in the Pines.** Dining choices are very limited on the North Rim,
but this is your best bet for a meal on a budget. Selections include pizza,
salads, deli sandwiches, hot dogs, rice bowls, and ice cream. Open for
breakfast, lunch, and dinner. ⊠*Grand Canyon Lodge, Bright Angel
Point, North Rim* ☎*877/386–4383 Ext. 766* ☰*AE, D, DC, MC, V*
♥*Closed mid-Oct.–mid-May.*

WHERE TO STAY

IN THE SOUTH RIM

$$ ⌂**El Tovar Hotel.** A registered National Historic Landmark, El Tovar
Fodor'sChoice was built in 1905 of Oregon pine logs and native stone. The hotel's
★ proximity to all of the canyon's facilities, its European hunting-lodge
atmosphere, and its renowned dining room make it the best place to
stay on the South Rim. It's usually booked well in advance (up to 13
months ahead), though it's easier to get a room during winter months.
Three suites (El Tovar, Fred Harvey, and Mary Jane Colter) and several
rooms have canyon views (these are booked early), but you can enjoy
the view anytime from the cocktail-lounge back porch. **Pros:** Historic
lodging just steps from the South Rim; fabulous lounge with outdoor
seating and canyon views; best in-park dining on-site. **Cons:** Books up
quickly, no Internet access. ⊠*Desert View Dr., Grand Canyon Village* ⌂*Box 699, Grand Canyon 86023* ☎ *888/297–2757 reservations
only, 928/638–2631* ⊕*www.grandcanyonlodges.com* ⌂*66 rooms, 12
suites* ⌖*In-room: refrigerator. In-hotel: restaurant, room service, bar,
no elevator, no-smoking rooms* ☰*AE, D, DC, MC, V.*

$$ ⌂**Kachina Lodge.** Located on the rim halfway between El Tovar and
Bright Angel Lodge, this motel-style lodge has many rooms with partial
canyon views ($10 extra). Although lacking the historical charm of the
neighboring lodges, these rooms are a good bet for families and are
within easy walking distance of dining facilities at El Tovar and Bright
Angel Lodge. There are also several rooms for people with physical dis-
abilities. There's no air-conditioning, but evaporative coolers keep the
heat at bay. Check in at El Tovar Hotel to the east. **Pros:** Partial canyon
views in half the rooms, family-friendly, accessible rooms. **Cons:** No
Internet access, check-in takes place at El Tovar Hotel, limited parking.
⊠*Desert View Dr., Grand Canyon Village* ⌂*Box 699, Grand Canyon
86023* ☎ *888/297–2757 reservations only, 928/638–2631* ⊕*www.
grandcanyonlodges.com* ⌂*49 rooms* ⌖*In-room: safe, refrigerator. In-
hotel: no-smoking rooms* ☰*AE, D, DC, MC, V.*

$ ⌂**Bright Angel Lodge.** Famed architect Mary Jane Colter designed this
♨ 1935 log-and-stone structure, which sits within a few yards of the can-
yon rim and blends superbly with the canyon walls. It offers a similar

5

GRAND CANYON NATIONAL PARK

location to El Tovar for about half the price. Accommodations are in motel-style rooms or cabins. Lodge rooms don't have TVs, and some rooms do not have private bathrooms. Scattered among the pines are 50 cabins, which do have TVs and private baths; some have fireplaces. Expect historic charm but not luxury. The Bright Angel Dining Room serves family-style meals all day and a warm apple grunt dessert large enough to share. The Arizona Room serves dinner only. Adding to the experience are an ice-cream parlor, gift shop, and small history museum with exhibits on Fred Harvey and Mary Jane Colter. **Pros:** Some rooms have canyon views, all are steps away from the rim; Internet kiosks and transportation desk for the mule ride check-in are in the lobby. **Cons:** The popular lobby is always packed, parking here is problematic, stairs throughout the building and lack of elevators make accessibility an issue. ⊠ *Desert View Dr., Grand Canyon Village* ⌂ *Box 699, Grand Canyon 86023* ☎ *888/297–2757 reservations only, 928/638–2631* ⊕ *www.grandcanyonlodges.com* ⬅ *37 rooms, 6 with shared toilet and shower, 13 with shared shower; 49 cabins* ♿ *In-room: no a/c (some), safe (some), refrigerator (some), no TV (some). In-hotel: 2 restaurants, bar, no elevator, public Internet, no-smoking rooms* ▤ *AE, D, DC, MC, V.*

$ **🔲 Maswik Lodge.** The lodge, named for a Hopi kachina who is said to
♻ guard the canyon, is 0.25 mi from the rim. Accommodations, nestled in the ponderosa pine forest, range from rustic cabins to more modern rooms. The cabins are the cheapest option but are available only spring through fall. Some rooms have air-conditioning, and the rest have ceiling fans. Teenagers like the lounge, where they can shoot pool, throw darts, or watch the big-screen TV. There is also an Internet room. Kids under 16 stay free. **Pros:** Larger rooms here than in historic lodgings, good for families, Internet access, affordable dining options. **Cons:** Plain rooms lack historic charm, tucked away from the rim in the forest. ⊠ *Grand Canyon Village* ⌂ *Box 699, Grand Canyon 86023* ☎ *888/297–2757 reservations only, 928/638–2631* ⊕ *www.grandcanyon lodges.com* ⬅ *250 rooms, 28 cabins* ♿ *In-room: no a/c (some), safe (some), refrigerator (some). In-hotel: restaurant, bar, no elevator, public Internet, no-smoking rooms* ▤ *AE, D, DC, MC, V.*

$ **🔲 Yavapai Lodge.** The largest motel-style lodge in the park is tucked in a piñon and juniper forest at the eastern end of Grand Canyon Village, near the RV park. The basic rooms are near the park's general store, the visitor center (0.5 mi), and the rim (0.25 mi). The cafeteria, open for breakfast, lunch, and dinner, serves standard park service food. An Internet room is available to guests. **Pros:** Transportation/activities desk on-site in the lobby, located near Market Plaza in Grand Canyon Village, forested grounds. **Cons:** No Internet access in rooms, farthest in-park lodging from the rim. ⊠ *Grand Canyon Village* ⌂ *Box 699, Grand Canyon 86023* ☎ *888/297–2757 reservations only, 928/638– 2961* ⊕ *www.grandcanyonlodges.com* ⬅ *358 rooms* ♿ *In-room: no a/c (some), refrigerator (some). In-hotel: restaurant, no elevator, public Internet, no-smoking rooms* ▤ *AE, D, DC, MC, V* ⊗ *Closed Jan. and Feb.*

¢   **Phantom Ranch.** In a grove of cottonwood trees on the canyon floor, Phantom Ranch is accessible only to hikers and mule trekkers. The wood-and-stone buildings originally made up a hunting camp built in 1922. There are 40 dormitory beds and 14 beds in cabins, all with shared baths. Seven additional cabins are reserved for mule riders, who buy their trips as a package. The mess hall–style restaurant, one of the most remote eating establishments in the United States, serves family-style meals, with breakfast, dinner, and box lunches available. Reservations, taken up to 13 months in advance, are a must for services and lodging. **Pros:** Only inner-canyon lodging option, fabulous canyon views, remote access limits crowds. **Cons:** Accessible only by foot or mule, few amenities. ⊠ *On canyon floor, at intersection of Bright Angel and Kaibab trails* ✉ *Box 699, Grand Canyon 86023* ☎ *303/297–2757 or 888/297–2757* ⊕ *www.grandcanyonlodges.com* 💤 *4 dormitories and 2 cabins for hikers, 7 cabins with outside showers for mule riders* ⚑ *In-room: no a/c, no phone, no TV. In-hotel: restaurant, no elevator, no-smoking rooms* ▤ *AE, D, DC, MC, V.*

IN THE NORTH RIM

$$ **Grand Canyon Lodge.** This historic property, constructed mainly in the
Fodor's Choice 1920s and '30s, is the premier lodging facility in the North Rim area.
★   The main building has limestone walls and timbered ceilings. Lodging options include small, rustic cabins; larger cabins (some with a canyon view and some with two bedrooms); and newer, traditional motel rooms. The best of the bunch are the log cabins 301 and 306, which have private porches perched on the lip of the canyon. Other cabins with fabulous canyon views include 305, 309, and 310. **Pros:** Steps away from gorgeous North Rim views, close to several easy hiking trails. **Cons:** As the only in-park North Rim lodging option, this lodge fills up fast; few amenities. ⊠ *Grand Canyon National Park, Hwy. 67, North Rim* ☎ *877/386–4383, 928/638–2611 May–Oct., 928/645–6865 Nov.–Apr.* ⊕ *www.grandcanyonforever.com* 💤 *44 rooms, 157 cabins* ⚑ *In-room: no a/c, refrigerator (some), no TV. In-hotel: 3 restaurants, bar, bicycles, no elevator, laundry facilities, public Internet, no-smoking rooms* ▤ *AE, D, MC, V* ⊘ *Closed mid-Oct.–mid-May.*

GRAND CANYON ESSENTIALS

For more on national parks, visit ⊕ *www.fodors.com.*

ADMISSION FEES & PERMITS

A fee of $25 per vehicle is collected at the east entrance near Cameron and at the south entrance near Tusayan for the South Rim and at the main entrance at the North Rim. Pedestrians and cyclists pay $12 per person. The fee pays for up to one week's access and is good for both rims. The Grand Canyon Pass, available for $50, gives unlimited access to the park for 12 months from the purchase date. The annual America the Beautiful—National Parks and Recreational Land Pass (☎ *888/ASK–USGS* ⊕ *store.usgs.gov/pass)* provides unlimited access to all national parks and federal recreation areas. Cost is $80 and they are valid for one year from the date of purchase.

Hikers descending into the canyon for an overnight stay need a backcountry permit, which can be obtained in person, by mail, or faxed by request (📪 *Box 129, Grand Canyon 86023* ☎ *928/638–7875* 🖷 *928/638–2125* 🖳 *$10, plus $5 per person per night* ⊕ *www.nps.gov/ grca*). Permits are limited, so make your reservation as far in advance as possible—they're taken up to four months ahead of arrival. A visit to the park's Web site will go far in preparing you for the permit process. Day hikes into the canyon or anywhere else in the national park do not require a permit; overnight stays at Phantom Ranch require reservations but no permits. Overnight camping in the national park is restricted to designated campgrounds.

ADMISSION HOURS
The South Rim is open 24/7, year-round. The North Rim is open midMay through mid-October, depending on the weather. Highway 67 from Jacob Lake is closed due to snowfall from around mid-October to mid-May, and during these times all facilities at the North Rim are closed. The entrance gates are open 24 hours, but are generally staffed from about 7 AM to 7 PM. The park is in the Mountain Time zone.

EMERGENCIES
In case of a fire or medical emergency, dial 911; from in-park lodgings, dial 9-911. To report a security problem, contact the Park Police (☎ 928/638–7805), stationed at all visitor centers. The **North Country Community Health Center** (⊠ *1 Clinic Rd., Grand Canyon Village* ☎ *928/638–2551*) is staffed by physicians from 8 AM–6 PM, seven days a week (reduced hours in winter). It does not have a pharmacy.

VISITOR INFORMATION
The Grand Canyon National Park's main orientation center, **Canyon View Information Plaza** (⊠ *East side of Grand Canyon Village, South Rim* ☎ *928/638–7888* ⊕ *www.nps.gov/grca* ⊙ *Daily 8–5*) provides pamphlets and resources to help plan your sightseeing. Park rangers are on hand to answer questions and aid in planning canyon excursions. A bookstore is stocked with books covering all topics on the Grand Canyon, and a daily schedule of ranger-led hikes and evening lectures is posted on a bulletin board inside. The information center can be reached by a short walk from Mather Point, by a short ride on the shuttle bus Village Route, or by a leisurely 1-mi walk on the Greenway Trail. At the **North Rim Visitor Center** (⊠ *Near the parking lot on Bright Angel Peninsula* ☎ *928/638–7888* ⊙ *Mid-May–mid-Oct., daily 8–6*) you can view exhibits, peruse the bookstore, and pick up useful maps and brochures.

Northeast
Arizona

WORD OF MOUTH

"Antelope Canyon...I remembered to take my tripod and it was needed. I must have taken more than 30 photos. The midday sun bouncing off the canyon walls and the hanging dust were truly amazing...The canyon is about 200 yards long and almost perfectly level from front to back. A very easy meandering walk and photo session. The curved walls and reflecting light made for quite a sight that should not be missed by anybody passing through the area."

—Myer

Updated
by Andrew
Collins

Northeast Arizona is a vast and magnificent land of lofty buttes, towering cliffs, and turquoise skies so clear that horizons appear endless. Most of the land in the area belongs to the Navajo and Hopi peoples, who adhere to ancient traditions based on spiritual values, kinship, and an affinity for nature. In many respects life on the Hopi Mesas has changed little during the last two centuries, and visiting this land can feel like traveling to a foreign country, or going back in time.

The Navajo Nation encompasses more than 27,000 square mi, an area that ranks larger than 10 of the 50 states. In its approximate center sits the nearly 3,000-square-mi Hopi Reservation, a series of adobe villages built on high mesas overlooking the cultivated land. On Arizona's northern and eastern borders, where the Navajo Nation continues into Utah and New Mexico, the Navajo and Canyon de Chelly national monuments contain haunting cliff dwellings of ancient people who lived in the area some 1,500 years ago. Glen Canyon Dam, which abuts the far northwestern corner of the reservation on U.S. 89, holds back more than 200 mi of emerald waters known as Lake Powell.

EXPLORING NORTHEAST ARIZONA

Relatively few visitors experience the vast, sweeping northeast quadrant of Arizona, which comprises the Navajo and Hopi reservations, but efforts to spend a few days here are rewarded with stunning scenery and the chance to learn about some of the world's most vibrant indigenous communities. This is part of the West's great Four Corners Region, home to the underrated and spectacular Canyon de Chelly National Monument as well as the dramatic buttes and canyons of Monument Valley. The one portion of the area outside tribal lands is Page, the anchor for exploring the 200 mi of shoreline that fringe crystalline Lake Powell.

ABOUT THE RESTAURANTS

Northeastern Arizona is a vast area with small hamlets and towns scattered miles apart, and there are few stores or restaurants along the highway. With the exception of Page, which has slightly more culinary variety, most of the region's restaurants serve basic but tasty Native American and Southwestern cuisine. Navajo and Hopi favorites include mutton stew, Hopi *piki* (paper-thin, blue-corn bread), and Navajo fry bread. Navajo tacos are fry bread piled with refried beans, ground beef, lettuce, tomato, scallions, cheese, avocado, sour cream, and salsa. Top the fry bread with butter, honey, and confectioner's sugar for a delicious dessert.

ABOUT THE HOTELS

Page also has the area's greatest concentration of lodgings, most of them fairly standard chain motels and hotels, but this base camp for exploring Lake Powell also has a few bed-and-breakfasts as well as houseboat rentals. You'll find a handful of well-maintained chains in the Navajo Nation, mostly in Kayenta, Chinle, Tuba City, and Window Rock. This is also a popular area for both tent and RV camping—you can obtain a list of campgrounds from the Page/Lake Powell Chamber of Commerce and the Navajo Nation Visitor Center.

TOP REASONS TO GO

Drive the Rim Roads at Canyon de Chelly: Visit one of the most spectacular natural wonders in the Southwest—it rivals the Grand Canyon for beauty. It's a must for photography buffs.

Go boating at Glen Canyon: Get to know this stunning, mammoth reservoir by taking a boat out on Lake Powell amid the towering cliffs.

Be petrified: Marvel at huge petrified logs and the dazzling colors of nature at Petrified Forest National Park.

Shop for handmade crafts on the Hopi Mesas: Pick up crafts by some of Arizona's leading Hopi artisans, who sustain their culture through the continuous occupation of the ancient villages on these mesas.

Take a jeep tour through Monument Valley: On an excursion through this 92,000-acre area, see firsthand the landscape depicted in such iconic western films as *Stagecoach* and *The Searchers*.

WHAT IT COSTS

	¢	$	$$	$$$	$$$$
Restaurants	under $8	$8–$12	$13–$20	$21–$30	over $30
Hotels	under $70	$70–$120	$121–$175	$176–$250	over $250

Restaurant prices are per person for a main course at dinner. Hotel prices are for a standard double in high season, excluding taxes and service charges.

THE PETRIFIED FOREST & THE PAINTED DESERT

PETRIFIED FOREST NATIONAL PARK

Northern Entrance: 54 mi east of Homolovi Ruins State Park and 27 mi east of Holbrook on I–40; Southern Entrance: 18 mi east of Holbrook on U.S. 180.

⊠*North Entrance: I–40, Milepost 311, 27 mi east of Holbrook, Petrified Forest* ☎*928/524–6228* ⊕*www.nps.gov/pefo* 🖅*$10 per vehicle or $5 per person on foot or bicycle, valid for 7 days* ⊙*Daily 8–5 Sept.–May and 7–7 June–Aug.*

Though named for its famous fossilized trees, Petrified Forest has something to see for history buffs of all stripes, from a segment of Route 66 to ancient dwellings to even more ancient fossils. And the good thing is, much of Petrified Forest's treasures can easily be viewed without a great amount of athletic conditioning. You can see a lot just by driving along the main road, from which historic sites are readily accessible. By combining a drive along the park road with a short hike here and there, and a visit to one of the park's landmarks, much can be seen in as little as half a day for those with limited time.

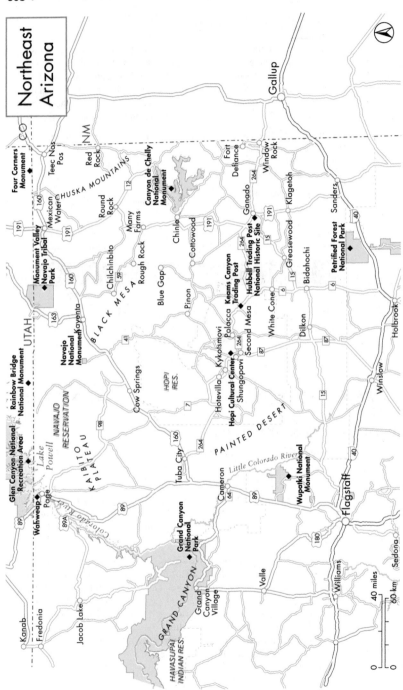

Northeast Arizona

HISTORIC SITES

Agate House. This eight-room pueblo is thought to have been built entirely of petrified wood 700 years ago. Researchers believe it might have been used as a temporary dwelling by seasonal farmers or traders from one of the area tribes. ⊠ *Rainbow Forest Museum parking area.*

Newspaper Rock. See huge boulders covered with petroglyphs believed to have been carved by the Pueblo Indians more than 500 years ago. ⊠ *6 mi south of Painted Desert Visitor Center.*

Painted Desert Inn National Historic Site. You'll find cultural history exhibits as well as the murals of Fred Kabotie, a popular 1940s artist whose work was commissioned by Mary Jane Colter. Native American crafts are displayed in this museum and mini visitor center. Check the schedule for daily events. ⊠ *2 mi north of Painted Desert Visitor Center* ☎ *928/524–6228* ⊕ *www.nps.gov/pefo* ⊠ *Free* ⊙ *Daily 8–5 Sept.– May and 7–7 June–Aug.*

Puerco Pueblo. This is a 100-room pueblo, built before 1400 and said to have housed ancestral Puebloan people. Many visitors come to see petroglyphs, as well as a solar calendar. ⊠ *10 mi south of Painted Desert Visitor Center.*

SCENIC STOPS

★ **Agate Bridge.** Here you'll see a 100-foot log spanning a 40-foot-wide wash. ⊠ *19 mi south of Painted Desert Visitor Center.*

Crystal Forest. Before they were stolen by looters, the fragments of petrified wood strewn here once held clear quartz and amethyst crystals. ⊠ *20 mi south of Painted Desert Visitor Center.*

★ **Giant Logs.** A short walk leads you past the park's largest log, known as "Old Faithful." It's considered the largest because of its diameter (9 feet, 9 inches), as well as how tall it once was. ⊠ *28 mi south of Painted Desert Visitor Center.*

Jasper Forest. More of an overlook than a forest, this spot has a large concentration of petrified trees in jasper or red. ⊠ *17 mi south of Painted Desert Visitor Center.*

The Tepees. Witness the effects of time on these cone-shaped rock formations colored by iron, manganese, and other minerals. ⊠ *8 mi south of Painted Desert Visitor Center.*

SCENIC DRIVE

Painted Desert Scenic Drive. A 28-mi scenic drive takes you through the park from one entrance to the other. If you begin from the north, the first 5 mi of the drive takes you along the edge of a high mesa, with spectacular views of Painted Desert. Beyond lies the desolate Painted Desert Wilderness Area. After the 5 mi point, the road crosses Interstate 40, then swings south toward Perco River across a landscape covered with sagebrush, saltbrush, sunflowers, and Apache plume. Past the river, the road climbs onto a narrow mesa leading to Newspaper Rock, a panel of Pueblo Indian rock art. Then the road bends southeast, enters a barren stretch, and passes tepee-shaped buttes in the distance. Next you come to Blue Mesa, roughly the park's midpoint and a good place to stop for views of petrified logs. The next stop on the drive is Agate Bridge, really a 100-foot log over a wide wash. The remaining

Petrified Forest
National Park

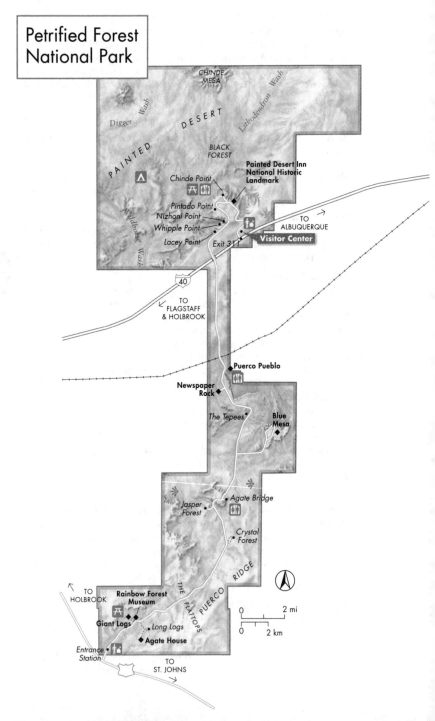

CHINDE MESA

DESERT

Digger Wash

Lithodendron Wash

PAINTED

BLACK FOREST

Wildhorse Wash

Chinde Point

Painted Desert Inn
National Historic
Landmark

Pintado Point

Nizhoni Point

Whipple Point

Lacey Point

Exit 311

Visitor Center

TO
ALBUQUERQUE

40

TO
FLAGSTAFF
& HOLBROOK

Puerco Pueblo

**Newspaper
Rock**

The Tepees

**Blue
Mesa**

Agate Bridge

Jasper
Forest

Crystal
Forest

PUERCO RIDGE

THE FLATTOPS

TO
HOLBROOK

**Rainbow Forest
Museum**

Giant Logs

Long Logs

Agate House

Entrance
Station

TO
ST. JOHNS

0   2 mi

0   2 km

overlooks are Jasper Forest and Crystal Forest, where you can get a further glimpse at the accumulated petrified wood. On your way out of the park, stop at the Rainbow Forest Museum for a rest and to shop for a memento. ⊠*Begins at Painted Desert Visitor Center.*

VISITOR CENTERS

Painted Desert Visitor Center. This is the place to go for general park information and an informative 20-minute film on the park. Proceeds from books purchased here fund the continuing research and interpretive activities for the park. ⊠*North entrance, off I–40, 27 mi east of Holbrook* 🕾*928/524–6228* ⊕*www.nps.gov/pefo* ☉*Daily 8–5 Sept.–May and 7–7 June–Aug.*

Rainbow Forest Museum and Visitor Center. The museum houses artifacts of early reptiles, dinosaurs, and petrified wood. Be sure to see Gertie, the skeleton of a phytosaur, a crocodile-like carnivore. ⊠*South entrance, off U.S. 180, 18 mi southeast of Holbrook* 🕾*928/524–6228* ☒*Free* ☉*Daily 8–5 Sept.–May, 7–7 June–Aug.*

SPORTS & THE OUTDOORS

HIKING

EASY **Crystal Forest.** The easy 0.8-mi loop leads you past petrified wood that once held quartz crystals and amethyst chips. ⊠*20 mi south of Painted Desert Visitor Center.*

Giant Logs. At 0.4 mi, Giant Logs is the park's shortest trail. The loop leads you to "Old Faithful," the park's largest log—it's 9 feet, 9 inches at its base, weighing 44 tons. ⊠*Directly behind Rainbow Forest Museum, 28 mi south of Painted Desert Visitor Center.*

Long Logs. While barren, the easy 0.6-mi loop reveals the largest concentration of wood in the park. ⊠*26 mi south of Painted Desert Visitor Center.*

☮ **Puerco Pueblo.** A relatively flat and interesting 0.3-mi trail takes you past remains of an ancestral home of the Pueblo people, built before 1400. The trail is paved and handicapped accessible. ⊠*10 mi south of Painted Desert Visitor Center.*

MODERATE **Agate House.** A fairly flat 1-mi trip takes you to an eight-room pueblo sitting high on a knoll. *See Historic Sites, What to See.* ⊠*26 mi south of Painted Desert Visitor Center.*

Blue Mesa. Although it's only 1-mi long and it's significantly steeper than the rest, this trail at the park's midway point is one of the most popular. ⊠*14 mi south of Painted Desert Visitor Center.*

Painted Desert Rim. The 1-mi trail is at its best in early morning or late afternoon, when the sun accentuates the brilliant red, blue, purple, and other hues of the desert and petrified forest landscape. ⊠*Tawa Point and Kachina Point, 1 mi north of Painted Desert Visitor Center.*

DIFFICULT **Kachina Point.** This is the trailhead for wilderness hiking. A 1-mi trail leads to the Wilderness Area, but from there you're on your own. With no developed trails, hiking here is cross-country style, but expect to see strange formations, beautifully colored landscape, and maybe, just maybe, a pronghorn antelope. ⊠*On northwest side of Painted Desert Inn Museum.*

6

WHERE TO STAY & EAT

There is no lodging or campgrounds within the Petrified Forest. Back-country camping is allowed if you obtain a free permit at the visitor center or museum; the only camping allowed is minimal-impact camping in a designated zone north of Lithodendron Wash in the Wilderness Area. Group size is limited to 8. RVs are not allowed. There are no fire pits or designated sites, nor is any shade available. Also note that if it rains, that pretty Painted Desert formation turns to sticky clay.

Dining in the park is limited to a cafeteria in the Painted Desert Visitor Center and snacks in the Rainbow Forest Museum. You may want to pack a lunch and eat at one of the park's picnic areas.

NAVAJO NATION EAST

CANYON DE CHELLY

Fodor'sChoice *30 mi west of Window Rock on AZ 264, then north 25 mi on*
★ *U.S. 191.*

Home to Ancestral Puebloans from AD 350 to 1300, the nearly 84,000-acre Canyon de Chelly (pronounced d'*shay*) is one of the most spectacular natural wonders in the Southwest. On a smaller scale, it rivals the Grand Canyon for beauty. Its main gorges—the 26-mi-long Canyon de Chelly ("canyon in the rock") and the adjoining 35-mi Canyon del Muerto ("canyon of the dead")—comprise sheer, heavily eroded sandstone walls that rise to 1,100 feet over dramatic valleys. Ancient pictographs and petroglyphs decorate some of the cliffs, and within the canyon complex there are more than 7,000 archaeological sites. Stone walls rise hundreds of feet above streams, hogans, tilled fields, and sheep-grazing lands.

You can view prehistoric sites near the base of cliffs and perched on high, sheltering ledges, some of which you can access from the park's two main drives along the canyon rims. The dwellings and cultivated fields of the present-day Navajo lie in the flatlands between the cliffs, and those who inhabit the canyon today farm much the way their ancestors did. Most residents leave the canyon in winter but return in early spring to farm.

The **visitor center** has exhibits on the history of the cliff dwellers and provides information on scheduled hikes, tours, and National Park Service programs offered throughout the summer months.

Both Canyon de Chelly and Canyon del Muerto have a paved rim drive with turnoffs and parking areas. Each drive takes a minimum of two hours—allow more if you plan to hike to White House Rim, picnic, or spend time photographing the sites. Overlooks along the rim drives provide incredible views of the canyon; be sure to stay on trails and away from the canyon edge, and to control children and pets at all times.

★ The **South Rim Drive** (36 mi round-trip with seven overlooks) of Canyon de Chelly starts at the visitor center and ends at **Spider Rock Overlook,** where cliffs plunge 1,000 feet to the canyon floor. The view here is of two pinnacles, Speaking Rock and Spider Rock; the latter rises about 800 feet from the canyon floor and is considered a sacred place. Other highlights on the South Rim Drive are Junction Overlook, where Canyon del Muerto joins Canyon de Chelly; White House Overlook, from which a 2½-mi round-trip trail leads to the **White House Ruin,** with dwelling remains of nearly 60 rooms and several kivas; and Sliding House Overlook, where you can see dwellings on a narrow, sloped ledge across the canyon. The carved and sometimes narrow trail down the canyon side to White House Ruin is the only access into Canyon de Chelly without a guide—but if you have a fear of heights, this may not be the hike for you.

The only slightly less breathtaking **North Rim Drive** (34 mi round-trip with four overlooks) of Canyon del Muerto also begins at the visitor center and continues northeast on Indian Highway 64 toward the town of Tsaile. Major stops include Antelope House Overlook, a large site named for the animals painted on an adjacent cliff; the Mummy Cave Overlook, where two mummies were found inside a remarkably unspoiled pueblo dwelling; and Massacre Cave Overlook, which marks the spot where an estimated 115 Navajo were killed by the Spanish in 1805. (The rock walls of the cave are still pockmarked from the Spaniards' ricocheting bullets.) ⊠*Indian Hwy. 7, 3 mi east of U.S. 191, Chinle* ☎*928/674–5500 visitor center* ⊕*www.nps.gov/cach* ⊠*Free* ☉*Daily 8–5.*

SPORTS & THE OUTDOORS

HIKING From late May through early September, free three-hour ranger-led hikes depart from the visitor center at 9 AM. Also at this time, two four-hour hikes (about $10 per person) leave from the visitor center and again in afternoon. Some trails are strenuous and steep; others are easy or moderate. Those with health concerns or a fear of heights should proceed with caution. Call ahead: hikes are occasionally canceled due to local customs or events.

Only one hike within Canyon de Chelly National Monument—the **White House Ruin Trail** on the South Rim Drive—can be undertaken without an authorized guide. The trail starts near White House Overlook and runs along sheer walls that drop about 550 feet. If you have concerns about height, be aware that the path gets narrow and somewhat slippery along the way. The hike is 2½ mi round-trip, and hikers should carry their own drinking water.

Private, guided hikes to the interior of the canyons cost about $15 per hour with a three-hour minimum for groups of up to four people. (Don't venture into the canyon without a guide or you'll face a stiff fine.) For overnights, you'll need a guide as well as permission to stay on private land. If you have a four-wheel-drive vehicle and want to drive yourself, guides will accompany you for a charge of about $15 an hour with a three-hour minimum for up to three vehicles. All Navajo guides are members of the **Tsegi Guide Association** (✉ *Canyon de Chelly Visitor Center, Indian Hwy. 7, Chinle* ☎ *928/674–5500*). You can hire a guide on the spot at the visitor center, or you can call ahead and make a reservation.

HORSEBACK
RIDING
★

Totsonii Ranch (✉ *South Rim Dr., Chinle* ☎ *928/755–2037* ⊕ *www.tot-soniiranch.com*), 13 mi from the visitor center at the end of the paved road, offers several types of tours into different parts of Canyon de Chelly: Canyon Rim (two hours), Three Turkey Ruins (four hours), Spider Rock (four hours), White House Ruins (six to seven hours), Canyon de Chelly overview (eight to nine hours), and one- and two-night treks. Some of these trips are geared only toward skilled adult riders, such as the Canyon Rim trips, which encounter steep terrain and offer amazing views. Spider Rock is a great choice for virtually any skill level and can be done in a half day—the ride leads right to the base of this 800-foot iconic pillar. Rates are $15 per hour per person plus $15 per hour per guide.

JEEP TOURS

Canyon de Chelly Tours (☎ *928/674–5433* ⊕ *www.canyondechellytours. com*) offers private jeep tours into Canyon de Chelly and arranges group tours and overnight camping in the canyon as well as late afternoon and evening tours. Entertainment such as storytellers, music, and Navajo legends can be arranged with advance reservation. Rates begin around $55 per person for three-hour tours, or $44 per hour per vehicle if you use your own SUV. Treks with **Thunderbird Lodge Canyon Tours** (✉ *Thunderbird Lodge Gift Shop, Indian Hwy. 7, Chinle* ☎ *928/674–5841 or 800/679–2473* ⊕ *www.tbirdlodge.com*), in six-wheel-drive vehicles, are available from late spring to late fall. Half-day tours are $43 and start at 9 AM and 1 or 2 PM daily; all-day tours cost $71 and include lunch.

WALKING
TOURS

Footpath Journey Tours (☎ *928/724–3366* ⊕ *www.footpathjourneys. com*) offers custom four- to seven-day treks into the canyon starting at $700 per person, not including food.

WHERE TO EAT

Chinle is the closest town to Canyon de Chelly. There are good lodgings with restaurants, as well as a supermarket and a campground. Be aware that you may be approached by panhandlers in the grocery store parking lot. In late August each year, Chinle is host to the Central Navajo Fair, a public celebration complete with a rodeo, carnival, and traditional dances.

WHERE TO STAY

$–$$

🏨 **Holiday Inn Canyon de Chelly.** Once Garcia's Trading Post, this hotel near Canyon de Chelly is less generic than you might expect: the exterior is territorial fort in style, although the rooms are predictably pastel and contemporary. Off the lobby there's a gift shop stocked with local Native American arts and crafts, plus a decent restaurant. **Pros:** Attractive, adobe-style building, nice pool and gym, the best of the area's restaurants. **Cons:** Not especially memorable decor, dull roadside setting. ✉ *Indian Hwy. 7* ⬚ *Box 1889, Chinle 86503* ☎ *928/674–5000 or 888/465–4329* ⊕ *www.holidayinn.com*

108 *rooms* In-room: *refrigerator, Wi-Fi. In-hotel: restaurant, gym, pool* AE, D, DC, MC, V.

$ **Thunderbird Lodge.** In an ideal ★ location within the national monument's borders, this pleasant establishment has stone-and-adobe units that match the site's original 1896 trading post. The cafeteria is in the original trading post and serves reasonably priced soups, salads, sandwiches, and entrées, including charbroiled steaks. The lodge

WORD OF MOUTH

"We enjoyed an afternoon with Thunderbird Lodge Canyon Tours—they take about 15 people in an open-top truck with bench seats. It's great for looking up and seeing a lot more than you can from a closed car. Our guide was extremely informative about Navajo history and lore." —Kayd

also offers jeep tours of Canyon de Chelly and Canyon del Muerto. **Pros:** Inside the actual park borders, steeped in history, tours offered right from hotel. **Cons:** Rustic decor, no high-speed Internet. *Indian Hwy. 7* Box 548, Chinle 86503 928/674–5841 or 800/679–2473 *www.tbirdlodge.com* 73 *rooms* In-hotel: *restaurant, no elevator* AE, D, DC, V.

THE HOPI MESAS

The Hopi occupy 12 villages in regions referred to as First Mesa, Second Mesa, and Third Mesa. Although these areas have similar languages and traditions, each has its own individual features. Generations of Hopitu, "the peaceful people," much like their Puebloan ancestors, have lived in these largely agrarian settlements of stone-and-adobe houses, which blend in with the earth so well that they appear to be natural formations. Television antennae, satellite dishes, and automobiles notwithstanding, these Hopi villages still exude the air of another time.

Descendants of the ancient Hisatsinom, the Hopi number about 12,000 people today. Their culture can be traced back more than 2,000 years, making them one of the oldest known tribes in North America. They successfully developed "dry farming" and grow many kinds of vegetables and corn (called maize) as their basic food—in fact the Hopi are often called the "corn people." They incorporate nature's cycles into most of their religious rituals. In the celebrated Snake Dance ceremony, dancers carry venomous snakes in their mouths to appease the gods and to bring rain. In addition to farming the land, the Hopi create fine pottery and basketwork and excel in wood carving of kachina dolls. **Inter Tribal Council of Arizona: Hopi Tribe** (928/734–3000 *www.itcaonline.com/tribes_hopi.html*).

KEAMS CANYON TRADING POST

❶ *43 mi west of Hubbell Trading Post on AZ 264.*

The trading post established by Thomas Keam in 1875 to do business with local tribes is now the area's main tourist attraction, offering a

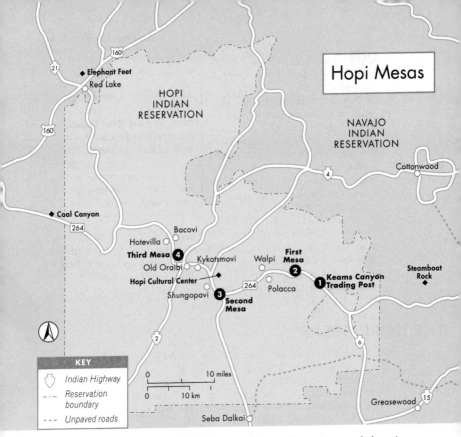

primitive campground, restaurant, service station, and shopping center, all set in a dramatic rocky canyon. An administrative center for the Bureau of Indian Affairs, Keams Canyon also has a number of government buildings. A road, accessible by passenger car, winds northeast 3 mi into the 8-mi wooded canyon. At **Inscription Rock**, about 2 mi down the road, frontiersman Kit Carson engraved his name in stone. There are several picnic spots in the canyon.

FIRST MESA

❷ *11 mi west of Keams Canyon, on AZ 264.*
★

First Mesa villages are renowned for their polychrome pottery and kachina-doll carvings. The first village that you approach is Polacca; the older and more impressive villages of Hano, Sichomovi, and Walpi are at the top of the sweeping mesa. From Polacca, a paved road (off AZ 264) angles up to a parking lot near the village of Sichomovi, and to the Punsi Hall Visitor Center. You must get permission at Punsi Hall to take the guided walking tour of Hano, Sichomovi, and Walpi. Admission is by tour only, so call ahead to find out when they're offered.

The older Hopi villages have structures built of rock and adobe mortar in simple architectural style. **Hano** actually belongs to the Tewa, a New

Mexico Pueblo tribe. In 1696 the Tewa Indians sought refuge with the Hopi on First Mesa after an unsuccessful rebellion against the Spanish in the Rio Grande Valley. Today, the Tewa live close to the Hopi but maintain their own language and ceremonies. **Sichomovi** is built so close to Hano that only the residents can tell where one ends and the other begins. Constructed in the mid-1600s, this village is believed to have been built to ease overcrowding at Walpi, the highest point on the mesa. **Walpi** (☎928/737–9556), built on solid rock and surrounded by steep cliffs, frequently hosts ceremonial dances. It's the most pristine of the Hopi villages, with cliff-edge houses and vast scenic vistas. Inhabited for more than 1,100 years (dating back to 900 AD), Walpi's cliff-edge houses seem to grow out of the nearby terrain. Today, only about 10 residents occupy this settlement, which has neither electricity nor running water; one-hour guided tours of the village are available. Note that Walpi's steep terrain makes it a less than ideal destination for acrophobes. ⊠*Punsi Hall Visitor Center, First Mesa* ☎*928/737–2262* ⊡*Guided First Mesa tours $8, Walpi tours $5* ⊗*First Mesa tours Nov.–mid-Mar., daily 9:30–4; mid-Mar.–Oct., daily 9–5, except when ceremonies are being held; Walpi tours by appointment.*

SECOND MESA

❸ *8 mi southwest of First Mesa, on AZ 264.*

The Mesas are the Hopi universe, and Second Mesa is the "Center of the Universe." **Shungopavi**, the largest and oldest village on Second Mesa, which was founded by the Bear Clan, is reached by a paved road angling south off AZ 264, between the junction of AZ 87 and the Hopi Cultural Center. The villagers here make silver overlay jewelry and coil plaques. Coil plaques are woven from galleta grass and yucca and are adorned with designs of kachinas, animals, and corn. The art of making the plaques has been passed from mother to daughter for generations, and fine coil plaques have become highly sought-after collector's items. The famous Hopi snake dances (closed to the public) are held here in August during even-numbered years. Two smaller villages are off a paved road that runs north from AZ 264, about 1/5 mi east of the Hopi Cultural Center. **Mishongnovi**, the easternmost settlement, was established in the late 1600s. For permission to visit **Sipaulovi**, which was originally at the base of the mesa before being moved to its present site in 1680, call the Sipaulovi Village Community Center (☎928/737–2570).

At the **Hopi Museum and Cultural Center**, you can stop for the night (the center has a motel), learn about the people and their reservation, and eat authentic Hopi cuisine. The museum here is dedicated to preserving the Hopi traditions and to presenting those traditions to non-Hopi visitors. A gift shop sells works by local Hopi artisans at reasonable prices, and a modest picnic area on the west side of the building is a pleasant spot for lunch with a view of the San Francisco Peaks. ⊠*AZ 264, Second Mesa* ☎*928/734–2401* ⊕*www.hopiculturalcenter. com* ⊡*Museum $3* ⊗*Mid-Mar.–Oct., weekdays 8–4:30, weekends 9–3; Nov.–mid-Mar., weekdays 8–4:30.*

THIRD MESA

4 *12 mi northwest of Second Mesa, on AZ 264.*

Third Mesa villages are known for their agricultural accomplishments, textile weaving, wicker baskets, silver overlay, and plaques. You'll find crafts shops and art galleries, as well as occasional roadside vendors, along AZ 264. The Hopi Tribal Headquarters and Office of Public Relations in Kykotsmovi should be visited first for necessary permissions to visit the villages of Third Mesa.

Kykotsmovi, at the eastern base of Third Mesa, is literally translated as "ruins on the hills" for the many sites on the valley floor and in the surrounding hills. Present-day Kykotsmovi was established by Hopi people from Oraibi—a few miles west—who either converted to Christianity or who wished to attend school and be educated. Kykotsmovi is the seat of the Hopi Tribal Government.

Old Oraibi, a few miles west and on top of Third Mesa at about 7,200 feet in elevation, is believed to be the oldest continuously inhabited community in the United States, dating from around AD 1150. It was also the site of a rare, bloodless conflict between two groups of the Hopi people; in 1906, a dispute, settled uniquely by a "push of war" (a pushing contest), sent the losers off to establish the town of Hotevilla. Oraibi is a dusty spot, and, as an act of courtesy, tourists are asked to park their cars outside and approach the village on foot.

Hotevilla and **Bacavi** are about 4 mi west of Oraibi, and their inhabitants are descended from the former residents of that village. The men of Hotevilla continue to plant crops and beautiful gardens along the mesa slopes. ⊠ *Cultural Preservation Office, AZ 264* ☎ *Box 123, Kykotsmovi 86039* ☎ *928/734–3000 or 928/734–2441* ⊕ *www.nau. edu/~hcpo-p* ☉ *Weekdays 8:30–5.*

MONUMENT VALLEY

MONUMENT VALLEY NAVAJO TRIBAL PARK

☾ *24 mi northeast of Kayenta, off U.S. 163.*

Fodor's Choice
★

For generations, the Navajo have grown crops and herded sheep in Monument Valley, considered to be one of the most scenic and mesmerizing destinations in the Navajo Nation. Within Monument Valley lies the 30,000-acre Monument Valley Navajo Tribal Park, where eons of wind and rain have carved the mammoth red-sandstone monoliths into memorable formations. The monoliths, which jut hundreds of feet above the desert floor, stand on the horizon like sentinels, frozen in time and unencumbered by electric wires, telephone poles, or fences—a scene virtually unchanged for centuries. These are the very same nostalgic images so familiar to movie buffs who recall the early Western films of John Wayne. A 17-mi self-guided driving tour on a dirt road (there's only one road, so you can't get lost) passes the memorable

Mittens and **Totem Pole** formations, among others. Drive slowly, and be sure to walk (15 minutes round-trip) from North Window around the end of Cly Butte for the views.

The **Monument Valley Visitor Center** has a small crafts shop and exhibits devoted to ancient and modern Native American history. Most of the independent guided tours here use enclosed vans and charge about $20 for 2½ hours. You can generally find Navajo guides—who will escort you to places that you are not allowed to visit on your own—in the center or through the booths in the parking lot. As of this writing, construction was underway on a new 74-room, three-story hotel and spa adjacent to the visitor center, which is slated to open in fall of 2008, just in time to celebrate the 50th anniversary of the tribal park. Both the hotel and visitor center sit on a gradual rise overlooking the valley, with big-sky views in every direction. The park also has a 99-site campground, which closes from early October through April. Call ahead for road conditions in winter. ✉*Visitor center, off U.S. 163, 24 mi north of Kayenta, Monument Valley* 🏢*Box 2520, Window Rock 86515* 🕾*435/727–5874 park visitor center, 928/871–6647 Navajo Parks & Recreation Dept.* ⊕*www.navajonationparks.org* 🎫*$5* 🕙*Visitor center May–Sept., daily 6 AM–8 PM; Mar. and Apr., daily 7–7; Oct.–Feb., daily 8–5.*

SPORTS & THE OUTDOORS

HIKING, HORSEBACK RIDING & JEEP TOURS

Jeep tours of the valley, from hour-long to overnight, can be arranged through Roland Cody Dixon at **Roland's Navajoland Tours** (🕾*520/697–3524 or 800/368–2785*); he offers cultural tours with crafts demonstrations, camping, and photography. **Sacred Monument Tours** (🕾*435/727–3218 or 928/380–4527* ⊕*www.monumentvalley.net*) has hiking, jeep, photography, and horseback-riding tours into Monument Valley. **Simpson's Trailhandler Tours** (🕾*435/727–3362* ⊕*www. trailhandlertours.com*) offers four-wheel-drive jeep tours as well as photography and hiking tours. **Totem Pole Tours** (🕾*435/727–3313 or 866/422–8687* ⊕*www.moab-utah.com/totempole*) offers jeep tours, some including entertainment and outdoor barbecues.

OFF THE BEATEN PATH

Four Corners Monument. An inlaid brass plaque marks the only point in the United States where four states meet: Arizona, New Mexico, Colorado, and Utah. Despite the Indian wares and booths selling greasy food, there's not much else to do here but pay a fee and stay long enough to snap a photo; you'll see many a twisted tourist trying to get an arm or a leg in each state. The monument is a 75-mi drive from Kayenta and is administered by the Navajo Nation Parks & Recreation Department. ✉*7 mi northwest of the U.S. 160 and U.S. 64 junction, Teec Nos Pos* 🕾*928/871–6647 Navajo Parks & Recreation Dept.* ⊕*www.navajonationparks.org* 🎫*$3* 🕙*Oct.–May, daily 8–5; June–Sept., daily 7 AM–8 PM.*

NAVAJO NATIONAL MONUMENT

Fodor'sChoice   *53 mi southwest of Goulding's Trading Post, 21 mi west of Kayenta.*
★   *From Kayenta, take U.S. 160 southwest to AZ 564, and follow signs 9 mi north to monument.*

At the Navajo National Monument, two unoccupied 13th-century cliff pueblos, Betatakin and Keet Seel, stand under the overhanging cliffs of Tsegi Canyon. The largest ancient dwellings in Arizona, these stone-and-mortar complexes were built by Ancestral Puebloans, obviously for permanent occupancy, but abandoned after less than half a century.

The well-preserved, 135-room **Betatakin** (Navajo for "ledge house") is a cluster of cliff dwellings that seem to hang in midair before a sheer sandstone wall. When discovered in 1907 by a passing American rancher, the apartments were full of baskets, pottery, and preserved grains and ears of corn—as if the occupants had been chased away in the middle of a meal. For an impressive view of Betatakin, walk to the rim overlook about ½ mi from the visitor center. Ranger-led tours (a 5-mi, four-hour, strenuous round-trip hike including a 700-foot descent into the canyon) leave once a day from late May to early September at 8 AM and return between noon and 1 PM. No reservations are accepted; groups of no more than 25 form on a first-come, first-served basis.

Keet Seel (Navajo for "broken pottery") is also in good condition in a serene location, with 160 rooms and five kivas. Explorations of Keet Seel, which lies at an elevation of 7,000 feet and is 8½ mi from the visitor center by foot, are restricted: only 20 people are allowed to visit per day, and only between late May and early September, when a ranger is present at the site. A permit—which also allows campers to stay overnight nearby—is required. ■ TIP→ Trips to Keet Seel are very popular, so reservations are taken up to two months in advance. Anyone who suffers from vertigo might want to avoid this trip: the trail leads down a 1,100-foot near-vertical rock face.

The **visitor center** houses a small museum, exhibits of prehistoric pottery, and a good crafts shop. Free campground and picnic areas are nearby, and rangers sometimes present campfire programs in summer. ⊠ *AZ 564, Black Mesa* ⊕ *HC 71, Box 3, Tonalea 86044* ☎ *928/672-2700* ⊕ *www.nps.gov/nava* ☜ *Free* ☉ *Apr.–Oct., weekdays 8–5, weekends 8–7; Nov.–Mar., daily 9–5; tours late May–early Sept.*

SPORTS & THE OUTDOORS

HIKING   Hiking is the best way for adventurous souls to see Keet Seel at the Navajo National Monument. It's a fairly strenuous hike to the sites, but if you're fit and leave early enough, it's well worth it to visit some of the best-preserved ancient dwellings in the Southwest. It's free, but the trail is open only from late May through early September, and you need to call ahead to make a reservation, usually at least two months in advance. ⊕ *Navajo National Monument, HC 71, Box 3, Tonalea 86044* ☎ *928/672-2366* ☜ *Free* ☉ *Apr.–Oct., weekdays 8–5, weekends 8–7; tours late May–early Sept.*

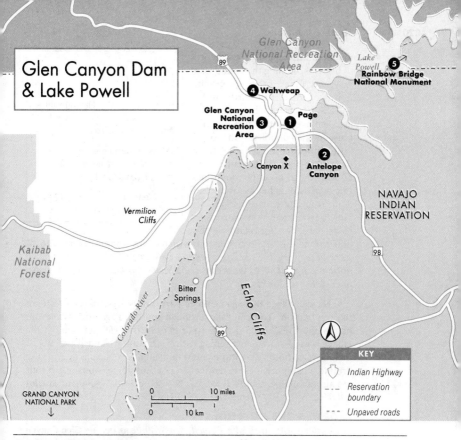

GLEN CANYON DAM & LAKE POWELL

PAGE

1 *90 mi west of the Navajo National Monument, 136 mi north of Flagstaff on U.S. 89.*

Built in 1957 as a Glen Canyon Dam construction camp, Page is now a tourist spot and a popular base for day trips to Lake Powell; it has also become a major point of entry to the Navajo Nation. The nearby Vermilion Cliffs are where the California condor, an endangered species, has been successfully reintroduced into the wild. The town's human population of nearly 7,100 makes it the largest community in far-northern Arizona, and most of the motels, restaurants, and shopping centers are concentrated along **Lake Powell Boulevard,** the name given to U.S. 89 as it loops through the business district. Each year, more than 3 million people come to play at Lake Powell.

At the corner of North Navajo Drive and Lake Powell Boulevard is the **John Wesley Powell Memorial Museum,** whose namesake led the first known expeditions down the Green River and the rapids-choked Colorado through the Grand Canyon between 1869 and 1872. Powell mapped and kept detailed records of his trips, naming the Grand Canyon and many other geographic points of interest in northern Arizona. Artifacts from his expeditions are displayed in the museum. The museum also doubles as the town's visitor information center. A travel desk dispenses information and allows you to book boating tours, raft trips, scenic flights, accommodations in Page, or Antelope Canyon tours. When you sign up for tours here, concessionaires give a donation to the nonprofit museum with no extra charge to you. ⊠6 N. Lake Powell Blvd. ☎928/645–9496 or 888/597–6873 ⊕www.powell museum.org ⊠$5 ⊙ Weekdays 9–5, Memorial Day–Labor Day also open Sat., call for hrs.

> ### LAKE POWELL FAST FACTS
>
> Lake Powell is 185 mi long with 2,000 mi of shoreline—longer than America's Pacific coast.
>
> This is the second-largest man-made lake in the nation and it took 17 years to fill.
>
> The Glen Canyon Dam is a 710-foot-tall wall of concrete.

The **Navajo Village Heritage Center** imparts an understanding of life on the reservation. You can take a guided tour of a traditional Navajo hogan and bread oven. For $55 per person (or $150 per family), the village hosts a 3½-hour "Evening with the Navajo–Grand Tour," which includes two hours of cultural entertainment and a Navajo taco dinner around a campfire. Less extensive (and expensive) versions of the tour are also available. ⊠531 Haul Rd. ☎928/660–0304 ⊕www.navajo-village.com ⊠$5 ⊙ Apr.–Oct., daily 10–3.

SPORTS & THE OUTDOORS

For water sports on Lake Powell, see Wahweap below. **Glen Canyon Recreation Area** (☎928/608–6200 ⊕www.nps.gov/glca) has a helpful Web site.

AIR TOURS   Page-based **American Aviation** (☎928/608–1060 or 866/525–3247 ⊕www.americanaviationwest.com) offers flightseeing tours of Monument Valley, Lake Powell and Rainbow Bridge, and Bryce.

FLOAT TRIPS   **Colorado River Discovery** (☎888/522–6644 ⊕www.raftthecanyon.com) offers waterborne tours, including a 5½-hour guided rafting excursion down a calm portion of the Colorado River on comfortable, motorized pontoon boats ($70). The scenery—multicolor-sandstone cliffs adorned with Native American petroglyphs—is spectacular. The trips are offered twice daily from April through September, and once a day March and October (no tours in winter). In 2008 the company also began offering full-day rowing trips along the river, using smaller boats maneuvered by well-trained guides ($155). These trips—offered Sunday, Monday, and Wednesday—are quieter and more low-key, and provide a more intimate brush with this magnificent body of water.

HIKING   The **Horse Shoe Bend Trail** (⊠Off U.S. 89) has some steep up and down paths and a bit of deep sand to maneuver; however, the views are well worth the hike. The trail leads up to a bird's-eye view of Glen Canyon and the Colorado River downstream from Glen Canyon Dam. There are some sheer drop-offs here, so watch children. To reach the trail, drive 4 mi south of Page on U.S. 89 and turn west onto a blacktop road 1/5 mi south of mile marker 545. It's a ¾-mi hike from the parking area to the top of the canyon.

WHERE TO EAT

★ $–$$ ✕**Dam Bar and Grille.** The Grille's vaguely industrial-looking decor is quite urbane for this part of the world, and the kitchen turns out filling, well-prepared food. Consider the 8-ounce cowboy steak topped with sautéed mushrooms and Swiss cheese, the smoked baby back ribs, the lobster salad, or the burger topped with bacon and cheddar. The Dam comprises a whole complex of establishments that also includes a sushi bar, coffeehouse, and nightclub. ⊠*644 N. Navajo Dr.* ☎*928/645–2161* ☰*AE, MC, V.*

$–$$ ✕**Fiesta Mexicana.** From the faux village-plaza decor, carved-wood booths, and piped-in mariachi music, this festive downtown eatery feels entirely predictable but quite pleasant. Part of a regional chain of Four Corners Mexican restaurants, Fiesta Mexicana prepares a nice range of traditional favorites, including particularly good chicken fajitas and massive margaritas. Dine on the covered patio for the best people-watching. ⊠*201 S. Lake Powell Blvd.* ☎*928/645–3999* ☰*AE, D, MC, V.*

WHERE TO STAY

★$ 🏨**Canyon Colors B&B.** Run by personable New England transplants Bev and Rich Jones, this desert-country B&B occupies a simple, modern house in a quiet residential neighborhood near downtown. The Sunflower and Paisley rooms, which can accommodate three and two, respectively, have queen beds and wood-burning stoves. The B&B also has an extensive video library, including many videos of Lake Powell and the Navajo Nation. **Pros:** Personal attention, peaceful setting, central location. **Cons:** Very small, need to book well ahead in summer. ⊠*225 S. Navajo Dr.* ⊡*Box 3657, 86040* ☎*928/645–5979 or 800/536–2530* ⊕*www.canyoncolors.com* ➘*2 rooms* ♤*In-room: refrigerator, VCR. In-hotel: public Internet, pool, no elevator* ☰*AE, MC, V* ⦿*BP.*

★$ 🏨**Days Inn & Suites.** Although part of an uneven chain of low-frills motels, the Page Days Inn is first-rate among budget-friendly properties in the region. The attractive Southwest-style building sits atop a plateau with expansive views of the region, although it doesn't directly view Lake Powell. Rooms are plainly furnished but have large windows or doors opening to small balconies. **Pros:** Many rooms have balconies, super-friendly staff, panoramic views. **Cons:** Need a car to get to downtown shopping and restaurants, rooms look rather ordinary, on a busy road at edge of town. ⊠*961 N. U.S. 89,* ☎*928/645–2800 or 877/525–3769* ⊕*www.daysinn.net* ➘*82 rooms* ♤*In-room: refrigerator, Wi-Fi. In-hotel: pool, some pets allowed* ☰*AE, D, MC, V* ⦿*CP.*

6

ANTELOPE CANYON

❷ *4 mi east of Page on the Navajo Reservation, on AZ 98.*
★

You've probably seen dozens of photographs of Antelope Canyon, a narrow, red-sandstone slot canyon with convoluted corkscrew formations, dramatically illuminated by light streaming down from above. And you're likely to see assorted shutterbugs waiting patiently for just the right shot of these colorful, photogenic rocks, which are actually petrified sand dunes of a prehistoric ocean that once filled this portion of North America. The best photos are taken at high noon, when light filters through the slot in the canyon surface. This is one place that you'll need to protect your camera equipment against blowing dust. Access to the canyon is limited to those on licensed tours. ✉ *AZ 98, Page* ✒ *Box 2520, Window Rock 86515* ☎ *928/871–6647 Navajo Parks & Recreation Dept.* ⊕ *www.navajonationparks.org* ✑ *$6, included in tour cost.*

ANTELOPE CANYON TOURS

Access to Antelope Canyon is restricted by the Navajo Tribe to licensed tour operators. The tribe charges a $6 per-person fee, included in the price of tours offered by the licensed concessionaires in Page. The easiest way to book a tour is in town at the John Wesley Powell Memorial Museum Visitor Center; you pay nothing extra for the museum's service. If you'd like to go directly to the tour operators, you can do that, too; visit ⊕ *www.navajonationparks.org/htm/antelopecanyon.htm* for a list of approved companies. Most companies offer 1½-hour sightseeing tours for about $25 to $30, or longer photography tours for $50. The best time to see the canyon is between 8 AM and 2 PM.

Antelope Canyon Adventures (☎ *928/645–5501 or 866/645–5501* ⊕ *www.jeeptour.com*) offers 1½-hour sightseeing tours and 2-hour photography tours.

Antelope Canyon Tours (☎ *928/645–9102 or 866/645–9102* ⊕ *www. antelopecanyon.com*) offers several tours daily from 8 AM to 3 PM for sightseers and photographers. The photo tour gives serious and amateur photographers the opportunity to wait for the right light to photograph the canyon and get basic information on equipment setup.

John Wesley Powell Memorial Museum Visitor Center (☎ *928/645–9496* ⊕ *www.powellmuseum.org*) arranges and books 1½-hour tours and 2-hour photography tours. Photo tours leave from Page at 8 and 9:30 AM and return about 2 PM. The shorter sightseeing tours leave frequently between 8 AM and 4 PM.

Overland Canyon Tours (☎ *928/608–4072* ⊕ *www.overlandcanyontours.com*) is one of only a few Native American–operated tour companies in Page. Tours include a narrative explaining the canyon's history and geology.

CANYON X   On private property, the isolated slot canyon known as Canyon X can
TOURS   be toured only by Navajo guide Harley Klemm and his company, Overland Canyon Tours, which also operates popular tours to Antelope

Canyon. Only one tour is given per day—departure times vary—and tours are offered by advance reservation only, with a limit of six participants. Because the area is rugged, children are not allowed, and participants should have good physical mobility to climb crevasses and some rough terrain.

GLEN CANYON NATIONAL RECREATION AREA

❸ Once you leave the Page business district heading northwest, the Glen Canyon Dam and Lake Powell behind it immediately become visible. This concrete-arch dam—all 5 million cubic feet of it—was completed in September 1963, its power plant an engineering feat that rivaled the Hoover Dam. The dam's crest is 1,560 feet across and rises 710 feet from bedrock and 583 feet above the waters of the Colorado River. When Lake Powell is full, it's 560 feet deep at the dam. The plant generates some 1.3 million kilowatts of electricity when each generator's 40-ton shaft is producing nearly 200,000 horsepower. Power from the dam serves a five-state grid consisting of Colorado, Arizona, Utah, California, and New Mexico and provides energy for some 1.5 million users.

With only 8 inches of annual rainfall, the Lake Powell area enjoys blue skies nearly year-round. Summer temperatures range from the 60s to the 90s. Fall and spring are usually balmy, with daytime temperatures often in the 70s and 80s, but chilly weather can set in. Nights are cool even in the summer, and in winter the risk of a cold spell increases, but all-weather houseboats and tour boats make for year-round cruising.

Just off the highway at the north end of the bridge is the **Carl Hayden Visitor Center,** where you can learn about the controversial creation of Glen Canyon Dam and Lake Powell and enjoy panoramic views of both. To enter the visitor center, you must go through a metal detector. Absolutely no bags are allowed inside. ⊠ *U.S. 89, 2 mi west of town, Page* ☎928/608–6404 ⊕*www.nps.gov/glca* ☜*$15 per vehicle or $7 per person (entering on foot or by bicycle), good for up to 7 days, $16 per week boating fee* ☉ *Visitor center June–Aug., daily 8–6; Sept.–Nov. and Mar.–May, daily 8–5; Dec.–Feb., daily 8–4.*

WAHWEAP

❹ *5 mi north of Glen Canyon Dam on U.S. 89.*

Most waterborne-recreational activity on the Arizona side of the lake is centered on this vacation village, where everything needed for a lakeside holiday is available: tour boats, fishing, boat rentals, dinner cruises, and more. The Lake Powell Resort has excellent views of the lake area and you can take a boat tour from the Wahweap Marina. Keep in mind that you must pay the Glen Canyon National Recreation Area entry fee (see above) upon entering Wahweap—this is true even if you're just passing through or having a meal at Lake Powell Resort.

❺ A boat tour to **Rainbow Bridge National Monument** is a great way to see the enormity of the lake and its incredible, rugged beauty. This 290-foot red-sandstone arch is the world's largest natural bridge and can be reached by boat or strenuous hike *(⇨See Hiking)*. The lake level is down due to the prolonged drought throughout the region, so expect a 1½-mi hike from the boat dock to the monument. The bridge can also be viewed by air. To the Navajos, this is a sacred area with deep religious and spiritual significance, so outsiders are asked not to hike underneath the arch itself. ☎928/608–6200 ⊕*www.nps.gov/rabr.*

SPORTS & THE OUTDOORS

BOAT TOURS   Excursions on double-decker scenic cruisers piloted by experienced guides leave from the dock of **Lake Powell Resort** (⊠*100 Lake Shore Dr., Wahweap* ☎928/645–2433 *or* 800/528–6154). The most popular tour is the full-day trip to Rainbow Bridge National Monument for $124 (a box lunch is included). There's also a 2½-hour sunset dinner cruise ($84) featuring a prime-rib dinner—vegetarian lasagna meals are available if ordered in advance. It's served on the fully enclosed decks of the 95-foot *Canyon King* paddle wheeler, a reproduction of a 19th-century bay boat.

BOATING   One of the most scenic lakes of the American West, Lake Powell has 186 mi of clear sapphire waters edged with vast canyons of red and orange rock. Ninety-six major side canyons intricately twist and turn into the main channel of Lake Powell, into what was once the main artery of the Colorado River through Glen Canyon. In some places the lake is 500 feet deep, and by June the lake's waters begin to warm and stay that way well into October.

An $80 million project begun in 2003 and under construction in four phases, **Antelope Point Marina** (⊘*BIA Hwy. N22B, Mile Marker 4, Navajo Nation 86040* ☎602/952–0114 ⊕ *www.antelopepointlakepowell.com*) will include a Navajo Cultural Center, artist studios, more than 300 wet slips for houseboats and watercraft, a floating marina village and restaurant, and 225 luxury casitas. As of this writing, the first two phases (infrastructure and the marina village) had been completed; the luxury casitas and cultural center are slated to open in 2010. At **Aramark's Lake Powell Resorts & Marinas** (☎928/645–1004 *or* 800/528–6154 ⊕*www.visitlakepowell.com*) houseboat rentals range widely in size, amenities, and price, depending upon season. *For more information on houseboats, see Houseboating in Where to Stay & Eat, below.* You may want to rent a powerboat or personal watercraft along with a houseboat to explore the many narrow canyons and waterways on the lake. A 19-foot powerboat for eight passengers runs approximately $380 and up per day. **Stateline Marina** (⊠*U.S. 89, State Line, UT* ☎928/645–1111), 1½ mi north of Lake Powell Resort, is part of

Aramark's Lake Powell Resorts & Marinas and site of the boat-rental office. It's here that you pick up rental houseboats, powerboats, kayaks, Jet Skis, and personal watercraft. There's also a public launch ramp if you're towing your own boat. **Wahweap Marina** (⊠ *100 Lake Shore Dr., Wahweap* ☎ *928/645–2433*) is the largest of the four full-service Lake Powell marinas run by Aramark's Lake Powell Resorts & Marinas. There are 850 slips and the most facilities, including a decent diner, public launch ramp, fishing dock, and a marina store where you can buy fishing licenses and other necessities. It's the only full-service marina on the Arizona side of the lake (the other three—Hite, Bullfrog, and Halls Crossing—are in Utah).

WHERE TO STAY & EAT

$$–$$$ ✗ **Rainbow Room.** The bi-level signature restaurant at the Lake Powell Resort occupies a cavernous round room affording 270-degree views of the lake, surrounding vermilion cliffs, and massive Navajo Mountain in the distance. Serving the best food in the region, the kitchen focuses on organic, healthful ingredients in producing such toothsome dishes as a Southwestern Cobb salad with crispy chicken, fire-roasted chiles, and smoked jalapeño-buttermilk dressing, and blue-corn-crusted pan-seared trout with pine-nut butter. ⊠ *100 Lake Shore Dr., 7 mi north of Page off U.S. 89, Wahweap* ☎ *928/645–2433* ▤ *AE, D, DC, MC, V.*

$$–$$$ ▦ **Lake Powell Resort.** This sprawling property consisting of several
Fodor$Choice one- and two-story buildings, run by Aramark, sits on a promontory
★ above Lake Powell and serves as the center for recreational activities in the area. The brightly colored Southwestern-style suites in the newest building are particularly attractive, and most have wonderful lake view. Restaurants include the airy Rainbow Room, a coffeehouse, and a seasonal pizza parlor. **Pros:** Stunning lake setting, couldn't be closer to the water, nice range of restaurants. **Cons:** Rooms aren't especially fancy, it can be a long way from your room to the restaurant and lobby. ⊠ *100 Lake Shore Dr., 7 mi north of Page off U.S. 89, Wahweap* ✉ *Box 1597, Page 86040* ☎ *928/645–2433 or 800/528–6154* ⊕ *www.lakepowell.com* ⇗ *350 rooms* ♿ *In-room: refrigerator. In-hotel: 3 restaurants, bar, pools, some pets allowed* ▤ *AE, D, DC, MC, V.*

NORTHEAST ARIZONA ESSENTIALS

To research prices, get advice from other travelers, and book travel arrangements, visit ⊕ *www.fodors.com.*

TRANSPORTATION

BY AIR

The only airline that offers service directly to northeastern Arizona is Great Lakes Aviation, which flies into Page Municipal Airport from Phoenix as well as Denver (with a stop in Farmington, New Mexico).

Contacts **Great Lakes Aviation** (☎ *800/554–5111* ⊕ *www.greatlakesav.com*). **Page Municipal Airport** (☎ *928/645–4337* ⊕ *www.cityofpage.org/airport.htm*).

BY BUS

In the unlikely event you end up in this part of the world without a car, bus travel is an option, albeit a not particularly practical one. The Navajo Transit System has extensive, fixed routes throughout the Navajo Reservation. The buses are modern, in good condition, and generally on time, but they do not make frequent runs, and when they do run they can be slow. Fares range from 70¢ for local rides to a high of $13.95 (Window Rock to Tuba City). This can be an up-close-and-personal way to travel through the Navajo Nation and meet the people who live here as they go about their daily business.

Contacts **Navajo Transit System** (☎ *928/729–4002* ⊕ *www.navajotransit.com*).

BY TRAIN

No passenger trains enter the Navajo or Hopi Reservation or stop at any of the other towns along its perimeter, but Amtrak calls on Winslow and Flagstaff, from which you can rent a car to explore the region.

VISITOR INFORMATION

Information **Glen Canyon Recreation Area** (☎ *928/608–6200* ⊕ *www.nps. gov/glca*). **Inter Tribal Council of Arizona: Hopi Tribe** (☎ *928/734–3000* ⊕ *www.itcaonline.com/tribes_hopi.html*). **Navajo Nation Tourism Office** (☎ *928/810–8501* ⊕ *www.discovernavajo.com*). **Page/Lake Powell Chamber of Commerce** (✉ *Box 727, 86040* ☎ *928/645–2741 or 888/261–7243* ⊕ *www. pagelakepowelltourism.com*).

Tucson

WITH SAGUARO NATIONAL PARK

WORD OF MOUTH

"If you want nightlife and shopping, go to Phoenix. If you want quiet, laid-back, beautiful surroundings with fabulous hiking opportunities, try Tucson."
—tucsonartist

"Sabino Canyon, the Desert Museum, St. Xavier Mission, and ballgames are all good local activities."
—CollegeMom

Updated by
Mara Levin

The Old Pueblo, as Tucson is affectionately known, is built upon a deep Native American, Spanish, Mexican, and Old West foundation. Arizona's second-largest city is both a bustling center of business and a relaxed university and resort town. Metropolitan Tucson has more than 850,000 residents, including thousands of snowbirds who flee colder climes to enjoy the sun that shines on the city more than 340 days out of 365.

The city has a tri-cultural (Hispanic, Anglo, Native American) population, and the chance to see how these cultures interact—and to sample their cuisines—is one of the pleasures of a visit. The city is particularly popular among golfers, but the area's many hiking trails will keep nonduffers busy, too. If the weather is too hot to stay outdoors comfortably, museums like the Arizona State Museum and the Center for Creative Photography offer a cooler alternative.

This college town has Mexican and Native American cultural influences, a striking landscape, and all the amenities of a resort town, as well as its fair share of ubiquitous strip malls and tract-home developments. High-tech industries have moved into the area, but the economy still relies heavily on tourism and the university—although, come summer, you'd never guess; when the snowbirds and students depart, Tucson can be a sleepy place.

EXPLORING TUCSON

The metropolitan Tucson area covers more than 500 square mi in a valley ringed by mountains—the Santa Catalinas to the north, the Santa Ritas to the south, the Rincons to the east, and the Tucson Mountains to the west. Saguaro National Park bookends Tucson, with one section on the far east side and the other out west near the world-class Arizona-Sonora Desert Museum. The central portion of the city has most of the shops, restaurants, and businesses, but not many tourist sights. Downtown's historical district and the neighboring University area are much smaller and easily navigated on foot. Up north in the Catalina Foothills, you'll find first-class resorts, restaurants, and hiking trails, most with spectacular views of the entire valley.

The central portion of Tucson—which has most of the shops, restaurants, and businesses—is roughly bounded by Craycroft Road to the east, Oracle Road to the west, River Road to the north, and 22nd Street to the south. The older downtown section, east of Interstate 10 off the Broadway-Congress exit, is smaller and easy to navigate on foot. Streets downtown don't run on any sort of grid, however, and many are one way, so it's best to get a good, detailed map. The city's Westside area is the vast region west of Interstate 10 and Interstate 19, which includes the western section of Saguaro National Park and the San Xavier Indian Reservation.

TOP REASONS TO GO

Cacti: Unique to this region, the saguaro is the quintessential symbol of the Southwest. The best places to see them up close are Saguaro National Park and Sabino Canyon.

Mexican food: Tucson boasts that it's the "Mexican Food Capital," and you won't be disappointed at any of the Mexican restaurants listed in this chapter.

The Arizona-Sonora Desert Museum: Anyone who thinks that museums are boring hasn't been here, where you can learn about the wildlife, plants, and geology of the region in a gorgeous, mostly out-door, setting.

Mission San Xavier del Bac: The "White Dove of the Desert" is the oldest building in Tucson. Ornate carvings and frescoes inside add to the mystical quality of this active parish on the Tohono O'odham reservation.

Strolling the U of A campus: Stop in at one of the five museums, then stroll University Boulevard and 4th Avenue for a taste of Tucson's hipper element.

DOWNTOWN

El Presidio Historic District, north of the Convention Center and the government buildings that dominate downtown, is an architectural thumbnail of the city's former self. The north–south streets Court, Meyer, and Main are sprinkled with traditional Mexican adobe houses sitting cheek by jowl with territorial-style houses, with wide attics and porches. Paseo Redondo, once called Snob Hollow, is the wide road along which wealthy merchants built their homes. The area most closely resembling 19th-century Tucson is the **Barrio Historico,** also known as Barrio Viejo. The narrow streets of this neighborhood, including Convent Avenue, have a good sampling of thick-wall adobe houses. The houses are close to the street, hiding the yards and gardens within. To the east of the Barrio Historico, across Stone Avenue, is the **Armory Park** neighborhood, mostly constructed by and for the railroad workers who settled here after the 1880s. The brick or wood territorial-style homes here were the Victorian era's adaptation to the desert climate.

Numbers in the text correspond to numbers in the margin and on the What to See in Downtown Tucson map.

❶ **"A" Mountain.** The original name of this mountain, Sentinel Peak, west of downtown came from its function as a lookout point for the Spanish, though the Pima village and cultivated fields that once lay at the base of the peak are long gone. In 1915 fans of the University of Arizona football team whitewashed a large "A" on its side to celebrate a victory, and the tradition has been kept up ever since—the permanent "A" is now red, white, and blue. During the day, the peak's a great place to get an overview of the town's layout; at night the city lights below form a dazzling carpet, but the teenage hangout–make-out scene may make some uncomfortable. ⌧ *Congress St. on Sentinel Peak Rd., Downtown.*

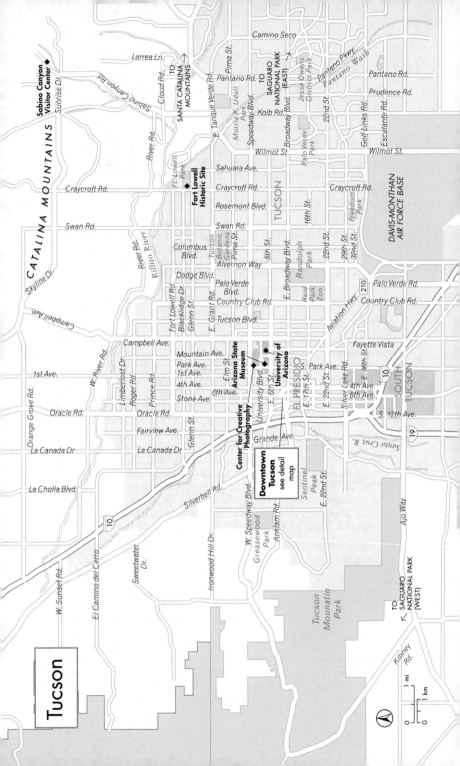

❷ El Tiradito (The Castaway). No one seems to know the details of the story behind this little shrine, but everyone agrees a tragic love triangle was involved. A bronze plaque indicates only that it's dedicated to a sinner who is buried here on unconsecrated ground. The candles that line the cactus-shrouded spot attest to its continuing importance in local Catholic lore. People light candles and leave *milagros* (miracles; little icons used in prayers for healing) for loved ones. A modern-day miracle: the shrine's inclusion on the National Register of Historic Places helped prevent a freeway from plowing through this section of the Barrio Historico. ⊠ *Main Ave. south of Cushing St., Downtown.*

❺ Pima County Courthouse. This Spanish colonial–style building with a mosaic-tile dome is among Tucson's most beautiful historic structures. Still in use, it was built in 1927 on the site of the original single-story adobe court of 1869; a portion of the old presidio wall can be seen in the south wing of the courthouse's second floor. At the side of the building, the county assessor's office has a diorama depicting the area's early days. ⊠ *115 N. Church Ave., between Alameda and Pennington Sts., Downtown* ⊕ *www.jp.co.pima.az.us* ⊠ *Free* ☉ *Weekdays 8–4:30, Sat. 8–noon.*

❸ Tucson Children's Museum. Youngsters are encouraged to touch and
☙ explore the science, language, and history exhibits here. They can key in on Little Tikes IBM computers or shop for healthy food in the Wellness Town Grocery Store. Dinosaur Canyon has mechanical prehistoric creatures, and there's an Enchanted Forest where toddlers can climb, build, and burn off steam. ⊠ *200 S. 6th Ave., Downtown* ☎ *520/792–9985* ⊕ *www.tucsonchildrensmuseum.org* ⊠ *$7* ☉ *Tues.–Sat. 10–5, Sun. noon–5.*

❹ Tucson Museum of Art and Historic Block. The five historic buildings on this
★ block are listed in the National Register of Historic Places. You can enter La Casa Cordova, the Stevens Home, the J. Knox Corbett House, and the Edward Nye Fish House but the Romero House, believed to incorporate a section of the presidio wall, is not open to the public. In the center of the museum complex, connecting the modern buildings to the surrounding historic houses, is the Plaza of the Pioneers, honoring Tucson's early citizens. The museum building, the only modern structure of the complex, houses a permanent collection of modern and contemporary art and hosts traveling shows.

Permanent and changing exhibitions of Western art fill the **Edward Nye Fish House,** an 1868 adobe that belonged to an early merchant, entrepreneur, and politician, and his wife. The building is notable for its 15-foot beamed ceilings and saguaro cactus–rib supports. There are free docent tours of the museum, and you can pick up a self-guided tour map of the El Presidio district. **La Casa Cordova,** one of the oldest buildings in Tucson, is also one of the best local examples of a Sonoran row house. This simple but elegant design is a Spanish style adapted to adobe construction. The oldest section of La Casa Cordova, constructed around 1848, has been restored to its original appearance and is the Mexican Heritage Museum. Furnishings of the Native American

7

"A" Mountain
(Sentinel Peak) . **1**

El Tiradito
(The
Castaway) **2**

Pima County
Courthouse **5**

Tucson
Children's
Museum **3**

Tucson
Museum
of Art and Historic
Block **4**

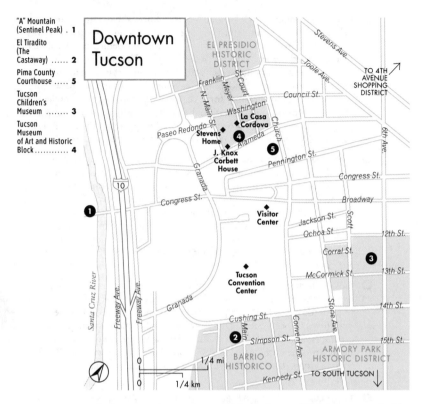

and pioneer settlers and an exhibit on the presidio's history are inside. The **J. Knox Corbett House** was built in 1906–07, and occupied by members of the Corbett family until 1963. The original occupants were J. Knox Corbett, successful businessman, postmaster, and mayor of Tucson, and his wife Elizabeth Hughes Corbett, an accomplished musician and daughter of Tucson pioneer Sam Hughes. Tucson's Hi Corbett field (the spring training field for the Colorado Rockies) is named for their grandnephew, Hiram. The two-story, Mission Revival–style residence has been furnished with Arts and Crafts pieces: Stickley, Roycroft, Tiffany, and Morris are among the more famous manufacturers represented. The **Stevens Home** was where the wealthy politician and cattle rancher Hiram Stevens and his Mexican wife, Petra Santa Cruz, entertained many of Tucson's leaders during the 1800s. A drought brought the Stevens's cattle ranching to a halt in 1893 and Stevens killed himself in despair after unsuccessfully attempting to shoot his wife (the bullet was deflected by the comb she wore in her hair). The 1865 house was restored in 1980 and now houses the Tucson Museum of Art's permanent collections of pre-Columbian, Spanish colonial, and Latin American folk art. Admission to the museum and all four homes is free on the first Sunday of every month. ■TIP→**There's free parking in a lot behind the museum at Washington and Meyer streets.**

⊠140 N. Main Ave., Downtown ☏*520/624–2333* ⊕*www.Tucson-MuseumofArt.org* ⊠*$8* ⊘*Tues.–Sat. 10–4, Sun. noon–4. Guided tours Oct.–May, Tues.–Sun.*

▌ NEED A
BREAK?

On the patio of the Stevens Home, part of the Tucson Museum of Art and Historic Block, **Cafe A La C'Arte** (⊠*150 N. Main Ave., Downtown* ☏*520/628–8533*) serves fanciful salads, soups, and sandwiches on weekdays from 11 to 3.

THE UNIVERSITY OF ARIZONA

The U of A (as opposed to rival ASU, in Tempe) is a major economic influence in Tucson, with a student population of more than 34,000. The land for the university was "donated" by a couple of gamblers and a saloon owner in 1891—their benevolence reputedly inspired by a bad hand of cards—and $25,000 of territorial (Arizona was still a territory back then) money was used to build Old Main, the original building, and hire six faculty members. Money ran out before Old Main's roof was placed, but a few enlightened citizens pitched in funds to finish it. Most of the city's populace was less than enthusiastic about the institution: they were disgruntled when the 13th Territorial Legislature granted the University of Arizona to Tucson and awarded Phoenix what was considered the real prize—an insane asylum and a prison.

The university's flora is impressive—it represents a collection of plants from arid and semiarid regions around the world. An extremely rare mutated, or "crested," saguaro grows at the northeast corner of the Old Main building. The long, grassy Mall in the heart of campus—itself once a vast cactus garden—sits atop a huge underground student activity center, and makes for a pleasant stroll on a balmy evening.

㊧ **Arizona Historical Society's Museum.** Flanking the entrance to the museum are statues of two men: Father Kino, the Jesuit who established San Xavier del Bac and a string of other missions, and John Greenaway, indelibly linked to Phelps Dodge, the copper-mining company that helped Arizona earn statehood in 1912. The museum houses the headquarters of the state Historical Society and has exhibits exploring the history of southern Arizona, the Southwest United States, and northern Mexico, starting with the Hohokam Indians and Spanish explorers. The harrowing "Life on the Edge: A History of Medicine in Arizona" exhibit gives a new appreciation of modern drugstores in present-day Tucson. Children enjoy the exhibit on copper mining (complete with an atmospheric replica of a mine shaft and camp) and the stagecoaches in the transportation area. The library has an extensive collection of historic Arizona photographs and sells inexpensive reprints. Admission is free on the first Saturday of every month. Park in the garage at the corner of 2nd and Euclid streets and get a free parking pass in the museum. *⊠949 E. 2nd St., University* ☏*520/628–5774* ⊕*www.arizonahistoricalsociety.org* ⊠*$5* ⊘*Tues.–Sat. 10–4; library weekdays 10–3, Sat. 10–1.*

Arizona State Museum. Inside the main gate of the university is Arizona's oldest museum, dating from territorial days (1893) and recognized as one of the world's most important resources for the study of Southwestern cultures. Exhibits in the original (south) building focus on the state's ancient history, including fossils and a fascinating sample of tree-ring dating. "Paths of Life: American Indians of the Southwest" is a permanent exhibit that explores the cultural traditions, origins, and contemporary lives of 10 native tribes of Arizona and Sonora, Mexico. ⊠*Park Ave. at University Blvd., University* ☎*520/621–6302* ⊕*www. statemuseum.arizona.edu* ⊠*Free* ☉*Mon.–Sat. 10–5, Sun. noon–5.*

★ **Center for Creative Photography.** Ansel Adams conceived the idea of a photographer's archive and donated the majority of his negatives to this museum. In addition to its superb collection of his work, the center has works by other major photographers including Paul Strand, W. Eugene Smith, Edward Weston, and Louise Dahl-Wolfe. Changing exhibits in the main gallery display selected pieces from the collection, but if you'd like to see the work of a particular photographer in the archives, call to arrange an appointment. ⊠*1030 N. Olive Rd., north of 2nd St., University* ☎*520/621–7968* ⊕*www.creativephotography. org* ⊠*Free* ☉*Weekdays 9–5, weekends noon–5.*

☾ **Flandrau Science Center and Planetarium.** Attractions include a 16-inch public telescope; the impressive Star Theatre, where a multimedia show brings astronomy to life; an interactive meteor exhibit; and a Mineral Museum, which displays more than 2,000 rocks and gems, some quite rare. Admission includes all exhibits and one planetarium show. ⊠*1601 E.University Blvd., University* ☎*520/621–4515, 520/621–7827 recorded message* ⊕*www.gotuasciencecenter.org* ⊠ *$5* ☉*Exhibits Thurs. and Fri. 9–3 and 6 PM–9 PM, Sat. noon–9, Sun. noon–5. Planetarium show times vary. Observatory Wed.–Sat. 7 PM–10 PM.*

4th Avenue. Students and counterculturists favor this ½-mi strip of 4th Avenue where vintage-clothing stores rub shoulders with ethnic eateries from Guatemalan to Greek. After dark, 4th Avenue bars pulse with live and recorded music. ⊠*Between University and 9th Sts.*

CENTRAL & EAST TUCSON

☾ **Colossal Cave Mountain Park.** This limestone grotto 20 mi east of Tucson (take Broadway Boulevard or 22nd Street East, to Colossal Cave Road) is the largest dry cavern in the world. Guides discuss the fascinating crystal formations and relate the many romantic tales surrounding the cave, including the legend that an enormous sum of money stolen in a stagecoach robbery is hidden here. Forty-five-minute cave tours begin every 30 minutes and require a ½-mi walk and climbing 363 steps. The park includes a ranch area with trail rides ($27 per hour), a gemstone-sluicing area, a small museum, nature trails, a butterfly garden, a snack bar, and a gift shop. Parking is $5 per vehicle. ⊠ *Old Spanish Trail, Eastside* ☎*520/647–7275* ⊕*www.colossalcave.com* ⊠ *$8.50* ☉*Oct.–mid-Mar., Mon.–Sat. 9–5, Sun. 9–6; mid-Mar.–Sept., Mon.–Sat. 8–6, Sun. 8–7.*

🌣 **Fort Lowell Park and Museum.** Fertile soil and proximity to the Rillito River once enticed the Hohokam to construct a village on this site. Centuries later, a fort (in operation from 1873–91) was built here to protect the fledgling city of Tucson against the Apaches. The former commanding officer's quarters has artifacts from military life in territorial days. Admission to the museum is free on the first Saturday of every month. The park has a playground, ball fields, tennis courts, and a duck pond. ✉ *2900 N. Craycroft Rd., Central* ☎ *520/885–3832* 💲 *Museum $3* ⊙ *Wed.–Sat. 10–4.*

> ### LONG LIVE ADOBE!
>
> Adobe—brick made of mud and straw, cured in the hot sun—was used widely as a building material in early Tucson because it provides natural insulation from the heat and cold and because it's durable in Tucson's dry climate. When these buildings are properly made and maintained, they can last for centuries. Driving around downtown Tucson, you'll see adobe houses painted in vibrant hues such as bright pink and canary yellow.

Pima Air and Space Museum. This huge facility ranks among the largest private collections of aircraft in the world. More than 200 airplanes are on display in hangars and outside, including a presidential plane used by both John F. Kennedy and Lyndon B. Johnson, a full-scale replica of the Wright brothers' 1903 Wright Flyer; the SR-71 reconnaissance jet; and a mock-up of the X-15, the world's fastest aircraft. World War II planes are particularly well-represented. Meander on your own or take a free walking tour of the hangars led by volunteer docents every day at 10:15. The open-air tram tour—an additional $5 fee—narrates all outside aircraft. Hour-long van tours of Aerospace Maintenance and Regeneration Center (AMARC)—affectionately called "The Boneyard"—at Davis-Monthan Air Force Base provide an eerie glimpse of hundreds of mothballed aircraft lined up in rows on a vast tract of desert. You must reserve in advance for the $6 AMARC tour, which is only available on weekdays. ✉ *6000 E. Valencia Rd., I-10, Exit 267, South* ☎ *520/574–0462* ⊕ *www.pimaair.org* 💲 *$13.50* ⊙ *Daily 9–5, last admission at 4.*

🌣 **Reid Park Zoo.** This small but well-designed zoo won't tax the children's—or your—patience. There are plenty of shady places to sit, a wonderful gift shop, and a snack bar to rev you up when your energy flags. The zoo's adorable newborns and the South American enclosure with its rain forest and exotic birds are popular. ■TIP➔**If you're visiting in summer, go early in the day when the animals are active.** The park surrounding the zoo has playground structures and a lake where you can feed ducks and rent paddleboats. ✉ *Reid Park, 1100 S. Randolph Way (off 22nd St.), Central* ☎ *520/791–3204* ⊕ *www.tucsonzoo.org* 💲 *$6* ⊙ *Daily 9–4.*

Tucson Botanical Gardens. The 5 acres are home to a variety of experiences: a tropical greenhouse; a sensory garden, where you can touch and smell the plants and listen to the abundant bird life; historical gardens that display the Mediterranean landscaping the property's original owners planted in the 1930s; a garden designed to attract birds; and a cactus garden. Other special gardens showcase wildflowers, Australian plants, and Native American crops and herbs. Call ahead to find out what's blooming. All paths are wheelchair accessible. ⊠ *2150 N. Alvernon Way, Central* ☎ *520/326–9686* ⊕ *www.tucsonbotanical.org* ⌨ *$7* ⊗ *Daily 8:30–4:30.*

CATALINA FOOTHILLS (NORTH)

★ **Sabino Canyon.** Year-round, but especially in summer, locals flock to Coronado National Forest to hike, picnic, and enjoy the waterfalls, streams, swimming holes, and shade trees. No cars are allowed, but a narrated tram ride (about 45 minutes round-trip) takes you up a WPA-built road to the top of the canyon; you can hop off and on at any of the nine stops or hike any of the numerous trails. There's also a shorter tram ride to adjacent Bear Canyon, where a much more rigorous but rewarding hike leads to the popular Seven Falls (it'll take about 1½ hours each way from the drop-off point, so carry plenty of water). If you're in Tucson near a full moon, take the special night tram and watch the desert come alive with nocturnal critters. ⊠ *Sabino Canyon Rd. at Sunrise Dr., Foothills* ☎ *520/749–2861 recorded tram information, 520/749–8700 visitor center* ⊕ *www.fs.fed.us/r3/coronado* ⌨ *$5 per vehicle; tram $3–$5* ⊗ *Visitor center weekdays 8–4:30, weekends 8:30–4:30; call for tram schedules.*

NORTHWEST TUCSON, THE WESTSIDE & THE SONORAN DESERT

☉ **Arizona–Sonora Desert Museum.** The name "museum" is a bit misleading since this delightful site is actually a beautifully planned zoo and botanical garden featuring the animals and plants of the Sonoran Desert. Hummingbirds, cactus wrens, rattlesnakes, scorpions, bighorn sheep, and prairie dogs all busy themselves in ingeniously designed habitats. An Earth Sciences Center has an artificial limestone cave and a hands-on meteor and mineral display. The coyote and javelina (wild, pig-like mammals with oddly oversized heads) exhibits have "invisible" fencing that separates humans from animals, and the Riparian Corridor section affords great underwater views of otters and beavers. The restaurants and gift shop, which carries books, jewelry and crafts, are outstanding. ⊠ *2021 N. Kinney Rd., Westside* ☎ *520/883–2702* ⊕ *www.desertmuseum.org* ⌨ *$12* ⊗ *Mar.–Sept., daily 7:30–5; Oct.–Feb., daily 8:30–5.*

Fodor's Choice

★ **Mission San Xavier del Bac.** The oldest Catholic church in the United States still serving the community for which it was built, San Xavier was founded in 1692 by Father Eusebio Francisco Kino, who established 22 missions in northern Mexico and southern Arizona. The current structure was made out of native materials by Franciscan missionaries between 1777 and 1797 and is owned by the Tohono O'odham tribe.

The beauty of the mission, with elements of Spanish, baroque, and Moorish architectural styles, is highlighted by the stark landscape against which it is set, inspiring an early-20th-century poet to dub it the White Dove of the Desert. Inside, there's a wealth of painted statues, carvings, and frescoes. Paul Schwartzbaum, who helped restore Michelangelo's masterwork in Rome, supervised Tohono O'odham artisans in the restoration of the mission's artwork, completed in 1997; Schwartzbaum has called the mission the Sistine Chapel of the United States. Mass is celebrated at 8:30 AM weekdays in the church and three times on Sunday morning. Call ahead for information about special celebrations.

In the spring and fall, those interested in visiting the area's historic missions can contact **Kino Mission Tours** (☎520/628–1269), which has professional historians and bilingual guides on staff.

Across the parking lot from the mission, San Xavier Plaza has a number of crafts shops selling the handiwork of the Tohono O'odham tribe, including jewelry, pottery, friendship bowls, and baskets with man-in-the-maze designs. ⊠1950 W. *San Xavier Rd., 9 mi southwest of Tucson on I–19, South* ☎520/294–2624 ⊕*www.sanxaviermission.org* ⊠*Free* ☉*Church daily 8–5, gift shop daily 8:30–5.*

OFF THE BEATEN PATH

Biosphere 2 Center. In the town of Oracle, about 30 minutes north of Tucson, this self-contained, closed ecosystem opened in 1991 as a facility to test nature technology and human interaction with it. The miniature world within Biosphere includes tropical rain forest, savanna, desert, thorn scrub, marsh, ocean, and agricultural areas, including almost 3,000 plant and animal species. A film and a large, rotating cutaway model in the visitor center explain the project, which included two "human missions" wherein scientists entered the ecosystem for extended periods of time—once for six months, once for two years. Guided walking tours, which last about two hours, take you inside some of the biomes, and observation areas let you peer in at the rest. A snack bar overlooks the Santa Catalina Mountains. ⊠AZ 77, Milepost 96.5, Oracle ☎520/838–6200 ⊕www.bio2.com ⊠$20 ☉Daily 9–4.

SAGUARO NATIONAL PARK

Updated by Mara Levin

   To reach the West Section of Saguaro National Park (Tucson Mountain District) from I–10, take exit 242 or exit 257, then Speedway Blvd. (the name will change to Gates Pass Rd.) west to Kinney Rd. and turn right. To reach the East Section of Saguaro (Rincon Mountain District) from I–10, take exit 257 or exit 275, then go east on Speedway Blvd. to Old Spanish Trail and turn right.

Standing sentinel in the desert, the towering saguaro is perhaps the most familiar emblem of the Southwest. Known for their height (often 50 feet) and arms reaching out in weird configurations, these slow-growing giants can take 15 years to grow a foot high and up to 75 years to grow their first arm. They are found only in the Sonoran Desert, and the largest concentration is in Saguaro National Park. In late spring (usually May), the succulent's top is covered with tiny white blooms—the Arizona state flower. The cacti are protected by state and federal laws, so don't disturb them.

Saguaro National Park preserves some of the densest stands of these massive cacti, which can live up to 200 years and weigh up to two tons. Today more than 90,000 acres include habitats stretching from the arid Sonoran Desert up to high mountain forests. The park is split into two sections, with Tucson sandwiched in the middle. Both districts are about a half-hour drive from central Tucson.

When should you go? Saguaro never gets crowded; however, most people visit in milder weather, October through April. December through February can be cool and prone to intermittent rain showers. The spring months from March through May offer bright, sunny days and desert wildflowers in bloom. Because of high temperatures, it's best to visit the park in the early morning or late afternoon from June through September. The intense heat found at lower elevations puts off most hikers, and lodging prices are much cheaper—rates at top resorts in Tucson drop by as much as 60%. The cooler temperatures from November to April are perfect for hiking and bird-watching throughout the park. ■TIP➜The wildlife, from bobcats to jackrabbits, is most active in the early morning and at dusk. In spring and summer lizards and snakes are out and about, but keep a low profile during the midday heat. ⊠*Saguaro West: 2700 N. Kinney Rd., 2 mi north of Arizona–Sonora Desert Museum entrance; Saguaro East: 3693 S. Old Spanish Trail* ☎*520/733–5158 Saguaro West, 520/733–5153 Saguaro East* ⊕*nps.gov/sagu* ☜*$10 per vehicle or $5 per person on foot or bike, good for 7 days* ☉*Visitor centers daily 9–5, park roads daily 7–sunset.*

SCENIC DRIVES Unless you're ready to lace up your hiking boots for a long desert hike, the best way to see Saguaro National Park is from the comfort of your car.

Bajada Loop Drive. This 6-mi drive winds through thick stands of saguaros and offers two picnic areas and a few short hikes, including one to a rock-art site. Although the road is unpaved and moderately bumpy, it's a worthwhile trade-off for access to some of the park's densest desert growth. It's one way between Hugh Norris Trail and Golden Gate Road, so if you want to make the complete circuit, travel counterclockwise. The road is susceptible to flash floods during the monsoon season, so check road conditions at the visitor center before proceeding. ⊠*Saguaro West.*

★ **Cactus Forest Drive.** This paved 8-mi drive provides a great overview of all Saguaro has to offer. The one-way paved road, which circles clockwise, also has several turnouts that make it easy to stop and linger over the scenery, new roadside displays, wide bicycle lanes, two picnic areas, and three easy nature trails. It's open from 7 AM to sunset daily. ⊠*Saguaro East.*

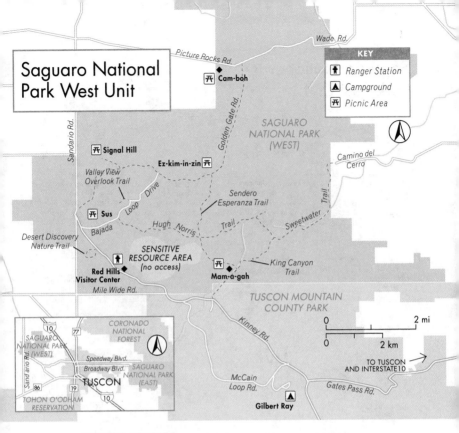

VISITOR CENTERS

Neither center serves coffee; they do sell bottled water.

Red Hills Visitor Center. Take in gorgeous views of nearby mountains and the surrounding desert from the center's large windows and shaded outdoor terrace. A spacious gallery is filled with educational exhibits, and a lifelike display simulates the flora and fauna of the region. A 15-minute slide show, "Voices of a Desert," offers a poetic, Native American perspective on the saguaro. Park rangers and volunteers provide maps and suggest hikes to suit your interests. A nicely appointed gift shop and bookstore add to the experience. ⊠*2700 N. Kinney Rd., Saguaro West* ☎*520/733–5158* ⊙*Daily 9–5.*

Saguaro East Visitor Center. Stop here to pick up free maps and printed materials on various aspects of the park, including maps of hiking trails and backcountry camping permits (Red Hills Visitor Center does not offer permits). Exhibits at the center are comprehensive, and a relief map of the park lays out the complexities of this protected landscape. A 15-minute "Home in the Desert" slide-show program gives the history of the region, and there is a short self-guided nature hike along the Cactus Garden Trail. A small, select variety of books and other gift items are sold here, too. ⊠*3693 S. Old Spanish Trail, Saguaro East* ☎*520/733–5153* ⊙*Daily 9–5.*

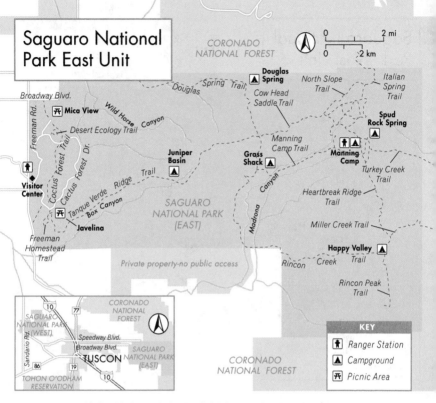

Saguaro National Park East Unit

CORONADO NATIONAL FOREST

Douglas Spring Trail

Douglas Spring ▲

Cow Head Saddle Trail

North Slope Trail

Italian Spring Trail

Broadway Blvd.

🅟 Mica View

Wild Horse Canyon

Desert Ecology Trail

Freeman Rd.

Cactus Forest Trail

Cactus Forest Dr.

Spud Rock Spring ▲

Juniper Basin ▲

Grass Shack ▲

Manning Camp Trail

🅟🅟▲ Manning Camp

Tanque Verde Ridge Trail

Box Canyon

Visitor Center ◆

Javelina 🅟

Freeman Homestead Trail

Turkey Creek Trail

SAGUARO NATIONAL PARK (EAST)

Madrona Canyon

Heartbreak Ridge Trail

Miller Creek Trail

Private property-no public access

Rincon Creek Trail

Happy Valley ▲

Rincon Peak Trail

0   2 mi
0   2 km

CORONADO NATIONAL FOREST

SAGUARO NATIONAL PARK (WEST)

10   77

Sandario Rd.

Speedway Blvd.

Broadway Blvd.

TUSCON

86   19

10

TOHON O'ODHAM RESERVATION

SAGUARO NATIONAL PARK (EAST)

CORONADO NATIONAL FOREST

KEY

🅟 Ranger Station

▲ Campground

🅟 Picnic Area

SPORTS & THE OUTDOORS

BICYCLING

Bajada Loop Drive. This 6-mi dirt road, starting north of the Red Hills Visitor Center in Saguaro West, has "washboards" worn into the ground by seasonal drainage, which make biking a challenge. You'll share the bumpy route with cars, but most of it is one way, and the views of saguaros set against the mountains are stunning. ⊠*Off Kinney Rd., 1.5 mi from Red Hills Visitor Center.*

Cactus Forest Drive. Expansive vistas of saguaro-covered hills in Saguaro East highlight this paved 8-mi loop road. Go slowly during the first few hundred yards because of an unexpectedly sharp curve. Snakes and javelinas traverse the roads. ⊠*Saguaro East Visitor Center.*

Cactus Forest Trail. Accessed from Cactus Forest Drive, the 2.5-mi trail near Saguaro East Visitor Center is a sand, single track with varied terrain. It's good for both beginning and experienced mountain bikers who don't mind sharing the path with hikers and the occasional horse, to whom bikers must yield. You'll see plenty of wildlife and older, larger saguaro alongside paloverde and mesquite trees. ⊠*1 mi south of Saguaro East Visitor Center on Cactus Forest Dr.*

CLOSE UP

East or West Saguaro?

Most visitors to Saguaro National Park choose one "side" of the park to tour, rather than both. Saguaro West, also known as the Tucson Mountain District, is the smaller, more-visited section of the park. Here you'll find a Native American video orientation to saguaros at the visitor center, hiking trails, an ancient Hohokam petroglyph site at Signal Hill, and a scenic drive through the park's densest desert growth. This section is near the Desert Museum, and many opt for combining these sights.

Saguaro East, also known as the Rincon Mountain District, is on the eastern side of Tucson in the Rincon Mountains, and encompasses 57,930 acres of designated wilderness, an easily accessible scenic loop drive, several easy and intermediate trails through the cactus forest, and opportunities for adventure and backcountry camping at six rustic campgrounds.

Also in the East part of the park is the Rincon Valley Area, a 4,011-acre expansion along the southern border of Saguaro's Rincon Mountain District with access to the area along Rincon Creek. The backcountry Saguaro Wilderness Area moves from desert scrublands at 3,000 feet to mixed conifer forests at 9,000 feet.

HIKING

EASY **Cactus Forest Trail.** This 2.5-mi one-way loop drive in the East district is open to pedestrians, bicyclists, and equestrians. It is an easy walk along a dirt path that passes historic lime kilns and a wide variety of Sonoran Desert vegetation. While walking this trail, keep in mind that it is the only off-road trail for bicyclists. ⊠*Saguaro East.*

Cactus Garden Trail. This 100-yard paved trail in front of the Red Hills Visitor Center is wheelchair accessible and has resting benches and interpretive signs about common desert plants. ⊠*Red Hills Visitor Center.*

☺ **Desert Discovery Trail.** Learn about plants and animals native to the region on this paved path in Saguaro West. The 0.5-mi loop is wheelchair accessible and has resting benches and ramadas (wooden shelters that supply shade for your table). ⊠*1 mi north of Red Hills Visitor Center.*

☺ **Desert Ecology Trail.** Exhibits on this 0.25-mi loop near the Mica View picnic area explain how local plants and animals subsist on a limited supply of water. ⊠*2 mi north of Saguaro East Visitor Center.*

☺ **Signal Hill Trail.** This 0.25-mi trail in Saguaro West is an easy, rewarding ascent to ancient petroglyphs carved a millennium ago by the Hohokam people. ⊠*4.5 mi north of Red Hills Visitor Center on Bajada Loop Dr.*

MODERATE **Douglas Spring Trail.** This challenging 6-mi trail leads almost due east into the Rincon Mountains. After a half mile through a dense concentration of saguaros you reach the open desert. About 3 mi in is Bridal Wreath Falls, worth a slight detour in early spring when melting snow creates a larger cascade. Blackened tree trunks at the Douglas Spring

7

Campground are one of the few traces of a huge fire that swept through the area in 1989. ⊠*Eastern end of Speedway Blvd., Saguaro East.*

Fodor'sChoice ★ **Hope Camp Trail.** Well worth the 5.6-mi round-trip trek, this Rincon Valley Area hike offers gorgeous views of the Tanque Verde Ridge and Rincon Peak. ⊠*From Camino Loma Alto trailhead to Hope Camp, Saguaro East.*

Sendero Esperanza Trail. You'll follow a sandy mine road for the first section of this 6-mi trail in Saguaro West, then ascend via a series of switchbacks to the top of a ridge where you'll cross the Hugh Norris Trail. Descending on the other side, you'll meet up with the King Canyon Trail. The Esperanza ("Hope") Trail is often rocky and sometimes steep, but rewards include remains of the Gould Mine, dating back to 1907. ⊠*1.5 mi east of intersection of Bajada Loop Dr. and Golden Gate Rd.*

Sweetwater Trail. In Saguaro West, this one-way trail is the only footpath with access to Wasson Peak from the eastern side of the Tucson Mountains. The trailhead is located at the. After climbing 3.4 mi it ends at King Canyon Trail. Long and meandering, this little-used trail allows more privacy to enjoy the natural surroundings than some of the more frequently used trails. ⊠ *Western end of El Camino del Cerro Rd., Saguaro West..*

Valley View Overlook Trail. On clear days you can spot the distinctive slope of Picacho Peak from this 1.5-mi trail in Saguaro West. Even on an overcast day you'll be treated to splendid vistas of Avra Valley. ⊠*3 mi north of Red Hills Visitor Center on Bajada Loop Dr.*

DIFFICULT Fodor'sChoice ★ **Hugh Norris Trail.** This 10-mi trail through the Tucson Mountains is one of the most impressive in the Southwest. It's full of switchbacks and some sections are moderately steep, but at the top of 4,687-foot Wasson Peak you'll enjoy views of the saguaro forest spread across the *bajada* (the gently rolling hills at the base of taller mountains). ⊠*2.5 mi north of Red Hills Visitor Center on Bajada Loop Dr.*

★ **Tanque Verde Ridge Trail.** Be rewarded with spectacular scenery on this 15.4-mi trail through desert scrub, oak, alligator juniper, and piñon pine at the 6,000-foot peak, where views of the surrounding mountain ranges from both sides of the ridge delight. ⊠*2 mi south of Saguaro East Visitor Center at Javelina picnic area.*

SPORTS & THE OUTDOORS

ADVENTURE & ECOTOURS

Baja's Frontier Tours (☎*520/887–2340 or 800/726–7231* ⊕*www.bajas frontiertours.com*) explores the natural and cultural history of Tucson and the surrounding area.

Southwest Trekking (⊠ *Box 57714, Tucson* ☎*520/296–9661* ⊕*www. swtrekking.com*) arranges top-notch guided mountain biking, hiking, and camping outings.

Sagauro National Park Flora & Fauna

The saguaro may be the centerpiece of Saguaro National Park, but more than 1,200 plant species, including 50 types of cactus, thrive in the park. Among the most common cacti here are the prickly pear, barrel cactus, and teddy bear cholla—so named because it appears cuddly, but rangers advise packing a comb to pull its barbed hooks from unwary fingers.

For many of the desert fauna, the saguaro functions as a high-rise hotel. Each spring, the Gila woodpecker and gilded flicker create holes in the cactus and then nest there. When they give up their temporary digs, elf owls, cactus wrens, sparrow hawks, and other avian life moves in, as do dangerous Africanized honeybees.

You're not likely to encounter the six species of rattlesnake and the Gila monster, a venomous lizard, that inhabit the park, but avoid sticking your hands or feet under rocks or into crevices. If you do get bitten, get to a clinic or hospital as soon as possible. Not all snakes pass on venom; 50% of the time, the bite is "dry" (nonpoisonous).

Sunshine Jeep Tours (☎520/742–1943 ⊕www.sunshinejeeptours.com) arranges trips into the Sonoran Desert outside Tucson in open-air, four-wheel-drive vehicles.

Trail Dust Adventures (☎520/747–0323 ⊕www.traildustadventures. com) offers Jeep tours that explore the desert and mountains outside of the city.

BALLOONING

Balloon America flies passengers above the Santa Catalinas on hot-air balloon tours (✉Box 31255, Tucson 85751 ☎520/299–7744 ⊕www.balloonrideusa.com) departing from the east side of Tucson from October through May.

Fleur de Tucson Balloon Tours (✉4635 N. Caida Pl., Tucson 85718 ☎520/529–1025 ⊕www.fleurdetucson.net), operates out of the northwest, has two flight options: over the Tucson Mountains and Saguaro National Park West, or over the Avra Valley.

BICYCLING

Tucson, ranked among America's top five bicycling cities by *Bicycling* magazine, has well-maintained bikeways, routes, lanes, and paths all over the city. Scenic-loop roads in both sections of Saguaro National Park offer rewarding rides for all levels of cyclists. Most bike stores in Tucson carry the monthly newsletter of the Tucson chapter of **GABA** (*Greater Arizona Bicycling Association* ✉Box 43273, Tucson 85733 ⊕www.bikegaba.org), which lists rated group rides, local bike rentals, and more. You can pick up a map of Tucson-area bike routes at the **Pima Association of Governments** (✉177 N. Church St., Suite 405, Downtown ☎520/792–1093).

Mountain bikes, comfort bikes, and road bikes can be rented by the day or week at **Fair Wheel Bikes** (✉1110 E. 6th St., University

☎520/884–9018). **Tucson Bicycles** (✉4743 E. Sunrise Dr., Foothills ☎520/577–7374) rents a selection of road and mountain bikes and organizes group rides of varying difficulty.

GOLF

For a detailed listing of the state's courses, contact the **Arizona Golf Association** (☎602/944–3035 or 800/458–8484 ⊕www.azgolf.org). The **Golf Stop Inc.** (✉1830 S. Alvernon Way, South ☎520/790–0941), a shop owned and run by two LPGA pros, can fit you with custom clubs, repair your old irons, or give you lessons. Tee off after 1 PM at many of Tucson's courses, and you can shave off nearly half the green fees. Some courses also have slightly lower fees Monday through Thursday.

MUNICIPAL COURSES One of Tucson's best-kept secrets is that the city's five low-price, municipal courses are maintained to standards usually found only at the best country clubs. To reserve a tee time at one of the city's courses, call the **Tucson Parks and Recreation Department** (☎520/791–4653 *general golf information, 520/791–4336 automated tee-time reservations ⊕www.tucsoncitygolf.com*) at least a week in advance.

Fodor'sChoice ★ **Randolph Park Golf Course–North Course** (✉600 S. Alvernon Way, Central ☎520/791–4161), a long, scenic 18-hole course that has hosted the LPGA Tour for many years, is the flagship of Tucson's municipal courses ($39 to walk, $49 with a cart).

RESORT COURSES **Hilton Tucson El Conquistador** (✉10000 N. Oracle Rd., Northwest ☎520/544–5000 ⊕www.hiltonelconquistador.com) has 45 holes of golf in the Santa Catalina foothills with panoramic views of the city ($120).

Fodor'sChoice ★ **Lodge at Ventana Canyon** (✉6200 N. Clubhouse La., Northeast ☎520/577–1400 or 800/828–5701) has two 18-hole Tom Fazio-designed courses ($209). Their signature hole, No. 3 on the mountain course, is a favorite of golf photographers. Guests staying up the road at Loews Ventana Resort also have privileges here.

★ **Omni Tucson National Golf Resort** (✉2727 W. Club Dr., Northwest ☎520/575–7540 ⊕www.tucsonnational.com), cohost of an annual PGA winter open, offers 27 holes and beautiful, long par 4s. The resort's orange-and-gold courses were designed by Robert Van Hagge and Bruce Devlin ($180).

Starr Pass Golf Resort (✉3645 W. Starr Pass Blvd., Westside ☎520/670–0400 ⊕www.jwmarriottstarrpass.com), with 18 magnificent holes in the Tucson Mountains, was developed as a Tournament Player's Course. Managed by Arnold Palmer, Starr Pass has become a favorite of visiting pros; playing its No. 15 signature hole has been likened to threading a moving needle ($185). Guests at the JW Marriott Starr Pass Resort have privileges here.

Westin La Paloma (✉3800 E. Sunrise Dr., Foothills ☎520/742–6000 ⊕www.westinlapalomaresort.com), in the Tucson foothills, is rated among the top resort courses by *Golf Digest*. The 27-hole layout was designed by Jack Nicklaus ($185).

HIKING

Catalina State Park (✉*11570 N. Oracle Rd., Northwest* ☎*520/628–5798* ⊕*www.pr.state.az.us*) is crisscrossed by hiking trails. One of them, the relatively easy, two-hour (5.5-mi round-trip) Romero Canyon Trail, leads to Romero Pools, a series of natural *tinajas,* or stone "jars," filled with water much of the year. The trailhead is on the park's entrance road, past the restrooms on the right side.

★ The Bear Canyon Trail in **Sabino Canyon** (✉*Sabino Canyon Rd. at Sunrise Dr., Foothills* ☎*520/749–8700* ⊕*www.fs.fed.us/r3/coronado*), also known as Seven Falls Trail, is a three-hour, 7.8-mi round-trip that is moderately easy and fun, crisscrossing the stream several times on the way up the canyon. Kids enjoy the boulder-hopping and all are rewarded with pools and waterfalls as well as views at the top. The trailhead can be reached from the parking area by either taking a five-minute Bear Canyon Tram ride or walking the 1.8-mi tram route.

The local chapter of the **Sierra Club** (✉*738 N. 5th Ave., University* ☎*520/620–6401*) welcomes out-of-towners on weekend hikes. The **Southern Arizona Hiking Club** (☎*520/751–4513* ⊕*www.sahcinfo.org*) leads weekend hikes of varying difficulty. For hiking on your own, a good source is **Summit Hut** (✉*5045 E. Speedway Blvd., Central* ☎*520/325–1554*), which has a collection of hiking reference materials and a friendly staff who will help you plan your trip. Packs, tents, bags, and climbing shoes can be rented and purchased here.

RODEO

In the last week of February, Tucson hosts **Fiesta de Los Vaqueros,** the largest annual winter rodeo in the United States, a five-day extravaganza with more than 600 events and a crowd of more than 44,000 spectators a day at the **Tucson Rodeo Grounds** (✉*4823 S. 6th Ave., South* ☎*520/294–8896* ⊕*www.tucsonrodeo.com*). The rodeo kicks off with a 2-mi parade of horseback riders (Western and fancy-dress Mexican *charro*), wagons, stagecoaches, and horse-drawn floats; it's touted as the largest nonmotorized parade in the world. Local schoolkids especially love the celebration—they get a two-day holiday from school. Daily seats at the rodeo vary from $8 to $14.

WHERE TO EAT

Tucson boldly proclaims itself to be the "Mexican Food Capital of the United States" and most of the Mexican food in town is Sonoran style. This means prolific use of cheese, mild peppers, corn tortillas, pinto beans, and beef or chicken. The majority of the best Mexican restaurants are concentrated in South Tucson and downtown, though some favorites have additional locations around town. If Mexican's not your thing, there are plenty of other options: you won't have any trouble finding excellent sushi, Indian, Thai, Italian, and Ethiopian food at reasonable prices.

WHAT IT COSTS					
	¢	$	$$	$$$	$$$$
Restaurants	under $8	$8–$12	$13–$20	$21–$30	over $30

Prices are per person for a main course.

DOWNTOWN TUCSON

AMERICAN

$ ✕**Cup Café.** This charming spot off the lobby of Hotel Congress is at the epicenter of Tucson's hippest downtown scene, but it's also a down-home, friendly place. Try the Gunpowder (eggs, potatoes, chorizo, and cheese) for breakfast or the Queer Steer Burger (a veggie burger) for lunch. The Heartbreaker appetizer (Brie melted over artichoke hearts and apple slices on a baguette) complements such entrées as chicken satay or "Tornados" of beef. Open until 10 PM weeknights and 1 AM weekends, it becomes interestingly crowded in the evening with patrons from Club Congress, the hotel nightclub. ⊠*Hotel Congress, 311 E. Congress St., Downtown* ☏*520/798–1618* ▤*AE, D, MC, V.*

MEXICAN

$$ ✕**Café Poca Cosa.** In what is arguably Tucson's most creative Mexican

Fodor'sChoice restaurant, the chef prepares recipes inspired by different regions of her

★ native country. The menu, which changes daily, might include chicken mole or pork *pibil* (made with a tangy Yucatecan barbecue seasoning). Servings are plentiful, and each table gets a stack of warm corn tortillas and a bowl of beans to share. Order the daily Plato Poca Cosa, and the chef will select one beef, one chicken, and one vegetarian entrée for you to sample. The bold-color walls are hung with Latin American art. ⊠*110 E. Pennington St., Downtown* ☏*520/622–6400* ▤*MC, V* ⊗*Closed Sun. and Mon.*

$ ✕**El Charro Café.** Started by Monica Flin in 1922, El Charro still serves splendid versions of the Mexican-American staples Flin claims to have originated, most notably chimichangas and cheese crisps. The *carne seca* chimichanga, made with beef dried on the premises—on the roof—is delicious. ⊠*311 N. Court Ave., Downtown* ☏*520/622–1922* ▤*AE, D, DC, MC, V.*

$ ✕**El Minuto Café.** Popular with local families and the business crowd at lunch, this bustling restaurant is in Tucson's Barrio Historico neighborhood and open until midnight Friday and Saturday and until 10 PM the rest of the week. For more than 50 years, El Minuto has served *topopo* salads (a crispy tortilla shell heaped with beans, guacamole, and many other ingredients), huge burritos, and green-corn tamales (in season) made just right. The spicy *menudo* (tripe soup) is reputed to be a great hangover remedy. ⊠*354 S. Main Ave., Downtown* ☏*520/882–4145* ▤*AE, D, DC, MC, V.*

SOUTHWESTERN

$$ ✕**Barrio.** Lively at lunchtime, this trendy grill serves the most innovative cuisine in the downtown area. Try a "little plate" of black tiger shrimp rubbed with tamarind paste, or stuffed Anaheim chile in red bell-pepper cream. Entrées are as varied as the simple but delicious

> **DID YOU KNOW?**
>
> Tucson is also the birthplace of the *chimichanga* (Spanish for "whatchamacallit"), a flour tortilla filled with chicken or beef, rolled and deep-fried.

fish tacos and the linguine with chicken, dried papaya, and mango in a chipotle-chardonnay cream sauce. Save room for an elegant dessert of fresh berries drenched in crème anglaise or a chilled chocolate custard topped with caramel. ⊠ *135 S. 6th Ave., Downtown* ☎ *520/629–0191* ⊟ *AE, D, DC, MC, V* ⊗ *Closed Mon. No lunch weekends.*

CENTRAL TUCSON

AMERICAN

$$ ✕**Kingfisher Bar and Grill.** Kingfisher is a standout for American cuisine. The emphasis is on fresh seafood, but the kitchen does baby back ribs and steak with equal success. Try the delicately battered fish-and-chips or the clam chowder on the late-night menu, served from 10 PM to midnight. Bright panels of turquoise and terra-cotta, black banquettes, and neon lighting make for a chic space. ⊠ *2564 E. Grant Rd., Central* ☎ *520/323–7739* ⊟ *AE, D, DC, MC, V* ⊗ *No lunch weekends.*

¢ ✕**Marlene's Hungry Fox.** Marlene's hungry customers have been coming here for good ol' fashioned breakfasts, served until 2 PM, since 1962. It's the home of the double yolk, meaning when you order one egg, you'll get two (and so on). You'll also get a real slice of Tucson life at this cheerful, unpretentious place decorated with cow and farm photos, and a spoon collection that lines the walls. ⊠ *4637 E. Broadway Blvd., Central* ☎ *520/326–2835* ⊟ *AE, D, MC, V* ⊗ *No dinner.*

ITALIAN

$ ✕**Zona 78.** Fresh food takes on a whole new meaning at this contemporary bistro emphasizing inventive pizzas, pastas, and salads. The casual interior's focal point is a huge stone oven, where the pies are fired with toppings like Australian blue cheese, kalamata olives, sausage, and even chicken with peanut sauce. Whole wheat crust is an option and there are also baked salmon and chicken entrées. The house-made mozzarella is delectable, either on top of a pizza or in a salad with organic tomatoes. ⊠ *78 W. River Rd., Central* ☎ *520/888–7878* ⊟ *AE, D, MC, V.*

MEXICAN

$ ✕**Molina's Midway.** Tucked into a side street just north of Speedway, this unassuming restaurant holds its own against any in South Tucson. Specialties include Sinchiladas (chicken or beef with chiles, cheese, and a cream sauce) and *carne asada* (chunks of mildly spiced steak) wrapped in soft corn or flour tortillas. Seating is plentiful and the service is friendly. ⊠ *1138 N. Belvedere, Central* ☎ *520/325–9957* ⊟ *AE, D, MC, V* ⊗ *Closed Mon.*

7

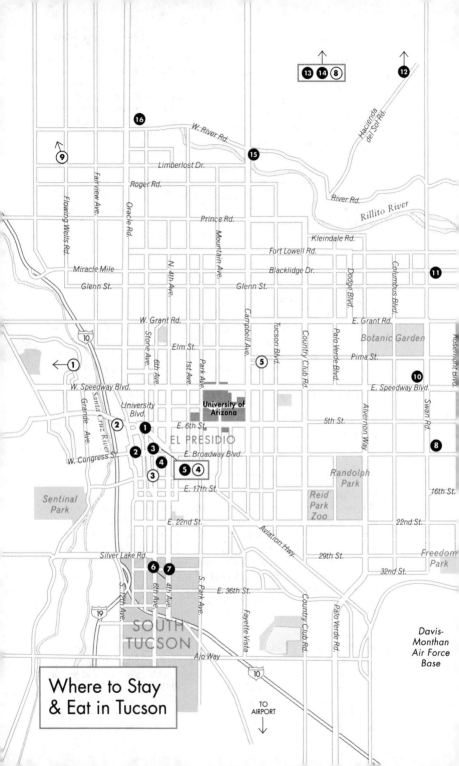

Where to Stay & Eat in Tucson

KEY

① Hotels
① Restaurants

Restaurants ▼	
Acacia	15
Barrio	4
Café Poca Cosa	3
Café Terra Cotta	13
Cup Café	5
El Charro Café	1
El Minuto Café	2
The Grill at Hacienda del Sol	12
Janos	14
Kingfisher Bar and Grill	9
Marlene's Hungry Fox	8
Mi Nidito	7
Micha's	6
Molina's Midway	10
Red Sky Cafe	11
Zona 78	16

Hotels ▼	
Arizona Inn	5
Canyon Ranch	6
Casa Tierra	1
Hotel Congress	4
Inn Suites Hotel & Resort	2
Loews Ventana Canyon Resort	7
The Royal Elizabeth Bed and Breakfast Inn	3
Westin La Paloma	8
White Stallion Ranch	9

7

River Rd.

Cloud Rd.

Ft. Lowell Park

Pantano Wash

Sabino Canyon Rd.

Canyon Rd.

E. Tanque Verde Rd.

Craycroft Rd.

Sahuara Ave.

Pantano Rd.

E. Broadway Blvd.

Wilmot St.

Palo Verde Park

Kolb Rd.

Prudence Rd.

Craycroft Rd.

Golf Links Rd.

Pantano Rd.

Prudence Rd.

0 — 2 miles
0 — 3 km

SOUTHWESTERN

$$ ✕ **Red Sky Cafe.** Trained in Paris, chef-owner Steve Schultz returned to Tucson to create his own contemporary cuisine, a fusion of French, Californian, and Southwestern flavors; the result is well-prepared, exquisitely presented meals. For a starter, try the foie gras with a potato pancake. Main courses, generously portioned, include soup or salad made with fresh (and often exotic) produce from the U of A's greenhouses. ⊠*Plaza Palomino, 2900 N. Swan Rd., Central* ☎*520/326–5454* ▤*AE, MC, V.*

CATALINA FOOTHILLS (NORTH)

SOUTHWESTERN

$$$$ ✕ **Janos.** Chef Janos Wilder was one of the first to reinvent Southwestern cuisine, and the menu, wine list, and service place this restaurant among the finest in the West. The hillside location on the grounds of the Westin La Paloma is a stunning backdrop for such dishes as sweet and spicy glazed quail with butternut-squash cannelloni, salmon with a scallop mousse served on polenta, and venison loin with chile-lime paste and pecans. Have a drink or a more casual meal of Caribbean fare next door at J Bar, a lively and lower-priced venue for sampling Janos's innovative cuisine. Twinkling city lights make patio seating a romantic choice here. ⊠ *Westin La Paloma, 3770 E. Sunrise Dr., Foothills* ☎*520/615–6100* ▤*AE, DC, MC, V* ⊘*Closed Sun. No lunch.*

Fodor's Choice
★

$$$ ✕ **Acacia.** One of Tucson's premier chefs, Albert Hall, opened his own restaurant in 2006 in one of the area's most artistic settings. A glass waterfall sculpture by local artist Tom Philabaum graces one wall and bold red-and-blue glass plates and stemware seem to float atop the tables. Roasted plum tomato–and–basil soup, a recipe from Albert's mom, is a favorite starter. Creative dishes like wild salmon with a pecan honey-mustard glaze and wood-fired quail filled with pancetta, mozzarella, roasted tomatoes, and Oaxacan risotto are among the many tempting entrées. Weekend evenings bring live jazz to the patio, which overlooks pretty, flower-filled St. Philip's Plaza. ⊠*4340 N. Campbell Ave., St. Philip's Plaza, Foothills* ☎*520/232–0101* ▤*AE, D, MC, V.*

$$$ ✕ **The Grill at Hacienda del Sol.** Tucked into the foothills and surrounded by flowering gardens, this special-occasion restaurant, a favorite among locals hosting out-of-town visitors, provides an alternative to the chile-laden dishes of most Southwestern nouvelle cuisine. Wild-mushroom bisque, pecan-grilled buffalo, and pan-seared sea bass are among the menu choices. Tapas (and most items on the full menu) can be enjoyed on the more casual outdoor patio, accented by live flamenco guitar music. The lavish Sunday brunch buffet is worth a splurge. ⊠*Hacienda del Sol Guest Ranch Resort, 5601 N. Hacienda del Sol Rd., Foothills* ☎*520/529–3500* ▤*AE, DC, MC, V.*

$$ ✕ **Café Terra Cotta.** Everything about this restaurant says Southwest—from the bright-orange-and-purple walls, large windows, and exposed beams to the contemporary art—but especially the food. Specialties include tortilla soup, shrimp flautas, and maple-leaf duck in a chocolate mole sauce. This is the ultimate casual and lively yet classy place

to dine in town; and happy-hour specials are a welcome find in the foothills. ⊠*3500 E. Sunrise Dr., Foothills* ☎*520/577–8100* ⊟*AE, D, DC, MC, V.*

SOUTH TUCSON

MEXICAN

$ ✕**Mi Nidito.** A perennial favorite among locals (be prepared to wait awhile), Mi Nidito—"my little nest"—has also hosted its share of visiting celebrities. Following President Clinton's lunch here, the rather hefty Presidential Plate (bean tostada, taco with barbecued meat, chiles rellenos, chicken enchilada, and beef tamale with rice and beans) was added to the menu. Top that off with the mango chimichangas for dessert, and you're talkin' executive privilege. ⊠*1813 S. 4th Ave., South* ☎*520/622–5081* ⊟*AE, DC, MC, V* ☉*Closed Mon. and Tues.*

$ ✕**Micha's.** Family-owned for 24 years, this local institution is a nondescript Mexican diner serving some of the best Sonoran classics this side of the border. House specialties include *machaca* (shredded beef) enchiladas and chimichangas, and *cocido,* a hearty vegetable-beef soup. Homemade chorizo spices up breakfast, which is served daily. A second location now brings this great food close to the university. ⊠*2908 S. 4th Ave., South* ☎*520/623–5307* ⊠*1220 E. Prince Rd., University* ☎*520/293–0375* ⊟*AE, DC, MC, V* ☉*No dinner Mon.*

7

WHERE TO STAY

When it comes to places to spend the night, the options in Tucson run the gamut: there are luxurious desert resorts, bed-and-breakfasts ranging from bedrooms in modest homes to private cottages nestled on wildlife preserves, as well as small to medium-size hotels and motels.

PLANNING INFORMATION

Summer rates (late May through September) are up to 60% lower than those in the winter. Note that unless you book months in advance, you'll be hard-pressed to find a Tucson hotel room at any price the week before and during the huge gem and mineral show, which is held the first two weeks in February. Also, resorts typically charge an additional daily fee for "use of facilities," such as pools, tennis courts, and exercise classes and equipment so be sure to ask what is included when you book a room.

WHAT IT COSTS					
	¢	$	$$	$$$	$$$$
Hotels	under $100	$100–$150	$151–$225	$226–$350	over $350

Prices are for a standard double in high season for two people.

DOWNTOWN TUCSON

$$ **The Royal Elizabeth Bed and Breakfast Inn.** Fans of Victoriana will adore this B&B in the Armory Park historic district. The inn, built in 1878, is beautifully furnished with period antiques and its six rooms are quite spacious. Gracious hosts Jeff and Charles take turns in the kitchen, preparing two-course breakfasts that might include chiles rellenos, a wild-mushroom frittata, or a fresh-fruit soufflé. **Pros:** Large and well-appointed rooms, a sense of privacy as well as B&B camaraderie. **Cons:** Pricey for downtown, neighbors aren't very lively (next door to a funeral home). ⊠ *204 S. Scott Ave., Downtown,* ☎ *520/670–9022* ⊕ *www.royalelizabeth.com* ➰ *6 rooms* ⌂ *In-room: VCR, Wi-Fi. In-hotel: pool, no-smoking rooms* ⊟ *AE, D, MC, V* ⦿ *BP.*

$ **Inn Suites Hotel & Resort.** Just north of the El Presidio district of downtown, this hotel—the term "resort" is a bit of a misnomer—is next to Interstate 10 but quiet nevertheless. The large, peach-and-green Southwestern-theme rooms, circa 1980, face an interior grassy courtyard with a sparkling pool and *palapas* (thatched open gazebos). Free daily extras such as a breakfast buffet, newspaper, and happy-hour cocktails make this a haven in the center of the city. **Pros:** Free breakfast and cocktails, affordable, kid-friendly. **Cons:** Little character, long walk to downtown restaurants. ⊠ *475 N. Granada Ave., Downtown,* ☎ *520/622–3000 or 877/446–6589* ⊕ *www.innsuites.com* ➰ *265 rooms, 35 suites* ⌂ *In-room: refrigerator, Wi-Fi In-hotel: restaurant, bar, pool, no-smoking rooms* ⊟ *AE, D, DC, MC, V* ⦿ *BP.*

¢   **Hotel Congress.** This hotel built in 1919 has been artfully restored to

Fodor's Choice   its original Western version of art deco. The gangster John Dillinger was

★   almost caught here in 1934 (apparently his luggage, filled with guns and ammo, was suspiciously heavy). Each room has a black-and-white tile bath and the original iron bed frames. The convenient location downtown means it can be noisy, so make sure you don't get a room over the popular Club Congress unless you plan to be up until the wee hours. A great place to stay for younger or more adventurous visitors, it's the center of Tucson's hippest scene. **Pros:** Convenient location, good restaurant, funky and fun. **Cons:** No air-conditioning, noise from nightclub. ⊠ *311 E. Congress St., Downtown,* ☎ *520/622–8848 or 800/722–8848* ⊕ *www.hotelcongress.com* ➰ *40 rooms* ⌂ *In-room: no TV. In-hotel: restaurant, bar, no-smoking rooms, no elevator* ⊟ *AE, D, MC, V.*

UNIVERSITY OF ARIZONA

$$$ **Arizona Inn.** Although near the university and many sights, the beau-

Fodor's Choice   tifully landscaped lawns and gardens of this 1930 inn seem far from

★   the hustle and bustle. The spacious rooms are spread over 14 acres in pink adobe-style casitas—most have private patios and some have fireplaces. The resort also has two luxurious two-story houses with their own heated pools and full hotel service. The main building has a library, a fine-dining restaurant, and a cocktail lounge where a jazz pianist plays. **Pros:** Unique historical property, emphasis on service. **Cons:** Rooms may not be modern enough for some, close to U of A Medical Center but long walk (1½ mi) to the main to campus. ⊠ *2200*

E. Elm St., University, ☎520/325–1541 or 800/933–1093 ⊕www. arizonainn.com ⟿70 rooms, 16 suites, 3 casitas ♿In-room: Ethernet. In-hotel: 2 restaurants, room service, bar, tennis courts, pool, gym, laundry service, no-smoking rooms ☰AE, DC, MC, V.

CATALINA FOOTHILLS (NORTH)

$$$$ **⊞Canyon Ranch.** The Canyon Ranch draws an international crowd of well-to-do health seekers to its superb spa facilities on 70 acres in the desert foothills. Two activity centers include an enormous spa complex and a Health and Healing Center, where dietitians, exercise physiologists, behavioral-health professionals, and medical staff attend to body and soul. Just about every type of physical activity is possible, from Pilates to guided hiking, and the food is plentiful and healthy. Rates include all meals, activities, taxes, and gratuities. There's a four-night minimum. **Pros:** A stay here can be a life-changing experience, gorgeous setting. **Cons:** Very pricey, not family-friendly. ⊠*8600 E. Rockcliff Rd., Foothills, ☎520/749–9000 or 800/742–9000 ⊕www.canyonranch. com ⟿240 rooms ♿In-room: refrigerator, Wi-Fi. In-hotel: restaurant, tennis courts, pools, gym, spa, laundry facilities, airport shuttle, no kids under 12, no-smoking rooms ☰AE, D, MC, V ⦿AI.*

$$$–$$$$ **⊞Loews Ventana Canyon Resort.** This is one of the most luxurious and prettiest of the big resorts, with dramatic stone architecture and an 80-foot waterfall cascading down the mountains. Rooms, facing either the Catalinas or the golf course and city, are modern and elegantly furnished in muted earth tones and light woods; each bathroom has a miniature TV and a double-wide tub. Dining options include everything from poolside snacks at Bill's Grill to fine Continental cuisine at the Ventana Room. The scenic Ventana Canyon trailhead is steps away, and there's a free shuttle to nearby Sabino Canyon. **Pros:** This place has everything: great golf, full spa, hiking, and even a kids' playground. **Cons:** Some rooms overlook the parking lot. ⊠*7000 N. Resort Dr., Foothills, ☎520/299–2020 or 800/234–5117 ⊕www.loewshotels.com ⟿384 rooms, 14 suites ♿In-room: refrigerator, Wi-Fi. In-hotel: 4 restaurants, room service, bar, golf courses, tennis courts, pools, gym, spa, bicycles, children's programs (ages 4–12), no-smoking rooms ☰AE, D, DC, MC, V.*

$$$–$$$$ **⊞Westin La Paloma.** Popular with business travelers and families, this sprawling resort offers views of the Santa Catalina Mountains above and the city below. It specializes in relaxation with an emphasis on fun: the huge pool complex has an impressively long waterslide, as well as a swim-up bar and grill for those who can't bear to leave the water. Kids' programs, including weekly "dive-in movies," make for a vacation the whole family can enjoy. The highly acclaimed Janos restaurant is on-site. **Pros:** Top-notch golf, tennis and spa, plush rooms, Janos/J Bar. **Cons:** So big it can feel crowded at pool areas and mazelike going to and from guest rooms. ⊠*3800 E. Sunrise Dr., Foothills, ☎520/742–6000 or 888/625–5144 ⊕www.starwood.com ⟿455 rooms, 32 suites ♿In-room: refrigerator, Wi-Fi. In-hotel: 4 restaurants, room service, bars, golf courses, tennis courts, pools, gym, spa, children's programs (ages 6 mos–12 yrs), no-smoking rooms ☰AE, D, DC, MC, V.*

7

NORTHWEST TUCSON

$$$-$$$$
Fodor'sChoice
★

⊞**White Stallion Ranch.** A 3,000-acre working cattle ranch run by the hospitable True family since 1965, this place is the real deal. You can ride up to four times daily, hike in the mountains, enjoy a hayride cookout, and compete in team cattle penning. Most rooms retain their original Western furniture, and newer deluxe rooms have whirlpool baths or fireplaces. A recently completed spa and fitness center bring even more comforts to this well-endowed but authentic setting. Rates include all meals, riding, and entertainment such as weekend rodeos, country line dancing, telescopic stargazing, and campfire sing-alongs. **Pros:** Solid dude ranch experience, very charming hosts, satisfying for families as well as singles or couples. **Cons:** Riding is very structured, no TVs, closed in summer. ⊠*9251 W. Twin Peaks Rd., Northwest,* ☎*520/297–0252 or 888/977–2624* ⊕*www.wsranch.com* ↩*24 rooms, 17 suites* ♿*In-room: no phone, no TV. In-hotel: bar, tennis courts, pool, gym, airport shuttle* ⊟*No credit cards* ⊘*Closed June–Aug.* ⊚*FAP.*

WEST OF TUCSON

$-$$
Fodor'sChoice
★

⊞**Casa Tierra.** For a real desert experience, head to this B&B on 5 acres near the Desert Museum and Saguaro National Park West. The last 1½ mi are on a dirt road. All rooms have private patio entrances and look out onto a lovely central courtyard. The Southwestern-style furnishings include Mexican *equipales* (chairs with pigskin seats) and tile floors. A full vegetarian breakfast served on fine china is included, and there's a media room in case you need a break from the quiet. There's a minimum stay of two nights. **Pros:** Peaceful, great southwest character. **Cons:** Very far from town. ⊠*11155 W. Calle Pima, Westside,* ☎*520/578–3058 or 866/254–0006* ⊕*www.casatierratucson.com* ↩*3 rooms, 1 suite* ♿*In-room: refrigerator, Wi-Fi, no TV. In-hotel: gym, no-smoking rooms* ⊟*AE, D, MC, V* ⊘*Closed mid-June–mid-Aug.* ⊚*BP.*

NIGHTLIFE & THE ARTS

The college and resort aspects of Tuscon contribute to the lively cultural and nightlife scene.

THE ARTS

The free *Tucson Weekly* (⊕*www.tucsonweekly.com*) and the "Caliente" section of the *Arizona Daily Star* (⊕*www.azstarnet.com*) both hit the stands on Thursday and have listings of what's going on in town.

Much of the city's cultural activity takes place at or near the **Tucson Convention Center** (⊠*260 S. Church St., Downtown* ☎*520/791–4101, 520/791–4266 box office* ⊕*www.tucsonconventioncenter.org*), which includes the Music Hall and the Leo Rich Theater. Dance, music, and other kinds of performances take place at the University of Arizona's **Centennial Hall** (✉ *1020 E. University Blvd., University* ☎ *520/621–3341* ⊕ *www.uapresents.org*).

One of Tucson's hottest rock-music venues, the **Rialto Theatre** (✉ *318 E. Congress St., Downtown* ☎ *520/798–3333* ⊕ *www.rialtotheatre.com*), was once a silent-movie theater but now reverberates with the sounds of jazz, folk, and world-music concerts, although the emphasis is on hard rock. Another recently refurbished old movie palace, the art deco **Fox Theatre** (✉ *17 W. Congress St., Downtown* ☎ *520/547–3040* ⊕ *www. foxtucsontheatre.org*) hosts film festivals and folk-rock concerts.

DANCE

Tucson shares its professional-ballet company, **Ballet Arizona** (☎ *888/322–5538* ⊕ *www.balletaz.org*), with Phoenix. Performances, from classical to contemporary, are held at the Music Hall in the Tucson Convention Center. The city's most established modern dance company, **Orts Theatre of Dance** (✉ *300 E. University Blvd., University* ☎ *520/624–3799* ⊕ *www.otodance.org*), incorporates trapeze flying into their dances. Outdoor and indoor performances are staged throughout the year.

MUSIC

A Wednesday-night chamber-music series is hosted by the **Arizona Friends of Chamber Music** (☎ *520/577–3769* ⊕ *arizonachambermusic. org*) at the Leo Rich Theater in the Tucson Convention Center from October through April. They also have a music festival the first week of March. The **Arizona Opera Company** (☎ *520/293–4336* ⊕ *www. azopera.com*), based in Tucson, puts on five major productions each year at the Tucson Convention Center's Music Hall. The **Arizona Symphonic Winds** (✉ *Tanque Verde and Sabino Canyon Rds., Northeast* ⊕ *www.azsymwinds.org*) has a spring–summer schedule of performances, many of which are held outdoors at Udall Park. Performances are usually at 7 PM, but you need to arrive at least an hour early. From May through September, the **Tucson Pops Orchestra** (☎ *520/722–5853* ⊕ *www.tucsonpops.org*) gives free concerts each Saturday evening at the De Meester Outdoor Performance Center in Reid Park. Arrive about an hour before the music starts (usually at 7 PM) to stake your claim on a viewing spot.

The **Tucson Symphony Orchestra** (✉ *443 S. Stone Ave., Downtown* ☎ *520/882–8585 box office, 520/792–9155 main office* ⊕ *www. tucsonsymphony.org*), part of Tucson's cultural scene since 1929, holds concerts in the Music Hall in the Tucson Convention Center and at sites in the Foothills and the Northwest as well.

Tucson's small but vibrant jazz scene encompasses everything from afternoon jam sessions in the park to Sunday jazz brunches at resorts in the Foothills. Call the **Tucson Jazz Society** (☎ *520/903–1265*) for information.

THEATER

Arizona's state theater, the **Arizona Theatre Company** (⊠*Temple of Music and Art, 330 S. Scott Ave., Downtown* ☎*520/622–2823 box office, 520/884–8210 company office* ⊕*www.aztheatreco.org*), performs classical pieces, contemporary drama, and musical comedy at the historic Temple of Music and Art from September through May. It's worth coming just to see the beautifully restored historic Spanish colonial–Moorish-style theater; dinner at the adjoining Temple Café is a tasty prelude.

The University of Arizona's **Arizona Repertory Theatre** (⊠*1025 N. Olive St., University* ☎*520/621–1162* ⊕*www.uatheatre.org*) has performances during the academic year. **Borderlands Theater** (⊠*40 W. Broadway, Downtown* ☎*520/882–7406* ⊕*www.borderlandstheater. org*) presents new plays about Southwest border issues—often multicultural and bilingual—at venues throughout Tucson, usually from late June through April.

NIGHTLIFE

BARS & CLUBS

BLUES & JAZZ **Boondocks** (⊠*3306 N. 1st Ave., Central* ☎*520/690–0991*) is the unofficial home of the Blues Heritage Foundation, hosting local and touring singer-songwriters.

COUNTRY & WESTERN An excellent house band gets the crowd two-stepping on Tuesday through Saturday nights at the **Maverick** (⊠*6622 E. Tanque Verde Rd., Eastside* ☎*520/298–0430*).

GAY & LESBIAN BARS **Ain't Nobody's Bizness** (⊠*2900 E. Broadway Blvd., Central* ☎*520/318–4838*) is the most popular lesbian bar in town. **IBT's (It's 'Bout Time)** (⊠*616 N. 4th Ave., University* ☎*520/882–3053*) is Tucson's most popular gay men's bar, with rock and disco DJ music and drag shows Wednesday and Saturday nights. Expect long lines on weekends.

ROCK & MORE **Club Congress** (⊠*Hotel Congress, 311 E. Congress St., Downtown* ★ ☎*520/622–8848*) is the main Friday venue for cutting-edge rock bands, with a mixed-bag crowd of alternative rockers, international travelers, and college kids. Saturday brings a more outrageous crowd dancing to an electronic beat.

★ The **Nimbus Brewing Company** (⊠*3850 E. 44th St., Southeast* ☎*520/745–9175*) is the place for acoustic blues, folk, and bluegrass, not to mention good, cheap food and microbrew beer.
Plush (⊠*340 E. 6th St., at 4th Ave., University* ☎*520/798–1298*) hosts alternative-rock bands like Camp Courageous and Greyhound Soul, as well as local performers with a loyal following.

SHOPPING

Much of Tucson's retail activity is focused around malls, but shops with more character and some unique wares can be found in the city's open plazas: St. Philip's Plaza (River Road and Campbell Avenue), Plaza Palomino (Swan and Fort Lowell roads), Casas Adobes Plaza (Oracle and Ina roads), and La Encantada (Skyline Drive and Campbell Avenue).

The 4th Avenue neighborhood near the University of Arizona—especially between 2nd and 9th streets—is fertile ground for unusual items in the artsy boutiques, galleries, and secondhand-clothing stores.

TUCSON ESSENTIALS

To research prices, get advice from other travelers, and book travel arrangements, visit ⊕www.fodors.com.

TRANSPORTATION

BY AIR

Tucson International Airport (TUS) is 8½ mi south of downtown, west of Interstate 10 off the Valencia exit. Many hotels provide courtesy airport shuttle service; inquire when making reservations.

Arizona Stagecoach carries groups and individuals between the airport and all parts of Tucson and Green Valley, for $9 to $38, depending on the location. If you're traveling light and aren't in a hurry, you can take a city Sun Tran bus to central Tucson. Bus 11, which leaves every half hour from a stop at the left of the lower level as you come out of the terminal, goes north on Alvernon Way, and you can transfer to most of the east–west bus lines from this main north–south road; ask the bus driver which one would take you closest to the location you need. You can also transfer to several lines from Bus 6, which leaves less frequently from the same airport location and heads to the Roy Laos center at the south of town.

Contacts **Arizona Stagecoach** (☎ *520/889–1000).* **Sun Tran** (☎ *520/792–9222).* **Tucson International Airport** (☎ *520/573–8000* ⊕ *www.tucsonairport.org).*

BY BUS

Within the city limits, public transportation, which is geared primarily to commuters, is available through Sun Tran, Tucson's bus system. On weekdays, bus service starts around 5 AM; some lines operate until 10 PM, but most go only until 7 or 8 PM, and weekend service is limited. A one-way ride costs $1; transfers are free, but be sure to request them when you pay your fare, unless exact change is required. An all-day pass costs $2. Those with valid Medicare cards can ride for 40¢. Call for information on Sun Tran bus routes.

Buses to Los Angeles, El Paso, Phoenix, Flagstaff, Douglas, and Nogales (Arizona) depart and arrive regularly from Tucson's Greyhound Lines terminal. For travel to Phoenix, Arizona Shuttle Service, Inc., runs express service from three locations in Tucson every hour on the hour, 4 AM to 9 PM every day; the trip takes about 2¼ hours. One-way fare is $24. They can also pick you up from your preferred destination. Call 24 hours in advance for reservations.

Information **Arizona Shuttle Service, Inc.** (☎ *520/795-6771*). **Greyhound Lines terminal** (✉ *471 W. Congress St., Downtown* ☎ *520/792-3475 or 800/229-9424* ⊕ *www.greyhound.com*). **Sun Tran** (☎ *520/792-9222*).

BY CAR

You'll need a car to get around Tucson and the surrounding area. Driving time from the airport to the center of town varies, but it's usually less than a half hour; add 15 minutes to any destination during rush hours (7:30 AM–9 AM and 4:30 PM–6 PM). Parking is not a problem in most parts of town, except near the university, where there are several pay lots.

From Phoenix, 111 mi northwest, Interstate 10 east is the road that will take you to Tucson. Also a major north–south traffic artery along the west side of town, Interstate 10 has well-marked exits all along the route.

BY TAXI

Taxi rates vary widely since they're unregulated in Arizona. It's always wise to inquire about the cost of a trip before getting into a cab.

Information **Allstate Taxi** (☎ *520/798-1111*). **Fiesta Taxi** (☎ *520/622-7777*). **Yellow Cab** (☎ *520/624-6611*).

BY TRAIN

Amtrak serves the city with westbound and eastbound trains six times a week.

Information **Amtrak** (✉ *400 E. Toole Ave., Downtown* ☎ *520/623-4442 or 800/872-7245* ⊕ *www.amtrak.com*).

CONTACTS & RESOURCES

EMERGENCIES

Hospitals **Columbia Northwest Medical Center** (✉ *6200 N. La Cholla Blvd., Northwest* ☎ *520/742-9000*). **St. Joseph's Hospital** (✉ *350 N. Wilmot Rd., Eastside* ☎ *520/873-3000*). **Tucson Medical Center** (✉ *5301 E. Grant Rd., Central* ☎ *520/327-5461*). **University Medical Center** (✉ *1501 N. Campbell Ave., University* ☎ *520/694-0111*); a teaching hospital with a first-rate trauma center.

VISITOR INFORMATION

Contacts **Metropolitan Tucson Convention and Visitors Bureau** (☎ *520/624-1817 or 800/638-8350* ⊕ *www.visittucson.org*).

Southern Arizona

WORD OF MOUTH

"We spent a week in Tucson and drove to Bisbee and Tombstone for a day…one of those times where the drive was as much a pleasure as the destination. We toured the mine, ate at the Bisbee Grille and walked around, then drove back to Tombstone…It's very touristy but that's OK. (Get it, OK, like corral.) I bought a nice pair of Navajo earrings at the Cochise Trading Post; seemed like the best place for quality and value."

—elizabeth_reed

Updated by
Mara Levin

Southern Arizona can do little to escape its cliché-ridden image as a landscape of cow skulls, tumbleweeds, dried-up riverbeds, and mother lodes—but it doesn't need to. The area that evokes such American dime-novel notions as Indian wars, vast land grants, and savage shoot-'em-ups is not simply another part of the Wild West drunk on romanticized images of its former self; local farmers and ranchers here evoke the self-sufficiency and ruggedness of their pioneer ancestors and revel in the area's rowdy past. Abandoned mining towns and sleepy Western hamlets dot a lonely landscape of rugged rock formations, deep pine forests, dense mountain ranges, and scrubby grasslands.

EXPLORING SOUTHERN ARIZONA

Southern Arizona ranges from the searing deserts surrounding Organ Pipe Cactus National Monument and the town of Yuma in the southwest to the soaring "Sky Islands" and rolling grasslands in the southeast. Towns are few and far between in the southwestern corner of the state where the desert and dry climate rule. In stark contrast, the varied terrain in the southeastern region ranges from pine-forested mountains and cool canyons to desert grasslands and winding river valleys. A complex network of highways links the many communities situated in this part of the state, where the next town or attraction is just over the hill, making the decision on which way you want to go next the hardest part of traveling.

ABOUT THE RESTAURANTS
In southern Arizona, cowboy fare is more common than haute cuisine. There are exceptions to the rule, though, especially in the wine-growing area of Sonoita and in the trendy town of Bisbee, both popular for weekend outings from Tucson. And, as one would expect, Mexican food dominates the menus on both sides of the border.

ABOUT THE HOTELS
There are plenty of chain hotels and major motels found throughout the southern region of Arizona, but why settle for boring basics in this beautiful and historic corner of the state? For the best experience, seek out an old-fashioned room in a historic hotel, a rustic casita at a working cattle ranch, or a spacious suite in a stunning bed-and-breakfast. There are a few scattered dude ranches found in the sweeping grasslands to the south, but not nearly as many as you'll find closer to metropolitan Tucson. It's usually not hard to find a room any time of the year, but keep in mind that prices tend to go up in high season (winter and spring) and down in low season (summer through early fall).

WHAT IT COSTS					
	¢	$	$$	$$$	$$$$
Restaurants	under $8	$8–$12	$13–$20	$21–$30	over $30
Hotels	under $70	$70–$120	$121–$175	$176–$250	over $250

Restaurant prices are per person for a main course at dinner. Hotel prices are for a standard double in high season, excluding taxes and service charges.

TOP REASONS TO GO

Tour Kartchner Caverns: The underground world of a living "wet" cave system is a rare and wonderful sensory experience. You'll see a multicolor limestone kingdom and probably feel "cave kiss" droplets grace your head; just don't touch anything.

Hike in the Chiricahuas: Stunning "upside-down" rock formations, flourishing wildlife, and relatively easy trails make for great hiking in this unspoiled region. The 3.4-mi Echo Canyon Loop Trail is a winner.

Explore Bisbee: Board the Queen Mine Train and venture into the life of a copper miner at the turn of the last century. Afterward, check out the narrow, hilly town's Victorian houses and thriving shops.

Bargain hunt in Nogales, Mexico: Shop for glassware, silver, leather, and pottery—and bargain with the sellers for 30% to 50% off the marked price. Park on the Arizona side and walk across the border to enjoy a different culture and spicy Sonoran-style Mexican food.

Stargaze at Kitt Peak: Clear skies and dry air provide ideal conditions for stargazing; the evening observation program, with top-notch telescopes and enthusiastic guides, is an excellent introduction to astronomy.

SOUTHEAST ARIZONA

TOMBSTONE

28 mi northeast of Sierra Vista via AZ 90, 24 mi south of Benson via AZ 80.

When prospector Ed Schieffelin headed out in 1877 to seek his fortune along the arid washes of San Pedro Valley, a patrolling soldier warned that all he'd find was his tombstone. Against all odds, his luck held out: he evaded bands of hostile Apaches, braved the harsh desert terrain, and eventually stumbled across a ledge of silver ore. The town of Tombstone was named after the soldier's offhand comment.

The rich silver lodes from the area's mines attracted a wide mix of fortune seekers ranging from prospectors to prostitutes and gamblers to gunmen. But as the riches continued to pour in, wealthy citizens began importing the best entertainment and culture that silver could purchase. Even though saloons and gambling halls made up two out of every three businesses on Allen Street, the town also claimed the Cochise County seat, a cultural center, and fancy French restaurants. By the early 1880s, the notorious boomtown was touted as the most cultivated city west of the Mississippi.

In 1881, a shootout between the Earp brothers and the Clanton gang ended with three of the "cowboys" (Billy Clanton and Tom and Frank McLaury) dead and two of the Earps (Virgil and Morgan) and Doc Holliday wounded. The infamous "Gunfight at the OK Corral" and the ensuing feud between the Earp brothers and the Clanton gang firmly

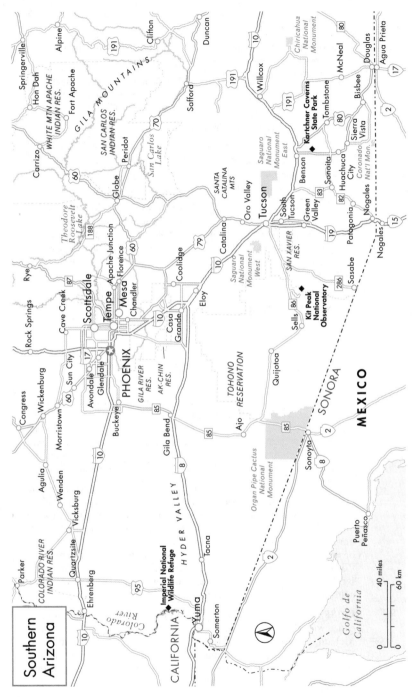

Southern Arizona

cemented Tombstone's place in the Wild West—even though the actual course of events is still debated by historians.

All in all, Tombstone's heyday only lasted a decade, but the colorful characters attached to the town's history live on—immortalized on the silver screen in such famous flicks as *Gunfight at the O.K. Corral, Tombstone,* and *Wyatt Earp.* The town's tourist industry parallels Hollywood hype. As a result, the main drag on Allen Street looks and feels like a movie set complete with gunning desperados, satin-bedecked saloon girls, and leather-clad cowboys. Today, the "Town Too Tough to Die" attracts a kitschy mix of rough-and-tumble bikers, European socialites, and pulp-fiction thrill seekers looking to walk the boardwalks of Tombstone's infamous past.

Start your tour of this tiny town and pick up a free discount pass at **Tombstone Visitor Center** (✉ *104 S. 4th St., at Allen St.* ☎ *520/457–3929* ⊕ *www.cityoftombstone.com* ⊙ *Daily 9–5*). There's a self-guided walking tour, but the best way to get the lay of the land is to take the 15-minute **stagecoach ride** ($10, $5 for kids) around downtown. Drivers relate a condensed version of Tombstone's notorious past. You'll also pass the Tombstone Courthouse and travel down Toughnut Street, once called Rotten Row—because of the lawyers who lived there.

For an introduction to the town's—and the area's—past, visit the **Tombstone Courthouse State Historic Park.** This redbrick 1882 county courthouse offers exhibits on the area's mining and ranching history and pioneer lifestyles; you can also see the restored 1904 courtroom and district attorney's office. The two-story building housed the Cochise County jail, a courtroom, and public offices until the county seat was moved to Bisbee in 1929. The stately building became the cornerstone of Tombstone's historic-preservation efforts in the 1950s and was Arizona's first operational state park. Today, you can relax with an outdoor lunch at the park's tree-shaded picnic tables. ✉ *219 E. Toughnut St., at 3rd St.* ☎ *520/457–3311* ⊕ *www.azstateparks.gov* 🖅 *$4* ⊙ *Daily 8–5.*

Originally a boardinghouse for the Vizina Mining Company and later a popular hotel, the **Rose Tree Inn Museum** has 1880s period rooms. Covering more than 8,600 square feet, the Lady Banksia rose tree, planted by a homesick bride in 1885, is reported to be the largest of its kind in the world. The best time to see the tree is in April when its tiny white roses bloom. Romantics can purchase a healthy clipping from the tree ($10.95 plus tax) to plant in their own yard. The museum might not look like much from the outside, but the collectibles and tree make this one of the best places to visit in town. ✉ *116 S. 4th St., at Toughnut St.* ☎ *520/457–3326* 🖅 *$5* ⊙ *Daily 9–5.*

Vincent Price narrates the dramatic version of the town's past in the **Historama**—a 26-minute multimedia presentation. At the adjoining **OK Corral,** a recorded voice-over details the town's famous shootout, while life-size figures of the gunfight's participants stand poised to shoot. A reenactment of the gunfight at the OK Corral is held daily at 2 PM. Photographer C.S. Fly, whose studio was next door to the

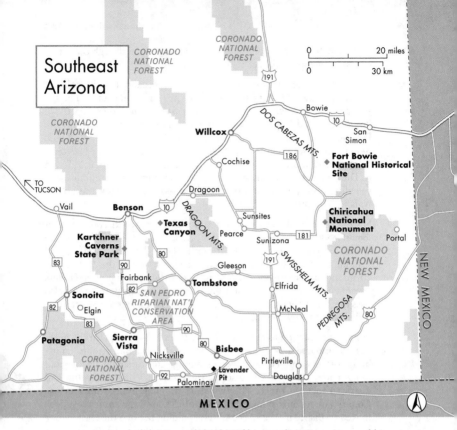

corral, didn't record this bit of history, but Geronimo and his pursuers were among the historic figures he did capture with his camera. Many of his fascinating Old West images may be viewed at the **Fly Exhibition Gallery.** ⊠*Allen St. between 3rd and 4th Sts.* ☎*520/457-3456* ⊕*www.ok-corral.com* ⊠*Historama, OK Corral, and Fly Exhibition Gallery $5.50, gunfight $2* ⊙*Daily 9–5; Historama shows on the half hr 9:30–4:30.*

Aficionados of the Old West have most likely seen the photograph of Billy Clanton in his coffin, which was taken after his demise at the infamous gunfight at the OK Corral. But Steve Elliott, owner of the **Tombstone Western Heritage Museum,** offers another glimpse of this cowboy—one with his eyes wide open. The 5"x 7" black-and-white photograph, taken by C. S. Fly in the 1880s, shows the Clantons, the McLaury brothers, and Billy Claiborne all saddled up and ready to ride. According to Elliott, it is the only known photograph of Billy Clanton taken while he was still among the living. Other relics of the Old West at the museum include 1880s dentist tools, clay poker chips, historic photographs, vintage firearms, and a stagecoach strongbox. ⊠*515 Fremont St., at 6th St.* ☎*520/457–3800* ⊠*$5* ⊙*Mon.–Sat. 10–5, Sun. 1–5.*

WHERE TO EAT

$–$$ ✕ **Lamplight Room.** The 1880s might have been a rough-and-tumble time for residents of Tombstone, but elegance found its way into the mining town—something reflected in its dining establishments. If you have the hankering to try some of the most elegant fare in town, dine at the Tombstone Boarding House Bed and Breakfast's Lamplight Room. The restaurant, decked out in Victorian finery, serves up period recipes and a complete Mexican menu at lunch and dinner. Wyatt Earp and Doc Holliday would feel right at home. ⊠ *108 N. 4th St.* ☎ *520/457–3716 or 877/225–1319* ▤ *D, MC, V.*

$ ✕ **Nellie Cashman's.** In 1882, a generous Tombstone pioneer opened a boardinghouse and restaurant catering to hard-rock miners. Named the "Angel of the Mining Camp," this kind-hearted entrepreneur was as well known for her hearty meals as for her good deeds. Today, her spirit lives on at Nellie Cashman's—an 1880s-style restaurant decked out with cheery mismatched tablecloths and historical photographs This homey favorite serves basic American food including biscuits and gravy, chicken-fried steak, and hefty hamburgers. The strawberry-rhubarb pie is worth the trip alone. ⊠ *117 5th St.* ☎ *520/457–2212* ▤ *AE, D, MC, V.*

WHERE TO STAY

$–$$ ▦ **Legends Bed & Breakfast.** Five blocks from the hubbub of Allen Street, this plain but serviceable hacienda, circa 1980—not 1880—has views of the Dragoon Mountains from the sun porch and hot tub. Two guestrooms furnished with Victorian antiques share a bath, and two larger rooms with fireplaces have private baths. Two separate common areas add to the comfortable feel of the place. **Pros:** Convenient to sights, quiet. **Cons:** Not much of the Wild West theme here, hot tub is directly off one of the bedrooms. ⊠ *210 N. 9th St.,* ☎ *520/457–3858 or 888/457–3858* ⊕ *www.legendsbandb.com* ⇲ *4 rooms* ♿ *In-room: VCR (some), no TV (some). In-hotel: no-smoking rooms, no elevator* ▤ *AE, D, MC, V* ⦿ *BP.*

★ $ ▦ **Tombstone Boarding House Bed & Breakfast.** This friendly B&B is actually two meticulously restored 1880s adobes that sit side by side: guests sleep in one house and go next door for a hearty country breakfast. The spotless rooms, all with private entrances, have period furnishings collected from around Cochise County. Even if you don't stay here, the Lamplight Room restaurant is worth a visit. **Pros:** Historical property, good breakfast. **Cons:** Small rooms, small bathrooms. ⊠ *108 N. 4th St.* ▢ *Box 906, 85638* ☎ *520/457–3716 or 877/225–1319* ⊕ *www.tombstoneboardinghouse.com* ⇲ *5 rooms* ♿ *In-room: no phone, no TV. In-hotel: restaurant, no-smoking rooms, no elevator, some pets allowed* ▤ *D, MC, V* ⦿ *BP.*

NIGHTLIFE

★ If you're looking to wet your whistle, stop by the **Crystal Palace** (⊠ *420 E. Allen St., at 5th St.* ☎ *520/457–3611*), where a beautiful mirrored mahogany bar, wrought-iron chandeliers, and tinwork ceilings date back to Tombstone's heyday. Locals come here on weekends to dance to live country-and-western music. Another hopping bar is **Big Nose**

Kate's Saloon (✉*Allen St. between 4th and 5th Sts.* ☎*520/457–3107* ⊕*www.bignosekate.com*). Occasionally an acoustic concert livens things up even more at this popular pub, once part of the original Grand Hotel built in 1881. Saloon girls encourage visitors to get into the 1880s spirit by dressing up in red-feather boas and dusters.

BISBEE

★ *24 mi south of Tombstone.*

Like Tombstone, Bisbee was a mining boomtown, but its wealth was in copper, not silver, and its success was much longer lived. The gnarled Mule Mountains aren't as impressive as some of the other mountain ranges in southern Arizona, but their rocky canyons concealed one of the richest mineral sites in the world.

Once known as the Queen of the Copper Camps, Bisbee is no longer one of the biggest cities between New Orleans and San Francisco. It was rediscovered in the early 1980s by burned-out city dwellers and revived as a kind of Woodstock West. The population is a mix of retired miners and their families, aging hippie jewelry makers, and enterprising restaurateurs and boutique owners from all over the country.

> ### WORD OF MOUTH
>
> "Stop in Bisbee and take the Copper Queen Mine tour, I think the kids would love it. You go down on an actual miner's tram into the mine, where it's always about 60 degrees—bring fleece! Retired miners strap helmets with lights on you and guide the tour—it's fascinating." —NewbE

If you want to head straight into town from U.S. 80, get off at the Brewery Gulch interchange. You can park and cross under the highway, taking Main, Commerce, or Brewery Gulch streets, all of which intersect at the large public parking lot next to the visitor center.

Bisbee Visitors Center is a good place to start your visit of this historic mining town. It offers up-to-date information on attractions, dining, lodging, tours and special events. ✉*2 Copper Queen Plaza* ☎*520/432–3554 or 866/224-7233* ⊕*www.discoverbisbee.com* ☯ *Weekdays 9–5, weekends 10–4*)

☙ For a lesson in mining history, take the **Copper Queen Mine Underground Tour.** The mine is less than ½ mi to the east of the Lavender Pit, across AZ 80 from downtown at the Brewery Gulch interchange. Tours are led by Bisbee's retired copper miners, who are wont to embellish their spiel with tales from their mining days. The 75-minute tours (you can't enter the mine at any other time) go into the shaft via a small open train, like those the miners rode when the mine was active. Before you climb aboard, you're outfitted in miner's garb—a yellow slicker and a hard hat with a light that runs off a battery pack. You may want to wear a sweater or light coat under your slicker because temperatures inside are cool. You'll travel thousands of feet into the mine, up a grade of 30 feet (not down, as many visitors expect). Those who are a bit claustrophobic might instead consider taking one of the van tours of the surface mines and historic district that depart from the building at the same times as the mine tours (excluding 9 AM). Reservations are suggested. ⊠*478 N. Dart Rd.* ☎*520/432–2071 or 866/432–2071* ⊕*www.queenminetour.com* ✉*Mine tour $12, van tour $10* ⊙*Tours daily at 9, 10:30, noon, 2, and 3:30.*

★ The **Bisbee Mining and Historical Museum** is in a redbrick structure built in 1897 to serve as the Copper Queen Consolidated Mining Offices. The rooms today are filled with exhibits, photographs, and artifacts that offer a glimpse into the everyday life of Bisbee's early mining community. Even though the exhibit "Bisbee: Urban Outpost on the Frontier" paints a flattering portrait of this Shady Lady's early years and the funky gift store gets in the groove with feathered ladies' hats and locally written books, most visitors will spend less than an hour taking in this dusty little museum. This was the first rural museum in the United States to become a member of the Smithsonian Institution Affiliations Program. ⊠*5 Copper Queen Plaza* ☎*520/432–7071* ⊕*www. bisbeemuseum.org* ✉*$7.50* ⊙*Daily 10–4.*

Bisbee's **Main Street** is alive and retailing. This hilly commercial thoroughfare is lined with appealing art galleries, antiques stores, crafts shops, boutiques, and restaurants—many in well-preserved turn-of-the-20th-century brick buildings.

Tom Mosier, a native of Bisbee, gives the **Lavender Jeep Tours** (⊠*45 Gila Dr.* ☎*520/432–5369*) for $25 to $49. He regales locals and visitors with tales of the town and its buildings, and tours of the surrounding region.

WHERE TO EAT

$$ ✕**Café Roka.** This is the deserved darling of the hip Bisbee crowd. The
★ constantly changing northern Italian–style evening menu is not extensive, but whatever you order—gulf shrimp tossed with lobster ravioli, roasted quail, New Zealand rack of lamb—will be wonderful. Portions are generous, and entrées include soup, salad, and sorbet. Exposed-brick walls and soft lighting form the backdrop for original artwork, and the 1875 bar hearkens to Bisbee's glory days. There's live jazz on Friday nights. ⊠*35 Main St.* ☎*520/432–5153* ▭*AE, MC, V* ⊙*Closed Sun.–Wed. No lunch.*

$–$$ ✕**The Bisbee Grille.** You might not expect diversity at a place with a reputation for having the best burger in town, but this restaurant delivers with salads, sandwiches, fajitas, pasta, salmon, steaks, and ribs. The dining room, built to resemble an old train depot, fills up fast on the weekends. ⊠*2 Copper Queen Plaza* ☎*520/432–6788* ▭*AE, D, MC, V.*

WHERE TO STAY

$–$$ ▦**School House Inn Bed & Breakfast.** You might flash back to your class-
Fodor's Choice room days at this B&B, a schoolhouse built in 1918 at the height of
★ Bisbee's mining days. Perched on the side of a hill, the two-story brick building has a pleasant outdoor patio shaded by an oak tree. The inn's rooms all have a theme—history, music, library, reading, arithmetic,

art, geography, and the principal's office—reflected in the decor. **Pros:** Well-preserved property, exceedingly friendly hosts, hearty vegetarian breakfasts. **Cons:** A mile walk or short drive into town. ⊠*818 Tombstone Canyon Rd.* ✆*Box 32, Bisbee 85603* ☎*520/432–2996 or 800/537–4333* ⊕*www.schoolhouseinnbb.com* ☞*6 rooms, 3 suites* ♨*In-room: no a/c, no phone, no TV, Wi-Fi. In-hotel: no kids under 10, no-smoking rooms, no elevator* ⊟*AE, D, MC, V* ⦿*BP.*

$ 🛏**Shady Dell Vintage Trailer Park.** For a blast to the past, stay in one of
Fodor'sChoice the funky, vintage aluminum trailers at this trailer park just south of
★ town. Choices include a 1952, 10-foot homemade unit and a 1951, 33-foot Royal Mansion. The entire collection is decked out 1950s style including vintage magazines, books, and vinyl records. Some have private bathrooms but only a few have private showers; the park restrooms are clean, with hot showers. Dot's Diner, on-site, serves burgers, fries, and milk shakes. **Pros:** Unique (how many vintage trailer-park hotels with a hip vibe are out there?), fun, cheap. **Cons:** Walking to the public restrooms in the middle of the night. ⊠*1 Old Douglas Rd.,* ☎*520/432–3567* ⊕*www.theshadydell.com* ☞*11 trailers* ♨*In-room: no a/c, no phone, kitchen, no TV. In-hotel: restaurant, laundry facilities, no kids under 10, no-smoking rooms* ⊟*MC, V.*

CHIRICAHUA NATIONAL MONUMENT

↻ *58 mi northeast of Douglas on U.S. 191 to AZ 181; 36 mi southeast*
Fodor'sChoice *of Willcox.*
★

Vast fields of desert grass are suddenly transformed into a landscape of forest, mountains, and striking rock formations as you enter the 12,000-acre Chiricahua National Monument. The Chiricahua Apache—who lived in the mountains for centuries and, led by Cochise and Geronimo, tried for 25 years to prevent white pioneers from settling here—dubbed it the Land of the Standing-Up Rocks. Enormous outcroppings of volcanic rock have been worn by erosion and fractured by uplift into strange pinnacles and spires. Because of the particular balance of sunshine and rain in the area, in April and May visitors will see brown, yellow, and red leaves coexisting with new green foliage. Summer in Chiricahua National Monument is exceptionally wet: from July through September there are thunderstorms nearly every afternoon. Few other areas in the United States have such varied plant, bird, and animal life. Deer, coatimundi, peccaries, and lizards live among the aspen, ponderosa pine, Douglas fir, oak, and cypress trees—to name just a few. Well worth the driving distance, this is an excellent area for bird-watchers, and hikers have more than 17 mi of scenic trails. The admission fee is good for seven days. Some of the most beautiful and untouched camping areas in Arizona are nearby, in the Chiricahua Mountains. ⊠*AZ 181, 36 mi southeast of Willcox* ☎*520/824–3560* ⊕*www.nps.gov/chir* 🎫*$5* ☉*Visitor center daily 8–4:30.*

TEXAS CANYON

Fodor'sChoice
★
16 mi west of Willcox off I–10.

A dramatic change of scenery along Interstate 10 will signal that you're entering Texas Canyon. The rock formations here are exceptional—huge boulders appear to be delicately balanced against each other.

Texas Canyon is the home of the **Amerind Foundation** (a contraction of "American" and "Indian"), founded by amateur archaeologist William Fulton in 1937 to foster understanding about Native American cultures. The research facility and museum are housed in a Spanish colonial revival–style structure designed by noted Tucson architect H.M. Starkweather. The museum's rotating displays of archaeological materials, crafts, and photographs give an overview of Native American cultures of the Southwest and Mexico. The adjacent Fulton–Hayden Memorial Art Gallery displays an assortment of art collected by William Fulton. Permanent exhibits include the work of O'odham women potters, an exquisite collection of Hopi kachina dolls, prized paintings by acclaimed Hopi artists, Pueblo pottery ranging from prehistoric pieces to modern ceramics, and archaeological exhibits on the Indian cultures of the prehistoric Southwest. The museum's gift shop has a superlative selection of Native American art, crafts, and jewelry. ⊠ *2100 N. Amerind Rd., 1 mi southeast of I–10, Exit 318, Dragoon* ☎ *520/586–3666* ⊕ *www.amerind.org* ⊠ *$5* ⊘ *Tues.–Sun. 10–4.*

KARTCHNER CAVERNS STATE PARK

Fodor'sChoice
★
9 mi south of Benson on AZ 90.

8

The publicity that surrounded the official opening of the Kartchner Caverns in November 1999 was in marked contrast to the secrecy that shrouded their discovery 25 years earlier and concealed their existence for 14 years. The two young men who stumbled into what is now considered one of the most spectacular cave systems anywhere played a fundamental role in its protection and eventual development. Great precautions have been taken to protect the wet-cave system—which comprises 13,000 feet of passages and two chambers as long as football fields—from damage by light and dryness.

The Discovery Center introduces visitors to the cave and its formations, and hour-long guided tours take small groups into the upper cave. Spectacular formations include the longest soda straw stalactite in the United States at 21 feet and 2 inches. The Big Room is viewed on a separate tour: it holds the world's most extensive formation of brushite moonmilk, the first reported occurrence of turnip shields, and the first noted

WORD OF MOUTH

"We live in Phoenix and take all visitors to Kartchner—they can never get enough. Take both tours! Each tour has features and formations unique to the other (bacon, straws, fried eggs, etc.), and taking both rather than one only adds 1½ hours to your day." —yotefan37 occurrence of birdsnest needle formations. Other funky and fabulous formations include brilliant red flowstone, rippling multihued stalactites, delicate white helictites, translucent orange bacon, and expansive mud flats. It's also the nursery roost for female cave myotis bats from April through September, during which time the lower cave is closed in an effort to foster the cave's unique ecosystem. Kartchner Caverns is a wet, "live" cave, meaning that water still rises up from the surface to increase the multicolor calcium carbonate formations already visible.

The total cavern size is 2.4 mi long, but the explored areas cover only 1,600 feet by 1,100 feet. The average relative humidity inside is 99%, so visitors are often graced with "cave kisses," water droplets from above. Because the climate outside the caves is so dry, it is estimated that if air got inside, it could deplete the moisture in only a few days, halting the growth of the speleothems that decorate its walls. To prevent this, there are 22 environmental monitoring stations that measure air and soil temperature, relative humidity, evaporation rates, air trace gases, and airflow inside the caverns. ■ **TIP➜ Tour reservations are required and should be made several months in advance.** If you're here and didn't make a reservation, you may be in luck: the park reserves 100 walk-up tickets each day, available on a first-come, first-served basis, for the Rotunda/Throne Room tour (arrive early for a shot at these). Hiking trails, picnic areas, and campsites are available on the park's 550 acres. ⊠ *AZ 90, 9 mi south of Exit 302 off I–10* ☏ *520/586–4100 information, 520/586–2283 tour reservations* ⊕ *www.pr.state.az.us* ✉ *$5 per vehicle up to people, $2 each additional person; Rotunda/Throne Room tours $18.95, Big Room tours $22.95* ☉ *Daily 7:30–6; cave tours, by reservation, daily 8–4.*

SOUTHWEST ARIZONA

NOGALES

15 mi south of Tumacácori, 63 mi south of Tucson on I–19 at the Mexican border.

Nogales, named for the walnut trees that grew along the river here, is actually two towns: the somewhat bland, industrial American city and the smaller Mexican town over the border. The American side was once a focal point for cattle shipping between Sonora and the United States. Today, Nogales reaps the benefits of NAFTA, with warehouses and trucking firms dedicated to the distribution of Mexican produce, making it one of the world's busiest produce ports. The American side depends on the health of the peso and the shoppers who cross the border from Mexico to buy American goods that they can't get in their country. The Mexican side has grown with the economic success of *maquiladoras,* factories that manufacture goods destined for the United States. There's a great deal of commerce between the two sides.

Some of this trade is in narcotics and undocumented workers, giving this border town a more edgy quality than its American counterpart. Bustling Nogales, Mexico can become fairly rowdy on weekend

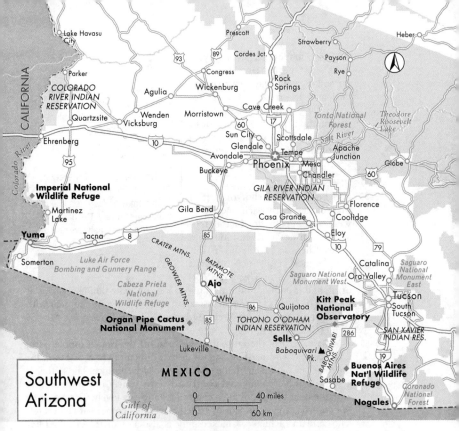

Southwest Arizona

0 ——— 40 miles
0 ——— 60 km

evenings, when underage Tucsonans head south of the border to drink. It has some good restaurants, however, and fine-quality crafts in addition to the usual souvenirs—and tourists as well as locals from Tucson and Phoenix enjoy a day trip of shopping and dining on the Mexico side. ■TIP→ **To make calls to Mexico use the prefix 011 along with the country code of 52.** Security on the American side of the border is very tight; don't even think about taking a firearm near the border. You'll also do better not to drive your car into Mexico: not only is there a very real possibility it may be stolen, but you'll face significant delays because of the thorough search you and your vehicle will receive upon returning. Most car-rental agencies allow you to take your rental into Mexico only if you buy their Mexican insurance packages. If you drive your own car into Mexico, you must purchase Mexico auto insurance for the duration of your stay. Be aware that road conditions in Mexico can be poor and that signs are in Spanish. This hassle is unnecessary, though, because you can cover Nogales in a day trip, and most of the good shopping is within easy walking distance of the border crossing. Park on the Arizona side, either on the street or, better yet, in one of many guarded lots that cost about $8 for the day (use the convenient public restrooms on the U.S. side before you cross). Keep in mind that all travelers must have a passport or other accepted secure document to enter or reenter the United States.

■TIP→ **Don't bother trading your dollars for pesos. Merchants prefer dollars and always have change on hand.** Be prepared for aggressive selling tactics and sometimes-disorienting hubbub, but locals are always glad to point you in the right direction, and almost all speak some English.

WHERE TO EAT

$–$$ ✕ **Elvira.** The free shot of tequila that comes with each meal will whet your appetite for Elvira's reliable fish dishes, chicken mole, and chiles rellenos. Tequila lovers can sample more than 100 different tequilas at the bar. This large, colorful, and friendly restaurant (divided into intimate dining areas) is at the foot of Avenida Obregón just south of the border and popular with those who visit Nogales often. ⊠ *Avda. Obregón 1, Nogales, Mexico* ☎ *631/312–4773* ▤ *MC, V.*

$–$$ ✕ **La Roca.** East of the railroad tracks and off the beaten tourist path,
★ La Roca is a favorite of Tucsonans. It isn't difficult to find, just look for the towering black sign to the east of the border entrance. The setting—a series of tiled rooms and courtyards in a stately old stone house, with a balcony overlooking a charming patio—is lovely. Try the *carne tampiqueña,* an assortment of grilled meats that comes with chiles rellenos and an enchilada. Chicken mole is also a favorite. ⊠ *Calle Elias 91, Nogales, Mexico* ☎ *631/312–0891* ▤ *MC, V.*

SHOPPING

The main shopping area is on the Mexican side, on Avenida Obregón, which begins a few blocks west (to your right) of the border entrance and runs north–south; just follow the crowds. You'll find handicrafts, furnishings, and jewelry here, but if you go off on some of the side streets, you might come across more interesting finds at better prices. Except at shops that indicate otherwise, bargaining is not only acceptable but expected. Playing this customary game can save you, on average, 50%, so don't be shy. The shops listed below tend to have fixed prices, so either buy here if you don't want to bargain at all, or note their prices and see if you can do better elsewhere.

KITT PEAK NATIONAL OBSERVATORY

56 mi southwest of Tucson; to reach Kitt Peak from Tucson, take I–10 to I–19 south, and then AZ 86. After 44 mi on AZ 86, turn left at AZ 386 junction and follow winding mountain road 12 mi up to observatory. In inclement weather, contact the highway department to confirm that the road is open.

Funded by the National Science Foundation and managed by a group of more than 20 universities, Kitt Peak National Observatory is part of the Tohono O'odham Reservation. After much discussion back in the late 1950s, tribal leaders agreed to share a small section of their 4,400 square mi with the observatory's telescopes. Among these is the McMath, the world's largest solar telescope, which uses piped-in liquid coolant. From the visitors' gallery you can see into the telescope's light-path tunnel, which goes down hundreds of feet into the mountain. Kitt Peak scientists use these high-power telescopes to conduct vital solar research and observe distant galaxies.

The visitor center has exhibits on astronomy, information about the telescopes, and hour-long guided tours ($4 per person) that depart daily at 10, 11:30, and 1:30. Complimentary brochures enable you to take self-guided tours of the grounds, and there's a picnic area about 1½ mi below the observatory. The observatory buildings have vending machines, but there are no restaurants or gas stations within 20 mi of Kitt Peak. The observatory offers a nightly observing program ($39 per person) except from July 15 to September 1; reservations are necessary. ✉ *AZ 386, Pan Tak* ☎ *520/318-8726, 520/318-7200 recorded message* ⊕ *www.noao.edu* 🎫 *$2* ⊗ *Visitor center daily 9–3:45.*

ORGAN PIPE CACTUS NATIONAL MONUMENT

32 mi southwest of Ajo; from Ajo, backtrack to Why and take AZ 85 south for 22 mi to reach the visitor center.

8

Organ Pipe Cactus National Monument, abutting Cabeza Prieta National Wildlife Refuge but much more accessible to visitors, is the largest habitat north of the border for organ-pipe cacti. These multi-armed cousins of the saguaro are fairly common in Mexico but rare in the United States. Because they tend to grow on south-facing slopes, you won't be able to see many of them unless you take one of the two scenic loop drives: the 21-mi **Ajo Mountain Drive** or the 53-mi **Puerto Blanco Drive**, both on winding, graded, one-way dirt roads.

■ TIP➔Be aware that Organ Pipe has become an illegal border crossing hot spot. Migrant workers and drug traffickers cross from Mexico under cover of darkness. At this writing, much of Puerto Blanco Drive has been closed indefinitely to the public. A two-way road that only travels 5 of the 53 mi on Puerto Blanco Drive is open, but the rest of the road will remain closed due to continuing concerns over its proximity to the U.S.–Mexico border. Even so, park officials emphasize that tourists have only occasionally been the victims of isolated property crimes—primarily theft of personal items from parked cars. Visitors are advised by rangers to keep valuables locked and out of plain view and not to initiate contact with groups of strangers whom they may encounter on hiking trails.

A campground at the monument has 208 RV (no hookups) and tent sites. Facilities include a dump station, flush toilets, grills, and picnic tables. ⊠*AZ 85* ☎*520/387–6849* ⊕*www.nps.gov/orpi* 🏷*$8 per vehicle* ☉*Visitor center daily 8–5.*

YUMA

170 mi northwest of Ajo.

Yuma's population swells during the winter months with retirees from cold climates who park their homes on wheels at one of the many RV communities. One fact may shed some light on why: according to National Weather Service statistics, Yuma is the sunniest city in the United States.

Most of the interesting sights in Yuma are at the north end of town.

Stop in at the **Yuma Convention and Visitors Bureau** (⊠*139 S. 4th Ave.* ☎*928/783–0071 or 800/293–0071* ⊕*www.visityuma.com* ☉*Weekdays 9–5, Sat. 9–4*) and pick up a walking-tour guide to the historic downtown area.

ↁ The most notorious tourist sight in town, **Yuma Territorial Prison,** now an Arizona state historic park, was built for the most part by the convicts who were incarcerated here from 1876 until 1909, when the prison outgrew its location. The hilly site on the Colorado River, chosen for security purposes, precluded further expansion.

Visitors gazing today at the tiny cells that held six inmates each, often in 115°F heat, are likely to be appalled, but the prison—dubbed the Country Club of the Colorado by locals—was considered a model of enlightenment by turn-of-the-20th-century standards: in an era when beatings were common, the hardest punishments meted out here were solitary confinement and assignment to a dark cell. The complex housed a hospital as well as Yuma's only public library, where the 25¢ that visitors paid for a prison tour financed the acquisition of new books.

The mess hall opened as a museum in 1940, and the entire prison complex was designated a state historic park in 1961. ⊠*1 Prison Hill Rd., near Exit 1 off I-8* ☎*928/783–4771* ⊕*www.azstateparks.gov* 🏷*$4* ☉*Daily 8–5.*

You can take a boat ride up the Colorado with **Yuma River Tours** (⊠*1920 Arizona Ave.* ☎*928/783–4400* ⊕*www.yumarivertours.com*). You can book 12- to 45-person jet-boat excursions through Smokey Knowlton, who has been exploring the area for more than 35 years.

WHERE TO EAT

$-$$ ✕**Chretin's Mexican Food.** A Yuma institution, Chretin's opened as a dance hall in the 1930s before it became one of the first Mexican restaurants in town in 1946. Don't be put off by the nondescript exterior or the entryway, which leads back past the kitchen and cashier's stand into three large dining areas. The food is all made on the premises, right down to the chips and tortillas. Try anything that features *machaca* (shredded spiced beef or chicken). ⊠485 S. 15th Ave. ☎928/782–1291 ⊟D, MC, V.

¢–$ ✕**Lutes Casino.** Almost always packed with locals at lunchtime, this ★ large, funky restaurant and bar claims to be the oldest pool hall and domino parlor in Arizona. It's a great place for a burger and a brew. If you can't choose between a cheeseburger and a hot dog, have both. The "Especial" combines these two American favorites and adds a generous dollop of Lutes' "special sauce." ⊠221 S. Main St. ☎928/782–2192 ⊟No credit cards.

WHERE TO STAY

$ 🏨**Best Western Coronado Motor Hotel.** This Spanish tile–roofed motor hotel was built in 1938 and has been well cared for. Bob Hope used to stay here during World War II, when he entertained the gunnery troops training in Yuma. Yuma Landing Restaurant & Lounge is on-site with an impressive collection of historical photos. **Pros:** Convenient to AZ 8 and a short walk to historic downtown area, full breakfast at restaurant. **Cons:** Some highway noise in rooms. ⊠233 S. 4th Ave., ☎928/783–4453 or 800/528–1234 ⊕www.bestwestern.com ⇆86 rooms ⚭In-room: refrigerator, DVD, dial-up. In-hotel: restaurant, bar, pool, laundry facilities, no elevator ⊟AE, D, DC, MC, V ⍟BP.

IMPERIAL NATIONAL WILDLIFE REFUGE

🕘 40 mi north of Yuma; from Yuma, take U.S. 95 north past the Proving Ground and follow the signs to the refuge.

A guided tour is the best way to visit the 25,765-acre Imperial National Wildlife Refuge, created by backwaters formed when the Imperial Dam was built. Something of an anomaly, the refuge is home both to species indigenous to marshy rivers and to creatures that inhabit the adjacent Sonoran Desert—desert tortoises, coyotes, bobcats, and bighorn sheep. Mostly, though, this is a major bird habitat. Thousands of waterfowl and shorebirds live here year-round, and migrating flocks of swallows pass through in spring and fall. During those seasons, expect to see everything from pelicans and cormorants to Canada geese, snowy egrets, and some rarer species. Canoes can be rented at Martinez Lake Marina, 3.5 mi southeast of the refuge headquarters. It's best to visit from mid-October through May, when it's cooler and the ever-present mosquitoes are least active. Kids especially enjoy the 1.3-mi Painted Desert Nature Trail, which winds through the different levels of the Sonoran Desert. From an observation tower at the visitor center you can see the river, as well as the fields being planted with rye and millet, on which the migrating birds like to feed. ⊠Martinez Lake Rd., Box 72217, Martinez Lake ☎928/783–3371 ⊕ refuges.fws.gov ⍰Free ⊙ Visitor center mid-Apr.–mid-Oct., weekdays 7:30–4; mid-Oct.–mid-Apr., weekdays 7:30–4, weekends 9–4.

SOUTHERN ARIZONA ESSENTIALS

To research prices, get advice from other travelers, and book travel arrangements, visit ⊕www.fodors.com.

TRANSPORTATION

BY AIR

Great Lakes Airlines flies direct from Phoenix to Sierra Vista. America West Express has direct flights to Yuma from Phoenix. Sky West, a United subsidiary, flies nonstop from Los Angeles to Yuma.

Contacts **America West Express** (☎800/235-9292 ⊕www.americawest.com). **Great Lakes Airlines** (☎800/554-5111 ⊕www.greatlakesav.com). **Sierra Vista Municipal Airport/Fort Huachuca** (✉2100 Airport Ave. ☎520/458-5775). **Sky West** (☎435/634-3000 ⊕www.skywest.com). **Yuma International Airport (YUM)** (☎928/726-5882 ⊕www.yumainternationalairport.com).

BY TAXI

Benson Taxi offers transport services in the Benson area. In Sierra Vista, Arizona World Shuttle provides local and regional transport, including service to and from the Tucson airport. Yuma City Cab has the best taxi service in Yuma.

Contacts **Arizona World Shuttle** (✉Sierra Vista ☎520/458-3330). **Benson Taxi** (✉Benson ☎520/586-1294). **Yuma City Cab** (✉Yuma ☎928/782-4444).

BY TRAIN

Amtrak trains run three times a week from Tucson east to the Benson depot and west to Yuma.

Contacts **Benson train station** (✉4th St. at San Pedro Ave., Benson) **Yuma train station** (✉281 Gila St., Yuma)

CONTACTS & RESOURCES

VISITOR INFORMATION

In Southeastern Arizona **Bisbee Visitor Center** (✉2 Copper Queen Plaza, Bisbee ☎520/432-3554 or 866/224-7233 ⊕www.discoverbisbee.com ☾Weekdays 9-5, weekends 10-4). **City of Tombstone Visitor Center** (✉104 S. 4th St., at Allen St., Tombstone ☎520/457-3929 ⊕www.cityoftombstone.com ☾Daily 9-5). **Patagonia Area Business Association Tourist Information Center** (✉317 McKeown Ave., Patagonia ☎520/394-0060 or 888/794-0060 ⊕www.patagoniaaz.com ☾Mon.-Sat. 10-5, Sun. 10-4) **Sierra Vista Convention and Visitors Bureau** (✉3020 E. Tacoma St., Sierra Vista ☎520/417-6960 or 800/288-3861 ⊕www.visitsierravista.com ☾Weekdays 8-5, Sat. 9-4).

In Southwestern Arizona **Nogales-Santa Cruz County Chamber of Commerce Visitor Center** (✉123 W. Kino Park Way, Nogales ☎520/287-3685 ⊕www.nogaleschamber.com ☾Weekdays 9-4). **Yuma Convention and Visitors Bureau** (✉139 S. 4th Ave., Yuma ☎928/783-0071 or 800/293-0071 ⊕www.visityuma.com ☾Weekdays 9-5, Sat. 9-4).

Moab & Southeastern Utah

WORD OF MOUTH

"I would not go out of my way for Monument Valley. The views are spectacular from afar. It's not a national park and doesn't have that solitude and wilderness feel. I didn't think it was worth the time to actually drive around each monument on a dusty, uninteresting road. Lake Powell is a marvel."

—travelottie

"I'd spend 3 nights in Moab—lots to see and do. Jeep trips, float trips, petroglyphs, Arches, Canyonlands, Dead Horse...Don't miss Moab."

—sharondi

By Janet
Buckingham

The first thing travelers to southeastern Utah notice is the color. Red, orange, purple, pink, creamy ivory, deep chocolate, and even shades of turquoise paint the landscape. Rocks jut and tilt first one way, then another. There's no flat canvas of color in this country, and near-vertical walls stand in the way of easy route-finding. Deep canyons, carved by wild Western rivers, crisscross the area. Rocks teeter on slim columns or burst like mushrooms from the ground. Snowcapped mountains stand in the distant horizon no matter which direction you look. The sky is more often than not blue in a region that receives only about eight inches of rain a year.

Embroidered through the region is evidence of the people who came before modern-day rock climbers and Mormons. Rock art as old as 4,000 years is etched or painted on canyon walls. The most familiar of these ancient dwellers are the Ancestral Puebloans, popularly known as Anasazi, who occupied the area between 700 and 2,000 years ago.

In modern-day southeastern Utah, Moab has become one of the state's liveliest small towns and the gateway to Arches and Canyonlands national parks. Surrounding the town, the area's unique and colorful geology calls out to mountain bikers, who love to ride over the humps of slickrock that act like natural highways in the wilderness. Thousands more take four-wheel-drive vehicles into the backcountry to drive the challenging network of roads left from mining days. Still others flock to the shores of the Colorado River, where they set out in rafts to tackle some of the largest white-water rapids in the country. With so many things to do, Moab has become a major tourist destination in the Southwest.

EXPLORING SOUTHEASTERN UTAH

I–70 is the speedway that gets you across Utah, but to dip into southeastern Utah, you'll need to use the main artery, U.S. 191, which runs south toward the Arizona border. The only road that stretches any distance westward across the region is Route 95, which dead ends at Lake Powell. No matter which of the state roads you use to explore the area, you're in for a treat. Here the earth is red, purple, and orange. The Manti–La Sal Mountains rise out of the desert-like ships. Mesas, buttes, and pinnacles interrupt the horizon in a most surprising way. But this is some of the most remote country in the United States, so services are sometimes far apart.

ABOUT THE RESTAURANTS

Since most people come to southeastern Utah to play on the rocks and rivers, casual is the *modus operandi* for dining. Whether you select an award-winning Continental restaurant or an outdoor patio grill, you can dress comfortably in shorts or jeans. Although you're in the middle of nowhere, there are some wonderful culinary surprises waiting for you, often with spectacular views as a bonus.

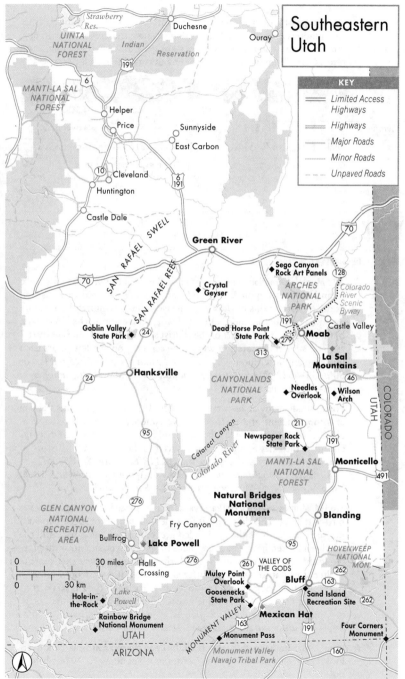

Southeastern Utah

KEY

═══	Limited Access Highways
═══	Highways
───	Major Roads
····	Minor Roads
---	Unpaved Roads

Strawberry Res.

UINTA NATIONAL FOREST

Duchesne

Ouray

Indian Reservation

6 191

MANTI-LA SAL NATIONAL FOREST

Helper
Price

Sunnyside
East Carbon

10 Cleveland
Huntington

Castle Dale

SAN RAFAEL SWELL

SAN RAFAEL REEF

Green River

70

Sego Canyon Rock Art Panels

128

ARCHES NATIONAL PARK

Colorado River Scenic Byway

Crystal Geyser

Goblin Valley State Park

24

Dead Horse Point State Park

Castle Valley

191
279 Moab

313

La Sal Mountains

Hanksville

24

CANYONLANDS NATIONAL PARK

Needles Overlook

46 Wilson Arch

COLORADO
UTAH

9

95

211

Cataract Canyon

Colorado River

Newspaper Rock State Park

191

Monticello

491

MANTI-LA SAL NATIONAL FOREST

Natural Bridges National Monument

GLEN CANYON NATIONAL RECREATION AREA

Fry Canyon

Blanding

HOVENWEEP NATIONAL MON.

Bullfrog
Lake Powell

276

0   30 miles
0   30 km

Halls Crossing

261 VALLEY OF THE GODS

95

Muley Point Overlook
Goosenecks State Park

Bluff 163

Sand Island Recreation Site 262

Hole-in-the-Rock

Lake Powell

Mexican Hat

Four Corners Monument

Rainbow Bridge National Monument

UTAH

163

MONUMENT VALLEY

Monument Pass

191

ARIZONA

Monument Valley Navajo Tribal Park

160

ABOUT THE HOTELS

Every type of lodging is available in southeastern Utah, from economy chain motels to B&Bs and high-end–high-adventure resorts. It's important to know when popular events are held, however, as motels and resorts can fill up weeks ahead of time during the busiest periods.

WHAT IT COSTS					
	¢	$	$$	$$$	$$$$
Restaurants	under $8	$8–$12	$13–$18	$19–$25	over $25
Hotels	under $70	$70–$110	$111–$150	$151–$200	over $200

Restaurant prices are for a main course at dinner, excluding sales tax of 7½%–8½%. Hotel prices are for two people in a standard double room in high season, excluding service charges and 11%–12¼% tax.

MOAB

EXPLORING MOAB

The **Moab Information Center,** right in the heart of town, is the best place to find information on Arches and Canyonlands national parks as well as other destinations in Utah's southeast. It has a wonderful bookstore operated by Canyonlands Natural History Association. The hours vary, but during the busiest part of the tourist season it's open until at least 7 PM, and sometimes later; in winter the center is open a few hours each morning and afternoon. ⊠ *Center and Main Sts.* ☎ *435/259–8825 or 800/635–6622* ⊕ *www.discovermoab.com* ⊙ *Mar.–Oct., daily 8–7; Nov.–Feb. hrs vary.*

For a small taste of history in the Moab area, stop by the **Museum of Moab.** Ancient and historic Native Americans are remembered in exhibits of sandals, baskets, pottery, and other artifacts. Other displays chronicle the early Spanish expeditions into the area and the history of uranium discovery and exploration. ⊠ *118 E. Center St.* ☎ *435/259–7985* ⊕ *www.moabmuseum.org* ☞ *$3* ⊙ *Apr.–Oct., weekdays 10–6, Sat. noon–6; Nov.–Mar., weekdays 10–3, Sat. noon–5.*

Scott M. Matheson Wetlands Preserve is the best place in the Moab area for bird-watching. This desert oasis is home to hundreds of species, including such treasures as the pied-billed grebe, the cinnamon teal, and the northern flicker. It's also a great place to spot beaver and muskrat playing in the water. A boardwalk winds through the preserve to a viewing shelter. Free nature walks are offered Saturday at 8 AM from March to May and from September to November. To reach the preserve, turn northwest off U.S. 191 at Kane Creek Boulevard and continue northwest approximately 2 mi. ⊠ *934 W. Kane Creek Blvd.* ☎ *435/259–4629* ⊕ *www.nature.org* ☞ *Free* ⊙ *Daily dawn–dusk.*

★ One of the finest state parks in Utah, **Dead Horse Point State Park** overlooks a sweeping oxbow of the Colorado River, some 2,000 feet below, as well as the upside-down landscapes of Canyonlands National Park. Dead Horse Point itself is a small peninsula connected to the main mesa by a narrow neck of land. As the story goes, cowboys used to drive wild horses onto the point and pen them there with a brush fence. Some were accidentally forgotten and left to perish. There's a modern visitor center and museum as well as a 21-site campground with drinking water and an overlook. ⊠ *34 mi west from Moab at end of Rte. 313* ☎ *435/259–2614, 800/322–3770 campground reservations* ⊕ *www. stateparks.utah.gov* ⊠ *$10 per vehicle* ⊗ *Daily 8–6.*

Fodor'sChoice The start of one of the most scenic drives in the country is found 2 mi
★ north of Moab off U.S. 191. The **Colorado River Scenic Byway—Route 128** runs along the Colorado River northeast to I–70. First passing through a high-walled corridor, the drive eventually breaks out into Professor Valley, home of the monoliths of Fisher Towers and Castle Rock, which you may recognize from various car commercials. The byway also passes the single-lane Dewey Bridge, which was in use from 1916 to 1986. Near the end of the 44-mi drive is the tiny town of Cisco. ⊠ *Rte. 128, from Moab to Cisco.*

★ If you're interested in Native American rock art, the **Colorado River Scenic Byway—Route 279** is a perfect place to spend a couple of hours. If you start late in the afternoon, the cliffs will be glowing orange as the sun sets. Along the first part of the route you'll see signs reading "Indian Writings." Park only in designated areas to view the petroglyphs on the cliff side of the road. At the 18-mi marker you'll see Jug Handle Arch on the cliff side of the road. Allow about two hours round-trip for this Scenic Byway drive. A few miles beyond this point, the road turns to four-wheel-drive only and takes you into the Island in the Sky District of Canyonlands. Do not continue on this road unless you are in a high-clearance four-wheel-drive vehicle with a full gas tank and plenty of water. ⊠ *Rte. 279, southwest of Moab.*

SPORTS & THE OUTDOORS

FOUR-WHEELING

There are thousands of miles of four-wheel-drive roads in and around Moab. The rugged terrain, with its hair-raising ledges, steep climbs, and smooth expanses of slickrock is the perfect place for drivers to test their mettle. There are abundant trails suitable for all levels of drivers. Seasoned 4X4 drivers might tackle the daunting **Moab Rim, Elephant Hill,** or **Poison Spider Mesa.** Novice drivers will be happier touring **Long Canyon, Hurrah Pass,** or, for those not afraid of precipitous cliff edges, the famous **Shafer Trail.** All of the routes offer spectacular scenery in the vast desert lands surrounding Moab. Expect to pay around $60 for a half-day tour, $100 for a full-day trip; multiday safaris usually start at around $500. Almost all of Moab's river-running companies also offer four-wheeling excursions.

For outfitters, see the Outfitters & Expeditions box.

GOLF

Moab Golf Course (✉2705 S. East Bench Rd.   ☎435/259–6488)is undoubtedly one of the most beautiful in the world. The 18-hole, par-72 course has lush greens set against a red-rock sandstone backdrop, a lovely visual combination that's been know to distract even the most focused golfer. Greens fees are $39 for 18 holes, including cart rental.

HIKING

Ramble through the desert near a year-round stream or get your muscles pumping with a hike up the side of a steep slickrock slope. Hiking is a sure way to fall in love with the high desert country, and there are plenty of hiking trails for all fitness levels. For a great view of the Moab valley and surrounding red rock country, hike up the steep **Moab Rim Trail.** For something a little less taxing, hike the shady, cool path of **Negro Bill Canyon,** which is off Route 129. At the end of the trail you'll find giant Morning Glory Arch towering over a cool pool created by a natural spring. If you want to take a stroll through the heart of Moab, hop on the **Mill Creek Parkway,** which winds along the creek from one side of town to the other. It's paved and perfect for bicycles, strollers, or joggers. For a taste of slickrock hiking that feels like the backcountry but is easy to access, try the **Corona Arch Trail,** off Route 279. You'll be rewarded with two large arches hidden from view of the highway. The Moab Information Center carries a free hiking trail guide to these and other trails. The many trails in the nearby Arches and Canyonlands national parks can get your boots moving in the right direction as well.

MOUNTAIN BIKING

Moab has earned a well-deserved reputation as the mountain-biking capital of the world, drawing riders of all ages off the pavement and onto rugged four-wheel-drive roads and trails. It's where the whole sport started and the area attracts bikers from all over the globe. One of the many popular routes is the **Slickrock Trail,** a stunning area of steep slickrock dunes a few miles east of Moab. Beginners should master the 2½-mi practice loop before attempting the longer, and very challenging, 10.3-mi loop. More moderate rides can be found on the **Gemini Bridges** or **Monitor and Merrimac** trails, both off U.S. 191 north of Moab. Klondike Bluffs, just north of Moab, is an excellent ride for novices. The Moab Information Center carries a free biking trail guide. Mountain bike rentals range from $38 for a good bike to $50 for a top-of-the-line workhorse. If you want to go on a guided ride, expect to pay between $120 to $135 per person for a half day, $155 to $190 for a full day, including the bike rental; you can save money by banding together with a larger group to keep the per-person rates down. Several companies offer shuttles to and from the trailheads.

For bike shops, shuttles, and tour companies, see the Outfitters & Expeditions box.

FodorsChoice
★

RIVER EXPEDITIONS

On the Colorado River northeast of Arches and very near Moab, you can take one of America's most scenic—yet unintimidating—river raft rides. This is the perfect place to take the family or to learn to kayak with the help of an outfitter. The river rolls by the red Fisher Towers as they rise into the sky in front of La Sal Mountains. A day trip on this stretch of the river will take you about 15 mi. Outfitters offer full- or half-day adventures here.

White-water adventures await more adventuresome rafters both upstream and down. Upriver, in narrow, winding Westwater Canyon near the Utah–Colorado border, the Colorado River cuts through the oldest exposed geologic layer on Earth. The result is craggy black granite jutting out of the water with red sandstone walls towering above. This section of the river is rocky and considered highly technical for rafters and kayakers, but it dishes out a great white-water experience in a short period of time. Most outfitters offer this trip as a one-day getaway, but you may also linger in the canyon as long as three days to complete the journey. A permit is required from the Bureau of Land Management (BLM) in Moab to run Westwater Canyon. Heart-stopping multiday trips through Cataract Canyon are for folks ready for a real adventure.

For rafting outfitters, see the Outfitters & Expeditions box.

WHERE TO EAT

★ $$–$$$$ ✗**Center Café.** This little jewel in the desert has a courtyard for outdoor dining. The mood inside is Spanish Mediterranean, made even more lovely by the fireplace. From grilled Black Angus beef tenderloin with caramelized onions and Gorgonzola, to roasted eggplant lasagna with feta cheese and Moroccan-olive marinara, there's always something on the contemporary menu to make your taste buds go "ah." Be sure to ask for the impressive wine list. ⊠ *60 N. 100 West St.* ☎ *435/259–4295* ▭ *D, MC, V* ☉ *Closed Dec.–Jan. No lunch.*

$–$$$$ ✗**Buck's Grill House.** For a taste of the American West, try the buffalo
Fodor's Choice meat loaf or elk stew served at this popular dinner spot. The steaks are
★ thick and tender, and the gravies will have you licking your fingers. A selection of Southwestern entrées, including duck tamales and buffalo chorizo tacos, round out the menu. Vegetarian diners, don't despair; there are some tasty choices for you, too. A surprisingly good wine list will complement your meal. Outdoor patio dining with the trickle of a waterfall will end your day perfectly. ⊠ *1393 N. U.S. 191* ☎ *435/259–5201* ▭ *D, MC, V* ☉ *Closed Thanksgiving–mid-Feb. No lunch.*

$–$$ ✗**Moab Brewery.** You can always find someone to talk to about canyon country adventure, since river runners, rock climbers, and locals all hang out here. There's a wide selection of menu choices, including fresh salads, creative sandwiches, and hot soups. Try the gyros salad for a taste of the Mediterranean. Last but not least, this hot spot serves the best brew in town. ⊠ *686 S. Main* ☎ *435/259–6333* ▭ *AE, D, MC, V.*

OUTFITTERS & EXPEDITIONS

BICYCLING

Chile Pepper Bikes. For bicycle rentals, repairs, and espresso, stop here before you hit the trails. ✉ 702 S. Main St., Moab ☎ 435/259–4688 or 888/677–4688 ⊕ www.chilebikes.com.

Moab Cyclery. Bike rentals and tours will get you rolling in canyon country. ✉ 391 S. Main St., Moab ☎ 435/259–7423 or 800/559–1978 ⊕ www.moabcyclery.com. **Poison Spider Bicycles.** This fully loaded shop is staffed by young, friendly bike experts. ✉ 497 N. Main St., Moab ☎ 435/259–7882 or 800/635–1792. **Rim Cyclery.** For full-suspension bike rentals and sales, solid advice on trails, and parts, equipment and gear, this is the oldest bike shop in town. ✉ 94 W. 100 North St., Moab ☎ 435/259–5333 or 888/304–8219 ⊕ www.rimcyclery.com.

Rim Tours. Trips include Gemini Bridges, the Slickrock Trail, Klondike Bluffs, and many other locations—including the White Rim Trail in Canyonlands. ✉ 1233 S. U.S. 191, Moab ☎ 435/259–5223 or 800/626–7335 ⊕ www.rimtours.com.

Western Spirit Cycling. This company offers fully supported, go-at-your-own-pace multiday bike tours throughout the region, including trips to the 140-mi Kokopelli Trail, which runs from Grand Junction, Colorado, to Moab. Guides versed in the geologic wonders of the area cook up meals worthy of the scenery each night. There's also the option to combine a Green River kayak trip with the three-night bike route. ✉ 478 Mill Creek Dr., Moab ☎ 435/259–8732 or 800/845–2453 ⊕ www.westernspirit.com.

FOUR-WHEELING

Coyote Land Tours. Let this company take you to backcountry where you could never wander on your own. Their big Mercedes Unimog vehicles cover some rough terrain while you sit back and enjoy the sights. ✉ 397 N. Main St., Moab ☎ 435/259–6649 ⊕ www.coyotelandtours.com.

Highpoint Hummer Tours. This outfitter does the driving while you gawk at the scenery as you travel off-road routes in an open-air Hummer ✉ 281 N. Main St., Moab ☎ 435/259–2972 or 877/486–6833 ⊕ www.highpointhummer.com.

MULTISPORT

Adrift Adventures. This outfitter can get you out on the Colorado or Green rivers for either day-long or multiday raft trips. Adrift also offers a unique combination horseback ride and river trip, movie-set tour, rock-art tours, and other 4X4 excursions. ✉ 378 N. Main, Moab ☎ 435/259–8594 or 800/874–4483 ⊕ www.adrift.net.

Coyote Shuttle. If you need a ride to or from your bicycle trailhead or river trip, call the Coyote. These folks also do shuttles to and from Green River for the train and bus service there. ✉ 397 N. Main, Moab ☎ 435/259–8656 ⊕ www.coyoteshuttle.com.

Moab Adventure Center. For a short trip on the Colorado River, a Hummer tour, scenic flight, national park tour, or rubber kayak rental, contact this reputable company. Its shop also sells gear and clothing. ✉ 225 S. Main St., Moab ☎ 435/259–7019 or 866/904–1163 ⊕ www.moabadventurecenter.com.

NAVTEC. A fast little boat by this outfit gets you down the Colorado River and through Cataract Canyon in one day. They also offer trips up to five days and 4X4 trips into nearby backcountry. Raft rentals are also available. ⊠ *321 N. Main St., Moab* ☎ *435/259–7983 or 800/833–1278* ⊕ *www.navtec.com.*

OARS. This company can take you rafting on the Colorado River and four-wheeling in the parks. ⊠ *543 N. Main St., Moab* ☎ *435/259–5865 or 800/342–5938* ⊕ *www.oarsutah.com.*

Red Cliffs Adventure Lodge. Take a horseback ride near one of Moab's working cattle ranches for a true Western experience. The lodge also offers guided rafting, hiking, and biking trips. ⊠ *Milepost 14, Rte. 128, Moab* ☎ *435/259–2002 or 866/812–2002* ⊕ *www.redcliffs lodge.com.*

Roadrunner Shuttle. Call for a ride to the airport or for a river or bike shuttle. They'll even take you to Salt Lake City or Grand Junction, Colorado, to catch a plane. ☎ *435/259–9402* ⊕ *www.roadrunnershuttle.com.*

Tag-A-Long Expeditions. This company holds more permits with the National Park Service and has been taking people into the white water of Cataract Canyon and Canyonlands longer than any other outfitter in Moab. They also run four-wheel-drive expeditions into the backcountry of the park as well as calm-water excursions on the Colorado River. They are the only outfitter allowed to take you into the park via both water and 4X4. Trips run from half day to six days in length. ⊠ *452 N. Main St., Moab* ☎ *435/259–8946 or 800/453–3292* ⊕ *www.tagalong.com.*

RIVER EXPEDITIONS

Canyon Voyages Adventure Company. This friendly, professional company is the only outfit that operates a kayak school. You can rent rafts and kayaks here. Inside the booking office is a great shop that sells river gear, outdoor clothes, hats, sandals, and backpacks. ⊠ *211 N. Main St., Moab* ☎ *435/259–6007 or 800/733–6007* ⊕ *www.canyon voyages.com.*

Holiday River Expeditions. You can rent a canoe or book a raft trip on the Green and Colorado rivers at this reliable company with decades of river experience. ⊠ *1055 E. Main St., Green River* ☎ *800/624–6323* ⊕ *www.bikeraft.com.*

Sheri Griffith Expeditions. This longtime Moab outfitter offers trips through the white water of Cataract, Westwater, and Desolation canyons. Specialty expeditions include river trips for women, writers, and families. They also offer more luxurious expeditions. ⊠ *2231 S. U.S. 191, Moab* ☎ *435/259–8229 or 800/332–2439* ⊕ *www.griffithexp.com.*

Tex's Riverways. The folks at Tex's will take very good care of you when you rent a canoe for a self-guided trip, and they can shuttle you to and from the Green or Colorado rivers. ⊠ *691 N. 500 West, Moab* ☎ *435/259–5101* ⊕ *www.texsriverways.com.*

ROCK CLIMBING

Desert Highlights. The only permitted canyoneering guide service in Arches, this outfitter can introduce you to the exciting sport of rock climbing. ⊠ *50 E. Center St., Moab* ☎ *435/259–4433 or 800/747–1342* ⊕ *www.deserthihglights.com.*

9

¢–$$ ✕**La Hacienda.** This family-run local favorite serves good south-of-the-border meals at an equally good price. The helpings are generous and the service is friendly. And yes, you can order a margarita. ⊠*574 N. Main St.* ☎*435/259–6319* ▤*AE, D, MC, V.*

¢–$$ ✕**Moab Diner.** For breakfast, lunch, and dinner, this is the place where old-time Moabites go. A mixture of good old-fashioned American food and Southwestern entrées gives you plenty to choose from. ⊠*189 S. Main St.* ☎*435/259–4006* ▤*D, MC, V.*

WHERE TO STAY

$$$$ ☒**Sorrel River Ranch.** This luxury ranch on the banks of the Colorado
Fodor'sChoice River 17 mi from Moab is the ultimate getaway. No matter which way
★ you look in a landscape studded with towering red cliffs, buttes, and spires, the vista is spectacular. Rooms are furnished with hefty log beds, tables, and chairs, along with Western art and Native American rugs. Some of the bathtubs even have views of the river and sandstone cliffs. For an extra cost, you can choose to relax in the spa with aromatherapy and a pedicure, go river rafting or mountain biking, or take an ATV out for a spin. At the **Sorrel River Grill** ($$–$$$$), the most scenic dining experience in the Moab area, the seasonal menu changes regularly to incorporate the freshest ingredients. ⊠*Rte. 128, Box K, mile marker 17.5,* ☎*435/259–4642 or 877/359–2715* ▤*435/259–3016* ⊕*www.sorrelriver.com* ⏎*32 rooms, 27 suites* ⚲*In-room: kitchen, VCR (some), Wi-Fi. In-hotel: restaurant, tennis court, pool, gym, spa, bicycles, laundry facilities, no-smoking rooms* ▤*AE, MC, V.*

★ $$$ ☒**Red Cliffs Adventure Lodge.** You can have it all at this gorgeous, classically Western lodge. The Colorado River rolls by right outside your door, and canyon walls reach for the sky in all their red glory; you can gaze at it all from your private riverfront patio. Rooms are Western in flavor, with log furniture, lots of wood, and Saltillo tile. Added attractions include an on-site winery, a movie memorabilia museum, as well as guided rafting, hiking, biking, and horseback-riding adventures into the desert. The setting is fabulous, but note that you're 14 mi from town. ⊠*Rte. 128, mile marker 14,* ☎*435/259–2002 or 866/812–2002* ⊕*www.redcliffslodge.com* ⏎*79 rooms, 30 cabins, 1 suite* ⚲*In-room: kitchen, VCR, Ethernet, Wi-Fi. In-hotel: restaurant, room service, pool, gym, no elevator, laundry facilities* ▤*AE, D, MC, V* ⎮◎⎮*CP.*

$$–$$$ ☒**Dream Keeper Inn.** Serenity is just a wish away at this B&B in a quiet
Fodor'sChoice Moab neighborhood, on large, shady grounds filled with flower and
★ vegetable gardens. The rooms line a hallway in the ranch-style home, and each opens onto the pool, patio, and courtyard area, where you may want to have your morning coffee. Or, you may prefer to have breakfast in the sunny indoor dining area. Some rooms have jetted tubs. **Pros:** Located on a quiet street. You can unwind in the shade near the pool. **Cons:** You'll have to leave the kids at home (which may not be a con for some). ⊠*191 S. 200 East, 84532* ☎*435/259–5998 or 888/230–3247* ▤*435/259–3912* ⊕*www.dreamkeeperinn.com* ⏎*6 rooms* ⚲*In-room: refrigerator, VCR, Wi-Fi. In-hotel: pool, no elevator, no kids under 15, no-smoking rooms* ▤*AE, D, MC, V* ⎮◎⎮*BP.*

WHERE TO CAMP

⚠ **Bureau of Land Management Campgrounds.** There are 342 sites at 18 different BLM campgrounds near Arches and Canyonlands national parks. Most of these are in the Moab area near Arches and Canyonlands' Island in the Sky District, along the Route 128 Colorado River corridor, on Kane Creek Road, and on Sand Flats Road. All sites are primitive, though Wind Whistle and Hatch Point do have water. Campsites go on a first-come, first-served basis. They are all open year-round. Credit cards are not accepted. ☎ *435/259–6111* ⊕ *www.blm. gov/utah/moab.*

★ ⚠ **Dead Horse Point State Park Campground.** A favorite of almost everyone who has ever camped here, either in RVs or tents, this mesa-top site fills up a little later in the day than the national park campgrounds. It is impressively set near the edge of a 2,000-foot cliff above the Colorado River. If you want to pay for your stay with a credit card you must do so during business hours (8–6 daily); otherwise you must pay in cash in the after-hours drop box. ⅃ *Flush toilets, dump station, drinking water, picnic tables, public telephone, ranger station* ⊋ *21 sites* ⊠ *Dead Horse Point State Park, Rte. 313, 18 mi off U.S. 191 (right outside the entrance to Canyonlands National Park)* ☎ *435/259–2614, 800/322–3770 reservations* ⊕ *www.stateparks.utah.gov* ▤ *MC, V.*

☾ ⚠ **Moab Valley RV Resort.** Near the Colorado River, with a 360-degree view, this campground seems to get bigger and better every year. Just 2 mi from Arches National Park, it's convenient for sightseeing, river rafting, and all types of area attractions and activities. On-site you can pitch some horseshoes, perfect your putting, or soak in the hot tub. Kids and parents alike will enjoy all the playgrounds, including a giant chess- and checkerboard. The place is spotlessly clean, with everything from tent sites to cottages. ⊠ *1773 N. U.S. 191, 84532* ☎ *435/259– 4469* ⊕ *www.moabvalleyrv.com* ⊋ *108 sites (62 with full hook-ups, 7 with water and electric only, 39 tent sites); 33 cabins* ⅃ *Flush toilets, full hookups, dump station, drinking water, guest laundry, showers, grills, picnic tables, electricity, public telephone, general store, play area, swimming (pool), Wi-Fi* ▤ *MC, V.*

Fodor'sChoice
★

★ ⚠ **Up the Creek Campground.** This neighborhood campground lies under big cottonwoods on the banks of Mill Creek. Even though you are near downtown, you'll feel like you're in the woods—the campground has walk-in tent sites only. ⊠ *210 E. 300 South, 84532* ☎ *435/259–6995* ⊕ *www.moabupthecreek.com* ⊋ *20 sites* ⅃ *Flush toilets, drinking water, showers, grills, picnic tables* ▤ *MC, V* ☾ *Mar.–Oct.*

9

CANYONLANDS NATIONAL PARK

Island in the Sky is 32 mi southwest of Moab via U.S. 191 and Rte. 313; Needles District is 76 mi southwest of Moab via U.S. 191 and Rte 211.

While Arches looks like Mars, Canyonlands resembles the moon. Mushroomlike rock formations rise randomly out of the ground, twisting into all manner of shapes: spires, pinnacles, buttes, and mesas. It's a desert landscape, but it's not devoid of water or color. The Green and Colorado rivers traverse the canyons, where the rich browns, verdant greens, and fresh yellows of the pinyon-juniper forests complement the deep reds, baby pinks, bright oranges, and milky whites of the rocks. The park's dirt roads appeal to mountain bikers, and the rising rapids of Cataract Canyon challenge rafters.

SCENIC DRIVES

Island in the Sky Park Road. This 12-mi long road connects to a 5-mi side road to the Upheaval Dome area. You can enjoy many of the park's vistas by stopping at the overlooks—get out of your car for the best views. Once you get to the park, allow about two hours to explore.

Needles District Park Road. You'll feel certain that you've driven into a picture postcard as you roll along the park road in the Needles District. Red mesas and buttes rise against the horizon, blue mountain ranges interrupt the rangelands, and the colorful red and white needles stand like soldiers on the far side of grassy meadows. The drive, about 10 mi one way, takes about half an hour.

WHAT TO SEE

SCENIC STOPS

★ **Grand View Point.** At the end of the main road of Island in the Sky, don't miss this 360-degree view that extends all the way to the San Juan Mountains in Colorado on a clear day. ⊠ *On the main road, 12 mi from the park entrance, Island in the Sky.*

★ **Mesa Arch.** Even though it can be crowded, you simply can't visit Island in the Sky without taking the quick ½-mi walk to Mesa Arch. The arch is above a cliff that drops nearly 1,000 feet to the canyon bottom. Views through Washerwoman Arch and surrounding buttes, spires, and canyons make this a favorite photo opportunity. ⊠ *On the main road, 6 mi from the park entrance, Island in the Sky.*

VISITOR CENTERS

Hans Flat Ranger Station. This remote spot is nothing more than a stopping point for permits, books, and maps before you strike out into the Maze District of Canyonlands. To get here, you must drive 46 mi on a dirt road that is sometimes impassable to two-wheel-drive vehicles. There's a pit toilet, but no water, food, or services of any kind. ⊠ *46 mi east of Rte. 24; 21 mi south and east of the Y-junction and Horseshoe Canyon kiosk on the dirt road, Maze* ☎ *435/259–2652* ⊙ *Daily 8–4:30.*

Island in the Sky Visitor Center. Stop and watch the orientation film and then browse the bookstore for information about the Canyonlands region. Exhibits help explain animal adaptations as well as some of the history of the park. ⊠ *Past the park entrance on the main park road, Island in the Sky* ☎ *435/259–4712* ⊙ *Daily 9–4:30 with expanded hrs Mar.–Oct.*

Needles District Visitor Center. This gorgeous building that blends into the landscape is worth seeing, even if you don't need the books, trail maps, or other information available inside. ⊠ *Less than 1 mi from the park entrance on the main park road, Needles* ☎ *435/259–4711* ⊘ *Daily 9–4:30 with expanded hrs Mar.–Oct.*

SPORTS & THE OUTDOORS

AIR TOURS

OUTFITTERS & EXPEDITIONS

Slickrock Air Guides. This company's regional tours give you an eagle's-eye view of the park, and you'll walk away with new respect and understanding of the word "wilderness." ⊠ *Canyonlands Air Field (also known as Grand County Airport), N. U.S. 191, near Moab* ☎ *435/259–6216 or 866/259–1626* ⊕ *www.slickrockairguides.com.*

BICYCLING

White Rim Road. Mountain bikers all over the world like to brag that they've ridden this 112-mi road around Island in the Sky. The trail's fame is well-deserved: it traverses steep roads, broken rock, and ledges as well as long stretches that wind through the canyons and look down onto others. There's always a good chance you'll see bighorn sheep here, too. Permits are not required for day use, but if you're biking White Rim without an outfitter you'll need careful planning and backcountry reservations (make them as far in advance as possible through the reservation office, ☎ 435/259–4351). Information about permits can be found at www.nps.gov/cany. There's no water on this route. White Rim Road starts at the end of Shafer Trail near Musselman Arch. ⊹ *Off the main park road about 1 mi from the entrance, then about 11 mi on Shafer Trail; or off Potash Rd. (Rte. 279) at the Jug Handle Arch turnoff about 18 mi from U.S. 191, then about 5 mi on Shafer Trail, Island in the Sky.*

See Four-Wheeling for more routes. For bike outfitters, see Outfitters & Expeditions box above.

BOATING & RIVER EXPEDITIONS

Seeing Canyonlands National Park from the river is a great and rare pleasure. Long stretches of calm water on the Green River are perfect for lazy canoe trips. In Labyrinth Canyon, north of the park boundary, and in Stillwater Canyon, in the Island in the Sky District, the river is quiet and calm and there's plenty of shoreside camping. The Island in the Sky leg of the Colorado River, from Moab to its confluence with the Green River and downstream a few more miles to Spanish Bottom, is ideal for both canoeing and for rides with an outfitter in a large, stable jet boat. If you want to take a self-guided flat-water float trip in the park you must obtain a $20 permit, which you have to request by mail or fax. Make your upstream travel arrangements with a shuttle company before you request a permit. For permits, contact the reservation office at park headquarters (☎ 435/259–4351).

Below Spanish Bottom, about 64 mi downstream from Moab, 49 mi from the Potash Road ramp, and 4 mi south of the confluence, the

Colorado churns into the first rapids of legendary Cataract Canyon, home of some of the best white water in the United States. Outfitters will take you for the ride of your life in this wild canyon, where the river drops more steeply than anywhere else on the Colorado River (in ¾ mi, the river drops 39 feet). You can join an expedition lasting anywhere from one to six days, or you can purchase a $30 permit for a self-guided trip from park headquarters.

For boating outfitters and rental companies, see Outfitters & Expeditions box above.

FOUR-WHEELING

Nearly 200 mi of challenging backcountry roads lead to campsites, trailheads, and natural and cultural features in Canyonlands. All of the roads require high-clearance, four-wheel-drive vehicles, and many are inappropriate for inexperienced drivers. Especially before you tackle the Maze, be sure that your four-wheel-drive skills are well honed and that you are capable of making basic road and vehicle repairs. Carry at least one full-size spare tire, extra gas, extra water, a shovel, a high-lift jack, and—October through April—chains for all four tires. Double-check to see that your vehicle is in top-notch condition, for you definitely don't want to break down in the interior of the park: towing expenses can exceed $1,000. For overnight four-wheeling trips you must purchase a $30 permit, which you can reserve in advance by contacting the Backcountry Reservations Office (☎435/259–4351). Cyclists share all roads, so be aware and cautious of their presence. Vehicular traffic traveling uphill has the right-of-way. It's best to check at the visitor center for current road conditions before taking off into the backcountry. You must carry a washable, reusable toilet with you in the Maze district and carry out all waste.

For guided 4X4 trips, see Outfitters & Expeditions box above.

★ **Elephant Hill.** The Needles route is so difficult—steep grades, loose rock, and stair-step drops—that many people get out and walk. In fact you can walk it faster than you can drive it. From Elephant Hill trailhead to Devil's Kitchen it's 3 ½ mi; from the trailhead to the Confluence Overlook, it's a 16-mi round-trip and requires at least eight hours. ✉ *Off the main park road, 7 mi from the park entrance, Needles.*

★ **White Rim Road.** Winding around and below the Island in the Sky mesa top, the dramatic 112-mi White Rim Road offers a once-in-a-lifetime driving experience. As you tackle Murphy's Hogback, Hardscrabble Hill, and more formidable obstacles, you will get some fantastic views of the park. A trip around the loop takes two to three days and you must make reservations almost a year in advance for an overnight campsite—unless you manage to snap up a no-show or cancellation. For reservation information call the Backcountry Reservation Office (☎435/259–4351). White Rim Road starts at the end of Shafer Trail near Musselman Arch. ✛ *Off the main park road about 1 mi from the entrance, then about 11 mi on Shafer Trail; or off Potash Rd. (Rte. 279) at the Jug Handle Arch turnoff about 18 mi from U.S. 191, then about 5 mi on Shafer Trail; Island in the Sky.*

HIKING

EASY **Aztec Butte Trail.** Chances are good you'll enjoy this hike in solitude. It begins level, then climbs up a steep slope of slickrock. The highlight of the 2-mi round-trip hike is the chance to see Ancestral Puebloan granaries. ⊠ *On Upheaval Dome Rd., about 6 mi from the park entrance, Island in the Sky.*

Grand View Point Trail. If you're looking for a level walk with some of the grandest views in the world, stop at Grand View Point and wander the 2-mi trail along the cliff edge. Most people just stop at the overlook and drive on, so the trail is not as crowded as you might think. On a clear day you can see up to 100 mi to the Maze and Needles districts of the park, the confluence of the Green and Colorado rivers, and each of Utah's major laccolithic mountain ranges: the Henrys, Abajos, and La Sals. ⊠ *On the main park road, 12 mi from the park entrance, Island in the Sky.*

Fodor'sChoice **Mesa Arch Trail.** By far the most popular trail in the park, this 2/3-mi ★ loop acquaints you with desert plants and terrain. The highlight of the hike is a natural arch window perched over an 800-foot drop below. The vistas of the rest of the park are nothing short of stunning. ⊠ *6 mi from the Island in the Sky Visitor Center.*

Slickrock Trail. If you're on this trail in summer, make sure you're wearing a hat, because you won't find any shade along the 2 2/5-mi round-trip trek across slickrock. This is one of the few front-country sites where you might see bighorn sheep. ⊠ *On the main park road, about 10 mi from the park entrance, Needles.*

Whale Rock Trail. If you've been hankering to walk across some of that pavement-smooth stuff they call slickrock, the hike to Whale Rock will make your feet happy. This 1-mi round-trip adventure, complete with handrails to help you make the tough 100-foot climb, takes you to the very top of the whale's back. Once you get there, you are rewarded with great views of Upheaval Dome and Trail Canyon. ⊠ *On Upheaval Dome Rd., 11 mi from the park entrance, Island in the Sky.*

MODERATE **Cave Spring Trail.** One of the best, most diverse trails in the park takes ★ ℭ you past a historic cowboy camp, prehistoric Native American petroglyphs, and great views along the way. About half of the trail is in shade, as it meanders under overhangs. Slanted, bumpy slickrock make this hike more difficult than others, and two ladders make the 3/5-mi round-trip walk even more of an adventure. Allow about 45 minutes. ⊠ *Off the main park road on Cave Springs Rd., 2 3//10 mi from the park entrance, Needles.*

DIFFICULT **Chesler Park Loop.** Chesler Park is a grassy meadow dotted with spires and enclosed by a circular wall of colorful "needles." One of Canyonlands' more popular trails leads through the area to the famous Joint Trail. The trail is 6 mi round-trip to the viewpoint. ⊠ *Elephant Hill trailhead, off the main park road, about 7 mi from the park entrance, Needles.*

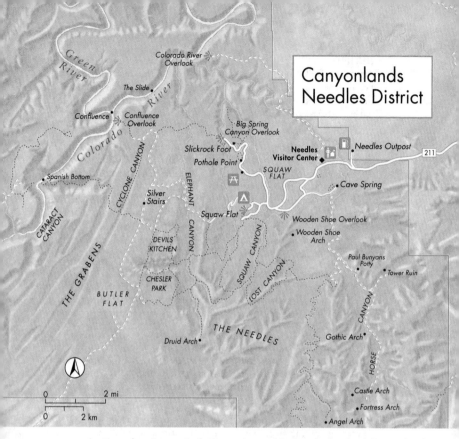

Canyonlands Needles District

Labels on map:
Green River · Colorado River Overlook · The Slide · Colorado River · Confluence · Confluence Overlook · Big Spring Canyon Overlook · Slickrock Foot · Pothole Point · Needles Visitor Center · Needles Outpost · 211 · SQUAW FLAT · Cave Spring · Spanish Bottom · CYCLONE CANYON · ELEPHANT CANYON · Silver Stairs · Squaw Flat · Wooden Shoe Overlook · Wooden Shoe Arch · CATARACT CANYON · DEVILS KITCHEN · SQUAW CANYON · LOST CANYON · Paul Bunyans Potty · Tower Ruin · THE GRABENS · CHESLER PARK · BUTLER FLAT · THE NEEDLES · Druid Arch · Gothic Arch · HORSE CANYON · Castle Arch · Fortress Arch · Angel Arch

0   2 mi
0   2 km

★ **Horseshoe Canyon Trail.** You arrive at this detached unit of Canyonlands National Park via a washboarded, two-wheel-drive dirt road. Park at the lip of the canyon and hike 6½ mi round-trip to the Great Gallery, considered by some to be the most significant rock-art panel in North America. Ghostly life-size figures in the Barrier Canyon style populate the amazing panel. The hike is moderately strenuous, with a 750-foot descent. Allow at least six hours for the trip and take a gallon of water per person. There's no camping allowed in the canyon, although you can camp on top near the parking lot. ⌧ *32 mi east of Rte. 24, Maze.*

★ **Joint Trail.** Part of the Chesler Park Loop, this well-loved trail follows a series of deep, narrow fractures in the rock. A shady spot in summer, it will give you good views of the Needles formations for which the district is named. The loop travels briefly along a four-wheel-drive road and is 11 mi round-trip; allow at least five hours to complete the hike. ⌧ *Elephant Hill trailhead, off the main park road, 7 mi from the park entrance, Needles.*

Syncline Loop Trail. Are you up for a long, full day of hiking? Try this 8-mi trail that circles Upheaval Dome. You not only get great views of the dome, you actually make a complete loop around its base. Stretches of the trail are rocky, rugged, and steep. ⌧ *On Upheaval Dome Rd., 11 mi from the park entrance, Island in the Sky.*

★ **Upheaval Dome Trail.** It's worth the steep hike to see this formation, which is either an eroded salt dome or a meteorite crash site. You reach the main overlook after just ½ mi, but you can double your pleasure by going on to a second overlook for a better view. The trail becomes steep and rough after the first overlook. Round-trip to the second overlook is 2 mi. ⊠*On Upheaval Dome Rd., 11 mi from the park entrance, Island in the Sky.*

ROCK CLIMBING

Canyonlands and many of the surrounding areas draw climbers from all over the world. Permits are not required, but because of the sensitive archaeological nature of the park, it's imperative that you stop at the visitor center to pick up regulations pertaining to the park's cultural resources. Popular climbing routes include Moses and Zeus towers in Taylor Canyon, and Monster Tower and Washerwoman Tower on the White Rim Road. Like most routes in Canyonlands, these climbs are for experienced climbers only.

For climbing outfitters, see Outfitters & Expeditions box above.

WHERE TO EAT

There are no dining facilities in the park itself. Needles Outpost, just outside the entrance to the park's Needles District, offers a snack bar with hamburgers and a small grocery store for picnicking necessities. Restaurants in Monticello and Blanding offer simple meals, and most do not serve alcohol. Your best bet for a variety of dining experiences, from microbreweries to fine dining or good home cooking, is in Moab. Moab delis and bakeries also can prepare fresh-made sandwiches to go.

PICNIC AREAS **Grand View Point.** Stopping here for a picnic lunch might be one of your more memorable vacation events. It's a gorgeous spot in which to recharge your energy and stretch your legs. There are picnic tables, grills, restrooms, and a little shade, if you sit near a juniper or pinyon. ⊠*12 mi from park entrance on the main road, Island in the Sky.*
Needles District Picnic Area. The most convenient picnic spot in the Needles District is a sunny location right near the roadway. There is one picnic table, but there are no grills, restrooms, water, or other amenities. ⊠*About 5 mi from the park visitor center, Needles.*
Upheaval Dome. Charming is a word that comes to mind to describe this picnic area nestled among the pinyon and juniper trees at the trailhead. There are no real vistas here, but the location is convenient to the Syncline Loop and Upheaval Dome trails. Amenities consist of picnic tables, grills, and restrooms without running water. ⊠*11 mi from the park entrance on Upheaval Dome Rd., Island in the Sky.*

9

WHERE TO STAY

There is no lodging inside Canyonlands. The towns of Monticello and Blanding offer basic motels, both family owned and national chains. Bluff also has motels and B&Bs and offers a quiet place to stay. A wide range of lodgings is available in Moab.

⚠ **Needles Outpost.** You may need to stop here for gas, supplies, or an icy drink and good meal after hiking, and you can also camp here. This privately run campground isn't as pretty or private as the others in and near Needles, but a chat with the owners will be a guaranteed hoot. ⊠*Rte. 211 about 1½ mi inside the park entrance, Needles* ☎*435/979–4007* ⌑*23 sites* ⅋*Flush toilets, dump station, drinking water, showers, fire grates, food service, service station* ▤*AE, D, MC, V* ⊙*Mid-Mar.–Oct.*

★ ⚠ **Squaw Flat Campground.** Squaw Flat is one of the best campgrounds in the National Park System. The sites are spread out in two different areas, giving each site almost unparalleled privacy. Each site has a rock wall at its back, and shade trees. The sites are filled on a first-come, first-served basis. ⊠*About 5 mi from the park entrance off the main road, Needles* ☎*435/259–7164* ⌑*25 sites* ⅋*Flush toilets, drinking water, fire pits, picnic tables* ▤*No credit cards.*

⚠ **Willow Flat Campground.** From this little campground on a mesa top, you can walk to spectacular views of the Green River. Most sites have a bit of shade from juniper trees. To get to Willow Flat you have to travel down a rough, washboarded road with tight and tricky turns. Since the drive is so difficult and only two sites are really suitable for RVs, RVers might prefer another campground. It is filled on a first-come, first-served basis only. ⊠*About 9 mi from the park entrance off the main park road, Island in the Sky* ☎*435/259–4712* ⌑*12 sites* ⅋*Pit toilets, drinking water, fire pits, picnic tables* ▤*No credit cards.*

CANYONLANDS ESSENTIALS

ACCESSIBILITY

There are currently no trails in Canyonlands that are accessible to people in wheelchairs, but Grand View Point and Buck Canyon Overlook at Island in the Sky are wheelchair accessible. The visitor centers at the Island in the Sky and Needles districts are also accessible, and the park's pit toilets are accessible with some assistance.

ADMISSION FEES

Admission is $10 per vehicle and $5 per person on foot, motorcycle, or bicycle, good for seven days. Your Canyonlands pass is good for all the park's districts. There's no entrance fee to the Maze District of Canyonlands. A $25 local park pass grants you admission to both Arches and Canyonlands for one year.

ADMISSION HOURS

Canyonlands National Park is open 24 hours a day, seven days a week, year-round. It is in the Mountain time zone.

EMERGENCIES

In the event of a fire or a medical emergency, dial 911 or contact a park ranger.

PERMITS

You need a permit for overnight backpacking, four-wheel-drive camping, mountain-bike camping, four-wheel-drive day use in Horse and Lavender canyons (Needles District), and river trips. You can get information on the Canyonlands reservation and permit system by visiting the park's Web site at ⊕*www.nps.gov/cany* or by calling the reservations office at ☎435/259–4351.

VISITOR INFORMATION

Contacts **Canyonlands National Park** (✉*2282 W. Resource Blvd., Moab, UT* ☎*435/719–2313, 435/259–4351 Backcountry Reservation Office* ⊕*www.nps. gov/cany*).

SOUTHEASTERN UTAH

GREEN RIVER

70 mi west of the Colorado state line via I–70.

Named for the river that runs through town, Green River, Utah, and its namesake are historically important. Early Indians used the river for centuries. The Old Spanish Trail also crossed the river, and the Denver and Rio Grande Railroad bridged the river here in 1883. Some say "the green" refers to the color of the water; others claim it's the vegetation along the river bank. Another story reports that it was named after a mysterious trapper named Mr. Green. Whatever the etymology, Green River remains a sleepy little town and a nice break from some of the more "hip" tourist towns in southern Utah.

Green River State Park is a shady retreat on the shores of the Green River. Best known for its 9-hole golf course, it's also a favorite of RV campers. It is the starting point for boaters drifting through Labyrinth and Stillwater Canyons on the Green River. ✉*450 S. Green River Rd.* ☎*435/564–3633, 800/322–3770 for campground reservations* ⊕*www.stateparks.utah.gov* 🎫*$7 per vehicle* ⊙*Summer, daily 6* AM–*10* PM; *winter, daily 8–5.*

The **Sego Canyon Rock Art Panels** are one of the most dramatic and mystifying rock-art sights in the area. On the canyon walls you can see large, ghostlike rock-art figures etched by Native Americans approximately 4,000 years ago. There's also art left by the Ute Indians from the 19th-century. Distinctive for their large anthropomorphic figures, and for horses, buffalo, and shields painted with red-and-white pigment, these rare drawings are some of the finest Ute pictographs in the region. The panels are 3½ mi off I–70 on a maintained gravel road. ✉*I–70, Exit 185, 25 mi east of Green River* ☎*435/259–6111 Bureau of Land Management Office in Moab.*

OFF THE BEATEN PATH

Crystal Geyser. The geyser erupts every 14 to 16 hours for about 30 minutes. The water shoots 80 to 100 feet high. On the banks of the Green River, 10 mi south of town, you'll get a good taste of backcountry on good, graded road. Mineral deposits have created a dramatic orange terrace surrounding the eruption site. The staff at the Green River Information Center, which is in the John Wesley Powell River History Museum, can provide detailed directions and updated road conditions.

SPORTS & THE OUTDOORS

RIVER FLOAT TRIPS   Bearing little resemblance to its name, Desolation Canyon acquaints those who venture down the Green River with some of the last true American wilderness. This journey takes you through a lush, verdant canyon where the rapids promise more laughter than fear and trembling. It's a favorite destination of canoe paddlers, kayakers, and beginning rafters. May through September raft trips through Gray-Desolation Canyon are popular and can be arranged by outfitters in Green River. South of town the river drifts at a lazier pace through Labyrinth and Stillwater canyons, and the 68-mi stretch of river that runs south to Mineral Bottom in Canyonlands National Park is best suited to canoes and motorized boats.

For river trip outfitters, see the Outfitters & Expeditions box.

WHERE TO STAY & EAT

¢–$$ ✕**Ben's Cafe.** At the local hot spot for homemade enchiladas you can also get a good porterhouse steak. This unpretentious restaurant on Green River's main thoroughfare offers plenty of choices at reasonable prices. ⊠*115 W. Main St.* ☎*435/564–3352* ▤*AE, D, DC, MC, V.*

★ ¢–$ ✕**Ray's Tavern.** Ray's is something of a Western legend and a favorite hangout for river runners. Stop here for great tales about working on the river as well as the coldest beer and the best all-beef hamburger in two counties. ⊠*25 S. Broadway* ☎*435/564–3511* ▤*AE, D, MC, V.*

$–$$ 🏨**Best Western River Terrace Hotel.** The setting, on the bank of the Green River, is conducive to a good night's rest. Comfortable, updated rooms are furnished with large beds, and the premises are clean. **Pros:** Riverside location is a real treat (be sure to request a river-view room). **Cons:** Nearby dining options are limited. ⊠*1740 E. Main St.,* ☎*435/564–3401 or 800/528–1234* 🖷*435/564–3403* ⊕*www.bestwestern.com* ◖*50 rooms* ♿*In-room: Wi-Fi. In-hotel: pool, no-smoking rooms* ▤*AE, D, DC, MC, V* ⍟*BP.*

MONTICELLO

53 mi south of Moab via U.S. 191.

Monticello, the seat of San Juan County, is a mostly Mormon community. This quiet town has seen some growth in recent years, mostly in the form of new motels made necessary by a steady stream of tourists venturing south from Moab, but it still offers very few dining or shopping opportunities. Nevertheless, with several inexpensive lodging choices, it's a more convenient alternative to Moab for those visiting the Needles District of Canyonlands National Park. At 7,000 feet, Monticello provides a cool respite from the summer heat of the desert, and it's at the doorstep of the Abajo Mountains. The highest point in the range, 11,360-foot Abajo Peak, is accessed by a road that branches off the graded, 22-mi Blue Mountain Loop (Forest Service Road 105, which begins in Monticello).

★ One of the West's most famous rock-art sites, **Newspaper Rock Recreation Site** contains Native American etchings that were engraved on the rock over the course of 2,000 years. Apparently, early pioneers and explorers to the region named the site Newspaper Rock because they believed the rock, crowded with drawings, constituted a written language with which early people communicated. Archaeologists now agree the petroglyphs do not represent language. The site is northwest of Monticello. ⊠*Rte. 211, about 15 mi west of U.S. 191.*

The Abajo Loop Scenic Backway (also known as Route 285 or Forest Road 079) climbs to 9,000 feet through the mountains between Monticello and Blanding. This route skirts the base of Abajo Peak and traverses 30 mi of mountainous terrain. The single-lane graded gravel or dirt road is rough and rocky. High clearance and stiff suspension are recommended. The route is impassable in winter and after rain storms. Allow at least three hours to drive this difficult but beautiful drive.

Before starting out on any trip into this rugged wilderness area, contact the **Manti–La Sal National Forest** (☎*435/587–3235*)to inquire about road conditions and to get further information about trails.

WHERE TO STAY & EAT

¢–$$ ✕**Homestead Steak House.** The folks here specialize in authentic Navajo fry bread and Navajo tacos. The popular—and big!—sheepherder's sandwich, is made with the fry bread and comes with your choice of beef, turkey, or ham and all the trimmings. No alcohol is served. ⊠*121 E. Center St.* ☎*435/678–3456* ▤*AE, D, MC, V.*

¢–$ 🏨**Days Inn.** One of the largest properties in Monticello, this is also one of the nicest, with a heated indoor pool and a hot tub that's just what the doctor ordered for soaking adventure-weary bodies. **Pros:** Management takes good care of the reliable chain rooms. **Cons:** Sits near the highway, so might be noisy (ask for a room on the back side). ⊠*549 N. Main St., Box 759,* ☎*435/587–2458* ▤*435/587–2191* ⊕*www. daysinn.com* ➥*43 rooms* &*In-room: refrigerator (some), Wi-Fi. In-hotel: pool, no elevator* ▤*AE, D, DC, MC, V* ⧌*CP.*

BLANDING

20 mi south of Monticello via U.S. 191.

Pioneers started settling along the base of the Abajo and Henry mountains near Blanding in 1897. Some of the stone buildings they raised still stand, and the town has a number of excellent museums that document the past. Thousands of ancient Pueblo ruins are scattered across the surrounding mesa top. You can't buy alcohol in this solidly Mormon town, and that includes even beer in grocery or convenience stores. Stock up in Monticello, 20 mi north on U.S. 191.

Stretch your legs while you learn about southeastern Utah in the **Blanding Visitor Center.** Maps, guidebooks, and regional books are for sale

9

here, and it's staffed by locals who really know the area. You'll see it right on the highway. ✉ *12 N. Grayson Pkwy.* ☎ *435/678–3662* ⊕ *www.blandingutah.org* ☾ *Apr.–Sept., Mon.–Sat. 8–8; Oct.–Mar., Mon.–Sat. 8–6.*

One of the nation's foremost museums dedicated to the Ancestral Puebloan Indians is at **Edge of the Cedars State Park.** The museum displays pots, baskets, spear points, and the only known metal implements from the Anasazi era in Utah. Behind the museum, you can visit an actual Anasazi ruin. ✉ *660 W. 400 North St.* ☎ *435/678–2238* ⊕ *www.stateparks.utah.gov* 🖃 *$6 per vehicle* ☾ *May–Sept., daily 9–6; Oct.–Apr., daily 9–5.*

☾ Road-weary travelers, especially children, will enjoy a stop at the **Dinosaur Museum,** the private collection of a family of working paleontologists. Skeletons, fossil logs, and footprints from all over the world are all on display. Hallways hold a collection of movie posters featuring Godzilla and other dinosaurlike monsters dating back to the 1930s. ✉ *754 S. 200 West St.* ☎ *435/678–3454* ⊕ *www.dinosaur-museum. org* 🖃 *$2* ☾ *Apr.–Oct., Mon.–Sat. 9–5.*

OFF THE BEATEN PATH

Hovenweep National Monument. For anyone with an abiding interest in the ancient Anasazi Indians, now called Ancestral Puebloans, a visit to this archaeological site is a must. Along a remote stretch of the Utah–Colorado border southeast of Blanding, Hovenweep features several unusual tower structures that may have been used for astronomical observations. A ½-mi walking tour, or a more rigorous 1½-mi hike into the canyon, allows you to see the ancient dwellings. A 32-site campground is available for overnighters in tents or small vehicles. ✉ *28 mi east of U.S. 191 on Rte. 262* ☎ *970/562–4282* ⊕ *www.nps.gov/hove* 🖃 *$6* ☾ *Daily 8* AM*–sunset.*

BLUFF

25 mi south of Blanding via U.S. 191.

Bluff, settled in 1880, is one of southeastern Utah's oldest towns. Mormon pioneers built a ranching empire that made the town at one time the richest per capita in the state. Although this early period of affluence has passed, several historic Victorian-style homes remain and can be seen on a short walking tour of the town. Pick up the free brochure "Historic Bluff by Bicycle and on Foot" at any business in town, and then take a walk through the era it describes. Most of the original homes from the 1880 town-site of Bluff City are part of the Bluff Historic District. In a dozen or so blocks are 42 historic structures, most built between about 1890 and 1905. On a windswept hill above town, gravestones bear the names of many of the town's first families.

Bluff is something of a supply point for residents of the Navajo Indian Nation, the largest Native American reservation, which lies just beyond the San Juan River. Bluff is a quiet place that has deliberately avoided the development that many nearby towns pursued. The San Juan River corridor and nearby canyons are rich with Native American rock art, dwellings, and other archaeological sites.

Three miles southwest of Bluff, the **Sand Island Recreation Site** has a large panel of Ancestral Puebloan rock art. The panel includes several large images of Kokopelli, the mischief maker from Pueblo Indian lore. ✉ *About 3 mi west of Bluff on U.S. 191* ☎ *435/587–1500 Monticello BLM office.*

OFF THE BEATEN PATH

Four Corners Monument. This marker represents the only place in the country where four states—Utah, Arizona, New Mexico, and Colorado—meet. Administered by the Navajo Nation, Four Corners offers not only a geography lesson but also a great opportunity to buy Native American jewelry and other traditional crafts directly from Navajo artisans. Bring cash, as credit cards and checks may not be accepted, particularly when buying from roadside displays or other impromptu marketplaces. To reach the monument, head south from Bluff on U.S. 191 for about 35 mi, to its junction with U.S. 160. (The U.S. 191–U.S. 160 junction is south of the Utah–Arizona border in the Navajo Nation.) Drive east on U.S. 160 for about 30 mi. At this point, U.S. 160 curves north to the monument site.

> ## TRAIL OF THE ANCIENTS
>
> As you head toward the southeast corner of Utah, you are not only entering the Four Corners Region of the United States, but approaching what is known as the "Trail of the Ancients." Route 95 is designated as such because it's rich with ancient Indian dwellings. Deep in the canyons of this area are petroglyphs, pictographs, and artifacts of the Ancestral Puebloan peoples. Enjoy looking but never touch, remove, or vandalize these historic sites or their artifacts; it's a federal offense to do so.

SPORTS & THE OUTDOORS

RIVER EXPEDITIONS

While somewhat calmer than the Colorado, the San Juan River offers some truly exceptional scenery and abundant opportunities to visit archaeological sites. It can be run in two sections: from Bluff to Mexican Hat, and from Mexican Hat to Lake Powell. Near Bluff (3 mi southwest on U.S. 191), the Sand Island Recreation Site is the launch site for most river trips. You'll find a primitive campground there. Permits from the Bureau of Land Management are required for floating on the San Juan River. For permits, contact the **Bureau of Land Management, Monticello Field Office** (⌂ *San Juan Resource Area, Box 7, Monticello, 84535* ☎ *435/587–1544* ⊕ *www.blm.gov/ut*).

Wild River Expeditions (✉ *101 Main St.* ☎ *435/672–2244 or 800/422–7654* ⊕ *www.riversandruins.com*)can take you out on the San Juan River on one- to eight-day float trips. This reliable outfitter is known for educational trips, which emphasize the geology, natural history, and archaeological wonders of the San Juan and its canyons.

WHERE TO STAY & EAT

$$–$$$ ╳ **Cow Canyon Trading Post.** Tiny but absolutely charming, this restaurant next to a classic trading post serves three dinner entrées daily. Meals are creative and diverse, with a touch of ethnic flair. Menu selections include a meat or vegetarian main with soup and salad. You can enjoy beer or wine with your meal. ⊠*U.S. 191 and Rte. 163* ☎*435/672–2208* ⊟*AE, D, MC, V* ⊘*Closed Nov.–Mar. No lunch.*

$ ⛄**Desert Rose Inn and Cabins.** Bluff's largest motel is truly a rose in the
Fodor'sChoice   desert. It's an attractive log-cabin-style structure with a front porch that
   ★   gives it a nostalgic touch, and all rooms are spacious and clean with
uncommonly large bathrooms. The cabins have small refrigerators and
microwaves. **Pros:** Beautiful motel with comfortable rooms. **Cons:** Has
no particular historic charm. ⊠*701 W. Main St. (U.S. 191), 84512*
☎*435/672–2303 or 888/475–7673* 🖷*435/672–2217* ⊕*www.desert
roseinn.com* 🛏*30 rooms, 6 cabins* ⚲*In-room: refrigerator (some),
Wi-Fi. In-hotel: no elevator, laundry facilities* ⊟*AE, D, MC, V.*

MEXICAN HAT

20 mi southwest of Bluff via U.S. 163.

Tiny Mexican Hat lies on the north bank of the San Juan River. Named
for a nearby rock formation, which you can't miss on the way into
town, Mexican Hat is a jumping-off point for visiting two geological
wonders: Utah's Goosenecks and Arizona's Monument Valley. Magnificent Monument Valley, stretching to the south into Arizona, is home
to many generations of Navajo farmers but is most recognizable from
old Westerns.

From the overlook in **Goosenecks State Park** (⊠*Rte. 316, off Rte. 261,
10 mi northwest of Mexican Hat)*you can peer down upon what geol-
ogists claim is the best example of an "entrenched meander" in the
world. The river's serpentine course resembles the necks of geese in
spectacular 1,000-foot-deep chasms. Although the Goosenecks of the
San Juan River is a state park, no facilities other than pit toilets are
provided, and no fee is charged.

The soaring red buttes, eroded mesas, deep canyons, and naturally
★   sculpted rock formations of **Monument Valley Navajo Tribal Park** are an
easy 21 mi drive south of Mexican Hat on U.S. 163 across Navajo land.
Monument Valley is a small part of the nearly 16-million acre Navajo
Reservation and is sacred to the Navajo Nation, or Diné (pronounced
din-*eh*, which means "the people"), as they refer to themselves. For
generations, the Navajo have grown crops and herded sheep in Monument Valley, considered to be one of the most scenic and mesmerizing
destinations in the Navajo Nation. Director John Ford made this amazing land of buttes, towering rock formations, and mesas popular when
he filmed *Stagecoach* here in 1938. The 30,000-acre Monument Valley
Navajo Tribal Park lies within Monument Valley. A 17-mi self-guided
driving tour on a dirt road (there's only one road, so you can't get lost)
passes the memorable **Mittens** and **Totem Pole** formations, among others. Drive slowly, and be sure to walk (15 minutes round-trip) from
North Window around the end of Cly Butte for the views. The park has
a 99-site campground, which closes from early October through April.
Be sure to call ahead for road conditions in winter. The Monument
Valley **visitor center** holds a small crafts shop and exhibits devoted to
ancient and modern Native American history. Most of the independent

guided tours here use enclosed vans, charge about $20 for 2½ hours, and will usually approach you in the parking lot; you can find about a dozen approved Navajo Native American guides in the center. They will escort you to places that you are not allowed to visit on your own. Bring your camera (and extra batteries) to capture this surreal landscape that constantly changes with the rising and setting sun. ⊠ *Visitor center, off U.S. 163, 21 mi south of Mexican Hat, Monument Valley* ☐ *Box 2520, Window Rock, 86515* ☎ *435/727–3353 park visitor center, 928/871–6647 Navajo Parks & Recreation Dept.* ⊕ *www. navajonationparks.org* ☑ *$5* ☉ *Visitor center May–Sept., daily 7–7; Oct.–Apr., daily 8–5.*

WHERE TO STAY

$$$ ☱ **Goulding's Lodge.** With spectacular views of Monument Valley from each room's private balcony, this motel often serves as headquarters for film crews. The lodge has handsome stucco buildings and all the rooms have balconies, coffeemakers, and hair dryers. The on-premises Stagecoach restaurant ($–$$$) serves the area favorite, a Navajo taco, or you can eat traditional American entrées; breakfasts are particularly good. Goulding's also conducts custom-guided tours of Monument Valley and provides Navajo guides into the backcountry. The lodge is 2 mi off U.S. 163, at the Monument Valley Tribal Park turnoff. **Pros:** This place is truly a slice of American history. And the views! **Cons:** It's miles from anything in any direction. ⊠ *Off U.S. 163, about 25 mi southwest of Mexican Hat, Box 360001, Monument Valley,* ☎ *435/727–3231* ☐ *435/727–3344* ⊕ *www.gouldings.com* ☚ *77 rooms* ☖ *In-room: refrigerator, DVD (some), VCR (some), Wi-Fi. In-hotel: restaurant, pool, no elevator, laundry facilities* ☐ *AE, D, DC, MC, V.*

NATURAL BRIDGES NATIONAL MONUMENT

33 mi north of Mexican Hat via Rtes. 261 and 275; 38 mi west of Blanding via Rtes. 95 and 275.

Nowhere but in Natural Bridges National Monument are three large river-carved bridges found so close together. When Elliot McClure, an early visitor, drove through the park in 1931, using the term "road" to describe the route into the Natural Bridges area was being generous. It's said the road was so bad that his car literally fell apart on the journey: First his headlights fell off. Next, his doors dropped off. Finally, his bumpers worked loose, and the radiator broke away.

Today a trip to see the three stone bridges is far less hazardous. All roads are paved, and a scenic 9-mi drive takes you to stops that overlook Sipapu, Owachomo, and Kachina bridges. Sipapu is the second-largest natural bridge in the world. Kachina is the most massive in the park. It was named for pictographs near its base that resemble katsina dolls. At 106-feet high and 9-feet thick, Owachomo Bridge is the smallest of the three. You'll need an hour or two to drive to overlooks of the natural bridges and remains of an Ancestral Puebloan structure, but if you have more time, you can also hike to each of the bridges on the uncrowded trails that are fragrant with the smell of sage. Sipapu and Kachina are fairly strenuous, with steep trails dropping into the canyon. Owachomo is an easy walk. The scientists among you should be sure to stop by the monument's array of solar panels, once the largest in the world; the solar energy helps keep Natural Bridges National Monument clean and quiet. ⊠*Rte. 275, off Rte. 95* ☎*435/692–1234* ⊕*www.nps.gov/nabr* ⊠*$6 per vehicle* ⊙*Daily 8 AM–sunset.*

LAKE POWELL

50 mi west of Natural Bridges National Monument (to Hall's Crossing) via Rte. 276.

Lake Powell, 185 mi long with 2,000 mi of shoreline—longer than America's Pacific coast—is the heart of the huge 1,255,400-acre Glen Canyon National Recreation Area. Created by the barrier of Glen Canyon Dam—a 710-foot wall of concrete in the Colorado River—Lake Powell took 17 years to fill. The second-largest man-made lake in the nation, Lake Powell extends through terrain so rugged it was the last major area of the United States to be mapped. It's ringed by red cliffs that twist off into 96 major canyons and countless inlets (most accessible only by boat) with huge, red-sandstone buttes randomly jutting from the sapphire waters. You could spend 30 years exploring the lake and still not experience everything there is to see. The Sierra Club has started a movement to drain the lake to restore water-filled Glen Canyon, which some believe was more spectacular than the Grand Canyon, but the lake is likely to be around for years to come, regardless of the final outcome of this plan.

The most popular thing to do at Lake Powell is rent a houseboat and chug leisurely across the lake, exploring coves and inlets. You'll have plenty of company, however, since thousands of people visit the lake during spring, summer, and fall. Fast motorboats, Jet Skis, and sailboats all share the lake. It's a popular spot for bass fishing, but you'll need a Utah fishing license from one of the marinas. Remember also that the lake extends into Arizona and if your voyage takes you across the state line, you'll need a fishing license that covers the southern end of the lake. Unless you love crowds and parties, it's best to avoid visiting during Memorial Day or Labor Day weekends. Because of drought conditions in the West, the level of water in Lake Powell has dropped significantly leading to the closure of boat ramps and marinas. It is important to check with the National Park Service for current water levels, closures, and other weather-related conditions.

Guided day tours are available for those who don't want to rent a boat. A popular full-day or half-day excursion sets out from the Bullfrog and Hall's Crossing marinas to **Rainbow Bridge,** the largest natural bridge in the world, and this 290-foot-high, 275-foot-wide arch is a breathtaking sight. The main National Park Service visitor center is at Bullfrog Marina; there's a gas station, campground, general store, and boat docks at the marina. ⊠*Bullfrog visitor center, Rte. 276* ☎*435/684–7400* ⊕*www.nps.gov/glca* ⊠*$15 per vehicle* ⊙*Hrs. vary; call for times.*

Hall's Crossing Marina is the eastern terminus of the **Lake Powell Ferry.** You and your car can float across a 3-mi stretch of the lake to the Bullfrog Basin Marina, from which it's an hour's drive north to rejoin Route 95. Ferries run seven days a week and depart on the even hour from Hall's Crossing and on the odd hour from Bullfrog. ⊠*Hall's Crossing Marina, Rte. 276* ☎*435/684–7000* ⌑*$20 per car* ⊙*Mid-May–mid-Sept., daily 8–7; mid-Sept.–Oct. and mid-Apr.–mid-May, daily 8–5; Nov.–mid-Apr., two trips per day (call for times).*

SPORTS & THE OUTDOORS

Boating and fishing are the major sports at Lake Powell. Conveniently, all powerboat rentals and tours are conducted by the same company, a division of Aramark called **Lake Powell Resorts & Marinas** (⊠*Bullfrog Marina* ⌑*Box 56909, Phoenix, 85079* ☎*800/528–6154* ⊕*www. lakepowell.com*). Daylong tours go to Rainbow Bridge, and there's also a Canyon Explorer tour that goes into some of the more interesting canyons. The company also rents houseboats, which are a popular option on Lake Powell.

OFF THE BEATEN PATH All of the landscape in this part of the country is strange and surreal, but **Goblin Valley State Park** takes the cake as the weirdest of all. As the name implies, the area is filled with hundreds of gnomelike rock formations. Colored in a dramatic orange hue, the goblins especially delight children. Short, easy trails wind through the goblins, and there's a small, but dusty, campground with modern restrooms and showers. ⊠*Rte. 24, 12 mi north of Hanksville* ☎*435/564–3633* ⊕*www.state parks.utah.gov* ⌑*$7 per vehicle* ⊙*Daily 8–sunset.*

SOUTHEASTERN UTAH ESSENTIALS

AIR TRAVEL

The nearest large airport to southeastern Utah is Walker Field Airport in Grand Junction, Colorado, 110 mi from Moab. It's served by Allegiant Air, American Eagle, Great Lakes Aviation, Sky West, United Express, and US Airways. Great Lakes Aviation also offers air service from Denver into Moab's Canyonlands Air Field.

Information **Canyonlands Air Field** (⊠*1 Airport Rd., Moab* ☎*435/259–0566*). **Walker Field Airport** (⊠*Grand Junction, CO* ☎*970/244–9100* ⊕*www.walker field.com*).

BUS TRAVEL

The only bus service in this part of Utah goes to Green River.

Information **Greyhound Lines** (☎*801/355–9579 or 800/231–2222* ⊕*www. greyhound.com*).

CAR TRAVEL

Information **Utah Highway Patrol** (☎*435/965–4684* ⊕*www.highwaypatrol.utah. gov*).**Utah State Road Conditions** (☎*511 toll-free within Utah*).

EMERGENCIES

Ambulance or Police **Emergencies** (☎*911*).

24-Hour Medical Care Allen Memorial Hospital (✉ *719 W. 4th North St., Moab* ☎ *435/259-7191*).**Blanding Medical Center** (✉ *930 N. 400 West St., Blanding* ☎ *435/678-3434*).**Green River Medical Center** (✉ *305 W. Main St., Green River* ☎ *435/564-3434*).**San Juan County Hospital** (✉ *364 W. 1st North St., Monticello* ☎ *435/587-2116*).

LODGING

Information **Moab Lodging and Central Reservations** (☎ *435/259-5125, 800/505-5343, or 800/748-4386* 🖶 *435/259-6079* ⊕ *www.moabutahlodging.com*).

CAMPING Information **Bureau of Land Management Moab Office** (☎ *435/259-6111* ⊕ *www.blm.gov*).**Manti-La Sal National Forest** (☎ *435/259-7155 Moab Ranger District, 435/587-2041 Monticello Ranger District* ⊕ *www.fs.fed.us/r4/mantilasal*). **Moab Information Center** (☎ *435/259-8825* ⊕ *www.discovermoab.com*).

VISITOR INFORMATION

Information **Blanding Chamber of Commerce** (✐ *Box 792, Blanding, 84511* ☎ *435/678-2539* ⊕ *www.blandingutah.org*).**Blanding Visitor Center** (✉ *12 N. Grayson, Blanding, 84511* ☎ *435/678-3662* ⊕ *www.blandingutah.org*).**BLM Grand Resource Area** (✐ *Box M, Moab, 84532* ☎ *435/259-8193* ⊕ *www.ut.blm. gov*).**Business Owners of Bluff** (⊕ *www.bluffutah.org*).**Grand County Travel Council** (✉ *125 E. Center St., Moab, 84532* ☎ *435/259-1370, 435/259-8825, or 800/635-6622* ⊕ *www.discovermoab.com*).**Green River Information Center** (✉ *885 E. Main St., Green River, 84525* ☎ *435/564-3427*).**San Juan County Community Development and Visitor Services** ✉ *117 S. Main St., Box 490, Monticello, 84535* ☎ *435/587-3235 or 800/574-4386* ⊕ *www.southeastutah.com*.

Arches National Park

The red rock landscape of Arches National Park awakens the spirit and challenges the imagination: balanced rocks teeter unthinkably on pedestals; sandstone arches—of which there are more than 2,000—frame the sky with peekaboo windows; and formations like the Three Penguins greet you at points throughout the 73,379-acre park. Far from a stereotypical beige-tone palette with the occasional cactus, the desert here is adorned with a rich tapestry of colors: red, orange, purple, pink, creamy ivory, deep chocolate, and even shades of turquoise. The Fiery Furnace burns like a wildfire at sunset, and acres of petrified sand dunes rise across the horizon.

Delicate Arch

WELCOME TO ARCHES NATIONAL PARK

TOP REASONS TO GO

★ **Unique terrain:** There's nowhere else on Earth that looks like this.

★ **Memorable snapshots:** You have to have a picture of Delicate Arch at sunset.

★ **Treasures hanging in the balance:** Landscape Arch is the longest open span in the world. Come quick! Due to its delicate nature, it could fall before you see it.

★ **Fiery Furnace:** A hike through this maze of rock walls and fins is sure to make you fall in love with the desert and appreciate nature at its most spectacular.

★ **Window to nature:** The park has the largest collection of natural arches in the world—more than 2,000. They make great frames through which to view moonrises, mountains, and more.

Balanced Rock

1 **Devil's Garden.** About 18 mi from the visitor center, this is the end of the road in Arches. Trails lead to Landscape Arch and numerous other natural rock windows. This area also has picnic tables, the park's only campground, and an amphitheater where campfire programs are held.

2 **Fiery Furnace.** This forbiddingly named area is so labeled because its orange spires of rock look much like tongues of flame, especially in the late-afternoon sun. About 14 mi inside from the visitor center, it's the site for ranger-guided walks.

3 **The Windows.** Reached on a spur 9 1/5 mi from the visitor center, this area of the park is where visitors with little time stop. Here you can see many of the park's natural arches from your car or on an easy rolling trail.

4 **Petrified Dunes.** Just a tiny pull-out about 5 mi from the visitor center, this scenic stop is where you can take pictures of acres and acres of petrified sand dunes.

5 **Courthouse Towers.** The Three Gossips, Sheep Rock, and Tower of Babel are the rock formations to see here. Enter this section of the park 3 mi past the visitor center. The Park Avenue Trail winds through the area, which was named for its steep walls and towers that look like buildings.

Bighorn Sheep

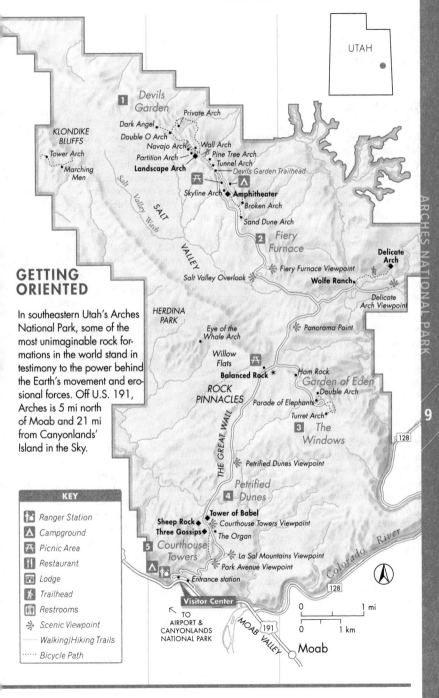

UTAH

1 **Devils Garden**

Private Arch

Dark Angel

Double O Arch

Navajo Arch · Wall Arch

Partition Arch · Pine Tree Arch

Landscape Arch · Tunnel Arch

Devils Garden Trailhead

KLONDIKE BLUFFS

Tower Arch

Marching Men

Salt Valley Wash

SALT VALLEY

Skyline Arch · **Amphitheater**

· Broken Arch

· Sand Dune Arch

2 **Fiery Furnace**

Delicate Arch

Fiery Furnace Viewpoint

Salt Valley Overlook · **Wolfe Ranch**

Delicate Arch Viewpoint

GETTING ORIENTED

In southeastern Utah's Arches National Park, some of the most unimaginable rock formations in the world stand in testimony to the power behind the Earth's movement and erosional forces. Off U.S. 191, Arches is 5 mi north of Moab and 21 mi from Canyonlands' Island in the Sky.

HERDINA PARK

Eye of the Whale Arch

Willow Flats

Balanced Rock *

ROCK PINNACLES

Panorama Point

Ham Rock

Garden of Eden

· **Double Arch**

Parade of Elephants ·

Turret Arch ·

3 **The Windows**

128

THE GREAT WALL

Petrified Dunes Viewpoint

Petrified

4 *Dunes*

Tower of Babel

Sheep Rock ◆ · Courthouse Towers Viewpoint

Three Gossips ◆ · The Organ

5 *Courthouse Towers*

La Sal Mountains Viewpoint

Park Avenue Viewpoint

· Entrance station

Colorado River

128

Visitor Center

← TO AIRPORT & CANYONLANDS NATIONAL PARK

MOAB VALLEY

191

Moab

KEY

🏠 *Ranger Station*

△ *Campground*

🌲 *Picnic Area*

🍴 *Restaurant*

🏨 *Lodge*

🚶 *Trailhead*

🚻 *Restrooms*

🔆 *Scenic Viewpoint*

····· *Walking/Hiking Trails*

······ *Bicycle Path*

0   1 mi

0   1 km

ARCHES NATIONAL PARK

9

ARCHES NATIONAL PARK PLANNER

When to Go

The busiest times of year at Arches are spring and fall. In the spring, blooming wildflowers and temperatures in the 70s bring the year's largest crowds. The crowds thin in summer as the thermostat approaches 100°F in July and then soars beyond that for about four weeks. In August, sudden, dramatic cloudbursts create rainfalls over red rock walls and dramatic skies for a part of the day.

Fall brings everybody back to the park because the weather is perfect—clear, warm days, and crisp, cool nights. October is the only autumn month that gets much rain, but even that isn't much, considering how little rain falls in the desert: an average of only 8 inches a year.

The park almost clears out in winter, and from December through February you can hike any of the trails in nearly perfect solitude. Though few realize it, winter can be the best time to visit this part of the country. Snow seldom falls in the valley beneath the La Sal Mountains, and when it does, Arches is a photographer's paradise, as snow drapes slickrock mounds and natural rock windows.

Getting There & Around

Interstate 70 is the speedway that gets you across Utah. To dip southeast toward Moab, veer off the interstate onto U.S. 191, a main artery running all the way south to the Arizona border, skirting Arches' western border, Moab, and the Monti-La Sal National Forest along the way. Alternatively, you can take Route 128, Colorado River Scenic Byway, traveling just east of Arches.

The nearest airport is Grand County Airport, also know as Canyonlands Field (☎435/259–7419), 18 mi north of Moab. Flights are very limited. The nearest train "station" is a solitary Amtrak stop in Green River, about 60 mi northwest of Moab. For train inquiries, call Amtrak (☎800/872–7245).

Branching off the main, 18-mi park road are two spurs, a 2½-mi one to The Windows section and a 1 3/5-mi one to the Delicate Arch trailhead and viewpoint. There are several four-wheel-drive roads in the park; always check at the visitor center for conditions before attempting to drive them. U.S. 191 tends to back up mid-morning to early afternoon.

Flora and Fauna

As in any desert environment, the best time to see wildlife in Arches is early morning or evening. Summer temperatures keep most animals tucked away in cool places, though lizards crawl around all day, so if you happen to be in the right place at the right time you'll spot one of the beautiful, turquoise-necklace-collared lizards. It's more likely you'll see the Western whiptail. Mule deer, jackrabbits, and small rodents such as pack rats are usually active in cool morning hours or near dusk. You may spot a lone coyote foraging day or night. The park protects a small herd of desert bighorns, and some of their tribe are often seen early in the morning grazing beside U.S. 191 south of the Arches entrance. If you are fortunate enough to encounter bighorn sheep, do not approach them. They have been known to charge human beings who attempt to get too close. The park's mule deer and small mammals such as chipmunks are very used to seeing people and may allow you to get close—but don't feed them.

By Janet
Buckingham

The red rock landscape of Arches National Park awakens the spirit and challenges the imagination: balanced rocks teeter unthinkably on pedestals; sandstone arches—of which there are more than 2,000—frame the sky with peekaboo windows; and formations like the Three Penguins greet you at points throughout the 73,379-acre park. Far from a stereotypical beige-tone palette with the occasional cactus, the desert here is adorned with a rich tapestry of colors: red, orange, purple, pink, creamy ivory, deep chocolate, and even shades of turquoise. The Fiery Furnace burns like a wildfire at sunset, and acres of petrified sand dunes rise across the horizon.

SCENIC DRIVES

Arches Main Park Road. Although they are not formally designated as such, the main park road and its two short spurs are scenic drives, and you can see much of the park from your car. The main road takes you through Courthouse Towers, where you can see Sheep Rock and the Three Gossips, then alongside the Great Wall and the Petrified Dunes. A drive to The Windows section takes you to Double Arch, North and South windows, and Turret Arch; you can see Skyline Arch along the roadside as you approach the campground. The road to Delicate Arch is not particularly scenic, but it allows you hiking access to one of the park's main features. Allow about two hours to drive the 36-mi round-trip, more if you explore the spurs and their features and stop at viewpoints along the way.

WHAT TO SEE

HISTORIC SITE

Wolfe Ranch. Built in 1906 out of Fremont cottonwoods, this rustic one-room cabin housed the Wolfe family after their first cabin was lost to a flash flood. In addition to the cabin you can see remains of a root cellar and a corral. Even older than these structures is the nearby Ute rock-art panel by the Delicate Arch trailhead. About 150 feet past the footbridge and before the trail starts to climb, you can see images of bighorn sheep as well as some smaller images believed to be dogs. To reach the panel, follow the narrow dirt trail along the rock escarpment until you see the interpretive sign. ⊠ *12 9/10 mi from the park entrance, 1 2/10 mi off the main road.*

SCENIC STOPS

Balanced Rock. One of the park's favorite sights, this rock has remained mysteriously balanced on its pedestal for who knows how long. The formation's total height is 128 feet, with the huge balanced rock rising 55 feet above the pedestal. A short loop (3/10 mi) around the base gives you an opportunity to stretch your legs and take photographs. ⊠ *9 1/5 mi from the park entrance on the main road.*

Fodor'sChoice
★
Delicate Arch. The familiar symbol of Arches National Park, if not for the entire state of Utah, Delicate Arch is tall enough to shelter a four-story building. The arch is a remnant of an Entrada sandstone fin;

ARCHES NATIONAL PARK

9

the rest of the rock has eroded and now frames the La Sal Mountains in the background. You can drive a couple of miles off the main road to view the arch from a distance, or you can hike right up to it. The trail is a moderately strenuous 3-mi round-trip hike. ⊠*13 mi from the park entrance, 2 1/5 mi off the main road.*

> ## WHAT'S AN ARCH?
>
> To be defined as an arch, a rock opening must be in a continuous wall of rock and have a minimum opening of 3 feet in any one direction. A natural bridge differs from an arch in that it is formed by water flowing beneath it.

Double Arch. In The Windows section of the park, Double Arch has appeared in several Hollywood movies, including *Indiana Jones and the Last Crusade*. Less than ¼ mi from the parking lot, the spectacular rock formation can be reached in about 10 minutes. ⊠*11 7/10 mi from the park entrance on the main road.*

★ **Landscape Arch.** This natural rock opening competes with Kolob Arch at Zion for the title of largest geologic span in the world. Measuring 306 feet from base to base, it appears as a delicate ribbon of rock bending over the horizon. In 1991 a slab of rock about 60 feet long, 11 feet wide, and 4 feet thick fell from the underside, leaving it even thinner. You can reach it by walking a rolling, gravel 1 3/5-mi-long trail. ⊠*Devils Garden, 18 mi from park entrance on the main road.*

☺ **Sand Dune Arch.** Kids love the trail to this arch because erosion has created a giant sandbox beneath the namesake arch. While it's an easy trail, remember that sand is difficult to walk in. A cautionary note: do not climb or jump off the arch; rangers have dealt with several accidents involving people who have done so. Allow about 15 minutes to walk the 3/10 mi to the arch and back to your car. The trail intersects with the Broken Arch Trail, so if you visit both arches, it's a 1½-mi round-trip. ⊠*16 mi from the park entrance on the main road.*

Skyline Arch. A quick walk from the parking lot gives you closer views and better photos of the arch. The short trail is 2/5 mi round-trip and only takes a few minutes to travel. ⊠*16½ mi from the park entrance on the main road.*

☺ **The Windows.** Many people with limited time to spend in the park drive to this area. Here you can see a large concentration of natural windows and walk a path that winds beneath them. ⊠*11 7/10 mi from the park entrance, 2½ mi off the main road.*

VISITOR CENTER

Arches Visitor Center. It's definitely worth stopping to see the interactive displays here; they'll make your sightseeing tour through the park more meaningful. Take time to view the 15-minute park film, *Secrets of the Red Rock,* and shop the bookstore for trail guides, books, and maps to enhance your visit. Exhibits inform you about geology, natural history, and Ancestral Puebloan presence in the Arches area. There is water in vending machines outside the center. ⊠*At the park entrance* ☎*435/719–2299* ☉*Hrs vary but generally 8 AM–5 PM daily, with extended hrs late spring through early fall.*

SPORTS & THE OUTDOORS

BICYCLING

There's outstanding mountain biking all around Arches National Park, but the park proper is not the best place to explore on two wheels. Bicycles are only allowed on established roads and since there are no shoulders, cyclists share the roadway with drivers and pedestrians gawking at the scenery. If you do want to take a spin in the park, try Willow Flats Road, the old entrance to the park. The road is about 6½-mi long one way and starts directly across from the Balanced Rock parking lot. It's a pretty ride on dirt and sand through slickrock, pinyon, and juniper country. You must stay on the road with your bicycle or you chance steep fines.

For bike rentals and expeditions, see Outfitters & Expeditions box above.

HIKING

EASY **Balanced Rock Trail.** You'll want to stop at Balanced Rock for photo opportunities, so you may as well walk the easy, partially paved trail around the famous landmark. This is one of the most accessible trails in the park and is suitable for small children and folks who may have difficulty walking. The trail is only 3/10 mi round-trip; you should allow 15 minutes for the walk. ⊠*Approximately 9 mi from the park entrance.*

Broken Arch Trail. An easy walk across open grassland, this loop trail passes Broken Arch, which is also visible from the road. The arch gets its name because it appears to be cracked in the middle, but it's not really broken. The trail is 2 mi round-trip, and you should allow about an hour for the walk. ⊠*End of Sand Dune Arch trail, 3/10 mi off the main park road, 11 mi from the park entrance.*

Double Arch Trail. Near the Windows Trail is this relatively flat trail that leads you to two massive arches that make for great photo opportunities. Although only ½ mi round-trip, you get a good taste of desert flora and fauna. ⊠*2½ mi from the main road on the Windows Section spur road.*

Park Avenue Trail. Walk under the gaze of Queen Nefertiti, a giant rock formation that some observers think has Egyptian-looking features. The nearby rock walls resemble a New York City skyline—hence the name Park Avenue. The trail is fairly easy, with only a short hill to navigate. It's 2 mi round-trip, or, if you are traveling with companions, you can have one of them pick you up at the Courthouse Towers Viewpoint, making it a 1-mi trek downhill. Allow about 45 minutes for the one-way journey. ⊠*On the main road, 2 mi from the park entrance.*

Sand Dune Arch Trail. Your kids will return to the car with shoes full of sand at this giant sandbox in the desert. It's a shady, quick hike that everyone in the family will enjoy. Set aside 30 minutes for this 2/5-mi walk. ⊠*On the main road, about 15½ mi from the park entrance.*

Windows Trail. One of everyone's favorite stops in the park also gives you an opportunity to get out and enjoy the desert air. Here you'll see three giant openings in rock and walk on a trail that leads you right through the holes. Allow about an hour on this gently inclined 1-mi round-trip hike. ⊠ *On the main road, 9½ mi from the park entrance.*

MODERATE
Fodor'sChoice
★

Devils Garden Trail. If you want to take a longer hike in the park, head out on this network of trails, where you can see a number of arches. You will reach Tunnel and Pine Tree arches after only 2/5 mi on the gravel trail, and Landscape Arch is 4/5 mi from the trailhead. Past Landscape Arch the trail changes dramatically, increasing in difficulty with many short, steep climbs. You will encounter some heights as you inch your way across a long rock fin. The trail is marked with rock cairns, and it's always a good idea to locate the next one before moving on. Along the way to Double O Arch, 2 mi from the trailhead, you can take short detours to Navajo and Partition arches. A round-trip hike to Double O takes from two to three hours. For a longer hike, include Dark Angel and/or return to the trailhead on the primitive loop. This is a difficult route through fins with a short side trip to Private Arch. If you hike all the way to Dark Angel and return on the primitive loop, the trail is 7 1/5 mi round-trip. Allow about five hours for this adventure, take plenty of water, and watch your route carefully. ⊠ *18 mi from the park entrance on the main road.*

Tower Arch Trail. In a remote, seldom-visited area of the park, this trail takes you to a giant rock opening. If you look beneath the arch you will see a 1922 inscription left by Alex Ringhoffer, who "discovered" this section of the park. Reach the trail by driving to the Klondike Bluffs parking area via a dirt road that starts at the main park road across from Broken Arch. Check with park rangers for road conditions before attempting the drive. Allow from two to three hours for this hike. ⊠ *24½ mi from the park entrance, 7 7/10 mi off the main road.*

DIFFICULT
★

Delicate Arch Trail. To see the park's most famous freestanding arch up close takes some effort. The 3-mi round-trip trail ascends a steep slickrock slope that offers no shade—it's very hot in summer. What you find at the end of the trail is, however, worth the hard work. You can walk under the arch and take advantage of abundant photo ops, especially at sunset. In spite of its difficulty, this is a very popular trail. Allow anywhere from one to three hours for this hike, depending on your fitness level and how long you plan to linger at the arch. The trail starts at Wolf Ranch. ⊠ *13 mi from the park entrance, 2 1/5 mi off the main road.*

★

Fiery Furnace Hiking. Rangers strongly suggest taking the guided hike through this area before you set out on your own, as there is no marked trail. A hike here is a challenging but fascinating trip through rugged terrain into the heart of Arches. The trail occasionally requires the use of hands and feet to scramble up and through narrow cracks and along narrow ledges above drop-offs. To hike this area on your own you must get a permit at the visitor center ($2). If you're not familiar with the

Furnace you can easily get lost and cause resource damage, so watch your step and use great caution. ⊠ *Off the main park road, about 15 mi from the visitor center.*

ROCK CLIMBING

Rock climbers travel from across the country to scale the sheer red rock walls of Arches National Park and surrounding areas. Most climbing routes in the park require advanced techniques. Permits are not required, but you are responsible for knowing park regulations and restricted routes. One popular route in the park is Owl Rock in the Garden of Eden (about 10 mi from the visitor center), which ranges in difficulty from 5.8 to 5.11 on a scale that goes up to 5.13+. Many climbing routes are available in the Park Avenue area, about 2 1/5 mi from the visitor center. These routes are also extremely difficult climbs. Before climbing, it's imperative that you stop at the visitor center and talk with a ranger.

For rock climbing outfitters, see Outfitters & Expeditions box above.

NEARBY TOWNS

Moab is the major gateway to both Arches and Canyonlands national parks. Here you'll find the area's greatest number of sports outfitters to help you enjoy the parks.

The next-closest town to Arches, about 47 mi to the northwest, is **Green River.** It's worth a visit for the **Crystal Geyser,** which erupts for 30 minutes every 14 to 16 hours.

See above for more information about these and other nearby towns.

WHERE TO EAT

Supermarkets, bakeries, and delis in downtown Moab will be happy to make you a sandwich to go. If you bring a packed lunch, there are several picnic areas from which to choose. *For dining recommendations in Moab see above.*

PICNIC AREAS **Balanced Rock.** The view is the best part of this picnic spot. There are no cooking facilities or water, but there are tables. If you sit just right you might find some shade under a small juniper; otherwise, this is an exposed site. Pit toilets are nearby. ⊠ *Opposite the Balanced Rock parking area, 9 1/5 mi from the park entrance on the main road.*

Devils Garden. There are grills, water, picnic tables, restrooms, and depending on the time of day, some shade from large junipers and rock walls. It's a good place for lunch before or after you go hiking. ⊠ *On the main road, 18 mi from the park entrance.*

WHERE TO STAY

Though there are no hotels or cabins in the park itself, in the surrounding area every type of lodging is available, from economy chain motels to B&Bs and high-end, high-adventure resorts. Campgrounds

ARCHES NATIONAL PARK

9

are in Moab and will generally provide services needed by RV travelers (⇨ *Where to Stay in Moab*).

⚠ **Devils Garden Campground.** This small campground is one of the most unusual—and gorgeous—in the national park system, and in the West, for that matter. Sites, which are tucked away into red rock outcroppings, are available on a first-come, first-served basis during the off-season, but March through October, when the campground gets full, campers are required to pre-register for a site; this can be done at the visitor center between 7:30 and 8 AM, or at the campground entrance station after 8 AM. Also March through October, up to 28 of the campsites can be reserved in advance (at least four but no more than 240 days prior) by contacting National Recreation Reservation Service (NRRS) via phone or online; there is a $9 booking fee. ✉ *18 mi from the park entrance on the main park road* ☎ *435/719–2299, 518/885–3639 or 877/444–6777 NRRS reservations* ☎ *435/259–4285* w*www.recreation.gov a 52 sites* ♿ *Flush toilets, drinking water, fire grates, picnic tables* ▭ *No credit cards.*

ARCHES ESSENTIALS

ACCESSIBILITY
Not all park facilities meet federally mandated ADA standards, but as visitation to Arches climbs, the park is making efforts to increase accessibility. Visitors with mobility impairments can access the visitor center, all restrooms throughout the park, and one campsite (#7) at the Devils Garden Campground. The Park Avenue Viewpoint is a paved path with a slight decline near the end, and both Delicate Arch and Balanced Rock viewpoints are partially hard surfaced.

ADMISSION FEES
Admission to the park is $10 per vehicle and $5 per person on foot, motorcycle, or bicycle, good for seven days. You must pay admission to Canyonlands separately. A $25 local park pass grants you admission to both the Arches and Canyonlands parks for one year.

ADMISSION HOURS
Arches National Park is open year-round, seven days a week, around the clock. It's in the Mountain time zone.

EMERGENCIES
Call 911 or contact a park ranger (on hand at the visitor center during operating hours). There are no first-aid stations in the park; report to the visitor center for assistance. The closest hospital is in Moab.

PERMITS
Permits are required for backcountry camping and for hiking without a park ranger in the Fiery Furnace. You can purchase a Fiery Furnace permit ($2 per person for adults, $1 for kids 7–12) at the visitor center.

VISITOR INFORMATION
Contacts **Arches National Park** (✉ *N. U.S. 191, Moab, UT* ☎ *435/719–2299, 435/719–2200, 435/719–2391 for the hearing-impaired* ⊕ *www.nps.gov/arch*).

Southwestern Utah

WORD OF MOUTH

"Cedar City is about the same distance and travel time to Springdale as St. George. It is a bit closer to the Kolob Canyon section of Zion, and probably about 30 minutes or so closer to Bryce than St. George. The drive between Cedar City and Bryce would be much better (scenery-wise) in fall than from Zion to Bryce. Cedar Breaks National Monument is not far from Cedar City and should be nice in fall, provided there isn't an early snowfall."

—BibE1

By John
Blodgett

Southwestern Utah is a land of adventure and contemplation, of adrenaline and retreat. It's not an either-or proposition; you rejuvenate whether soaking at a luxury spa or careening on a mountain bike down an alpine single-track headed straight for an aspen tree. The land settlers tamed for planting cotton and fruit is now a playground for golfers, bikers, and hikers. Arts festivals and concerts under canyon walls have smoothed the rough edges hewn by miners and the boomtowns that evaporated as quickly as they materialized. Ruins, petroglyphs, pioneer graffiti, and ghost towns—monuments to what once was—beckon new explorers. The region's secrets reveal themselves to seekers, yet some mysteries remain elusive—the paradox of the bustling world that lies hidden under the impression of spare, silent, and open space.

EXPLORING SOUTHWESTERN UTAH

ABOUT THE RESTAURANTS

Traditional and contemporary American cuisines are most common, followed closely by those with Mexican and Southwestern influences. Around St. George, there are a number of restaurants that serve seafood; keep in mind that at nicer restaurants, the fish is flown in daily from the West Coast; at the less expensive locales, the fish is usually frozen. Because this is conservative Utah, don't presume a restaurant serves beer, much less wine or cocktails, especially in the smaller towns. Dress tends to be casual.

ABOUT THE HOTELS

Southwestern Utah is steeped in pioneer heritage, and you'll find many older homes that have been refurbished as bed-and-breakfasts. Green Gate Village in St. George, a collection of pioneer homes gathered from around the state, is an excellent example. The area also has its share of older independent motels in some of the smaller towns. Most of the major hotel and motel chains have opened up at least one facility in the region. The high season is usually summer, and logic dictates that the closer you want to be to a major attraction, the further in advance you have to make reservations. If you are willing to find a room upward of an hour from your destination, perhaps with fewer amenities, you may be surprised not only by same-day reservations in some cases, but also much lower room rates. Panguitch has some particularly good options for budget and last-minute travelers.

WHAT IT COSTS				
¢	$	$$	$$$	$$$$
Restaurants under $8	$8–$12	$13–$18	$19–$25	over $25
Hotels under $70	$70–$110	$111–$150	$151–$200	over $200

Restaurant prices are for a main course at dinner, excluding sales tax of 7½%–8½%. Hotel prices are for two people in a standard double room in high season, excluding service charges and 11%–12¼% tax.

SOUTHWESTERN UTAH TOP 5

To Go With the (Lava) Flow: As you hike along the lower trails of Snow Canyon State Park, look up to see ridges capped in lava from eruptions possibly as recent as 20,000 years ago.

To Sit in a Stagecoach: Check out the one restored stagecoach that visitors can hop aboard at Iron Mission State Park Museum.

To Camp Beneath the Aspens: The 26 campgrounds in Dixie National Forest might seem like a lot, but it's still easy to lose yourself amidst the forest's two million acres.

To Pay Your Respects to the Bard: Watch the likes of Othello on a stage that replicates the Old Globe Theatre during the Utah Shakespearean Festival.

To Watch Where a Dinosaur Stepped: The St. George Dinosaur Discovery Site at Johnson Farm would be developed real estate if a backhoe hadn't unearthed ancient footprints in 2000.

UTAH'S DIXIE

Mormon pioneers from the American South settled this part of Utah to grow cotton and brought the name Dixie with them. Some thought the move was a gamble, but the success of the settlement may be measured in the region's modern-day definition of risk: hopping the border to nearby Mesquite, Nevada, to roll the dice. St. George is often the hottest place in the state, but the Pine Valley Mountains and Brian Head offer alpine relief and summer recreation.

CEDAR CITY

250 mi southwest of Salt Lake City via I–15 south.

Rich iron-ore deposits here grabbed Mormon leader Brigham Young's attention, and he ordered a Church of Jesus Christ of Latter-day Saints (LDS) mission established. The first ironworks and foundry opened in 1851 and operated for only eight years; problems with the furnace, flooding, and hostility between settlers and American Indians eventually put out the flame. Residents then turned to ranching and agriculture for their livelihood, and Cedar City thrived thereafter.

Cedar City calls itself "The Festival City." The Southern Utah University campus hosts the city's major event, the Utah Shakespearean Festival, which has been stretching its season longer and longer as its reputation has grown. Though better known for festivals than recreation, the city is well placed for exploring the Brian Head area.

In winter the primary access roads to Brian Head and Cedar Breaks National Monument are either closed occasionally for snow removal (Route 143 from the north and east) or closed for the season (Route 148 from the south). Call the Cedar City office of the Utah Department of Transportation at ☎435/865–5500 for current road conditions.

10

WHAT TO SEE

Inside the Iron County Visitor Center, the **Daughters of the Utah Pioneers Museum** displays pioneer artifacts such as an old trundle sewing machine, an antique four-poster bed, and photographs of old Cedar City and its inhabitants. ⊠*582 N. Main St.* ☎*435/586–4484* ⬚*Free* ⊗ *Weekdays 1–4.*

The **Iron Mission State Park Museum** is a memorial to the county's iron-industry heritage. Explore the bullet-scarred stagecoach that ran in the days of Butch Cassidy, plus tools and other mining artifacts. A log cabin built in 1851—the oldest standing home in southern Utah—and a collection of wagon wheels and farm equipment are displayed outside. Local artisans demonstrate pioneer crafts. ⊠*635 N. Main St.* ☎*435/586–9290* ⬀*www.stateparks.utah.gov* ⬚*$3* ⊗ *Mid-May–mid-Sept., daily 9–6; mid-Sept.–Oct. and Mar.–mid-May, daily 9–5; Nov.–Feb., Mon.–Sat. 9–5.*

SPORTS & THE OUTDOORS

The **Dixie National Forest** (⊠*1789 N. Wedgewood La.* ☎*435/865–3700* ⬀*www.fs.fed.us/dxnf*)administers an area encompassing almost 2 million acres, stretching 170 mi across southwestern Utah, and containing 26 designated campgrounds. The forest is popular for such activities as horseback riding, fishing, and hiking.

THE ARTS

FodorsChoice
★

From June to October, the **Utah Shakespearean Festival** (☎*435/586–7880 or 800/752–9849* ⬀*www.bard.org*)puts on plays by the Bard and others, drawing tens of thousands over the course of the season. The outdoor theater at Southern Utah University is a replica of the Old Globe Theatre from Shakespeare's time, showcasing Shakespearean costumes and sets during the season. Call ahead for a schedule of performances.

WHERE TO EAT & STAY

★ **$$–$$$$**   ✕ **Milt's Stage Stop.** This dinner spot in beautiful Cedar Canyon is known for its 12-ounce rib-eye steak, prime rib, fresh crab, lobster, and shrimp dishes. In winter, deer feed in front of the restaurant as a fireplace blazes away inside. A number of hunting trophies decorate the rustic building's interior, and splendid views of the surrounding mountains delight patrons year-round. ⊠*Cedar Canyon, 5 mi east of town on Rte. 14* ☎*435/586–9344* ⊟*AE, D, DC, MC, V* ⊗ *No lunch.*

¢–$ ✕ **The Pastry Pub.** Don't be fooled by the name—coffee and tea are the only brews on tap here, and sandwiches and salads join pastries on the chalkboard menu. Build a sandwich of meat, egg, cheese, and more on a bagel, croissant, sliced bread, or make it a wrap (five flavors available). Festival-goers, take note: this is the best bet for a late-night bite after the show. ⊠*86 W. Center St.* ☎*435/867–1400* ⊟*AE, D, MC, V* ⊗ *Closed Sun.*

$ ⛺ **Bard's Inn Bed and Breakfast.** Rooms in this restored turn-of-the-20th-century house are named after heroines and heroes in Shakespeare's plays. There are antiques throughout and handcrafted quilts grace the beds. Hosts Jack and Audrey prepare a full breakfast that includes

PLANNING YOUR TRIP

WHEN TO GO

Year-round, far southwestern Utah is the warmest region in the state; St. George is usually the first city to break 100°F every year, and even the winters remain mild at lower desert elevations. Despite the heat, most people visit from June to September, making the off-season a pleasantly uncrowded experience for those willing and able to travel from fall to spring. Incidentally, Utahns from the north tend to stay away from the southern parts of the state during peak months for the very reasons—intense, dry heat and unyielding sun—that attract so many travelers from out of state. If you decide to brave the heat, wear sunscreen and drink lots of water, regardless of your activity level.

Farther east, around Cedar Breaks National Monument, elevations approach and surpass 9,000 feet, making for more temperamental weather, intermittent and seasonal road closures due to snow, and downright cold nights well into June. At this altitude, the warm summer sun is perfectly balanced by the coolness of the alpine forests during the day.

GETTING THERE & AROUND

Getting around Southwestern Utah is usually straightforward. The region's biggest cities, Cedar City and St. George, spring up alongside I-15, the major north–south travel corridor to the west. Farther east, U.S. 89 is a more scenic north–south route with access to Bryce Canyon National Park, the east side of Zion National Park, and the Kanab area. Routes 14 and 9 are the major east–west connectors between the two main highways, with Route 9 being the primary access to Springdale and Zion National Park. ■TIP→ However, be warned: if you need to travel between I-15 and U.S. 89 via Route 9 during the day, you must pay the $25 admission fee to Zion National Park even if you do not plan to stop and visit. Access to the massive and remote Grand Staircase–Escalante National Monument is via Route 12 to the north and U.S. 89 to the south.

fresh home-baked breads such as Amish friendship bread and croissants, plus fruit, juices, and shirred eggs. Bone up on your Shakespeare before attending a play by reading from a supply of on-site Cliffs Notes. **Pros:** Close to the festival grounds, dining options nearby. **Con:** Rooms fill up in advance during festival season. ⊠ *150 S. 100 West St.,* ☎ *435/586–6612* ⊕ *www.bardsbandb.com* ➶ *7 rooms* ⚒ *In-room: no phone, refrigerator (some), Wi-Fi. In-hotel: no elevator, public Internet, public Wi-Fi, airport shuttle, no-smoking rooms* ⊟ *AE, MC, V.*

$–$$ ⊞ **Best Western Town & Country Inn.** Actually two buildings directly across the street from each other, this two-story motel has good amenities and a friendly staff. You can easily walk the few blocks to the Shakespearean Festival and the downtown shopping district. **Pro:** Conveniently located near downtown. **Con:** Can get crowded during festival season. ⊠ *189 N. Main St.,* ☎ *435/586–9900 or 800/493–4089* 🖷 *435/586–1664* ⊕ *www.bwtowncountry.com* ➶ *157 rooms* ⚒ *In-room: refrigerator, Ethernet (some), Wi-Fi. In-hotel: 2 restaurants, pools, no elevator, laundry facilities, airport shuttle, no-smoking rooms* ⊟ *AE, D, DC, MC, V* �Ⓞ*CP.*

10

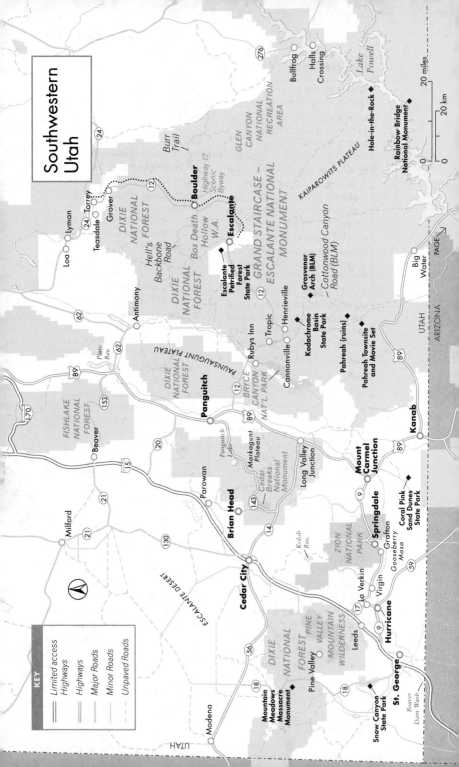

Southwestern Utah

KEY

═══ Limited access Highways
═══ Highways
─── Major Roads
─── Minor Roads
- - - Unpaved Roads

0   20 miles
0   20 km

UTAH

UTAH
ARIZONA

PAGE

FISHLAKE NATIONAL FOREST

ESCALANTE DESERT

DIXIE NATIONAL FOREST

PINE VALLEY MOUNTAIN WILDERNESS

DIXIE NATIONAL FOREST

PAUNSAUGUNT PLATEAU

DIXIE NATIONAL FOREST

Hell's Backbone Road

DIXIE NATIONAL FOREST

Burr Trail

Box Death Hollow W.A.

Highway 12 Scenic Byway

GRAND STAIRCASE – ESCALANTE NATIONAL MONUMENT

KAIPAROWITS PLATEAU

GLEN CANYON NATIONAL RECREATION AREA

Lake Powell

Cedar Breaks National Monument

Markagunt Plateau

Gooseberry Mesa

ZION NATIONAL PARK

BRYCE CANYON NAT'L. PARK

Cottonwood Canyon Road (BLM)

Milford

Modena

St. George

Snow Canyon State Park

Mountain Meadows Massacre Monument

Pine Valley

Leeds

Hurricane

Virgin

La Verkin

Springdale

Grafton

Cedar City

Brian Head

Parowan

Beaver

Panguitch

Panguitch Lake

Piute Res.

Antimony

Loa

Lyman

Teasdale

Torrey

Grover

Boulder

Escalante

Escalante Petrified Forest State Park

Rubys Inn

Tropic

Cannonville

Henrieville

Kodachrome Basin State Park

Grosvenor Arch (BLM)

Pahreah (ruins)

Pahreah Townsite and Movie Set

Long Valley Junction

Mount Carmel Junction

Coral Pink Sand Dunes State Park

Kanab

Big Water

Bullfrog

Halls Crossing

Hole-in-the-Rock

Rainbow Bridge National Monument

Kolob Res.

Beaver Dam Wash

18

18

56

130

21

21

170

15

20

153

143

14

89

62

62

89

12

12

9

9

17

59

276

24

24

12

89

89

Cedar Breaks National Monument

Cedar Breaks National Monument, a natural amphitheater similar to Bryce Canyon, spans almost 3 mi and plunges 2,000 feet into the Markagunt Plateau. Short alpine hiking trails along the rim and thin crowds make this a wonderful summer stop. Although its roads may be closed in winter due to heavy snow, the monument stays open for cross-country skiing and snowmobiling.

It's never crowded here, and most people who visit are content to photograph the monument from one of the handful of overlooks alongside the road—which means the intrepid hiker, skier, or snowshoer can easily find solitude along the trails. In fact, winter is one of the best times to visit, when snow drapes the red-orange formations; though call ahead for road conditions and keep in mind that all visitor facilities are closed from October through late May.

⌧ *Rte. 148, 9 mi south of Brian Head* ☎ *435/586–9451* ⊕ *www.nps. gov/cebr* ✉ *$4 per person* ☾ *Visitor center June–early-Oct., daily 8–6.*

ST. GEORGE

50 mi southwest of Cedar City via I–15.

Believing the mild year-round climate ideal for growing cotton, Brigham Young dispatched 309 LDS families in 1861 to found St. George. They were to raise cotton and silkworms and to establish a textile industry, to make up for textile shortages resulting from the Civil War. The area was subsequently dubbed "Utah's Dixie," a name that stuck even after the war ended and the "other" South could once again provide cotton to Utah. The settlers—many of them originally from southern states—found the desert climate preferable to northern Utah's snow, and they remained as farmers and ranchers. Crops included fruit, molasses, and grapes for wine that the pioneers sold to nearby mining communities. St. Georgians now number more than 60,000, many of whom are retirees attracted by the hot, dry climate and the numerous golf courses. But historic Ancestor Square, the city's many well-preserved, original pioneer and Mormon structures, and a growing shopping district make St. George a popular destination for families, as well.

Numbers in the margin correspond to the St. George map.

WHAT TO SEE

Mormon leader Brigham Young spent the last five winters of his life in the warm, sunny climate of St. George. Built of adobe on a sandstone-and-basalt foundation, **Brigham Young Winter Home** has been restored to its original condition. A portrait of Young hangs over one fireplace, and furnishings authentic to the late-19th-century time period have been donated by supporters. Guided tours are available. ⌧ *67 W. 200 North St.* ☎ *435/673–5181* ✉ *Free* ☾ *Daily 9–6.*

★ ❹ Chances are the **Rosenbruch Wildlife Museum** in St. George is unlike any museum you've ever seen. This modern 25,000-square-foot facility displays more than 300 species of wildlife (stuffed) from around the

10

Brigham Young's
Winter Home **1**

St. George
Dinosaur Discovery
Site at Johnson
Farm **6**

Rosenbruch
Wildlife
Museum **4**

St. George
Tabernacle **3**

St. George
Temple **2**

Snow Canyon
State Park........**5**

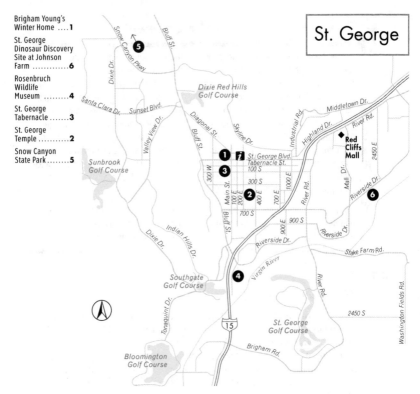

globe, displayed in an uncanny representation of their native habitat—the plains of Africa, the forests of North America, and the mountains of Asia. A wheelchair-accessible pathway of almost ¼ mi winds through the different environments. Two waterfalls cascade from a two-story mountain, and more than 50 hidden speakers provide ambient wildlife and nature sounds. Before your tour, check out the video presentation in the 200-seat theater, and be sure not to miss the massive bug collection. ⊠ *1835 Convention Center Dr.* ☎ *435/656–0033 www.rosenbruch.org* ⊠ *$8* ⊙ *Mon. noon–9, Tues.–Sat. 10–6.*

★ ❺   Red Navajo sandstone mesas and formations are crowned with black lava rock, creating high-contrast vistas from either end of **Snow Canyon State Park.** From the campground you can scramble up huge sandstone mounds and overlook the entire valley. ⊠ *1002 Snow Canyon Dr., Ivins, 8 mi northwest of St. George* ☎ *435/628–2255* ⊕ *www.stateparks.utah.gov* ⊠ *$5* ⊙ *Daily 6 AM to 10 PM.*

☾ ❻   Follow footsteps cast in stone millions of years ago at **St. George Dinosaur Discovery Site at Johnson Farm,** where property development came to a halt when the ancient prints from the Jurassic period were unearthed in 2000. To reach the tracks, take 700 South Street east to Foremaster Drive and continue past the sod farm. ⊠ *2180 E. Riverside Dr.* ☎ *435/574–3466* ⊕ *www.dinotrax.com* ⊠ *$3* ⊙ *Mon.–Sat. 10–6.*

③ Mormon settlers began work on the **St. George Tabernacle** in June 1863, a few months after the city of St. George was established. Upon completion of the sandstone building's 140-foot clock tower 13 years later, Brigham Young formally dedicated the site. This is one of the best-preserved pioneer buildings in the entire state, and is still used for public meetings and programs for the entire community. ⊠ *18 S. Main St.* ☎ *435/673–5181* ⊙ *Mon. 9–6.*

② The red-sandstone **St. George Temple,** plastered over with white stucco, was completed in 1877 and served as a meeting place for both Mormons and other congregations. It's still in use today, and though only Mormons can enter the temple, a visitor center next door offers guided tours for everyone. ⊠ *250 E. 400 South St.* ☎ *435/673–5181* ☜ *Free* ⊙ *Visitor center daily 9–9.*

> ### GUIDED HIKE TO BRYCE OR ZION
>
> Join **Southern Utah Scenic Tours** (☎ *435/867–8690 or 888/404–8687* ⊕ *www.utahscenictours.com)* for an all-day tour from Cedar City to either Zion National Park or Bryce National Park, including a short, easy-to-moderate hike. The price includes pick-up and drop-off at your hotel; snacks and lunch; and all applicable park fees.

OFF THE BEATEN PATH

Beaver Dam Wash. Utah's lowest point happens to mark the convergence of the Colorado Plateau, the Great Basin, and the Mojave Desert. In this overlapping of ecosystems, you'll find a large diversity of plants and animals, especially of birds. In the southern part of the wash stands the greatest concentration of Joshua trees in the area. To get here, take Route 18 north of St. George and turn west onto Route 8, the paved road that runs 12 mi through Santa Clara. ⊠ *12 mi southwest of Shivwits on Old Hwy. 91* ☎ *801/539–4001* ☜ *Free.*

SPORTS & THE OUTDOORS

BICYCLING The folks at **Bicycles Unlimited** (⊠ *90 S. 100 East St.* ☎ *888/673–4492* ⊕ *www.bicyclesunlimited.com)* are a font of information on mountain biking in southern Utah. They rent bikes and sell parts, accessories, and guidebooks.

GOLF **Bloomington** (⊠ *3174 E. Bloomington Dr.* ☎ *435/673–2029)* offers a striking combination of manicured fairways and greens beneath sandstone cliffs. **Dixie Red Hills** (⊠ *645 W. 1250 North St.* ☎ *435/634–5852)* has 9 holes. The 18-hole **Entrada** (⊠ *2537 W. Entrada Trail* ☎ *435/986–2200)* is Utah's first Johnny Miller Signature Course. **St. George Golf Club** (⊠ *2190 S. 1400 East St.* ☎ *435/634–5854)* is a popular 18-hole course with challenging par-3 holes.

Water provides challenges at **Southgate Golf Club** (⊠ *1975 S. Tonaquint Dr.* ☎ *435/628–0000)*, with several holes bordering ponds or crossing the Santa Clara River. Designed by Ted Robinson, fairway features at **Sunbrook** (⊠ *2366 Sunbrook Dr.* ☎ *435/634–5866)* include rock walls, lakes, and waterfalls.

10

HIKING **Snow Canyon State Park** (⊠*8 mi northwest of St. George on Rte. 18*
★ ☎*435/628–2255* ⊕*www.stateparks.utah.gov*)has several short trails
and lots of small desert canyons to explore.

THE ARTS

Spend a few quiet hours out of the Dixie sun at the **St. George Art
Museum** (⊠*47 E. 200 North St.* ☎*435/627–4525*). The permanent collection celebrates local potters, photographers, painters, and more. Special exhibits highlight local history. A rotating series of musicals such as
Joseph and the Amazing Technicolor Dream Coat and *Les Misérables*
entertain at **Tuacahn** (⊠*1100 Tuacahn Dr., Ivins* ☎*435/652–3200 or
800/746–9882* ⊕*www.tuacahn.org*), an outdoor amphitheater nestled
in a natural sandstone cove.

WHERE TO EAT

★ ¢–$ ✕**Bear Paw Coffee Company.** The menu is full of flavor, with elements of
Southwestern, Tex-Mex, American, and Italian cuisines all represented,
but breakfast is the star of the show here (served all day, every day).
The coffee is hot, the teas loose, the juice fresh, and the servers smiling.
Home brewers (of coffee and tea, that is) can get their fresh beans and
leaves here, too. ⊠*75 N. Main St.* ☎*435/634–0126* ▤*AE, D, MC,
V* ⊗*No dinner.*

$$$–$$$$ ✕**Painted Pony.** Patio dining and local art hanging on the walls provide
suave accompaniment to the creative meals served in this downtown
restaurant. Be sure to try the Dixie pork chop or the bacon-wrapped
duck. ⊠*2 W. St. George Blvd., Ancestor Sq.* ☎*435/634–1700* ▤*AE,
D, MC, V* ⊗*No lunch Sun.*

$$$–$$$$ ✕**Sullivan's Rococo Steakhouse & Inn.** Specializing in beef and seafood,
this St. George restaurant is known for its prime rib, but its vistas
are worthy noting, too. It sits atop a hill overlooking town, so you
can enjoy spectacular views right from your table. ⊠*511 Airport Rd.*
☎*435/628–3671* ▤*AE, D, MC, V.*

WHERE TO STAY

★ $–$$$$ ▥**Green Gate Village Historic Inn.** Step back in time in these restored
pioneer homes dating to the 1860s. The inn takes its name from the
green gates and fences that surrounded the homes of St. George's LDS
leaders in the late 1800s. The last remaining original gate is displayed
in the inn's garden and served as a model for those now surrounding
Green Gate Village. Behind the gates is a village of nine fully restored
pioneer homes filled with antique furnishings and modern amenities.
Guests with children need to get prior approval from the management.
Pros: Each building is the real historic deal. Location is close to taber-
nacle and downtown walking tour. **Cons:** Village-like setting might not
appeal to those seeking privacy. ⊠*76 W. Tabernacle St.,* ☎*435/628–
6999 or 800/350–6999* ⊕*www.greengatevillageinn.com* �*4 rooms,
10 suites* ⚭*In-room: kitchen (some), refrigerator, DVD (some), VCR,
Wi-Fi (some). In-hotel: 2 restaurants, room service, pool, gym, spa, no
elevator, public Internet, parking (no fee), no-smoking rooms* ▤*AE,
D, MC, V* ⏴⏵*BP.*

$$$$ ⌂ **Red Mountain Spa.** Located near the mouth of Snow Canyon, this
Fodor's Choice   active resort is a retreat designed for fitness and rejuvenation. Breakfast
★   and lunch buffets list the nutritional contents of each item, while dinner
is a more traditional sit-down experience. But it's not just about the
food; there are fitness classes, hikes, yoga, and plenty of other activities
that leave you with a healthy glow. The well-appointed rooms aren't
especially large, but with so many things to do, you won't want to
lounge around your room anyway. **Pros:** Down-to-earth spa experience, healthy food. **Cons:** You might feel guilty if you don't wake up at
dawn to hit the gym or the trails. ⊠ *1275 E. Red Mountain Cir., Ivins,
7 mi northwest of St. George,* ☎ *435/673–4905 or 800/407–3002*
⊕ *www.redmountainspa.com* ⬚ *82 rooms, 24 suites* ⌂ *In-room: safe,
Ethernet. In-hotel: 2 restaurants, tennis court, pools, gym, spa, water
sports, bicycles, no elevator, laundry facilities, concierge, public Internet, airport shuttle, some pets allowed, no kids under 12, no-smoking
rooms* ⊟ *AE, D, MC, V* ⏐◯⏐ *FAP.*

HURRICANE

17 mi northeast of St. George via I–15 north and Rte. 9 east.

An increasing number of lodging establishments makes Hurricane a
fine alternate base for exploring Dixie. Nearby Gooseberry Mesa is one
of the best places to mountain bike in Utah.

SPORTS & THE OUTDOORS

BICYCLING   The mountain biking trails on **Gooseberry Mesa,** off Route 59 south
★   of Hurricane, rival those of world-famous Moab on the other side of
southern Utah, yet don't have the hordes of fat-tire fanatics. Come here
for solitary and technical single-track challenges.

GOLF   Hurricane has **Sky Mountain** (⊠ *1030 N. 2600 West St.* ☎ *888/345–
5551*), one of the state's most scenic 18-hole golf courses. Many fairways are framed by red-rock outcroppings; the course has a front-tee
view of the nearby 10,000-foot Pine Valley Mountains.

WHERE TO EAT & STAY

★ ¢   ✕ **Main Street Café.** One of the best cups of coffee in Dixie is poured right
here in Hurricane. A full espresso bar will satisfy "caffiends," while
vegetarians and others can choose from salads, sandwiches, breakfast burritos, homemade breads, and desserts. Sit inside to admire the
works of local artists, or share the patio with the hummingbirds. ⊠ *138
S. Main St.* ☎ *435/635–9080* ⊟ *MC, V* ⊗ *Closed Sun. No dinner.*

¢   ⌂ **Comfort Inn Zion.** Golfers will appreciate the package deals available
with nearby courses, and everyone benefits from being fairly close to
Zion National Park, which is a 35-mi drive away. If the hot southern
Utah sun has sapped your energy, a dip in the pool will wake you
for your next adventure. **Pro:** Minutes from two 18-hole golf courses.
Con: Location in a newly developed area lacks charm. ⊠ *43 N. 2600
West,* ☎ *435/635–3500 or 800/635–3577* ⊟ *435/635–7224* ⊕ *www.
comfortinnzion.com* ⬚ *53 rooms* ⌂ *In-room: Wi-Fi. In-hotel: pool, no
elevator, laundry facilities, public Internet, public Wi-Fi, no-smoking
rooms* ⊟ *AE, D, MC, V* ⏐◯⏐ *CP.*

10

SPRINGDALE

21 mi east of Hurricane via Rte. 9.

Springdale's growth has followed that of next-door neighbor Zion National Park, the most popular park destination in Utah and one of the most popular in the United States. Hotels, restaurants, and shops keep popping up, yet the town still manages to maintain its small-town charm. And oh, that view! Many businesses along Zion Park Boulevard, the main drag, double as shuttle stops for the bus system that carts tourists into the jaw-dropping sandstone confines of Zion Canyon, the town's main attraction.

THE ARTS

NIGHTLIFE The **O.C. Tanner Amphitheater** (⊠*Lion Blvd., Springdale* ☎*435/652–7994* ⊕*www.dixie.edu/tanner*)is set amid huge sandstone boulders at the base of the enormous red cliffs spilling south from Zion National Park. In summer, live concerts are held each weekend, when everything from local country-music bands to the Utah Symphony Orchestra takes to the stage.

WHERE TO EAT

$$–$$$$ ✕**Bit & Spur Restaurant and Saloon.** This restaurant has been a legend
Fodor'sChoice in Utah for more than 25 years. The house favorites' menu lists tradi-
★ tional Southwestern dishes like *flautas verde* (deep-fried burritos with tomatillo salsa), but the kitchen also gets creative. Try the *bistec asado* (chile-rubbed steak) or pasta with rosemary cream sauce. When the weather is nice, arrive early so you can eat outside and enjoy the lovely grounds and views. ⊠*1212 Zion Park Blvd.* ☎*435/772–3498* ⊟*AE, D, MC, V* ⊘*No lunch.*

¢–$ ✕**Sol Foods.** For a quick, healthful meal any time of day, stop here for organic, ethnic, and gourmet food items. Daily specials include spanakopita, quiche, lasagna, and salads. They can also prepare picnic baskets or box lunches for your day in the park. Nearby is Sol's ice cream parlor, with hand-dipped ice cream cones, banana splits, and espresso. The patio seating is near the Virgin River, with views into the park. There is public Wi-Fi available, and beer is served. ⊠*95 Zion Park Blvd.* ☎*435/772–0277* ⊟*MC, V.*

$$–$$$$ ✕**Spotted Dog Cafe at Flanigan's Inn.** Named in honor of the family dog of Springdale's original settlers, this contemporary American restaurant offers dinner entrées such as regional red mountain trout and tenderloin of pork. Breakfast is also served, and the sidewalk patio fills quickly. ⊠*428 Zion Park Blvd.* ☎*435/772–0700* ⊟*AE, MC, V, D* ⊘*No lunch.*

★ $$–$$$$ ✕**The Switchback Grille.** Crowded with locals and tourists alike, this restaurant is known for its wood-fired pizzas, ribs, and vegetarian dishes. Favorites include corn-crusted Utah mountain trout and crown rack of barbecue ribs. The vaulted ceilings make the dining room feel open and comfortable. They're open for breakfast; both lunch and more casual dinner items are served next door at Switchback Jack's Sports Grill. ⊠*1149 Zion Park Blvd.* ☎*435/772–3700* ⊟*AE, D, MC, V.*

$-$$ ✕**Zion Pizza and Noodle Co.** The "Cholesterol Hiker" and veggie-friendly "Good for You" pizzas and the selection of microbrews put some pizzazz into the menu at this casual restaurant in a former church building. Whether you dine indoors or in the beer garden, you can also order pasta dishes like linguine with pesto, mushrooms, and fresh tomatoes. ✉*868 Zion Park Blvd.* ☎*435/772–3815* ▭*No credit cards* ⊘*Closed Dec.–Feb.*

WHERE TO STAY

$-$$ 🏨**Best Western Zion Park Inn.** This spacious and modern facility has large rooms. The Switchback Grille will get you going in the morning with a hearty breakfast, and since the inn is a stop on the park shuttle route, take one step out the door and you're on your way to Zion Canyon. **Pros:** Restaurants serve some of Springdale's tastiest fare. On-site liquor store is only place in town that sells wine by the bottle. **Con:** Not for the quaint-at-heart. ✉*1215 Zion Park Blvd., Box 800,* ☎*435/772–3200 or 800/934–7275* ⊕*www.zionparkinn.com* ⤶*120 rooms, 6 suites* ♿*In-room: refrigerator, Ethernet, Wi-Fi. In-hotel: 2 restaurants, pool, laundry facilities, public Internet, public Wi-Fi, some pets allowed, no-smoking rooms* ▭*AE, D, DC, MC, V.*

★ $$–$$$ 🏨**Cliffrose Lodge and Gardens.** Flowers adorn the 5-acre grounds of this friendly, charming lodge. Comfortable rooms will keep you happy after a long hike, and from your balcony you can continue to enjoy views of the towering, colorful cliffs. The Virgin River runs right along the property, so you can have a picnic or barbecue out back to the sound of rushing water. The Cliffrose is within walking distance of the Zion Canyon visitor center and shuttle stop. **Pro:** It's the closest lodging to Zion's South Entrance. **Con:** You'll need to book early in high season. ✉*281 Zion Park Blvd., Box 510,* ☎*435/772–3234 or 800/243–8824* ⊕*www.cliffroselodge.com* ⤶*29 rooms, 10 suites* ♿*In-room: refrigerator, Wi-Fi. In-hotel: pool, laundry facilities, no-smoking rooms* ▭*AE, D, MC, V.*

$$–$$$$ 🏨**Desert Pearl Inn.** You may never want to leave this comfortable inn,
Fodor's Choice where every room has vaulted ceilings, thick carpets, cushy throw pil-
★ lows, Roman shades, oversize windows, and sleeper sofas, as well as a large balcony or patio overlooking either the Virgin River or the pool. The pool area is exceptionally well landscaped and fully equipped, with a double-size hot tub and a shower–and–rest room block. **Pro:** Spacious, condo-like rooms. **Con:** Fills up early during high season. ✉*707 Zion Park Blvd.84767* ☎*435/772–8888 or 888/828–0898* ⊕*www. desertpearl.com* ⤶*69 rooms, 4 suites* ♿*In-room: safe, kitchen, refrigerator, DVD, VCR, Ethernet, dial-up, Wi-Fi. In-hotel: pool, laundry facilities, public Internet, no-smoking rooms* ▭*AE, D, MC, V.*

$$–$$$ 🏨**Flanigan's Inn, Spa, and Café.** Close to the park with canyon views, this rustic country inn has contemporary furnishings. The pool area

10

is small but scenic. You can walk to the Zion visitor center from here (it's a few blocks), though the shuttle to the canyon stops on the property. **Pro:** Close to Zion Canyon Theatre. **Con:** Not centrally located to downtown. ⊠*428 Zion Park Blvd.84767* ☎*435/772–3244 or 800/765–7787* ⊕*www.flanigans.com* ↩*28 rooms, 4 suites, 2 villas* ⚭*In-room: refrigerator, DVD, VCR (some), dial-up, Wi-Fi. In-hotel: restaurant, bar, pool, spa, no elevator, parking (no fee), no-smoking rooms.* ⊟*AE, D, MC, V.*

CAMPING   ⚠**Zion Canyon Campground & RV Park.** About a half mile from the south entrance to the park, this campground is surrounded on three sides by the canyon's rock formations. Many of the sites are on the river. ⚭*Flush toilets, full hookups, dump station, drinking water, guest laundry, showers, fire grates, picnic tables, food service, electricity, public telephone, general store, play area, swimming (river), Wi-Fi* ↩*110 RV sites, 110 tent sites* ⊠*479 Zion Park Blvd.* ☎*435/772–3237* 🖷*435/772–3844* ⊕*www.zioncamp.com* ⊟*D, MC, V.*

ALONG U.S. 89

MT. CARMEL JUNCTION

13 mi east of Zion National Park via Rte. 9 east.

Little more than where Route 9 meets U.S. 89, Mt. Carmel Junction does offer some funky small-town lodging for those willing to stay about 15 minutes east of Zion National Park's east entrance. But don't miss the studio of Maynard Dixon, the artist many consider the finest painter of the American West.

WHAT TO SEE

The **Maynard Dixon Home and Studio** was the final residence of the best-known painter of the American West, who died here in 1946. The property and log cabin structure are now maintained by the nonprofit Thunderbird Foundation for the Arts, which gives tours and schedules artist workshops and retreats. ⊠*2 mi north of Mt. Carmel Junction on U.S. 89, mile marker 84, Mt. Carmel* ☎*435/648–2653 or 801/533–5330* ⊕*www.thunderbirdfoundation.com* 🎫*$20* ⊗*Tours by appointment only May–Oct., Mon.–Sat.*

WHERE TO STAY

$ 🖥**Best Western East Zion Thunderbird Lodge.** A quick 13 mi east of Zion National Park, this red-adobe motel is a good option if lodging in Springdale has filled, or if you want to be within an hour's drive of Bryce Canyon National Park as well. Surrounded by the Zion Mountains and bordered by a scenic golf course, the rooms are spacious and bright. **Pro:** A convenient base for visiting Zion and Bryce (and even the North Rim of the Grand Canyon). **Con:** No attractions within walking distance. ⊠*Junction of U.S. 89 and Rte. 9, Box 5531, 84755* ☎*435/648–2203 or 888/848–6358* ⊕*www.bestwestern.com* ↩*62 rooms* ⚭*In-room: kitchen (some), Ethernet (some), Wi-Fi. In-*

hotel: restaurant, golf course, pool, spa, no elevator, laundry facilities, public Internet, no-smoking rooms ☐*AE, D, DC, MC, V.*

¢–$ 🏨**Golden Hills Motel.** This clean and simple establishment right at Mt. Carmel Junction is an inexpensive and no-frills lodging option. Its funky pink-and-blue roadside diner serves good, basic country-style fare like country-fried steak, liver and onions, and homemade breads and pies. Some rooms in this ground-level facility are on the riverside. **Pro:** One of the most affordable lodgings in the vicinity of Zion National Park. **Con:** Because prices are so reasonable, you'll need to reserve early. ✉*Junction of U.S. 89 and Rte. 9* ☎*435/648–2268 or 800/648–2268* ⊕*www.goldenhillsmotel.com* ➽*30 rooms* ⌂*In-room: refrigerator, DVD (some), Wi-Fi. In-hotel: restaurant, pool, gym, bicycles, no elevator, laundry facilities, public Internet, public Wi-Fi, some pets allowed, no-smoking rooms* ☐*MC, V.*

🕒 $$–$$$$ 🏨**Zion Ponderosa Ranch Resort.** This multipursuit resort on an 8,000-acre ranch just east of Zion National Park offers activities from horseback riding to spa treatments, and just about everything in between. Lodging options include suites that sleep six and luxurious mountain homes for up to 13. Hearty meals are included. ✉*5 mi. north of route marker 46 on North Fork Country Rd., Mount Carmel* ☎*800/293–5444* ⊕*www.zionponderosa.com* ➽*16 suites, 8 cabins, 17 houses* ⌂*In-room: kitchen (some), DVD (some), Wi-Fi (some). In-hotel: restaurant, tennis courts, pool, spa, bicycles, children's programs (ages 4–11)* ☐*AE, D, MC, V* ⎔*EP, AP* ⊘*Closed Dec.–Feb.*

KANAB

17 mi southeast of Mt. Carmel Junction via U.S. 89 south.

Kanab is Hollywood's vision of the American West. Soaring vermilion sandstone cliffs and sagebrush flats with endless vistas have lured filmmakers to this area for more than 75 years. The welcoming sign at city limits reads "Greatest Earth on Show"—Kanab has been used as a setting in more than 100 movies and television shows. Abandoned film sets have become tourist attractions, and old movie posters or still photographs are a decorating staple at local businesses. In addition to a movie-star past, Kanab is ideally positioned as a base for exploration. With major roads radiating in four directions, it offers easy access to three national parks, three national monuments (including Grand Staircase–Escalante), two state parks, and several historic sites.

FUN EVENT

The nostalgic **Western Legends Roundup** (☎*800/733–5263*)is for anyone who loves cowboys, pioneer life, or American Indian culture. For four days every August, Kanab fills with cowboy poets and storytellers, musicians, Western arts-and-crafts vendors, and American Indian dancers and weavers.

SPORTS & THE OUTDOORS

Eroding sandstone formed the sweeping expanse of pink sand at **Coral Pink Sand Dunes State Park.** Funneled through a notch in the rock, the wind picks up speed and carries grains of sand into the area. Once the wind slows down, the sand is deposited, creating this giant playground for dune buggies, ATVs, and dirt bikes. A small area is fenced off for walking, but the sound of wheeled toys is always with you. Children love to play in the sand, but before you let them loose, check the surface temperature; it can become very hot. ⊠ *Yellowjacket and Hancock Rds., 12 mi off U.S. 89, near Kanab* ☎*435/648–2800* ⊕*www.state parks.utah.gov* ⊒*$6* ☉*Daily, dawn–dusk.*

WHERE TO EAT

¢–$ ✕**Fernando's Hideaway.** Fernando's mixes the best margarita for miles—it's mighty fine with a quesadilla as a warm-up for dinner. The house salsa is chunky and fresh-tasting, and menu items are available as dinner platters or à la carte. Steaks and seafood will please those with a hankering for American food. Accommodations are made for vegetarians. Colorful Mexican folk art adorns the bright dining room, and the patio may encourage you to linger with another margarita. ⊠*332 N. 300 West St.* ☎*435/644–3222* ⊟*AE, MC, V* ☉*Closed Oct.–mid-Feb.*

★ $$–$$$$ ✕**Rocking V Cafe.** Fresh fish, including mahimahi when available, arrives several times a week at this respected café that prides itself on "slow food." Buffalo tenderloin is a favorite, but vegetarians and vegans have plenty of choices, as well. Save room for dessert—the crème brûlée is perfectly prepared. Lunch offers a more casual selection of wraps, sandwiches, burgers, and salads. A full liquor license supports a decent wine and beer list, but cocktails are limited to standards such as margaritas. The Web site is a must-read—trust us. ⊠*97 W. Center St.* ☎*435/644–8001* ⊟*MC, V* ☉*Closed Jan.–late Mar.*

PANGUITCH

67 mi north of Kanab via U.S. 89.

An elevation of 6,650 feet helps this town of 1,600 residents keep its cool. Main Street is lined with late-19th-century buildings, and its early homes and outbuildings are noted for their distinctive brick architecture. Decent amenities, inexpensive lodging (mainly strip motels), and an excellent location 24 mi northwest of Bryce Canyon National Park make Panguitch a comfortable launching pad for recreation in the area.

WHERE TO EAT & STAY

★ $–$$ ✕**Cowboy's Smokehouse Café.** Stuffed animal trophies and hundreds of business cards and photographs from customers line the walls at this barbecue joint. Specialties include mesquite-smoked beef, pork, turkey, and chicken, and a sauce with no fewer than 15 secret ingredients. Try homemade peach, apricot, or cherry cobbler if you have room for dessert. Breakfast is served, too. ⊠*95 N. Main St.* ☎*435/676–8030* ⊟*MC, V* ☉*Closed Sun.*

☾ ¢–$ 🖼 **Marianna Inn Motel.** Rooms at this clean, family-friendly, one-story motel have up to four beds; those with whirlpool baths are $25 extra. You can barbecue your own supper on one of the grills and eat your meal on the covered patio. Relax afterward on a hammock

Quilted Support

During the bitter winter of 1864, Panguitch residents were on the verge of starvation. A group of men from the settlement set out over the mountains to fetch provisions from the town of Parowan, 40 mi away. When they hit waist-deep snow drifts they were forced to abandon their oxen. Legend says the men, frustrated and ready to turn back, laid a quilt on the snow and knelt to pray. Soon they realized the quilt had kept them from sinking into the snow. Spreading quilts before them as they walked, leapfrog style, the men traveled to Parowan and back, returning with life-saving provisions. Every June, the four-day **Quilt Walk Festival** (☎ *435/676–2418* ⊕ *www.quiltwalk.com*) commemorates the event with quilting classes, a tour of Panguitch's pioneer homes, crafts shows, and a dinner-theater production in which the story is acted out.

or in the summer-only outdoor spa. **Pro:** Distance from Bryce means reservations typically are easier to come by. **Con:** Some may find Panguitch too sleepy. ⊠ *699 N. Main St. 84759 ☎ 435/676–8844 ⊕ www.mariannainn.com ⬅32 rooms ⬥In-room: refrigerator (some). In-hotel: no elevator, some pets allowed, no-smoking rooms* ⊟ *AE, D, DC, MC, V.*

¢   📺 **Panguitch Inn.** This quiet inn occupies a 100-year-old, two-story building a few blocks from downtown restaurants and shops. Rooms are simple and no-frills, but clean. **Pro:** Covered indoor parking. **Con:** Rooms don't match building's quaintness. ⊠ *50 N. Main St., 84759 ☎ 435/676–8871 ⊕ www.panguitchinn.com ⬅25 rooms ⬥In-room: Wi-Fi. In-hotel: no-smoking rooms ⊗ Closed Nov.–Mar.* ⊟ *AE, D, DC, MC, V.*

GRAND STAIRCASE–ESCALANTE NATIONAL MONUMENT

10

Encompassing 1.7 million acres in south-central Utah, the Grand Staircase–Escalante National Monument has three distinct sections—the Grand Staircase, the Kaiparowits Plateau, and the Canyons of the Escalante—offer remote backcountry experiences hard to find elsewhere in the Lower 48. Waterfalls, shoulder-width slot canyons, American Indian ruins and petroglyphs, and improbable colors all characterize this wilderness. Straddling the northern border of the monument, the small towns of Escalante and Boulder offer access, information, outfitters, lodging, and dining to adventurers. The highway that connects them, Route 12, is one of the most scenic stretches of road in the Southwest.

The monument is popular with backpackers and hard-core mountain bike enthusiasts. You can explore the rocky landscape, which represents some of America's last wilderness, via dirt roads with a four-wheel-drive vehicle; most roads depart from Route 12. Roadside views into the monument are most impressive from Route 12 between Escalante and Boulder. It costs nothing to enter the park, but fees apply for camping and backcountry permits.

Monument Contact Information ⊠ *Escalante Interagency Visitor Center, 755 W. Main St.* ☎*435/826–5499* ⊕*www.ut.blm.gov/monument.*

ESCALANTE

47 mi east of Bryce Canyon National Park entrance via Rte. 12 east.

Though the Dominguez and Escalante expedition of 1776 came nowhere near this area, the town's name does honor the Spanish explorer. It was bestowed nearly a century later by a member of a survey party led by John Wesley Powell, charged with mapping this remote area. These days Escalante has modern amenities and is a western gateway to the Grand Staircase–Escalante National Monument.

WHAT TO SEE

Escalante Petrified Forest State Park. Created to protect a huge repository of fossilized wood and dinosaur bones, this park has two short interpretive trails to educate visitors. There's an attractive swimming beach at the park's Wide Hollow Reservoir, which is also good for boating, fishing, and birding. ⊠*710 N. Reservoir Rd.* ☎*435/826–4466* ⊕*www.stateparks.utah.gov* ☜*$5* ☉*Daily 8* AM–*10* PM.

NEED A BREAK?

A fine place to stop along the way for the view (and a brew) is **Kiva Koffeehouse** (⊠*Near mile marker 74 on Rte. 12, 13 mi east of Escalante* ☎ *435/826–4550*), constructed by a local artist and inventor when in his 80s. He quarried the sandstone for the walls and floors on this very site and spent two years finding and transporting the 13 Douglas-fir logs surrounding the structure. It's open from April to October, and there are two rooms for rent in a cabin below.

SCENIC DRIVE

FodorsChoice
★

Keep your camera handy and steering wheel steady along **Highway 12 Scenic Byway** between Escalante and Loa, near Capitol Reef National Park. Though the highway starts at the intersection of U.S. 89, west of Bryce Canyon National Park, the stretch that begins in Escalante is one of the most spectacular. The road passes through Grand Staircase–Escalante National Monument and on to Capitol Reef along one of the most scenic stretches of highway in the United States. Be sure to stop at the scenic overlooks; almost every one will give you an eye-popping view. Don't get distracted, though; the paved road is twisting and steep, and at times climbs over a hogback with sheer drop-offs on both sides.

SPORTS & THE OUTDOORS

BICYCLING

A good long-distance mountain-bike ride in the isolated Escalante region follows the 44-mi **Hell's Backbone Road** from Escalante to Boulder. The grade is steep and, if you're driving, a four-wheel-drive vehicle is recommended, but the views of Box Death Hollow make it all worthwhile.

The road leaves from the center of town. Inquire about road conditions before departing.

HIKING Some of the best backcountry hiking in the area lies 15 mi east of Escalante on Route 12, where the **Lower Escalante River** carves through striking sandstone canyons and gulches. You can camp at numerous sites along the river for extended trips, or you can spend a little time in the small park where the highway crosses the river. With a guided tour from **Utah Canyons** (✉ *325 W. Main St.* ☎ *435/826–4967* ⊕ *www.utah canyons.com*), you can slip into the slot canyons with confidence or end a day of adventure by watching a sunset from the rim of a canyon.

OUTFITTER & Canyoneering and hiking are the focus of **Excursions of Escalante,** where
EXPEDITION tours are custom-fit to your schedule and needs. All necessary gear is provided, and tours last from one to eight days. ✉ *125 E. Main St.* ☎ *800/839–7567* ⊕ *www.excursions-escalante.com* ☉ *Wed.–Mon. 8–5 or by appointment.*

WHERE TO EAT & STAY

¢–$ ✕**Esca-Latte Coffee Shop & Cafe.** Fuel up for your hike with the best coffee in town. When you're hot and spent after your day of exploration, there's no better place to sit back and relax with friends. Try a turkey sub or homemade pizza with a cold draft microbrew, or opt for a salad. Watch hummingbirds fight the wind at the feeders while dining on the patio. ✉ *310 W. Main St.* ☎ *435/826–4266* ▭ *AE, D, MC, V.*

★ $$ ▦**Escalante's Grand Staircase Bed & Breakfast Inn.** Rooms have skylights, tile floors, log furniture, and murals reproducing area petroglyphs. You can relax on the outdoor porches or in the library, or make use of the rental bikes to explore the adjacent national monument. **Pro:** Southwestern rusticity with modern flair. **Con:** Escalante's wonderful remoteness may not be for everyone. ✉ *280 W. Main St., Box 657, Escalante,* ☎ *435/826–4890 or 866/826–4890* ⊕ *www.escalantebnb. com* ⇆ *8 rooms* ⚿ *In-room: no a/c, no phone, no TV, Wi-Fi. In-hotel: no elevator, public Wi-Fi, no kids under 12, no-smoking rooms* ▭ *AE, D, MC, V* ⦿|*BP.*

10

SOUTHWESTERN UTAH ESSENTIALS

TRANSPORTATION

BY AIR

SkyWest flies to **St. George Municipal Airport** (✉ *317 S. Donlee Dr., St. George* ☎ *435/634–5822* ⊕ *www.sgcity.org/airport*), and operates as a carrier for both United Express and Delta Connection flights. Las Vegas's **McCarran International Airport** (✉ *5757 Wayne Newton Blvd., Las Vegas* ☎ *702/261–5211* ⊕ *www.mccarran.com*) is 116 mi from St. George; the **St. George Shuttle** (✉ *915 Bluff St.* ☎ *435/628–8320 or 800/933–8320* ⊕ *www.stgshuttle.com*) makes nine trips a day between it and St. George.

BY BUS

Greyhound Lines (☎ *800/229-9424* ⊕ *www.greyhound.com*) serves the I–15 corridor, making stops in Parowan and St. George.

BY CAR

I–15 is the main route into southwestern Utah, from Las Vegas to the southwest and Salt Lake City to the northeast. U.S. 89, which leads to Kanab, is a good, well-traveled road with interesting sights, as well as gas stations and convenience stores. Routes 143 and 14 are the main east–west connecting routes. Some mountain curves can be expected on these roads, and winter months may see hazardous conditions and occasional closures in the higher elevations around Brian Head and Cedar Breaks. Contact the **Utah Department of Transportation** (☎ *801/965-4000* ⊕ *www.dot. state.ut.us*) for construction delays and road conditions.

CONTACTS & RESOURCES

EMERGENCIES

In most towns, call ☎911 for police, fire, and ambulance service. In rural areas, the **Utah Highway Patrol** (☎ *435/634-2890*) has jurisdiction, as do county sheriff departments.

CAMPING

Most of the **Utah State Parks** (✉ *1594 W. North Temple, Salt Lake City* ☎ *801/538-7220* ⊕ *www.stateparks.utah.gov*) have camping facilities, and **Dixie National Forest** (✉ *1789 N. Wedgewood Ln., Cedar City84720* ☎ *435/865-3700* ⊕ *www. fs.fed.us/dxnf*)contains many wonderful sites. The **Utah Bureau of Land Management** (✉ *345 East Riverside Dr., St. George 84720* ☎ *435/688-3200* ⊕ *www.blm. gov/ut*) also runs campgrounds in the area.

VISITOR INFORMATION

Contacts Garfield County Travel Council (✉ *55 S. Main St., Panguitch* ☎ *800/444-6689* ⊕ *www.brycecanyoncountry.com*). **Iron County Visitors Center** (⌂ *581 N. Main St., Cedar City, 84720* ☎ *800/354-4849* ⊕ *www.scenicsouthern utah.com*). **Kane County Office of Tourism** (⌂ *78 S. 100 East St., Kanab, 84741* ☎ *800/733-5263* ⊕ *www.visitsouthernutah.com*). **St. George Area Convention & Visitors Bureau** (✉ *1835 Convention Center Dr., St. George* ☎ *800/869-6635* ⊕ *www.utahstgeorge.com*). **Utah Office of Tourism** (✉ *300 N. State St., Salt Lake City* ☎ *800/200-1160* ⊕ *www.utah.com*).

Bryce Canyon National Park

Bryce is a visitor favorite among Utah's national parks. The park was named for Ebenezer Bryce, a pioneer cattleman and the first permanent settler in the area (who called the canyon "a helluva place to lose a cow").

Bryce Canyon is known for its fanciful "hoodoos," best viewed at sunrise or sunset, when the light plays off the red rock. In geological terms, Bryce is actually an amphitheater, not a canyon. The hoodoos in the amphitheater took on their unusual shapes because the top layer of rock—"cap rock"—is harder than the layers below it. If erosion undercuts the soft rock beneath the cap too much, the hoodoo will tumble. But Bryce will never be without hoodoos, because as the amphitheater's rim recedes, new hoodoos are formed.

WELCOME TO BRYCE CANYON

Inspiration Point at Bryce Canyon

TOP REASONS TO GO

★ **Hoodoos Galore:** Bryce Canyon attracts visitors for its hundreds, if not thousands, of brightly colored, limestone spires, more commonly known as hoodoos.

★ **Famous Fresh Air:** To say the air around Bryce Canyon is rarified is not an exaggeration. With some of the clearest skies anywhere, the park offers views that, on a clear day, extend 200 mi and into three states.

★ **Spectacular Sunrises & Sunsets:** The deep orange and crimson hues of the park's hoodoos are intensified by the light of the sun at either end of the day.

★ **Getting into the Zone(s):** Bryce Canyon's elevation range—2,000 feet—is such that it spans three climatic zones: spruce/fir forest, ponderosa pine forest, and pinyon pine/juniper forest. The result is a park rich in biodiversity.

★ **Gaspworthy Geology:** A series of horseshoe-shaped amphitheaters comprise much of the park, and are the focus of most scenic turnouts.

Spire in Bryce Canyon

1 Bryce Amphitheater. Here is the park's densest collection of attractions, including the historic Bryce Canyon National Park Lodge and the points Sunrise, Sunset, and Inspiration. Paria View looks far south into Grand Staircase–Escalante National Monument.

2 Under-the-Rim Trail. Though it more or less parallels most of the scenic drive and accesses many popular sites, from Bryce Point to the vicinity of Swamp Canyon, this trail is the best way to reach the Bryce Canyon backcountry. A handful of primitive campgrounds line the route.

Hoodoo Towers

3 Rainbow and Yovimpa Points. The end of the scenic road, but not of the scenery, here you can hike a trail to see some ancient bristlecone pines and look south into Grand Staircase–Escalante National Monument.

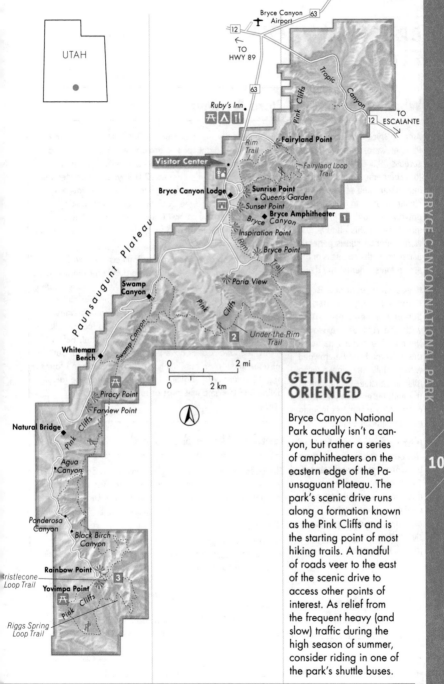

10

GETTING ORIENTED

Bryce Canyon National Park actually isn't a canyon, but rather a series of amphitheaters on the eastern edge of the Paunsaguant Plateau. The park's scenic drive runs along a formation known as the Pink Cliffs and is the starting point of most hiking trails. A handful of roads veer to the east of the scenic drive to access other points of interest. As relief from the frequent heavy (and slow) traffic during the high season of summer, consider riding in one of the park's shuttle buses.

BRYCE CANYON PLANNER

When to Go

Around Bryce Canyon National Park, elevations approach and surpass 9,000 feet, making for temperamental weather, intermittent and seasonal road closures due to snow, and downright cold nights well into June. At this altitude, the warm summer sun is perfectly balanced by the coolness of the alpine forests during the day.

If you choose to see Bryce Canyon in July, August, or September, you'll be visiting with the rest of the world. During these months, traffic on the main road can be crowded with cars following slow-moving RVs, so consider taking one of the park buses from the visitor center. Also in summer, lodging may be difficult to find.

If it's solitude you're looking for, come to Bryce any time between October and March. The snow may be flying, but imagine the multihued rocks under an icing of white. Strap on snowshoes or cross-country skis, and you might just have a trail all to yourself.

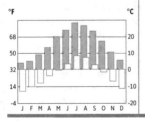

Flora & Fauna

Due to elevations approaching 9,000 feet, many of Bryce Canyon's 400 plant species are unlike those you'll see at less lofty places. Look at exposed slopes and you might catch a glimpse of the gnarled, 2,000-year-old bristlecone pine. More common, and far younger, are the Douglas fir, ponderosa pine, and the quaking aspen, most striking in its bright golden fall color. No fewer than three kinds of sagebrush—big, black, and fringed—grow here, as well as the blue columbine.

Their reputation as a pest among Southern Utah ranchers notwithstanding, the Utah prairie dog is designated a threatened species. Be cautious around them. Though cute and seemingly approachable, they might bite if you get too close, and the bacteria that causes bubonic plague has been found on their fleas. Other animals include elk, black-tailed jackrabbits, and the desert cottontail. Below 7,000 feet, black bear have been seen in the trees, but infrequently. It's far more likely you'll see the soaring forms of golden and bald eagles, or perhaps a peregrine falcon diving into the amphitheaters at speeds approaching 200 mph.

Getting There & Around

The closest major cities to Bryce Canyon are Salt Lake City and Las Vegas, each about 270 mi away. The nearest commercial airport is 80 mi west in Cedar City, Utah. The park is reached via Route 63, just 3 mi south of the junction with Highway 12.

You can see the park's highlights by driving along the well-maintained road running the length of the main scenic area. Bryce has no restrictions on automobiles, but in the summer you may encounter heavy traffic and full parking lots. A shuttle bus system operates from mid-May through September. It is free, though you still must pay the park entrance fee. The shuttle departs from the staging area off Highway 12 about 3 mi north of the park entrance every 10 to 15 minutes. Stops include Best Western Ruby's Inn, the North Campground, the visitor center, and all major overlooks in the northern portion of the park.

SCENIC DRIVE

Fodor'sChoice **Main Park Road.** One of the delights of Bryce Canyon National Park
★ is that much of the park's grandeur can be experienced from scenic
overlooks along its main thoroughfare, which meanders 18 mi from
the park entrance south to Rainbow Point. Allow two to three hours
to travel the entire 36 mi round-trip. The road is open year-round, but
may be closed temporarily after heavy snowfalls to allow for clear-
ing. Major overlooks are rarely more than a few minutes' walk from
the parking areas, and many let you see more than 100 mi on clear
days. All overlooks lie east of the road—to keep things simple (and left
turns to a minimum), you can proceed to the southern end of the park
and stop at the overlooks on your northbound return. Trailers are not
allowed beyond Sunset Campground. Day users may park trailers at
the visitor center or other designated sites; check with park staff for
parking options. RVs can drive throughout the park, but vehicles longer than 25 feet are not allowed at Paria View.

WHAT TO SEE

SCENIC STOPS

Agua Canyon. When you stop at this overlook in the southern section
of the park, pick out among the hoodoos the formation known as the
Hunter, which actually has a few small hardy trees growing on its cap.
The plays of light and colorful contrasts are especially noticeable here.
⊠ *12 mi south of park entrance.*

Bryce Point. After absorbing views of the Black Mountains and Navajo
Mountain, you can follow the trailhead for the Under-the-Rim-Trail
and go exploring down in the amphitheater to the cluster of top-heavy
hoodoos known collectively as the Hat Shop. Along the Peekaboo
Loop Trail, which also descends from this point, is the **Wall of Windows.** Openings carved into a wall of rock illustrate the drama of erosion that formed Bryce Canyon. ⊠ *5½ mi south of park entrance on
Inspiration Point Rd.*

★ **Fairyland Point.** At the scenic overlook closest to the park entrance (look
for the sign marking the route off the main park road), there are splendid views of Fairyland Amphitheater and its delicate, fanciful forms.
The Sinking Ship and other formations stand before the grand backdrop of the Aquarius Plateau and distant Navajo Mountain. ⊠ *1 mi
off main park road, 1 mi north of visitor center.*

Inspiration Point. Not far at all (3/10 mi) east along the Rim Trail from
Bryce Point is Inspiration Point, site of a wonderful panorama and one
of the best places in the park to see the sunset. ⊠ *5½ mi south of park
entrance on Inspiration Point Rd.*

★ **Natural Bridge.** Despite its name, this formation is actually an arch
carved in the rock by rain and frost erosion; true natural bridges must
be bored out by streams and rivers. Pine forests are visible through the
span of the arch. ⊠ *11 mi south of park entrance.*

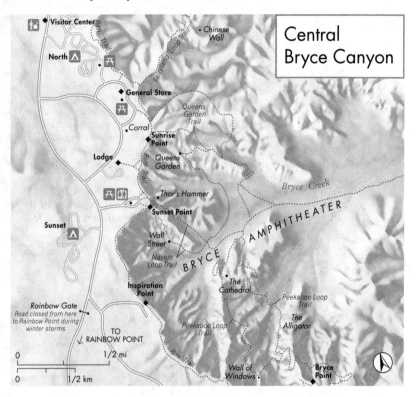

Central
Bryce Canyon

Rainbow and Yovimpa Points. While Rainbow Point's orientation allows a view north along the southern rim of the amphitheater and east into Grand Staircase–Escalante National Monument, the panorama from Yovimpa Point spreads out to the south and on a clear day you can see as far as 100 mi to Arizona. Yovimpa Point also has a shady and quiet picnic area with tables and restrooms. The Bristlecone Loop Trail connects the two viewpoints and leads through a grove of bristlecone pine trees. There are informative displays on flora, fauna, and geological history at Rainbow Point. ⊠ *18 mi south of park entrance.*

★ **Sunrise Point.** Named for its stunning views at dawn, this overlook is a popular stop for the summer crowds that come to Bryce Canyon and is the starting point for the Queen's Garden Trail and the Fairyland Loop Trail. You have to descend the Queen's Garden Trail to get a regal glimpse of **Queen Victoria,** a hoodoo that appears to sport a crown and glorious full skirt. The trail is popular and marked clearly, but moderately strenuous. ⊠ *2 mi south of park entrance near Bryce Canyon National Park Lodge.*

Sunset Point. Bring your camera to watch the late-day sun paint its magic on the hoodoos here. You can only see **Thor's Hammer,** a delicate formation similar to a balanced rock when you hike 521 feet down into the amphitheater on the Navajo Loop Trail. ⊠*2 mi south of park entrance near Bryce Canyon National Park Lodge.*

VISITOR CENTER

Bryce Canyon Visitor Center. You can visit with park rangers, watch a video about Bryce Canyon, study exhibits, or shop for informative books, maps, and other materials at this spacious visitor center. First aid, emergency, and lost-and-found services are offered here, and rangers dole out backcountry permits. If you want coffee, head to nearby Ruby's Inn. ⊠*1 mi south of park entrance* ☎*435/834–5322* ⊕*www.nps.gov/brca* ☉*May–Sept., daily 8–8; Apr. and Oct., daily 8–6; Nov.–Mar., daily 8–4:30.*

SPORTS & THE OUTDOORS

AIR TOURS

Bryce Canyon Airlines & Helicopters. For a once-in-a-lifetime view of Bryce Canyon National Park, join professional pilots and guides for a helicopter ride over the park. Flights depart from Ruby's Inn Heliport. ☎*435/834–8060* ⊕*www.rubysinn.com/bryce-canyon-airlines.html* ☎*$59–$349.*

HIKING

EASY **Bristlecone Loop Trail.** Hike through dense spruce and fir forest to exposed cliffs where ancient bristlecone pines somehow manage to survive the elements; some of the trees here are more than 1,700 years old. You might see yellow-bellied marmots and blue grouse, critters not found at lower elevations in the park. The popular 1-mi trail takes about an hour to hike. ⊠*Rainbow Point, 18 mi south of park entrance.*

Queen's Garden Trail. This hike is the easiest into the amphitheater and therefore the most crowded. Allow two to three hours to hike the 2 mi down and back. ⊠*Sunrise Point, 2 mi south of park entrance.*

MODERATE **Navajo Loop Trail.** A steep descent via a series of switchbacks leads to Wall Street, a narrow canyon with high rock walls and towering fir trees. The northern end of the trail brings Thor's Hammer into view. Allow one to two hours on this 1½-mi trail. ⊠*Sunset Point, 2 mi south of park entrance.*

★ **Navajo/Queen's Garden Combination Loop.** By walking this extended 3-mi loop, you can see some of the best of Bryce; it takes two to three hours. The route passes fantastic formations and an open forest of pine and juniper on the amphitheater floor. Descend into the amphitheater from Sunset Point on the Navajo Trail and ascend via the less demanding Queen's Garden Trail; return to your starting point via the Rim Trail. ⊠*Sunset and Sunrise points, 2 mi south of park entrance.*

DIFFICULT **Fairyland Loop Trail.** Hike into whimsical Fairyland Canyon on this strenuous but uncrowded 8-mi trail. It winds around hoodoos, across trickles of water, and finally to a natural window in the rock at Tower Bridge, 1½ mi from Sunrise Point and 4 mi from Fairyland Point. The pink-and-white badlands and hoodoos surround you the whole way.

10

Allow four to five hours round trip. You can pick up the loop at Fairyland Point or Sunrise Point. ⊠*Fairyland Point, 1 mi off main park road, 1 mi south of park entrance; Sunrise Point, 2 mi south of park entrance.*

HORSEBACK RIDING

OUTFITTERS & EXPEDITIONS

Canyon Trail Rides. Via horse or mule descend to the floor of the Bryce Canyon amphitheater. Most who take this expedition have no riding experience, so don't hesitate to join in. A two-hour ride ambles along the amphitheater floor to the Fairy Castle before returning to Sunrise Point. The half-day expedition follows Peekaboo Trail, winds past the Fairy Castle and the Alligator, and passes the Wall of Windows before returning to Sunrise Point. To reserve a trail ride, call or stop by their desk in the lodge. ⊠*Bryce Canyon National Park Lodge* ☎*435/679–8665.*

> ## PICNICKING IN THE PARK
>
> **North Campground(** ⊠*About ¼ mi south of the visitor center)*, a shady, alpine setting among ponderosa pine, has picnic tables and grills.
>
> At the southern end of the park, shady and quiet **Yovimpa Point** (⊠*18 mi south of the park entrance)* this spot looks out onto the 100-mi vistas from the rim. There are tables and restrooms.

WHERE TO EAT

ABOUT THE RESTAURANTS

Dining options in the park proper are limited to Bryce Canyon National Park Lodge; the nearby Ruby's Inn complex is your best eating bet close by. For other dining options outside the park, *see above.*

$$–$$$ ✕**Bryce Canyon National Park Lodge.** Set among towering pines, this rustic old lodge is the only place to dine within the park. The simple breakfast menu features eggs, flapjacks, and lighter fare such as oatmeal and granola. For dinner, try the red canyon grilled trout almandine or the cherry-glazed pork chops. Reservations are essential for dinner. ⊠*About 2 mi south of the park entrance* ☎*435/834–8760* ⊕*www.brycecanyonlodge.com* ⌂*Reservations essential (for dinner)* ▤*AE, D, DC, MC, V* ⊘*Closed Nov.–Mar.*

WHERE TO STAY

ABOUT THE HOTELS

Lodging options in Bryce Canyon include both rustic and modern amenities, but all fill up fast in summer. The big advantage of staying here is proximity, though Bryce Canyon National Park Lodge also has views.

ABOUT THE CAMPGROUNDS

Campgrounds in Bryce Canyon fill up fast, especially during the summer, and are family friendly. All are drive-in, except for the handful of backcountry sites that only backpackers and gung-ho day hikers ever see. Most are first-come, first-served during the high season, but call to inquire about those available for reservation. A $5 backcountry permit, available from the visitor center, is required for camping in the park's interior, allowed only on Under-the-Rim Trail and Rigg's Spring Loop, both south of Bryce Point. Campfires are not permitted.

$$$

Fodor'sChoice

★

Bryce Canyon National Park Lodge. A few feet from the amphitheater's rim and trailheads is this rugged stone-and-wood lodge. You have your choice of suites on the lodge's second level, motel-style rooms in separate buildings (with balconies or porches), and cozy lodgepole-pine cabins, some with cathedral ceilings and gas fireplaces. Reservations are hard to come by, so call several months ahead. Horseback rides into the park's interior can be arranged in the lobby. Reservations are essential for dinner at the lodge restaurant. **Pro:** Fine Western-style lodging with bright orange hoodoos are only a short walk away. **Con:** Closed in the winter. ⊠ *2 mi south of park entrance,* ☎ *435/834–5361 or 888/297– 2757* 🖶 *435/834–5464* ⊕ *www.brycecanyonlodge.com* ➚ *114 rooms, 3 suites* ⌂ *In-room: no a/c, no TV. In-hotel: restaurant, no elevator, no-smoking rooms* ▭ *AE, D, MC, V* ☾ *Closed Nov.–Mar.*

★ **$$–$$$**

Best Western Ruby's Inn. North of the park entrance and housing a large restaurant and gift shop, this is "Grand Central Station" for visitors to Bryce. Rooms vary in age, with sprawling wings added as the park gained popularity. All of the guest rooms are consistently comfortable and attractive, however. Centered between the gift shop and restaurant, the lobby of rough-hewn log beams and poles sets a Southwestern mood. **Pro:** Has it all—general store, post office, campground, restaurants, gas and more. **Con:** Expansion has caused it to lose some of its charm. ⊠ *1000 South Rte. 63, Box 640001, Bryce* ☎ *435/834–5341 or 866/866–6616* 🖶 *435/834–5265* ⊕ *www.rubysinn.com* ➚ *368 rooms, 6 suites* ⌂ *In-room: refrigerator, Ethernet, dial-up, Wi-Fi. In-hotel: 2 restaurants, pools, bicycles, laundry facilities, concierge, public Internet, public Wi-Fi, airport shuttle, some pets allowed, no-smoking rooms* ▭ *AE, D, DC, MC, V.*

CAMPING

North Campground. A cool, shady retreat in a forest of ponderosa pines, this is a great home base for your exploration of Bryce Canyon. You're near the general store, Bryce Canyon National Park Lodge, trailheads, and the visitor center. Reservations are accepted at 32 sites from May through September; the remaining 75 are available on a first-come, first-served basis. The campground usually fills by early afternoon in July, August, and September. ⊠ *Main park road, ½ mi south of visitor center* ☎ *435/834–5322, 877/444–6777 reservations* ⊕ *www. recreation.gov* ➚ *107 sites, 47 for RVs* ⌂ *Flush toilets, dump station (closed during winter), drinking water, fire grates, picnic tables, public telephone, general store* ▭ *No credit cards* ☾ *Daily.*

Sunset Campground. This serene alpine campground is within walking distance of Bryce Canyon National Park Lodge and many trailheads. All sites are filled on a first-come, first-served basis. The campground fills by early afternoon in July, August, and September, so get your campsite before you sightsee. Reservations not accepted. ⊠ *Main park road, 2 mi south of visitor center* ☎ *435/834–5322* ➚ *101 sites, 49 for RVs* ⌂ *Flush toilets, dump station, drinking water, fire grates, picnic tables, public telephone, general store* ▭ *No credit cards* ☾ *May–Oct.*

10

BRYCE CANYON NATIONAL PARK

BRYCE CANYON ESSENTIALS

ACCESSIBILITY

Most park facilities were constructed between 1930 and 1960. Some have been upgraded for handicap accessibility, while others can be used with some assistance. Because of the park's natural terrain, only a ½-mi section of the Rim Trail between Sunset and Sunrise points is wheelchair accessible. The 1-mi Bristlecone Loop Trail at Rainbow Point has a hard surface and could be used with assistance, but several grades do not meet standards. Handicapped parking is marked at all overlooks and public facilities. Accessible campsites are available at Sunset Campground.

ADMISSION FEES

The entrance fee is $25 per vehicle for a seven-day pass and $12 for pedestrians, bicyclists, or motorcyclists. An annual Bryce Canyon park pass, good for one year from the date of purchase, costs $30. This pass can also be used on the park shuttle. If you leave your private vehicle outside the park, the one-time entrance fee, including transportation on the shuttle, is $12.

EMERGENCIES

In an emergency, dial 911. To contact park police or if you need first aid, go to the visitor center or speak to a park ranger. (In the summer months only, there is also first aid at Bryce Canyon National Park Lodge.)

VISITOR INFORMATION

Contacts **Bryce Canyon National Park** ✏ *Box 640201, Bryce Canyon, UT 84764* ☎ *435/834–5322* ⊕ *www.nps.gov/brca.*

Zion National Park

The walls of Zion Canyon soar more than 2,000 feet above the valley below, but it's the character, not the size, of the sandstone forms that defines the park's splendor. The domes, fins, and blocky massifs bear the names and likenesses of cathedrals and temples, prophets and angels. But for all Zion's grandeur, trails that lead deep into side canyons and up narrow ledges on the sheer canyon walls reveal a subtler beauty. Tucked among the monoliths are delicate hanging gardens, serene spring-fed pools, and shaded spots of solitude. So diverse is this place that 85% of Utah's flora and fauna species are found here.

The park comprises two distinct sections—Zion Canyon, and the Kolob Plateau and Canyons. Most people restrict their visit to the better-known Zion Canyon, especially if they have only one day to explore.

WELCOME TO ZION NATIONAL PARK

TOP REASONS TO GO

★ **To Hike Where Angels Land:** Though not for the timid or the weak, the Angels Landing Trail culminates in one of the park's most astounding viewpoints.

★ **To Leave Traffic Behind:** During the busy summer season, cars are no longer allowed in Zion Canyon, allowing for a relaxing and scenic shuttle bus ride.

★ **To Veg Out:** Zion Canyon is home to approximately 900 species of plants, more than anywhere else in Utah.

★ **To Take the Subway:** Only the hardiest of hikers venture through the pools and tunnels of the Subway in the Zion Canyon backcountry.

★ **To Experience Highs & Lows:** Zion Canyon area geography ranges from mountains to desert, offering a diverse selection of places to explore.

1 Zion Canyon. This area defines Zion National Park for most people. Free shuttle buses are the only vehicles allowed in the crowded high season. The backcountry is accessible via the West Rim Trail and The Narrows, and 2,000-foot cliffs rise all around.

2 Zion-Mount Carmel Highway. Everyone loves driving through the tunnel hewn from stone, even RVers who have to pay a fee and get a ranger escort. Canyon Overlook Trail provides a quick overlook of the West Temple and other majestic formations.

Map labels:
exit 42
exit 40
Horse Ranch Mountain
Visitor Center
Double Arch Alcove
Nagunt Mesa
Kolob Canyons Viewpoint
3 Kolob Canyons
Kolob Arch
La Verkin Creek
15
Firepit Knoll
Lower Kolob Plateau
Spendlove Knoll
0   2 mi
0   2 km
Kolob Terrace Road
Virgin
9

The Virgin River

3 Kolob Canyons. The quiet northwest corner of Zion, this area lets you see some of the park's attractions, such as the West Temple, from an angle many visitors never witness. Kolob Arch is easily reached via a relatively short trail.

Hiking through the river in Zion Narrows

4 Lava Point. Infrequently visited, this area has a primitive campground and nearby are two reservoirs that provide the only significant fishing opportunities in Zion National Park. Lava Point Overlook provides a view of Zion Canyon from the north.

UTAH

GETTING ORIENTED

The heart of Zion Canyon National Park is Zion Canyon itself, which follows the North Fork of the Virgin River for 6½ mi beneath cliffs that approach 2,000 feet in elevation. The Kolob area is considered by some to be superior in beauty, and you aren't likely to run into any crowds here. Both sections hint at the extensive backcountry beyond, open for those with the stamina, time, and the experience to go off the beaten paths of the park.

ZION NATIONAL PARK

10

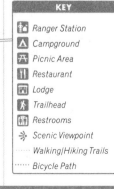

KEY	
🛈	Ranger Station
⛺	Campground
🌲	Picnic Area
🍴	Restaurant
🏨	Lodge
🚶	Trailhead
🚻	Restrooms
⁂	Scenic Viewpoint
⋯⋯	Walking/Hiking Trails
⋯⋯	Bicycle Path

Upper Kolob Plateau

Lava Point
Lava Point
Viewpoint

4

Horse Pasture

West Rim Trail

Plateau

Viewpoint

Left Fork

The Narrows

Orderville Canyon
Mountain of
Mystery

Temple of
Sinawava

ght Fork

Zion Canyon

Weeping Rock
Angels Landing
Great White Throne
The Grotto
Emerald Pools
Trails
Zion Lodge

The Sentinel
Shuttle Bus
(summer only)
East Entrance

Altar of Sacrifice

Court
of the
Patriarchs

9

The West Temple
Canyon Junction

Zion Human History Museum
Tunnel
Zion–Mount Carmel Hwy.

2

Parunuweap Canyon

Rockville

ZION NATIONAL PARK PLANNER

When to Go

Zion is the most heavily visited national park in Utah, receiving nearly 2.5 million visitors each year. **Most visitors come between April and October,** when upper Zion Canyon is accessed only by free shuttle bus to reduce traffic congestion.

Summer in the park is hot and dry except for sudden cloudbursts, which can create flash flooding and spectacular waterfalls. Expect afternoon thunderstorms between July and September. In the summer sun, wear sunscreen and drink lots of water, regardless of your activity level. Winters are mild at lower desert elevations, so consider planning your visit for some time other than peak season. You can expect to encounter winter driving conditions November through March, and although most park programs are suspended, winter is a wonderful and solitary time to see the canyons. During these months the shuttle does not operate.

⚠ **Extreme highs in Zion can often exceed 100°F in July and August.**

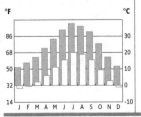

Getting There & Around

In southwestern Utah, not far from the Nevada border, Zion National Park is closer to Las Vegas (158 mi) than to Salt Lake City (310 mi). The nearest commercial airport is 46 mi away in St. George, Utah. Off Route 9, the park is 21 mi east of Interstate 15 and 24 mi west of U.S. 89.

November through March, private vehicles are allowed on Zion's main park road, Zion Canyon Scenic Drive. From April through October, however, it is closed to private vehicles. During this time, the park's easy-to-use shuttle system ferries people into the canyon from the Zion Canyon Visitor Center, where the parking lot is typically full, 10 to 3 daily, May through September. To avoid parking hassles, leave your car in the nearby town of Springdale and ride the town shuttle to the park entrance where you can connect with the park shuttle. Town shuttle stops are at Majestic View, Driftwood Motel, Quality Inn, Bit & Spur Restaurant, Zion Park Inn, Bumbleberry Inn, Pizza and Noodle Company, Zion Canyon Clothing, Flanigan's Inn, and Zion Giant Screen Theater. The shuttles are free, but you must pay the park entrance fee.

If you enter or exit Zion via the east entrance you will have the privilege of driving a gorgeous, twisting 24-mi stretch of the Zion–Mount Carmel Highway (Route 9). Two tunnels, including the highway's famous 1 1/10-mi tunnel, lie between the east park entrance and Zion Canyon. The tunnels are so narrow that vehicles more than 7 feet, 10 inches wide or 11 feet, 4 inches high require traffic control while passing through. Rangers, who are stationed at the tunnels 8 AM to 8 PM daily, April through October, stop oncoming traffic so you can drive down the middle of the tunnels. Large vehicles must pay an escort fee of $15 at either park entrance. West of the tunnels the highway meets Zion Canyon Scenic Drive at Canyon Junction, about 1 mi north of the Zion Canyon Visitor Center.

SCENIC DRIVES

★ **Kolob Canyons Road.** From Interstate 15 you get no hint of the beauty that awaits you on this 5-mi road. Most visitors gasp audibly when they get their first glimpse of the red canyon walls that rise suddenly and spectacularly out of the earth. The scenic drive winds amid these towers as it rises in elevation, until you reach a viewpoint that overlooks the whole Kolob region of Zion National Park. The shortest hike in this section of the park is the Middle Fork of Taylor Creek Trail, which is 2 7/10 mi one way to Double Arch Alcove, and gets fairly rugged toward the end (⇨ *Hiking in the Sports & the Outdoors section*). During heavy snowfall Kolob Canyons Road may be closed. ⊠ *Kolob Canyons Rd. east of I–15, Exit 40.*

★ **Zion–Mount Carmel Highway & Tunnels.** Two narrow tunnels lie between the east park entrance and Zion Canyon on this breathtaking 24-mi stretch of Route 9. As you travel through solid rock from one end of the longest (1 1/10 mi) tunnel to the other, portals along one side provide a few glimpses of cliffs and canyons, and when you emerge on the other side you find that the landscape has changed dramatically. The tunnels are so narrow that large vehicles more than 7 feet, 10 inches wide or 11 feet, 4 inches high require traffic control while passing through, available 8 AM–8 PM daily, April–October, and must pay a $15 escort fee. ⊠ *Zion–Mount Carmel Rte. 9, about 5 mi east of Canyon Junction.*

WHAT TO SEE

HISTORIC SITES

★ **Zion Human History Museum.** Enrich your visit with a stop here, where you'll get a complete overview of the park with special attention to human history. Exhibits explain how settlers interacted with the geology, wildlife, plants, and unpredictable weather in the canyon from prehistory to the present. A 22-minute film plays throughout the day. ⊠ *Zion Canyon Scenic Dr., 1 mi north of south entrance* ☎ *435/772– 3256, ext. 168* ⊕ *www.nps.gov/zion/HHMuseum.htm* ☜ *Free* ☽ *Late May–early Sept., daily 9–7; early May and early-Sept.–mid-Oct., daily 10–6; Mar.–Apr. and late Oct., daily 10–5.*

Zion Lodge. The Union Pacific Railroad constructed the first Zion National Park Lodge in 1925, with buildings designed by architect Stanley Gilbert Underwood. A fire destroyed the original building, but it was rebuilt to recapture some of the look and feel of the first building. The original Western-style cabins are still in use today. Among giant cottonwoods across the road from the Emerald Pools trailhead, the lodge houses a restaurant, snack bar, and gift shop. ⊠ *Zion Canyon Scenic Dr., about 3 mi north of Canyon Junction* ☎ *435/772–7700* ⊕ *www.zionlodge.com.*

SCENIC STOPS

Checkerboard Mesa. The distinctive pattern on this huge, white mound of sandstone was created by a combination of vertical fractures and the exposure of horizontal bedding planes by erosion. ⊠ *Zion–Mount Carmel Hwy., 1 mi west of the east entrance.*

★ **Court of the Patriarchs.** This trio of peaks bears the names of, from left to right, Abraham, Isaac, and Jacob. Mount Moroni is the reddish peak on the far right, which partially blocks your view of Jacob. You can see the Patriarchs better by hiking a half mile up Sand Bench Trail. ⊠ *Zion Canyon Scenic Dr., 1½ mi north of Canyon Junction.*

Great White Throne. Towering over the Grotto picnic area near Zion Lodge is this massive 6,744-foot rock peak. ⊠ *Zion Canyon Scenic Dr., about 3 mi north of Canyon Junction.*

★ **Weeping Rock.** A short, paved walk leads up to this flowing rock face, where wildflowers and delicate ferns thrive near a spring-fed waterfall that seeps out of a cliff. In fall, this area bursts with color. The 1/5-mi trail to the west alcove takes about 25 minutes round-trip. It is paved, but too steep for wheelchairs. ⊠ *Zion Canyon Scenic Dr., about 4 mi north of Canyon Junction.*

VISITOR CENTERS

Kolob Canyons Visitor Center. At the origin of Kolob Canyons Road, this park office has a small bookstore plus exhibits on park geology and helpful rangers to answer questions. ⊠ *Exit 40 off I–15* ☎ *435/586–9548* ☽ *Oct.–Apr., daily 8–4:30; May–Sept., daily 8–5.*

Zion Canyon Visitor Center. Unlike most national park visitor centers, which are filled with indoor displays, Zion's presents most of its information in an appealing outdoor exhibit. Beneath shade trees beside a gurgling brook, displays help you plan your stay and introduce you to the area's geology, flora, and fauna. Inside, a large bookstore operated by the Zion Natural History Association sells field guides and other publications. **Ranger-guided shuttle tours** of Zion Canyon depart from the parking lot and travel to the Temple of Sinawava, with several photo-op stops along the way. The tour schedule and free tour tickets are available inside. You can also pick up backcountry permits here. ⊠ *At south entrance, Springdale* ☎ *435/772–3256, ext. 616* ⊕ *www.nps.gov/zion* ☽ *Apr.–May and Sept.–mid-Oct., daily 8–6; June–Aug., daily 8–7; mid-Oct.–Mar., daily 8–5.*

SPORTS & THE OUTDOORS

AIR TOURS

Bryce Canyon Airlines & Helicopters. For a once-in-a-lifetime view of Zion National Park, join professional pilots and guides for an airplane ride over the park (and Bryce Canyon National Park during the same flight). Flights depart from Ruby's Inn Heliport near Bryce Canyon National Park. There is a two-person minimum. ☎ *435/834–8060* ⊕ *www.rubysinn.com/bryce-canyon-airlines.html* ▧ *$175 per person.*

HIKING

Permits are required for overnight climbs and backcountry camping. The maximum size of a group hiking into the backcountry is 12 people. The cost for a permit for 1–2 people is $10; 3–7 people, $15; and 8–12 people, $20. Permits and hiking information are available at the Zion Canyon Visitor Center.

EASY **Emerald Pools Trail.** Two small waterfalls cascade (or drip, in dry weather) into pools at the top of this relatively easy trail. The way is paved up to the lower pool and is suitable for baby strollers and wheelchairs with assistance. Beyond the lower pool, the trail becomes rocky and steep as you progress toward the middle and upper pools. A less crowded and exceptionally enjoyable return route follows the Kayenta Trail connecting on to the Grotto Trail. Allow 50 minutes round-trip to the lower pool and 2½ hours round-trip to the middle and upper pools. ⊠ *Zion Canyon Scenic Dr., about 3 mi north of Canyon Junction.*

Grotto Trail. This flat and very easy trail takes you from Zion Lodge to the Grotto picnic area, traveling for the most part along the park road. Allow 20 minutes or less for the walk. If you are up for a longer hike, and have two to three hours, connect with the Kayenta Trail after you cross the footbridge, and head for the Emerald Pools. You will begin gaining elevation, and it's a steady, steep climb to the pools. ⊠ *Zion Canyon Scenic Dr., about 3 mi north of Canyon Junction.*

Pa'rus Trail. This 2-mi walking and biking path parallels and occasionally crosses the Virgin River, starting at South Campground and proceeding north along the river to the beginning of Zion Canyon Scenic Drive. It's paved and gives you great views of the Watchman, the Sentinel, the East and West Temples, and Towers of the Virgin. Dogs are allowed on this trail as long as they are leashed. Cyclists must follow traffic rules on this heavily used trail. ⊠ *Canyon Junction, ½ mi north of south entrance.*

Riverside Walk. Beginning at the Temple of Sinawava shuttle stop at the end of Zion Canyon Scenic Drive, this easily enjoyed 1-mi round-trip stroll shadows the Virgin River. The river gurgles by on one side of the trail; on the other, wildflowers bloom out of the canyon wall in fascinating hanging gardens. This is the park's most trekked trail; it is paved and suitable for baby strollers and for wheelchairs with assistance. A round-trip walk takes between one and two hours. The end of the trail marks the beginning of the Narrows Trail. ⊠ *Zion Canyon Scenic Dr., 5 mi north of Canyon Junction.*

MODERATE **Canyon Overlook Trail.** It's a little tough to locate this trailhead, but you'll find it if you watch for the parking area just east of Zion–Mount Carmel tunnel. The trail is moderately steep but only 1 mi round-trip; allow an hour to hike it. The overlook at trail's end gives you views of the West and East Temples, Towers of the Virgin, the Streaked Wall, and other Zion Canyon cliffs and peaks. ⊠ *Rte. 9, east of Zion–Mount Carmel Tunnel.*

Watchman Trail. For a view of the town of Springdale and a look at lower Zion Creek Canyon and the Towers of the Virgin, take the moderately strenuous hike that begins on a service road east of Watchman Campground. Some springs seep out of the sandstone to nourish hanging gardens and attract wildlife here. There are a few sheer cliff edges on this route, so children should be supervised carefully. Allow two hours for this 3-mi hike. ⊠ *East of Rte. 9 (main park road), on access road inside south entrance.*

DIFFICULT **Angels Landing Trail.** Truly one of the most spectacular hikes in the park,
Fodor'sChoice this trail is an adventure for those not afraid of heights. On your ascent
★ you must negotiate Walter's Wiggles, a series of 21 switchbacks built out of sandstone blocks, and traverse sheer cliffs with chains bolted into the rock face to serve as handrails. In spite of its hair-raising nature, this trail attracts many people. Small children should skip it, however, and older children should be carefully supervised. Allow 2½ hours round-trip if you stop at Scout's Lookout, and four hours if you keep going to where the angels (and birds of prey) play. ⊠ *Zion Canyon Scenic Drive, about 4½ mi north of Canyon Junction.*

★ **Narrows Trail.** On a hot, clear day there are few things more enjoyable than a walk in the river. This route does not follow a trail or path; rather, you are walking on the riverbed, no matter how much water is in it. The gateway of the Narrows admits adventurous souls deeper into Zion Canyon than most visitors go. As beautiful as it is, this hike is not for everyone. To see the Narrows you must wade upstream through chilly water and over uneven, slippery rocks. Just to cross the river, you must walk deliberately and slowly using a walking stick. Be prepared to swim, as chest-deep holes may occur even when water levels are low. Like any narrow desert canyon, this one is famous for sudden flash flooding even when skies are clear. *Before attempting to hike into the Narrows, check with park rangers about the likelihood of flash floods.* A day trip up the lower section of the Narrows is 6 mi one way to the turnaround point. Allow at least five hours round-trip. ⊠ *At the end of Riverside Walk.*

HORSEBACK RIDING

OUTFITTERS & **Canyon Trail Rides.** These friendly folks have been around for years,
EXPEDITIONS and they are the only outfitter for trail rides inside the park. Anyone over age seven can participate in guided rides along the Virgin River. The horses work from late March through October; you may want to make reservations ahead of time. ⊠ *Across the road from Zion Lodge* ☎ *435/679–8665* ⊕ *www.canyonrides.com* ⊠ *$30–$65.*

WHERE TO EAT

ABOUT THE RESTAURANTS

There is only one full-service restaurant in Zion National Park, so for more dining options, head for the nearby town of Springdale (⇨ *above*), which has the area's best restaurants.

PICNICKING IN THE PARK

⏱ **The Grotto.** A shady lunch retreat with lots of amenities—drinking water, fire grates, picnic tables, and restrooms—the Grotto is ideal for families. A short walk takes you to Zion Lodge, where you can pick up fast food. ✉ *Zion Canyon Scenic Dr., 3½ mi north of Canyon Junction.*

Kolob Canyons Viewpoint. Enjoy the views while you have your lunch at the picnic table. Restrooms and drinking water are available at the Kolob Canyons Visitor Center.

✉ *Kolob Canyons Rd., 5 mi from Kolob Canyons Visitor Center.*

⏱ **Zion Nature Center.** On your way to or from the Junior Ranger Program feed your kids at the Nature Center picnic area. When the nature center is closed, you can use the restrooms in South Campground. ✉ *Near the entrance to South Campground ½ mi north of the south entrance* ☎ *435/772–3256.*

$$–$$$ ✕ **Red Rock Grill at Zion Lodge.** This is the only full-service restaurant inside the park. A rustic reproduction of the original lodge dining room, the restaurant is hung with historic photos. You can dine on the patio overlooking the front lawn of the lodge. A good selection of steak, fish, and poultry is offered for dinner, and lunch includes sandwiches and salads. Breakfast is also served. ✉ *Zion Canyon Scenic Dr., 3¼ mi north of Canyon Junction* ☎ *435/772–7760* ⊕ *www.zionlodge. com* ⚖ *Reservations essential (for dinner)* ▱ *AE, D, DC, MC, V.*

¢ ✕ **Castle Dome Café.** Right next to the Zion Lodge shuttle stop and adjoining the gift shop, this small fast-food restaurant defines convenience. Hikers on the go can grab a banana or a sandwich here, or you can while away an hour with ice cream on the sunny patio. ✉ *Zion Canyon Scenic Dr., 3¼ mi north of Canyon Junction* ☎ *435/772–7700* ⊕ *www.zionlodge.com* ▱ *AE, D, DC, MC, V.*

WHERE TO STAY

ABOUT THE HOTELS

Lodging within Zion is very limited and rustic. Still, in the summer high season, you'll want to make reservations if you want to stay in or close to the park. Nearby Springdale has many lodging options, from quaint smaller motels and bed-and-breakfasts, to upscale hotels with modern amenities and riverside rooms.

ABOUT THE CAMPGROUNDS

Campgrounds within Zion National Park are family friendly, convenient, and quite pleasant, but in the high season they do fill up fast. Your best bet is to reserve ahead of time whenever possible. Backcountry camping in the park is an option for overnight backpackers, but make sure to get a permit at the Zion Canyon Visitor Center.

$$$ ▤ **Zion Lodge.** Although the original lodge burned down in 1966, the rebuilt structure convincingly re-creates the classic look of the old inn. Knotty pine woodwork and log and wicker furnishings accent the lobby.

10

ZION NATIONAL PARK

Lodge rooms are modern but not fancy, and the historic Western-style cabins have gas-log fireplaces. This is a place of quiet retreat, so there are no TVs—kids can amuse themselves outdoors on the abundant grassy lawns. The lodge is within easy walking distance of trailheads, horseback riding, and, of course, the shuttle stop, all of which are less than ½ mi away. **Pro:** Prime location in the heart of Zion Canyon. **Con:** Reservations tend to fill far in advance. Make yours at least six months ahead. ⊠*Zion Canyon Scenic Dr., 3¼ mi north of Canyon Junction* ☎*435/772–7700, 888/297–2757 reservations* ☎*435/772–7790* ⊕*www.zionlodge.com* ✎*122 rooms, 6 suites* ⚿*In-room: refrigerator (some), no TV, dial-up. In-hotel: 2 restaurants, bar, public Internet, no-smoking rooms* ⊟*AE, D, MC, V* ⦿|*EP.*

CAMPING   ⚠ **South Campground.** All the sites here are under big cottonwood trees, granting campers some relief from the summer sun. The campground operates on a first-come, first-served basis, and sites are usually filled before noon each day during high season. ⊠*Rte. 9, ½ mi north of south entrance* ✎*127 sites* ⚿*Flush toilets, dump station, drinking water, fire grates, picnic tables* ☎*435/772–3256* ⊟*No credit cards* ⊙*Mar.–Oct.*

★   ⚠ **Watchman Campground.** This large campground on the Virgin River operates on a reservation system from April to October, but you do not get to choose your own site. ⊠*Access road off Zion Canyon Visitor Center parking lot* ☎*435/772–3256, 877/444–6777 reservations* ⊕*www.recreation.gov* ✎*152 sites, 63 with hook-ups* ⚿*Flush toilets, partial hookups (electric), dump station, drinking water, fire grates, picnic tables* ⊟*D, MC, V.*

ZION NATIONAL PARK ESSENTIALS

ACCESSIBILITY
Both visitor centers, all shuttle buses, and Zion Lodge are fully accessible to wheelchairs. Several campsites (sites A24 and A25 at Watchman Campground and sites 103, 114, and 115 at South Campground) are reserved for people with disabilities, and two trails—Riverside Walk and Pa'rus Trail—are accessible with some assistance.

ADMISSION FEES
Entrance to Zion National Park is $25 per vehicle. People entering on foot or by bicycle pay $12 per person (not to exceed $25 per family) or $20 per motorcycle. Entrance to the Kolob Canyons section of the park costs $25, and includes access to Zion Canyon.

EMERGENCIES
In the event of an emergency, dial 911, report to a visitor center, or contact a park ranger at 435/772–3322. The nearest hospitals are in St. George, Cedar City, and Kanab. In Springdale, **Zion Canyon Medical Clinic** (⊠*120 Zion Blvd.* ☎*435/772–3226* ⊙*Mid-May–mid-Oct., Tues.–Sat. 9–5*) accepts walk-in patients.

VISITOR INFORMATION
Contacts Zion National Park (⊠*Springdale, UT 84767-1099* ☎*435/772–3256* ⊕*www.nps.gov/zion*).

Southwest Colorado

WORD OF MOUTH

"The scenery on the drive back to Durango was one of the most spectacular views we have ever seen—had to make several stops."

—LvSun

Revised &
Updated by
Ann Miller &
Kyle Wagner

The ruddy or red-hue rocks found in much of the state, particularly in the southwest, give Colorado its name. The region's terrain varies widely—from yawning black canyons and desolate monochrome moonscapes to pastel deserts and mesas, glistening sapphire lakes, and wide expanses of those stunning red rocks. It's so rugged in the southwest that a four-wheel-drive vehicle or hiker's sturdiness is necessary to explore much of the wild and beautiful backcountry.

The region's history and people are as colorful as the landscape. Southwestern Colorado, as well as the "Four Corners" neighbors of northwestern New Mexico, northeastern Arizona, and southeastern Utah, was home to the Ancestral Puebloan peoples formerly known as Anasazi, meaning "ancient ones." They constructed impressive cliff dwellings in what are now Mesa Verde National Park, Ute Mountain Tribal Park, and other nearby sites. This wild and woolly region, dotted with rowdy mining camps and boomtowns, also witnessed the antics of such notorious outlaws as Butch Cassidy, who embarked on his storied career by robbing the Telluride Bank in 1889, and Robert "Bobby" Clark, who hid out in Creede from the James Gang after he shot Jesse in the back.

EXPLORING SOUTHWEST COLORADO

Southwest Colorado is the land beyond the interstates. It's a landscape of towering mountains, arid mesa-and-canyon country, and roiling rivers. Old mining roads, legacies of the late 19th and early 20th centuries when gold and silver mining was ascendant, lead through drop-dead gorgeous mountain valleys to the rugged high country. However, much of this part of the state is designated as wilderness area—including the nearly 1-million-acre Weminuche Wilderness, the state's largest protected area—which means that no roads may be built and no wheeled or motorized vehicles are permitted.

ABOUT THE RESTAURANTS

With dining options ranging from creative contemporary cuisine in the posh ski resorts of Telluride to no-frills American fare in down-home ranching communities, no one has any excuse to visit a chain restaurant here. The leading chefs are tapping into the region's local bounty, so you can find innovative recipes for ranch-raised game, lamb, and trout. Many serve only locally raised, grass-fed meats. Olathe sweet corn is a delicacy enjoyed across the state in restaurants and grocery stores. Seasonal produce is always highlighted on the best menus.

ABOUT THE HOTELS

No matter what you're looking for in vacation lodging—luxurious slope-side condominium, landmark inn in a historic town, riverside cabin, quaint bed-and-breakfast inn, budget motel, or chock-full-of-RVs campground—southwest Colorado has it in abundance. In ski resorts, especially, the rates vary from season to season. Some properties close in fall once the aspens have shed their golden leaves, open in winter when the lifts begin running, close in spring after the snow melts, and open again in mid-June.

TOP REASONS TO GO

11

The Colorado Trail: Bike, hike, or photograph the more than 500 mi of volunteer-maintained trail traversing six wilderness areas and eight mountain ranges from Durango to Denver, with breathtaking views of old-growth forests alternating with wildflower-covered meadows, lakes, and creeks.

Mountain Biking Crested Butte: There's a reason the Mountain Bike Hall of Fame resides here—the town is one of the birthplaces of fat-tire biking, and the up-close mountain scenery, sweet single-track, and the sheer variety of trails and terrain are a testament to the reason of its location.

Durango & Silverton Narrow Gauge Railroad: This year-round, nine-hour journey along the Animas River from Durango to Silverton will take you back in time. The train is powered by coal and steam and the railroad line has been in continuous operation since 1882. The views include dramatic canyons and the sweeping panoramas of the San Juan National Forest.

Downhill Skiing and Snowboarding at Telluride Ski Resort: There's rarely a wait to get at the sweeping, groomed trails and seemingly endless tree runs and moguls available at this, the largest collection of 14,000-foot mountains in the country. Expansive views, varied terrain, and remote slopes that hold powder add to the experience.

WHAT IT COSTS					
	¢	$	$$	$$$	$$$$
Restaurants	under $8	$8–$12	$13–$18	$19–$25	over $25
Hotels	under $80	$80–$120	$121–$170	$171–$230	over $230

Restaurant prices are for a main course at dinner, excluding 5.9%–8.1% tax. Hotel prices are for two people in a standard double room in high season, excluding service charges and 7.6%–9.9% tax.

TIMING

Southwest Colorado, like the rest of the state, is intensely seasonal. Snow begins falling in the high country in late September or early October, and by Halloween seasonal closures turn most unpaved roads into routes for snowmobiles. The San Juan Mountains are the snowiest region of the Colorado Rockies, with average annual snowfalls approaching 400 inches in some spots. Winter lingers well into the season that is called spring on the calendar—the greatest snowfalls generally occur in March and April. Skiing winds down in early to mid-April, and ski towns virtually shut down until summer. Durango, a college town, keeps rolling throughout the year.

In mid-April the snow in the higher elevations begins to melt. Cresting streams offer thrilling, if chilling, white-water rafting and kayaking. Hiking trails become accessible, and wildflowers begin their short, intense season of show. Summer is glorious in the mountains, with brilliant sunshine in cobalt blue skies. Late summer brings brief and often

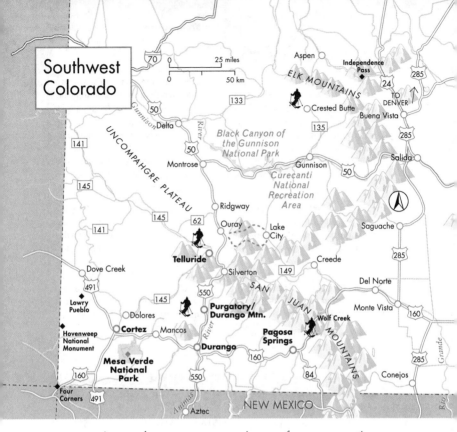

Southwest Colorado

intense showers on many an August afternoon, sometimes accompanied by dramatic thunder and lightning. Summer tourism winds down after Labor Day and shuts down completely in October and the cycle begins again. Spring and fall are the best times to visit the harsh dry climate of the mesa-and-canyon country around the Four Corners.

TELLURIDE

66 mi south of Montrose, 125 mi north of Durango.

Tucked like a jewel in a tiny valley caught between azure sky and gunmetal mountains is Telluride, once so inaccessible that it was a favorite hideout for desperadoes such as Butch Cassidy, who robbed his first bank here in 1889. The savage but beautiful terrain of the San Juan Mountains, with peaks like 14,157-foot Mount Sneffels, and rivers, like the San Miguel, now attracts mountain people of a different sort—alpinists, snowboarders, freestylers, mountain bikers, and freewheeling four-wheelers—who attack any incline, up or down, and do so with abandon.

Although the resort and the town are distinct areas, you can travel between them via a 2.5-mi, over-the-mountain gondola, one of the most beautiful commutes in Colorado. The gondola makes a car unnecessary for local transportation; both the village and the town are pedestrian friendly. This innovative form of public transportation operates summer and winter from early morning until late at night, and unless you have skis or a snowboard, the ride is free.

WORD OF MOUTH

"Personally I would spend 2 days in Durango, then spend a ½ day and do the Million-Dollar Highway drive up to Telluride. Telluride is gorgeous! The walk up to Tomboy (the old mine above the town) is beautiful." —steviegene

Telluride has two off-seasons, when most restaurants and many lodgings are closed. Nearly everyone flees town after the ski area shuts down in mid-April, to return in early or mid-June. The town closes up from late September or early October until ski season gets going in late November to early December.

The 1887 brick **San Miguel County Courthouse** (✉ *301 Colorado Ave.*) was the county's first courthouse, and it still operates as one today.

William Jennings Bryan spoke at the **New Sheridan Hotel & Opera House** (✉ *231 W. Colorado Ave.* ☎ *970/728–4351*) during his 1896 presidential campaign. The opera house, added in 1914 and completely redone in 1996, is now home to the thriving Sheridan Arts Foundation.

In the old Miner's Hospital, **Telluride Historical Museum** was constructed in 1888 and carefully restored in 2000. Exhibits on the town's past, including work in the nearby mines and techniques practiced by doctors who once practiced here, are on display. ✉ *201 W. Gregory Ave.* ☎ *970/728–3344* ⊕ *www.telluridemuseum.org* ✉ *$5* ☾ *Tues., Wed., Fri., and Sat. 11–5; Thurs. 11–7; Sun. 1–5.*

Operated by local thespian Ashley Boling, **Historic Tours of Telluride** (☎ *970/728–6639*) provides humorous walking tours around the downtown streets, adding anecdotes about infamous figures such as Butch Cassidy and Jack Dempsey.

★ U.S. 550 and Route 62 fan out from Ridgway to form one of the country's most stupendously scenic drives, the **San Juan Skyway.** The roadway weaves through a series of Fourteeners (a Rockies term for peaks reaching more than 14,000 feet) and picturesque mining towns. U.S. 550 continues south to historic Ouray and over Red Mountain Pass to Silverton and Durango. Take Route 62 west and Route 145 south to see the extraordinary cliff dwellings of Mesa Verde National Park. U.S. 160 completes the San Juan Skyway circuit to Durango. In late September and early October this route offers some of the most spectacular aspen viewing in the state.

Fodor'sChoice **DOWNHILL SKIING & SNOWBOARDING**

★ **Telluride** is really two ski areas in one. For many years, Telluride had a reputation as being an experts-only ski area. Indeed, the north-facing trails are impressively steep and long, and by spring the moguls are massive. The terrain accessed by Chairlift 9, including the famed Spiral Staircase and the Plunge, is for experts only (although one side of the Plunge is groomed so advanced skiers can have their turn).

But then there is the other side—literally—of the ski area, the gently sloping valley called Goronno Basin, with long runs excellent for intermediates and beginners. On the ridge that wraps around the ski area's core is the aptly named See Forever, a long cruiser that starts at 12,255 feet and seems to go on and on. Below that are numerous intermediate runs and a phenomenal terrain park called Sprite Air Garden, designed for snowboarders. Near Goronno Basin is another section that includes super-steep, double-diamond tree runs on one side and glorious cruisers on the other.

> ### NOTHING FEST
>
> Telluride is famous for its seemingly endless stream of festivals—so much so that its nickname is "Festival City." In 1991, a resident wrote a tongue-in-cheek letter to the city requesting that a Nothing Festival be implemented to give the citizens a break. Much to everyone's surprise, it was. During the festival, as listed on the Web site ⊕ *www.nothingfestival.com*, "Sunrises and sunsets as normal." T-shirts with a special logo are for sale each year and festivalgoers are encouraged to tie a piece of string on their wrists to indicate nonparticipation.

Slide through a Western-style gate and you come to Prospect Bowl, a 733-acre expansion that includes three chairlifts and a network of runs subtly cut around islands of trees. One cluster of intermediate runs is served by a swift high-speed quad. The terrain runs the gamut from almost-flat, beginner terrain to double-diamond fall-away chutes, cliff bands, and open glades. ⊠ *565 Mountain Village Blvd.,* ☎ *970/728–6900 or 800/778–8581* ⊕ *www. tellurideskiresort.com* ⊙ *Late Nov.–early Apr., daily 9–4.*

FACILITIES   3,530-foot vertical drop; 1,700 skiable acres; 24% beginner, 38% intermediate, 38% advanced/expert; 2 gondolas, 7 high-speed quad chairs, 2 triple chairs, 2 double chairs, 2 surface lifts, 1 moving carpet. (☎ *970/728–7425*).

LESSONS &   The **Telluride Ski & Snowboard School** (⊠ *565 Mountain Village Blvd.*
PROGRAMS   ☎ *800/801–4832* ⊕ *www.tellurideskiresort.com*) offers half-day group clinics beginning at $55. Lessons for first-timers are available for alpine and telemark skiers, as well as snowboarders. A five-hour clinic with rentals and restricted lift tickets costs $115. Children's programs for ages 3 to 12 are $120 a day for lifts, lessons, and lunch. Telluride was a pioneer in creating Women's Week programs, five days of skills-building classes with female instructors. Sessions are scheduled for February and March.

LIFT TICKETS   The one-day walk-up rate is $85. On multiday, advance-purchase tickets the daily rate can drop as low as $59.

RENTALS   Equipment rentals are available at **Paragon Ski and Sport** (⊠ *236 S. Oak St.* ☎ *970/728–4581* ⊕ *www.paragontelluride.com*). Beginner packages (skis, boots, and poles) are $22 a day, and top-of-the-line packages are $42 a day. Paragon also rents telemark and cross-country gear, as well as snowshoes and snowblades.

Ski rentals are available from the ubiquitous **Telluride Sports** (✉ *150 W. Colorado Ave.* ☎*970/728–4477 or 800/828–7547* ⊕*www.telluride sports.com*). Complete packages (skis, boots, and poles) start at around $28. There are 10 other locations in the area.

NORDIC SKIING

BACKCOUNTRY SKIING Among the better backcountry skiing routes is the **San Juan Hut System** (✉ *224 E. Colorado Ave.,* ☎*970/626–3033* ⊕*www.sanjuanhuts.com*). It leads toward Ridgway along the Sneffels Range. The five huts in the system are about 7 mi apart and are well equipped with beds, blankets, wood-burning stoves, and cooking stoves. Previous backcountry experience is not essential to ski here, though it's highly recommended. Rental equipment is available, and reservations are recommended at least two weeks in advance. The San Juan Hut System also offers a guide service as an introduction to the backcountry tracks.

TRACK SKIING **Telluride Nordic Center** (✉ *Town park* ☎*970/728–1144* ⊕*www. telluridetrails.org*) gives you access to 10 mi of cross-country trails. The areas around Molas Divide and Mesa Verde National Park are extremely popular. The center also rents equipment for both adults and children.

The **Topaten Touring Center** (☎*970/728–7517*), near the Chair 10 unload), offers 6.25 mi of trails groomed for cross-country skiing and snowshoeing in a high-mountain setting.

OTHER SPORTS & THE OUTDOORS

Telluride Outside (✉ *121 W. Colorado Ave.* ☎*970/728–3895 or 800/831–6230* ⊕*www.tellurideoutside.com*) organizes a variety of summer and winter activities in the Telluride area, including hot-air ballooning, sleigh rides, snowmobile tours, mountain-biking trips, and even winter fly-fishing excursions.

FISHING For an afternoon in some of the finest backcountry wilderness around, as well as a plethora of rainbow, cutthroat, brown, and brook trout, head for the beautiful San Miguel and Delores rivers. Anyone older than 16 needs a Colorado fishing license, which you can obtain at local sporting-goods stores. See ⊕*www.wildlife.state.co.us/fishing* for more information.

Telluride Outside (✉ *121 W. Colorado Ave.* ☎*970/728–3895 or 800/831–6230* ⊕*www.tellurideoutside.com*), Colorado's second-largest fishing-guide service, offers guided fly-fishing trips from its fly-fishing store, the Telluride Angler.

FOUR-WHEELING The Tomboy Road, accessed directly from North Fir Street at the edge of town, leads to one of the country's most interesting mining districts. It went down in history in 1901 when the Western Federation of Miners organized a strike at Tomboy Mine. The state militia was eventually called in to put an end to the strike. The ruins of Tomboy Mine, Tomboy Mill, and parts of the town of Tomboy are all that remain of those turbulent times. The road offers fabulous views of Bridal Veil Falls and passes through the Social Tunnel on its way to the high country. After 7.5 mi, the road crests over 13,114-foot-high Imogene Pass, the highest pass road in the San Juan Mountains. If you continue down the other side, you will end up near Yankee Boy Basin near Ouray.

Dave's Mountain Tours (⌂ *Box 2736, Telluride 81435* ☎*970/728–9749* ⊕*www.telluridetours.com*) conducts summer jeep tours over Imogene Pass and other historic areas. If you want an in-town adventure, go on the Segway historical tour. Dave's offers snowmobile tours in season.

GLIDER RIDES   Offering an unusual look at the San Juans, **Telluride Soaring** (☎*970/209–3497*) operates out of the Telluride Regional Airport. Rates are about $110 per half hour, $160 per hour; rides are offered daily, weather permitting.

HIKING   The peaks of the rugged San Juan Mountains around Telluride require some scrambling, occasionally bordering on real climbing, to get to the top. A local favorite is Mount Wilson, a roughly 4,000-vertical-foot climb for which only the last 400 vertical feet call for a scramble across steep, shale slopes. July and August are the most likely snow-free months on this 8-mi round-trip hike.

Sound a bit too grueling? An immensely popular 2-mi trail leads to **Bear Creek Falls.** The route is also used by mountain bikers. On the opposite side of the valley, the 3-mi **Jud Wiebe Trail** begins as an excellent hike that is often passable from spring until well into fall. From here you have amazing views of Utah's LaSal Mountains. For more-ambitious hikers, the Jud Wiebe Trail links with the 13-mi Sneffels Highline Trail. This route leads through wildflower-covered meadows. Another trail leads to 425-foot **Bridal Veil Falls,** the state's highest cascade. It tumbles lavishly from the head of a box canyon. A beautifully restored power-house sits beside the falls.

HORSEBACK   Roudy Roudebush rode through America's living rooms courtesy of
RIDING   a memorable television commercial in which he and his horse, Cindy, trotted right up to the bar at the New Sheridan Hotel. Roudy is now riding Cindy's son, Golly, and you can join them. His slogan has long been "Gentle horses for gentle people, fast horses for fast people, and for people who don't like to ride, horses that don't like to be rode." **Ride with Roudy** (☎*970/728–9611* ⊕*www.ridewithroudy.com*) is in a barn on an old ranch 6 mi from Telluride. Trail rides pass through aspen groves and across open meadows with views of the Wilson Range. Winter rides leave from Roudy's other ranch, in Norwood. Hour-long rides cost about $35.

MOUNTAIN   Having a fully equipped hut awaiting at the end of a tough day of
BIKING   mountain biking 35 mi makes the **San Juan Hut System** (✉*224 E. Colo-rado Ave.,* ☎*970/626–3033* ⊕*www.sanjuanhuts.com*) the backcoun-try biker's choice. The system operates two 215-mi routes, one from Telluride to Moab, Utah, the other from Durango to Moab. Dirt roads, desert slick rock, and canyon country—the areas along the way where there are canyons to explore, such as in Moab and Grand Junction—

11

are all part of the experience, and the huts supply the beds, blankets, wood-burning stoves, and cooking stoves, which cuts down on what you need to haul on your bike.

RAFTING There are plenty of rapids around Telluride. **Telluride Outside** (⊠ *121 W. Colorado Ave.* ☎ *970/728–3895 or 800/831–6230* ⊕ *www.tellurideoutside.com*) explores the Gunnison, Dolores, Colorado, and Animas rivers.

ROCK CLIMBING Many people would consider being suspended from a wall of ice or a sheer cliff to be a bizarre form of torture. For those who think it might be fun, **Fantasy Ridge Mountain Guides** (⊠ *28 Village Ct.,* ☐ *Box 405, Placerville 81430* ☎ *970/728–3546* ⊕ *www.fantasyridge.com*) offers introductory ice-climbing and rock-climbing courses. A three-day ice-climbing course costs about $900 (lodging included). Rock-climbing classes range from hourly instruction costing $25 to five-day programs that start at $1,120. Many use the famous Ophir Wall. Fantasy Ridge also guides Fourteener climbs and other expeditions in the San Juan Mountains.

WHERE TO EAT

$$$$ ✕**Allred's.** After riding up in the gondola, diners are still astounded by the views from this mountainside eatery. Try the free-range Canadian veal chop with potato-chanterelle hash, or the seared yellowfin tuna with vegetable risotto, fried oyster mushrooms, and red pepper au jus. The bittersweet chocolate cake and the passion-fruit sorbet will send you home smiling. ⊠ *Top of San Sophia gondola* ☎ *970/728–7474* ⊟ *AE, D, MC, V* ☉ *Closed early Apr.–early June and Oct.–late Nov. No lunch.*

★ $$$$ ✕**Cosmopolitan.** Hotel Columbia, a sleek lodge at the base of the gondola, is home to this elegant restaurant specializing in dishes such as salmon with a spicy dipping sauce and seared tuna with coconut-vanilla rice. Try the New Orleans–style beignets with a cappuccino for dessert, cheekily listed as "coffee and donuts" on the menu. For a romantic evening, book a table for two in the cozy wine cellar. ⊠ *300 W. San Juan Ave.* ☎ *970/728–1292* ☖ *Reservations essential* ⊟ *AE, MC, V* ☉ *Call for seasonal closings. No lunch.*

$$$$ FodorsChoice ★ ✕**La Marmotte.** With its rough brick walls, lacy curtains, and baskets overflowing with flowers or strings of garlic bulbs, this romantic bistro would be right at home in Provence. Fish dishes, such as seared Alaska salmon in a red wine sauce, are particularly splendid. ⊠ *150 W. San Juan Ave.* ☎ *970/728–6232* ☖ *Reservations essential* ⊟ *AE, D, MC, V* ☉ *Closed mid-Apr.–early June, Oct.–late Nov., and Tues. mid-June–Sept. No lunch.*

$$$ ✕**Honga's Lotus Petal & Tea Room.** A local favorite, this tearoom serves up Japanese-, Thai-, and Balinese-influenced fare in a restored Victorian. The sushi bar is one of the best in town. Though the place caters mostly to vegetarians, it also puts free-range chicken and organic beef on the menu. Blackened tofu is the signature dish, and the crowds go wild for the crunchy shrimp roll and pineapple-coconut curry. Don't leave town without sampling the addictive pot stickers. ⊠ *135 E. Colorado Ave.* ☎ *970/728–5134* ⊟ *AE, MC, V* ☉ *Closed early Apr.–late May and mid-Oct.–late Nov.*

$$ ✘**Fat Alley BBQ.** Messy, mouthwatering ribs and Carolina-style pulled-pork sandwiches are complemented by delectable side dishes such as red beans and rice, baked sweet potatoes, and snap-pea and feta salad. More than a dozen beers, 30 bourbons, and a few wines are available, in addition to homemade iced tea and pink lemonade. A few long tables flanked by benches let you dine family-style and old skis adorn the walls at this no-frills joint. ✉*122 S. Oak St.* ☎*970/728–3985* ⛄*Reservations not accepted* ☰*AE, MC, V.*

$ ✘**Baked in Telluride.** Racks of fresh-baked breads, rolls, bagels, donuts, and other pastries are on display everywhere in this bakery, which also makes heavenly pasta sauces (check out the Alfredo), pizzas, and huge, inexpensive salads. Get it to go or sit in one of the tables in the back. ✉*127 S. Fir St.* ☎*970/728–4705* ☰*AE, MC, V.*

¢ ✘**Maggie's Bakery & Café.** A little spot with a blue awning and a couple of tables set up outside, Maggie's often has the front door propped open and the smell of fresh-baked fruit pies and oatmeal cookies lures customers in. You can grab breakfast and lunch here as well as a sweet treat (the sticky buns are the best), including piled-high sandwiches, pizza, and soup. They also make their own jams. ✉*217 E. Colorado Ave.* ☎*970/728–3334* ☰*No credit cards* ☽*No dinner.*

WHERE TO STAY

★ **$$$$** 🏨**Hotel Columbia Telluride.** It's hard to go wrong with views of the mountains, the gondola, and the San Miguel River. Play oversize checkers in your charmingly decorated rustic-chic room with a fireplace or walk out the front door and wander around town. They will store your mountain bike or your skis, and with the gondola right there, it's easy to access just about anything. The Cosmopolitan restaurant (*see Where to Eat above*) housed in this hotel is one of the best in town and the complimentary breakfast there is above average. **Pros:** stunning views; charming, spacious rooms; convenient to gondola. **Cons:** some street noise, must keep your shutters closed or gondola riders can see right in. ✉*300 W. San Juan Ave.,* ☎*800/201–9505* ⊕*www.columbiatelluride. com* ⇝*21 rooms* ⛄*In room: no a/c, VCR, Wi-Fi. In hotel: restaurant, concierge, parking (no fee), no-smoking rooms* ☰*AE, D, MC, V.*

$$$$ 🏨**Hotel Telluride.** The rooms are far more upscale than the pricing would suggest, and the building itself looks like an old stone mansion nestled against the mountain. All of the rooms have San Juan views from a patio or balcony, and a complimentary breakfast buffet is offered at the Bistro, a lodge-style eatery on-premises. The fitness center has been nicely updated, massages are offered in the spa, and the hot tubs on the roof are delightful when it's snowing. **Pros:** terrific value, abundant breakfast, romantic hot tubs. **Cons:** hot tubs often taken, hotel fills up in season. ✉*199 N. Cornet St.,* ☎*866/468–3504* ⊕*www.thehotel telluride.com* ⇝*59 rooms, 2 suites* ⛄*In room: safe, refrigerator, Wi-Fi. In hotel: restaurant, bar, gym, spa, concierge, public Wi-Fi, no-smoking rooms* ☰*AE, D, MC, V.*

$$$$ 🏨**Inn at Lost Creek.** A grand stone-and-wood structure with the architecture of a European alpine lodge, this rambling five-story, luxury lodge is next to the Mountain Village Gondola (which carries you to downtown Telluride) and just two blocks from the conference center.

You can literally ski out the front door. Most of the rooms are suites with balconies, ideal for a romantic getaway, and the rooftop spa is a nice extra. **Pros:** ski in ski out, romantic, convenient location. **Cons:** pricey, rooftop spa usually crowded. ☒*119 Lost Creek La., Mountain Village* ☎*970/728–5678 or 888/601–5678* ⊕*www.innatlostcreek. com* ⤳*29 suites, 3 studios* ⚷*In-room: kitchen (some), DVD, VCR, Wi-Fi. In-hotel: restaurant, bar, gym, spa, laundry facilities, airport shuttle, no-smoking rooms* ⊟*AE, D, DC, MC, V.*

$$$ ⊡**The Peaks Resort & Golden Door Spa.** The somewhat forbidding exterior at this luxury resort no longer seems worth mentioning when you first catch sight of Mount Wilson, the peak pictured on every can of Coors. Make sure to ask for a room with a balcony. The rooms are sizable, decorated in Norwegian wood and muted shades of green. The range of activities here is vast, from an indoor pool to tennis courts— there's even an indoor climbing wall. And then there are the invigorating, revitalizing treatments at the five-story Golden Door Spa. More than 55 treatments are offered in the 44 private rooms, from skin-tightening wraps to muscle-taming massages. **Pros:** spacious rooms, great views, something for everyone. **Cons:** easy to feel overwhelmed, popular activities are often booked well in advance. ☒*136 Country Club Dr.,* ☎*970/728–6800 or 800/789–2220* ⊕*www.thepeaksresort. com* ⤳*174 rooms, 32 suites* ⚷*In-room: no a/c, VCR, ethernet, Wi-Fi. In-hotel: 2 restaurants, room service, bar, tennis courts, pools, gym, spa, no-smoking rooms* ⊟*AE, DC, MC, V* ⊘*Closed early Apr.–mid-May and mid-Oct.–mid-Nov.*

CONDOS **Telluride Central Reservations** (☎*800/525–3455* ⊕*www.visittelluride. com*) handles all the properties at Telluride Mountain Village, and several more in town. **Telluride Rentals** (☎*800/970–7541* ⊕*www.telluride-rentals.com*) rents several top-notch accommodations.

PURGATORY

20 mi south of Silverton via U.S. 550; 25 mi north of Durango via U.S. 550.

North of the U.S. 160 and U.S. 550 junction are two well-known recreational playgrounds: the ravishing golf course and development at the Lodge at Tamarron, and Purgatory at Durango Mountain Resort. Purgatory, as everyone still calls this ski area despite its recent name change, is about as down-home as a ski resort can get. The clientele includes cowboys, families, and college students on break.

DOWNHILL SKIING & SNOWBOARDING

★ **Purgatory at Durango Mountain Resort** (formerly known simply as Purgatory) has plenty of intermediate runs and glade and tree skiing. What's unique about Purgatory is its stepped terrain: lots of humps and dips and steep pitches followed by virtual flats. This trail profile makes it easier for skiers and snowboarders to stay in control (or simply get their legs back under them after they've conquered a section a little steeper than they might be accustomed to). A great powder day on the mountain's backside will convince anyone that Purgatory isn't just "Pleasant Ridge," as it's somewhat condescendingly known in Crested Butte and Telluride. ⊠*U.S. 550* ☎*970/247–9000 or 800/568–3275* ⊕*www.durangomountainresort.com* ☉*Late Nov.–early Apr., daily 9–4.*

FACILITIES 2,029-foot vertical drop; 1,200 skiable acres; 23% beginner, 51% intermediate, 26% advanced; 1 high-speed 6-passenger chair, 1 high-speed quad chair, 4 triple chairs, 3 double chairs, 1 surface lift, and 1 moving carpet (beginners' lift).

LESSONS & PROGRAMS Durango Mountain Resort's **Adult Adventure School** (☎*970/385–2149*) offers 2½-hour group lessons for everyone from newcomers to experts at 9:45 AM and 1:15 PM each day during the season. The cost is $49. There are also daily lessons in snow biking and twice-monthly lessons in telemark skiing.

Teaching children to ski or snowboard is a cinch at **Kids Mountain Adventure** (☎*970/385–2149*). There are three age-appropriate classes for kids 3 to 12 years old. There's also child care for those between two months and three years. A full day costs $87.

LIFT TICKETS The at-the-window rates are $60 to $65 for a one-day lift ticket. A Guaranteed to Green ski package, which means that they promise you will be able to ski from top to bottom on a green run by the end of it, is a good deal for beginner skiers, as it combines a half-day morning lesson with an all-day lift ticket. The cost is $165.

RENTALS **Bubba's Boards** (⊠*Village Plaza* ☎*970/259–7377 or 866/860–7377*) is Durango Mountain Resort's full-service snowboard shop. Rentals begin at $29 per day.

Performance Peak (☎*970/247–9000*) rents top-of-the-line demo and retail skis and boots from K2, Salomon, Dynastar, Volkl, Nordica, Dolomite, and Rossignol; full packages (skis, boots, and poles) begin at $39. Snowshoe rentals are $12. The shop also offers custom boot fitting, ski tuning, and equipment repair.

Purgatory Rentals (⊠*Village Center* ☎*970/385–2182*) offers skis, boots, and poles, as well as other equipment. Rates begin at $21 per day for the basic package, rising to $29 for the high-performance package.

OTHER SPORTS & THE OUTDOORS

GOLF **Glacier Club at Tamarron.** Near the spectacular Hermosa Cliffs, this splendid course has 27 holes of scenic masters-level golf. This club, part of the Lodge at Tamarron, is considered one of the country's top resort courses. ⊠*40290 U.S. 550* ☎*970/375–8300 or 866/375–8300* ⊕*www.theglacierclub.com* ⚐*Reservations essential* ⚑*18 holes. Yards: 6,885/5,330. Par: 72/72. Green Fee: $69/$125.*

SNOWMOBILING **Snowmobile Adventures** (⊠*Village Center* ☎*970/247–9000 or 970/385–2110*) offers guided snowmobile tours on more than 60 mi of nearby trails.

WHERE TO STAY & EAT

11

★ $$$ ✕**Sow's Ear.** It's a toss-up between the Ore House in downtown Durango and this watering hole in the Silverpick Lodge for the area's "best steak house" award. The Sow's Ear has the edge, though, for its great views of the mountain. If you prefer more action, there's also an open kitchen in the dining area where you can view your meal being prepared. The mouthwatering, fresh-baked jalapeño-cheese rolls and honey-wheat rolls, and creative entrées such as blackened filet mignon are a few more reasons Sow's Ear leads the pack. Complement your meal with a selection from their extensive domestic wine list. ⊠*48475 U.S. 550* ☎*970/247–3527* ⚐*Reservations essential* ▤*AE, D, MC, V* ⊘*Closed mid-Mar.–Memorial Day and Labor Day–mid-Dec.*

$ ✕**Olde Schoolhouse Cafe & Saloon.** The pizza and calzones are made with homemade dough and fresh ingredients, and the local SKA brew is on tap in this funky building, now far astray from its scholarly roots. There are darts, a pool table, even an old shuffleboard, and later in the evening this becomes the local hangout for conversation and relaxation. ⊠*46778 Hwy. 550, Durango* ☎*970/259–2257* ▤*MC, V* ⊘*No lunch weekdays.*

$$$ ▦**Lodge at Tamarron.** This handsome lodge, on 750 acres surrounded by the San Juan National Forest, fits in beautifully with the natural environment. The sprawling main lodge seems to be an extension of the nearby Hermosa Cliffs. The well-appointed rooms are a blend of frontier architecture and Southwestern decor, and nearly all feature a fireplace, a full kitchen, and a private terrace. The lodge is famed for the Glacier Club at Tamarron, and tennis and horseback riding are also popular pastimes. **Pros:** ability to cook your own food, stunning setting, multiple activities make it a great family spot. **Con:** pricey. ⚓ *18 mi north of Durango on U.S. 550* ⚐*Drawer 3131, 81302* ☎*970/259– 2000, 800/982–6103, or 800/525–0892* ⊕*www.lodgeattamarron.com* ⬐*412 rooms* ⚐*In-hotel: 2 restaurants, bar, golf course, tennis courts, pool, spa, no-smoking rooms* ▤*AE, D, DC, MC, V.*

$$ ▦**Purgatory Village Hotel at Durango Mountain Resort.** This comfortable slope-side lodging has generously proportioned rooms decorated with contemporary furnishings. If you want a bit of pampering, the one- and two-bedroom condos have wood-burning fireplaces and whirlpool baths. **Pros:** slope-side location, good restaurants, reasonable price considering locale. **Con:** in season, the hotel is very chaotic. ⊠*1 Skier Pl.,* ☎*970/385–2100 or 800/982–6103* ⊕*www.durangomountainresort. com* ⬐*133 rooms* ⚐*In-room: no a/c, kitchen (some). In-hotel: 2 restaurants, bar, pool, public Wi-Fi, no-smoking rooms* ▤*AE, D, MC, V.*

CONDOS There are 110 apartments at **Cascade Village** (⊠*50827 U.S. 550, Purgatory* ☎*970/259–3500 or 800/982–6103*), about 1.5 mi north of the ski area.

EN
ROUTE

U.S. 550 toward Durango parallels the Animas River and the tracks of Durango & Silverton Narrow Gauge Railroad. Scenes from *Butch Cassidy and the Sundance Kid* were filmed in this canyon.

DURANGO

25 mi south of Purgatory via U.S. 550; 45 mi east of Cortez via U.S. 160; 62 mi west of Pagosa Springs via U.S. 160.

Wisecracking Will Rogers had this to say about Durango: "It's out of the way and glad of it." His statement is a bit unfair, considering that as a railroad town Durango has always been a cultural crossroads and melting pot (as well as a place to raise hell). Laid out at 6,500 feet along the winding Animas River, with the San Juan Mountains as backdrop, the town was founded in 1879 by General William Palmer, president of the all-powerful Denver & Rio Grande Railroad, when nearby Animas City haughtily refused to donate land for a depot. Within a decade Durango had completely absorbed its rival. The booming town quickly became the region's main metropolis and a gateway to the Southwest. A walking tour of the historic downtown bears eloquent witness to Durango's prosperity during the late 19th century. The northern end of Main Avenue offers the usual assortment of cheap motels and fast-food outlets, all evidence of Durango's present status as the major hub for tourism in the area.

The intersection of 13th Avenue and Main Avenue (locals also refer to it as Main Street) marks the northern edge of Durango's **National Historic District**. Old-fashioned streetlights line the streets, casting a warm glow on the elegant Victorians now filled with upscale galleries, restaurants, and the occasional factory outlet store. The three-story sandstone **Newman Building** (⊠ *8th St. and Main Ave.*) is one of the elegant edifices restored to their original grandeur. Dating from 1887, the **Strater Hotel** (⊠ *7th St. and Main Ave.*) is a reminder of when this town was a stop for many people headed west. Awash in flocked wallpaper and lace, the hotel's Diamond Belle Saloon is dominated by a gilt-and-mahogany bar. A player piano and scantily clad waitresses call to mind an old-time honky-tonk. The **Durango Depot** (⊠ *4th St. and Main Ave.*), dating from 1882, is a must for those who dream of riding the rails.

The **3rd Avenue National Historic District** (known simply as "The Boulevard"), two blocks east of Main Avenue, contains several Victorian residences, ranging from the imposing mansions built by railroad barons to more-modest variations erected by well-to-do merchants. The hodgepodge of styles veers from Greek revival to Gothic Revival to Queen Anne to Spanish Colonial and Mission designs.

The most entertaining way to relive the halcyon days of the Old West is to take a ride on the **Durango & Silverton Narrow Gauge Railroad**, a nine-hour, round-trip journey along the 45-mi railway to Silverton. You'll travel in comfort in lovingly restored coaches or in the open-air cars called gondolas as you listen to the train's shrill whistle as it chugs along. You get a good look at the Animas Valley, which in some parts is broad and green and in others is narrow and rimmed with rock. The train runs from mid-May to late October, with four departures daily between June and August and one daily at other times. A shorter excursion—to Cascade Canyon—is available in winter. ⊠479

Main Ave. ☎*970/247–2733 or 888/872–4607* ⊕*www.durango train.com* ◫*$65.*

About 7 mi north of Durango, **Trimble Hot Springs** is a great place to soak your aching bones, especially if you've been doing some hiking. The complex includes an Olympic-size swimming pool and three natural mineral pools ranging from 83°F to 107°F. Massage and spa treatments are also available. ✉*County Rd. 203 off U.S. 550* ☎*970/247–0212* ⊕*www. trimblehotsprings.com* ◫*$15* ☉*June–Aug., daily 8 AM–11 PM; Sept.–May, daily 10–10.*

High on a mesa southeast of Durango, **Fort Lewis College** brings a bit of culture to the Four Corners area. The Center for Southwest Studies gallery has rotating

LEAP OF FAKE

The famous scene in the 1969 movie *Butch Cassidy and the Sundance Kid*, where Paul Newman and Robert Redford—playing Cassidy and the Kid, respectively—jump off a 30-foot cliff, was shot 13 mi north of Durango at Baker's Bridge. It draws visitors to the site to see the dramatic drop, but some are disappointed to find that the camera angle and much manipulation of the rapids conspired to make it seem more dangerous. In reality, the actors were shot jumping onto a platform 6 feet down, and the real jump into the Animas River was done by stuntmen. The river shot was taken later in California.

exhibitions of contemporary artists, Native American treasures, and Western-cultural collections. **Art Gallery** (☉*Weekdays 10–4*) is a beautifully lighted contemporary space showcasing the creations of a creative and diverse student body. ✉*1000 Rim Dr.* ☎*970/247–7184* ⊕*www.fortlewis.edu.*

SPORTS & THE OUTDOORS

Contact the rangers of the **San Juan National Forest** (✉*15 Burnett Ct.,* ☎*970/247–4874* ⊕*www.fs.fed.us/r2/sanjuan*) for information about rock climbing and other outdoor activities in the San Juan Mountains.

The **San Juan Public Lands Center** (✉*15 Burnett Ct.,* ☎*970/247–4874* ☉*Weekdays 8–5*) gives out information on hiking, fishing, and camping, as well as cross-country skiing, snowshoeing, and snowmobile routes. This office also stocks maps and guidebooks.

BICYCLING With a healthy college population and a generally mild climate, Durango is extremely bike friendly and a destination for single-track enthusiasts. Many locals consider bikes to be their main form of transportation. The bike lobby is active, the trail system is well developed, and mountain biking is a particularly popular recreational activity.

Get an overview of the scene at ⊕*www.trails2000.org*, home of the very active local advocacy trail group. Although everybody in town seems to be an expert, a good place to go for advice and maps before you head off is **Mountain Bike Specialists** (✉*949 Main Ave.* ☎*970/247–4066* ⊕*www.mountainbikespecialists.com*), where you can also rent a bike, arrange a tour, or get hooked up with the trail of your dreams.

To get around town, start with the **Animas River Trail,** which parallels the river from North City Park to the south part of town along a 5-mi route. It is the main artery linking up with other trail systems. With its many access points, you might consider it rather than driving around town, especially on a busy weekend.

Everybody likes the **Hermosa Creek Trail,** an intermediate-to-difficult 20-mi jaunt. It has a couple of steep spots and switchbacks, but it rolls through open meadows, towering aspen and pine forests, and along the sides of mountains before dumping out in a parking lot in Hermosa, 9 mi north of Durango. Don't try it too early in the season while the snow is melting because there are two creek crossings. Starting at the same spot as the Hermosa Creek Trail is the Lime Creek Trail, which will test you as it mostly follows the old stage road; it covers 11 mi from Purgatory to Silverton. ✛ *Trailhead: Take Hwy. 550 north 28 mi from Durango. Look for parking lot on right, north of Cascade Village near Purgatory..*

CLIMBING   **SouthWest Adventure Guides** (✉ *1205 Camino del Rio* ☎ *970/259–0370 or 800/642–5389* ⊕ *www.mtnguide.net*) is a climbing school that takes you to some of the area's most beautiful peaks. Other programs include rock climbing, ice climbing, Nordic skiing, snowshoeing, and mountaineering.

FISHING   In business since 1983, **Duranglers** (✉ *923 Main Ave.* ☎ *970/385–4081 or 888/347–4346* ⊕ *www.duranglers.com*) sells rods and reels, gives fly-fishing lessons, and runs custom trips to top fishing spots in the area, including the San Juan River in nearby northern New Mexico.

GOLF   **Dalton Ranch Golf Club.** About 6 mi north of Durango, Dalton Ranch is a Ken Dye–designed 18-hole championship course with inspiring panoramas of red-rock cliffs. Dalton's Grill has become a popular hangout for locals who like watching the resident elk herd take its afternoon stroll, especially in late fall and winter. The golf season here is early April to late October, weather permitting. ✉ *589 County Rd. 252, off U.S. 550* ☎ *970/247–8774* ⊕ *www.daltonranch.com* ⚒ *Reservations essential* ⛳ *18 holes. Yards: 6,934/5,539. Par: 72/72. Green Fee: $59–$89.*

Hillcrest Golf Course. Hillcrest is an 18-hole public course perched on a mesa near the campus of Fort Lewis College. The course is open from February to December, weather permitting. ✉ *2300 Rim Dr.* ☎ *970/247–1499* ⚒ *Reservations essential* ⛳ *18 holes. Yards: 6,838/5,252. Par: 71/71. Green Fee: $30.*

HIKING   Hiking trails are ubiquitous around Durango. Many trailheads around the edges of town lead to backcountry settings, and the San Juan Forest has plenty of mind-boggling walks and trails for those who want to backpack into wilderness. Before you go, check the local hiking organization, **Trails2000** (⊕ *www.trails2000.org*) for directions, information, and news about hiking in and around Durango.

If you're cramped for time, try the 0.66-mi **Animas View Overlook Trail** for spectacular views. It passes interpretive signs on geology, history, and flora before bringing you to a precipice with an unparalled view of the valley in which Durango sits and the Needle Mountains. It's the only wheelchair-accessible trail in the area, and you can picnic there, too.

The **Lion's Den Trail** hooks up with the **Chapman Hill Trail** west of Fort Lewis College for a nice moderate hike, climbing switchbacks that take you away from city bustle and hook up with the **Rim Trail**.

Fodor'sChoice ★ The **Colorado Trail** starts not far north of Durango and goes all the way to Denver. Though you're not obliged to go that far, just a few miles in and out will give you a taste of this epic trail, which winds through mountain ranges and high passes and some of the most amazing scenery in any mountains. ⊕*www.coloradotrail.org.*

HORSEBACK RIDING **Southfork Stables & Outfitters** (⊠*28481 U.S. 160* ☎*970/259–4871*) offers guided trail rides in summer and one-hour trips to view an elk herd in winter. You can also take part in cattle drives.

RAFTING **Durango Rivertrippers** (⊠*720 Main Ave.* ☎*970/259–0289 or 800/292–2885* ⊕*www.durangorivertrippers.com*) runs two- and four-hour trips down the Animas River, as well as 2- to 10-day wilderness expeditions on the Dolores River.

WHERE TO EAT

$$$$ ✕**Chez Grand-mère.** It's hard to decide whether to work your way through the à la carte menu or go with a prix-fixe dinner. Either way, the French and Belgian dishes served in the sweet dining room made to look, yes, just like Grandma's, are as comforting as you'd expect; try the succulent crab cakes, grilled squab, roast lamb, or lobster and shrimp sausages. The chef makes some of the ingredients himself, like the vinegar for the vinaigrettes, forages for local mushrooms, and makes a point of tracking down top-quality produce and meats. ⊠*3 Depot Pl.* ☎*970/247–7979* ☖*Reservations essential* ▭*AE, D, MC, V* ⊘*Closed Sun. and Mon. No lunch.*

$$$$ ✕**Ore House.** Durango is a meat-and-potatoes kind of town, and this is Durango's idea of a steak house. The aroma of beef smacks you in the face as you walk past. This local favorite serves enormous slabs of aged Angus that are hand cut daily. If you're watching your cholesterol, better "steer" clear. ⊠*147 E. College Dr.* ☎*970/247–5707* ▭*D, MC, V.*

$$$$ ✕**Red Snapper.** If you're in the mood for fresh fish, head to this congenial spot, which is full of saltwater aquariums. Try the oysters Durango, with jack cheese and salsa; salmon Wellington; or snapper Monterey, with jack cheese and tarragon. Delicious steaks and prime rib are also available. The salad bar is enormous. ⊠*144 E. 9th St.* ☎*970/259–3417* ▭*AE, MC, V* ⊘*No lunch weekends.*

$$$ ✕**Ariano's Northern Italian Restaurant.** In a dimly lighted room plastered with local art, this northern Italian restaurant offers a selection of pastas that are made fresh daily. Try the veal scaloppine with fresh sage and garlic or the fettuccine Alfredo. ⊠*150 E. College Dr.* ☎*970/247–8146* ▭*AE, D, DC, MC, V* ⊘*No lunch.*

$$$ ✕**East by Southwest.** Pan-Asian food with a strong Japanese bent gets a bit of a Latin treatment in this snazzy but comfortable space. Steaks (using Kobe beef), sushi and sashimi, tempura, and other traditional

dishes are attractively presented and layered with complementary flavors; the seven-course tasting menu is a smart way to try it all. The sake, beer, and wine selections are well varied, and the tea and tonic bar is fun, too. ⊠*160 E. College Dr.* ☎*970/247–5533* ⊗*No lunch Sun.*

$$ ✗**Carver's Bakery & Brew Pub.** The "Brews Brothers," Bill and Jim Carver, have about eight beers on tap at any given time, including such flavors as Raspberry Wheat Ale, Jackrabbit Pale Ale, and Colorado Trail Nut Brown Ale. If you're feeling peckish, try one of the bread bowls filled with soup or salad. There's a patio out back where you can soak up the sun. From breakfast to the wee hours, the place is always hopping. ⊠*1022 Main Ave.* ☎*970/259–2545* ⚓*Reservations not accepted* ⊟*AE, D, MC, V.*

$$ ✗**Cyprus Café.** In warm weather, sit on the patio to listen to live jazz, and the rest of the time cozy up to your fellow diners in this tiny space. Mediterranean food receives upscale treatment here, from chicken breasts stuffed with artichokes, feta, and mint to rigatoni layered with shrimp, spinach, and ricotta to a salt-roasted duck that makes your mouth water when it hits the table. The wine list is small, eclectic, and reasonably priced. Lunch is also interesting; try the wild salmon with caramelized onions or chicken sausage with fresh mozzarella sandwiches. ⊠*725 E. 2nd Ave.* ☎*970/385–6884* ⊟*AE, D, MC, V.*

$$ ✗**Ken & Sue's Place.** This might well be Durango's favorite restaurant. Locals are wild for the artfully prepared contemporary cuisine enlivened with a light touch of Asian and Southwestern accents. Try the pistachio nut–crusted grouper with vanilla-rum butter, or lemon-pepper linguine. ⊠*636 Main Ave.* ☎*970/385–1810* ⊟*AE, D, DC, MC, V* ⊗*No lunch weekends.*

$ ✗**Brickhouse Cafe & Coffee Bar.** Great lattes await at this popular little place set in a restored historic house with wonderful landscaping. Don't miss the malted buttermilk waffles, pigs in a blanket, or big burgers. Breakfast and lunch are served all day. ⊠*1849 Main Ave.* ☎*970/247–3760* ⊟*AE, D, MC.*

$ ✗**Olde Tymer's Café.** If you're longing to meet a local, look no farther than the bustling Olde Tymer's, located in a beautiful old building with an inviting patio in the back. The hamburger is a huge specimen on a fat, fresh bun, and folks swear by the piled-high salads and sandwiches. ⊠*100 Main Ave.* ☎*970/259–2990* ⊟*AE, D, MC, V.*

WHERE TO STAY

$$$ 🏨**Strater Hotel.** The grand dame of Durango's hotels opened for busi-

FodorśChoice ness in 1887, and a loving restoration has returned her luster. Inside,

★ the Diamond Belle Saloon glitters with crystal chandeliers, rustic oak beams, and plush velvety curtains. The individually decorated rooms are exquisite: after all, the hotel owns the country's largest collection of Victorian walnut antiques and has its own wood-carving shop to create exact period reproductions. Your room might have entertained Butch Cassidy, Louis L'Amour (he wrote *The Sacketts* here), Francis Ford Coppola, John Kennedy, or Marilyn Monroe (the latter two stayed here at separate times). **Pros:** location right in the thick of things, space has Old West feel, they will safely store your mountain bike for you. **Con:** when the bar downstairs gets going, rooms right above it get no peace. ⊠*699 Main Ave.,* ☎*970/247–4431 or 800/247–4431* ⊕*www.strater.com* ⟿*93 rooms* ⟳*In-room: dial-up, Wi-Fi (some). In-hotel: restaurant, room service, bar, no-smoking rooms* ⊟*AE, D, DC, MC, V* �‖*CP.*

★ $$ 🏨**New Rochester Hotel.** This one-time flophouse is funky yet chic, thanks to the mother-and-son team of Diane and Kirk Komick, who rescued some of the original furnishings. Marquee-lighted movie posters from Hollywood Westerns line the airy hallways, and steamer trunks, hand-painted settees, wagon-wheel chandeliers, and fluffy quilts in the rooms contribute to a laid-back retro vibe. Windows from Denver & Rio Grande Railroad carriages convert the back porch into a parlor car, and gas lamps add a warm glow to the courtyard. A full gourmet breakfast, with plenty of coffee and several varieties of tempting mini-muffins and scones is included. The owners also run the nearby Leland House B&B. **Pros:** inviting atmosphere, large rooms. **Con:** can be noisy. ⊠*726 E. 2nd Ave.,* ☎*970/385–1920 or 800/664–1920* ⊕*www.rochesterhotel. com* ⟿*13 rooms, 1 suite* ⟳*In-hotel: restaurant, no elevator, some pets allowed, no-smoking rooms* ⊟*MC, V* �‖*BP.*

GUEST RANCH 🏨**Wilderness Trails Ranch.** It's only an hour's drive to Durango, but this
$$$$ family-owned and -operated guest ranch, nestled in the Upper Pine River valley, on the borders of the Piedra and Weminuche wilderness areas, might as well be a lifetime away. The riding programs are the main attraction here; guests are individually matched with horses to fit their experience and comfort level. Other activities include hiking, rafting, waterskiing, and fishing. Cozy log cabins, complete with gas stoves, modern baths, and terry robes, are arranged in a semicircle around the main lodge, campfire ring, and pool; Cordon Bleu–trained chefs are at the helm in the dining room, which has views of the mountains and busy hummingbird feeders through large picture windows. **Pros:** very friendly owners, family friendly, gorgeous setting. **Con:** minimum stay required. ⊠*23486 County Rd. 501, Bayfield* ☎*970/247– 0722 or 800/527–2624* ⊕*www.wildernesstrails.com* ⟿*10 cabins* ⟳*In-room: no phone, refrigerator, no TV. In-hotel: bar, pool, no elevator, children's programs (ages 3–17), no-smoking rooms* ⊟*D, MC, V* ◷*Closed Oct.–May* �‖*FAP.*

NIGHTLIFE & THE ARTS

BARS & CLUBS Even though it opened more than a century ago, the hottest spot in town is still the **Diamond Belle Saloon** (⊠*699 Main Ave.* ☎*970/247– 4431*). The honky-tonk player piano and waitresses dressed as 1880s saloon girls pack them in to this spot in the Strater Hotel. **Lady Falconburgh's Barley Exchange** (⊠*640 Main Ave.* ☎*970/382–9664*) is a favorite with locals. The pub serves more than 140 types of beer. Taste many fine brews, including True Blonde Ale, Mexican Logger Octoberfest, and Pinstripe Red Ale, at **Ska Brewery & Tasting Room** (⊠*545 Turner Dr.* ☎*970/247–5792* ⊕*www.skabrewing.com*). The Bodo Park brewery is open from noon to 7 PM weekdays and from noon to 3 PM on Saturday.

DINNER The **Bar D Chuckwagon** (⊠*8080 County Rd. 250, E. Animas Valley*
SHOWS ☎*970/247–5753 or 888/800–5753* ⊕*www.bardchuckwagon.com*)

serves up mouthwatering barbecued beef, beans, and biscuits. Many people head to this spot 9 mi from Durango to hear the Bar D Wranglers sing.

PAGOSA SPRINGS

62 mi east of Durango via U.S. 160.

Although not a large town, Pagosa Springs has become a major center for outdoor sports. Hiking, biking, and cross-country skiing opportunities abound not far from the excellent ski area of Wolf Creek. It has no lodging facilities, so Pagosa Springs is a logical place to stay.

With water ranging in temperature from 84°F to 114°F, the **Springs Resort** is a great place to relax. There are 17 outdoor tubs, a Mediterranean-style bathhouse, private rooms for massage therapy and spa treatments, a mountain sports shop, and an organic café. ✉*165 Hot Springs Blvd.* ☎*800/225–0934* ⊕*pagosahotsprings.com* ✍*$17* ⏱*June 12–Sept. 6, daily 7* AM*–1* AM*; Sept. 7–June 11, Sun.–Thurs. 7* AM*—11* PM*, Fri. and Sat. 7* AM*–1* AM* ▤*AE, D, DC, MC, V.*

DOWNHILL SKIING & SNOWBOARDING

With more than 450 average inches of snow annually, **Wolf Creek Ski Area** is Colorado's best-kept white-powder secret. It's set in 1,600 acres of Forest Service land in the San Juan Wilderness. The trails are designed to accommodate any level of ability and traverse every kind of ski terrain in ever-changing conditions, from wide-open bowls to steep glades, with a commanding view of remote valleys and towering peaks.

Because there are no overnight accommodations and it's a family-owned business, Wolf Creek has a reputation as a laid-back place for those with an aversion to lift lines and the faster-paced, better-known ski areas.

Arguably the best area stretches back to Horseshoe Bowl from the Waterfall area, serviced by the Alberta Lift. The more intrepid will want to climb the Knife Ridge Staircase to the more-demanding Knife Ridge Chutes. Just below is the groomed Sympatico, which runs down a gentler ridge and through dense forest below the Alberta Lift. The 50 trails run the gamut from wide-open bowls to steep glades.

Lodging options from rustic log cabins, bed-and-breakfasts, and motels in all price ranges are nearby along or off Highway 160: Creede, South Fork, and Monte Vista on the east and Pagosa Springs on the west. ✉*U.S. 160 at top of Wolf Creek Pass* ☎*970/264–5629* ⊕*www.wolf creekski.com* ⏱*Early Nov.–mid-Apr., daily 8:30–4.*

FACILITIES   1,604-foot vertical drop; 1,600 skiable acres; 20% beginner, 35% intermediate, 25% advanced, 20% expert; 1 quad, 2 triples, 2 doubles, 2 surface lifts.

LESSONS & **Wolf Creek Ski School** holds group lessons—$55 for four hours and $40
PROGRAMS for two-hour sessions. First-day beginner packages (ages nine and up)
are $47 ($57 snowboard). Private, one-hour lessons are $65 ($95 for
two). Children over four can join the Wolf Pups program, which includes
lift tickets and lunch. It's $45 for a half day, $55 for a full day.

LIFT TICKETS The walk-up rate is $48 for adults, $36 for half day, with three-day
lift passes for $141.

RENTALS **Wolf Creek Ski Rental,** in the Sports Center Building across from the
ticket office, rents skis and boards. Adult sets (skis, boots, poles) are
$14–$31 and $18 for telemark. Boards are $26 with or without boots;
boot rentals are $10.

OTHER SPORTS & THE OUTDOORS

GOLF **Pagosa Springs Golf Club.** The 27 championship holes here can be played
in three combinations, essentially creating three 18-hole courses. A
bonus is the gorgeous mountain scenery. The regular season runs from
May 15 to October 15. Cart rental is $15 for 18 holes. Reservations are
recommended during peak season. ⊠ *1 Pine Club Pl.* ☎ *970/731–4755*
⊕ *www.golfpagosa.com* ⅃ *27 holes. Yards: 5,074/7,228. Par: 71/72.
Green Fee: $49–$79.*

HIKING Pagosa Springs sits in a wondrous landscape, and there's no better way
to enjoy its isolated natural beauty than to experience it from a trail.
Around here, trails pass through green forests and along cold mountain
streams or mountain plateaus. Don't forget comfortable shoes, water,
a map, and warm, wet-weather clothing—conditions can deteriorate
quickly any month of the year.

If you aren't used to it, high altitude can catch you off guard. Drink
plenty of water to help stave off the effects of altitude sickness—
dizziness, shortness of breath, headache, and nausea. Slather on the
sunscreen—it's easy to get sunburned up here. And, in summer, an early
morning start is best, as afternoon thunderstorms are frequent and a
danger above the tree line.

The **Piedra Falls Trail** is a leisurely half-hour, 1.2-mi stroll through the
scenic landscape of the San Juan Mountains to the falls, which tumble
down a narrow wedge cut through volcanic rocks and boulders. Up
close, the falls are quite wet and from anywhere they are quite noisy.
⊠ *Pagosa Ranger District, San Juan National Forest* ☎ *970/264–2268*
⊕ *www.fs.fed.us/r2/sanjuan.*

For serious hikers and backpackers, the **Continental Divide Trail** (⊕ *www.
cdtrail.org*) passes through 80 mi of the Weminuche Wilderness near
the Wolf Creek summit.

WHERE TO STAY & EAT

¢ ✕ **Elkhorn Café.** Filling and fiery Mexican fare (try the stuffed sopaipillas), as well as the usual burgers and chili fries, makes this a popular
drop-in spot for locals. Fill up on a breakfast burrito before attack-
ing the Wolf Creek bowls. ⊠ *438 Main St.* ☎ *970/264–2146* ▭ *AE,
D, MC, V.*

★ **$-$$**   ⬚**Springs Resort.** Wrap yourself in a big white spa robe and head directly for the pools. Multiple soaking pools are terraced on several levels overlooking the San Juan River, and hotel guests have 24-hour access. Pick your temperature (from Tranquility to Lobster Pot), and relax. Rooms are standard but comfortable, and the larger configurations have lots of space and kitchenettes. **Pros:** proximity to hot springs, can cook your own meals. **Con:** service can be indifferent. ✉*165 Hot Springs Blvd.,* ☎*800/225–0934* ⊕*www.pagosahotsprings.com* ⬚*46 rooms, 4 suites* ⬚*In-room: kitchen (some). In-hotel: pool, spa, some pets allowed, no-smoking rooms* ⊟*D, MC, V.*

$ ⬚**Davidson's Country Inn B&B.** This three-story log cabin is on a 32-acre working ranch in the middle of Colorado's San Juan Mountains. It's just north of Pagosa Springs, meaning you can stay here and still enjoy the slopes at the Wolf Creek Ski Area. Rooms are comfortable and crammed with family heirlooms and antiques. A full breakfast is included, although not for cabin guests. **Pros:** beautiful setting, family friendly, feels like a getaway. **Con:** a bit off the beaten path. ✉*2763 U.S. 160,* ☎*970/264–5863* ⊕*www.davidsonsinn.com* ⬚*1 cabin; 8 rooms, 4 with bath* ⬚*In-room: no a/c, no TV. In hotel: no elevator, no-smoking rooms* ⊟*AE, D, MC, V* ⎁*BP.*

CORTEZ

45 mi west of Durango via U.S. 160.

The northern escarpment of Mesa Verde and the volcanic blisters of the La Plata Mountains to the west dominate sprawling Cortez. A series of Days Inns, Dairy Queens, and Best Westerns, the town has a layout that seems to have been determined by neon-sign and aluminum-siding salesmen of the 1950s. Hidden among these eyesores, however, are fine galleries and a host of secondhand shops that can yield surprising finds.

The exterior of the excellent **Cortez Cultural Center** has been painted to resemble the cliff dwellings of Mesa Verde. Exhibits focus on regional artists and artisans, the Ute Mountain branch of the Ute tribe, and various periods of Ancestral Puebloan culture. The Cultural Park at the Cortez Cultural Center contains an authentic Navajo hogan and a Ute tepee. The park itself is open 9 to 5; admission is free. Summer evenings there are Native American dances; sandpainting, rug weaving, and pottery-making demonstrations; theatrical events; and storytelling. ✉*25 N. Market St.* ☎*970/565–1151* ⊕*www.cortezculturalcenter.org* ⬚*Free* ⊙*June–Aug., Mon.–Sat. 10–10; Sept.–May, Mon.–Sat. 10–5.*

Visitor information is available at the **Colorado Welcome Center** (✉*Cortez City Park, 928 E. Main St.* ☎*970/565–3414 or 800/253–1616* ⊕*www.mesaverdecountry.com*).

Native American guides at **Ute Mountain Tribal Park** lead grueling hikes into this dazzling repository of Ancestral Puebloan ruins, including the majestic Tree House cliff dwelling and enchanting Eagle's Nest petroglyphs. Tours usually start at the Ute Mountain Pottery Plant, 15 mi south of Cortez, on U.S. 491. Overnight camping can also be arranged. ✉ *Box 109, Towaoc 81334* ☎ *970/565–3751* ⊕ *www.ute mountainute.com.*

Crow Canyon Archaeological Center promotes understanding and appreciation of Ancestral Puebloan culture by guiding visitors through excavations and botanical studies in the region. Also included in the weeklong programs are day trips to isolated canyon sites and hands-on lessons in weaving and pottery-making with Native American artisans. ✉ *23390 County Rd. K,* ☎ *970/565–8975 or 800/422–8975* ⊕ *www.crowcanyon.org.*

A brass plaque set on a granite platform surrounded by four state flags marks the only spot where four states—Colorado, Arizona, Utah, and New Mexico—meet at a single point. **Four Corners Monument** (✉ *U.S. 160* ☎ *No phone* ⊕ *www.navajonationparks.org* ✉ *$3 per vehicle* ⊗ *Sept.–May, daily 8–5; May–Sept., daily 7–8*) is photo-op country. Snacks and souvenirs are sold by Native Americans from rickety wood booths. To get here, travel south from Cortez on U.S. 160 for about 40 mi. You can't miss the signs.

OFF THE
BEATEN
PATH

Mud Creek Hogan. This endearing bit of classic American kitsch features more than a dozen enormous arrows stuck in the ground to mark the spot of a hokey trading post and museum, where you get the feeling that everything is for sale. The grounds are adorned with tepees and a giant plastic horse. Beside the shop is a re-creation of a frontier town, complete with saloon, hotel, bank, jail, and livery station. Don't breathe too hard or you'll blow the town over: The paper-thin buildings don't exist past the facades. ✉ *East U.S. 160 from Mesa Verde National Park* ☎ *970/533–7117.*

WHERE TO STAY & EAT

$$ ✕ **Nero's.** Chef Richard Gurd's menu features a spicy "Cowboy" steak, and exotic lasagna and shrimp dishes, the most popular being shrimp with artichoke hearts in lemon sauce. The decor is Southwestern accented with regional art. ✉ *303 W. Main St.* ☎ *970/565–7366* ⊟ *AE, D, DC, MC, V.*

¢ ⊞ **Anasazi Motor Inn.** This is definitely the nicest motel on the strip, mostly because its air-conditioned rooms are spacious and pleasantly decorated in desert colors. The pool is a godsend after a long drive. **Pros:** clean, reasonably priced. **Con:** nothing fancy. ✉ *640 S. Broadway,* ☎ *970/565–3773 or 800/972–6232* 🖷 *970/565–1027* ⊕ *www. anasazimotorinn.com* ⮌ *86 rooms* ♿ *In-room: refrigerator (some). In-hotel: restaurant, bar, pool, no elevator, airport shuttle, no-smoking rooms* ⊟ *AE, D, DC, MC, V.*

SOUTHWEST COLORADO ESSENTIALS

TRANSPORTATION

BY AIR

Telluride is notorious for being one of the hardest ski resorts in the country to fly into, mainly because the elevation of Telluride Regional Airport (TEX) is well above 9,000 feet. A little turbulence, a few clouds, and the next thing you know you're landing at Montrose Airport, 67 mi away, and taking a shuttle to Telluride. Telluride Airport welcomes flights from America West, Frontier, Great Lakes Aviation, and United.

The Durango–La Plata Airport (DRO) is your closest option for Silverton, Durango, Pagosa Springs, Mesa Verde National Park, and the Four Corners region. It's served by America West Express, Delta, US Airways, and United Express.

Something to consider for travel to the Four Corners region, given your location and airline schedules, is to at least check into flying to Albuquerque instead of Denver. The Albuquerque International Sunport (ABQ) is host to many of the major airlines and is closer than Denver.

Information Albuquerque International Sunport (ABQ) (☎ 505/244-7700 ⊕ www.cabq.gov/airport). **Durango–La Plata Airport (DRO)** (☎ 970/247-8143 ⊕ www.durangoairport.com). **Telluride Regional Airport (TEX)** (☎ 970/728-5313 ⊕ www.tellurideairport.com).

TRANSFERS Several companies offer transportation between the airports and the resorts. Shuttles average $15–$30 per person. In Crested Butte, Gunniston, and Montrose try Alpine Express. Advance reservations may be required. Telluride Express serves Telluride Regional Airport. In Durango, the best service is Durango Transportation.

Contacts Alpine Express (☎ 970/641-5074 or 800/822-4844 ⊕ alpine expressshuttle.com). **Durango Transportation** (☎ 970/247-4161 or 800/626-2066). **Telluride Express** (☎ 970/728-6000 or 888/212-8294 ⊕ www.tellurideexpress.com).

BY BUS

If you're traveling between the major towns, Greyhound is your best bet. In Crested Butte, Mountain Express shuttles regularly between the town and the ski area every 15 minutes during ski season. The Galloping Goose loops around Telluride every 15 minutes in summer and winter, less often in the off-season. Durango Lift has regular bus service up and down Main Street, as well as to Purgatory during ski season.

Contacts Durango Lift (☎ 970/259-5438). **Galloping Goose** (☎ 970/728-5700). **Greyhound** (☎ 800/231-2222). **Mountain Express** (☎ 970/349-5616).

BY CAR

Telluride is 330 mi southwest of Denver. There is no such thing as a direct route, but the fastest is probably U.S. 285 south to U.S. 50 west to Montrose. Take U.S. 550 south to Ridgway. From Ridgway, take Route 62 west to Placerville and Route 145 south to Telluride.

In winter, the only way out of Crested Butte is to head toward Gunnison, because the alternate route to Aspen, Kebler Pass over Route 133, is closed.

Getting to the remote Four Corners region is a bit simpler. If you're entering Colorado from the south, U.S. 550, U.S. 160, and U.S. 491 lead to the Four Corners region. From the east or west, I–70 (U.S. 6) intersects U.S. 50 in Grand Junction; U.S. 550 runs south to the San Juan Mountains and Four Corners from Montrose. From the Denver area, take Interstate 25 to Interstate 70 west for a long drive to U.S. 50.

Information American Automobile Association of Colorado (☎866/625-3601 ⊕www.aaacolo.com). **Colorado Road Report** (☎877/315-7623). **Colorado State Patrol** (☎970/249-4392 ⊕www.csp.state.co.us).

BY TAXI

In most resort towns you'll need to call for a cab. The wait is seldom more than 15 minutes.

Contacts Durango Transportation (☎970/259-4818). **Telluride Shuttle & Taxi** (☎970/728-6668). **Telluride Transit** (☎970/728-6000).

BY TRAIN

The Durango & Silverton Narrow Gauge Railroad can take you from Durango to Silverton in lovingly restored coaches. The train runs from mid-May to late-October, with four departures daily from June to August and only one in the other months.

Contact Durango & Silverton Narrow Gauge Railroad (✉479 Main Ave. ☎970/247-2733 or 888/872-4607 ⊕www.durangotrain.com 💲$65).

CONTACTS & RESOURCES

EMERGENCIES
Ambulance or Police (☎911).

24-Hour Medical Care Gunnison Valley Hospital (✉711 N. Taylor ☎970/641-1456 ⊕www.gvh-colorado.org). **Mercy Medical Center** (✉375 E. Park Ave., Durango ☎970/247-4311 ⊕www.mercydurango.org). **Montrose Memorial Hospital** (✉800 S. 3rd St. ☎970/249-2211 ⊕www.montrosehospital.com). **Southwest Memorial Hospital** (✉1311 N. Mildred St., Cortez ☎970/565-6666 ⊕www.swhealth.org). **Telluride Medical Center** (✉500 W. Pacific Ave. ☎970/728-3848 ⊕www.telluridemedicalcenter.org).

VISITOR INFORMATION
Contact Southwest Colorado Travel Region (☎800/933-4340 ⊕www.swcolotravel.org).

Crested Butte & Gunnison Crested Butte–Mount Crested Butte Chamber of Commerce (✉601 Elk Ave., Crested Butte ☎970/349-6438 or 800/545-4505 ⊕www.cb.chamber.com). **Crested Butte Snow Report** (☎888/442-8883). **Crested Butte Vacations** (✉Box 5700, Mount Crested Butte, 81225 ☎970/349-2222 or 888/223-3530 ⊕www.skicb.com). **Gunnison County Chamber of Commerce** (✉500 E. Tomichi Ave., Gunnison 81230 ☎970/641-1501 or 800/274-7580 ⊕www.gunnisonchamber.com).

Durango, Silverton & Pagosa Springs **Durango Chamber Resort Association** (⊠ 111 S. Camino del Rio, Durango ☎ 970/247-0312 or 800/525-8855 ⊕ www.durango.org). **Pagosa Springs Chamber of Commerce** (⊠ 402 San Juan St., ☎ 970/264-2360 or 800/252-2204 ⊕ www.pagosaspringschamber. com). **Silverton Chamber of Commerce** (⊠ 414 Greene St., ☎ 970/387-5654 or 800/752-4494 ⊕ www.silvertoncolorado.com). **Wolf Creek Snow Report** (☎ 800/754-9653).

Four Corners **Cortez Area Chamber of Commerce** (⊠ 928 E. Main St., Cortez ☎ 970/565-3414 ⊕ www.mesaverdecountry.com). **Mesa Verde Country** (⊡ Box HH, Cortez 81321 ☎ 800/253-1616 ⊕ www.mesaverdecountry.com).

Lake City & Creede **Creede Chamber of Commerce** (⊠ 1207 N. Main St., Creede 81130 ☎ 800/327-2102 ⊕ www.creede.com). **Lake City Chamber of Commerce** (⊠ 800 N. Gunnison Ave., ☎ 800/569-1874 ⊕ www.lakecity.com).

Telluride **Telluride and Mountain Village Visitor Services** (⊠ 630 W. Colorado Ave., Box 653, Telluride ☎ 970/728-3041 or 800/525-3455 ⊕ www.visittelluride. com). **Telluride Ski Resort** (⊠ 565 Mountain Village Blvd., ☎ 970/728-6900 or 866/287-5015 ⊕ www.tellurideskiresort.com). **Telluride Snow Report** (☎ 970/728-7425).

Mesa Verde National Park

Unlike most national parks of the west, Mesa Verde earned its status from its rich cultural history rather than its geological treasures. President Theodore Roosevelt established it in 1906 as the first national park to "preserve the works of man." The Ancestral Puebloan people, who lived in the region from roughly 600 to 1300, left behind more than 4,800 archaeological sites spread out over 80 square mi. Their ancient dwellings, set high into the sandstone cliffs, are the heart of the park.

WELCOME TO MESA VERDE NATIONAL PARK

TOP REASONS TO GO

★ **Ancestral Mansions:** Explore Cliff Palace and the Long House, each with more than 100 rooms. They are among the 600 cliff dwellings tucked into Mesa Verde.

★ **Pueblo Places:** View kivas, petroglyphs, wall paintings, and more. More than 4,800 archaeological sites and 3 million objects of the Ancestral Puebloans have been unearthed at Mesa Verde.

★ **Geological Goodies:** Get low and look close; the desert landscape has a story to tell. Ripple marks suggest the area was once covered with water, turtleback weathering notes the effects of erosion, and flower-pattern solution rills reveal the power of acidic rain on the sandstone's structure.

★ **Bright Nights:** Gaze into the sky's starry depths. With no major cities nearby to reflect light at night, the Four Corners area is an ideal place to be an amateur astronomer.

1 Morefield Campground. Near the entrance, this large campground is a natural center of operations for any visitor to Mesa Verde. It includes a village area with a gas station and grocery store. The park's best-known sites are farther in, but there are a few hiking trails close by.

2 Far View Visitor Center. About a 45-minute drive from Mesa Verde's entrance, the main visitor center is near the park's only overnight lodge (seasonal), and from where you can access 12-mi Wetherill Mesa Road (seasonal) to the west and 12-mi Mesa Top Loop Road to the south.

3 Chapin Mesa. In many ways the heart of Mesa Verde, this southern swath is where the famous 150-room Cliff Palace dwelling is located, as well as some scenic overlooks.

COLORADO

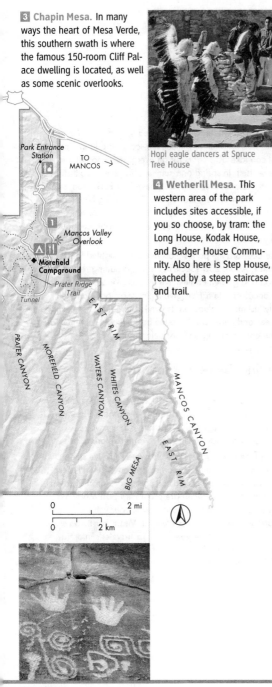

Park Entrance Station
TO MANCOS →

Mancos Valley Overlook

1

Morefield Campground

Prater Ridge Trail

Tunnel

PRATER CANYON

MOREFIELD CANYON

WATERS CANYON

WHITES CANYON

EAST RIM

MANCOS CANYON

BIG MESA

EAST RIM

0   2 mi
0   2 km

Hopi eagle dancers at Spruce Tree House

4 Wetherill Mesa. This western area of the park includes sites accessible, if you so choose, by tram: the Long House, Kodak House, and Badger House Community. Also here is Step House, reached by a steep staircase and trail.

GETTING ORIENTED

Perhaps no other area offers as much evidence into the Ancestral Puebloans' existence as Mesa Verde National Park. Several thousand archaeological sites have been found, and research is ongoing to discover more. The carved-out homes and assorted artifacts, displayed at the park's Chapin Mesa Archeological Museum, belonged to ancestors of today's Hopi, Zuni, and Pueblo tribes, among others. Due to the sensitive nature of these remnants, hiking in the park is restricted to designated trails, and certain cliff dwellings may only be accessed under accompaniment of a ranger during the peak summer season.

KEY	
👫	Ranger Station
⛺	Campground
🎪	Picnic Area
🍴	Restaurant
🏠	Lodge
🚶	Trailhead
🚻	Restrooms
⇟	Scenic Viewpoint
⋯⋯	Walking/Hiking Trails
⋯⋯	Bicycle Path

MESA VERDE NATIONAL PARK

Petroglyphs

MESA VERDE NATIONAL PARK PLANNER

When to Go

The best times to visit the park are late May, early June, and most of September, when the weather is fine but the summer crowds have thinned. Mid-June through August are Mesa Verde's most crowded months. In July and August you must stop at the Far View Visitor Center to purchase tickets for the Balcony House, Cliff House and Long House tours. At times, the lines at the museum and visitor center may last for 15 to 20 minutes. Afternoon thunder showers are common in July and August.

The mesa gets as many as 100 inches of snow in winter. Snow may fall as late as May and as early as October, but there's rarely enough to hamper travel. In winter, the Wetherill Mesa Road and Far View Lodge are closed, but the sight of the sandstone dwellings sheltered from the snow in their cliff coves is spectacular.

AVG. HIGH/LOW TEMPS

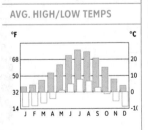

Flora & Fauna

Since 2000, wildfires have claimed thousands of Mesa Verde's acres. Visitors will see the scars for a long time, as it can take 300 years for an evergreen woodland to restore itself. In spring and summer, however, you'll still see brightly colored blossoms, like the yellow Perky Sue, sage, yucca, and mountain mahogany. Sand-loving blue lupines are seen along the roadways in the higher elevations, and bright-red Indian paintbrushes are scattered throughout the rocky cliffs.

Mule deer are the park's most frequently sighted larger animals. About 200 species of birds, including red-tailed hawks and golden eagles, live in Mesa Verde, as does the poisonous prairie rattler (give it plenty of space and it'll likely just mosey along on its way). The animals seek shade in trees and under brush, so the best times to spot them are in the early morning and just before dusk.

Getting There & Around

The park is located off U.S. 160, between Cortez and Durango in what's known as the Four Corners. The nearest bus station and regional airport are 35 mi away in Durango, Colorado, a small city worth exploring.

Most of the scenic drives at Mesa Verde involve steep grades and hairpin turns, particularly on Wetherill Mesa. Vehicles over 8,000 pounds or 25 feet are prohibited on this road. Towed vehicles are prohibited past Morefield Campground. Check the condition of your vehicle's brakes before driving the road to Wetherill Mesa. For the latest road information, tune your radio to Traveler's Information Station at 1610 AM, or call the ranger station at ☎970/529–4461. Off-road vehicles are prohibited in the park.

SCENIC DRIVES

By John
Blodgett
Updated by
Lois Friedland

Mesa Top Loop Road. This 6-mi drive skirts the scenic rim of Chapin Mesa, reaching several of Mesa Verde's most important archaeological sites. Two of the parks' most impressive viewpoints are also on this road: Navajo Canyon Overlook and Sun Point Overlook, from which you can see Cliff Palace, Sunset House, and other dwellings. ⊙ *Daily 8* AM*–sunset.*

Park Entrance Road. The main park road leads you from the entrance to Far View Visitor Center, on 15 mi of switchbacks, which reveal far-ranging vistas of the surrounding areas. You can stop at a couple of pretty overlooks along the way, but hold out for Park Point, which, at the mesa's highest elevation (8,572 feet), affords unobstructed 360-degree views.

WHAT TO SEE

HISTORIC SITES

Many of the historic sites are clustered along specific drive loops. **Step House, Long House, Badger House Community,** and **Kodak House** are all on the **Wetherill Mesa** loop. There are three driving loops on **Chapin Mesa.** The shortest one goes to the **Chapin Mesa Archeological Museum** and **Spruce House.** A second loop goes to the **Sun Temple, Square Tower House,** and **Mesa Top** sites. The third loop includes the **Cliff Palace** and the **Balcony House.**

Badger House Community. A self-guided walk takes you through a group of subterranean dwellings, called pit houses, and aboveground storage rooms. The community dates to 650, the Basket Maker period, and covers 7 acres of land. Most of the pit houses and kivas—religious or ceremonial rooms—were connected by an intricate system of tunnels, some up to 41 feet long. Allow about an hour to see all the sites. ⊠ *On Wetherill Mesa Rd.,* ✛ *12 mi from the Far View Visitor Center* ⊙ *Memorial Day–Labor Day, daily 8–4:30.*

� ★ **Balcony House.** The stonework of this 40-room cliff dwelling, which once housed about 40 or 50 people, is impressive, but you're likely to be even more awed by the skill it took to reach this place. Perched in a sandstone alcove 600 feet above the floor of Soda Canyon, Balcony House seems almost suspended in space. Even with the aid of modern steps and a partially paved trail, today's visitors must climb two wooden ladders (the first one 32 feet high) to enter. Surrounding the house are a courtyard with a parapet wall and the intact balcony for which the house is named. A favorite with kids, the dwelling is only accessible on a ranger-led tour. Youngsters love climbing the ladders, crawling through the tunnels, and clambering around its nooks and crannies. Purchase your ticket at the Far View Visitor Center. ⊠ *On Cliff Palace Loop Rd.,* ✛ *8.5 mi southeast of the Far View Visitor Center* ⊠ *$3* ⊙ *Late May–mid-Oct., daily 9–5.*

Fodor's Choice ★ **Cliff Palace.** This was the first major Mesa Verde dwelling seen by cowboys Charlie Mason and Richard Wetherill in 1888. It is also the largest, containing about 150 rooms and 23 kivas on three levels. The tour involves a steep downhill hike and four ladders. Purchase tickets at the Far View Visitor Center for the one-hour, ranger-led tour through this dwelling. ⊠ *On Cliff Palace Loop Rd., ✚ 7 mi south of the Far View Visitor Center* ⌨ *$3* ⊙ *Mid-May–mid-Oct., daily 9–5.*

Far View Sites Complex. This is believed to have been one of the most densely populated areas in Mesa Verde, comprising as many as 50 villages in a 0.5-square-mi area at the top of Chapin Mesa. Most of the sites here were built between 900 and 1300. Begin the self-guided tour at the interpretive panels in the parking lot, then proceed down a 0.5-mi, level trail. ⊠ *On the park entrance road, ✚ 1.5 mi south of the Far View Visitor Center* ⊙ *Mid-May–mid-Oct., daily 8–6:30.*

Long House. Excavated in 1959 through 1961, this Wetherill Mesa cliff dwelling is the second largest in Mesa Verde. It is believed that about 150 people lived in Long House, so named because of the size of its cliff alcove. The spring at the back of the alcove is still active today. The ranger-led tour begins a short distance from the parking lot and takes about 1½ hours; purchase tickets for the tour at the Far View Visitor Center. ⊠ *On Wetherill Mesa Rd., ✚ 12 mi from the Far View Visitor Center* ⌨ *$3* ⊙ *Memorial Day–Labor Day, daily 10–4.*

Spruce Tree House. The best-preserved site in the park, this dwelling contains 130 living rooms and eight kivas. It's the only dwelling where you can actually enter a kiva, via a short ladder, just as the original inhabitants did. Tours are self-guided, but a park ranger is on-site to answer questions. The short trail starts behind the Chapin Mesa Archeological Museum and descends 170 feet—you'll find yourself puffing on the way back up, but it's worth the effort. The site is open year-round, with guided tours from mid-November to early March. ⊠ *On the park entrance road, ✚ 5 mi south of the Far View Visitor Center* ⊙ *Mar.–Nov., daily 9–5.*

Step House. So named because of a crumbling prehistoric stairway leading up from the dwelling, Step House on Wetherill Mesa is reached via a paved, though steep, trail. The house is one of the least-visited dwellings in the park. ⊠ *On Wetherill Mesa Rd., ✚ 12 mi from the Far View Visitor Center* ⊙ *Memorial Day–Labor Day, daily 8–4:30.*

Sun Temple. Although researchers assume the Sun Temple on the Cliff Palace Loop was probably a ceremonial structure, they are unsure of the purpose of this complex, which has no doors or windows in most of its chambers. ⊠ *On Cliff Palace Loop Rd., ✚ 8 mi south of the Far View Visitor Center* ⊙ *Daily 8–sunset.*

Triple Village Pueblo Sites. Three dwellings built atop each other from 750 to 1150 at first look like a mass of jumbled walls, but an interpretive panel helps identify them. The 325-foot trail from the walking area is paved and wheelchair accessible. ⊠ *On Mesa Top Loop Rd., ✚ 8 mi south of the Far View Visitor Center* ⊙ *Daily.*

SCENIC STOPS

Cedar Tree Tower. A self-guided tour takes you to, but not through, a tower and kiva built between 1100 and 1300 and connected by a tunnel. The tower-and-kiva combinations in the park are thought to have been either religious structures or signal towers. ⊠ *On the park entrance road,* ✛ *4 mi south of the Far View Visitor Center* ⊙ *Daily.*

Kodak House Overlook. Get an impressive view into Kodak House and its several small kivas from here. The house, closed to the public, was named for a Swedish researcher who stored his Kodak camera here in 1891. ⊠ *On Wetherill Mesa Rd. 1,* ✛ *2 mi from the Far View Visitor Center* ▧ *$3 at Far View Visitor Center* ⊙ *Memorial Day–Labor Day, daily.*

Soda Canyon Overlook. Get your best view of Balcony House here and read interpretive panels about the house and canyon geology. ⊠ *On Mesa Top Loop Rd.,* ✛ *9 mi south of the Far View Visitor Center* ⊙ *Daily.*

VISITOR CENTERS

★ **Chapin Mesa Archeological Museum.** The museum tells the entire story of the cliff-dwelling people and gives as complete an understanding as possible of the Basket Maker and Ancestral Puebloan cultures through detailed dioramas and exhibits, including original textiles, sandals, and kiva jars. ⊠ *On the park entrance road,* ✛ *5 mi south of the Far View Visitor Center* ☎ *970/529–4465* ▧ *Free* ⊙ *Apr.–mid-Oct., daily 8–6:30; mid-Oct.–Mar., daily 8–5.*

★ **Far View Visitor Center.** Buy tickets for the Cliff Palace, Balcony House, and Long House ranger-led tours here. An extensive selection of books and videos on the history of the park are also for sale. Rangers are on hand to answer questions and explain the history of the Ancestral Puebloans. ✛ *15 mi south of the park entrance* ☎ *970/529–5036* ⊙ *Mid-Apr.–mid-Oct., daily 8–5.*

SPORTS & THE OUTDOORS

HIKING

EASY **Knife Edge Trail.** Take this trail for an easy 2-mi (round-trip) walk around the north rim of the park. If you stop at all the flora identification points that the trail guide pamphlet suggests, the hike should take about 1½ to 2 hours. The patches of asphalt you're likely to spot along the way are leftovers from Knife Edge Road, built in 1914 as the main entryway into the park.

♨ **Soda Canyon Overlook Trail.** One of the easiest and most rewarding strolls in the park, this little trail travels 1.5 mi round-trip through the forest on almost completely level ground. The overlook is an excellent point from which to photograph the cliff dwellings. The trailhead is about 0.25 mi past the Balcony House parking area.

MODERATE **Farming Terrace Trail.** This 30-minute, 0.5-mi loop beginning and ending on the spur road to Cedar Tree Tower, meanders through a series of check dams the Ancestral Puebloans built in order to create farming terraces.

Fodor's Choice
★ **Petroglyph Point Trail.** The highlight of this 2.8-mi loop is the largest and best-known group of petroglyphs in Mesa Verde. Since the trail offshoots from Spruce Tree House Trail, it is only accessible when Spruce Tree House is open, March through November, daily 9–5.

Spruce Canyon Trail. If you want to venture down into the canyon, this is your trail. It's only 2 mi long, but you can go down about 300 feet in elevation. It is only accessible when Spruce Tree House is open, from March through November, daily 9–5, and registration is required.

DIFFICULT **Prater Ridge Trail.** This loop, which starts and finishes at Morefield Campground, is the longest hike (7.8-mi round-trip) you can take inside the park and affords fine views of Morefield Canyon to the south and the San Juan Mountains to the north.

> **ANTSY POTS**
>
> Anthills contribute an important ingredient to the pottery that vastly improved the Basket Maker standard of living. Pueblo potters, as did their ancestors, collect the small pebbles from the ants' nests to grind up and use as temper, the material added to clay to prevent the vessels from cracking as they dry.

EDUCATIONAL OFFERINGS

RANGER PROGRAMS

ARAMARK. The park concessionaire provides half-day ranger-guided tours of the Mesa Top Loop Road sites from mid-April through mid-October. The tours depart in vans or buses from Far View Terrace. Tours cover the history, geology, and excavation process in Mesa Verde. ⌖*ARAMARK Mesa Verde, Box 277, Mancos 81328* ☎*970/564–4300 or 800/449–2288* ⊕*www.visitmesaverde.com* ✍*$49* ☼*Mid-Apr.–mid-Oct., daily.*

Evening Ranger Campfire Program. A park ranger presents a different 45-minute program or slide presentation each night of the week. ⊠*Morefield Campground Amphitheater,* ⊹*4 mi south of the park entrance* ☎*970/529–4465* ☼*Memorial Day–Labor Day, daily 9 PM–9:45 PM.*

Ranger-Led Tours. Balcony House, Cliff Palace, and Long House can only be explored on a ranger-led tour; each lasts about an hour. Buy tickets for these at Far View Visitor Center the day of the tour, or at the Morefield Campground Ranger Station the evening before the tour, 5 PM to 8:30 PM. ☎*970/529–4465* ✍*$3 per tour* ☼*Mid-Apr.–mid-Oct.*

WHERE TO EAT

$$$ ✕**Metate Room.** Tables in this Southwestern-style dining room are can-
★ dlelit and cloth covered, but the atmosphere remains casual. A wall of windows affords wonderful Mesa Verde vistas. The menu includes American staples like steak and seafood, but game meats such as quail, venison, and rabbit occasionally appear as well. Try Anasazi beans and

mesa bread to start. ⊠*Far View Lodge,* ⊕*across from the Far View Visitor Center* ☎*AE, D, DC, MC, V* ⊗*Closed late Oct.–early Apr. No lunch.*

¢ ✗**Far View Terrace.** This full-service cafeteria offers great views, plentiful choices, and reasonable prices. Fluffy blueberry pancakes are often on the breakfast menu. Dinner options might include a Navajo taco piled high with all the fixings. Don't miss the creamy malts and homemade fudge; a shot at the espresso bar will keep you going all day. ⊠*On Mesa Top Loop Rd.,* ⊕*across from the Far View Visitor Center* ☎*970/529–4444* ▤*D, MC, V* ⊗*Closed late Oct.–early Apr.*

¢ ✗**Knife Edge Café.** An all-you-can-eat pancake breakfast is served every morning from 7:30 to 10 at this café in Morefield Campground. ⊕*4 mi south of the park entrance* ☎*970/565–2133* ▤*AE, D, MC, V* ⊗*Closed Labor Day–Memorial Day. No lunch or dinner.*

¢ ✗**Spruce Tree Terrace.** A limited selection of hot food and sandwiches is all you'll find at this cafeteria, but the patio is pleasant, and since it's across the street from the Chapin Mesa Archeological Museum, it's convenient. The Terrace is also the only food concession open year-round. ⊠*On the park entrance road,* ⊕*4 mi from the Far View Visitor Center* ☎*970/529–4521* ▤*AE, D, DC, MC, V* ⊗*No dinner Dec.–Feb.*

WHERE TO STAY

★ $$ ▦ **Far View Lodge.** Talk about a view—many rooms in the older buildings have private balconies, from which you can admire the neighboring states of Arizona, Utah, and New Mexico up to 100 mi in the distance. The Kiva rooms in the newer buildings have handcrafted furniture and are more comfortable but do not have the views. In either building, quarters are motel-style and basic, with a Southwestern touch. Talks by guest speakers on various park topics and multimedia shows on the Ancestral Puebloans are held occasionally. The hotel also offers enthusiastically guided tours of the park. The Metate Room, the lodge's main dining room, is acclaimed for its fine steaks and excellent Southwestern fare. ⊕*15 mi southwest of the park entrance, across from the Far View Visitor Center* ⊡*Reservations: ARAMARK Mesa Verde, Box 277, Mancos 81328* ☎*970/564–4300 or 800/449–2288* ⊕*www. visitmesaverde.com* ⊷*150 rooms* ⟡*In-room: refrigerator (some). In-hotel: restaurant, bar, laundry facilities, some pets allowed, no-smoking rooms* ▤*AE, D, DC, MC, V* ⊗*Closed mid-Oct–mid-Apr.*

CAMPGROUNDS
& RV PARKS

$$$

FodorsChoice

★

△**Morefield Campground.** With about 400 shaded campsites, access to trailheads, and plenty of amenities, the only campground in the park is an appealing mini-city for campers. Reservations are accepted for all sites. ⊕*4 mi from the park entrance* ⊡*Box 277, Mancos 81328* ☎*970/564–4300 or 800/449–2288* ⊕*www.visitmesaverde.com* ⊷*380 sites, 15 with hookups* ⟡*Flush toilets, full hookups for RVs, drive campsites for cars, dump station, drinking water, guest laundry, showers, fire grates, grills, picnic tables, food service, electricity, public telephone, general store, ranger station, service station* ▤*AE, D, DC, MC, V* ⊗*Late-Apr.–mid-Oct.*

MESA VERDE ESSENTIALS

ACCESSIBILITY

Steep cliffs, deep canyons, narrow trails, and hard-to-reach archaeo-logical sites mean accessibility is limited within Mesa Verde. Service dogs cannot be taken into Balcony House, Cliff Palace, or Long House because of ladders in those sites. None of these sites is accessible to those with mobility impairments. If you have heart or respiratory ailments, you may have trouble breathing in the thin air at 7,000 to 8,000 feet. Wheelchairs with wide-rim wheels are recommended on trails, some of which do not meet legal grade requirements. For the hearing impaired, park videos are open captioned. Mesa Top Loop Road provides the most comprehensive and accessible view of all the archaeological sites.

ADMISSION FEES

At this writing, a seven-day vehicle permit costs $15 between Memorial Day and Labor Day; this summer fee is scheduled to increase to $20 in 2009. The rest of the year, the permit is $10. An annual permit for Mesa Verde is $30. Ranger-led tours of Cliff Palace, Long House, and Balcony House are $3 per person.

ADMISSION HOURS

The facilities open each day at 8 AM and close at sunset from Memorial Day through Labor Day. The rest of the year, the facilities close at 5. Wetherill Mesa, all the major cliff dwellings, and Morefield ranger station are open only from Memorial Day through Labor Day, Far View Visitor Center, Far View Lodge, and Morefield Campground are open mid-April through mid-October.

EMERGENCIES

To report a fire or call for aid, dial 911 or 970/529–4465. First-aid stations are located at Morefield Campground, Far View Visitor Center, and Wetherill Mesa.

VISITOR INFORMATION

Mesa Verde National Park (🖃 *Box 8, Mesa Verde, 81330-0008* ☎ *970/529–4465* 🌐 *www.nps.gov/meve).*

West Texas

WORD OF MOUTH

"The drive west on I-10 from Ozona is spectacular classic West Texas scenery, with the sky as big and blue as you can imagine. We diverted briefly to get a spectacular view of the Pecos River valley from an overlook above Sheffield...Soon the spectacular array of scores of 200-foot-tall spinning wind turbines was visible on the horizon on the mesas far to the north of I-10...They added an odd but graceful modern touch to the seemingly ageless Pecos River Valley terrain."

—MRand

By Jennifer
Edwards

AS SOON AS VISITORS SET their soles on the dry-as-the-Sahara soil of West Texas, they'll realize they've entered a world set apart from the rest of the Lone Star State. Remote from urban population centers, isolated within the northern plains of the Chihuahua Desert, West Texas lives by its own rules, not unlike Australia's Outback. It's a land of flat and rugged beauty and twisted vegetation like the kind that might float on the bottom of the sea. Cacti rise like coral, and ground squirrels, horned lizards, and serpents wiggle like eels among the mesquite bushes populating the landscape—the same mesquite that bequeaths its poignant, smoky taste to everything from fajitas to barbecue chips.

WEST TEXAS TOP 5

■ **Jumping Jackrabbits:** Wildlife runs the gamut, from prairie dogs to roadrunners.

■ **Bumpy El Paso:** View the striking Franklin Mountains that rise up from the city.

■ **Tex-Mex Culture:** Neither entirely Mexican nor entirely Texan, it's a mishmash of both.

■ **Tumbling About:** There just might be more tumbleweeds here than people. It rolls all about, so be careful when you drive.

■ **Park It:** Visit Big Bend National Park, the region's gem.

West Texas is a land of severe beauty, with clutches of exquisiteness and quiet civilization—a rural, traditional culture that has an equal mix of Old West and Old Mexico. Cowboy hats are worn here not for fashion, but for duty: "cowboy" and "cowhand" are occupational titles of many folk, as is "oilman." Working cowboys roam the plains and make fires at night, and there are still cattle drives to the south.

While in West Texas, visitors should look for the rolling tumbleweed and such wildlife as roadrunners and gigantic jackrabbits.

EXPLORING WEST TEXAS

Interstates 10 and 20, along with highways 87, 277, and 90, are the main roads traversing the region. I–10 connects the region's largest city, El Paso, home to the Fort Bliss Military Reservation with the towns of San Angelo, and Pecos, Midland, and Odessa via I–67 and I–20 respectively. From Pecos, home to what may well be the nation's oldest rodeo, travelers can slip south on Highway 17 to the unique culture mix that defines Marfa, and then south on Highway 118 to Alpine in the Fort Davis mountains and Big Bend National Park.

ABOUT THE RESTAURANTS

Tex-Mex, Mexican, and Southern cooking are what this region does best. In general, steer away from East Asian; stick with items like country-fried steaks, barbecue, and Mexican dishes like burritos, *asado* (a tangy dish, often pork, cooked in oil and ground-up chiles), *chiles rellenos* (raw green chiles that are stuffed with meat, cheeses, and spices and then baked; can be hot or mild), and *barbacoa* (slow-cooked beef seasoned with tangy marinade). (Note that some barbacoa is actually from the head of the cow [called *barbacoa de cabeza*].) For the best

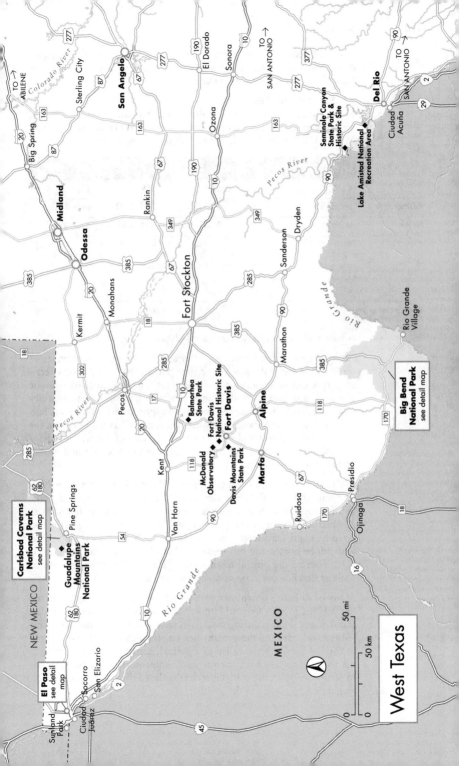

West Texas

fare, look past professional decor and instead search out the less glamorous restaurants. Tacos *al pastor* (country-style) are often a delicious highlight of more authentic eateries.

ABOUT THE HOTELS

Major chains, such as Hilton, Holiday Inn, Days Inn, and Comfort Inn, are represented in the major population centers of El Paso, Odessa, and Midland. It can be difficult to find lodging in smaller towns.

WHAT IT COSTS					
	¢	$	$$	$$$	$$$$
Restaurants	under $8	$8–$12	$13–$20	$21–$30	over $30
Hotels	under $50	$50–$100	$101–$150	$151–$200	over $200

Restaurant prices are per person for a main course at dinner. Hotel prices are per night for two people in a standard double room in high season, excluding taxes and service charges. Lodging tax rate is 6 percent statewide with an additional county tax, which varies by county.

EL PASO

About 306 mi west of Midland via I–20 and I–10.

Fabled El Paso, just barely in Texas and in fact on Mountain Time (rather than Central), was at one time part of the New Mexico Territory. It is still an important crossing point for those entering from or departing for Mexico. One glance at a map will show why this city along the Rio Grande has become the transportation and business hub for southern New Mexico and West Texas, as well as a destination for outdoor adventurers and history buffs. The mix of American Indian, Spanish, and American cultures is evident in the city's art and music, architecture, and cuisine.

El Paso lies between the southern end of the Rockies and the northern terminus of Mexico's Sierra Madre, making it a major stopping point on the southern route west during the California gold rush. In 1850 the downtown area was sparsely settled, with a dirt trail leading to the Rio Grande. Eight years later there was an established roadway populated with adobe homes and businesses, and not long after that San Jacinto Plaza became the official town square. The arrival of the railroad in 1888 sealed El Paso's fate as a vital city of the West.

Many of El Paso's downtown gems, such as the historically protected Plaza Hotel (one of Conrad Hilton's first hotels), unfortunately today stand empty. Hotels during the 1950s were often full, sometimes with Hollywood stars and the wealthy heading for a cheap and easy divorce in Ciudad Juárez (often called just Juárez), across the river. Adding to the town's bravado back then were live alligators in the plaza pond. (A sculpture of writhing alligators has replaced the real reptiles, which ended their residency in the 1960s.)

Chamizal National
Memorial **6**

El Paso Desert
Botanical
Gardens **1**

El Paso Museum
of Art **4**

Franklin Mountains
State Park **2**

Hueco Tanks
Historic Site **7**

Magoffin Home
State Historical
Park **5**

Mission Ysleta ...**8**

Presidio Chapel
San Elizario **9**

San Elizario County
Jail **10**

Wyler Aerial
Tramway **3**

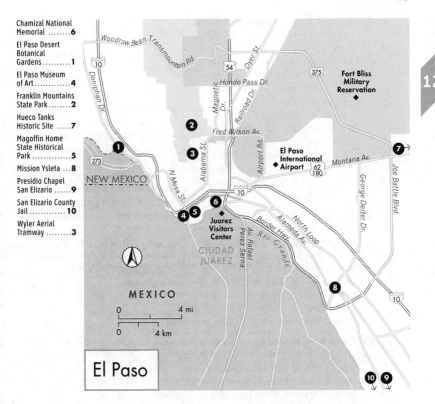

12

El Paso

Sixteenth-century Spanish explorer Don Juan de Oñate dubbed the entire Rio Grande Valley Paso del Rio del Norte ("the pass through the river of the north")—from which El Paso derives its name. Oñate was so grateful that the expedition of about 500 ragged colonists had reached the Rio Grande that he ordered his people to don their best clothes for a feast of thanksgiving on April 30, 1598—a celebration that preceded the arrival of the pilgrims in Massachusetts by nearly a quarter century.

WHAT TO SEE

❻ Chamizal National Memorial. In 1964 nearly a century of dispute between Texas and Mexico, caused by the shifting banks of the Rio Grande, came to an end. Both the United States and Mexico founded memorials within their borders to commemorate this event. Texas created a 55-acre park, on formerly Mexican land, with a visitor center, three galleries, drama festivals, and long walking paths. Across the border, easily accessed by the Bridge of the Americas, is the Mexican counterpart, the 800-acre Parque Chamizal. ⊠*800 S. San Marcial* ☎*915/532–7232* ⊕*www.nps.gov/cham* ⊠*Free* ☉*Daily 5 AM–10 PM.*

❶ **El Paso Desert Botanical Gardens.** Located in Keystone Heritage Park, these gardens juxtapose the exotic—an Asian-style koi pond and little waterfall—with native cacti and other succulents set against the backdrop of the northern Chihuahua Desert. There's even a natural wetlands area. ✉ *4200 Doniphan Rd.* ☎ *915/584–0563* 🌐 *www.elpasobotanicalgardens.org* 🎫 *$2* ⏲ *Sept.–May, Sat. and Sun. noon–3; June–Aug., Sat. and Sun. 8–11* AM.

❹ **El Paso Museum of Art.** The museum features a striking array of Spanish and native art, from Picasso and Goya to Southwest artists Tom Lea and Henrietta Wyeth. ✉ *1 Arts Festival Plaza* ☎ *915/532–1707* 🌐 *www.elpasoartmuseum.com* 🎫 *Free* ⏲ *Tues., Wed., 9–5, Thurs. 9–9, Fri., Sat. 9–5, Sun. noon–5.*

OH, THE BLISS!

Fort Bliss Army Base has gone from mounted cavalry stationed amid adobe-style houses to modern soldiers living in a high-tech base. It encompasses more than one million acres. And though it's an active base with air defense training schools and brigades, it remains tourist friendly. On site are a free history museum and a museum filled with Old West replicas of buildings and military items from the 1850s through 1860s, when the base was located in Magoffinsville.Bring a driver's license and insurance card/documentation and proof of registration.

❼ **Hueco Tanks Historic Site.** This park, named after natural, water-holding stone basins called *huecos,* is internationally renowned for its rock climbing and is a big draw for lovers of the pictographs left by the Apache, Kiowa, and Jornada Mogollon tribes who dwelt here. Due to past vandalism of the petroglyphs, rangers now accompany visitors to the sensitive areas of the park, and reservations for tours (such as the pictograph tour, as well as birding and bouldering tours) are required. Rock climbing without a guide is an option, and so is camping, since park staff are located throughout the park and keep an eye on visitors' activities. From downtown El Paso, take U.S. 62/180 32 mi northeast, turn north on Ranch Road 2775; follow signs. **TIP→ Call two days before your trip, as the number of visitors allowed is limited. Reservations are required to get in the park, unless visitors are among the first ten at the door when the park opens at 8** AM. ✉ *6900 Hueco Tanks Rd., No. 1, El Paso* ☎ *915/857–1135 or 800/792–1112, option 3* 🎫 *$4 per person, per day; camping $12–$16* ⏲ *Oct.–Apr., daily 8–6; May–Sept., Mon.–Thurs. 8–6, Fri.–Sun. 7–7. Tours times for the more protected areas vary* ✍ *Reservations required.*

❺ **Magoffin Home State Historical Park.** This 19-room Territorial-style adobe home near downtown El Paso was erected in 1875 by early El Paso pioneer Joseph Magoffin, and occupied by the Magoffin family for 110 years. The city of El Paso grew out of Magoffinsville, a town started by this prominent and powerful family that vastly influenced the area by encouraging trade, organizing area merchants, establishing perhaps the first alfalfa crop in the region, and later leasing buildings for the incipient Fort Bliss. ✉ *1120 Magoffin St., follow signs off I–10; westbound* *traffic takes Cotton St. exit; eastbound traffic takes Downtown exit to Kansas St.* ☎915/533–5147 💲$3 🕒Tues.–Sun. 9–5.

8 Mission Ysleta. Around 1681, Spanish refugees from the Pueblo Revolt **Fodor'sChoice** in and around Santa Fe established this *ysleta* (small island) mission. ★ Like other old missions in the area, Ysleta is still an active church. Guided tours of the mission are available from downtown El Paso via Sun Metro Buses and the El Paso-Juárez Trolley Co. Nearby, the Tigua Indian Reservation sells Tigua pottery, jewelry, and art. ⊠*Old Pueblo Rd. at Zaragosa and Alameda, take Zaragosa exit off I–10, east of El Paso* ☎915/859–9848 💲Free 🕒Mon.–Sat. 9–5; Sun. openings vary with church schedule.

9 Presidio Chapel San Elizario. This 1789 Spanish fortress provided set- ★ tlers protection from raiding Comanches and Apaches. It was near this site that the expedition of Spanish explorer Don Juan de Oñate stopped to conduct a thanksgiving celebration in 1598. It's located in the San Elizario Historical District, 17 mi southeast of downtown El Paso. Tours are conducted on-site by friendly volunteers but feature only the museum, and not the church. The **El Paso Mission Trail Association** (☎915/534–0677) offers more extensive tours. ■TIP➡Call ahead if you're planning to visit the church. The father might be able to leave it open a bit later than 11. ⊠*1556 San Elizario Rd., San Elizario* ☎915/851–1682 💲Free 🕒Tues.–Sat. 10–2, Sun. 10–noon (visitor center and museum); Mon.–Fri. 10–11 (church).

10 San Elizario County Jail. Thought to have been built as a private residence in the early 1800s, this adobe building at some point became El Paso County's first courthouse and jail, and, according to Pat Garrett's book *Authentic Life of Billy the Kid,* was the only jail the Kid broke *into,* which he did in order to free his friend Melquiades Segura. ⊠*On Main Street (100 yards west of the chapel), San Elizario* ☎915/851–1682 San Elizario Genealogy and Historical Society 💲Free guided tours of jail and plaza beginning at the Los Portales building 🕒Tues.–Sun. 10–2, and after hrs by special arrangement.

3 Wyler Aerial Tramway. Touted as the only public-accessible tram in 🐾 Texas, this tramway totes visitors up 5,632-foot Ranger Peak, which ★ provides a striking view of three states, two nations, and 7,000 square mi. ⊠*1700 McKinley Ave.* ☎915/566–6622 💲$7 🕒Sun.–Mon. and Thurs. noon–6, Fri.–Sat. noon–8.

ACROSS THE BORDER

If what you want is a quick and easy Mexican experience, Ciudad Juárez, is just across the Rio Grande from El Paso, but venture here only after careful consideration (*see tip below*). If you do go, walking across the border is easy enough, but taking the **El Paso-Juárez Trolley Co. Border Jumper** (⊠1 *Civic Center Plaza, El Paso* ☎915/544–0061 💲$12.50 🕒Departs hourly 10 AM to 5 PM) makes it all so much easier.

Built in the style of a *pueblito* (small pueblo), Ajuua! (⊠162 N. Efren Ornelas, Av. Lincoln and Av. 16 de Septiembre ☎52–656/616–6935 ⌹AE, MC, V) is a popular stopover for trolley passengers. The traditional Mexican dishes are reliably good, as are the margaritas. On weekend evenings, expect mariachi bands and colorfully costumed dancers. It's customary to tip the mariachi's leader a dollar or two. For shopping, **Avenida de Juárez** features artisan-oriented stores with handwoven shawls and hand-embroidered *huipiles,* the traditional blouses worn by indigenous Mexican women. The **plaza**, with its lovely cathedral, and the Spanish architecture of the wealthier neighborhoods make for scenic walks among some areas of the city.

Despite the town's attractiveness, the harsh reality is that this is the last stop along a long route for hundreds of thousands of Latin Americans trying to get into the United States to work. Poverty is ever-present. The murder rate is extremely high right now as well. ■TIP→ The more than a decade-long string of serial murders of women has caused legitimate concern. Travelers of all genders should be mindful of this and no one should travel alone. Drug violence also is wreaking havoc here with safety and tourism. Please exercise great caution, and check travel warnings on the Department of State Web site (⊕ *www.state.gov*).

SPORTS & THE OUTDOORS

❷ **Franklin Mountains State Park.** Within the park's 37 square mi are hik-
★ ing, mountain-biking, and horseback-riding trails, all offering amazing views of the city below. Plans are in the works for 100 mi more of trails. Rock climbing is permitted. This is a good place to get up close and personal with native species like foxes and kestrels and bluebirds, as well as plants found nowhere else in Texas, like the stout barrel cactus. Limited camping is available for tents; there are five RV sites. Tours are offered on the first and third weekends of the month; call ahead to reserve a space. ⊠ *1331 McKelligon Canyon Rd.* ☎ *915/566–6441* 🖼 *$4, additional for camping* ⊙ *Daily 8–5.*

THE ARTS

Like most cosmopolitan cities, El Paso offers a spectrum of arts and entertainment experiences, including theaters and performance halls hosting native dance performances, ballet, opera, and Shakespearean plays—as well as productions both for kids and by kids. For nightlife, free outdoor concerts on summer Fridays feature jazz, salsa, classical, and rock music (check out ⊕ *www.elpasocvb.com* for more details). Musicians introduce a similar and lively mix in El Paso's revitalized downtown area—the place to go for clubbing and bar hopping.

☽ **El Paso KIDS-N-CO.** This theater company is dedicated to teaching kids ages 5 and up the finer parts of the art, which its troupe then present during four annual children's productions like "The Ugly Duckling" and "Charlotte's Web." Visitors can wander into the headquarters for a tour or a glimpse of rehearsals during business hours. ⊠ *1301 and 1305 Texas Ave.* ☎ *915/315–1455* ⊕ *www.kidsnco.org* ⊙ *Mon.–Sat. 9–3; performance times vary.*

12

WHERE TO EAT

Some restaurants capitalize on the mountainous surroundings, dry heat, and low humidity of the area with outdoor tables. If dining alfresco, bring a light jacket; though the area can broil in the noontime sun, its desert nature brings in chill temperatures at night.

DID YOU KNOW?

Did you know that El Pasoans claim the cocktail classic known as the margarita was invented in a Juárez bar called Tommy's Place? Stories about the origin of the famous cocktail abound, but nobody really knows for sure if this one is a myth or a reality.

$$$–$$$$
★

✕**Café Central.** The old saw "evolve or perish" has served this restaurant well. In 1918 Café Central opened in Juárez and served alcohol (and tasty food) to the Prohibition-weary masses from the United States. Once Prohibition ended, the café moved north across the border, changed hands, and became part of the local scene. Today, bold decoration, an airy courtyard, and innovative Southwestern–Asian food combine to make this urbane eatery a popular destination for the city's hip crowds. The menu changes seasonally, according to the availability of ingredients. Although you can enjoy a gourmet experience for about fifteen bucks by ordering a soup and a salad, it's worth the splurge to explore other menu options. Lunch is a bit less expensive than dinner, yet equally tantalizing. ⊠*Texas Tower, 109 N. Oregon St.* ☎*915/545–2233* ⚇*Reservations required* ▤*AE, D, DC, MC, V* ⊗*Closed Sun.*

$$–$$$$
☺
Fodor'sChoice
★

✕**Cattleman's Steakhouse.** Twenty miles east of El Paso, this is pretty much in the middle of nowhere, but it's worth the trip, as much for the quirky theme rooms as for the terrific steaks. Consistently voted a local favorite, the succulent steaks are so tender they almost melt in your mouth. The mesquite-smoked barbecue and seafood on the menu are as tempting as the steaks—note that strict vegetarians won't find a happy meal here. A children's zoo, playground, lake walk, hayrides (on Sunday), and a movie set are among the numerous nonculinary diversions. It opens at 12:30 PM on weekends. ⊠*Exit 49 off I–10 (follow signs), Fabens* ☎*915/544–3200* ⚇*Reservations not accepted* ▤*AE, D, MC, V* ⊗*No lunch Mon.–Fri.*

¢–$

✕**Leo's.** The Mexican food at Leo's four El Paso locations is repeatedly voted a favorite by locals. Enchiladas, tacos, combination plates, and fluffy sopaipillas are served in helpings that will leave you stuffed—that is, if you can elbow your way through the crowds and get a table. ⊠*5103 Montana St.* ☎*915/566–4972* ⊠*5315 Hondo Pass* ☎*915/757–9025* ⊠*315 Mills Ave.* ☎*915/544–1001* ⊠*7520 Remcon Circle* ☎*915/833–1189* ▤*AE, D, MC, V.*

$$–$$$
★

✕**The Magic Pan.** The chefs at the Magic Pan dish up fusion cuisine, like Tex/Italian blend mesquite chicken penne. However, they also serve classy Asian standbys such as sesame-crusted ahi tuna and distinctly domestic selections like Angus rib eye. A strong Southwestern current underlies many of the dishes. Dine outside and take in the desert breeze. ⊠*5034 Doniphan, inside Placita Santa Fe* ☎*915/581–2121* ⊕*www.magicpanrestaurant.com* ⚇*Reservations required for dinner* ▤*AE, D, MC, V* ⊗*No lunch Tues.–Sun., no dinner Wed.–Sat.*

$-$$$ ✕**The State Line.** Named for its position on the border of El Paso and New Mexico, The State Line is a popular place with those who relish its tangy barbecue. The barbecued ribs and smoked chicken are fabulous here. Bring an appetite, because the trimmings include generous helpings of potato salad, coleslaw, and beans. Drinks are served in an outdoor courtyard, where you can wait for your table. ⊠*1222 Sunland Park Dr., Sunland Park exit off I–10* ☎*915/581–3371* ⌔*Reservations not accepted* ⊟*AE, D, DC, MC, V.*

WHERE TO STAY

$-$$ 🏨**Camino Real Hotel, El Paso.** The grande dame of downtown hotels, the stunner here is the enormous 1912 Tiffany-designed, stained-glass dome suspended above the bar. The rooms are large and airy, with marble-top desks and many antique furnishings. The Dome Restaurant ($$) offers fine dining, and brunch is popular at the more casual Azulejo (¢–$). It's in a fantastic location, across the street from the art museum and civic center, and 15 minutes from the airport. **Pros:** Refurbished and historic. **Cons:** Parking isn't free, Wi-Fi doesn't always work well from room (works in lobby though). ⊠*101 S. El Paso St.* ☎*915/534–3000 or 800/769–4300* ⊕*www.caminoreal.com/elpaso* ⮐*359 rooms* ⌂*In-hotel: 2 restaurants, room service, pool, gym, airport shuttle, parking (fee), some pets allowed (fee), public Wi-Fi, no-smoking rooms. In-room: Wi-Fi* ⊟*AE, D, DC, MC, V.*

$-$$
Fodor's Choice
★   🏨**Holiday Inn Sunland Park.** This Holiday Inn, on a hill with 6.5 acres near Sunland Park Racetrack, has outdoor courtyards; the Southwestern-style rooms have ironing boards, hair dryers, and coffeemakers. Breakfast buffets are served in the Sierra Grille Restaurant, and a Sunday brunch is available from 11 to 2. The service from the staff is attentive and noteworthy. **Pros:** There's a nice, well-maintained gym, and room service. **Cons:** Some rooms are on the small side. ⊠*900 Sunland Park Dr.* ☎*915/833–2900 or 800/658–2744* ⊕*www.holidayinn.com* ⮐*178 rooms* ⌂*In-room: dial-up. In-hotel: restaurant, bar, pool, no-smoking rooms* ⊟*AE, D, DC, MC, V.*

GUADALUPE MOUNTAINS NATIONAL PARK

Off U.S. 62/180, about 110 mi northeast of El Paso and 40 mi southwest of Carlsbad Caverns National Park.

Guadalupe Mountains National Park is a study in extremes: it has mountaintop forests but also rocky canyons; arid deserts and yet a stream that winds through verdant woods. The park is home to the Texas madrone tree, found commonly only here and in Big Bend National Park. Guadalupe Mountains National Park also has the distinction of hosting the loftiest spot in Texas: 8,749-foot Guadalupe Peak. The mountain dominates the view from every approach, but it's just one member of a rugged range carved by wind, water, and time.

More than 86,000 acres of mountains, canyons, woods, and desert house an incredible diversity of wildlife, including hallmark Southwestern species like roadrunners and long-limbed jackrabbits, who run so fast they appear to float on their enormous, black-tipped ears.

Park Contact Information ⓘ *Guadalupe Mountains National Park, HC 60, Box 400, Salt Flat, 79847* ☎*915/828–3251* ⊕*www.nps.gov/gumo* ✉*Gate admission, free; camping, $8 per site.*

12

WHAT TO SEE

HISTORIC SITES

☾ **Frijole Ranch Museum.** You'll find displays and photographs depicting ranch life and early park history inside this old ranch-house museum. Hiking trails are adjacent to the shady, tree-lined grounds. Some of the trails, which are easy to travel and great for kids, lead to the **Manzanita Spring.** ✉*Access road 1 mi northeast of Headquarters Visitors Center* ☎*915/828–3251* ✉*Free* ☾*Call for hours.*

★ **Pinery Bitterfield Stage Station Ruins.** In the mid-1800s passengers en route from St. Louis or San Francisco would stop for rest and refreshment this structure, one of the stops along the old Bitterfield Overland Mail stagecoach route. A paved ¾-mi round-trip trail leads here from the Headquarters Visitors Center, or you can drive directly here. ✉*½ mi east of Headquarters Visitors Center.*

SCENIC STOP

Fodor's Choice **McKittrick Canyon.** A desert creek flows through this canyon, which is
★ lined with walnut, maple, and other trees that explode into brilliant colors each fall. Call the visitor center to find out the progress of the colorful fall foliage; the spectacular changing of the leaves can often take until November, depending on the weather. You're likely to spot mule deer heading for the water here. ✉*4 mi off U.S. 62/180, about 7 mi northeast of Headquarters Visitor Center* ☾*Highway gate open Nov.–Apr., daily 8–4:30; May–Sept., daily 8–6.*

SPORTS & THE OUTDOORS

BIRD-WATCHING

More than 300 species of birds have been spotted in the park, including the ladder-backed woodpecker, Scott's oriole, Say's phoebe, and white-throated swift. Many non-native birds—such as fleeting humming birds and larger but less graceful turkey vultures—stop at Guadalupe during spring and fall migrations. **Manzanita Springs,** located near the Frijole Ranch Museum, is an excellent birding spot. Books on birding are available at the Pine Springs station; visitors might find the Natural History Association's birding checklist for Guadalupe Mountains National Park especially helpful. It will be easy to spot the larger birds of prey circling overhead, such as keen-beaked golden eagles and swift, red-tailed hawks. Be on the lookout for owls in the **Bowl** area, and watch for swift-footed roadrunners in the desert areas (they're quick, but not as speedy as their cartoon counterpart).

HIKING

No matter which trail you select, be sure to pack wisely—the park doesn't sell anything. This includes the recommended gallon of water per day per person, as well as sunscreen and hats. (Bring a five, too—that's the additional cost to use the trails, payable at the visitor centers.) The area has a triple-whammy as far as sun ailments are concerned: it's very open, very sunny, and has a high altitude (which makes sunburns more likely). Slather up. And be sure to leave Fido at home—few of the park's trails allow pets. For overnight backpacking trips, you must get a free permit from either the Headquarters Visitor Center (☎915/828–3251) or the **Dog Canyon Ranger Station** (☎505/981–2418).

EASY   The easiest McKittrick trail is the 1-mi **McKittrick Nature Loop.** Signs
☪   along the way explain the geological and biological history of the area.
Fodor's Choice   The trail is handicapped accessible and great for little ones. Plus, you
★   can see the canyon's signature foliage in the late fall.

MODERATE   **El Capitan/Salt Basin Overlook Trails** form a popular loop through the low
★   desert. El Capitan skirts the base of El Capitan peak for about 3.5 mi, leading to a junction with Salt Basin Overlook. The 4.5-mi Salt Basin Overlook trail begins at the Pine Springs trailhead and has views of the stark, white salt flat below and loops back onto the El Capitan Trail. Though moderate, the 11.3-mi round-trip is not recommended during the intense heat of summer, since there is absolutely no shade. ✉*Behind Headquarters Visitor Center at Pine Springs campground.*

☪   **Smith Spring Trail** departs from the Frijole Ranch trailhead. The trail, a round-trip walk of 2.2 mi, takes you through a shady oasis where you're likely to spot mule deer alongside a spring and a small waterfall. Allow 1½ hours to complete the walk. This is a good hike for older kids, whose legs won't tire as easily. ✉*Access road 1 mi northeast of Headquarters Visitors Center.*

DIFFICULT   Cutting through forests of pine and Douglas fir, **The Bowl** is considered
★   one of the most gorgeous trails in the park. The strenuous 9-mi round-trip—which can take up to 10 hours, depending on your pace—begins at the Pine Springs trailhead. This is where rangers go when they want to enjoy themselves. Don't forget to drink (and bring) lots of water!

ALPINE, MARFA & THE DAVIS MOUNTAINS

Nestled amid the plum and tan beauty of the Davis Mountains is a duo of cities increasingly known for their hipness as much as for their oddity. Originally ranching towns, Marfa and Alpine have held on to their deep Southwestern roots while getting a facelift from wealthy East Coasters who have established an incredibly influential arts foundation in the area and who continue to trickle in.

In Marfa the Chinati Foundation (founded by Donald Judd) attracts thousands of New Yorkers during its open house every year, creating a demand for book stores, coffee shops, art galleries, and bistros that wouldn't look out of place in Manhattan or Los Angeles. In nearby

Alpine there isn't quite as much urban foot traffic, but there are enough visitors to elicit fine Southwestern eateries. Historic Alpine is also a place that gubernatorial and senatorial hopefuls come to stump in. Maybe it's because their venue of choice—Railroad Blues—has to be one of the quirkiest and most laid-back bars you'll ever hope to find.

And when all that hipness starts to sizzle in the desert sun, you can quench your sizzling skin in the clear, cool spring water of Balmorhea State Park, about 40 mi south of Pecos on Highway 10.

ALPINE & MARFA

Marfa is about 200 mi southeast of El Paso; Alpine is about 80 mi north of Big Bend National Park.

WHAT TO SEE

Museum of the Big Bend. This West Texas haven for art lovers and cowboy poets is under renovation and expansion, but it remains open, with 5,000 feet of space holding exhibits on cowboys and conquistadors. There's also an annual show of ranching handiwork (like saddles, reins, and spurs) held in conjunction with the Cowboy Poetry Gathering each February. ⊠ *Sul Ross State University Campus, just off the westbound lane of Holland Avenue, the city's (two-way) main drag. Alpine* ☎ *432/837–8143* ⊕ *www.sulross.edu/~museum* ☜ *Donations accepted* ☉ *Tues.–Sat. 9–5, Sun. 1–5.*

NIGHTLIFE & THE ARTS

Fodor'sChoice ★ Young, hip, modern, and undeniably cool, the **Ballroom Marfa** (⊠ *198 E. San Antonio St., Marfa* ☎ *432/729–3600.* ⊕ *www.ballroommarfa.org* ☜ *$5, sometimes more for certain events* ☉ *Thurs.–Sun. noon–6 (later when there's a live performance)* is part gallery, part performance-art and live-music venue. The **Chinati Foundation** (⌂ *Box 1135, Marfa* ☎ *432/729–4362* ⊕ *www.chinati.org* ☜ *$10* ☉ *By guided tour only, Wed.–Sun. at 10 AM and 2 PM)* changes its exhibits regularly. People fly from all over the country to see the collection, and the foundation conducts tours of its huge contemporary-art holdings by appointment. Getting to the museum is tricky; get directions by phone or online.

Fodor'sChoice ★ **Railroad Blues** (⊠ *504 W. Holland Ave., Alpine* ☎ *432/837–3103* ⊕ *www.railroadblues.com*), a cozy wooden bar thick with atmosphere and Texas music, is home to live music artists, kooky characters, and live, spontaneous dancing. Watch couples two-step and see if you can pick up the moves. Acts generally go on at 10 PM on weekends.

FORT DAVIS AREA

24 mi south of Alpine.

WHAT TO SEE

☺ ★ **McDonald Observatory Visitors Center.** There's plenty to do here: check out exhibits, examine sunspots and flares safely via video or peer into the research telescopes. After nightfall, the observatory offers "star parties." Kids get a discount on admission. ⊠ *Hwy. 118 north through*

Seeing the Lights

Nobody knows what they are. Nobody knows where they came from. And, to many's frustration, nobody knows when they'll appear.

There are folks who have lived in the 2,100-soul town of Marfa all their lives and never once seen the famous Marfa lights. Meanwhile, some visitors have happened upon the spectacle their very first night in town.

Those who have seen the lights all share similar accounts. They're balls that glimmer and glow along the horizon or on mountainsides. They float and they grow and they shrink, seeming almost to breathe. They split apart and merge together. And they change colors many times before disappearing into wherever it is they've come from.

Though the lights have been here for hundreds of years, scientists have yet to offer a viable explanation for what causes the ghostly lights. They've proffered ideas such as swamp gas, moonlight on minerals in the earth, or atmospheric conditions that play on the eye. Marfa residents have long ceased to care, however; they'd rather just enjoy the mystery and continue to celebrate it annually with their well-attended Marfa Lights Festival (☎432/729–4942 or 800/650–9696, www.marfacc.com/marfa_lights.htm), which is during Labor Day weekend.

Alpine and Fort Davis, Fort Davis ☎432/426–3540 ⊕www.mcdonald observatory.org ☑$8 ($10 for star party).

Fort Davis National Historic Site. Tucked snug in the Davis Mountains, Fort Davis is regarded as one of the best surviving examples of Old West frontier posts. Troops were garrisoned here to protect travelers and mail coaches from American Indian depredations. ⊠*Off Hwy. 118, Fort Davis ☎432/426–3224, Ext. 20 ⊕www.nps.gov/foda ☉Daily 8–5 ☑$3 for a 7-day pass.*

SPORTS & THE OUTDOORS

Balmorhea State Park. Slide out of the broiling sun and into the waters of Solomon Spring in this paved artesian pool. The park, just outside Balmorhea, is open seven days a week year-round, 8 AM to sunset (and later for pre-arranged night-scuba diving). ⌂*Box 15, Toyahvale79786 ☎432/375–2370 ☑$5 Oct.–Apr.; $7 May–Sept.*

EN ROUTE
As you travel from the Davis Mountains north toward Odessa, you pass by the small town of Pecos, at the intersection of Highway 17 and I–20, about 75 mi north of Fort Davis. The highlight here is **The West of the Pecos Rodeo** (⊠*Exit 42 off I–20, Pecos ☎Chamber of commerce, 800/588–2855 ⊕www.pecosrodeo.com ☑$12.50 in advance, $15 at the door*), held in late July each year, features rodeo events, then post-rodeo all-night dancing to country and Tejano music. Rodeo events take place throughout town, but the main event is conducted at Buck Jackson Rodeo Arena.

MIDLAND-ODESSA

284 mi east of El Paso via I–10 and I–20, and 76 mi east of Pecos via I–20, and 350 mi west of Fort Worth via I—20.

The oil crazy city of Midland during the '80s could well have been the setting for TV's "Dallas." Many of its surrounding fields are lined with pumpjacks, iron devices that resemble sipping-bird toys as they pull the oil from the earth. Midland is considered the hometown of the Bush family, who frequently come back to visit. Often grouped with Midland as a sort of West Texas metroplex (albeit on a much smaller scale than the Big D metroplex), the football-manic city of Odessa lies just 20 mi west of Midland. It is the origin of the *Friday Night Lights* book and movie, and the hometown of the "Heroes" TV show cheerleader character Claire Bennet. Texas native Tommy Lee Jones often comes to West Texas to film his epics about life along the border.

Both cities have a lot to offer in terms of theater, museums, shopping, and culture—from rodeos and barn dances to lively Mexican events like the Ballet Folklorico, Fiesta West Texas, Cinco de Mayo, and Diez y Seis de Septiembre, as well as mariachi competitions.

WHAT TO SEE

Bush Childhood Home. In 1948 George H. W. and Barbara Bush moved with two-year-old George W. to Odessa, Texas. They lived there for a brief spell, moved to California briefly, and then returned to Texas, only this time settling in Midland. Though they lived in several homes, this one, measuring 1,655 square feet and inhabited in 1951, is one of the area's best-preserved. Daily tours are offered. Hear and read interpretive information such as interviews culled from childhood friends of the Bushes, and view photo exhibits and original furnishings in the home's museum. ✉*1412 W. Ohio Ave., Midland* ☎*866/684–4380* ⊕*www.bushchildhoodhome.org* ✉*Donations accepted* ۞*Tues.–Sat. 10–5, Sun. 2–5; tour times vary.*

Petroleum Museum. The 60,000 square feet of this multistage museum make for a pleasant afternoon viewing murals of early oil-field life, taking in an explanation of the origins of the vast oil reserves in West Texas, and enjoying lots of award-winning artwork. The cherry on top: the Chapparal cars—the cutting edge, mostly1960s racers that were named after the fleet bird commonly known as the roadrunner. One of the models on display won the Indy 500 in 1980. ✉*1500 I–20 W, Midland* ☎*432/683–4403* ⊕*www.petroleummuseum.org* ✉*$8* ۞*Mon.–Sat. 10–5, Sun. 2–5.*

Meteor Crater and Museum. Yeah, it's a hole in the ground. But it's a *HUGE* hole in the ground—the second-largest impact crater in the United States and the sixth-largest meteor crater in the world. Tours of the crater are self-guided; a museum about the attraction is also on-site. ✉*Exit 108 off I–20/3100 Meteor Crater Rd., Odessa* ☎*432/381– 0946* ✉*Donations accepted* ۞*Daily 9–6 (crater); Mon.–Sat. 10–5, Sun. 1–5 (museum).*

Friday Night Lights: Football as Religion

There are two main ways to socialize in the Panhandle. No, make that three. There's church. There's football. Then there's the church of football—one faith in these parts on which most everyone can agree.

That's a bit of a stereotype, agreed, but one reinforced with glee throughout the small towns and large cities of Texas. Fall's a time of great expectation, and not just because of the changing of the leaves or the cooling of the sizzle. Let the season begin! Parents of players or parents who know the parents of high-school and college football players often schedule their weekends around attending the game. Texans are staunchly patriotic, and are wholeheartedly devoted to their state, their hometowns, and their families. Attending the game is a way for them to show support for all four.

In this part of the world high-school football is as important as NFL, and college football is pretty up there,

too. Little Joey playing first string or the Cowboys' Tony Romo getting distracted by his girlfriend is equally big news. Sportswriters are assigned exclusively to cover high-school football games, and journalists from all over the state will travel to attend the state finals if their team is in them; so will families and supporters.

Football can also be political. As in other places, mayoral hopefuls and those running for office know the games are a good time to network, but it goes beyond that. Rooting for an NFL team from "up north" that's playing a Texas team seems disrespectful somehow. And tensions arise between family members rooting for, say, the Texas Tech Red Raiders over the University of Texas Longhorns (That liberal city! It isn't even *part* of Texas!).

But in the end, it's all in good fun, and Texans will good-naturedly make fun of their football obsession. Just don't block the view.

NIGHTLIFE

Dos Amigos Cantina. A combination rodeo ring and rock-'n-roll stage, Dos Amigos is the place to go for outdoor and indoor concerts, a Bud, and some interesting local action. The area's strategic location along the long stretch from Dallas to El Paso helps it net a wide range of performers, on the road to larger cities, including Morrissey, Deftones, Chevelle, and other popular acts. It also hosts a lot of Texas country-and-western artists and indy artists still on the make. ⊠*4700 Golder Ave., Odessa* ☎*432/368–7556* ⊕*www.dosamigoscantina.com* ⊠*Concert prices vary; no cover on non-music nights.*

The Ranch. The Ranch is in many ways Dos Amigos's Midland counterpart, except that the fare on its stage is almost always cowboy hat–wearing country artists—and some of the best in Texas at that. Drinks are also cheaper here, and make for a nice accompaniment to a nice, authentic Texan ballad. ⊠*4400 N. Big Spring St., Midland* ☎*432/620–0114* ⊕*www.theranchmidland.com* ⊠*Concert prices vary; no cover on non-music nights.*

WHERE TO EAT

¢–$$ ✕**Doña Anita's.** Despite the plain decor, the cooks serve fantastic, homey
Fodor's Choice food. It's said that this is a favorite eatery when the Bush family's in
★ town. Maybe that's because there are a ton of Tex-Mex faves on the
menu, from fajitas to flautas, and even the waitresses complain about
getting plump from trying them all. ✉*305 W. Florida Ave., Midland*
☎*432/683–6727* ✆*No dinner Sun.* ▭*AE, D, MC, V.*

¢–$ ✕**Delicias.** Delicias is, in a word, delicious. Period. Every dish, from the
★ *menudo* (that quintessential, spicy Mexican stew made with beef tripe
and hominy) to fajitas, is well prepared and maybe just a little deli-
ciously greasy. Locals, including native and first-generation Mexican
families, fill up the restaurant at lunch and dinner. ✉*716 W. 8th St.,
Odessa* ✆*Closed Sun.* ☎*432/580–8306* ▭*D, MC, V.*

SAN ANGELO

112 mi southeast of Midland.

In the late 1800s the all-black regiments known respectfully by Ameri-
can Indians as the Buffalo Soldiers kept travelers and settlers in West
Texas safe from attack by hostile Indian tribes. The protection they
provided from Fort Concho was effective enough that a rowdy town
sprang up on the opposite bank of the Concho River. In those days,
the frontier town that would later become San Angelo was known for
prostitution, gambling, and illicit revelry in general.

Immortalized in gunslinger ballads and given nods in Old West novels,
the town has grown up. These days the fort has become a historic land-
mark and the town is home to a university, Angelo State, a beautiful
fine arts museum, a bordello museum, and fun little shops along the
Concho River. It also has some hidden gems, like the artists' commune
known as the Chicken Farm and a colony of Mexican free-tail bats that
fly in clouds from the Foster Road Bridge. It's also known for native
sons Los Lonely Boys, who snagged a Grammy in 2005.

WHAT TO SEE

Fort Concho National Historic Landmark. An important frontier post, Fort
Concho protected settlers and travelers in West Texas from hostile
American Indian tribes. It was also home to the Buffalo Soldiers until
it was decommissioned in 1889 after decades of service. The museum
preserves many of the fort's original 28 buildings, which face each
other in a square shape. ✉*630 S. Oakes St.* ☎*325/657–4444* ⊕*www.
fortconcho.com* ✆*$3 (self-guided tour), $5 (guided tour)* ✆*Mon.–Sat.
9–5, Sun. 1–5 (museum), Mon.–Fri. 8–5 (trading post).*

OFF THE BEATEN PATH
In a state peppered with caverns, limestone caves, and sinkholes, many
remain undiscovered, others are still being explored. Many of them,
particularly those open to the public, contain rock twisted by water
into beautiful shapes and eerily lifelike clusters of forms that can resem-
ble faces, mushrooms, waves, or—in the case of the **Caverns of Sonora**—
a beautiful and diaphanous butterfly. It's partly for this reason that
many consider these caverns the most beautiful in the world. In fact,

the founder of the National Speleological Society has quipped that its beauty can't be exaggerated, "not even by a Texan." Guides conduct a nearly two-hour-long tour, as well as special classes for kids that feature real fossil digs. The caverns are located 10 mi outside of Sonora.

OFF THE BEATEN PATH

Fodor's Choice ★ **Alamo Village**—It's not possible to run out of activities on this huge, historic movie set surrounded by miles of ranch. There's a museum commemorating John Wayne, who filmed *The Alamo* here in 1959, and the goings-on for guests include horse races, gunfighter skits, and an Indian museum flush with artifacts. ✉ *7 mi north of Brackettville on Hwy. 674, Brackettville* ☎ *325/653–4936* ⊕ *www.thealamovillage.homestead.com/alamovillage.html* ⛁ *$10.75* ⊙ *Daily 9–6.*

WEST TEXAS ESSENTIALS

Research prices, get travel advice, and book your trip at fodors.com.

TRANSPORTATION

BY AIR

The El Paso and Midland airports keep West Texas serviced and hopping. Most of the major airlines fly to the El Paso Airport, 7 mi from downtown. The petite but busy Midland Airport is served by Southwest, American Eagle, and Continental Express. Continental has thrice daily flights between Del Rio and Houston.

Contacts **Del Rio International Airport** (✉ *1104 W. 10th St., Del Rio* ☎ *830/774–8538*). **El Paso International Airport** (✉ *6701 Convair Rd., El Paso* ☎ *915/780–4749* ⊕ *www.elpasointernationalairport.com*). **Midland International Airport** (✉ *9506 LaForce Blvd., Midland* ☎ *432/560–2200* ⊕ *www.flymaf.com*).

BY BUS & TRAIN

Greyhound Lines (☎ *800/231–2222* ⊕ *www.greyhound.com*) connects Alpine, El Paso, Marfa, Midland, Odessa, and Pecos. **Amtrak** (☎ *800/872–7245* ⊕ *www.amtrak.com*) stops in Del Rio, Sanderson, Alpine, and El Paso.

CONTACTS & RESOURCES

EMERGENCIES

In an emergency, dial 911 (from Mexico dial 066).

VISITOR INFORMATION

Alpine Chamber of Commerce (✉ *106 N. 3rd St., Alpine* ☎ *800/561–3735 or 432/837–2326* ⊕ *www.alpinetexas.com*). **El Paso Convention and Visitors Bureau** (✉ *1 Civic Center Plaza, El Paso* ☎ *915/534–0601 or 800/351–6024* ⊕ *www.elpasocvb.com*). **Marfa Chamber of Commerce** (✉ *207 N. Highland St., Marfa* ☎ *800/650–9696* ⊕ *www.marfacc.com*). **Midland Chamber of Commerce** (✉ *109 N. Main St., Midland* ☎ *800/624–6435* ⊕ *www.midlandtxchamber.com*). **Odessa Convention and Visitors Bureau** (✉ *700 N. Grant St., Ste. 200, Odessa* ☎ *800/780–4678* ⊕ *www.odessacvb.com*). **San Angelo Chamber of Commerce** (✉ *418 W. Ave. B, San Angelo* ☎ *325/655–4136* ⊕ *www.sanangelo.org*).

Big Bend National Park

Cradled in the warm, southwestern elbow of Texas, the 801,163 acres of Big Bend National Park hang suspended above the deserts of northern Mexico. From the craggy, bald Chisos Mountains rising up to 8,000 feet to the flat and stark plains of the Chihuahua Desert, Big Bend is one of the nation's most geographically diverse parks, with the kind of territory that inspired Hollywood's first Western sets. Visitors can ride the rapids of the Rio Grande, trek through the classic, Old West landscape, and marvel at the moonscape that skirts Boquillas, Mexico.

WELCOME TO BIG BEND

TOP REASONS TO GO

★ **Varied Terrain:** Visit gilded desert, a fabled river, bird-filled woods, and mountain spirals all in the same day.

★ **Wonderful Wildlife:** Catch sight of the park's extremely diverse number of animals, including several dozen shy mountain lions and about the same number of lumbering bears.

★ **Bird-watching:** Spy a pied-billed grebe or another member of the park's more than 400 bird species, including the Lucifer hummingbird and the unique-to-this-area pato Mexicano (Mexican duck).

★ **Hot spots:** Dip into the natural hot springs (105°F) near Rio Grande Village.

★ **Mile-high Mountains:** Lace up those hiking boots and climb the Chisos Mountains, reaching 8,000 feet skyward in some places and remaining cool even during the most scorching Southern summer.

1 North Rosillos. Dinosaur fossils have been found in this remote, northern portion of the park. Made up primarily of back roads, this is where nomadic warriors traveled into Mexico via the Comanche Trail.

2 Chisos Basin. This bowl-shaped canyon amid the Chisos Mountains is at the heart of Big Bend. It's the place to watch a sunset and begin a hike.

3 Castolon. Just east of Santa Elena Canyon, this historic district was once used by ranchers and the U.S. military, earning it a place on the National Register of Historic Places.

4 Rio Grande Village. Tall, shady cottonwoods highlight the park's eastern entrance along the Mexican border and Rio Grande. It's popular with RVers and bird-watchers.

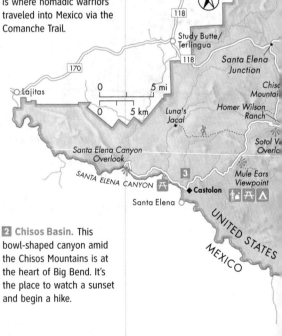

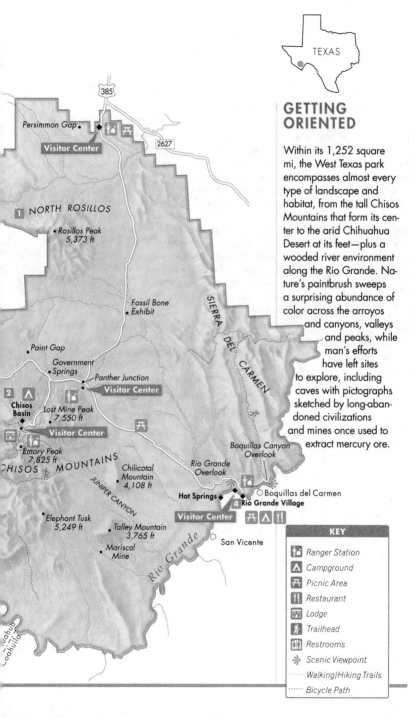

12

BIG BEND NATIONAL PARK

TEXAS

GETTING ORIENTED

Within its 1,252 square mi, the West Texas park encompasses almost every type of landscape and habitat, from the tall Chisos Mountains that form its center to the arid Chihuahua Desert at its feet—plus a wooded river environment along the Rio Grande. Nature's paintbrush sweeps a surprising abundance of color across the arroyos and canyons, valleys and peaks, while man's efforts have left sites to explore, including caves with pictographs sketched by long-abandoned civilizations and mines once used to extract mercury ore.

Persimmon Gap
Visitor Center
385
2627

1 NORTH ROSILLOS
Rosillos Peak
5,373 ft

SIERRA DEL CARMEN

Fossil Bone
Exhibit

Paint Gap
Government
Springs
Panther Junction
Visitor Center

2 Chisos
Basin
Lost Mine Peak
7,550 ft
Visitor Center

Emory Peak
7,825 ft
CHISOS MOUNTAINS
Chilicotal
Mountain
4,108 ft

JUNIPER CANYON

Boquillas Canyon
Overlook

Rio Grande
Overlook

Hot Springs
4 Rio Grande Village
Boquillas del Carmen
Visitor Center

Elephant Tusk
5,249 ft
Talley Mountain
3,765 ft
Mariscal
Mine
San Vicente

Rio Grande

Chihuahua
Coahuila

KEY	
🚻	Ranger Station
△	Campground
⊼	Picnic Area
🍴	Restaurant
▨	Lodge
🚶	Trailhead
🚻	Restrooms
⋟	Scenic Viewpoint
······	Walking/Hiking Trails
······	Bicycle Path

BIG BEND PLANNER

When to Go

There is never a bad time to make a Big Bend foray—except during Thanksgiving, Christmas, and Spring Break. During these holidays, competition for rooms at the Chisos Mountain Lodge and campsites is fierce—with reservations for campsites and rooms needed up to a year in advance.

Depending on the season, Big Bend sizzles or drizzles, steams up collars or chills fingertips. Many shun the park in the summer, because temperatures skyrocket (up to 120°F in some areas), and the Rio Grande dips.

In winter, temperatures rarely dip below 30°F. During those few times the mercury takes a dive, visitors might be rewarded with a rare snowfall.

Temperatures vary throughout the park, the mountains routinely 5–10 degrees cooler than the rest of the park, and the sweltering stretches of Rio Grande 5–10 degrees warmer.

AVG. HIGH/LOW TEMPS

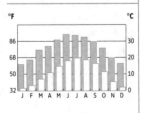

Flora & Fauna

Because Big Bend contains habitats as diverse as spent volcanoes, slick-sided canyons, and the Rio Grande, it follows that species here are extremely diverse, too. Among the park's most notable residents are endangered species like the agave cactus–eating Mexican long-nosed bat, shadow-dappled peregrine falcon, and fat-bellied horned lizard. More than 400 species of birds wing throughout the park, including the black-capped vireo and the turkey vulture, which boasts a 6-foot wingspan. In the highlands several dozen mountain lions lurk, while black bears loll in the crags and valleys. Your chances of spotting the reclusive creatures are rare, though greater in the early morning. If you do encounter either, stand tall, shout, and look as scary as possible.

Supremely adapted to the arroyos, valleys, and slopes, the plants range from the brightly colored hedgehog cactus (found only in the Chisos) to the towering rasp of the giant dagger yucca. Also here are 65 types of cacti—so watch where you tread.

Getting There & Around

Big Bend is 39 mi south of Marathon, off U.S. 385; 76 mi south of Alpine, off Route 118; and 50 mi east of Presidio, off Route 170. The nearest airport is in Midland, 3½ hours north of the park. The bus takes you as far as Marathon, and the train as far as Alpine.

Paved park roads have twists and turns, some very extreme in higher elevations. Four-wheel-drive vehicles are needed for many of the backcountry roads. At parking areas take valuables with you.

SCENIC DRIVES

★ **Chisos Basin Road.** Panoramic vistas, a restaurant with an up-close view of the mountains, and glimpses of the Colima warbler (found only in Big Bend) await in the forested Chisos Basin. On the drive up, you're likely to spot lions and bears as well as white-tailed deer amid juniper trees and pinyon pines. Due to the road's sharp curves, avoid this drive if you're in an RV longer than 24 feet. ⊠ *South from Chisos Basin Junction, 7 mi southwest of Chisos Basin Junction and 9 mi southwest of Panther Junction.*

Fodor'sChoice **Ross Maxwell Scenic Drive.** This route takes you 30 mi through pyramid-
★ shaped volcanic mountains. If you don't mind a little grate in your gait from the gravel that blankets the road, you can make this drive a loop by starting out at the west park entrance and turning southwest onto Old Maverick Road (unpaved) for 12.8 mi to the Santa Elena Canyon overlook—where you can get a taste of the lowland desert. (*Note: If you're in an RV, don't even attempt Old Maverick Road. The road isn't paved and is rough going in some spots.*)

SCENIC STOPS

★ **Chisos Basin.** Panoramic vistas, a restaurant with an up-close view of the mountains, and glimpses of the Colima warbler (found only in Big Bend) await in the forested Chisos Basin. This central site also has hiking trails, a lodge, a campground, a grocery store, and a gift shop. ⊠ *Off Chisos Basin Rd., 7 mi southwest of Chisos Basin Junction and 9 mi southwest of Panther Junction.*

Rio Grande Village. Don't be fooled by the name—there's no real village here. There is, however, a campground, RV park, and amphitheater, as well as a boat launch on the Rio Grande. A grove of giant cottonwood trees alongside the river makes for cooling shadows in this hot, southern area of the park, and the grassy picnic area is highly recommended for birders. A visitor center (with a small bookstore), gasoline, and groceries are available. Note: this area is closed during summer's leaf-curling heat. ⊠ *22 mi southeast of Panther Junction.*

★ **Santa Elena Canyon.** The finale of a short hike (1.7 mi round-trip), is a spectacular view of the Rio Grande and cliffs that rise 1,500 feet to create a natural box. ⊠ *30 mi southwest of Santa Elena Junction via Ross Maxwell Scenic Dr.; 14 mi southwest of Rte. 118 via Old Maverick Rd.*

VISITOR CENTERS

Castolon Visitor Center. Here you'll find some of the most hands-on exhibits the park has to offer, with touchable fossils, plants, and implements used by the farmers and miners who settled here in the 1800s and early 1900s. ⊠ *In the Castolon Historic District, southwest side of the park, at the end of the Ross Maxwell Scenic Dr.* ☎ *432/477–2271* ⊙ *Nov.–May, daily 10–noon and 1–5.*

Fodor'sChoice **Chisos Basin Visitor Center.** The center is one of the bettter-equipped, as
★ it offers an interactive computer exhibit, a bookstore, camping supplies, picnic fare, and some produce. There are plenty of nods to the

wild, with natural resource and geology exhibits and a larger-than-life representation of a mountain lion. ✉ *Off Chisos Basin Rd., 7 mi southwest of Chisos Basin Junction and 9 mi southwest of Panther Junction* 🕾 *432/477–2264* 🕾 *Nov.–Mar., daily 9–3:30, closed for lunch; Apr.–Oct., daily 9 AM–4:30 PM, closed for lunch.*

Panther Junction Visitor Center. At this writing, the park's main visitor center was undergoing renovations; however, the center will remain open throughout the construction. Planned improvements include an enlarged bookstore and new, touchable exhibits on the park's mountain, river, and desert environments. Nearby, a gas station offers limited groceries such as chips, premade sandwiches, and picnic items. ✉ *30 mi south of U.S. 385 junction leading to north park boundary* 🕾 *432/477–1158* 🕾 *Daily 8–6.*

Persimmon Gap Visitor Center. Complete with exhibits and a bookstore, this visitor center is the northern boundary gateway into miles of flatlands that surround the more scenic heart of Big Bend. Dinosaur fossils have been found here; none are on display in the center, but the **Fossil Bone Exhibit** is located on the road between Persimmon Gap and Panther Junction. ✉ *3 mi south of U.S. 385 junction* 🕾 *432/477–2393* 🕾 *Daily 9–4:30, closed for lunch.*

Rio Grande Village Visitor Center. Opening days and hours are sporadic here, but if you do find this center open, then view videos of Big Bend's geological and natural features at its minitheater. There are also exhibits dealing with the Rio Grande. ✉ *22 mi southeast of Panther Junction* 🕾 *432/477–2271* 🕾 *Daily 8:30–4. Closed May through Oct.*

SPORTS & THE OUTDOORS

BIRD-WATCHING

Situated on north–south migratory pathways, Big Bend is home to at least 434 different species of birds—more than any other national park. In fact, the birds that flit, waddle, soar, and swim in the park represent more than half the bird species found in North America, including the Colima warbler, found nowhere else. To glimpse darting hummingbirds, turkey vultures, and golden eagles, look to the Chisos Mountains. To spy woodpeckers, scaled quail (distinctive for dangling crests), and the famous Colima, look to the desert scrub. And for cuckoos, cardinals, and screech owls, you must prowl along the river.

BOATING & RAFTING

The 118 mi of the Rio Grande that border the park form its backbone, defining the vegetation, landforms, and animals found at the park's southern rim. By turns shallow and deep, the river flows through stunning canyons and picks up speed over small and large rapids. Most outfitters, renting rafts, canoes, and kayaks, are in the communities of Study Butte, Terlingua, and Lajitas just west of the park boundary, off Route 170.

MULTISPORT OUTFITTERS

Big Bend River Tours. Tours that explore the Rio Grande include rafting, canoeing, and hiking and horseback trips combined with a river float. Rafting tours include gourmet or music themes. ✍️ *Box 317, Terlingua 79852* ☎ *800/545–4240* ⊕ *www.bigbendrivertours.com.*

Desert Sports. From rentals—mountain bikes, boats, rafts, and inflatable kayaks—to experienced guides for mountain-bike touring, boating, and hiking, this outfitter has it covered. ✍️ *Box 448, Terlingua 79852* ☎ *432/371–2727 or 888/989–6900* ⊕ *www.desertsportstx.com.*

Far Flung Outdoor Center. Call these pros for personalized trips via rafts and 4x4s. Tailored trips include gourmet rafting tours with cheese and wine served on checkered tablecloths alongside the river, and sometimes spectacular star-viewing at night. ✍️ *Box 377, Terlingua 79852* ☎ *800/839–7238* ⊕ *www. farflungoutdoorcenter.com.*

Red Rock Outfitters. This outfitter sells gear and leads rafting, canoeing, horseback-riding, and mountain-biking excursions, plus Jeep and ATV tours. ✍️ *HC 70 Box 400, Lajitas 79852* ☎ *432/424–5170.*

HIKING

EASY **Chihuahuan Desert Nature Trail.** A windmill and spring form a desert oasis, a refreshing backdrop to a ½-mi, hot and flat nature trail; wild doves are abundant, the hike is pleasant, and kids will do just fine. Keep an eye out for the elf owl, one of the sought-after birds on the park's "Top 10" list. ✉ *Dugout Wells, 5 mi southeast of Panther Junction.*

Rio Grande Village Nature Trail. This ¾-mi trail is short and easy yet packs a powerful wildlife punch. The village is considered one of the best spots in the park to see rare birds, and the variety of other wildlife isn't in short supply either. Keep a lookout for coyotes, javelinas (they look like wild pigs), and other mammals. Although this is a good trail for kids to lay their tootsies on, it isn't the most remote, so expect higher traffic. Restrooms (open year-round) are nearby, and the trail can be done in less than an hour, even when lingering. The first ¼ mi is wheelchair accessible. ✉ *22 mi southeast of Panther Junction.*

MODERATE **The Lost Mine Trail.** Set aside about two hours to leisurely explore the nature of the Chisos Mountains along this elevation-climbing 4.8 mi round-trip trail. It starts at 5,400 feet, one of the highest elevations in the park, and climbs to an even higher vantage point. Though the air is thinner, all but the smallest kids should enjoy this trail because of the sweeping cliff view at the end of the first mile. ✉ *Begin at mile marker 5 on the Basin Rd.*

DIFFICULT **Chisos Basin Loop Trail.** A forested area and higher elevations give you some sweeping views of the lower desert and distant volcanic mountains on this 1.6-mi round-trip hike. The elevation in the pass where the trail begins is 5,400 feet; the highest point on the trail is 7,825 feet. What makes this trail difficult is not the length, but the climb. Set aside about an hour. ✉ *7 mi southwest of Chisos Basin Junction.*

Fodor'sChoice **Santa Elena Canyon Trail.** This moderate-to-difficult trail is worth every
★ bead of sweat. The finale of the 1.7-mi round-trip, which crosses Terlingua Creek, is a spectacular view of the Rio Grande and cliffs that
rise 1,500 feet to create a natural box. Try to end up there near sunset,
when the dying sun stains the cliffs a rich red-brown chestnut—its
beauty can inspire poetry. ⊠ *8 mi west of Castolon, accessible via Ross
Maxwell Scenic Dr. or Old Maverick Rd.*

WHERE TO EAT & STAY

You can reserve a spot at the park's four developed sites from November 15 to April 15 ($14 per night); sites are first-come, first-served dur-
ing the off season. Make reservations at ☎877/444–6777 or ⊕*www.
reserveusa.com.* Pick up a free permit if you're camping at the park's
primitive backcountry sites.

$$ ☷**Chisos Mountains Lodge.** Views of desert peaks and staying in the
Ⓒ cooler, forested section of Big Bend's higher elevations more than make
up for the spartan rooms. With ranger talks just next door at the visi-
tor center, miles of easy hiking paths, and plenty of wildlife, this is a
great place for kids. Make advance reservations during busy times,
such as Thanksgiving and Spring Break. Guests can rent a TV/VCR
and movies. At its restaurant (¢–$$), views of the imposing Chisos
Mountains are a pleasant accompaniment to nicely prepared (but not
fancy) fare such as chicken-fried steak and hamburgers. ⊠ *7 mi southwest of Chisos Basin Junction and 9 mi southwest of Panther Junction*
☎*432/477–2291* ⌂*72 rooms* ⌂ *In-room: no phone, no TV. In-hotel:
restaurant, some pets allowed, no-smoking rooms* ☰*AE, D, DC, MC,
V. $100–$120 per night for double occupancy.*

BIG BEND ESSENTIALS

ACCESSIBILITY
Visitor centers and some campsites and restrooms at Rio Grande Village
and Chisos Basin are wheelchair accessible. A TDD line (☎432/477–
2370) is available at park headquarters at Panther Junction Visitor
Center. Wheelchair-accessible hiking trails include the Founder's Walk
and Panther Path at Panther Junction; Window View Trail at Chisos Basin; and Rio Grande Village Nature Trail boardwalk. The Rio
Grande and Chisos Basin amphitheaters also are accessible.

ADMISSION FEE
The $20 gate fee covers you for seven consecutive days.

EMERGENCIES
Dial 911 or 432/477–1188. Medical services are just outside the park
in tiny communities along Route 170.

VISITOR INFORMATION
Contacts Big Bend National Park ⌂ *Box 129, Big Bend National Park, 79834*
☎*432/477–2251* ⊕ *www.nps.gov/bibe.*

Carlsbad Caverns National Park

On the surface, Carlsbad Caverns National Park is deceptively normal—but all bets are off once visitors set foot in the elevator, which plunges 75 stories underground. The country beneath the surface is part silky darkness, part subterranean hallucination. The snaky, illuminated walkway seems less like a trail and more like a foray across the river Styx and into the Underworld. Within more than 14 football fields of subterranean space are hundreds of formations that alternately resemble cakes, soda straws, ocean waves, and the large, leering face of a mountain troll.

WELCOME TO CARLSBAD CAVERNS

TOP REASONS TO GO

★ **300,000 hungry bats:** Every night and every day, bats wing to and from the caverns in a swirling, visible tornado.

★ **Take a guided tour through the underworld:** Plummet 75 stories underground, and step into enormous caves hung with stalactites and bristling with stalagmites.

★ **Living Desert Zoo and Gardens:** More preserve than zoo, this 1,500-acre park houses scores of rare species, including endangered Mexican wolves and Bolson tortoises, and now boasts a new black bear exhibit.

★ **Birding at Rattlesnake Springs:** Nine-tenths of the park's 330 bird species, including roadrunners, golden eagles, and acrobatic cave swallows, visit this green desert oasis.

★ **Pecos River:** The Pecos River, a Southwest landmark, flows through the nearby town of Carlsbad. The river is always soothing, but gets festive for holiday floaters when riverside homeowners lavishly decorate their homes.

1 Bat Flight. Cowboy Jim White discovered the caverns after noticing that a swirling smokestack of bats appeared there each morning and evening. White is long gone, but the 300,000-member bat colony is still here, snatching up 3 tons of bugs a night. Watch them leave at dusk from the amphitheater located near the park visitor center.

2 Carlsbad Caverns Big Room Tour. Travel 75 stories below the surface to visit the Big Room, where you can traipse beneath a 255-foot-tall ceiling and take in immense and eerie cave formations. Situated directly beneath the park visitor center, the room can be accessed via quick-moving elevator or the natural cave entrance.

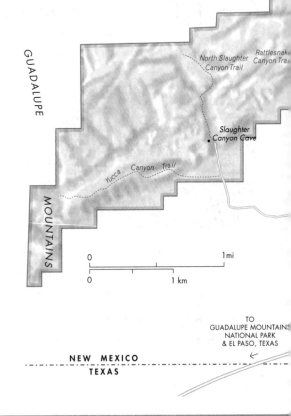

GUADALUPE

MOUNTAINS

North Slaughter Canyon Trail

Rattlesnake Canyon Tra.

Slaughter Canyon Cave

Yucca Canyon Trail

0   1 mi
0   1 km

TO GUADALUPE MOUNTAINS NATIONAL PARK & EL PASO, TEXAS

NEW MEXICO
TEXAS

3 Living Desert Zoo and Gardens. Endangered river cooters, Bolson tortoises, and Mexican wolves all roam in the Living Desert Zoo and Gardens. You can also skip alongside roadrunners and slim wild turkeys in the park's aviary, or visit a small group of cougars. The Living Desert is located within the town of Carlsbad, New Mexico, 23 mi to the north of the park.

4 The Pecos River. In the town of Carlsbad, a river runs through it—the Pecos River, that is. The river, a landmark of the Southwest, skims through town and makes for excellent boating, waterskiing, and fishing in some places. In the winter, residents gussy up dozens of riverside homes for the holiday season.

12

CARLSBAD CAVERNS NATIONAL PARK

GETTING ORIENTED

To get at the essence of Carlsbad Caverns National Park, you have to delve below the surface— literally. Most of the park's key sights are underground in a massive network of caves (there are 113 in all, although not all are open to visitors; a variety of tours leave from the visitor center). The park also has a handful of trails above ground, where you can experience the Chihuahua Desert and some magnificent geological formations.

Walnut Canyon Desert Dr.

2 • Cavern Entrance

Visitor Center 1

Whites City

TO CARLSBAD ↗
3 4

5 Rattlesnake Springs

418

62
180

5 Rattlesnake Springs. Despite 30,000-plus acres in which to roam, nine-tenths of the park's 330-plus species of birds show up at Rattlesnake Springs at one time or another—probably because it's one of the very few water sources in this area.

KEY	
🏚	Ranger Station
⬛	Campground
🎋	Picnic Area
🍴	Restaurant
🖼	Lodge
🚶	Trailhead
🚻	Restrooms
⇘	Scenic Viewpoint
-----	Walking/Hiking Trails
·····	Bicycle Path

CARLSBAD CAVERNS PLANNER

When to Go

While the desert above may alternately bake or freeze, the caverns remain in the mid-50s; the fantastic formations don't change with the seasons either. If you're coming to see the Mexican free-tailed bat, however, come between spring and late fall.

Getting There & Around

Carlsbad Caverns is 27 mi southwest of Carlsbad, New Mexico, and 35 mi north of Guadalupe Mountains National Park via U.S. 62/180. The nearest full-service airport is in El Paso, 154 mi away. The 9.5-mi Walnut Canyon Desert Drive loop is one-way. It's a curvy, gravel road and is not recommended for motor homes or trailers. Be alert for wildlife such as mule deer crossing roadways, especially in early morning and at night.

AVG. HIGH/LOW TEMPS

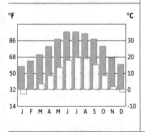

Flora & Fauna

Without a doubt, the park's most prominent and popular residents are Mexican free-tailed bats. These bats have bodies that barely span a woman's hand, yet sport wings that would cover a workingman's boot. Female bats give birth to a single pup each year, which usually weighs more than a quarter of what an adult bat does. Their tiny noses and big ears enable them to search for the many tons of bugs they consume over their lifetime. Numbering nearly a third of a million, these tiny creatures are the park's mascot.

Famous fanged flyers aside, there is much more wildlife to recommend in the park. One of New Mexico's best birding areas is at Rattlesnake Springs. Summer and fall migrations give you the best chance of spotting the most varieties of the more than 330 species of birds. Lucky visitors may spot a golden eagle, a rare visitor, or get the thrill of glimpsing a brilliant, gray-and-crimson vermilion flycatcher.

Snakes generally appear in summer. ■TIP➔ **If you're out walking, be wary of different rattlesnake species, such as banded-rock and diamondbacks. If you see one, don't panic. Rangers say they are more scared of us than we are of them. Just don't make any sudden moves, and slowly walk away or back around the vipers.**

This area is also remarkable because of its location in the Chihuahua Desert, which sprouts unique plant life. There are thick stands of raspy-leaved yuccas, as well as the agave (mescal) plants that were once a food source for early Apache tribes. The leaves of this leggy plant are still roasted in sand pits by Apache elders during traditional celebrations.

In spring, thick stands of yucca plants unfold yellow flowers on their tall stalks. Blossoming cacti and desert wildflowers are one of the natural wonders of Walnut Canyon. You'll see bright red blossoms adorning ocotillo plants, and sunny yellow blooms sprouting from prickly pear cactus.

WHAT TO SEE

SCENIC STOPS

The Big Room. With a floor space equal to about 14 football fields, this underground focal point of Carlsbad Caverns clues visitors in to just how large the caverns really are. Its caverns are close enough to the trail to cause voices to echo, but the chamber itself is so vast voices don't echo far; the White House could fit in just one corner of the Big Room, and wouldn't come close to grazing the 255-foot ceiling. The 1-mi loop walk on a mostly level, paved trail is self-guided. An audio guide is also available from park rangers for a few dollars. ⊠ *At the visitor center* 🖾 *$6; free for kids under 15* ⊗ *Memorial Day–Labor Day, daily 8–5 (last entry into the Natural Entrance is at 3:30; last entry into the elevator is at 5); Labor Day–Memorial Day, daily 8:30–3:30 (last entry into the Natural Entrance at 2; last entry into the elevator at 3:30).*

Natural Entrance. A self-guided, paved trail leads from the natural cave entrance. The route is winding and sometimes slick from water seepage aboveground. A steep descent of about 750 feet takes you about a mile through the main corridor and past features such as the Bat Cave and the Boneyard. (Despite its eerie name, the formations here don't look much like femurs and fibulas; they're more like spongy bone insides.) Iceberg Rock is a 200,000-ton boulder that dropped from the cave ceiling some millennia ago. After about a mile, you'll link up underground with the 1-mi Big Room trail and return to the surface via elevator. ⊠ *At the visitor center* 🖾 *$6* ⊗ *Memorial Day–Labor Day, daily 8:30–3:30; Labor Day–Memorial Day, daily 9–2.*

Rattlesnake Springs. Enormous cottonwood trees shade the picnic and recreation area at this cool oasis near Black River. The rare desert wetland harbors butterflies, mammals, and reptiles, as well as 90% of the park's 330 bird species. Don't let its name scare you; there may be rattlesnakes here, but not more than at any other similar site in the Southwest. Overnight camping and parking are not allowed. Take U.S. 62/180 5.5 mi south of White's City and turn west onto Highway 418 for 2.5 mi. ⊠ *Hwy. 418.*

VISITOR CENTER

A 75-seat theater offers an engrossing film about the different types of caves, as well as an orientation video that explains cave etiquette. Some of the rules include staying on paths so you don't get lost; keeping objects and trash in your pockets and not on the ground; and not touching the formations. Besides laying down the ground rules, visitor center exhibits offer a primer on bats, geology, wildlife, and the early tribes and nomads that once lived in and passed through the Carlsbad Caverns area. Friendly rangers staff an information desk, where tickets and maps are sold. Two gift shops also are on the premises. ⊠ *7 mi west of park entrance at White's City, off U.S. 62/180* ☎ *505/785–2232* ⊗ *Labor Day–Memorial Day, daily 8–5; Memorial Day–late Aug., daily 8–7.*

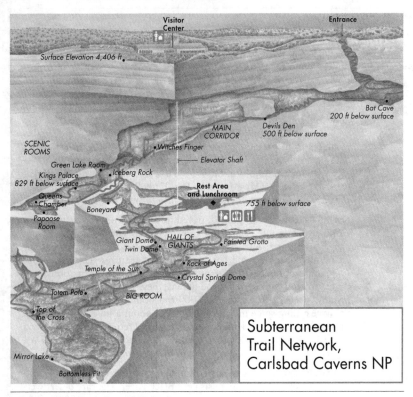

Surface Elevation 4,406 ft

Visitor Center

Entrance

Bat Cave
200 ft below surface

MAIN CORRIDOR

Devils Den
500 ft below surface

SCENIC ROOMS

Witches Finger

Elevator Shaft

Green Lake Room
Kings Palace
829 ft below surface
Iceberg Rock

Rest Area and Lunchroom

755 ft below surface

Queens Chamber
Boneyard

Papoose Room

Giant Dome
Twin Dome
HALL OF GIANTS

Painted Grotto

Temple of the Sun

Rock of Ages

Crystal Spring Dome

Totem Pole
BIG ROOM

Top of the Cross

Mirror Lake

Bottomless Pit

Subterranean Trail Network, Carlsbad Caverns NP

SPORTS & THE OUTDOORS

HIKING

All hikers are advised to stop at the visitor center information desk for current information about trails; those planning overnight hikes must obtain a free backcountry permit. Trails are poorly defined, but can be followed with a topographic map.

SPELUNKING

Carlsbad Caverns is famous for the beauty and breadth of its inky depths, as well as for the accessibility of some of its largest caves. All cave tours are ranger led, so safety is rarely an issue in the caves, no matter how remote. There are no other tour guides in the area, nor is there an equipment retailer other than the Wal-Mart located in Carlsbad, 23 mi away. Depending on the difficulty of your cave selection (Spider Cave is the hardest to navigate), you'll need at most knee pads, flashlight batteries, sturdy pants, hiking boots with ankle support, and some water.

Hall of the White Giant. Plan to squirm through some tight passages for long distances to access a very remote chamber, where you'll see towering, glistening white formations that explain the name of this feature. This strenuous, ranger-led tour lasts about four hours. Steep drop-offs might elate you—or make you queasy. Wear sturdy hiking shoes, and pick up four AA batteries for your flashlight before you come. Visitors must be at least 12 years old. ⊠ *At the visitor center* ☎ *800/967–2283* ✆ *$20* ⚓ *Reservations essential* ⊘ *Tour Sat. at 1.*

King's Palace. Throughout King's Palace, you'll see leggy "soda straws" large enough for a giant to sip and multi-tiered curtains of stone—sometimes by the light of just a few flashlights. The mile-long walk is on a paved trail, but there's one very steep hill. This ranger-guided tour lasts about 1½ hours and gives you the chance to experience a blackout, when all lights are extinguished. While advance reservations are highly recommended, this is the one tour you might be able to sign up for on the spot. Children under 4 aren't allowed on this tour. ⊠ *At the visitor center* ☎ *800/967–2283* ✆ *$8* ⊘ *Tours Labor Day–Memorial Day, daily 10 and 2; Memorial Day–Labor Day, daily 10, 11, 2, and 3.*

Left Hand Tunnel. Lantern light illuminates the easy walk on this detour in the main Carlsbad Cavern, which leads to Permian Age fossils—indicating that these caves were hollowed from the Permian Reef that still underlies the Guadalupe Mountain range above. The guided tour over a packed, dirt trail lasts about two hours. It's a moderate trek that older kids can easily negotiate, but children under 6 aren't allowed. ⊠ *At the visitor center* ☎ *800/967–2283* ✆ *$8* ⊘ *Tour daily at 9.*

Lower Cave. Fifty-foot vertical ladders and a dirt path will take you into undeveloped portions of Carlsbad Caverns. It takes about half a day to negotiate this moderately strenuous side trip led by a knowledgeable ranger. Children younger than 12 are not allowed on this tour. ⊠ *At the visitor center* ☎ *800/967–2283* ✆ *$20* ⚓ *Reservations essential* ⊘ *Tour weekdays at 1.*

★ **Slaughter Canyon Cave.** Discovered in the 1930s by a local goatherd, this cave is one of the most popular secondary sites in the park, about 23 mi southwest of the main Carlsbad Caverns and visitor center. Both the hike to the cave mouth and the tour will take about half a day, but it's worth it to view the deep cavern darkness as it's punctuated only by flashlights and, sometimes, headlamps. From the Slaughter Canyon parking area, give yourself 45 minutes to make the steep ½-mi climb up a trail leading to the mouth of the cave. Arrange to be there a quarter of an hour earlier than the appointed time. You'll find that the cave consists primarily of a single corridor, 1,140 feet long, with numerous side passages.

You can take some worthwhile pictures of this cave. Wear hiking shoes with ankle support, and carry plenty of water. You're also expected to bring your own two-D-cell flashlight. Children under age 6 are not permitted. It's a great adventure if you're in shape and love caving. ⊠ *End of Hwy. 418, 10 mi west of U.S. 62/180* ☎ *800/967–2283* ✆ *$15* ⚓ *Reservations essential* ⊘ *Tours Memorial Day–Labor Day, daily 10 and 1; post–Labor Day–Dec., weekends at 10; Jan.–Memorial Day, weekends 10 and 1.*

Spider Cave. Visitors may not expect to have an adventure in a cavern system as developed and well stocked as Carlsbad Caverns, but serious cavers and energetic types have the chance to clamber up tight tunnels, stoop under overhangs, and climb up steep, rocky pitches. This backcountry cave is listed as "wild," a clue that you might need a similar nature to attempt a visit.

> **FLYING BLIND**
>
> Bats use a type of sonar system called echolocation to orient themselves and locate their insect dinners at night. About 15 species of bats live in Carlsbad Caverns, although the Mexican free-tailed is the most predominant.

Plan to wear your warm, but least-favorite clothes, as they'll probably get streaked with grime. You'll also need soft knee pads, 4 AA batteries, leather gloves, and water. The gloves and pads are to protect you on long, craggy clambers and the batteries are for your flashlight. It will take you half a day to complete this ranger-led tour noted for its adventure. Visitors must be at least 12 years old and absolutely not claustrophobic. ⊠*Meet at visitor center* ☎*800/967–2283* ⊠*$20* ⚲*Reservations essential* ☉*Tour Sun. at 1.*

OUTFITTERS & EXPEDITIONS
Spelunkers who wish to explore both developed and wild caves are in luck; park rangers lead visitors on six different tours, including **The Hall of the White Giant** and **Spider Cave,** known for its tight twists and grimy climbs. Reservations are required at least a day in advance. If you're making reservations 21 days or more before your visit, you can send a check; 20 days or less, and you must pay by credit card over the phone or online. ☎*800/967–2283* ⊕*www.nps.gov/archive/cave/tour-gui. htm.* Those who want to go it alone outside the more established caverns can get permits and information about 10 backcountry caves from the **Cave Resources Office** (☎*505/785–2232 Ext. 363*). Heed rangers' advice for these remote, undeveloped, nearly unexplored caves.

RANGER PROGRAMS

Fodor'sChoice ★
Evening Bat Flight Program. In the amphitheater at the Natural Cave Entrance (off a short trail from main parking lot) a ranger discusses the park's batty residents before the creatures begin their sundown exodus. The bats aren't on any predictable schedule, so times are a little iffy. ⊠*Natural Cave Entrance, at the visitor center* ⊠*Free* ☉*Mid-May–mid-Oct., nightly at sundown.*

WHERE TO EAT & STAY

ABOUT THE RESTAURANTS

Choice isn't an issue inside Carlsbad Caverns National Park because there are just three dining options—the surface-level café, the underground restaurant, and the bring-it-in-yourself option. Luckily, everything is reasonably priced (especially for national park eateries). More dining options are available outside the park in White's City and Carlsbad.

ABOUT THE HOTELS

The only overnight option within the arid, rugged park is to make your own campsite in the backcountry, at least half a mile from any trail.

Outside the park, however, options expand. White's City, which is less than 10 mi to the east of the park, contains two motels. Both are near the boardwalk that connects shopping and entertainment options. In Carlsbad, there are even more choices, but many of the hotels here are aging and not particularly well maintained—so don't expect a mint on your pillow. Still, most are clean, if less than opulent.

ABOUT THE CAMPGROUNDS

Backcountry camping is by permit only (no campfires allowed) in the park; free permits can be obtained at the visitor center, where you can also pick up a map of areas closed to camping. You'll need to hike to campsites. There are no vehicle or RV camping areas in the park. Commercial sites can be found in White's City and Carlsbad.

WHERE TO EAT

¢–$ ✕ **Carlsbad Caverns Restaurant.** This comfy, diner-style restaurant has the essentials—hamburgers, sandwiches, and hot roast beef. ⊠ *Visitor center, 7 mi west of U.S. 62/180 at the end of the main park road* ☎ *505/785–2281* ▤ *AE, D, MC, V* ⊙ *Closes at 6:30 Memorial Day weekend–Labor Day, then at 5 after Labor Day.*

¢–$ ✕ **Underground Lunchroom.** Grab a treat, soft drink, or club sandwich for a quick break. Service is quick, even when there's a crowd. ⊠ *Visitor center, 7 mi west of U.S. 62/180 at the end of the main park road* ☎ *505/785–2281* ▤ *AE, D, MC, V* ⊙ *No dinner. Closes at 5 Memorial Day weekend–Labor Day, then at 3:30 after Labor Day.*

CARLSBAD CAVERNS ESSENTIALS

ACCESSIBILITY

Portions of the paved Big Room trails in Carlsbad Caverns are accessible to wheelchairs. A map defining appropriate routes is available at the visitor center information desk. Strollers are not permitted on trails (use a baby pack instead). Individuals who may have difficulty walking should access the Big Room via elevator. The TDD number is 888/530–9796.

ADMISSION FEES

No fee is charged for parking or to enter the aboveground portion of the park. It costs $6 to descend into Carlsbad Cavern either by elevator or through the Natural Entrance. Costs for special tours range from $7 to $20 plus general admission.

CAVE TOURS

From Memorial Day weekend through Labor Day, tours are conducted from 8:30 to 5; the last entry into the cave via the Natural Entrance is at 3:30, and the last entry into the cave via the elevator is at 5. From Labor Day until Memorial Day weekend, tours are offered from 8:30

to 3:30; the last entry into the cave via the Natural Entrance is at 2, and the last entry into the cave via the elevator is 3:30. Carlsbad Caverns is in the Mountain Time Zone.

EMERGENCIES

In the event of a medical emergency, dial 911, contact a park ranger, or report to the visitor center. To contact park police dial 505/785–2232, locate a park ranger, or report to the visitor center. Carlsbad Caverns has trained emergency medical technicians on duty and a first-aid room. White's City has emergency medical technicians available to respond to medical emergencies. A full-service hospital is in nearby Carlsbad.

VISITOR INFORMATION

Contacts **Carlsbad Caverns National Park** ✉ *3225 National Parks Hwy., Carlsbad, NM* ☎ *505/785–2232, 800/967–2283 reservations for special cave tours, 800/388–2733 cancellations* ⊕ *www.nps.gov/cave.*

Las Vegas

"Vegas has changed enormously in the 10 years I've been visiting, and not always for the better. The growth in huge, corporate resorts means the personal touch is being forgotten. For all that, it's still the most jaw-dropping, ridiculous, fun place to visit. Would I go every year? No. Would I go every two years? Actually, yes."

—GrahamC

By Swain
Schep

Washington, D.C., may be America's seat of power, but if you want its seat of promise, it just might reside in the land of oversize coin cups in slot pits, where particular ATMs only dispense $100 bills and all-you-can-eat buffets challenge you to eat your weight in jumbo shrimp, Alaskan crab legs, and prime rib. And the promise takes many forms, 24/7. Whether you go for the volcanic excess and passionate consumerism of the Strip, the more humble (but still neon-bathed) downtown experience, or the grittier locals joints, Las Vegas promises wealth, excitement, and a temporary sense of importance to all who visit.

For the millions of visitors who make the trek to Las Vegas every year, the city offers an ever-increasing array of sights, sounds, and experiences to play on their unsatisfied needs. We desire travel to exotic locales, so we stay in a hotel modeled after one, like the Mirage or the Venetian. We want to experience adventure, so we play casino games: a good adrenaline proxy for physical risk. Just for a moment we want to own and consume finer things than we have, so we visit opulent restaurants and visit any of several concentrations of high-end shopping districts, looking to buy items that would be just beyond our reach back in the "real" world.

Beyond and to some degree within the spectacle, the people of Las Vegas are quintessentially American. It shines through in the out-of-staters who settled in Southern Nevada for a million different reasons over the years, who deal blackjack and drive cabs. But also evident is the melting pot; Las Vegas is the city on the hill for immigrants from all over the world. For visitors and many locals as well, Las Vegas knows what you want and doles it out in spades. It's both exotic and comfortably familiar at the same time. But the city goes beyond merely reflecting American tastes and ideals; it consumes, amplifies, and blasts them out at high volume.

EXPLORING LAS VEGAS

WHO WILL ESPECIALLY LOVE THIS TRIP?

Groups: You don't have to be with a bachelor or bachelorette party to have fun here. Any excuse that brings together a loosely connected group of people ready to have a good time will do. Friendships get cemented (and occasionally severed), love blossoms (and occasionally wilts), but the stories of your trip will echo for a long time.

Couples: Yes, couples—real life, thought-they-knew-everything-about-each-other couples. And it's not so he can play golf at the 18-hole, 6,994 yard par-71 Bali Hai Golf Club while she's miles away shopping at Fashion Outlets Las Vegas in Primm, NV. Playing a game together like Blackjack spurs stress-free interaction that is hard to come by in other environments. You'll remember that it's fun to have fun together.

Singles: Vegas used to be a city where men outnumbered women by a wide margin. No more. Vegas is as much of a hook-up town as there is anywhere. Try the pool at the Hard Rock Hotel on a Saturday afternoon if you're on the prowl. Or make friends playing Blackjack at the Party Pit at Harrah's. At night, dress to impress and you just might get in to Pure in Caesar's Palace where you can dance the night away.

Serious Gamblers: You won't find higher stakes anywhere in the United States. And if your goal is to play poker for 55 out of the 60 hours you're in town, there's a seat open for you right now at the Bellagio Poker Room among others. Nevada's also the only state in the union with legal sports betting, and you'll love picking the point spreads, then kicking back in a comfy chair to watch the games at places like the Mandalay Bay Race and Sports Book.

Foodies: Southern Nevada has a high concentration of fine restaurants with some world-famous chefs. Have a pizza by Wolfgang Puck at the Venetian's Postrio. But gustatory pleasures can be found off the Strip, too, like Nora's Wine Bar.

Sun Worshippers: Vegas gets 300 days of sun a year, so rain checks are rare at the local golf courses. A quick trip out of the city limits and you can find yourself rock climbing, hiking, or exploring a ghost town. Or if you'd prefer a more leisurely approach to your vacation, the swimming pools at the megaresorts offer everything from swim-up gambling to poolside cabanas.

Shutterbugs: Sure there's the gaudy architecture and volcanic spectacles of the Las Vegas Strip. But don't let your f-stop there. Get out of town to the stunning environs; just over the hills are mountains, forests, nature preserves, lakes, dams, and wildlife.

Families: You might occasionally be forced to cover their eyes and ears, but the underage crowd loves the video game arcades, and the wide variety of roller coasters like X-Scream atop the Stratosphere.

WHEN IS THE BEST TIME TO VISIT?

First-time visitors tend to gravitate to the Strip, and that means a lot of walking. If you go in the summer, be prepared to face the dry afternoon heat, which can climb into the low 100s. Wear sunscreen and drink lots of water. If you can't stand the heat, the only shot you have to get out of the kitchen is to go between October and April.

At no time of year is weather in Las Vegas particularly bad. Sure it gets hot in the summer, and winter nights can get downright cold. But if you prepare well, and bring clothes that suit your planned activities, you'll be fine.

If you suffer from agoraphobia (fear of crowds) you should consider an alternate destination entirely. You will wait in lines and bump shoulders with others no matter when you go. The only hint of "quiet time" to be had is in the middle of the week. If you're able to take off work, you'll get cheaper flights, better hotel rates, and lower minimum bets at the tables.

TOP 5 REASONS TO GO

The Spectacle: In the old days, reason one would be gaming, but these days you can gamble—in one form or another—in nearly every state in the union. Las Vegas is a place you must see even if you've never rolled dice in your life outside of that Yahtzee game that ended in tears at your 4th grade birthday party.

The Adrenaline: The variety of gambling and entertainment outlets, the level of stakes, the quality of dealers, the sheer numbers of players at the tables, and the overall energy radiating from the Strip and its environs makes Vegas a unique kind of rush.

The People: They're sometimes beautiful and famous, sometimes they're middle-of-the-road, and sometimes they're beyond description. But no matter what they're always fascinating to observe. It's not just a people-watcher's paradise, Vegas provides a fantastic opportunity to interact. Belly up to a craps table and you'll see why.

The Food: The days of the $4.95 steak dinner are over. But that's a good thing; in their place have come scores of world-class restaurants of all cuisines. And you don't have to go to a five-star restaurant to get excellent chow; some folks swear the casino coffee shops and taco stands offer the best grub in the city. And, friends, you can take a pass on some of the buffets, but don't pass them all. The dinner buffet at the Bellagio is a triple threat: classy, plentiful, and good.

The Smiles: When people go to Las Vegas they come alive, because the city provides so many opportunities to become a slightly different person. You'll rarely get reminders of your daily routine, because the sometimes flamboyant, sometimes seedy Vegas is like nowhere else you've ever been. And that's precisely the idea.

On the other hand, if you want to spin up the excitement meter as high as it can go, travel to Las Vegas on New Years Eve, St. Patrick's Day, or during one of the long summer-holiday weekends (Memorial Day, July 4, Labor Day). You may have to fight for space at a craps table, but once you're in there and rolling dice, you'll be at the center of your own little party.

Big crowds gravitate to Las Vegas for headline sporting events, and the hotels will usually take advantage of the surges with higher rates. Booking early may save you heartburn on a busy weekend, but it's not likely to save you much money.

Any NFL playoff weekend will fill the casinos with jersey-wearing yahoos, culminating in Superbowl Sunday in early February. NASCAR visits Las Vegas in spring, bringing race fans out of the woodwork and into the casinos and restaurants. College basketball's March Madness is sure to swell the casinos as do the NBA playoffs in May and June. Then there are the headline boxing matches—if there is such a thing anymore—along with the Super Bowl in early February. Another big event is December's National Finals Rodeo—the "Super Bowl" of the bull-riding set.

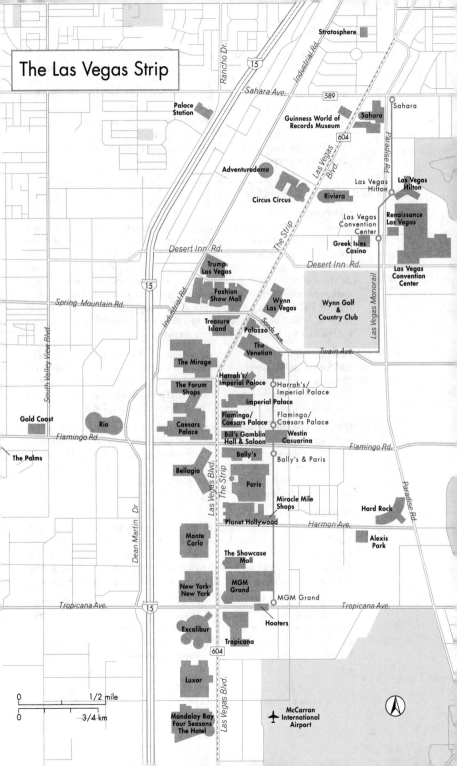

It's not just sports enthusiasts that can affect your stay in Las Vegas. The city is a prime destination for conventions and exhibitions, and when the big ones roll through town, they bring exhibitors and visitors that crowd the hotels and restaurants. In its heyday, Comdex brought a quarter of a million people to town, but that show is no longer an annual Vegas tradition. These days it's the Consumer Electronics Show that brings the most visitors to Vegas, drawing more than 100,000 people in for its week's run of showing off the newest in personal gadgetry.

HOW SHOULD I GET THERE?

DRIVING

There's nothing quite like a road trip to Vegas. Opportunities abound for fun along the way, whether you're traveling the old Route 66 from somewhere in the heartland, driving through the Mojave desert from Los Angeles, or finding your way to Vegas from points farther. If you can time it right, the night approach is magical. After twisting through darkened mountain passes and driving across vast salt flats, the first hint of Las Vegas is an unearthly glow rising from the distant desert horizon, which at last gives way to a carnival of twinkling neon as you see the city for the first time from across the valley.

Las Vegas is a drivable weekend destination for residents of Southern California and Arizona. Los Angelenos will take I–15 through Barstow. Phoenix residents don't have the luxury of a straight shot to Las Vegas. The best they can do is wind through the notoriously dangerous U.S. 93 that makes its way through Wikieup before meeting I–40.

If you're coming from farther away, you'd better plan on staying the night somewhere. For those approaching from the east on I–40, why not take a moment to contemplate your life at the South Rim of the Grand Canyon? Or if you're coming from the northwest down I–15, clear your head for a night at St. George, Utah, on the edge of the stunning Zion National Park.

FLYING

Las Vegas is served by most of the major domestic carriers through McCarran International Airport, the sixth busiest airport in the U.S., which sits on the east side of the south end of the Strip. Scheduled flights and charters also flow through McCarran from several different countries including Mexico, Canada, and scattered cities in Europe.

Most passengers have to deal with a brief tram ride between the main terminal and the gate complexes. If you're flying in at the start of a busy weekend the taxi line snakes through the loading zone and can look daunting to a weary traveler anxious to hit the tables. The good news is that it moves pretty fast. Limousines and hotel shuttles (both direct and indirect) are available as well.

Getting out of Las Vegas has its challenges as well. Monday usually sees a mass exodus of weekend visitors, which can clog even the most efficient ticketing and airport security operations. You can do yourself

CLOSE UP

How to Snack

When in Vegas you're at the hub of a glorious food galaxy. It's akin to New York City because you're always within a few yards and a few minutes of a hot meal 24 hours a day. But just because Las Vegas is home to award-winning eateries doesn't mean visitors have to make every meal a sit-down event.

Newer hotels offer the spectrum of fast-food options inside the facilities. The Starbucks phenomenon has fully penetrated the casino scene, and if your hotel doesn't have the name brand, there will be some analog serving lattes and bagels over a countertop. Most Strip and Downtown resort hotels offer several typecast restaurants, including a high-end continental joint, perhaps a steak house, and/or some kind off yummy ethnic chow. In addition, snackers will almost always find a 24-hour coffee shop to keep you knee deep in breakfast food, sandwiches, and desserts. **Mr. Lucky's 24/7 Café** at the Hard Rock Hotel (*4455 Paradise Rd., 702/693–5000*) is the best in the city, offering a diverse menu to table and counter customers. The similarly named but unrelated **24/7** at the Palms (*4321 W Flamingo Rd., 702/942–7777*) is worth the side trip off the Strip for the meat loaf alone.

If your goal is to get local fare, you'll need to remove yourself from within 100 yards of any neon whatsoever. Las Vegas has great restaurants, but they're strictly for the tourists. Las Vegas is an immigrant city, with a fifth of the populace being foreign-born, so try the ethnic fare. **Nora's Wine Bar & Osteria** is a modern Italian experience with a live jazz trio on weekends and a special computer-controlled wine-serving system to complement the Sicilian accented menu. Locals also turn to **Mimmo Ferraro's Italian** for a quieter night out. **Big Mama's Rib Shack** (*2230 W. Bonanza, 702/597–1616*) is a not-so-well-kept secret a few miles outside of Downtown, offering much more than yummy hickory-cooked barbeque; there are creole items (red beans and rice) and authentic Georgia soul food (chitlins), too. The strong Far East influence can be felt in the Las Vegas gastronomic scene at locals favorites **Joyful House**—the best Cantonese food in the state—and the nontraditional **Firefly**, a tapas house blending Asian, Spanish, and Latin influences. Vegetarians, as is their lot in life, must often find Indian food for a full vegetarian menu. In Las Vegas that means **Shalimar**. For dessert, you can't go wrong at **Luv It Frozen Custard.**

13

---

several favors to make life easier: use electronic ticketing and check-in, be aware of security regulations when you pack your bag, and get to the airport two hours early.

TRAIN

Train travel is seriously underrated in this age of instant gratification and impatience. Since you're breaking some rules on this trip, why not take a little extra time in getting there by hopping on Amtrak's South-west Chief? Rolling between Los Angeles and Chicago, the Chief stops in Needles, California, where Amtrak provides connecting bus service to both Laughlin and Las Vegas. Nothing could be finer.

CLAIM TO FAME

Oh boy. If you don't know what the Las Vegas claim to fame is, perhaps a trip to Poughkeepsie is more your speed.

The town may exude promise, but it was built on sin. Consider that the basic premise of the city's slogan, "What happens here, stays here" is that you're good-naturedly encouraged to lie about your trip should anyone ask about it. And there's a reason for that: what happens here usually stays there because it's likely illegal where you live. While bars all across America are closing at 1 or 2 AM, alcohol consumption in Las Vegas continues into the breakfast hours completely unhindered. If you're thinking about getting married, the waiting period in this state is exactly the length of time it takes you to fill out the appropriate forms.

And let's get this straight: prostitution, while legal in some parts of Nevada, is not legal in Las Vegas, despite all the advertising for, well, sex in the city.

Debauchery and matrimony aside, the main course in this town is, of course, gambling. Every light hanging from all the magnificent buildings, as well as every fountain, pirate ship, and volcano is paid for with gamblers' losses in games of chance. In fact most of the public works in the state of Nevada could be described the same way. The limits are higher than just about anywhere else, and the range of bets you can make is broader as well, from card games to sporting events two continents away to the outcome of elections. Gambling makes Vegas go.

HOW DO I GET AROUND?

Las Vegas is a walking town. You can find broad sidewalks, escalators, and moving walkways all over town. In addition, the Strip has recently sprouted a series of pedestrian bridges to make it easier than ever to cross the busy intersections and get to the next megaresort. Just be aware that distances can be deceiving. It may well seem like you're just next door to Caesar's Palace, but by the time you find your way out of your own hotel, walk along the busy sidewalks of the Strip, and travel the long moving sidewalks leading into Caesar's, you'll find 20 minutes have elapsed.

When your dogs give out, you can take the monorail or taxis to your next destination. Or better yet, maybe you're lucky enough to be staying at a hotel with a luxury spa, like the Spa Wynn Las Vegas, where you can treat your aching feet to a deep tissue massage.

BY CAR

If you've driven into town, or gotten a rental at the airport, a car can come in handy in Las Vegas. Parking at the casinos is usually free and plentiful. Just beware of the Strip at night; it can turn into a parking lot of bass thumpers, cruisers, and gawkers. Stick to the routes behind the casinos if you know what's good for you.

And there's plenty to do well outside of town, so take full advantage of your automotive resources by exploring the magnificent countryside around Las Vegas. There's more to it than desert scrub. Consider one of several government-operated nature preserves and parks like Mt. Charleston or Red Rock Canyon, just west of town. Take the tour at Hoover Dam, or rent a boat at Lake Mead. In the winter months you can even go skiing in Lee Canyon at Las Vegas Ski and Snowboard Resort.

BY MONORAIL

The Las Vegas monorail opened in 2004 and runs along 4 mi of track from the MGM Grand to stops at Bally's, Flamingo, and Harrah's before taking a jog to the east and stopping at stations near the Convention Center, Las Vegas Hilton, and the Sahara. This is by no means the scenic route, as the train runs along the backside of the hotels rather than the Strip. You may save some time, but it doesn't come cheap. A one-way ticket is $5, regardless of your entry and exit point. Discounts are available if you buy in bulk.

There is talk of extending the monorail to Downtown via the Stratosphere tower, and another link will take passengers to the airport. But for now, those projects are on ice until the monorail crowd works out funding details.

BY TAXI

This isn't New York, so don't think you can hail a cab standing on any street corner. Taxis are no longer permitted to pick up or drop off passengers on the Strip, the place you're most likely to discover an intense dislike of walking. If you're on the Strip and need a cab, just walk into the nearest hotel. Almost all of them have clearly marked taxi stands where an attendant will hail a waiting cab on your behalf. (Be polite: give him or her a buck.) Rates are reasonable given the level of convenience, but visit a cash machine before you hop in, as most Las Vegas cabs inexplicably don't take plastic. Taxi-stand lines can get long on weekend nights, so if you have a tight itinerary and the economics make sense, you might consider arranging a car service of some kind through your hotel concierge.

WHERE SHOULD I FOCUS MY ENERGY?

If you're here for 1 day: Try the spicy scrambled eggs for brunch at the Mesa Grill at Caesar's Palace to get you started off right. Then make a complete lap of Las Vegas Blvd, North to the Wynn, then South to the Mandalay and Luxor, drinking in the sights and sounds of the Strip.

If you're here for 2 days: Catch a show if you're in town for a night. Even during the weekdays you can see some great standing acts, like comic magician Mac King at Harrah's, or a Broadway-lite show like *The Producers* at Paris Las Vegas.

If you're here for 3 days: You'll be here long enough to get a good feel for what a Vegas all-nighter is really like, so belly up to a midnight card game at Hard Rock Hotel, then sleep it off in a poolside Cabana. By the third day you shouldn't even have to use your Blackjack crib sheet anymore.

HISTORY YOU CAN SEE

Unexpectedly, perhaps, the city has several fine collections of art, artifacts, and culturally important pieces. Consider the masters on display at the Guggenheim Hermitage Collection at the Venetian or the Bellagio Gallery of Fine Art, showing the works of Faberge, Warhol, and Picasso, to name a few.

If you're after local flavor, you can get a whiff of Vegas's history by going downtown, where the original casinos stood. Outside of town, Lake Mead and Hoover Dam are each amazing landmarks as well as living reminders of the great public works projects of the New Deal. Boulder City, originally a temporary village created for the workers on the dam in the 1930s, thrives today and has an interesting Hoover Dam Museum, detailing the history of that project and its effect on the area. A dam tour, into the bowels of the turbines and spillways is well worth the history buff's time, too, and kids love it.

If you're here for 4 days: The Main Street Experience downtown is a (mostly) wholesome spot for people weary of the crowds on the Strip. Take the time to learn a more challenging table game like Craps or Pai Gow. It helps when you're playing at lower stakes at the El Cortez Hotel downtown as you suck in that authentic Vegas vibe.

If you're here for 5 days: See some of the countryside. Tour the Hoover Dam just south of town and spend some time at Boulder Beach on Lake Mead. When night falls, pick out a Cirque du Soleil show to see; there are at least five to choose from on most nights. We recommend Mystere at Treasure Island.

If you're here for 6 days: Why not see the weirder side of Las Vegas? Go bowling at the Suncoast Hotel, then consider the nuclear option: the Atomic Testing Museum. Head out west to spend a night at the Little A'Le'Inn on Highway 375 in Lincoln County, better known as the Extraterrestrial Highway for its history of UFO sightings and proximity to the ever-spooky Area 51.

If you're here for 7 days or more: Surely you can't gamble for a week straight, right? Drive out to the new glass-floored Grand Canyon Skywalk. It extends 70 feet out over the gorge, providing you an unobstructed view a mile straight down. Follow that up with a night in Laughlin, the mini-Vegas on the Arizona border with a charm and style all its own.

WHAT ARE THE TOP EXPERIENCES?

The Football Weekend: For the true pigskin faithful, there are few better places to spend a fall weekend than in the loving embrace of a Las Vegas sports book, with a fist full of betting slips to invest you in the gridiron events like never before. Surrounded by boisterous fans, colossal video screens, and clockwork cocktail waitresses, you'll think you've died and gone to your living room...in heaven. Football

STRANGE BUT TRUE

- Las Vegas is making dramatic changes to its image and appeal. Fewer than 1 visitor in 10 actually comes to Las Vegas for the purpose of gambling.

- All the same, 87% of visitors to Las Vegas report they gambled when they were there.

- The average bankroll for Las Vegas gamblers is about $600.

- Gambling was illegal in Las Vegas between 1910 and 1931.

- Las Vegas was recently voted the "meanest city in america" toward homeless people.

- The Stratosphere Tower is the tallest building west of the Mississippi River.

- The high-end suite atop the Hard Rock Hotel has its own bowling lane.

- New York City may never sleep, but Las Vegas is one of two major cities in the country with no closing laws. The other? New Orleans.

- If you're at the casino sports book hoping to bet on the local teams, you can forget it. Casinos don't offer bets for or against UNLV, and if a professional sports league plays an exhibition game in Vegas, that game will not be available for betting.

contests make ideal anchor events for groups traveling together; a moment when everyone can pause for two hours together of screaming at professional athletes. Make plans to get into town Friday evening, and don't even think about leaving before Tuesday morning so you don't miss any of the college or NFL action. You can't go wrong camping out at the Mandalay Bay sports book with plenty of cushy lounge chairs and a snack bar within arm's reach. If you're traveling with a crowd, Paris and Red Rocks have hundreds of seats with individual TVs. Pick your month wisely and you'll get a bonus; September and October has baseball, and November and beyond have basketball.

Celeb Sightings: Actors, rock stars, and athletes are people, too (sort of), and they are drawn to Southern Nevada for the same Dionysian reasons everyone else is: the resorts are palatial, the gambling is a rush, the restaurants are exceptional, and there's always another party to attend. Besides, Vegas offers the ideal setting for a famous person to be rich and famous, with its crowds of onlookers just dying to gawk at somebody of interest. So if you're on a first-name basis with your favorite stars (you know: Brad, Angelina, Leonardo) or perhaps your subscription to People just expired, head to Sin City and play a game of "I Spy: Celebrity Challenge." Start at the Hard Rock Hotel and count Baldwin brothers in the Circle Bar or over tuna tataki at Nobu. Then jump in a cab and head to any watering hole at the HRH's archrival across town: the Palms. If you time it just right, you can catch a Hilton-sister centered squabble just as dessert arrives at spectacular Alizé, with its unbroken view of the valley from 55 floors up. And in case you were worried, the well-known and well-born don't restrict themselves to off-strip locations either. You'll practically have to fight through the reality TV stars at Caesar's Palace famous Forum Shops, where Spago is as good a place to spend your 15 minutes as any. And if you're willing to dive deep into the A-list scene, Vegas nightclubs and boogie joints are always awash in rockers and athletes on steroid suspension. Boy-banders are known to congregate at Treasure Island's Tangerine, and then go right upstairs to ultrahip sushi and gathering spot Social House. Or you can always try the hottest clubs in town: Pure at Caesar's Palace, or Tao at Mandalay Bay. Since you're on a first name basis with the stars, you should have no trouble getting in!

Bachelor/Bachelorette Party: For the soon-to-be-wed, Las Vegas offers an unforgettable opportunity for making a final stand in the name of bachelor- or bachelorette-hood. Forget the celebrities; for this one weekend, you're the star. But before we get too deep into the fantasy, keep in mind that the friends who volunteered to come with you aren't coming for you, they're coming for Vegas. There's something for everyone in your pack, but at the same time it's the perfect destination for group activities: lounge together, eat together, and play together in any of the activities readymade for a group of six to eight people. If you're all staying at a full-service resort hotel like Bellagio or Venetian, nobody has to stray very far to get exactly what they want, be it food, shopping, spa services, or something else. That gives prenuptial parties a sense of cohesion that isn't available in New Orleans, Miami, or New York. Boys can be boys at the local golf courses (among other manly activities). Girls can be girls at any of a dozen deluxe spas, like Spa Wynn. If titillation is the order of the day, girls will enjoy their time watching Thunder from Down Under, the male revue at Excalibur. The bachelor party will, in all likelihood, choose to skip the PG-13 rated dance reviews and head straight to Spearmint Rhino, an international-chain topless joint. Then there's the over-the-top side of Las Vegas that can contribute to the party getting really out of hand: the guys might do something extreme like Flyaway Indoor Skydiving *(702/731–4768)* or get after-hours pedicures at AMP Salon (the Palms) by lingerie-clad technicians (all on the up-and-up, we assure you). Meanwhile, the ladies might take a pole-dancing lesson, or take a shopping detour at Serge's Showgirl Wigs *(953 Sahara Ave., 702/732–1015)*. Both parties might wind up at the Palms' in-house Hart & Huntington Tattoo parlor *(702/942–7040)* for a permanent reminder of this weekend. Anything is possible.

BEST BETS

TOURS

Gray Line. Several bus companies offer Las Vegas city and neon-light tours, but Gray Line is among the best; excursions may take you into Red Rock Canyon, Lake Mead, Colorado River rafting, Hoover Dam, and Valley of Fire; longer trips go to different sections of the Grand Canyon(☎702/384–1234 or 800/634–6579 ⊕*www.graylinelasvegas.com*).

Helicopter Tours. Helicopters do two basic tours in and around Las Vegas: a brief flyover of the Strip and a several-hour trip out to the Grand Canyon and back.

Operators **Maverick Helicopters Tours** (☎ *702/261–0007 or 888/261–4414* ⊕ *www.maverickhelicopter.com*). **Papillon Grand Canyon Helicopters** (☎ *702/736–7243 or 888/635–7272* ⊕ *www.papillon.com*). **Sundance Helicopters** (☎ *702/736–0606 or 800/653–1881* ⊕ *www.helicoptour.com*).

Monorail. Begun in 1995 and greatly expanded in 2004, the monorail stretches from MGM Grand, on the south, to the Sahara, to the north, with several stops in between, and makes the 4-mi trip in about 14 minutes. To head farther south to Mandalay Bay, walk across the Strip and pick up the small, free monorail at the Excalibur. To the north, a downtown monorail extension is in the planning stages but completion is several years away. Also, although it's a fairly short walk (10 minutes tops) between the Mirage and Treasure Island casinos, you can also get between them on the free tram that runs roughly every 10 to 15 minutes, 9 AM–1 AM.

The monorail runs Monday–Thursday 7 AM–2 AM, Friday–Sunday 7 AM–3 AM. Fares are $5 for one ride, $9 for two rides, $35 for 10 rides, $15 for a one-day pass, and $40 for a three-day pass. You can purchase tickets at station vending machines or in advance online. (☎ *702/699–8200* ⊕ *www.lvmonorail.com*).

WHERE TO EAT

	WHAT IT COSTS				
	¢	$	$$	$$$	$$$$
Restaurants	under $10	$10–$20	$20–$30	$30–$40	over $40

Prices are per person for a main course at dinner.

$$$$ **✕Alex.** Super chef Alessandro Stratta serves his high-end French Riviera cuisine to the well-heeled at this drop-dead-gorgeous dining room, **Fodor's Choice** reached via a grand staircase. Stratta's four-course prix-fixe menu ★ ($145) and seasonal tasting menu ($325, with wine pairings) are not for the meek of wallet, but the artfully presented food here absolutely delivers. Specialties include foie gras ravioli in a truffle bouillon with duck confit salad and wild turbot with salsifis (an herb whose edible root has an oysterlike taste), black truffles, almonds, and a red wine sauce. Dessert tends toward the fanciful, including a wonderful chocolate-banana malt with caramel–and–macadamia brittle ice cream. This is one Vegas restaurant you might want to dress your best for—jackets aren't required but are suggested. ⊠ *Wynn Las Vegas, 3131 Las Vegas Blvd. S, North Strip* ☎ *702/248–3463* ⚉ *Reservations essential* ☰ *AE, D, DC, MC, V* ⊘ *Closed Mon. No lunch.*

$$$$ **✕Aureole.** Celebrity chef Charlie Palmer re-created his famed New ★ York restaurant for Mandalay Bay. He and designer Adam Tihany added a few playful, Las Vegas–style twists: a four-story wine tower,

LIKE A LOCAL

With so many casinos, Las Vegas is home to a thousand and one words, customs, and mores that stem from the business and the insane volumes of cash that change hands between tourists and the house every minute of every day. You'll observe casino personnel performing odd rituals with their hands to "show" anyone watching them they aren't stealing.

And that's just the beginning. The gambling scene can feel a little like a club you don't belong to sometimes; especially if you've never played before. But don't worry, you'll pick it up fast. Here are some quick tips for getting along in a Las Vegas casino:

■ Don't cheat—yes it's possible, and yes, you can get into big trouble for it.

■ Don't chat—if you're at a table game, using a cellular phone or handheld device will get you booted from the table.

■ Don't hand money to dealers. Nobody in Vegas can take money directly from your hand, so when you want to buy chips, put your bills down on the table halfway between you and the casino employee.

■ Do your homework. If you don't have a chance to learn how to play your game of choice prior to arrival, make your first foray at a less-crowded table, where the dealer will have time to explain what's happening to you.

■ Don't linger: if you're not enjoying yourself, if you don't like the dealer or the people you're playing next to, or if you think they don't like you. Just get up and leave.

for example, holds 10,000 bottles that are reached by "wine fairies" who are hoisted up and down via a system of electronically activated pulleys. Seasonal specialties on the fixed-price menu might include French onion soup with foie gras, truffles, and Sonoma squab topped with seared foie gras and served in a preserved-cherry jus. For dessert try innovative offerings like citrus-scented cheesecake with huckleberry compote or crème brûlée ice cream with maple–brown sugar sauce. ⊠ *Mandalay Bay Resort & Casino, 3950 Las Vegas Blvd. S, South Strip* ☎ *702/632–7401* ⚑ *Reservations essential* ▤ *AE, D, DC, MC, V* ⊘ *No lunch.*

$$$$ ✕ **Delmonico Steakhouse.** Hammy showbiz chef Emeril Lagasse gives the
★   New Orleans touch to this big city–style steak house at the Venetian. Enter through 12-foot oak doors; you can find a subdued modern interior that creates a feeling of calm, and friendly but professional staff members who set you at ease. Consider the classic steak tartare with Dijon emulsion or the panfried oysters with shrimp, mushrooms, and spinach pasta for starters, and such entrées as grilled rack of lamb with parsnip potatoes and port wine–cherry reduction, or the tender bone-in rib steak. Don't miss the apple–and–cheddar cheese bread pudding for dessert. ⊠ *Venetian Resort-Hotel-Casino, 3355 Las Vegas Blvd. S, Center Strip* ☎ *702/733–5000* ⚑ *Reservations essential* ▤ *AE, D, DC, MC, V.*

$$$$ ✕**Le Cirque.** This sumptuous restaurant, a branch of the New York City
FodorśChoice landmark, is one of the city's best. The mahogany-lined room is all the
★ more opulent for its size: in a city of mega-everything, Le Cirque seats
only 80 under its drooping silk-tent ceiling. Even with a view of the
hotel's lake and its mesmerizing fountain show, you'll only have eyes
for your plate when your server presents dishes such as the roasted venison loin, braised rabbit in Riesling, or grilled monkfish tournedos. The
wine cellar contains about 1,000 premium selections representing every
wine-producing region of the world. Although men aren't required to
wear a jacket and tie, most do. ⊠*Bellagio Las Vegas, 3600 Las Vegas
Blvd. S, Center Strip* ☎*702/693–8100* ⌖*Reservations essential* ☐*AE,
D, DC, MC, V* ☉*No lunch.*

$$$$ ✕**Picasso.** This restaurant, adorned with the artist's original works,
★ raised the city's dining scene a notch when it opened. Although it's still
much adored, some believe it may be resting a bit on its laurels, and
that chef Julian Serrano doesn't change his menu often enough. The
artful, innovative cuisine is based on French classics but also has strong
Spanish influences. Appetizers on the seasonal menu might include
warm quail salad with sautéed artichokes and pine nuts or poached
oysters with osetra caviar and vermouth sauce. Sautéed medallions of
fallow deer, roasted milk-fed veal chop, or roasted almond–and–honey
crusted pigeon might appear as entrée choices. Dinners are prix fixe,
with four- or five-course menus. ⊠*Bellagio Las Vegas, 3600 Las Vegas
Blvd. S, Center Strip* ☎*702/693–8105* ⌖*Reservations essential* ☐*AE,
D, DC, MC, V* ☉*Closed Tues. No lunch.*

$$$–$$$$ ✕**André's French Restaurant.** This second location of André's French Res-
★ taurant serves food that's as excellent as that at the downtown original
but in a more spectacular room packed with lavish Louis XVI furnish-
ings. Specialties here include filet mignon tartare prepared tableside
with potato pancakes and arugula salad, and seared venison loin with
crème fraîche polenta, Napa cabbage, Granny Smith apples, and bing
cherry chutney. The clubby cigar bar has an amazing selection of ports.
(⇨*André's French Restaurant in Downtown.*) ⊠*Monte Carlo Resort
and Casino, 3770 Las Vegas Blvd. S, South Strip* ☎*702/798–7151*
⌖*Reservations essential* ☐*AE, DC, MC, V* ☉*No lunch.*

$$–$$$$ ✕**Eiffel Tower Restaurant.** The must-do restaurant of Paris Las Vegas is a
★ room with a view, all right—it's about a third of the way up the hotel's
half-scale Eiffel Tower replica, with views from all four glassed-in sides
(request a Strip view when booking for the biggest wow factor—it
overlooks the fountains at Bellagio, across the street). But patrons are
often pleasantly surprised that the food here measures up to the setting.
The French-accented menu includes appetizers of cold smoked salmon,
sea scallops, and Russian caviar. On the entrée list, you find Atlantic
salmon in pinot noir sauce, lobster thermidor, roasted rack of lamb
Provençal, and filet mignon in mushroom sauté. ⊠*Paris Las Vegas,
3655 Las Vegas Blvd. S, Center Strip* ☎*702/948–6937* ⌖*Reservations
essential* ☐*AE, D, DC, MC, V.*

$$–$$$$ ✕**Nobu.** Chef Nobu Matsuhisa has replicated the decor and menu of
★ his Manhattan Nobu in this slick restaurant with bamboo pillars, a
seaweed wall, and birch trees. Imaginative specialties include spicy

13

ON THE WAY

Always worth the stop, the South Rim of the **Grand Canyon** sits about an hour north of the freeway in Arizona. Visitors can take a quick view of the gorge at the visitor center, or take part in any number of more exciting activities, like camping, mule rides, or guided tours.

If **Meteor Crater** was in Ohio it would be front-page news, but because this 50,000-year-old hole-in-the-ground happens to be right next to the world's most famous hole in the ground (see above), it gets forgotten. About 30 mi east of Flagstaff, all 4,000 feet wide and 550 feet deep of the Crater sits right off I-40, making it much more convenient than the Grand Canyon for a quick stop.

The **Lost City Museum** is petroglypherrific! Coming in from the

Northeast on I-15, travelers will pass through Overton at about 200 mi out from Vegas. This small archaeology and geology museum has been around for more than 70 years, with well-conceived exhibits on the area's Paiute Indian history, among other things.

Route 66 came closest to Las Vegas between Barstow, then Needles, California to Oatman and Kingman, Arizona. Adventurers can go out and find pieces of the original two-lane road. Art, photographs, Americana, and other wonders await at Barstow's relatively new Route 66 "Mother Road" Museum (760/255–1890). Oatman offers a mining town-turned-offbeat tourist trap feel, and comes complete with burros, saloons, and staged gunfights. No wonder Clark Gable and Carole Lombard honeymooned there in 1939.

sashimi, monkfish pâté with caviar, sea-urchin tempura, and scallops with spicy garlic. For dessert there's a warm chocolate soufflé. ⊠ *Hard Rock Hotel and Casino, 4455 Paradise Rd., Paradise Road* ☎ *702/693–5000* ⊟ *AE, D, DC, MC, V* ⊗ *No lunch.*

$–$$$$ ✕ **Spago Las Vegas.** His fellow chefs stood by in wonder when Wolf-
★ gang Puck opened this branch of his famous Beverly Hills eatery in the culinary wasteland that was Las Vegas in 1992, but Spago Las Vegas has become a fixture in this ever-fickle city, and it remains consistently superb. The less expensive Café, which overlooks the busy Forum Shops at Caesars, is great for people-watching; inside, the dinner-only Dining Room is more intimate. Both menus are classic Puck. In the Café, sample white-bean cassoulet with chicken sausage and whole-grain mustard. Top picks in the Dining Room include porcini mushroom ravioli with Muscovy duck confit and white-truffle foam, and coriander-crusted yellowfin tuna with a lemongrass, coconut, and sea urchin sauce. ⊠ *Forum Shops at Caesars, 3500 Las Vegas Blvd. S, Center Strip* ☎ *702/369–6300* ⊟ *AE, D, DC, MC, V.*

$$–$$$ ✕ **Verandah.** Informal, peaceful, and refined, this beautifully decorated
★ though somewhat overlooked gem at the Four Seasons offers the perfect antidote to the noisier and flashier restaurants elsewhere at Mandalay Bay. It's easy to carry on a conversation outside on the tropically landscaped terrace or inside the dining room with its muted colors and candlelit tables. Service here rivals any in town, and the presentation

and quality of the innovative dishes leaves nothing to be desired, especially considering the comparatively reasonable prices. You might start with the smoked salmon–and–potato galette with celery-root rémoulade and lemon essence, followed by mushroom-truffle gnocchi with broad beans or pistachio-crusted New Zealand snapper with roasted corn, pearl pasta, and citrus sauce. Many of Mandalay Bay's best restaurants don't serve breakfast or lunch—Verandah does an admirable job with both. ⊠*Four Seasons Hotel, 3960 Las Vegas Blvd. S, South Strip* ☎*702/632–5000* ⊟*AE, D, DC, MC, V.*

13

$–$$$ ✕**Mon Ami Gabi.** This French-inspired steak house that first earned ★ acclaim in Chicago has became much beloved here in Vegas. It's the rare restaurant with sidewalk dining on the Strip—enjoy the views of nearby casinos and the parade of curious passersby. For those who prefer a less lively environment, a glassed-in conservatory just off the street conveys an outdoor feel, and still-quieter dining rooms are inside, adorned with chandeliers dramatically suspended three stories above. The specialty of the house is steak frites, offered four ways: classic, au poivre, bordelaise, and Roquefort. The skate with garlic fries and caper-lemon butter is also excellent. This place is a favorite for Sunday brunch. ⊠*Paris Las Vegas, 3655 Las Vegas Blvd. S, Center Strip* ☎*702/944–4224* ⊟*AE, D, DC, MC, V.*

$ ✕**Tides Oyster Bar.** For affordable seafood, this futuristic incarnation ★ of a '50s coffee shop does the trick. The space is groovy and inviting, with blue mosaic columns soaring above the dining space, and a long counter facing the kitchen, where you can sit on a blond-wood bar stool and slurp clams and oysters on the half shell or a dinner-size bowl of gumbo. A particular specialty is the traditional crab roast, prepared in an old-timey steam kettle with tomato, herbs, butter, and brandy. ⊠*Red Rock Casino, Resort and Spa, 11011 W. Charleston Blvd., Summerlin* ☎*702/797–7576* ⊟*AE, D, DC, MC, V.*

¢–$ ✕**'Wichcraft.** Skip the drab fast-food court at MGM and grab a bite at this futuristic space with marble-top café tables, vibrant lime-green walls, and blond-wood floors. The creative sandwiches include Sicilian tuna with fennel, black olives, and lemon juice on a baguette, and meat loaf with bacon, cheddar, and tomato relish on a roll. It's a great option for breakfast, too—try a roll stuffed with a fried egg, bacon, blue cheese, and greens. Although it's possible to make this an early dinner option, keep in mind that it closes at 6 on weekdays, 8 on Friday and Saturday. ⊠*MGM Grand Hotel and Casino, 3799 Las Vegas Blvd. S, South Strip* ☎*702/891–3166* ⌂*Reservations not accepted* ⊟*AE, D, DC, MC, V.*

WHERE TO STAY

The lodgings we list are the cream of the crop in each price category. Properties are assigned price categories based on the range between their least and most expensive standard double rooms at high season (excluding holidays).

Assume that hotels operate on the European Plan (EP, with no meals) unless we specify that they use the Continental Plan (CP, with a continental breakfast), Modified American Plan (MAP, with breakfast and dinner), or the Full American Plan (FAP, with all meals).

WHAT IT COSTS					
	¢	$	$$	$$$	$$$$
Hotels	under $60	$60–$129	$130–$200	$200–$270	over $270

All prices are for a standard double room for two people, excluding 10% tax.

$$–$$$$
Fodor'sChoice
★

Bellagio Las Vegas. This is a hard place to land good deals, although it never hurts to check the hotel's Web site for specials: rates average $250 to $300 much of the year, but during slower weeks you can usually snag a room for around $170 to $180 (competitive in comparison with other high-end Strip properties). If it's pampering you're after, stay in the Spa Tower, which has impressive rooms and suites as well as an expanded full-service spa and salon—suites have steam showers and soaking tubs. Rooms in the original hotel tower are super snazzy, with luxurious fabrics and Italian marble. Elegant Italian provincial furniture surrounds either a single king-size bed or two queen-size beds. Bellagio has one of the higher staff-to-guest ratios in town, which results in visibly more solicitous service than you might expect at such an enormous property. Because this is an adult-oriented resort, few of its amenities are geared toward kids. ⊠3600 Las Vegas Blvd. S, Center Strip, ☎702/693–7111 or 888/987–6667 ⊕www.bellagio.com ⇌3,421 rooms, 512 suites ⊟AE, D, DC, MC, V.

$$–$$$$
★

Hard Rock Hotel. It's impossible to forget you're in the Hard Rock, no matter where you go in this rock-fixated joint: even the hall carpeting is decorated with musical notes. The rooms are large, with sleek furnishings, Bose CD-stereos, and flat-screen plasma TVs that show continuous music videos on one channel. Some beds have leather headboards, bathrooms have stainless-steel sinks, and the double French doors that serve as floor-to-ceiling windows actually open. The Hard Rock's pool area—a tropical beach–inspired oasis with a floating bar, private cabanas, and poolside blackjack—is a favorite filming location for MTV and popular TV shows. Very crowded (but fun) public areas offer plenty of opportunities for people-watching. It's possible to score reasonable rates here on weeknights—the Hard Rock has definitely lost a bit of its arrogance, thanks to all those competing hipster-infested hotels in town, and works harder to please guests. The Rock Spa is one of the coolest places in town to get a massage. ⊠4455 Paradise Rd., Paradise Road, ☎702/693–5000 or 800/473–7625 ⊕www.hardrockhotel.com ⇌583 rooms, 64 suites ⊟AE, D, DC, MC, V.

$$–$$$$
★

Red Rock Casino Resort Spa. Opened in 2006 on the western edge of Las Vegas suburbia, near Red Rock canyon, is this swanky golden-age Vegas throwback—there are crystal chandeliers throughout (an interesting contrast to earthy sandstone walls and teak-marble floors), a large pool area, a 16-screen movie theater, a vast selection of excellent restaurants (some with outdoor patios), and rooms with floor-to-ceiling glass windows and 42-inch TVs. An early 2007 expansion added another 450 rooms. The sports book has its own

VIP area and three video walls that can combine into one huge screen. ⊠*11011 W. Charleston Blvd., Summerlin,* ↗*805 rooms, 45 suites* ☎*702/797–7777 or 866/767–7773* ⊕*www.redrocklasvegas.com* ≣*AE, D, DC, MC, V.*

$$–$$$$
Fodor'sChoice
★

Venetian. Some of the Strip's largest and plushest suites are found at this elegant, gilded resort that's a hit with foodies, shoppers, and high rollers. It's all about glitz and wow effect here, which makes it a popular property if you're celebrating a special occasion or looking for the quintessential over-the-top Vegas experience. The 700-plus-square-foot guest quarters, richly adorned in a modified Venetian style, have a sunken living room with dining table and convertible sofa, walk-in closets, separate shower and tub, three telephones (including one in the bathroom), and 27- or 36-inch TVs. The even posher Venezia Tower has a concierge floor, private entrance, fountains, and gargantuan suites with mosaic walls, vaulted ceilings, and carved marble accents. Service here, at one time a bit uneven, has improved markedly in recent years. ⊠*3355 Las Vegas Blvd. S, Center Strip,* ☎*702/414–1000 or 888/883–6423* ⊕*www.venetian.com* ↗*4,027 suites* ≣*AE, D, DC, MC, V.*

$$–$$$$
Fodor'sChoice
★

Wynn Las Vegas. Decked out with replicas of pieces from Steve Wynn's acclaimed art collection, the princely rooms, averaging a whopping 650 square feet, offer spectacular views through wall-to-wall floor-to-ceiling windows. Rest your head at night on custom pillow-top beds with 320-thread-count linens, and stay plugged into the world with cordless phones—bedside drapery and climate controls are another nice touch. The superposh Tower Suites Parlor and Salon units have use of a separate pool and lanai and have such opulent amenities as granite wet bars, separate powder rooms, 42-inch flat-screen TVs, and walk-in closets. Even relatively minor touches, such as richly appointed armchairs with ottomans and giant, fluffy Turkish towels, speak to the sheer sumptuousness of this place. ⊠*3131 Las Vegas Blvd. S, Center Strip,* ☎*702/770–7100 or 888/320–9966* ⊕ *www.wynnlasvegas.com* ↗*2,359 rooms, 357 suites* ≣*AE, D, DC, MC, V*

$–$$$$

Golden Nugget Hotel and Casino. New owners took over the Golden Nugget in 2003 and again in 2005; since that time, the place has continued to rank as downtown's leading property, although it doesn't have quite the flair it did back when Steve Wynn operated it. Among its neighbors, the hotel has the biggest and best pool. The well-kept rooms are modern and comfortable, with desks, high-speed Internet, armoires, and marble bathrooms. Casino policies are inconsistent, but a popular permanent poker room is likely to last. ⊠*129 E. Fremont St., Downtown,* ☎*702/385–7111 or 800/634–3454* ⊕*www.goldennugget.com* ↗*1,805 rooms, 102 suites* ≣*AE, D, DC, MC, V.*

$–$$$$
★

Mandalay Bay. The main hotel at the Mandalay Bay Resort & Casino (THEhotel and the Four Seasons are the others) is the least fabulous of the three, but it's still a first-rate property with cavernous rooms. Bathrooms have understated, elegant stone floors and counters as well as deep soaking tubs with separate showers. The breezy, low-key decor is luxurious without being overbearing. ⊠*3950 Las Vegas Blvd. S, South Strip,* ☎*702/632–7777 or 877/632–7700* ⊕*www.mandalaybay.com* ↗*3,215 rooms, 1,100 suites* ≣*AE, D, DC, MC, V.*

$-$$$$ ▦ **Monte Carlo Resort and Casino.** The Strip could use more places like
☺   this: it's handsome but not ostentatious, and they haven't skimped on
★   the rooms, which are outfitted with elegant cherrywood furnishings. If
you have kids, it's a good alternative to Excalibur: family-friendly perks
include a kiddie pool and a mini-"water park." There's a decent selec-
tion of restaurants (among them, Andre's) and the casino is so orderly
you can follow a carpeted "road" from one end to the other. The pool
was handsomely renovated in 2006. ⊠*3770 Las Vegas Blvd. S, South
Strip,* ☎*702/730–7777 or 888/529–4828* ⊕*www.montecarlo.com*
⇖*2,743 rooms, 259 suites*⊟*AE, D, DC, MC, V.*

$-$$$$ ▦ **Paris.** Midpriced among the Center Strip's high-profile resorts, Paris
actually offers more elegant digs—even in its standard units, which
have marble baths with separate tubs and showers—than some of its
pricier and more talked-about competitors, although some find the
heavy-handed decor a little busy. Every room has custom-designed fur-
niture with Franco-inspired decorative elements and artwork, and east-
facing rooms overlook the magnificent fountains and lagoon across the
street at Bellagio. Otherwise, your room may overlook the pleasant
pool area. Suites add more space, of course, plus considerably more
dashing red, beige, and gold furniture and rich fabrics. The fabulous
buffet serves dishes from five French regions. The other dining options
are mostly quite good, a couple of them excellent, although none is
truly a showstopper, save perhaps for Mon Ami Gabi bistro. A mas-
sive octagonal pool sits in the shadows of the ersatz Eiffel Tower, on
the hotel rooftop—it could use a little more shade, but it's surrounded
by neatly tended gardens. ⊠*3655 Las Vegas Blvd. S, Center Strip,*
☎*702/739–4111 or 877/796–2096* ⊕*www.paris-lv.com* ⇖*2,621
rooms, 295 suites*⊟*AE, D, DC, MC, V.*

NIGHTLIFE & THE ARTS

FodorśChoice   **Body English.** An increasingly competitive nightclub environment sent
★   Hard Rock reps scouring Europe's hottest nightspots in search of a
winning design to replace the previous dance emporium. The chosen
theme seems to be "1970s decadent English rock aristocracy's living
room," and it works. As wallflowers swill brandy, very sexy singles
gyrate on the dance floor under a huge crystal chandelier said to be
valued at $250,000. Meanwhile, you can find celebs (and there tend
to be a lot of them, depending on the event—one time we were there,
Jenna Jameson and Jenny McCarthy were purring at each other) hang
out in VIP areas that overlook the action. Sunday night is when the
grooviness soars for the weekly party night. ⊠*Hard Rock Hotel and
Casino, 4455 Paradise Rd., Paradise Road*☎*702/693–5000.*

★   **Crown & Anchor Pub.** Not far from the Strip, this friendly British-style
pub caters to the university crowd. Grab a Guinness, Newcastle, or
Blackthorn Cider from the very, very, very extensive drinks menu,
play a game of darts, or settle in and grab some grub. ⊠*1350 E.
Tropicana Ave., University District*☎*702/739–8676* ⊕*www.crown
andanchorlv.com.*

VITAL STATS

■ Las Vegas is home to 538,653 people plus about a million and a half more outside the city limits.

■ The city is disproportionately foreign-born with 20% of citizens hailing from outside the country as opposed to 12% nationally.

■ MGM Grand is the world's largest hotel in terms of rooms. Luxor is third. (In case you're wondering, some hotel in Thailand is second.)

■ Las Vegas is one of the fastest-growing cities in the United States;

more than 5,000 people move here every month.

■ The valley was discovered by Europeans by a Spanish Expedition in 1826 that noted the many springs in the area. Mormon missionaries moved in before the Civil War and the city was incorporated in 1905 after it had become an important railroad center.

■ Las Vegas averages 294 days of sun per year with an average daytime high of 80°.

13

Ghostbar. Perched on the penthouse level of the Palms, this apex of ultralounges has rock music, glamorous patrons, glowing lights, and a glassed-in view of the city. Step outside and you can find that the nice outdoor deck is cantilevered over the side of the building, with a Plexiglas platform that allows revelers to look down 450 feet below. Because of the laughably complicated process to get in the door, some might find this spot frustrating (although, with the right blend of patience and good humor, getting inside can be highly entertaining). ⊠*The Palms, 4321 W. Flamingo Rd., West Side* ☎*702/938–2666 or 702/492–3960* ⊕*www.n9negroup.com.*

Fodor'sChoice ★ **Mix at THEhotel.** Floor-to-ceiling windows, an appealing curved bar, an equally appealing staff—what could top all that? An outdoor deck that offers stunning views of the Strip, that's what. At this spot atop THEhotel at Mandalay, even the glass-walled restrooms give you a window onto the city. Black leather accented by red lighting creates a hipper-than-thou vibe. ⊠*Mandalay Bay Resort & Casino, 3590 Las Vegas Blvd. S, South Strip* ☎*877/632–9500.*

Fodor'sChoice ★ **Peppermill's Fireside Lounge.** Many visitors to Sin City looking for a bit of ring-a-ding-ding leave disappointed, finding the frequently swinging wrecking ball has left behind little but massive movie-set-like resort-casinos to dominate the landscape. But benign neglect has preserved this shagadelic lounge, one of the town's truly essential nightspots. Near the old Stardust Hotel, this evergreen ironic-romantic getaway serves food, but what you're really here for is the must-see-to-believe firepit, the crazy waitress outfits, and the lethally alcoholic Scorpion cocktail. The Pep showed up in the Martin Scorsese film *Casino.* ⊠*2985 Las Vegas Blvd. S, Center Strip* ☎*702/735–7635* ⊕*www.peppermilllasvegas.com.*

Fodor'sChoice ★ **PURE.** Although other clubs are newer and flashier, PURE still takes the cake for best all-around shake appeal. In addition to its super-cool Tuesday night party and alluring crowd, it's got a secret weapon in its outdoor terrace, one complete with waterfalls, private cabanas, dance floor, and a view that places you not high above but right in the middle of the action on the Strip. Indoor types party in a cream-color main room or in the smaller Red Room, which is a special VIP area. For the deejay mavens out there, red-hot spinmeister (and former Nicole Richie beau) DJ AM is in residence. It connects to the fabulous Pussycat Dolls Lounge if you need a breather. ⊠ *Caesars Palace, 3500 Las Vegas Blvd. S, Center Strip* ☎ *702/731–7873.*

SHOPPING

BEST MALLS

★ **Fashion Show Mall.** It's impossible to miss this swanky, fashion-devoted mall due to one big element: The Cloud, a futuristic steel shade structure that looms high above the mall's entrance. Ads and footage of the mall's own fashion events are continuously projected onto the eye-catching architecture (think Times Square à la Las Vegas). The inside of the mall is sleek, spacious, and airy, a nice change from some of the claustrophobic casino malls. The mall delivers on its name—fashion shows are occasionally staged in the Great Hall on an 80-foot-long catwalk that rises from the floor. Not everything here is overpriced. Although you do find many of the same stores that are at the casino malls, such as Louis Vuitton, there's also a smattering of different fare; trendy clothes boutique Talulah G.; and the only bookstore on the Strip, Waldenbooks. Neiman Marcus, Saks Fifth Avenue, two Macy's stores, Bloomingdale's Home, Nordstrom, and Dillard's serve as the department-store anchors. Fashion Show is next to the New Frontier. ⊠ *3200 Las Vegas Blvd. S, North Strip* ☎ *702/369–8382* ⊕ *www.thefashionshow.com.*

Fodor'sChoice The **Forum Shops at Caesars** resemble an ancient Roman streetscape,
★ with immense columns and arches, two central piazzas with fountains, and a cloud-filled ceiling with a sky that changes from sunrise to sunset over the course of three hours. The Festival Fountain (in the west wing of the mall) puts on its own show every hour on the hour daily starting at 10 AM: a robotic, pie-eyed Bacchus hosts a party for friends Apollo, Venus, and Mars, complete with lasers, music, and sound effects; at the end, the god of wine and merriment delivers—what else?—a sales pitch for the mall. The "Atlantis" show (in the east wing) is even more amazing: Atlas, king of Atlantis, can't seem to pick between his son, Gadrius, and his daughter, Alia, to assume the throne. A struggle for control of the doomed kingdom ensues amid flame and smoke. If you can tear yourself away from the animatronic wizardry, you can find designer shops and the old standbys. For fashionistas, there are all the hard-hitters: Christian Dior, Gucci, Fendi, Pucci, Louis Vuitton, Tod's, and Valentino (whew!). Pick up your diamonds at Harry Winston, Bulgari, or Chopard, or go for a sparkling handbag at Judith Leiber. If your purse strings are a little tighter, there's always the ubiquitous Gap or Abercrombie stores. The mall is open late (until 11 Sunday through Thursday, until midnight Friday and Saturday). ⊠ *Caesars Palace, 3500 Las Vegas Blvd. S, Center Strip* ☎ *702/896–5599 Appian Way, 702/893–4800 Forum Shops* ⊕ *www.forumshops.com.*

Fodor'sChoice **The Venetian.** The **Grand Canal Shoppes** are *the* most elegant—and
★ fun—shopping experience on the Strip. Duck into shops like Burberry
or Lladró as you amble under blue skies alongside a Vegas-ified Grand
Canal. Eventually, all the quaint bridges and walkways lead you to St.
Mark's Square, which is full of little gift-shop carts and street performers. If you're loaded down with bags, hail a gondola—it's one of the
kitschiest experiences in any of the megamalls ($15 per person). Two
must-see stores are Il Prato, which sells unique Venetian collectibles,
including masks, stationery sets, and pen-and-inkwell sets, and Ripa de
Monti, which carries luminescent Venetian glass. Also, because Arizona's famous Canyon Ranch spa has an outpost here, there's the don't-
miss Canyon Ranch Living Essentials shop, full of cookbooks, body
products, and spa robes. The mall is open late (until 11 Sunday through
Thursday, until midnight Friday and Saturday). ⊠ *Venetian Resort-
Hotel-Casino, 3355 Las Vegas Blvd. S, Center Strip* ☎ *702/733–5000*
⊕ *www.venetian.com.*

ONLY IN VEGAS

★ **Bonanza "World's Largest Gift Shop."** OK, so it may not, in fact, be the
world's largest, but it's the town's largest—and for that matter, the
town's best—souvenir store. Although it has most of the usual junk,
it also stocks some unusual junk. Dying for a pair of fuzzy pink dice
to hang on your car's rearview mirror? They've got 'em in spades.
Can't go home without your own blinking "Welcome to Fabulous Las
Vegas" sign? Or the coveted Elvis aviator sunglasses complete with
black sideburns? Or how about a mechanical card shuffler, dealer's
green visor, and authentic clay poker chips for poker nights back home?
They're all right here. The store is so huge that you won't feel trapped,
as you might in some of the smaller shops. It's open until midnight,
and it's across from the Sahara. ⊠ *2460 Las Vegas Blvd. S, North
Strip* ☎ *702/385–7359* ⊕ *www.worldslargestgiftshop.com.*

Gambler's Book Shop. GBC is the world's largest independent bookstore specializing in books about 21, craps, poker, roulette, and all the
other games of chance, as well as novels about casinos, biographies
of crime figures, and anything else that relates to gambling and Las
Vegas. ⊠ *630 S. 11th St., Downtown* ☎ *702/382–7555 or 800/522–
1777* ⊕ *www.gamblersbook.com.*

The Liberace Museum Store. The store stocks the maestro's CDs and videos,
jewelry, and, in case you're running low, his signature candelabras. ⊠ *1775
E. Tropicana Ave., East Side* ☎ *702/798–5595* ⊕ *www.liberace.org.*

☾ **Star Trek Store.** Inside the Star Trek Experience, Trekkies salivate over
★ this collection of Federation merchandise: uniforms, Tribbles (Trekkies
know what this is), rare artwork, and the "Original Series Communica-
tor." There's also a large collection of Starfleet Academy Merchandise.
You may come across rare props from the original series and its string
of sequels. These very rare collectibles include a $5,000 life-size Borg
Queen. Check out the bargains at Ferengi Liquidations. ⊠ *Las Vegas
Hilton, 3000 Paradise Rd., Paradise Road* ☎ *888/697–8735* ⊕ *www.
startrekexp.com.*

13

SPORTS & THE OUTDOORS

GOLF

Bali Hai Golf Club. The calling card of this 7,002-yard par-71 is its convenience to the Strip; the tee for the first hole is a few minutes' walk from the Mandalay Bay. The course was designed to mimic a South Pacific paradise, with white sand, palm trees, and exotic plants perched on volcanic outcroppings. The clubhouse includes a pro shop and the well-regarded Cili Restaurant, but beware there's no practice facility and the proximity to the airport can be distracting depending on how cooperative Air Traffic Control is being the day you're there. Greens fees start at around $200 for the twilight specials, and well North of $325 on weekends. *5160 Las Vegas Blvd. S.,* ☎*888/427–6678* ⊕*www. balihaigolfclub.com.*

★ **Reflection Bay Golf Club.** Fifteen miles from the Strip and minutes from the Hyatt resort, the 7,261-yard par-72 Jack Nicklaus–designed Reflection Bay has a beautiful location fronting Lake Las Vegas, with 10 mi of lakefront beach. MiraLago Lakeside Mediterranean Café, in the elegant clubhouse, has a large patio overlooking the lake. Weekday greens fees are $275; $295 on weekends. Twilight rates are $160 weekdays and $180 weekends. Guests at Lake Las Vegas hotels pay about $60 less per round. ✉*75 MonteLago Blvd., Henderson* ☎*702/740–4653* ⊕*www.lakelasvegas.com.*

Shadow Creek Las Vegas. It will cost you a pretty penny, but the back nine of this exclusive course is a memorable parade of sublimely proportioned holes that will challenge your decision-making as much as your swing. The 7,239-yard par-72 was originally built by casino mogul Steve Wynn before being sold to MGM. Appropriately enough, it's still frequented by Hollywood A-Listers. If you can stand being among shallow movie stars for an afternoon, you'll enjoy a magical setting of Tom Fazio–architected waterfalls and pine trees, incongruously placed amid the sandy flats of North Las Vegas. *3 Shadow Creek Dr.* ☎*866/260–0069* ⊕*www.shadowcreek.com.*

HIKING & CAMPING

Floyd Lamb Park. Now a Las Vegas city park, this 2,000-acre swath of green in Northwest Las Vegas offers walking paths, picnic tables, several stock ponds for fishing, the Tule Springs archeological sites, and a gun club for shooters. Open Daily 7–7. 9200 Tule Springs Rd. ☎*702/486–5413*

Mt. Charleston. In winter Las Vegans crowd the upper elevations of the Spring Mountains to throw snowballs, sled, cross-country ski, and even slide downhill at a little ski area. In summer they return to wander the high trails and escape the valley's 115°F heat (temperatures are at least 20°F cooler than in the city), and maybe even make the difficult hike to Mt. Charleston, the range's high point. Easier trails lead to seasonal waterfalls or rare, dripping springs where dainty columbine and stunted aspens spill down ravines and hummingbirds zoom. Or they might lead onto high, dry ridges where ancient bristlecone trees have become twisted and burnished with age. For camping information contact the **U.S. Forest Service** (☎702/515–5400). For recorded snow reports and winter road conditions call the **Las Vegas Ski and Snowboard Resort** (☎702/593–9500).

Red Rock Canyon National Conservation Area. Go West on Charleston Blvd and before long you're in the Bureau of Land Management-controlled territory of Red Rock Canyon, featuring a research center, picnic areas, hiking trails, vistas, scenic roads, and a rock-climber's paradise. Visitor Center hours are 8am–4:30pm daily. ☎702/363–1921 ⊕www.balihaigolfclub.com.

13

WATER SPORTS

Lake Mead, which is actually the Colorado River backed up behind the Hoover Dam, is the nation's largest man-made reservoir: it covers 229 square mi, is 110 mi long, and has an irregular shoreline that extends for 550 mi. You can get information about the lake's history, ecology, recreational opportunities, and the accommodations available along its shore at the **Alan Bible Visitors Center** (☎702/293–8990 ⊕www.nps.gov/lame/visitorcenter/ ☉Daily 8:30–4:30). People come to Lake Mead to swim: **Boulder Beach** is the closest to Las Vegas, only a mile or so from the visitor center.

Angling and houseboating are favorite pastimes; marinas strung along the Nevada shore rent houseboats, personal watercraft, and ski boats. The lake is regularly stocked with a half-million rainbow trout, and at least a million fish are harvested every year. You can fish here 24 hours a day, year-round (except for posted closings). You must have a fishing license (details are on the National Park Service Web site), and if you plan to catch and keep trout, a separate trout stamp is required. Divers can explore the murk beneath, including the usually submerged foundations of St. Thomas, a farming community that was inundated in 1938. ⊕www.nps.gov/lame 🎟$5 per vehicle, good for 5 days; lake-use fees $10 first vessel, $5 additional vessel, good for 1–5 days.

VISITOR INFORMATION

Before you go to Las Vegas, contact the city and state tourism offices for general information. When you get there, you might want to visit the Las Vegas Convention and Visitors Authority (3150 Paradise Road), next door to the Las Vegas Hilton, for brochures and general information. Hotels and gift shops on the Strip have maps, brochures, pamphlets, and free-events magazines—*What's On in Las Vegas, Showbiz,* and *Las Vegas Today*—that list shows and buffets and offer discounts to area attractions.

The *Las Vegas Advisor,* a monthly print newsletter and online Web site, keeps up-to-the-minute track of the constantly changing Las Vegas landscapes of gambling, accommodations, dining, entertainment, Top Ten Values (a monthly list of the city's best deals), complimentary offerings, coupons, and more and is an indispensable resource for any Las Vegas visitor. Send $5 for a sample issue, or buy a 72-hour membership to the *Advisor's* online version by logging on to ⊕*www.lasvegasad visor.com*. Annual print memberships cost $50, and online memberships cost $37 per year.

Las Vegas Advisor (☎*702/252–0655* ⊕*www.lasvegasadvisor.com*).
Las Vegas Convention and Visitors Authority (☎*702/892–0711 or 877/847–4858* ⊕*www.visitlasvegas.com*).
Nevada Commission on Tourism (☎*775/687–4322 or 800/638–2328* ⊕*www.travelnevada.com*).

American Southwest Essentials

PLANNING TOOLS, EXPERT INSIGHT,
GREAT CONTACTS

There are planners and there are those who, excuse the pun, fly by the seat of their pants. We happily place ourselves among the planners. Our writers and editors try to anticipate all the issues you may face before and during any journey, and then they do their research. This section is the product of their efforts. Use it to get excited about your trip to the American Southwest, to inform your travel planning, or to guide you on the road should the seat of your pants start to feel threadbare.

GETTING STARTED

We're really proud of our Web site: Fodors.com is a great place to begin any journey. Scan Travel Wire for suggested itineraries, travel deals, restaurant and hotel openings, and other up-to-the-minute info. Check out Booking to research prices and book plane tickets, hotel rooms, rental cars, and vacation packages. Head to Talk for on-the-ground pointers from travelers who frequent our message boards. You can also link to loads of other travel-related resources.

▌RESOURCES

ONLINE TRAVEL TOOLS

ALL ABOUT THE USA
Safety Transportation Security Administration (TSA ⊕ www.tsa.gov)

Time Zones Timeanddate.com (⊕ www.timeanddate.com/worldclock) can help you figure out the correct time anywhere.

Weather Accuweather.com (⊕ www.accuweather.com) is an independent weather-forecasting service with good coverage of hurricanes. **Weather.com** (⊕ www.weather.com) is the Web site for the Weather Channel.

▌THINGS TO CONSIDER

GEAR

SHIPPING LUGGAGE AHEAD
Imagine traveling with only a carry-on in tow. Shipping your luggage in advance via an air-freight service is a great way to cut down on backaches, hassles, and stress—especially if your packing list includes strollers, car seats, etc. There are some things to be aware of, though.

First, research carry-on restrictions; if you absolutely need something that isn't practical to ship and isn't allowed in carry-ons, this strategy isn't for you. Second, plan to send your bags several days in advance. Third, plan to spend some money: it will cost at least $100 to send

a small piece of luggage, a golf bag, or a pair of skis to a domestic destination, much more to places overseas.

Some people use Federal Express to ship their bags, but this can cost even more than air-freight services. All these services insure your bag (for most, the limit is $1,000, but you should verify that amount); you can, however, purchase additional insurance for about $1 per $100 of value.

Contacts Luggage Concierge (☎ 800/288–9818 ⊕ www.luggageconcierge.com). **Luggage Express** (☎ 866/744–7224 ⊕ www.usxpluggageexpress.com). **Luggage Free** (☎ 800/361–6871 ⊕ www.luggagefree.com). **Sports Express** (☎ 800/357–4174 ⊕ www.sportsexpress.com) specializes in shipping golf clubs and other sports equipment. **Virtual Bellhop** (☎ 877/235–5467 ⊕ www.virtualbellhop.com).

TRIP INSURANCE
What kind of coverage do you honestly need? Do you even need trip insurance at all? Take a deep breath and read on.

We believe that comprehensive trip insurance is especially valuable if you're booking a very expensive or complicated trip (particularly to an isolated region) or if you're booking far in advance. Who knows what could happen six months down the road? But whether or not you get insurance has more to do with how comfortable you are assuming all that risk yourself.

Comprehensive travel policies typically cover trip-cancellation and interruption,

Trip Insurance Resources

INSURANCE COMPARISON SITES		
Insure My Trip.com	800/487–4722	www.insuremytrip.com
Square Mouth.com	800/240–0369	www.quotetravelinsurance.com
COMPREHENSIVE TRAVEL INSURERS		
Access America	866/807–3982	www.accessamerica.com
CSA Travel Protection	800/873–9855	www.csatravelprotection.com
HTH Worldwide	610/254–8700 or 888/243–2358	www.hthworldwide.com
Travelex Insurance	888/457–4602	www.travelex-insurance.com
Travel Guard International	715/345–0505 or 800/826–4919	www.travelguard.com
Travel Insured International	800/243–3174	www.travelinsured.com
MEDICAL-ONLY INSURERS		
International Medical Group	800/628–4664	www.imgglobal.com
International SOS	215/942–8000 or 713/521–7611	www.internationalsos.com
Wallach & Company	800/237–6615 or 504/687–3166	www.wallach.com

letting you cancel or cut your trip short because of a personal emergency, illness, or, in some cases, acts of terrorism in your destination. Such policies also cover evacuation and medical care. Some also cover you for trip delays because of bad weather or mechanical problems as well as for lost or delayed baggage. Another type of coverage to look for is financial default—that is, when your trip is disrupted because a tour operator, airline, or cruise line goes out of business. Generally you must buy this when you book your trip or shortly thereafter, and it's only available to you if your operator isn't on a list of excluded companies.

Expect comprehensive travel insurance policies to cost about 4% to 7% or 8% of the total price of your trip (it's more like 8%–12% if you're over age 70). A medical-only policy may or may not be cheaper than a comprehensive policy. Always read the fine print of your policy to make sure that you are covered for the risks that are of most concern to you.

Compare several policies to make sure you're getting the best price and range of coverage available.

■TIP→ OK. You know you can save a bundle on trips to warm-weather destinations by traveling in the rainy season. But there's also a chance that a severe storm will disrupt your plans. The solution? Look for hotels and resorts that offer storm/hurricane guarantees. Although they rarely allow refunds, most guarantees do let you rebook later if a storm strikes.

BOOKING YOUR TRIP

❙ ONLINE

You really have to shop around. A travel wholesaler such as Hotels.com or Hotel-Club.net can be a source of good rates, as can discounters such as Hotwire or Priceline, particularly if you can bid for your hotel room or airfare. Indeed, such sites sometimes have deals that are unavailable elsewhere. They do, however, tend to work only with hotel chains (which makes them just plain useless for getting hotel reservations outside of major cities) or big airlines (so that often leaves out upstarts like jetBlue and some foreign carriers like Air India).

Also, with discounters and wholesalers you must generally prepay, and everything is nonrefundable. And before you fork over the dough, be sure to check the terms and conditions, so you know what a given company will do for you if there's a problem and what you'll have to deal with on your own.

■TIP➡ **To be absolutely sure everything was processed correctly, confirm reservations made through online travel agents, discounters, and wholesalers directly with your hotel before leaving home.**

Booking engines like Expedia, Travelocity, and Orbitz are actually travel agents, albeit high-volume, online ones. And airline travel packagers like American Airlines Vacations and Virgin Vacations—well, they're travel agents, too. But they may still not work with all the world's hotels.

An aggregator site will search many sites and pull the best prices for airfares, hotels, and rental cars from them. Most aggregators compare the major travel-booking sites such as Expedia, Travelocity, and Orbitz; some also look at airline Web sites, though rarely the sites of smaller budget airlines. Some aggregators also compare other travel products, including complex packages—a good thing, as you can sometimes get the best overall deal by booking an air-and-hotel package.

❙ WITH A TRAVEL AGENT

If you use an agent—brick-and-mortar or virtual—you'll pay a fee for the service. And know that the service you get from some online agents isn't comprehensive. For example Expedia and Travelocity don't search for prices on budget airlines like jetBlue, Southwest, or small foreign carriers. That said, some agents (online or not) *do* have access to fares that are difficult to find otherwise, and the savings can more than make up for any surcharge.

A knowledgeable brick-and-mortar travel agent can be a godsend if you're booking a cruise, a package trip that's not available to you directly, an air pass, or a complicated itinerary including several overseas flights. What's more, travel agents that specialize in a destination may have exclusive access to certain deals and insider information on things such as charter flights. Agents who specialize in types of travelers (senior citizens, gays and lesbians, naturists) or types of trips (cruises, luxury travel, safaris) can also be invaluable.

■TIP➡ **Remember that Expedia, Travelocity, and Orbitz are travel agents, not just booking engines. To resolve any problems with a reservation made through these companies, contact them first.**

Complain about the surcharges all you like, but when things don't work out the way you'd hoped, it's nice to have an agent to put things right.

Agent Resources American Society of Travel Agents (☎703/739–2782 ⊕www.travelsense.org).

Online Booking Resources

AGGREGATORS

Kayak	www.kayak.com	also looks at cruises and vacation packages.
Mobissimo	www.mobissimo.com	
Qixo	www.qixo.com	also compares cruises, vacation packages, and even travel insurance.
Sidestep	www.sidestep.com	also compares vacation packages and lists travel deals.
Travelgrove	www.travelgrove.com	also compares cruises and packages.

BOOKING ENGINES

Cheap Tickets	www.cheaptickets.com	a discounter.
Expedia	www.expedia.com	a large online agency that charges a booking fee for airline tickets.
Hotwire	www.hotwire.com	a discounter.
lastminute.com	www.lastminute.com	specializes in last-minute travel the main site is for the U.K., but it has a link to a U.S. site.
Luxury Link	www.luxurylink.com	has auctions (surprisingly good deals) as well as offers on the high-end side of travel.
Onetravel.com	www.onetravel.com	a discounter for hotels, car rentals, airfares, and packages.
Orbitz	www.orbitz.com	charges a booking fee for airline tickets, but gives a clear breakdown of fees and taxes before you book.
Priceline.com	www.priceline.com	a discounter that also allows bidding.
Travel.com	www.travel.com	allows you to compare its rates with those of other booking engines.
Travelocity	www.travelocity.com	charges a booking fee for airline tickets, but promises good problem resolution.

ONLINE ACCOMMODATIONS

Hotelbook.com	www.hotelbook.com	focuses on independent hotels worldwide.
Hotel Club	www.hotelclub.net	good for major cities worldwide.
Hotels.com	www.hotels.com	a big Expedia-owned wholesaler that offers rooms in hotels all over the world.
Quikbook	www.quikbook.com	offers "pay when you stay" reservations that let you settle your bill at checkout, not when you book.

OTHER RESOURCES

Bidding For Travel	www.biddingfortravel.com	a good place to figure out what you can get and for how much before you start bidding on, say, Priceline.

Online Booking Resources

CONTACTS		
Forgetaway		www.forgetaway.weather.com
Home Away	512/493–0382	www.homeaway.com
Interhome	954/791–8282 or 800/882–6864	www.interhome.us
Vacation Home Rentals Worldwide	201/767–9393 or 800/633–3284	www.vhrww.com
Villas International	415/499–9490 or 800/221–2260	www.villasintl.com

■ ACCOMMODATIONS

Most hotels and other lodgings require you to give your credit-card details before they will confirm your reservation. If you don't feel comfortable e-mailing this information, ask if you can fax it (some places even prefer faxes). However you book, get confirmation in writing and have a copy of it handy when you check in.

Be sure you understand the hotel's cancellation policy. Some places allow you to cancel without any kind of penalty— even if you prepaid to secure a discounted rate—if you cancel at least 24 hours in advance. Others require you to cancel a week in advance or penalize you the cost of one night. Small inns and B&Bs are most likely to require you to cancel far in advance. Most hotels allow children under a certain age to stay in their parents' room at no extra charge, but others charge for them as extra adults; find out the cutoff age for discounts.

■TIP→ Assume that hotels operate on the European Plan (EP, no meals) unless we specify that they use the Breakfast Plan (BP, with full breakfast), Continental Plan (CP, continental breakfast), Full American Plan (FAP, all meals), Modified American Plan (MAP, breakfast and dinner) or are all-inclusive (AI, all meals and most activities).

BED & BREAKFASTS

Reservation Services **Bed & Breakfast.com** (☎512/322–2710 or 800/462–2632 ⊕www. bedandbreakfast.com) also sends out an online newsletter. **Bed & Breakfast Inns Online** (☎615/868–1946 or 800/215–7365 ⊕www. bbonline.com). **BnB Finder.com** (☎212/432–7693 or 888/547–8226 ⊕www.bnbfinder.com).

HOME EXCHANGES

Exchange Clubs **Home Exchange.com** (☎800/877–8723 ⊕www.homeexchange. com); $59.95 for a 1-year online listing. **HomeLink International** (☎800/638–3841 ⊕www.homelink.org); $90 yearly for Web-only membership; $140 includes Web access and two catalogs. **Intervac U.S.** (☎800/756–4663 ⊕www.intervacus.com); $78.88 for Web-only membership; $126 includes Web access and a catalog.

■ AIRLINE TICKETS

Most domestic airline tickets are electronic. With an e-ticket the only thing you receive is an e-mailed receipt citing your itinerary and reservation and ticket numbers.

The greatest advantage of an e-ticket is that if you lose your receipt, you can simply print out another copy or ask the airline to do it for you at check-in. You usually pay a surcharge (up to $50) to get a paper ticket, if you can get one at all.

The sole advantage of a paper ticket is that it may be easier to endorse over to another airline if your flight is canceled and the airline with which you booked can't accommodate you on another flight.

■TIP→ Discount air passes that let you travel economically in a country or region

Car-Rental Resources

AUTOMOBILE ASSOCIATIONS		
U.S.: American Automobile Association (AAA)	315/797–5000	www.aaa.com; most contact with the organization is through state and regional members.
National Automobile Club	650/294–7000	www.thenac.com; membership is open to California residents only.
MAJOR AGENCIES		
Alamo	800/462–5266	www.alamo.com.
Avis	800/331–1084	www.avis.com.
Budget	800/472–3325	www.budget.com.
Enterprise	800/261–7331	www.enterprise.com
Hertz	800/654–3001	www.hertz.com.
National Car Rental	800/227–7368	www.nationalcar.com.

must often be purchased before you leave home. In some cases you can only get them through a travel agent.

▋ RENTAL CARS

When you reserve a car, ask about cancellation penalties, taxes, drop-off charges (if you're planning to pick up the car in one city and leave it in another), and surcharges (for being under or over a certain age, for additional drivers, or for driving across state or country borders or beyond a specific distance from your point of rental). All these things can add substantially to your costs. Request car seats and extras such as GPS when you book.

Rates are sometimes—but not always—better if you book in advance or reserve through a rental agency's Web site. There are other reasons to book ahead, though: for popular destinations, during busy times of the year, or to ensure that you get certain types of cars (vans, SUVs, exotic sports cars).

▋TIP→ Make sure that a confirmed reservation guarantees you a car. Agencies sometimes overbook, particularly for busy weekends and holiday periods.

CAR-RENTAL INSURANCE

Everyone who rents a car wonders whether the insurance that the rental companies offer is worth the expense. No one—including us—has a simple answer. It all depends on how much regular insurance you have, how comfortable you are with risk, and whether or not money is an issue.

If you own a car and carry comprehensive car insurance for both collision and liability, your personal auto insurance will probably cover a rental, but read your policy's fine print to be sure. If you don't have auto insurance, then you should probably buy the collision- or loss-damage waiver (CDW or LDW) from the rental company. This eliminates your liability for damage to the car.

Some credit cards offer CDW coverage, but it's usually supplemental to your own insurance and rarely covers SUVs, minivans, luxury models, and the like. If your coverage is secondary, you may still be liable for loss-of-use costs from the car-rental company (again, read the fine print). But no credit-card insurance is valid unless you use that card for *all* transactions, from reserving to paying the final bill.

■TIP→Diners Club offers primary CDW coverage on all rentals reserved and paid for with the card. This means that Diners Club's company—not your own car insurance—pays in case of an accident. It *doesn't* mean that your car-insurance company won't raise your rates once it discovers you had an accident.

You may also be offered supplemental liability coverage; the car-rental company is required to carry a minimal level of liability coverage insuring all renters, but it's rarely enough to cover claims in a really serious accident if you're at fault. Your own auto-insurance policy will protect you if you own a car; if you don't, you have to decide whether you are willing to take the risk.

U.S. rental companies sell CDWs and LDWs for about $15 to $25 a day; supplemental liability is usually more than $10 a day. The car-rental company may offer you all sorts of other policies, but they're rarely worth the cost. Personal accident insurance, which is basic hospitalization coverage, is an especially egregious rip-off if you already have health insurance.

■TIP→You can decline the insurance from the rental company and purchase it through a third-party provider such as Travel Guard (www.travelguard.com)—$9 per day for $35,000 of coverage. That's sometimes just under half the price of the CDW offered by some car-rental companies.

■ VACATION PACKAGES

Packages *are not* guided excursions. Packages combine airfare, accommodations, and perhaps a rental car or other extras (theater tickets, guided excursions, boat trips, reserved entry to popular museums, transit passes), but they let you do your own thing. During busy periods packages may be your only option, as flights and rooms may be sold out otherwise.

Packages will definitely save you time. They can also save you money, particularly in peak seasons, but—and this is a really big "but"—you should price each part of the package separately to be sure. And be aware that prices advertised on Web sites and in newspapers rarely include service charges or taxes, which can up your costs by hundreds of dollars.

■TIP→Some packages and cruises are sold only through travel agents. Don't always assume that you can get the best deal by booking everything yourself.

Each year consumers are stranded or lose their money when packagers—even large ones with excellent reputations—go out of business. How can you protect yourself?

First, always pay with a credit card; if you have a problem, your credit-card company may help you resolve it. Second, buy trip insurance that covers default. Third, choose a company that belongs to the United States Tour Operators Association, whose members must set aside funds to cover defaults. Finally, choose a company that also participates in the Tour Operator Program of the American Society of Travel Agents (ASTA), which will act as mediator in any disputes.

You can also check on the tour operator's reputation among travelers by posting an inquiry on one of the Fodors.com forums.

Organizations American Society of Travel Agents (ASTA ☎703/739–2782 or 800/965–2782 ⊕www.astanet.com). **United States Tour Operators Association** (USTOA ☎212/599–6599 ⊕www.ustoa.com).

■TIP→Local tourism boards can provide information about lesser-known and small-niche operators that sell packages to only a few destinations.

TRANSPORTATION

▌BY AIR

■TIP➜If you travel frequently, look into the TSA's Registered Traveler program. The program, which is still being tested in several U.S. airports, is designed to cut down on gridlock at security checkpoints by allowing prescreened travelers to pass quickly through kiosks that scan an iris and/or a fingerprint. How sci-fi is that?

Airlines & Airports Airline and Airport Links.com (⊕www.airlineandairportlinks. com) has links to many of the world's airlines and airports.

Airline Security Issues Transportation Security Administration (⊕www.tsa.gov) has answers for almost every question that might come up.

AIR TRAVEL RESOURCES IN THE USA

FLIGHTS

Airline Contacts Alaska Airlines (☎800/252–7522 or 206/433–3100 ⊕www.alaskaair.com). **American Airlines** (☎800/433–7300 ⊕www.aa.com). **ATA** (☎800/435–9282 or 317/282–8308 ⊕www.ata.com). **Continental Airlines** (☎800/523–3273 for U.S. and Mexico reservations, 800/231–0856 for international reservations ⊕www.continental.com). **Delta Airlines** (☎800/221–1212 for U.S. reservations, 800/241–4141 for international reservations ⊕www.delta.com). **jetBlue** (☎800/538–2583 ⊕www.jetblue.com). **Northwest Airlines** (☎800/225–2525 ⊕www.nwa.com). **Southwest Airlines** (☎800/435–9792 ⊕www. southwest.com). **Spirit Airlines** (☎800/772–7117 or 586/791–7300 ⊕www.spiritair.com). **United Airlines** (☎800/864–8331 for U.S. reservations, 800/538–2929 for international reservations ⊕www.united.com). **USAirways** (☎800/428–4322 for U.S. and Canada reservations, 800/622–1015 for international reservations ⊕www.usairways.com).

▌BY BUS

Bus Information Greyhound Lines, Inc. (☎800/231–2222 ⊕www.greyhound.com)

▌BY TRAIN

Information Amtrak (☎800/872–7245, 800/523–6590 TDD/TTY ⊕www.amtrak.com).

FOR INTERNATIONAL TRAVELERS

CURRENCY

The dollar is the basic unit of U.S. currency. It has 100 cents. Coins are the penny (1¢); the nickel (5¢), dime (10¢), quarter (25¢), half-dollar (50¢), and the very rare golden $1 coin and even rarer silver $1. Bills are denominated $1, $5, $10, $20, $50, and $100, all mostly green and identical in size; designs and background tints vary. You may come across a $2 bill, but the chances are slim.

CUSTOMS

Information **U.S. Customs and Border Protection** (⊕ www.cbp.gov).

DRIVING

Driving in the United States is on the right. Speed limits are posted in miles per hour (usually between 55 mph and 70 mph). Watch for lower limits in small towns and on back roads (usually 30 mph to 40 mph). Most states require front-seat passengers to wear seat belts; many states require children to sit in the back seat and to wear seat belts. In major cities rush hour is between 7 and 10 AM; afternoon rush hour is between 4 and 7 PM. To encourage carpooling, some freeways have special lanes, ordinarily marked with a diamond, for high-occupancy vehicles (HOV)—cars carrying two people or more.

Highways are well paved. Interstates—limited-access, multilane highways designated with an "I–" before the number—are fastest. Interstates with three-digit numbers circle urban areas, which may also have other limited-access expressways, freeways, and parkways. Tolls may be levied on limited-access highways. U.S. and state highways aren't necessarily limited-access, but may have several lanes.

Gas stations are plentiful. Most stay open late (24 hours along major highways and in big cities) except in rural areas, where Sunday hours are limited and where you may drive for long stretches without a refueling opportunity. Along larger highways, roadside stops with restrooms, fast-food restaurants, and sundries stores are well spaced. State police and tow trucks patrol major highways. If your car breaks down on an interstate, pull onto the shoulder and wait for help, or have your passengers wait while you walk to an emergency phone (available in most states). If you carry a cell phone, dial *55, noting your location on the small green roadside mileage marker.

ELECTRICITY

The U.S. standard is AC, 110 volts/60 cycles. Plugs have two flat pins set parallel to each other.

EMBASSIES

Contacts **Australia** (☎ 202/797–3000 ⊕ www.austemb.org). **Canada** (☎ 202/682–1740 ⊕ www.canadianembassy.org). **United Kingdom** (☎ 202/588–7800 ⊕ www.britainusa.com).

EMERGENCIES

For police, fire, or ambulance, dial 911 (0 in rural areas).

HOLIDAYS

New Year's Day (Jan. 1); Martin Luther King Day (3rd Mon. in Jan.); Presidents' Day (3rd Mon. in Feb.); Memorial Day (last Mon. in May); Independence Day (July 4); Labor Day (1st Mon. in Sept.); Columbus Day (2nd Mon. in Oct.); Thanksgiving Day (4th Thurs. in Nov.); Christmas Eve and Christmas Day (Dec. 24 and 25); and New Year's Eve (Dec. 31).

MAIL

You can buy stamps and aerograms and send letters and parcels in post offices. Stamp-dispensing machines can occasionally be found in airports, bus and train stations, office buildings, drugstores, and convenience stores. U.S. mail boxes are stout, dark blue steel bins; pickup schedules are posted inside the bin (pull down the handle to see them). Parcels weighing more than a pound must be mailed at a post office or at a private mailing center.

Within the United States a first-class letter weighing 1 ounce or less costs 42¢; each additional ounce costs 17¢. Postcards cost 27¢. Postcards or 1-ounce airmail letters to most countries costs 94¢; postcards or 1-ounce letters to Canada or Mexico cost 72¢.

To receive mail on the road, have it sent c/o General Delivery at your destination's main post office (use the correct five-digit ZIP code). You must pick up mail in person within 30 days, with a driver's license or passport for identification.

Contacts DHL (☎800/225–5345 ⊕www. dhl.com). **Federal Express** (☎800/463–3339 ⊕www.fedex.com). **Mail Boxes, Etc./ The UPS Store** (☎800/789–4623 ⊕www. mbe.com). **United States Postal Service** (⊕www.usps.com).

PASSPORTS & VISAS

Visitor visas aren't necessary for citizens of Australia, Canada, the United Kingdom, or most citizens of European Union countries coming for tourism and staying for fewer than 90 days. If you require a visa, the cost is $100, and waiting time can be substantial, depending on where you live. Apply for a visa at the U.S. consulate in your place of residence; check the U.S. State Department's special Visa Web site for further information.

Visa Information Destination USA (⊕www.unitedstatesvisas.gov).

PHONES

Numbers consist of a three-digit area code and a seven-digit local number. Within many local calling areas you dial only the seven digits; in others you dial "1" first and all 10 digits—just as you would for calls between area-code regions. The same is true for calls to numbers prefixed by "800," "888," "866," and "877"—all toll-free. For calls to numbers prefixed by "900" you must pay—usually dearly.

For international calls, dial "011" followed by the country code and the local number. For help, dial "0" and ask for an overseas operator. Most phone books list country codes and U.S. area codes. The country code for Australia is 61, for New Zealand 64, for the United Kingdom 44. Calling Canada is the same as calling within the United States, whose country code, by the way, is 1.

For operator assistance, dial "0." For directory assistance, call 555–1212 or occasionally 411 (free at many public phones). You can reverse long-distance charges by calling "collect"; dial "0" instead of "1" before the 10-digit number.

Instructions are generally posted on pay phones. Usually you insert coins in a slot (usually 25¢–50¢ for local calls) and wait for a steady tone before dialing. On long-distance calls the operator tells you how much to insert; prepaid phone cards, widely available in various denominations, can be used from any phone. Follow the directions to activate the card (there's usually an access number, then an activation code), then dial your number.

CELL PHONES

The United States has several GSM (Global System for Mobile Communications) networks, so multiband mobiles from most countries (except for Japan) work here. Unfortunately, it's almost impossible to buy a pay-as-you-go mobile SIM card in the U.S.—which allows you to avoid roaming charges—without also buying a phone. That said, cell phones with pay-as-you-go plans are available for well under $100. The cheapest ones with decent national coverage are the GoPhone from Cingular and Virgin Mobile, which only offers pay-as-you-go service.

Contacts Cingular (☎888/333–6651 ⊕www.cingular.com). **Virgin Mobile** (☎No phone ⊕www.virginmobileusa.com).

ON THE GROUND

▌ COMMUNICATIONS

INTERNET

Contacts **Cybercafes** (⊕www.cybercafes.com) lists over 4,000 Internet cafés worldwide.

▌ EATING OUT

RESERVATIONS & DRESS

Regardless of where you are, it's a good idea to make a reservation if you can. We only mention them specifically when reservations are essential (there's no other way you'll ever get a table) or when they are not accepted. For popular restaurants, book as far ahead as you can (often 30 days), and reconfirm as soon as you arrive. (Large parties should always call ahead to check the reservations policy.) We mention dress only when men are required to wear a jacket or a jacket and tie.

Online reservation services make it easy to book a table before you even leave home. OpenTable covers most states, including 20 major cities, and has limited listings in Canada, Mexico, the United Kingdom, and elsewhere. DinnerBroker has restaurants throughout the United States as well as a few in Canada.

Contacts **OpenTable** (⊕www.opentable.com). **DinnerBroker** (⊕www.dinnerbroker.com).

CREDIT CARDS

Throughout this guide, the following abbreviations are used: **AE**, American Express; **D**, Discover; **DC**, Diners Club; **MC**, MasterCard; and **V**, Visa.

It's a good idea to inform your credit-card company before you travel, especially if you're going abroad and don't travel internationally very often. Otherwise, the credit-card company might put a hold on your card owing to unusual activity—not a good thing halfway through your trip. Record all your credit-card numbers—as well as the phone numbers to call if your cards are lost or stolen—in a safe place, so you're prepared should something go wrong. Both MasterCard and Visa have general numbers you can call (collect if you're abroad) if your card is lost, but you're better off calling the number of your issuing bank, since MasterCard and Visa usually just transfer you to your bank; your bank's number is usually printed on your card.

Reporting Lost Cards **American Express** (☎800/528-4800 in U.S., 336/393-1111 collect from abroad ⊕www.americanexpress.com). **Diners Club** (☎800/234-6377 in U.S., 303/799-1504 collect from abroad ⊕www.dinersclub.com). **Discover** (☎800/347-2683 in U.S., 801/902-3100 collect from abroad ⊕www.discovercard.com). **MasterCard** (☎800/627-8372 in U.S., 636/722-7111 collect from abroad ⊕www.mastercard.com). **Visa** (☎800/847-2911 in U.S., 410/581-9994 collect from abroad ⊕www.visa.com).

TRAVELER'S CHECKS

Some consider this the currency of the cave man, and it's true that fewer establishments accept traveler's checks these days. Nevertheless, they're a cheap and secure way to carry extra money, particularly on trips to urban areas. Both Citibank (under the Visa brand) and American Express issue traveler's checks in the United States, but Amex is better known and more widely accepted; you can also avoid hefty surcharges by cashing Amex checks at Amex offices. Whatever you do, always keep track of all the serial numbers in case the checks are lost or stolen.

Contacts **American Express** (☎888/412-6945 in U.S., 801/945-9450 collect outside of U.S. to add value or speak to customer service ⊕www.americanexpress.com).

INDEX

A

A (shop), 70
Abiquiu, NM, 155—157
Adobe Bar, 190
Agate Bridge, 307
Agate House, 307
Air tours
Bryce Canyon National Park, 441
Grand Canyon National Park, 288
Northeast Arizona, 320
Southeastern Utah, 389
Zion National Park, 450
Air travel, 558—559, 561. ⇨See also transportation under specific destinations
Alamo Village, 508
Albuquerque, NM, 22—26
the arts, 62—64
dining, 42—52
exploring, 26—42
lodging, 52—61
nightlife, 61—62
price categories, 43, 53
shopping, 67—72
side trips, 72—82
sports & outdoors, 64—67
transportation, 24—25
visitor information, 25
when to go, 23—24
Albuquerque Aquarium, 27
Albuquerque BioPark, 27—29
Albuquerque International Balloon Fiesta, 39—40
Albuquerque Museum of Art and History, 29
Alex×, 539
Alexander's Inn ⬚, 117
Alhambra (shop), 196
Alley Cantina, 190
Alpine, TX, 503, 508
American Artists Gallery House Bed & Breakfast ⬚, 183
American International Rattlesnake Museum, 29, 32
Amerind Foundation, 369
"A" Mountain, 329
Amsterdam (bar), 248
Amusement parks, 64
Andaluz ⬚, 53
Anderson-Abruzzo International Balloon Museum, 39
Anderson Valley Vineyards, 40
Andiamo×, 101
André's French Restaurant×, 541
Andrew Smith Gallery, 135
Angel Fire, NM, 205—206
Angel Fire Resort, 206
Angels Landing Trail, 452
Antelope Canyon, 322—323
Apple Tree×, 176

Aquariums, 27
Aqua Santa×, 101
Archdiocese of Santa Fe Museum, 94—95
Arches National Park, 405—414
accessibility, 414
admission procedures, 414
dining, 413
drives and sites, 409—410
emergencies, 414
flora and fauna, 408
lodging, 413—414
sports & outdoors, 411—413
transportation, 408
visitor center, 410
visitor information, 414
when to go, 408
Arizona. ⇨See North–Central Arizona; Northeast Arizona; Phoenix/Scottsdale/Tempe, AZ; Southern Arizona; Tucson, AZ
Arizona Biltmore Resort & Spa ⬚, 237, 240
Arizona Center, 210
Arizona Doll and Toy Museum, 212
Arizona Historical Society's Museum, 333
Arizona Inn ⬚, 352—353
Arizona Mining and Mineral Museum, 211
Arizona Science Center, 210—211
Arizona Snowbowl, 257
Arizona-Sonora Desert Museum, 336
Arizona State Museum, 334
Arizona State University, 219—220
Armory Park, 329
Art galleries and museums
Albuquerque, 29, 37, 38, 68—69
North-Central Arizona, 275
Phoenix area, 212, 214, 216, 217, 218, 220, 221
Santa Fe, 91—92, 97—98, 99, 100, 135—137, 138, 142—143
Southwestern Colorado, 469
Southwestern Utah, 424
Taos, 167—169, 172, 193—195
Tucson, 331—333, 334
West Texas, 496
Art Gallery, 469
Artichoke Cafe×, 43
ASU Karsten Golf Course, 222
Atalaya Trail, 133
Aureole×, 539—540
Austing Haus ⬚, 198—199
Axis/Radius (club), 248

AZ 88×, 233
Aztec×, 101

B

Back at the Ranch (shop), 140
Badger House Community, 485
Balcony House, 485
Ballooning
Albuquerque, 39—40, 64—65
Phoenix area, 221
Taos, 191
Tucson, 343
Ballroom Marfa, 503
Balmorhea State Park, 504
Bandelier National Monument, 151—152
Barelas Coffee House×, 43
Baseball, 66—67
Basketball, 67
Bavarian, The ⬚, 199
Bear Paw Coffee Company×, 424
Beaver Dam Wash, 423
Bellagio Las Vegas ⬚, 544
Bell Rock, 265—266
Bent Street Cafe & Deli×, 176—177
Bernalillo, NM, 76—77
Best Western Ruby's Inn ⬚, 443
Bicycling. ⇨See also Mountain biking
Albuquerque, 65
Arches National Park, 411
Grand Canyon National Park, 294
Phoenix area, 221—222
Saguaro National Park, 340
Santa Fe, 131—132
Southeastern Utah, 384, 389
Southwestern Colorado, 469—470
Southwestern Utah, 423, 425, 432—433
Taos, 191
Tucson, 343—344
Bien Shur×, 46
Big Bend National Park, 509—516
accessibility, 516
admission fee, 516
emergencies, 516
flora and fauna, 512
lodging, 516
scenic drives and stops, 513
sports & outdoors, 514—516
transportation, 512
visitor centers, 513—514
visitor information, 516
when to go, 512
Big Room, The, 521
Biltmore Fashion Park, 249
Biosphere 2 Center, 337
Bird-watching
Albuquerque, 65

Big Bend National Park, 514
Santa Fe, 132
West Texas, 501
Bisbee, AZ, 366—368
Bisbee Mining and Historical
  Museum, 367
Bit & Spur Restaurant and
  Saloon✕, 426
Blanding, UT, 397—398, 404
Blue Window Bistro✕, 150
Bluff, UT, 398—400, 404
Blumenschein Home and
  Museum, 167
Boating
  Big Bend National Park, 514
  Northeast Arizona, 324—325
  Southeastern Utah, 389—390,
    403
  Southern Arizona, 374
Bobcat Bite✕, 102
Bobcat Inn ☷, 124
Bode's (shop), 156
Body English (club), 546
Bonanza "World's Largest Gift
  Shop," 549
Booking your trip, 556—560
Bowl, The, 502
Bradbury Science Museum, 149
Brigham Young Winter Home,
  421
Bright Angel Point, 293
Bright Angel Trail, 290
Broken Saddle Riding Co., 82
Bryce Canyon National Park,
  435—444
  accessibility, 444
  admission fees, 444
  dining, 442
  drives and stops, 439—441
  emergencies, 444
  flora and fauna, 438
  lodging, 442—443
  sports & outdoors, 441—442
  transportation, 438
  visitor center, 441
  visitor information, 444
  when to go, 438
Bryce Canyon National Park
  Lodge ☷, 443
Buck's Grill House✕, 383
Bumble Bee's Baja Grill✕,
  102, 104
Bush Childhood Home, 505
Bus travel, 561. ⇨*See also*
  transportation under specific
  destinations
Byzantium✕, 177

C

Cactus Forest Drive, 338
Café Central✕, 499
Cafe Pasqual's✕, 104
Café Poca Cosa✕, 346
Café Roka✕, 367
Camelback Mountain and Echo
  Canyon Recreation Area, 223

Canyon Colors B&B ☷, 321
Canyon de Chelly, 310—313
Canyonlands National Park,
  387—395
Canyon Wren ☷, 270
Carlsbad Caverns National
  Park, 517—526
  accessibility, 525
  admission fees, 525
  cave tours, 525—526
  dining, 524, 525
  emergencies, 526
  flora and fauna, 520
  lodging, 525
  Ranger programs, 524
  scenic stops, 521
  sports & outdoors, 522—524
  transportation, 520
  visitor center, 521
  visitor information, 526
  when to go, 520
Car rentals, 559—560
Carson National Forest, 201
Car travel, 562. ⇨*See also*
  transportation under specific
  destinations
Casa de las Chimenas ☷,
  183—184
Casa Escondida ☷, 161
Casa Rondeña Winery, 40
Casas de Sueños ☷, 56
Casa Tierra ☷, 354
Catalina State Park, 345
Cathedral Rock, 266
Cathedral Rock Trail, 266
Cattleman's Steakhouse✕, 499
Caverns of Sonora, 507—508
Caves
  *Carlsbad Caverns National
    Park,* 521, 522—524,
    525—526
  North-Central Arizona, 257,
    271—272
  Southern Arizona, 369—370
  Tucson, 334
  West Texas, 507—508
Cave Spring Trail, 391
Cedar Breaks National Monu-
  ment, 421
Cedar City, UT, 417—419
Cedar Crest, NM, 78—80
Cell phones, 563
Center Café✕, 383
Center for Creative Photogra-
  phy, 334
Cerrillos, NM, 82
Chamizal National Memorial,
  495
Chapel of the Holy Cross,
  266
Chapin Mesa Archaeological
  Museum, 487
Char's Has the Blues, 247
Chelsea's Kitchen✕, 226
Chihuahuan Desert Nature
  Trail, 515
Chimayó, NM, 160—161

Chiricahua National Monu-
  ment, 368
Chisos Basin, 513
Chisos Basin Loop Trail, 515
Chisos Basin Road, 513
Chisos Basin Visitor Center,
  513—514
Chocolate Maven✕, 104
Chocolate Turtle B&B ☷, 75
Churches
  Albuquerque, 35—36, 72, 74
  North-Central Arizona, 266
  Santa Fe, 94—95, 96—97,
    99—100, 160
  Southwestern Utah, 423
  Taos, 172, 174
  Tucson, 331, 336—337
  West Texas, 497
Church of San Geronimo, 174
Church Street Café✕, 46
Cinnamon Morning B&B ☷, 59
Ciudad Juárez, Mexico,
  497—498
Clafoutis✕, 104—105
Classic Century Square Antique
  Mall, 69
Cliff Palace, 485—486
Cliffrose Lodge and Gar-
  dens ☷, 427
Cliff's Amusement Park, 64
Coleman Gallery Contemporary
  Art, 69
Colorado. ⇨*See* Southwestern
  Colorado
Colorado River Scenic Byways,
  381
Colorado Trail, 471
Colossal Cave Mountain Park,
  334
Compound, The✕, 105
Copper Queen Mine Under-
  ground Tour, 366—367
Coral Pink Sand Dunes State
  Park, 429—430
Cordova, NM, 162
Coronado State Monument, 76
Coronado State Park, 76
Corrales, NM, 74—75
Cortez, CO, 476—477
Cosmopolitan✕, 463
Cottage Place✕, 261
Country Furnishings of Taos,
  197
Court of the Patriarchs, 450
Cowboy's Smokehouse Café✕,
  430
Cowgirl (bar), 127
Credit cards, 564
Creede, CO, 480
Crested Butte, CO, 479
Cristo Rey Church, 95
Crow Canyon Archaeological
  Center, 477
Crown & Anchor Pub, 546
Crystal Geyser, 395—396
Crystal Palace, 365

Currency, 562
Customs, 562

D

Dahl & DiLuca ✕, 269—270
Dam Bar and Grille ✕, 321
Daughters of the Utah Pioneers Museum, 418
Days Inn & Suites ⬚, 321
Dead Horse Point State Park, 380—381, 387
Dead Horse Ranch State Park, 272
De La Tierra ✕, 177
Delicate Arch, 409—410
Delicate Arch Trail, 412
Delicias ✕, 507
Delmonico Steakhouse ✕, 540
Desert Botanical Garden, 214
Desert Pearl Inn ⬚, 427
Desert Rose Inn and Cabins ⬚, 400
Desert View and Watchtower, 286
Design Center, 137
Devils Garden Campground, 414
Devils Garden Trail, 412
D.H. Lawrence Ranch and Memorial, 203
Diego's Cafe ✕, 106
Dining, 7, 564. ⇨ Also specific destinations
Dinosaur Museum, 398
Dixie National Forest, 418
Doña Anita's ✕, 507
Don Gaspar Inn ⬚, 117
Double Take at the Ranch (shop), 140
Dream Keeper Inn ⬚, 386
Durango, CO, 468—474, 480
Durango & Silverton Narrow Gauge Railroad, 468—469

E

Eagle Nest Lake State Park, 204
Edge of the Cedars State Park, 398
Edward Nye Fish House, 331
Eiffel Tower Restaurant ✕, 541
Elaine's, A Bed and Breakfast ⬚, 79
El Capitan/Salt Basin Overlook Trails, 502
Electricity, 562
Elephant Hill, 390
El Farol (bar), 127
El Farolito ✕, 158
El Mesón & Chispa Tapas Bar ✕, 106
El Monte Sagrado ⬚, 185
El Museo Cultural de Santa Fe, 98—99
El Paragua Restaurant ✕, 154—155

El Paso, TX, 494—500, 508
El Paso Desert Botanical Garden, 496
El Paso Museum of Art, 496
El Patio ✕, 47
El Rancho de las Golondrinas, 147
El Rey Inn ⬚, 124—125
El Santuario de Chimayó, 160
El Tiradito, 331
El Tovar Hotel ✕ ⬚, 298, 299
El Zaguan, 96
Embassies, 562
Embassy Suites Hotel Albuquerque ⬚, 56—57
Emergencies, 562
Arches National Park, 414
Big Bend National Park, 516
Bryce Canyon National Park, 444
Carlsbad Caverns National Park, 526
Grand Canyon National Park, 302
Mesa Verde National Park, 490
Southeastern Utah, 403—404
Southwestern Colorado, 479
Southwestern Utah, 434
Tucson, 358
West Texas, 508
Zion National Park, 454
Encanto Park, 211
Enchanted Circle, 200—201
Enchanted Forest Cross-Country Ski Area, 204
Enchantment Resort ⬚, 270
Escalante, UT, 432—433
Escalante Petrified Forest State Park, 432
Escalante's Grand Staircase Bed & Breakfast Inn ⬚, 433
Española, NM, 153—155
Española Valley Fiber Arts Center, 154
Evening Bat Flight Program, 524
evo Gallery, 136
¡Explora!, 32

F

Fairmont Scottsdale Princess ⬚, 241
Fairyland Point, 439
Far View Lodge ⬚, 489
Far View Sites Complex, 486
Far View Visitor Center, 487
Fashion Show Mall, 548
FEZ ✕, 228
Fiery Furnace Hiking, 412—413
Firehouse Collection, 167
Fishing
Las Vegas, 551
Santa Fe, 132
Southeastern Utah, 403
Southwestern Colorado, 461, 470

Taos, 191—192
Flagstaff, AZ, 255, 257—264
Flandrau Science Center and Planetarium, 334
Florence Hawley Ellis Museum of Anthropology, 157
Flying Star ✕, 47
Football
Albuquerque, 67
West Texas, 506
Fort Concho National Historic Landmark, 507
Fort Davis, TX, 503—504
Fort Lewis College, 469
Fort Lowell Park and Museum, 335
Fort Verde State Historic Park, 271
Forum Shops at Caesars, 548
Four Corners Monument, 317, 399, 477
Four Peaks Brewing Company, 248
Four Seasons Scottsdale at Troon North ⬚, 241
Four-wheeling
North-Central Arizona, 268
Northeast Arizona, 312, 317
Southeastern Utah, 381, 384, 390
Southwestern Colorado, 461—462
Franklin Mountains State Park, 498
Frijole Ranch Museum, 501
Fuller Lodge, 149—150

G

Galisteo, NM, 146
Galisteo Inn ⬚, 146
Gardens
Albuquerque, 27
Phoenix area, 214
Santa Fe, 96
Tucson, 335—336
West Texas, 496
Genoveva Chavez Community Center, 131
Georgia O'Keeffe Museum (Abiquiu), 156
Georgia O'Keeffe Museum (Santa Fe), 91
Gerald Peters Gallery, 136
Geronimo ✕, 107
Ghost Ranch Education and Retreat Center, 157
Ghost Ranch Piedra Lumbre Education and Visitor Center, 157—158
Giant Logs, 307
Giggling Springs, 152—153
Glen Canyon National Recreation Area, 323
Glider rides, 462
Goblin Valley State Park, 403
Gold Canyon Golf Club, 222
Golden, NM, 79

Gold Street Caffè ✕, 47
Golf
Albuquerque, 65—66, 73, 80
Las Vegas, 550
North-Central Arizona,
267—268
Phoenix area, 222—223
Santa Fe, 132, 148
Southeastern Utah, 382
Southwestern Colorado, 466,
470, 475
Southwestern Utah, 423, 425
Taos, 192, 206
Tucson, 344
Gooseberry Mesa, *425*
Goosenecks State Park, *400*
Governor Bent Museum, *167*
Grand Canyon Lodge ✕ ⛺,
293, 299, 301
Grand Canyon National Park,
279—302
admission, 301—302
dining, 297, 298—299
drives, sites and stops, 284,
286—288, 291, 293—294
emergencies, 302
flora and fauna, 282
lodging, 297—298, 299—301
North Rim, 280, 291—295
planning your trip, 283
price categories, 297
Ranger programs, 288, 294
South Rim, 280, 284—291
sports & outdoors, 288—291,
294—295
transportation, 283
visitor information, 302
West Rim and Havasu Canyon,
281, 295—297
when to go, 282
Grand Staircase-Escalante
National Monument,
431—433
Grand View Point, *388*
Grayhawk Country Club, *222*
Greasewood Flats (club), *248*
Green Gate Village Historic
Inn ⛺, *424*
Green River, UT, *395—396, 404*
Green River State Park, *395*
Gruet Winery, *40—41*
Guadalajara Grill ✕, *178*
Guadalupe Mountains National
Park, *500—502*
Gunnison, CO, *479*

H

Hacienda del Sol ⛺, *185*
Hacienda Nicholas ⛺, *118*
Hard Rock Hotel ⛺, *544*
Harry's Roadhouse ✕, *108*
Harwood Museum, *167—168*
Havasu Canyon, *296—297*
Havasupai Tribe, *296—297*
Health clubs, *192*
Heard Museum, *211—212*

Heartline Café ✕, *269*
Hermits Rest, *286*
High Road to Taos, *159—162*
Highway *67, 291*
Highway 12 Scenic Byway, *432*
Hiking
Albuquerque, 66
Arches National Park,
411—413
Big Bend National Park,
515—516
Bryce Canyon National Park,
441—442
Carlsbad Caverns National
Park, 522
Grand Canyon National Park,
288—290, 294—295
Las Vegas, 550—551
Mesa Verde National Park,
487—488
North-Central Arizona, 260—
261, 268, 276
Northeast Arizona, 309, 311—
312, 317, 318, 320—321
Phoenix area, 223, 226
Saguaro National Park,
341—342
Santa Fe, 132—133, 150—151
Southeastern Utah, 382,
391—393
Southwestern Colorado, 462,
470—471, 475
Southwestern Utah, 424, 433
Taos, 199—200
Tucson, 345
West Texas, 498, 502
Zion National Park, 451—452
Historama, *363—364*
Historic Taos Inn ⛺, *185—186*
Holiday Inn Sunland Park ⛺,
500
Holidays, *562*
Hope Camp Trail, *342*
Hopi Mesas, *313—316*
Hopi Museum and Cultural
Center, *315*
Hopi Point, *286*
Horseback riding
Albuquerque, 82
Bryce Canyon National Park,
442
North-Central Arizona, 268
Northeast Arizona, 312, 317
Phoenix area, 226
Santa Fe, 133, 146
Southwestern Colorado, 462,
471
Taos, 199—200
West Texas, 498
Zion National Park, 452
Horseshoe Canyon Trail, *392*
Hotel Columbia Telluride ⛺,
464
Hotel Congress ⛺, *352*
Hotel Santa Fe ⛺, *118*
Houses of historic interest

Phoenix area, 212, 214—215,
218—219
Santa Fe, 96, 156
Southwestern Utah, 421, 428
Taos, 167, 168, 203
Tucson, 331—333
West Texas, 496—497, 505
Hovenweep National Monu-
ment, *398*
Hualapai Tribe, *295*
Hueco Tanks Historic Site, *496*
Hugh Norris Trail, *342*
Huhugam Heritage Center, *214*
Hurricane, UT, *425*
Hyatt Regency Tamaya ⛺, *77*

I

Imperial National Wildlife Ref-
uge, *375*
Indian Pueblo Cultural Center,
32
India Palace ✕, *108*
Inn of the Anasazi ✕ ⛺, *108,*
119
Inn of the Five Graces ⛺,
119—120
Inn of the Governors ⛺, *120*
Inn of the Turquoise Bear ⛺,
120
Inn on La Loma Plaza ⛺, *186*
Inn on the Alameda ⛺,
120—121
Institute of American Indian
Arts (IAIA), *91*
Insurance, *554—555, 559—560*
International Folk Art Market,
97
Internet access, *564*
Iron Mission State Park
Museum, *418*
Isleta Pueblo, *72—73*

J

Jade Bar, *247*
James Kelly Contemporary, *136*
Janos ✕, *350*
J.D. Challenger Gallery, *194*
Jeep tours. ⇨*See*
Four-wheeling
Jémez Spring Bath House, *152*
Jémez Springs, NM, *152—153*
Jémez State Monument, *152*
Jerome, AZ, *273—274*
Jerome State Historic Park, *274*
J. Knox Corbett House, *332*
John Wesley Powell Memorial
Museum, *319—320*
Joint Trail, *392*
Jonson Gallery, *37*
Joseph's Table ✕, *179*

K

Kanab, UT, *429—430*
Kartchner Caverns State Park,
369—370

Kasha-Katuwe Tent Rocks National Monument, 148
Keams Canyon Trading Post, 313—314
Kierland Commons, 250
KiMo Theatre, 32—33, 63
Kit Carson Home and Museum, 168
Kit Carson Park, 168
Kitt Peak National Observatory, 372—373
Kolb Studio, 284
Kolob Canyons Road, 449
Kuaua Pueblo, 76

L
La Bellavia✕, 262
La Boca✕, 108—109
La Casa Cordova, 331—332
La Choza✕, 109
Lady Banksia rose tree, 363
La Fonda, 91
La Grande Orange✕, 227
La Hacienda✕, 234—235
La Hacienda de los Martínez, 171
Lake City, CO, 480
Lake Mead, 551
Lake Powell, 319, 320, 323—325, 402—403
Lake Powell Resort ⌂, 325
La Marmotte✕, 463
Lambert's of Taos✕, 179
La Mesa (shop), 139
Landscape Arch, 410
La Roca✕, 372
Las Vegas, NV, 528—529
  dining, 533, 539—543
  gambling scene, 540
  itineraries, 535—536
  lodging, 543—546
  nightlife, 546—548
  price categories, 539, 544
  shopping, 548—549
  sports & outdoors, 550—551
  top experiences, 530, 536—538
  tours, 538—539
  transportation, 532—535
  visitor information, 551—552
  when to go, 529—530, 532
L'Auberge de Sedona✕ ⌂, 269, 270
Laughing Lizard Inn and Cafe ⌂, 153
Lava River Cave, 257
Le Cirque✕, 541
Léona's Restaurante✕, 160—161
Linda Durham Gallery, 136
Little America of Flagstaff ⌂, 262
Little Tree B&B ⌂, 189
Llama trekking, 192
Lodge at Ventana Canyon, 344
Lodging, 7, 558. ⇨ Also specific destinations
Long House, 486

Lon's at the Hermosa✕, 229—230
Los Alamos, NM, 149—151
Los Alamos Historical Museum, 150
Los Poblanos Inn ⌂, 59—60
Lowell Observatory, 257, 259
Lutes Casino✕, 375

M
Mabel Dodge Luhan House ⌂, 187
Madeleine Inn ⌂, 122
Madrid, NM, 80—81
Magic Pan✕, 499
Magoffin Home State Historical Park, 496—497
Mail and shipping, 562—563
Main Park Road, 439
Main Street Café✕, 425
Mandalay Bay ⌂, 545
Manti-La Sal National Forest, 397
Marfa, TX, 503, 504, 508
Margaret Moses Gallery, 72
Maria's New Mexican Kitchen✕, 109
Mariscos la Playa✕, 109—110
Matador (bar), 127—128
Mather Point, 287
Mauger Estate B&B Inn ⌂, 58
Maxwell Museum of Anthropology, 37—38
May Café✕, 49
Maynard Dixon Home and Studio, 428
McDonald Observatory Visitors Center, 503—504
McKittrick Canyon, 501
McKittrick Nature Loop, 502
Meal plans, 7, 558
Medizona✕, 233
Mesa Arch, 388
Mesa Arch Trail, 391
Mesa Southwest Museum, 221
Mesa Verde National Park, 481—490
  accessibility, 490
  admission procedures, 490
  dining, 488—489
  drives and sites, 485—487
  emergencies, 490
  flora and fauna, 484
  lodging, 489
  Ranger programs, 488
  sports & outdoors, 487—488
  transportation, 484
  visitor centers, 487
  visitor information, 490
  when to go, 484
Metate Room✕, 488—489
Meteor Crater and Museum, 505
Mexican Hat, UT, 400—401
Mexico border crossings
  Southern Arizona, 370—372
  West Texas, 497—498

Midland, TX, 505—507, 508
Mill Avenue Shops, 250
Millicent Rogers Museum, 172
Milt's Stage Stop✕, 418
Mine Museum, 274
Mineshaft Tavern✕, 81
Mine tours, 366—367
Mission Cafe✕, 110
Mission San Xavier del Bac, 336—337
Mission Ysleta, 497
Mix at THEhotel (club), 547
Moab, UT, 380—387
Moab Valley RV Resort, 387
Mon Ami Gabi✕, 543
Monica's El Portal✕, 49
Monte Carlo Resort and Casino ⌂, 546
Montez Gallery, 139
Montezuma Castle National Monument, 271
Montezuma Well, 271—272
Monticello, UT, 396—397
Monument Valley Navajo Tribal Park, 316—317, 400—401
Mooney Falls, 297
Morefield Campground, 489
Mountain biking
  North-Central Arizona, 261, 268—269
  Southeastern Utah, 382
  Southwestern Colorado, 462—463
  West Texas, 498
Mt. Carmel Junction, UT, 428—429
Mount Elden Trail System, 259
Mud Creek Hogan, 477
Mule rides, 290—291, 295
Museo Chicano, 212
Museum of Archaeology & Material Culture, 78—79
Museum of Indian Arts and Culture, 97
Museum of International Folk Art (MOIFA), 97—98
Museum of Moab, 380
Museum of Northern Arizona, 259
Museum of Spanish Colonial Art, 98
Museum of the Big Bend, 503
Museums. ⇨See also Art galleries and museums
  air and space, 335
  in Albuquerque, 29, 32, 33, 34—35, 36, 37—38, 39, 42, 78—79, 81
  auto racing, 42
  ballooning, 39
  Carson, 168
  children's, 98, 331
  cowboys, 364, 503
  Hispanic culture, 98—99, 212
  history, 29, 92, 94, 150, 167, 214, 218, 275, 307, 333, 380, 459

Holocaust, 34
human history, 449
iron industry, 418
in Mesa Verde National Park, 487
meteor craters, 505
military life, 335, 507
mining, 81, 211, 274, 367
Native American culture, 37—38, 78—79, 97, 98, 157, 211—212, 215—216, 315, 334, 369, 487
natural history, 34—35, 221, 259, 309
in North-Central Arizona, 259, 260, 274, 275
in Northeast Arizona, 307, 309, 315, 319—320
oil industry, 505
O'Keeffe, 156
paleontology, 157, 398
in Phoenix area, 210—212, 214, 215—216, 218, 221
pioneer life, 260, 418
Powell, 319—320
ranch life, 501
rattlesnakes, 29, 32
religious artifacts, 94—95
in Santa Fe, 92, 94—95, 98, 149, 150, 156
science, 32, 33, 34—35, 149, 210—211, 214
in Southeastern Utah, 380, 398
in Southern Arizona, 363, 364, 367, 369
in Southwestern Colorado, 459
in Southwestern Utah, 418, 421—422
in Taos, 167, 168
toys, 79, 212
in Tucson, 331, 333, 334, 335
turquoise, 36
in West Texas, 501, 503, 505, 507
wildlife, 421—422
in Zion National Park, 449
Mystery Castle, 214—215

N

Narrows Trail, 452
National Hispanic Cultural Center, 33—34
National Museum of Nuclear Science & History, 33
Native American sites
Albuquerque, 32, 37—38, 71—73, 77—79
Grand Canyon National Park, 295, 296
Mesa Verde National Park, 485—486, 487
North-Central Arizona, 262, 263, 264, 271, 272—273, 275
Northeast Arizona, 307, 310—311, 313—318, 320

Phoenix area, 211—212, 214, 215—216
Santa Fe, 91, 97, 98, 142—143, 157
Southeastern Utah, 395, 397, 398, 399, 400—401
Southern Arizona, 369
Southwestern Colorado, 476, 477
Taos, 173—174, 176, 197
Tucson, 334
Nativo Lodge Hotel 🏨, 60
Natural Bridge, 439
Natural Bridges National Monument, 401—402
Navajo Falls, 296—297
Navajo National Monument, 318
Navajo/Queen's Garden Combination Loop, 441
Navajo Village Heritage Center, 320
Nedra Matteucci Galleries, 136
New Mexico. ⇨See Albuquerque, NM; Santa Fe, NM; Taos, NM
New Mexico History Museum, 92, 94
New Mexico Holocaust & Intolerance Museum, 34
New Mexico Museum of Art, 91—92
New Mexico Museum of Natural History and Science, 34—35
New Mexico State Capitol, 96
New Rochester Hotel 🏨, 473
New Sheridan Hotel & Opera House, 459
Newspaper Rock, 307
Newspaper Rock Recreation Site, 397
Nobu ✕, 541—542
Nogales, AZ, 370—372
North-Central Arizona, 254. ⇨See also Grand Canyon National Park
dining, 254—255
Flagstaff area, 255, 257—264
lodging, 254—255
price categories, 254
Sedona and Oak Creek Canyon, 264—271
transportation, 277—278
Verde Valley, Jerome and Prescott, 271—277
visitor information, 278
Northeast Arizona, 8, 304
dining, 304, 305
Glen Canyon Dam and Lake Powell, 319—325
Hopi Mesas, 313—316
lodging, 304, 305
Monument Valley, 316—318
Navajo Nation East, 310—313
Petrified Forest and Painted Desert, 305—310

price categories, 305
transportation, 325—326
visitor information, 326
Northern Arizona University Observatory, 259—260
Northlight Gallery, 220

O

Oak Creek Canyon, 266—267
Observatories
North-Central Arizona, 257, 259—260
Southern Arizona, 372—373
West Texas, 503—504
Odessa, TX, 505—507, 508
O'Farrell Hats, 140
Ojo Caliente, NM, 158—159
OK Corral & Stable, 226
O'Keeffe Cafe ✕, 110
Old Coal Mine Museum, 81
Oldest House, 96
Old Santa Fe Inn 🏨, 122
Omni Tucson National Golf Resort, 344
Online travel tools, 554, 556, 557—558
Oracle, AZ, 337
Organ Pipe Cactus National Monument, 373—374
Orilla Verde Recreation Area, 188
Orlando's ✕, 180
Orpheum Theatre, 212

P

Package vacations, 560
Packing tips, 554
Page, AZ, 319—321
Pagosa Springs, CO, 474—476, 480
Painted Desert, 307—308
Painted Desert Inn National Historic Site, 307
Panguitch, UT, 430—431
Papago Park, 215
Parks. ⇨See also Arches National Park; Big Bend National Park; Bryce Canyon National Park; Carlsbad Caverns National Park; Grand Canyon National Park; Mesa Verde National Park; Zion National Park
Albuquerque, 27—29, 41, 76
North-Central Arizona, 260, 267, 271, 272
Northeast Arizona, 305, 307—310
Phoenix area, 211, 215, 216
Santa Fe, 144
Southeastern Utah, 380—381, 387—395, 398, 400, 403
Southern Arizona, 369—370
Southwestern Colorado, 476—477

Southwestern Utah, 418, 422, 429—430, 432
Taos, 168, 201, 202—203, 204
Tucson, 329, 334, 337—342, 345
West Texas, 496, 498, 500—502, 504
Paseo del Bosque Bike Trail, 65
Passports, 563
Patina (shop), 142
Pecos, TX, 504
Pecos National Historic Park, 144
Peñasco, NM, 162
Peppermill's Fireside Lounge, 547
Petrified Forest National Park, 305, 307—310
Petroglyph National Monument, 41
Petroglyph Point Trail, 488
Petroleum Museum, 505
Phippen Museum of Western Art, 275
Phoenician, The 🏨, 241—242
Phoenician Golf Club, 222
Phoenix Art Museum, 212, 214
Phoenix Museum of History, 214
Phoenix/Scottsdale/Tempe, AZ, 8, 208
the arts, 244—246
dining, 208—209, 224—225, 226—236
exploring, 209—221
lodging, 208—209, 236—244
Main Street Arts District, 217
nightlife, 246—249
Old Town Scottsdale, 217—218, 250
price categories, 209
shopping, 249—250
spas, 242
sports & outdoors, 221—223, 226
transportation, 251—252
visitor information, 252
Phoenix Zoo, 215
Phones, 563
Picasso ✕, 541
Pima Air and Space Museum, 335
Pima County Courthouse, 331
Pinery Bitterfield Stage Station Ruins, 501
Pioneer Museum, 260
Plaza Café ✕, 110—111
Point Sublime, 294
Powell Memorial, 284
Prairie Star ✕, 76
Prescott, AZ, 275—277
Presidio Chapel San Elizario, 497

Price categories
Albuquerque, 43, 53
Grand Canyon National Park, 297

Las Vegas, 539, 544
North-Central Arizona, 254
Northeast Arizona, 305
Phoenix area, 209
Santa Fe, 100, 117
Southeastern Utah, 380
Southern Arizona, 360
Southwestern Colorado, 457
Southwestern Utah, 416
Taos, 176, 183
Tucson, 346, 351
West Texas, 494
Pueblo Grande Museum and Cultural Park, 215—216
Puerco Pueblo, 307
PURE (club), 547—548
Purgatory, CO, 465—467
Purgatory at Durango Mountain Resort, 465—466
Pyramid Cafe ✕, 111

Q

Questa, NM, 202—203
Quilt Walk Festival, 431

R

Rafting
Big Bend National Park, 514
Grand Canyon National Park, 291
Northeast Arizona, 320
Santa Fe, 133—134
Southwestern Colorado, 463, 471
Taos, 192—193
Railroad Blues (club), 503
Railroads
North-Central Arizona, 273
Santa Fe, 99
Southwestern Colorado, 468—469
Rainbow Bridge National Monument, 323—324
Rainbow Forest Museum and Visitor Center, 309
Rainbow Man (shop), 143
Rainbow Ryders, 65
Rancho de San Juan 🏨, 155
Rancho Pinot Grill ✕, 234
Ranchos de Taos, 171
Randall Davey Audubon Center, 132
Randolph Park Golf Course-North Course, 344
Range Cafe & Bakery ✕, 77
Rawhide Western Town and Steakhouse, 246
Ray's Tavern ✕, 396
Red Cliffs Adventure Lodge 🏨, 386
Red Mountain Spa 🏨, 425
Red River, NM, 203—205
Red River Hatchery, 203
Red Rock Casino Resort Spa 🏨, 544—545
Reflection Bay Golf Course, 550

Reid Park Zoo, 335
Rhythm Room (club), 247
Rim Trail, 289—290
Rio Grande Botanic Garden, 27
Rio Grande Gorge Bridge, 172—173
Rio Grande Nature Center State Park, 41
Rio Grande Zoo, 27—28
Riordan State Historic Park, 260
River expeditions, 383, 385, 389—390, 396, 399
Robert Nichols Gallery, 143
Rock climbing
Arches National Park, 413
North-Central Arizona, 260—261
Southeastern Utah, 385, 393
Southwestern Colorado, 463, 470
West Texas, 498
Rocking V Cafe ✕, 430
Rodeos
Tucson, 345
West Texas, 504
Rooftop Pizzeria ✕, 111
Rosenbruch Wildlife Museum, 421—422
Rose Tree Inn Museum, 363
Ross Maxwell Scenic Drive, 513
Rosson House, 212
Royal Palms Resort & Spa 🏨, 240
Ruth Hall Museum of Paleontology, 157

S

Sabino Canyon, 336, 345
Sabroso ✕, 180
Saguaro National Park, 337—342, 343
St. Augustine church, 72
St. Francis Cathedral Basilica, 94—95
St. George, UT, 421—425
St. George Art Museum, 424
St. George Dinosaur Discovery Site at Johnson Farm, 422
St. George Tabernacle, 423
St. George Temple, 423
Salinas Pueblo Missions National Monument, 74
Sally's Mesquite Grill and BBQ ✕, 270
San Angelo, TX, 507—508
Sanctuary on Camelback Mountain 🏨, 240
Sandia Crest, 79
Sandia Golf Club, 66
Sandia Park, NM, 78—80
Sandia Peak Aerial Tramway, 41—42
Sandia Resort & Casino 🏨, 60—61
Sand Island Recreation Site, 399

San Elizario County Jail, *497*
San Felipe de Neri Catholic Church, *35—36*
San Francisco de Asís Church, *172*
San Francisco Volcanic Field, *263—264*
San Geronimo Lodge ☷, *188*
San Juan National Forest, *469*
San Juan Skyway, *459*
San Marcos Cafe ✕, *82*
San Miguel County Courthouse, *459*
San Miguel Mission, *96—97*
San Purísima Concepción de Cuarac, *74*
Santacafé ✕, *112*
Santa Elena Canyon, *513*
Santa Elena Canyon Trail, *516*
Santa Fe, NM, *84—85*
the arts, *126—127, 128—131*
dining, *100—116*
exploring, *90—100*
lodging, *116—126*
nightlife, *126—128*
planning your time, *87, 90*
price categories, *100, 117*
shopping, *135—143*
side trips, *144—162*
sports & outdoors, *131—134*
transportation, *86*
visitor information, *86*
when to go, *85*
Santa Fe Chamber Music Festival, *129*
Santa Fe Children's Museum, *98*
Santa Fe Clay, *99*
Santa Fe Depot, *257*
Santa Fe Farmers Market, *142*
Santa Fe Mountain Sports, *134*
Santa Fe Opera, *130*
Santa Fe Sage Inn ☷, *124*
Santa Fe Southern Railway, *99*
Santo Domingo Pueblo, *77—78*
Santo Niño de Atocha, *160*
Santuario de Guadalupe, *99—100*
School House Inn Bed & Breakfast ☷, *367—368*
Scott M. Matheson Wetlands Preserve, *380*
Scottsdale, AZ. ➪See Phoenix/ Scottsdale/Tempe, AZ
Scottsdale Center for the Arts, *218*
Scottsdale Fashion Square, *250*
Scottsdale Historical Museum, *218*
Scottsdale Museum of Contemporary Art, *218*
Sea Saw ✕, *234*
Sedona, AZ, *265—271*
Sedona Golf Resort, *267—268*
Sego Canyon Rock Art Panels, *395*

Shady Dell Vintage Trailer Park ☷, *368*
Sharlot Hall Museum, *275*
Shed, The ✕, *112*
Shemer Arts Center, *216*
Shidoni Foundry and Galleries, *137*
Shohko ✕, *112*
Silverton, CO, *480*
SITE Santa Fe, *100*
Skiing
Albuquerque, *80*
North-Central Arizona, *261*
Santa Fe, *134, 151*
Southwestern Colorado, *459—461, 465—466, 474—475*
Taos, *200, 204—205, 206*
Slate Street Cafe ✕, *50*
Slaughter Canyon Cave, *523*
Slide Rock State Park, *267*
Smoki Museum, *275*
Snoopy Rock, *267*
Snowboarding
North-Central Arizona, *261*
Southwestern Colorado, *459—460, 465—466, 474—475*
Snow Canyon State Park, *422, 424*
Snowmobiling, *466*
Soda Dam, *152*
Sorrel River Ranch ☷, *386*
Southeastern Utah, *378.* ➪See also Arches National Park
Canyonlands National Park, *387—395*
dining, *378, 380*
emergencies, *403—404*
lodging, *380, 404*
Moab, *380—387*
outfitters and expeditions, *384—385*
price categories, *380*
southeast region, *395—403*
transportation, *403*
visitor information, *404*
Southern Arizona, *360—361*
dining, *360*
lodging, *360*
price categories, *360*
Southeast Arizona, *361—370*
Southwest Arizona, *370—375*
transportation, *376*
visitor information, *376*
South Kaibab Trail, *290*
South Mountain Park, *216, 223*
Southwestern Colorado, *456.* ➪See also Mesa Verde National Park
Cortez, *476—477*
dining, *456, 457*
Durango, *468—474, 480*
emergencies, *479*
lodging, *456, 457*
Pagosa Springs, *474—476, 480*
price categories, *457*
Purgatory, *465—467*
Telluride, *458—465, 480*

transportation, *478—479*
visitor information, *479—480*
when to go, *457—458*
Southwestern Utah, *416.* ➪See also Bryce Canyon National Park; Zion National Park
dining, *416*
emergencies, *434*
Grand Staircase-Escalante National Monument, *431—433*
lodging, *416, 434*
price categories, *416*
transportation, *419, 433—434*
U.S. 89, *428—431*
Utah's Dixie, *417—428*
visitor information, *434*
when to go, *419*
Sow's Ear ✕, *467*
Spago Las Vegas ✕, *542*
Spanish Table (shop), *141*
Spelunking, *522—524*
Springdale, UT, *426—428*
Springs Resort ☷, *474, 476*
Spruce Tree House, *486*
Squaw Flat Campground, *394*
Stakeout Grill and Bar ✕, *180*
Star Trek Store, *549*
Step House, *486*
Strater Hotel ☷, *472—473*
Sugar Nymphs Bistro ✕, *162*
Sunrise Point, *440*
Sunset Crater Volcano National Monument, *263—264*
Sun Temple, *486*
Switchback Grille ✕, *426*
Symbols, *7*

T

Taliesin West, *218—219*
Tamarind Institute, *38*
Tanque Verde Ridge Trail, *342*
Taos, NM, *164—165*
the arts, *189—191*
dining, *175, 176—181*
exploring, *167—174, 176*
lodging, *181—189*
nightlife, *189—190*
planning your time, *166*
price categories, *176, 183*
shopping, *193—197*
side trips, *200—206*
sports & outdoors, *191–193*
transportation, *166*
visitor information, *166*
when to go, *165*
Taos Art Museum at the Fechin House, *168—169*
Taos Cow ✕, *181*
Taos Pueblo, *173—174, 176*
Taos Ski Valley, *198—200*
T. Cook's at the Royal Palms ✕, *231*
Tecolote Cafe ✕, *112*
Telluride, CO, *458—465, 480*

Telluride Historical Museum, 459
Tempe, AZ. ⇨See Phoenix/Scottsdale/Tempe, AZ
Tempe Center for the Arts, 221
Tempe Town Lake, 221
Ten Thousand Waves ⌶, 126
Texas. ⇨See West Texas
Texas Canyon, 369
315 Restaurant & Wine Bar ✕, 100
Thunderbird Lodge ⌶, 313
Tia Sophia's ✕, 112—113
Tides Oyster Bar ✕, 543
Tingley Beach, 28—29
Tinkertown Museum, 79
Todos Santos (shop), 141
Tombstone, AZ, 361, 363—366
Tombstone Boarding House Bed & Breakfast ⌶, 365
Tombstone Courthouse State Historic Park, 363
Tombstone Western Heritage Museum, 364
Touchstone Inn ⌶, 188
Tournament Players Club of Scottsdale, 222
Trading Post Cafe ✕, 181
Train travel, 561. ⇨See also transportation under specific destinations
Travel agents, 556
Traveler's checks, 564
Trimble Hot Springs, 469
Trip insurance, 554—555
Triple Village Pueblo Sites, 486
Troon North, 222—223
Tsankawi, 150—151
Tucson, AZ, 328
the arts, 354—356
dining, 345—351
emergencies, 358
exploring, 329—342
lodging, 348—349, 351—354
nightlife, 356
price categories, 346, 351
shopping, 356—357
sports & outdoors, 342—345
transportation, 357—358
visitor information, 358
Tucson Botanical Gardens, 335—336
Tucson Children's Museum, 331
Tucson Museum of Art and Historic Block, 331—333
Tune Up ✕, 113, 116
Turquoise Museum, 36
Turquoise Trail, 78—82
Tuzigoot National Monument, 272—273

U

University of Arizona, 333—334
University of New Mexico, 37—38

Unser Racing Museum, 42
Upheaval Dome Trail, 393
Up the Creek Campground, 387
Utah. ⇨See Southeastern Utah; Southwestern Utah
Utah Shakespearean Festival, 418
Ute Mountain Tribal Park, 476—477

V

Venetian ⌶, 545
Venetian Grand Canal Shoppes, 549
Verandah ✕, 542—543
Verde Canyon Railroad, 273
Verde Valley, 271—273
Via Delosantos ✕, 232
Visas, 563
Visitor information
Albuquerque, 25
Arches National Park, 414
Big Bend National Park, 516
Bryce Canyon National Park, 444
Carlsbad Caverns National Park, 526
Grand Canyon National Park, 302
Las Vegas, 551—552
Mesa Verde National Park, 490
North-Central Arizona, 278
Northeast Arizona, 326
Phoenix area, 252
Santa Fe, 86
Southeastern Utah, 404
Southern Arizona, 376
Southwestern Colorado, 479—480
Southwestern Utah, 434
Taos, 166
Tucson, 358
West Texas, 508
Zion National Park, 454

W

Wahweap, AZ, 323—325
Walnut Canyon National Monument, 263
Watchman Campground, 454
Weeping Rock, 450
Wells Fargo History Museum, 214
Western Legends Roundup, 429
Westin Kierland Resort & Spa ⌶, 243
West of the Pecos Rodeo, 504
West Texas, 492. ⇨See also Big Bend National Park; Carlsbad Caverns National Park

Alpine, Marfa, and the Davis Mountains, 502—504
dining, 492, 494
El Paso, 494—500, 508
emergencies, 508
Guadalupe Mountains National Park, 500—502
lodging, 494
price categories, 494
San Angelo, 507—508
transportation, 508
visitor information, 508
Weyrich Gallery, 69
Wheelwright Museum of the American Indian, 98
When to go, 20
White House Ruin, 311
White Rim Road, 390
White Stallion Ranch ⌶, 354
Wildlife preserves
Southeastern Utah, 380
Southern Arizona, 375
Wild Rivers Recreation Area, 202—203
Wild west shows, 246
Wineries, 40—41
Wolfe Ranch, 409
Wupatki National Monument, 264
Wyler Aerial Tramway, 497
Wynn Las Vegas ⌶, 545

Y

Yavapai Observation Station, 288
Yuma, AZ, 374—375
Yuma Territorial Prison, 374

Z

Zia Diner ✕, 116
Zinc Wine Bar & Bistro ✕, 52
Zion Human History Museum, 449
Zion Lodge, 449
Zion-Mount Carmel Highway & Tunnels, 449
Zion National Park, 445—454
accessibility, 454
admission fees, 454
dining, 452—453
drives and sites, 449—450
emergencies, 454
lodging, 453—454
sports & outdoors, 450—452
transportation, 448
visitor centers, 450
visitor information, 454
when to go, 448
Zoos
Albuquerque, 27—28
Phoenix area, 215
Tucson, 335, 336

NOTES

ABOUT OUR WRITER

Since moving to Utah in 1996, writer and photojournalist John Blodgett has explored almost every corner of the Beehive State. It was in the silent canyons and wide-open lands of sage brush in the southern portion of the state, though, that John discovered a new muse. He has written for *Utah Business, Salt Lake, City Weekly, Digital IQ, Utah Home & Garden, Catalyst,* and assorted Fodor's titles. He constructed the introductory planning material for this guide.